Conference on Empirical Methods in Natural Language Processing 2019 and the 9th International Joint Conference on Natural Language Processing (EMNLP-IJCNLP 2019)

System Demonstrations

Hong Kong, China
3-7 November 2019

ISBN: 978-1-7138-0068-2

EMNLP-IJCNLP 2019

The 2019 Conference on
Empirical Methods in Natural Language Processing
And the 9th International Joint Conference on
Natural Language Processing

Proceedings of System Demonstrations

November 3 – 7, 2019
Hong Kong, China

Introduction

Welcome to the proceedings of the system demonstrations session. This volume contains the papers of the system demonstrations presented at the 2019 Conference on Empirical Methods in Natural Language Processing and 9th International Joint Conference on Natural Language Processing (EMNLP-IJCNLP), which was held in Hong Kong, China on November 3-7, 2019.

The system demonstrations session includes papers describing systems ranging from early research prototypes to mature production-ready software. We received 110 submissions, 22 of which were either invalid or withdrawn by the authors. Of the 88 valid submissions, 44 were selected for inclusion in the proceedings after review of three members of the program committee, achieving an overall acceptance rate of 40%.

We thank all authors for their submissions, and the 130 members of the program committee for their timely and thoughtful reviews. In addition, EMNLP-IJCNLP 2019 has a Best Demo Award for the first time, and the best paper award was selected among outstanding papers following a second round of reviewing by five senior members of the program committee who are due a special recognition for their efforts.

Ruihong Huang and Sebastian Padó
EMNLP-IJCNLP 2019 System Demonstration Co-Chairs

Table of Contents

ABSApp: A Portable Weakly-Supervised
Aspect-Based Sentiment Extraction System

Oren Pereg[1], Daniel Korat[1], Moshe Wasserblat[1], Jonathan Mamou[1], Ido Dagan[2]
[1]Intel AI Lab, Petah Tikva, Israel
[2]Department of Computer Science, Bar-Ilan University, Ramat Gan, Israel
[1]`firstname.lastname@intel.com`
[2]`dagan@cs.biu.ac.il`

Abstract

We present ABSApp, a portable system for weakly-supervised aspect-based sentiment extraction [1]. The system is interpretable and user friendly and does not require labeled training data, hence can be rapidly and cost-effectively used across different domains in applied setups. The system flow includes three stages: First, it generates domain-specific aspect and opinion lexicons based on an unlabeled dataset; second, it enables the user to view and edit those lexicons (weak supervision); and finally, it enables the user to select an unlabeled target dataset from the same domain, classify it, and generate an aspect-based sentiment report. ABSApp has been successfully used in a number of real-life use cases, among them movie review analysis and convention impact analysis.

1 Introduction

Aspect Based Sentiment Analysis (ABSA) is the task of extracting, from a given corpus, opinion targets (aspect terms) and the sentiment expressed towards them. For example, in the sentence *"The dessert was incredible"*, the aspect term is *dessert* and the sentiment towards it is positive. This fine-grained trait of ABSA makes it an effective application for measuring and monitoring the ratio between positive and negative opinions expressed towards specific aspects of a product or service.

Most work around ABSA focused on supervised sequence tagging based systems. Liu et al. (2015) showed promising results when the training and the inference data are from the same domain. However, this approach is typically not robust across different domains since aspect terms from two different domains are usually semantically different hence separated in the embedding

---

[1]A demo video of ABSApp is available at `https://drive.google.com/open?id=1BLk0xkjIOqyRhNy4UQEFQpDF_KR_NMAd`.

vector space. For example, frequent aspect terms in the restaurant domain, like *food, menu, starters* and *salad,* have little or no semantic relatedness to frequent aspect terms in the laptop domain, like *screen size, keyboard* and *battery life*. In addition to aspect terms, many opinion terms are also domain-specific. For example, opinion terms like *tasty (positive), yummy (positive), flavorful (positive)* and *tasteless (negative)* are specific to the restaurant domain whereas opinion terms like *lightweight (positive), durable (positive), compatible (positive)* and *heavy (negative)* are specific to the laptop domain. This makes domain-agnostic ABSA a challenging task, with little work addressing it.

A recent line of work is based on transfer-learning methods, in which labeled data from a source domain is used for training a model to classify data in a target domain. Ding et al. (2017) and Wang and Jialin Pan (2018) proposed using supervised RNNs for cross-domain aspect term extraction and for aspect and opinion term co-extraction. This approach showed encouraging results, however it requires a considerable amount of labeled data from the source domain which is often not practical in applied settings due to cost or legal considerations (relevant data is usually not available for commercial use).

Another approach towards domain robustness is based on unsupervised methods. Hu and Liu (2004) used association rules and Qiu et al. (2011) used syntactic rules for aspect and opinion term co-extraction. Industrial setups usually lack labeled data for training and this is where unsupervised methods excel. However, these methods can be noisy (see the ABSApp-unsup baseline in Table 2). In this paper we show that weak supervision, namely a short manual process of editing lexicons that were generated by an unsupervised method, produces results that are comparable to

Proceedings of the 2019 EMNLP and the 9th IJCNLP (System Demonstrations), pages 1–6
Hong Kong, China, November 3 – 7, 2019. ©2019 Association for Computational Linguistics

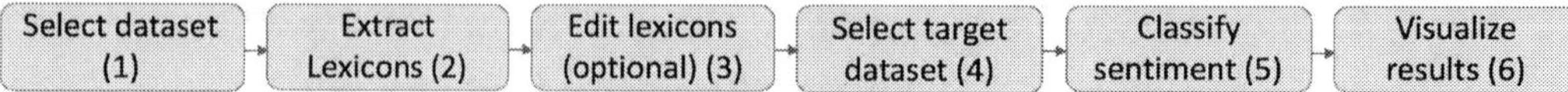

Figure 1: ABSApp workflow.

transfer-learning based supervised methods.

The contribution of this paper is twofold. First, it presents ABSApp, a practical weakly-supervised system that does not require labeled data for training, hence can be rapidly and cost-effectively used across different domains for producing fine-grained sentiment reports. Second, it introduces a workflow that enables users to weakly-supervise the system, thus enhancing its precision. This workflow enables users to select an unlabeled input dataset from a completely new domain, produce domain-specific aspect and opinion lexicons, and edit the lexicons. The user can then select an unlabeled target dataset from the same domain, classify it, and obtain a detailed report regarding the positive and negative sentiments expressed towards each aspect in the corpus and browse through the results.

Our system has been successfully deployed in several real-life use cases. One of them is the analysis of social media opinions towards specific aspects of movies, preformed in collaboration with a major entertainment content provider. Another use case involves measuring the impact of social events, like conventions and conferences, based on opinions published in social media posts.

The system is distributed as open source software under the Apache license as part of NLP Architect by Intel AI Lab.[2]

2 System Workflow

This section describes the workflow of ABSApp, as depicted in Figure 1.

Steps 1 & 2: Selecting a Dataset and Extracting Lexicons. The first step of the flow is to select an input dataset for lexicon extraction, performed by clicking the *Extract lexicons* button shown in Figure 2. Once a dataset is selected, the system performs the lexicon extraction process. This step extracts aspect terms and produces an aspect lexicon. In addition, this step extracts candidate opinion terms, filters them and estimates their polarity, producing an opinion lexicon (see Section 3.1).

Step 3: Lexicon Editing. Figure 2 shows the aspect and opinion lexicon management (editing) user interface. The user can choose to edit an aspect lexicon or an opinion lexicon that was generated in step 2. As shown in Figure 2, in which the *Aspect Lexicon* has been selected, the *Term* column displays the aspect terms while the *Alias1-3* columns display aspect terms that have the same semantic meaning.

Upon selecting a specific aspect, the *Examples* view on the right-hand side of Figure 2 displays text snippets from the input dataset that include this term (highlighted in blue). The *Examples* view enables the user to verify that the selected term indeed functions as an aspect term in various contexts in the domain. Based on this, the user can delete (by unchecking the term's checkbox), add or modify the lexicon items. The recommended best practice is to keep relevant aspect terms and delete non-relevant aspect terms. For example, keep terms like 'service' and 'decor' and delete terms like 'time' and 'city' from an aspect lexicon related to restaurant reviews.

In addition, the user can group together synonym aspects like 'drinks' and 'beverages' (see Figure 2). Finally, the user can save the edited lexicon. The opinion lexicon editor (not shown) functions similarly to the aspect lexicon editor except that it includes a *Polarity* column and a *Score* column (see Section 3.1) instead of the *Alias* columns. Both the polarity and the score can be edited by the user.

Steps 4 & 5: Selecting a Target Dataset and Performing Sentiment Classification. A target dataset and its classification are performed by clicking the *Classify* button in Figure 2. Once the dataset is selected the system starts the sentiment classification process (see Section 3.2).

Step 6: Results Visualization. Figure 3 shows the output of the sentiment classification process. The upper part of the figure displays the count of positive and negative sentiment mentions detected in the target dataset towards each aspect, as green and red bars. Hovering over a green(red) bar displays the count of the positive(negative) senti-

---

[2] http://nlp_architect.nervanasys.com/ absa.html

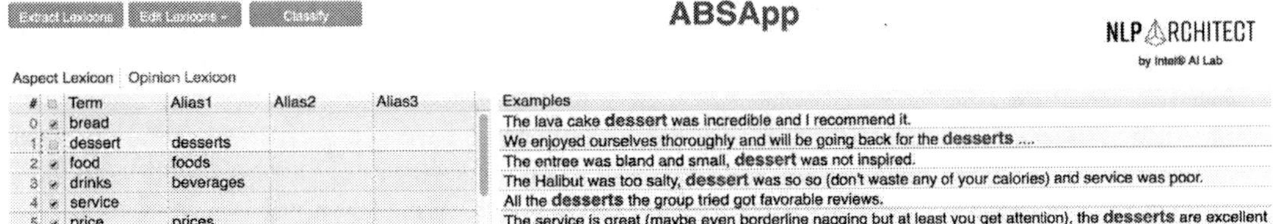

Figure 2: ABSApp user interface for aspect and opinion lexicons management. The figure displays an aspect lexicon related to the restaurants domain.

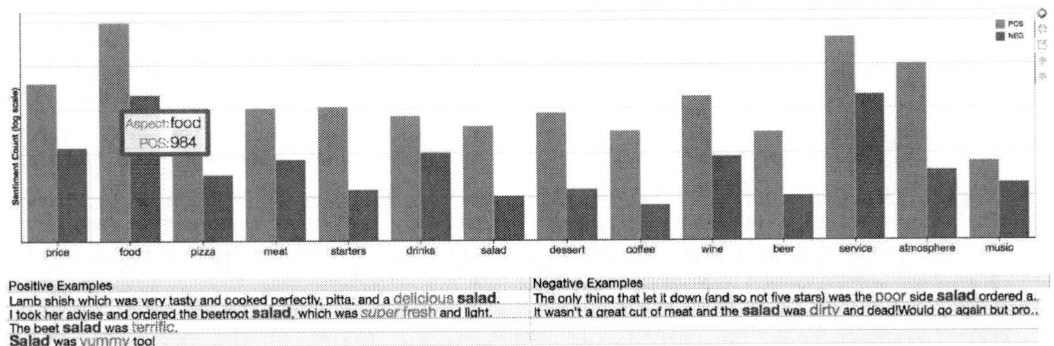

Figure 3: ABSApp user interface for displaying the accumulated amount of positive & negative sentiment per aspect (top) and sentences containing sentiment towards a specific aspect (bottom).

ment mentions towards a specific aspect (see the blue rectangle in Figure 3). The displayed value is an aggregation of the sentiment mention count towards the aspect term and towards all of its *Alias* terms (as in Figure 2).

Upon clicking a bar related to a specific aspect, a list of sentences containing positive and negative sentiment towards that aspect is displayed with the aspect terms colored blue and the positive and negative opinion terms colored green and red, respectively (lower part of Figure 3). This view enables the user to drill-down into the results and extract further insight.

3 Algorithmic Components

Our algorithmic approach is based on using unlabeled data from a new target domain to co-extract aspect and opinion terms, in order to generate domain-specific aspect and opinion lexicons (Section 3.1). Those lexicons are then used to extract aspect-opinion sentiment mentions in datasets from the same domain (Section 3.2).

3.1 Lexicon Extraction

Pre-processing. The first lexicon extraction step includes applying tokenization, part-of-speech tagging [3] and dependency parsing to the input data. For dependency parsing, we used the Bi-LSTM parser proposed by Kiperwasser and Goldberg (2016).

Aspect and Opinion Term Extraction. This step is based on applying the bootstrap opinion and aspect term co-extraction using the dependency relation rules algorithm, proposed by Qiu et al. (2011). The bootstrap process is initialized with a seed lexicon of generic opinion terms. New aspect and opinion terms are extracted based on the seed lexicon and the dependency relation rules. The extracted terms are then added to the seed lexicon, and used for extracting additional terms in the next iteration. In order to initialize the bootstrap process, we used the opinion lexicon generated by Hu and Liu (2004), which contains around 6800 opinion terms along with their sentiment polarity. Table 1 shows two of the 8 rules that are used along with example sentences. The example for rule *R1* illustrates the extraction of the aspect term *decor* based on the known opinion term *nice*, while the example for rule *R2* illustrates the extraction of the opinion term *tasty* based on the

---

[3]Performed by spaCy (https://spacy.io/).

known aspect term *food*.

RuleID	Rule	Example
R1	$O \xrightarrow{amod} A(NN)$	nice decor
		(nice $\xrightarrow{amod}$ decor)
R2	$A \xrightarrow{nsubj} O(ADJ)$	the food was super tasty
		(food $\xrightarrow{nsubj}$ tasty)

Table 1: Examples of the opinion and aspect terms extraction rules. O represents an opinion term and A represents an aspect term.

Opinion Lexicon Scoring and Filtering. This step aims to filter the noisy candidate opinion terms extracted by the bootstrap process. It is based on using an MLP classifier for generating a score that represents the probability that a candidate is indeed an opinion term. Candidate opinion terms are qualified as opinion terms if their classification score exceeds a threshold [4].

The MLP classifier input features consists of the candidate term word embedding[5] and the mean, standard-deviation, maximum and minimum word-embedding cosine similarities between the candidate term and a pre-determined set of generic opinion terms. The MLP consists of a single hidden layer and is trained once for a binary classification task using manually labeled data that consists of a set of opinion terms (positive class) and a set of non-opinion terms (negative class) from a specific domain[6]. Once the model is generated it is then used for grading candidate opinion terms extracted in other domains. It is reasonable to use such model across domains, since the classification features represent semantic similarity levels that are robust across domains.

Opinion Polarity Estimation The goal of this step is to set the binary sentiment polarity (positive or negative) of the opinion terms. Following Pablos et al. (2016), an opinion term polarity is assigned based on estimating whether it is semantically closer to a set of generic positive opinion terms or to a set of generic negative opinion terms. To produce those sets we used a subset of 47 positive terms and a subset of 47 negative terms derived from the opinion lexicon generated by Hu and Liu (2004). The semantic similarity between an opinion term and a positive or negative set is estimated by averaging the cosine similarity of the embedding of the opinion term and the embedding of each one of the terms in the positive or negative set.

In this module we used pre-trained embeddings[5] which produce overall good results but raise a drawback; some opinion terms may convey different sentiment polarities in different domains (e.g. 'delicate movie' (positive) vs. 'delicate cellphone' (negative)), while a pre-trained embeddings setup is only capable of setting a single polarity per opinion term. A suggested solution is to adapt the embeddings to the target domain or to use context embeddings. We intend to address this challenge in future work.

3.2 Sentiment Classification

Sentiment classification uses the opinion and aspect lexicons for detecting aspect-opinion pairs (sentiment mentions) within the input target dataset, and determining their sentiment polarity. Aspect-opinion pairs are extracted based on detecting a direct or second-order dependency relation of any type, between them. The aspect-opinion pair polarity is assigned according to the polarity of the opinion term. This step also uses a pre-determined negation lexicon containing negation terms. Upon detecting a direct dependency relation between a negation term and the opinion term, the aspect-opinion pair polarity is reversed.

4 Evaluation

Our evaluation objective is to show that the different algorithmic steps, namely, lexicon extraction and sentiment classification, produce usable results. An additional objective is to show that weak supervision of an aspect lexicon that was generated in an unsupervised manner produces comparable results to the recent transfer-learning based methods (Ding et al., 2017; Wang and Jialin Pan, 2018). For this purpose, we leveraged the data of SemEval 2014 task 4 (Pontiki et al., 2014), which tests the two main ABSA sub-tasks: aspect term extraction and aspect term polarity detection.

Datasets. The performance of the algorithm was evaluated using data from two different domains: restaurant reviews and laptop reviews. Those two domains are disjoint and therefore demonstrate

---

[4]The threshold's value was empirically determined based on precision-recall tradeoff.

[5]We used Stanford Glove embeddings `https://nlp.stanford.edu/projects/glove/`

[6]This training data can be downloaded from `https://github.com/NervanaSystems/nlp-architect/blob/master/nlp_architect/models/absa/train/lexicons/RerankTrainingData.csv`

the robustness of our system. Following previous work, the restaurant reviews dataset consists of the restaurant reviews from SemEval 2014 task 4 subtask 1 (Pontiki et al., 2014) and from SemEval 2015 task 12 subtask 1 (Pontiki et al., 2015). The laptop domain consists of the laptop reviews from SemEval 2014 task 4 subtask 1. The gold data includes manual labeling of the spans of aspect term mentions within each sentence in the dataset as well as the sentiment polarity (positive, negative, conflict or neutral) related to each aspect. The two domains consist of a total of 5841 and 3614 sentences, respectively.

Experimental Setup. Following the first two subtasks of the SemEval 2014 task 4, our experiment is split into two parts: First, we evaluate aspect term extraction by generating an aspect lexicon, using it for detecting aspect terms within the test set and comparing it against the gold labels. Second, we evaluate the sentiment polarity detected towards each extracted aspect by comparing between the aspect-opinion pairs detected with their assigned polarity and the gold labels.

The data from each domain was randomly split into 75% training and 25% testing. The training data was used (ignoring its annotation) for generating the domain-specific opinion and aspect lexicons according to workflow steps 1-3 of Figure 1. As a baseline to the aspect term extraction evaluation, we tested the unsupervised output of ABSApp, in which the lexicons were not manually edited. We also tested the weakly-supervised output of the system, in which the aspect lexicon was edited ; this manual process, which took about 15 minutes, involved deleting aspects that are non-relevant to the domain (see step 3 in Section 2 for detailed description of this process).

Following the settings in prior aspect term extraction work, only exact matches between the predicted aspects and gold labels are counted as correct. We also added a more lenient metric where partial matches are counted as correct, since, for many practical usages, partial matches are sufficient for extracting valuable insight. For example, in the restaurant domain, 'service' and 'waiting service' can be counted as the same aspect. This lenient metric was also used for the aspect term polarity evaluation task.

Results. Table 2 shows an F1 score evaluation of the aspect term extraction task. It includes a comparison between the unsupervised output

of the system ('ABSApp-unsup'), its weakly-supervised output ('ABSApp-wksup') and two transfer-learning based methods: 'Hier-joint' by Ding et al. (2017) and 'RNSCN' by Wang and Jialin Pan (2018). 'ABSApp-wksup Ln' represents the weakly-supervised system lenient matches.

It is noticeable from Table 2 that the results of the unsupervised output of the system ('ABSApp-unsup') are noisy, but that the weakly-supervised output results ('ABSApp-wksup') are quite comparable to the cited transfer-learning based methods, however, the latter require annotated data from a source domain (the results shown are averaged across tests using data from 2 different annotated source domains), whereas ABSApp relies on a short weak supervision process but does not require any labeled data, which is often unavailable in applied industrial settings.

Table 3 shows an evaluation of the weakly-supervised ABSApp lenient performance of the aspect term polarity task. This task relates to the sentiment polarity (positive, negative) detected towards each extracted aspect mention, hence it reflects the quality of both algorithmic components: aspect and opinion lexicon extraction (Section 3.1) and sentiment classification (Section 3.2).

It is seen from Table 3 that although the recall in both tests is not high (because it reflects correct detection of an aspect term, an opinion term and a relation between them), the precision is above 70%. Such precision is often sufficient for practical purposes. Note that there is no transfer-learning work related to the aspect term polarity task, therefore no benchmarks to other systems are shown.

Model	Restaurants	Laptops
Hier-Joint†	48.0	34.2
RNSCN†	51.5	45.9
ABSApp-unsup	43.5	23.2
ABSApp-wksup	51.1	40.1
ABSApp-wksup Ln	66.9	58.2

Table 2: Aspect term extraction evaluation (F1 score). † average performance over evaluations using different random dataset splits of the test data, as reported by Wang and Jialin Pan (2018).

Domain	Precision	Recall	F1 score
Restaurants	70.3	44.5	54.6
Laptops	72.7	27.6	40.1

Table 3: Weakly-supervised ABSApp aspect term polarity evaluation.

5 Field Use Cases

This section describes two use cases in which AB-SApp has been successfully used.

Movie Reviews Analysis. One of the main predictors for the commercial success of a movie is the estimated hype effect of the movie's pre-release in social media as measured using sentiment analysis (Natarajan et al., 2019). ABSApp was used in collaboration with a major entertainment content provider for analyzing audience opinion in social media towards movies and trailers. The system detected the different characters, actors, scenes and music as aspects, and produced fine-grained sentiment reports periodically. These reports were used to fine-tune the content of future movie trailer releases.

Convention Impact Analysis. Analysis of sentiment towards different aspects is useful also for measuring the impact of professional events, determining user impressions, and acting accordingly. ABSApp was used during the 2018 Intel AI development convention in San Francisco [7] to extract aspects related to the convention and to analyze the sentiment towards them based on Twitter feeds. The system detected aspects like sessions, keynotes, demos, venue, etc., and provided the event organizers with valuable information regarding the level of positive/negative sentiment towards them. In addition, it enabled organizers to browse through sentences containing sentiment towards specific aspects and draw conclusions as to what should be changed and what should be continued at current and future conventions.

6 Conclusion

We presented ABSApp, a weakly-supervised system for Aspect Based Sentiment Analysis. We showed that weak supervision of lexicons, which were generated in an unsupervised manner, produces comparable results to recent supervised transfer-learning based methods. This enables, rapid and cost-effective use across different domains in applied setups where labeled data is often unavailable.

References

Ying Ding, Jianfei Yu, and Jing Jiang. 2017. Recurrent neural networks with auxiliary labels for cross-domain opinion target extraction. In *Association for the Advancement of Artificial Intelligence*, pages 3436–3442.

Minqing Hu and Bing Liu. 2004. Mining opinion features in customer reviews. In *American Association for Artificial Intelligence*.

Eliyahu Kiperwasser and Yoav Goldberg. 2016. Simple and accurate dependency parsing using bidirectional lstm feature representations. *Transactions of the Association for Computational Linguistics*, 4:313–327.

Pengfei Liu, Shafiq Joty, and Helen Meng. 2015. Fine-grained opinion mining with recurrent neural networks and word embeddings. In *Proceedings of the 2015 Conference on Empirical Methods in Natural Language Processing, EMNLP 2015*, pages 1433–1443.

V. Anantha Natarajan, K SaiHarsha, and M Santhosh Kumar. 2019. Box-office revenue estimation for telugu movie industry using predictive analytic techniques. *International Journal of Recent Technology and Engineering (IJRTE)*, 7(6):896–902.

Aitor García Pablos, Montse Cuadros, and German Rigau. 2016. A comparison of domain-based word polarity estimation using different word embeddings. In *Proceedings of the Tenth International Conference on Language Resources and Evaluation (LREC 2016)*, pages 54–60, Portorož, Slovenia. European Language Resources Association (ELRA).

Maria Pontiki, Dimitris Galanis, Haris Papageorgiou, Suresh Manandhar, and Ion Androutsopoulos. 2015. SemEval-2015 task 12: Aspect based sentiment analysis. In *Proceedings of the 9th International Workshop on Semantic Evaluation (SemEval 2015)*, pages 486–495, Denver, Colorado. Association for Computational Linguistics.

Maria Pontiki, Dimitris Galanis, John Pavlopoulos, Harris Papageorgiou, Ion Androutsopoulos, and Suresh Manandhar. 2014. SemEval-2014 task 4: Aspect based sentiment analysis. In *Proceedings of the 8th International Workshop on Semantic Evaluation (SemEval 2014)*, pages 27–35, Dublin, Ireland. Association for Computational Linguistics.

Guang Qiu, Bing Liu, Jiajun Bu, and Chun Chen. 2011. Opinion word expansion and target extraction through double propagation. *Comput. Linguist.*, 37(1):9–27.

Wenya Wang and Sinno Jialin Pan. 2018. Recursive neural structural correspondence network for cross-domain aspect and opinion co-extraction. In *Proceedings of the 56th Annual Meeting of the Association for Computational Linguistics*, pages 1–11.

---

[7] `https://newsroom.intel.com/press-kits/2018-ai-devcon/#gs.bejr0q`

AllenNLP Interpret:
A Framework for Explaining Predictions of NLP Models

Eric Wallace[1]   Jens Tuyls[2]   Junlin Wang[2]   Sanjay Subramanian[1]
Matt Gardner[1]   Sameer Singh[2]
[1]Allen Institute for Artificial Intelligence   [2]University of California, Irvine
ericw@allenai.org, sameer@uci.edu

Abstract

Neural NLP models are increasingly accurate but are imperfect and opaque—they break in counterintuitive ways and leave end users puzzled at their behavior. Model interpretation methods ameliorate this opacity by providing explanations for specific model predictions. Unfortunately, existing interpretation codebases make it difficult to apply these methods to new models and tasks, which hinders adoption for practitioners and burdens interpretability researchers. We introduce AllenNLP Interpret, a flexible framework for interpreting NLP models. The toolkit provides interpretation primitives (e.g., input gradients) for any AllenNLP model and task, a suite of built-in interpretation methods, and a library of front-end visualization components. We demonstrate the toolkit's flexibility and utility by implementing live demos for five interpretation methods (e.g., saliency maps and adversarial attacks) on a variety of models and tasks (e.g., masked language modeling using BERT and reading comprehension using BiDAF). These demos, alongside our code and tutorials, are available at https://allennlp.org/interpret.

1 Introduction

Despite constant advances and seemingly superhuman performance on constrained domains, state-of-the-art models for NLP are imperfect: they latch on to superficial patterns (Gururangan et al., 2018), reflect unwanted social biases (Doshi-Velez and Kim, 2017), and significantly underperform humans on a myriad of tasks. These imperfections, coupled with today's advances being driven by (seemingly black-box) neural models, leave researchers and practitioners scratching their heads, asking, *"why did my model make this prediction?"*

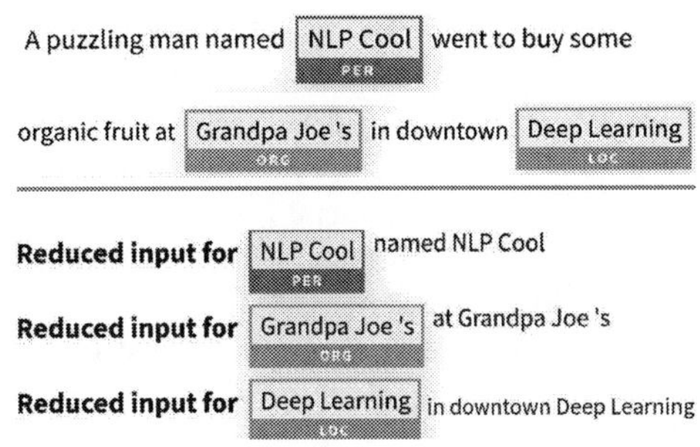

Figure 1: An interpretation generated using AllenNLP Interpret for NER. The model predicts three tags for an input (top). We interpret each tag separately, e.g., input reduction (Feng et al., 2018) (bottom) removes as many words as possible without changing a tag's prediction. Input reduction shows that the words "named", "at", and "in downtown" are sufficient to predict the People, Organization, and Location tags, respectively.

Instance-level interpretation methods help to answer this question by providing explanations for specific model predictions. These explanations come in many flavors, e.g., visualizing a model's local decision boundary (Ribeiro et al., 2016), highlighting the saliency of the input features (Simonyan et al., 2014), or adversarially modifying the input (Ebrahimi et al., 2018). Interpretations are useful to illuminate the strengths and weaknesses of a model (Feng et al., 2018), increase user trust (Ribeiro et al., 2016), and evaluate hard-to-define criteria such as safety or fairness (Doshi-Velez and Kim, 2017).

Many open-source implementations exist for instance-level interpretation methods. However, most codebases focus on computer vision, are model- or task-specific (e.g., sentiment analysis), or contain implementations for a small number of interpretation methods. Thus, it is difficult for practitioners to interpret *their* model. As a re-

7

Proceedings of the 2019 EMNLP and the 9th IJCNLP (System Demonstrations), pages 7–12
Hong Kong, China, November 3 – 7, 2019. ©2019 Association for Computational Linguistics

sult, model developers rarely leverage interpretations and thus lack a robust understanding of their system. The inflexibility of existing interpretation codebases also burdens interpretability researchers—they cannot easily evaluate their methods on multiple models.

We present AllenNLP Interpret, an open-source, extensible toolkit built on top of AllenNLP (Gardner et al., 2018) for interpreting NLP models. The toolkit makes it easy to apply existing interpretation methods to *new models*, as well as develop *new interpretation methods*. The toolkit consists of three contributions: a suite of interpretation techniques implemented for broad classes of models, model- and task-agnostic APIs for developing new interpretation methods (e.g., APIs to obtain input gradients), and reusable front-end components for interactively visualizing the interpretations.

AllenNLP Interpret has numerous **use cases**. Our external website shows demos of:

- *Uncovering Model Biases:* A SQuAD model relies on lexical overlap between the words in the question and the passage. Alternatively, a textual entailment model infers contradiction on observing the word "politics" in the hypothesis.
- *Finding Decision Rules:* A named entity recognition model predicts the location tag when it sees the phrase "in downtown".
- *Diagnosing Errors:* A sentiment model incorrectly predicts the positive class due to the trigram "tony hawk style".

2 Interpreting Model Predictions

This section introduces an end user's view of our toolkit, i.e., the available interpretations, models, and visualizations.

2.1 What Are Instance-Level Interpretations

AllenNLP Interpret focuses on two types of interpretations: gradient-based saliency maps and adversarial attacks. We choose these methods for their flexibility—gradient-based methods can be applied to any differentiable model.

Saliency maps explain a model's prediction by identifying the importance of the input tokens. Gradient-based methods determine this importance using the gradient of the loss with respect to the tokens (Simonyan et al., 2014).

Adversarial attacks provide a different lens into a model—they elucidate its capabilities by exploit-ing its weaknesses. We focus on methods that modify tokens in the input (e.g., replace or remove tokens) in order to change the model's output in a desired manner.

2.2 Saliency Map Visualizations

We consider three saliency methods. Since our goal is to interpret why the model made *its* prediction (not the ground-truth answer), we use the model's own output in the loss calculation. For each method, we reduce each token's gradient (which is the same dimension as the token embedding) to a single value by taking the L_2 norm.

Vanilla Gradient This method visualizes the gradient of the loss with respect to each token (Simonyan et al., 2014). Figure 2 shows an example interpretation of BERT (Devlin et al., 2019).

Integrated Gradients Sundararajan et al. (2017) introduce integrated gradients. They define a baseline x', which is an input absent of information (we use a sequence of all zero embeddings). Word importance is determined by integrating the gradient along the path from this baseline to the original input.

SmoothGrad Smilkov et al. (2017) average the gradient over many noisy versions of the input. For NLP, we add small Gaussian noise to every embedding and take the average gradient value.

2.3 Adversarial Attacks

We consider two adversarial attacks: replacing words to change the model's prediction (HotFlip) and removing words to maintain the model's prediction (Input Reduction).

Untargeted & Targeted HotFlip We consider word-level substitutions using HotFlip (Ebrahimi et al., 2018). HotFlip uses the gradient to swap out words from the input in order to change the model's prediction. It answers a sensitivity question: *how would the prediction change if certain words are replaced?* We also extend HotFlip to a targeted setting, i.e., we substitute words in order to change the model's prediction to a *specific* target prediction. This answers an almost counterfactual question: *what words should be swapped in order to cause a specific prediction?*

We closely follow the original HotFlip algorithm: replace tokens based on a first-order Taylor

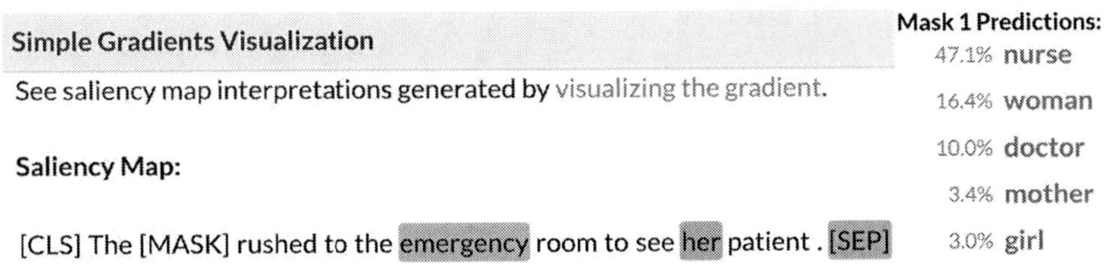

Simple Gradients Visualization

See saliency map interpretations generated by visualizing the gradient.

Saliency Map:

[CLS] The [MASK] rushed to the emergency room to see her patient . [SEP]

Mask 1 Predictions:

47.1% **nurse**

16.4% **woman**

10.0% **doctor**

3.4% **mother**

3.0% **girl**

Figure 2: A saliency map generated using Vanilla Gradient (Simonyan et al., 2014) for BERT's masked language modeling objective. BERT predicts the [MASK] token given the input sentence; the interpretation shows that BERT uses the gendered pronoun "her" and the hospital-specific "emergency" to predict "nurse".

approximation of the loss around the current token embeddings.[1] Figure 3 shows an example of a HotFlip attack on sentiment analysis.

Input Reduction Feng et al. (2018) introduce input reduction. They remove as many words as possible from the input *without* changing a model's prediction. Input reduction works by iteratively removing the word with the smallest gradient value. We classify input reduction as an "adversarial attack" because the resulting inputs are usually nonsensical but cause high confidence predictions (Feng et al., 2018). Figure 1 shows an example of reducing an NER input.

2.4 Currently Available Models

The toolkit currently interprets six tasks which cover a wide range of input-output formats and model architectures.

- **Reading Comprehension** using the SQuAD (Rajpurkar et al., 2016) and DROP (Dua et al., 2019) datasets. We use NAQANet (Dua et al., 2019) and BiDAF models (Seo et al., 2017).

- **Masked Language Modeling** using the transformer models available in Pytorch Transformers[2], e.g., BERT (Devlin et al., 2019), RoBERTa (Liu et al., 2019), and more.

- **Text Classification** and **Textual Entailment** using BiLSTM and self-attention classifiers.

- **Named Entity Recognition (NER)** and **Coreference Resolution**. These are examples of tasks with complex input-output structure; we can use the same function calls to analyze each predicted tag (e.g., Figure 1) or cluster.

3 AllenNLP Interpret Under the Hood

This section provides implementation details for AllenNLP Interpret: how we compute the token embedding gradient in a model-agnostic way, as well as the available front-end interface. Figure 4 provides an overview of our software implementation and the surrounding AllenNLP ecosystem.

3.1 Model-Agnostic Input Gradients

Existing Classes in AllenNLP Models in AllenNLP are of type Model (a thin wrapper around a PyTorch Module). The Model wrapper includes a forward() function, which runs the model and optionally computes the loss if a label is provided.

Obtaining predictions from an AllenNLP Model is simplified via the Predictor class. This class provides a model-agnostic way for obtaining predictions: call predict_json() with a JSON containing raw strings and it will return the model's prediction. For example, passing {"input": "this demo is amazing!"} to a sentiment analysis Predictor will receive positive and negative class probabilities in return.

Our AllenNLP Extension The core backbone of our toolkit is an extension to the Predictor class that allows interpretation methods to compute input gradients in a model-agnostic way. Creating this extension has two main implementation challenges: (1) the loss (with the model's *own predictions* as the labels) must be computed for widely varying output formats (e.g., classification, tagging, or language modeling), and (2) the gradient of this loss with respect to the token embeddings must be computed for widely varying embedding types (e.g., word vectors, ELMo (Peters et al., 2018) embeddings, BERT embeddings).

Predictions to Labeled Instances To handle challenge (1), we leverage the fact that all mod-

---

[1] We also adapt HotFlip to contextual embeddings; details provided in Section 3.2.

[2] https://github.com/huggingface/pytorch-transformers

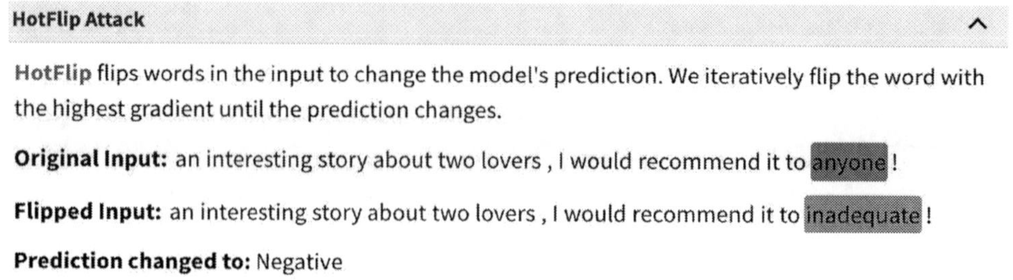

Figure 3: A word-level HotFlip attack on a sentiment analysis model—replacing "anyone" with "inadequate" causes the model's prediction to change from Positive to Negative.

els will return a loss if a label is passed to their forward() function. We first query the model with the input to obtain its prediction. Next, we convert this prediction into a set of "labeled examples" using a function called predictions_to_labeled_instances(). For categorical predictions (e.g., classification, span prediction), this function returns a single instance with the label set to the model's argmax prediction.

For tasks with structured outputs (e.g., NER, coref), this function returns multiple instances, where each instance is used to compute the loss for a different part of the output. For example, there are separate instances for each of the three NER tags predicted in Figure 1. Separating out the instances allows us to have more fine-grained interpretations—we can analyze one part of the overall prediction rather than interpreting the entire tag sequence.

Embedding-Agnostic Gradients To handle difficulty (2)—computing the gradients of varying token embeddings—we rely on the abstractions of AllenNLP. In particular, AllenNLP uses a Token-Embedder interface to converts token ids into embeddings. We can thus compute the gradient for any embedding method by registering a PyTorch backward gradient hook on the model's TokenEmbedder function.

Our end result is a simple API for computing input gradients for any model: call predictions_to_labeled_instances() and then get_gradients().

3.2 Context-Independent Embedding Matrix for Deep Embeddings

The final implementation difficulty arises from the fact that contextual embeddings such as ELMo and BERT do not have an "embedding matrix" to search over (their embeddings are context-

dependent). This raises difficulties for methods such as Hotflip (Section 2.3) that require searching over a discrete embedding matrix. To solve this, we create a context-independent matrix that contains the features from the model's last context-independent layer. For instance, we pass all of the words from a particular task's training set into ELMo and save the features from its context-independent Char-CNN into a "word embedding matrix". This allows us to run HotFlip for contextual embeddings while still capturing context information since the gradient backpropagates through the contextual layers.

3.3 Frontend Visualizations

We interactively visualize the interpretations using the AllenNLP Demo, a web application for running AllenNLP models. We add HTML and JavaScript components that provide visualizations for saliency maps and adversarial attacks. These components are reusable and greatly simplify the process for adding new models and interpretation methods (Section 4). For example, a single line of HTML code can create the visualizations shown in Figures 1–3. Note that visualizing the interpretations is not required—AllenNLP Interpret can be run in an offline, batch manner. This is useful for aggregating interpretation results, e.g., as in Feng et al. (2018) and Wallace et al. (2018).

4   Adding a Model or Interpretation

This section describes the high-level process for adding new analysis methods or AllenNLP models to our toolkit.

New Interpretation We provide a tutorial for adding a new analysis method to our toolkit. In particular, it walks through the three main requirements for adding SmoothGrad:

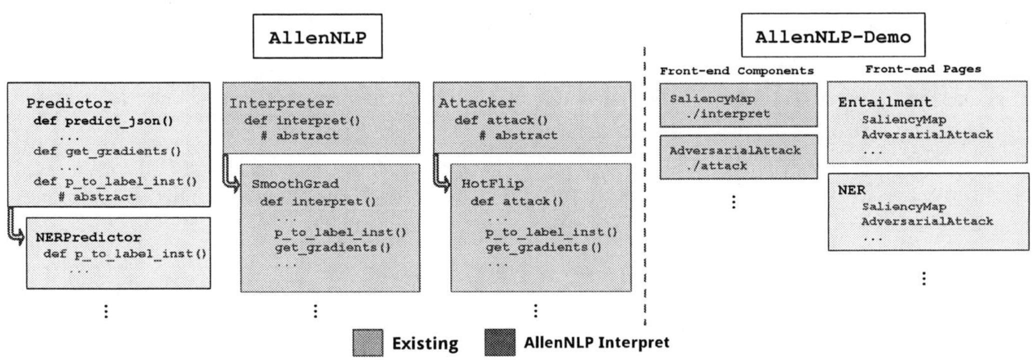

Figure 4: **System Overview:** Our toolkit (in blue) and the surrounding AllenNLP ecosystem. The only model-specific code is a simple function called predictions_to_labeled_instances() (abbreviated as p_to_label_inst()), which is added to the model's Predictor class (e.g., for an NER model's predictor; left of figure). This function allows input gradients to be calculated using get_gradients() in a model-agnostic manner (e.g., for use in SmoothGrad or HotFlip; middle left of Figure). On the front-end (right of Figure), we create reusable visualization components, e.g., for visualizing saliency maps or adversarial attacks.

1. Implementing SmoothGrad in AllenNLP, using predictions_to_labeled_instances() and get_gradients() (requires adding about ten lines of code to the vanilla gradient method).
2. Adding a SmoothGrad Interpreter to the demo back-end (about five lines of code).
3. Adding the HTML/JavaScript for saliency visualization (requires making a one-line call to the reusable front-end components).

New Model We also provide a tutorial for interpreting a new model. If your task is already available in the demos (e.g., text classification), you need to change a *single* line of code to replace the demo model with your model. If your task is not present in the demos, you will need to:

1. Write the predictions_to_labeled_instances() function for your model (consists of three lines for classification).
2. Create a path to your model in the demo's back-end (about 5-10 lines of code).
3. Add a front-end page to visualize the model and interpretation output. This is simplified by the reusable front-end components (consists of copy-pasting code templates).

5   Related Work

Alternative Interpretation Methods We focus on gradient-based methods (saliency maps and adversarial attacks) but numerous other instance-level model interpretation methods exist. For example, a common practice in NLP is to visualize attention weights (Bahdanau et al., 2015) or to isolate the effect of individual neurons (Karpathy et al., 2016). We focus on gradient-based methods because they are applicable to many models.

Existing Interpretation Toolkits In computer vision, various open-source toolkits exist for explaining and attacking models (e.g., Papernot et al. (2016); Ozbulak (2019), inter alia); some toolkits also include interactive demos (Norton and Qi, 2017). Similar toolkits for NLP are significantly scarcer, and most toolkits focus on specific models or tasks. For instance, Liu et al. (2018), Strobelt et al. (2019), and Vig (2019) visualize attention weights for specific NLP models, while Lee et al. (2019) apply adversarial attacks to reading comprehension systems. Our toolkit differs because it is flexible and diverse; we can interpret and attack any AllenNLP model.

6   Conclusion

We presented AllenNLP Interpret, an open-source toolkit that facilitates the interpretation of NLP models. The toolkit is flexible—it enables the development and evaluation of interpretation methods across a wide range of NLP models and tasks.

The toolkit is continually evolving—we will continue to implement new interpretation methods and models as they become available. We welcome open-source contributions, and we hope the toolkit is useful for model developers and interpretability researchers alike.

Acknowledgements

The authors thank Shi Feng, the members of UCI NLP, and the anonymous reviewers for their valuable feedback. We also thank the developers of AllenNLP for their help with constructing our toolkit, especially Joel Grus. This work is supported in part by NSF Grant IIS-1756023.

References

Dzmitry Bahdanau, Kyunghyun Cho, and Yoshua Bengio. 2015. Neural machine translation by jointly learning to align and translate. In *ICLR*.

Jacob Devlin, Ming-Wei Chang, Kenton Lee, and Kristina Toutanova. 2019. BERT: pre-training of deep bidirectional transformers for language understanding. In *NAACL*.

Finale Doshi-Velez and Been Kim. 2017. Towards a rigorous science of interpretable machine learning. *arXiv preprint arXiv:1702.08608*.

Dheeru Dua, Yizhong Wang, Pradeep Dasigi, Gabriel Stanovsky, Sameer Singh, and Matt Gardner. 2019. DROP: A reading comprehension benchmark requiring discrete reasoning over paragraphs. In *NAACL*.

Javid Ebrahimi, Anyi Rao, Daniel Lowd, and Dejing Dou. 2018. HotFlip: White-box adversarial examples for text classification. In *ACL*.

Shi Feng, Eric Wallace, Alvin Grissom II, Mohit Iyyer, Pedro Rodriguez, and Jordan Boyd-Graber. 2018. Pathologies of neural models make interpretations difficult. In *EMNLP*.

Matt Gardner, Joel Grus, Mark Neumann, Oyvind Tafjord, Pradeep Dasigi, Nelson Liu, Matthew Peters, Michael Schmitz, and Luke Zettlemoyer. 2018. AllenNLP: A deep semantic natural language processing platform. In *ACL Workshop for NLP Open Source Software*.

Suchin Gururangan, Swabha Swayamdipta, Omer Levy, Roy Schwartz, Samuel R. Bowman, and Noah A. Smith. 2018. Annotation artifacts in natural language inference data. In *NAACL*.

Andrej Karpathy, Justin Johnson, and Li Fei-Fei. 2016. Visualizing and understanding recurrent networks. In *ICLR Workshop Track*.

Gyeongbok Lee, Sungdong Kim, and Seung-won Hwang. 2019. QADiver: Interactive framework for diagnosing QA models. In *AAAI Demonstrations*.

Shusen Liu, Tao Li, Zhimin Li, Vivek Srikumar, Valerio Pascucci, and Peer-Timo Bremer. 2018. Visual interrogation of attention-based models for natural language inference and machine comprehension. In *EMNLP*.

Yinhan Liu, Myle Ott, Naman Goyal, Jingfei Du, Mandar Joshi, Danqi Chen, Omer Levy, Mike Lewis, Luke Zettlemoyer, and Veselin Stoyanov. 2019. Roberta: A robustly optimized bert pretraining approach. *arXiv:1907.11692*.

Andrew P Norton and Yanjun Qi. 2017. AdversarialPlayground: A visualization suite showing how adversarial examples fool deep learning. In *2017 IEEE VizSec Symposium*.

Utku Ozbulak. 2019. Pytorch CNN visualizations. https://github.com/utkuozbulak/pytorch-cnn-visualizations.

Nicolas Papernot, Fartash Faghri, Nicholas Carlini, Ian Goodfellow, Reuben Feinman, Alexey Kurakin, Cihang Xie, Yash Sharma, Tom Brown, Aurko Roy, et al. 2016. Technical report on the CleverHans v2.1.0 adversarial examples library. *arXiv:1610.00768*.

Matthew E. Peters, Mark Neumann, Mohit Iyyer, Matt Gardner, Christopher Clark, Kenton Lee, and Luke Zettlemoyer. 2018. Deep contextualized word representations. In *NAACL*.

Pranav Rajpurkar, Jian Zhang, Konstantin Lopyrev, and Percy Liang. 2016. SQuAD: 100,000+ questions for machine comprehension of text. In *EMNLP*.

Marco Tulio Ribeiro, Sameer Singh, and Carlos Guestrin. 2016. Why should I trust you?: Explaining the predictions of any classifier. In *KDD*.

Min Joon Seo, Aniruddha Kembhavi, Ali Farhadi, and Hannaneh Hajishirzi. 2017. Bidirectional attention flow for machine comprehension. In *ICLR*.

Karen Simonyan, Andrea Vedaldi, and Andrew Zisserman. 2014. Deep inside convolutional networks: Visualising image classification models and saliency maps. In *ICLR*.

Daniel Smilkov, Nikhil Thorat, Been Kim, Fernanda B. Viégas, and Martin Wattenberg. 2017. SmoothGrad: removing noise by adding noise. In *ICML Workshop on Visualization for Deep Learning*.

Hendrik Strobelt, Sebastian Gehrmann, Michael Behrisch, Adam Perer, Hanspeter Pfister, and Alexander M Rush. 2019. Seq2Seq-Vis: A visual debugging tool for sequence-to-sequence models. *IEEE TVCG*.

Mukund Sundararajan, Ankur Taly, and Qiqi Yan. 2017. Axiomatic attribution for deep networks. In *ICML*.

Jesse Vig. 2019. Visualizing attention in transformer-based language models. *arXiv:1904.02679*.

Eric Wallace, Shi Feng, and Jordan Boyd-Graber. 2018. Interpreting neural networks with nearest neighbors. In *EMNLP 2018 Blackbox NLP Workshop*.

ALTER: Auxiliary Text Rewriting Tool for Natural Language Generation

Qiongkai Xu   **Chenchen Xu**
The Australian National University
Data61 CSIRO
Qiongkai.Xu@anu.edu.au
Chenchen.Xu@anu.edu.au

Lizhen Qu
Laboratory for Dialogue Research
Monash University
Lizhen.Qu@monash.edu

Abstract

In this paper, we describe *ALTER*, an auxiliary text rewriting tool that facilitates the rewriting process for natural language generation tasks, such as paraphrasing, text simplification, fairness-aware text rewriting, and text style transfer. Our tool is characterized by two features, i) recording of word-level revision histories and ii) flexible auxiliary edit support and feedback to annotators. The text rewriting assist and traceable rewriting history are potentially beneficial to the future research of natural language generation.

1 Introduction

Generative modeling of editing text with respect to control attributes, coined *GMETCA*, has seen increasing progress over the past few years. Such a generative task is referred to as *style transfer*, when the control attributes indicate a change of writing styles (Mir et al., 2019; Fu et al., 2018). This generative task subsumes also gender obfuscation (Reddy and Knight, 2016), authorship obfuscation (Shetty et al., 2018), and text simplification (Xu et al., 2015), when the control attributes indicate protection of gender information, protection of authorship, and simplifying the content and structure of the text, respectively.

The research on *GMETCA* are impeded by the lack of standard evaluation practices (Mir et al., 2019; Tikhonov and Yamshchikov, 2018). Different evaluation methods make system comparison across publications difficult. In light of this, Mir et al. (2019); Fu et al. (2018) proposed both human evaluation and automated methods to judge style transfer models on three aspects: a) style transfer intensity; b) content preservation; c) naturalness. However, it is still difficult to reach an agreement on how to measure to what extent a generated text satisfy all three criterion. Moreover, the

lack of human generated gold references hinders the progress of related research, as they i) automate error analysis as in (Li et al., 2018); ii) avoid repeated efforts in user studies to check if system outputs reproduce human-like editing. Therefore, it is beneficial to collect gold references, human edited text, as test corpora for those emerging tasks.

The collection of gold references can be conducted on a crowd-sourcing platform, such as Amazon Mechanical Turk[1], or through existing writing tools (Goldfarb-Tarrant et al., 2019). However, the existing crowd-sourcing platforms and annotation tools do not have the flexibility to add task-specific classifiers and language models, which are widely used for evaluating *GMETCA* models (Mir et al., 2019). As pointed out by Dow et al. (2011), it is important to incorporate task-specific feedback to achieve the improvement of user engagement and quality of results. Feedback is particularly important for *GMETCA* according to our user study (details in Section 4.1), because annotators fail to capture the weak associations between certain textual patterns and attribute values. For example, for gender obfuscation on *'The dessert is yummy!'*, people can easily overlook the implicit indicator *'yummy'* of female authors.

To tackle the aforementioned challenges, we design *ALTER*, an **A**uxi**L**iary **TE**xt **R**ewriting tool, to collect gold references for *GMETCA*. Our tool contains multiple models to provide feedback on rewriting quality and also allows easy incorporation of more task-specific evaluation models. In addition, our tool has a module to record word-level revision histories with edit operations. The revisions are decomposed into a sequence of word-level edit operations, such as insertions (I), deletions (D), and replacements (R), as illus-

---

[1] https://www.mturk.com/

13

Proceedings of the 2019 EMNLP and the 9th IJCNLP (System Demonstrations), pages 13–18
Hong Kong, China, November 3 – 7, 2019. ©2019 Association for Computational Linguistics

Ori: My husband and I enjoy LA Hilton Hotel.
P_1: Family enjoy LA Hilton Hotel. (Rs)
P_2: Family enjoy Hilton Hotel in LA. (Ro)
P_3: All family members enjoy Hilton Hotel in LA. (I)
P_4: All family members love Hilton Hotel in LA. (Rv)

(a) Revision history 1 (RH1)

Ori: My husband and I enjoy LA Hilton Hotel.
P_1: My husband and I love LA Hilton Hotel. (Rv)
P_2: My husband and I love Hilton Hotel. (D)
P_3: My husband and I love Hilton Hotel in Los Angeles. (I)
P_4: My husband and I love Hilton Hotel in LA. (Ro)
P_5: Family love Hilton Hotel in LA. (Rs)
P_6: All family members love Hilton Hotel in LA. (I)

(b) Revision history 2 (RH2)

Table 1: Two revision histories, RH1 and RH2, from 'My husband and I enjoy LA Hilton Hotel.' to 'All family members love Hilton Hotel in LA.'. Although the overall transformations of RH1 and RH2 are similar, they follow different revision histories.

trated in Table 1. The benefits of revision histories are three-fold. Firstly, revision histories can provide supervision signals for the generative models, which consider rewriting as applying a sequence of edit operations on text (Li et al., 2018; Guu et al., 2018). Secondly, revision histories can potentially provide deep insights regarding cognitive process and human edit behaviours in varying demographic groups. For example, in Table 1, human writers could prefer replacing the subject (Rs) and the object (Ro) as RH1 than replacing the verb (Rv) as RH2. Statistics on revision histories could provide supporting evidence about related assumptions. Thirdly, there are often multiple gold references for the same text. It is more accessible using revision histories to acquire multiple references than rewriting every reference from scratch. As shown in Table 1, P3, P4 in RH1 and P1, P3, P4 and P6 in RH2 are all valid revisions of the original sentence.

To sum up, our contributions are:

- We implemented a tool *ALTER*, which is capable of providing instant task-specific feedback on rewriting quality for *GMETCA*.

- *ALTER* records revision histories with edit operations, which are useful for comparing and analyzing human edit behaviours.

The code of *ALTER* is publicly available under MIT license at `https://github.com/xuqiongkai/ALTER`. A screencast video demo of our system is provided at Google drive.

2 Related Work

Our work is related to the research on edit history of text and assistant text rewriting.

Document-level edit records were used as data to analyze the evolution of knowledge base (Ferschke et al., 2011; Medelyan et al., 2009) and retrieve sentence paraphrases (Max and Wisniewski, 2010). In contrast, our work focuses on word-level edit operations with order. We believe such paradigm introduces more linguistic features, that will benefit both linguistic and social behavior research. Recently, there has been a series of work on conducting edit operations on text to advance automatic natural language generation (Guu et al., 2018; Li et al., 2018). We believe the real-world human rewriting history collected by our system will strengthen these works.

A writing assistant has been proposed to facilitate users, organizing and revising their document. Zhang et al. (2016) proposed to detect the writers' purpose in the revised sentences. Goldfarb-Tarrant et al. (2019) developed a collaborative human-machine story-writing tool that assists writers with story-line planning and story-detail writing. The assistant and feedback generally improved the user engagement and the quality of generated text in those works.

3 ALTER

In this section, we describe the design of *ALTER*, an auxiliary text rewriting tool that is able to i) provide instant task-specific feedback to encourage user engagement, and ii) trace the word-level revision histories. We demonstrate an example of adapting our system on a *GMETCA* task, namely generating the gender-aware rewritten text, which is i) semantically relevant, ii) grammatically fluent, and iii) gender neutral.

3.1 System Overview

Figure 1 depicts the overall architecture of *ALTER*, which consists of a rewriting module, an administrative module, and multiple machine assistance services. The rewriting module offers annotators a user friendly interface for editing a given sentence with instant feedback. The feedback and revision histories in the interface are provided by the machine assistance services. Moreover, the administrative module provides administrators an interface for user management and assigning target

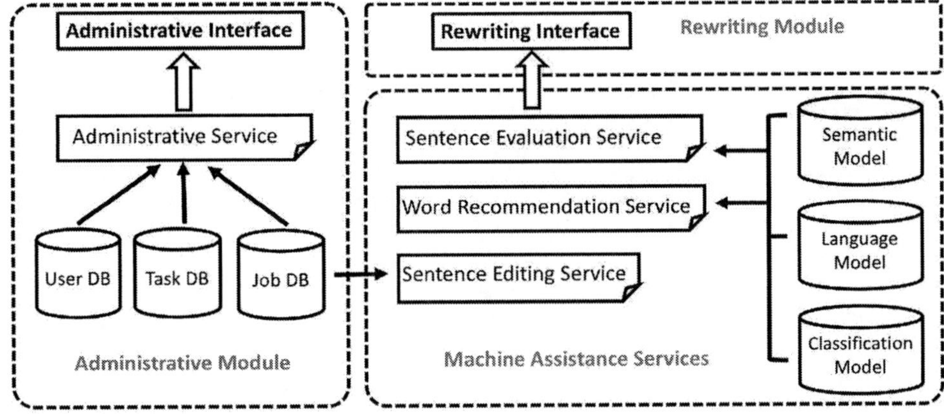

Figure 1: System architecture of the Auxiliary Text Rewriting Tool (ALTER).

tasks, which are basically a set of sentences for rewriting, as *jobs* to individual annotators.

ALTER is based on an easy-to-extend web-based framework that follows the Model-View-Controller (Krasner et al., 1988) software design pattern. The models are the wrappers of the databases (DB). The controller decides what should be displayed on the interfaces, which are considered as the views. This flexible design enables various feedback providers to be easily plugged in and out, making it possible to support different text generation tasks. The front-end is developed with React[2] that enables cross-platform support for major operating systems.

3.2 Rewriting Interface

Figure 2 illustrates a screenshot of the annotator interface. In the left column, there is a list of jobs, which are the sentences assigned to the annotator. The completed jobs are marked in blue. An annotator starts with selecting an incomplete job from the job list, which will be shown in the auxiliary edit panel in the right column. We support two edit modes:

- **Direct typing mode**: Annotators can directly type a whole sentence into the text input field. This mode is provided for the annotators who prefer typing to clicking. To save time, the original sentence is copied to the input field as default value.

- **Auxiliary mode**: Annotators can click on a word shown above the text input field, and choose one of the edit operations from a set,

$S = \{$*Word Typing, Deletion, Substitution, Reordering*$\}$. If the annotator chooses *Substitution*, he can select to show a list of words in the gray panel recommended by either word similarity or a pre-trained language model. In this mode, the annotator receives feedback from the upper right corner. Each feedback is a numerical score computed by a feedback provider based on the current sentence. After each edition, a record is added to the revision history below, with the corresponding edit operation and the modified sentences. The annotators are also allowed to roll back the sentences to a previous status by clicking the corresponding record in a history.

3.3 Machine Assistance Services

The machine assistance services in our system include feedback providers and word recommendation services. The machine assistance services can be categorized as sentence-level and word-level.

At the sentence-level, we provide automatic sentence evaluation scores as feedback. In our current system, we consider evaluation metrics widely used in style transfer and obfuscation of demographic attributes (Mir et al., 2019; Zhao et al., 2018; Fu et al., 2018).

- **PPL**. PPL denotes the perplexity score of the edited sentences based on the language model BERT[3] (Devlin et al., 2019).

- **WMD**. WMD is the word mover distance (Kusner et al., 2015) between the origi-

---

[2] https://reactjs.org

[3] https://github.com/google-research/bert

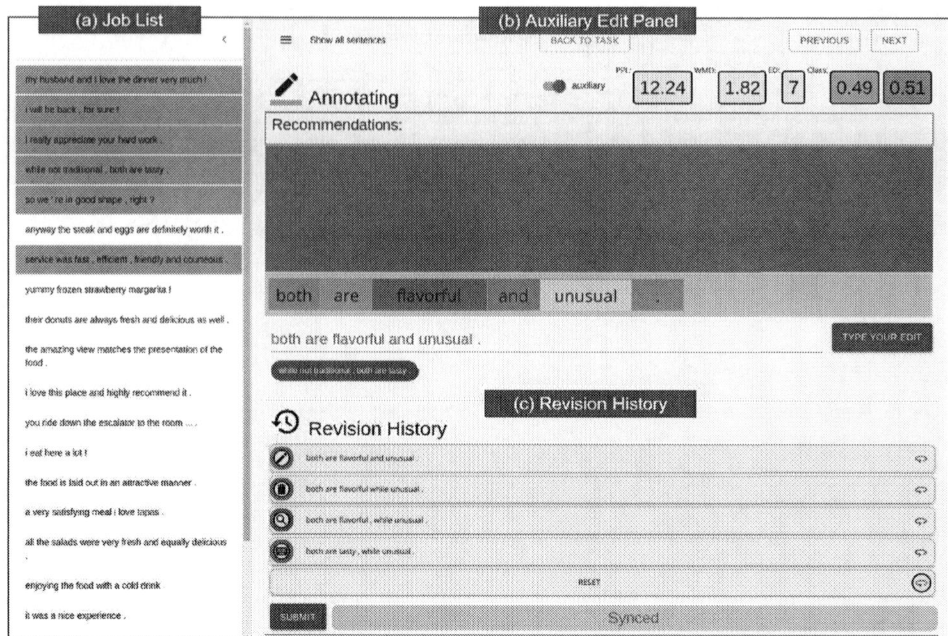

Figure 2: The Auxiliary Text Rewriting Interface is composed of (a) a job list, (b) an auxiliary edit panel and (c) a list of the revision history of current job.

nal sentence and the edited sentence based on Google's pre-trained Word2Vec model[4].

- **ED**. ED denotes the word edit distance between the original sentence and the rewritten sentence.

- **Class**. Class denotes the probability of the attribute value given the edited sentence. It is used to measure style transfer intensity or the degree of obfuscation. In our user study, we employ a transformer-based (Vaswani et al., 2017) binary classifier trained on the **Gender** (Reddy and Knight, 2016) corpus, which contains 2.6M balanced training samples.

At the word-level, we provide two word recommendation services for word substitution, which are based on word embedding similarity and language model, respectively. We include also a word-level feedback provider, which characterizes the contributions of individual words to the sentence-level classification results.

- **Word Similarity Recommendation**. Given a selected word, this service recommends a list of words ranked by the cosine similarity

computed based on pre-trained Google word embeddings.

- **Language Model Recommendation**. The services apply a pre-trained language model BERT to the context around the selected word to predict top-k most likely words.

- **Salience**. This module utilizes the sentence classifier trained on the Gender corpus to compute a salience score for each word. A salience score is defined as $S(X, i) = P(Y|X) - P(Y|X \setminus x_i)$, where $P(Y|X)$ denotes the probability of an attribute value Y given the input sentence X, and $X \setminus x_i$ denotes the sentence X excluding the ith word.

4 User Study

We conduct empirical studies to demonstrate i) annotators fail to capture certain textual patterns leading to worse estimation accuracy than the classifier; ii) *ALTER* improves user engagement; iii) machine assistance consistently collects more references per sentence than asking annotators directly typing edited sentences. Both studies are based on the *Gender* (Reddy and Knight, 2016) dataset, which consists of reviews from Yelp annotated with the gender of the authors. In the first

[4]https://code.google.com/archive/p/word2vec

study, we ask annotators to estimate the gender of authors given a sentence. In the second study, We consider a privacy-aware text rewriting task. We ask annotators to rewrite sentences that i) leak less gender information, ii) maximally preserve content; iii) are grammatically fluent.

4.1 Awareness of Gender Information

In the first study, we compare the accuracy of predicting gender information between two human annotators and the classifier[5]. Both of them predict the authors' gender of 300 sentences randomly sampled from the test set. Human annotators obtain merely 66.0 of accuracy on average, while the classifier achieves 77.3. We have carefully investigated the prediction results and the sampled sentences. We found out that it is indeed difficult for humans to estimate correctly the authors' gender based on a short piece of text, e.g.,"the food is delicious" and "the people were nice". Both examples are perceived as neutral for our annotators. Apart from human failure to capture weak associations between certain textual patterns and gender, we conjecture that the bias in the corpus may help the classifier achieve better performance.

4.2 User Engagement

In this study, three graduate students are invited to rewrite 100 sentences randomly selected from the test set of the Gender corpus. All students take two steps to rewrite each sentence:

1. In the *direct typing mode*, type the edited sentence directly in the input field .

2. In the *auxiliary mode*, improve the edited sentence from the first step when necessary. The annotators are instructed that i) it is fine to leave the sentences as they are if feedback do not provide useful clues; ii) all feedback and recommendations are machine generated, thus not perfect.

We consider the two-step approach to compare the differences between the two modes while minimizing individual differences between annotators.

We analyze the revision history collected in the second step, and found out that feedback indeed leads to significant improvement of user engagement. In the second step, 89.67% of the sentences

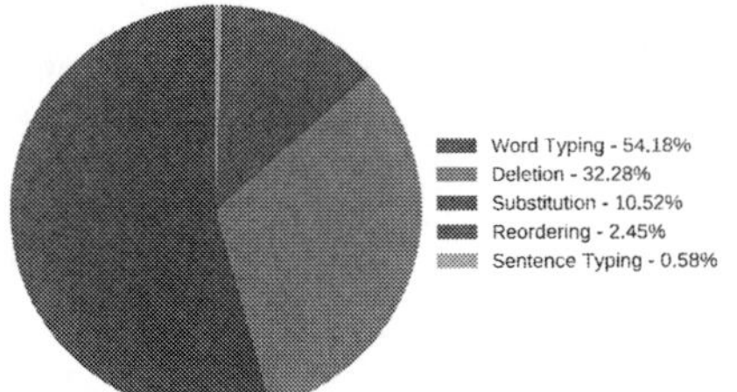

Figure 3: Distribution of operations in revision history by Word Typing, Deletion, Substitution, Reordering and Sentence Typing.

were modified in the auxiliary mode. The average number of edit operations in the second step is 4.63, showing the willingness of writers to further edit the text under auxiliary mode. The distribution of edit operations is illustrated in Figure 3, *word typing* and *deletion* are clearly the most popular edit operations. Word recommendation services are also effective, contributing more than 10% of the new edits in the auxiliary mode.

The references collected in the second step result in less leakage of gender information than the ones in the first step. We measure the leakage of gender information by applying the transformer-based classifier on references collected in both steps. We compute averaged *entropy* score, $-\sum_i p_i \log p_i$, based on the predication of each class p_i. Higher *entropy* indicates better obfuscation of gender. The sentences collected in the first step and the second step achieve 0.347 and 0.535 respectively. The entropy of the sentences collected in the first step is just 0.027 better than that of the original sentences.

We further investigate the revision histories, and find more gold references per sentence in the second step than in the first step. We consider semantically relevant and grammatically fluent sentences as valid references. The average number of the valid references generated in auxiliary mode is 3.79, while we can merely obtain one reference per sentence in the direct typing mode.

5 Conclusion and Future Work

In this paper, we demonstrate our auxiliary text rewriting tool *ALTER* to collect gold references for *GMETCA*, assisted with word-level revision histories and task-specific instant feedback. In the future, we will apply *ALTER* to collect high-quality benchmarks for *GMETCA*.

---

[5]We use a linear SVM model trained on **Gender**.

Acknowledgement

This project is supported by the partnership between ANU and Data61/CSIRO. We also gratefully acknowledge the funding from Data61 scholarship that supports Qiongkai Xu and Chenchen Xu's PhD research.

References

Jacob Devlin, Ming-Wei Chang, Kenton Lee, and Kristina Toutanova. 2019. Bert: Pre-training of deep bidirectional transformers for language understanding. In *Proceedings of the 2019 Conference of the North American Chapter of the Association for Computational Linguistics: Human Language Technologies, Volume 1 (Long and Short Papers)*, pages 4171–4186.

Steven Dow, Anand Kulkarni, Brie Bunge, Truc Nguyen, Scott Klemmer, and Björn Hartmann. 2011. Shepherding the crowd: managing and providing feedback to crowd workers. In *CHI'11 Extended Abstracts on Human Factors in Computing Systems*, pages 1669–1674. ACM.

Oliver Ferschke, Torsten Zesch, and Iryna Gurevych. 2011. Wikipedia revision toolkit: efficiently accessing wikipedia's edit history. In *Proceedings of the 49th Annual Meeting of the Association for Computational Linguistics: Human Language Technologies: Systems Demonstrations*, pages 97–102.

Zhenxin Fu, Xiaoye Tan, Nanyun Peng, Dongyan Zhao, and Rui Yan. 2018. Style transfer in text: Exploration and evaluation. In *Thirty-Second AAAI Conference on Artificial Intelligence*.

Seraphina Goldfarb-Tarrant, Haining Feng, and Nanyun Peng. 2019. Plan, write, and revise: an interactive system for open-domain story generation. In *Proceedings of the 2019 Conference of the North American Chapter of the Association for Computational Linguistics (Demonstrations)*, pages 89–97.

Kelvin Guu, Tatsunori B Hashimoto, Yonatan Oren, and Percy Liang. 2018. Generating sentences by editing prototypes. *Transactions of the Association of Computational Linguistics*, 6:437–450.

Glenn E Krasner, Stephen T Pope, et al. 1988. A description of the model-view-controller user interface paradigm in the smalltalk-80 system. *Journal of object oriented programming*, 1(3):26–49.

Matt Kusner, Yu Sun, Nicholas Kolkin, and Kilian Weinberger. 2015. From word embeddings to document distances. In *International Conference on Machine Learning*, pages 957–966.

Juncen Li, Robin Jia, He He, and Percy Liang. 2018. Delete, retrieve, generate: a simple approach to sentiment and style transfer. In *Proceedings of the 2018 Conference of the North American Chapter of the Association for Computational Linguistics: Human Language Technologies, Volume 1 (Long Papers)*, pages 1865–1874.

Aurélien Max and Guillaume Wisniewski. 2010. Mining naturally-occurring corrections and paraphrases from wikipedia's revision history. In *LREC*.

Olena Medelyan, David Milne, Catherine Legg, and Ian H Witten. 2009. Mining meaning from wikipedia. *International Journal of Human-Computer Studies*, 67(9):716–754.

Remi Mir, Bjarke Felbo, Nick Obradovich, and Iyad Rahwan. 2019. Evaluating style transfer for text. In *Proceedings of the 2019 Conference of the North American Chapter of the Association for Computational Linguistics: Human Language Technologies, Volume 1 (Long and Short Papers)*, pages 495–504.

Sravana Reddy and Kevin Knight. 2016. Obfuscating gender in social media writing. In *Proceedings of the First Workshop on NLP and Computational Social Science*, pages 17–26.

Rakshith Shetty, Bernt Schiele, and Mario Fritz. 2018. A4nt: Author attribute anonymity by adversarial training of neural machine translation. In *27th {USENIX} Security Symposium ({USENIX} Security 18)*, pages 1633–1650.

Alexey Tikhonov and Ivan P. Yamshchikov. 2018. What is wrong with style transfer for texts? *CoRR*, abs/1808.04365.

Ashish Vaswani, Noam Shazeer, Niki Parmar, Jakob Uszkoreit, Llion Jones, Aidan N Gomez, Łukasz Kaiser, and Illia Polosukhin. 2017. Attention is all you need. In *Advances in neural information processing systems*, pages 5998–6008.

Wei Xu, Chris Callison-Burch, and Courtney Napoles. 2015. Problems in current text simplification research: New data can help. *Transactions of the Association for Computational Linguistics*, 3:283–297.

Fan Zhang, Rebecca Hwa, Diane Litman, and Homa B Hashemi. 2016. Argrewrite: A web-based revision assistant for argumentative writings. In *Proceedings of the 2016 Conference of the North American Chapter of the Association for Computational Linguistics: Demonstrations*, pages 37–41.

Junbo Zhao, Yoon Kim, Kelly Zhang, Alexander Rush, and Yann LeCun. 2018. Adversarially regularized autoencoders. In *International Conference on Machine Learning*, pages 5897–5906.

Applying BERT to Document Retrieval with Birch

Zeynep Akkalyoncu Yilmaz, Shengjin Wang, Wei Yang, Haotian Zhang, and **Jimmy Lin**
David R. Cheriton School of Computer Science
University of Waterloo

Abstract

We present Birch, a system that applies BERT to document retrieval via integration with the open-source Anserini information retrieval toolkit to demonstrate end-to-end search over large document collections. Birch implements simple ranking models that achieve state-of-the-art effectiveness on standard TREC newswire and social media test collections. This demonstration focuses on technical challenges in the integration of NLP and IR capabilities, along with the design rationale behind our approach to tightly-coupled integration between Python (to support neural networks) and the Java Virtual Machine (to support document retrieval using the open-source Lucene search library). We demonstrate integration of Birch with an existing search interface as well as interactive notebooks that highlight its capabilities in an easy-to-understand manner.

1 Introduction

The information retrieval community, much like the natural language processing community, has witnessed the growing dominance of approaches based on neural networks. Applications of neural networks to document ranking usually involve multi-stage architectures, beginning with a traditional term-matching technique (e.g., BM25) over a standard inverted index, followed by a reranker that rescores the candidate list of documents (Asadi and Lin, 2013).

Researchers have developed a panoply of neural ranking models—see Mitra and Craswell (2019) for a recent overview—but there is emerging evidence that BERT (Devlin et al., 2019) outperforms previous approaches to document retrieval (Yang et al., 2019c; MacAvaney et al., 2019) as well as search-related tasks such as question answering (Nogueira and Cho, 2019; Yang et al., 2019b).

We share with the community Birch,[1] which integrates the Anserini information retrieval toolkit[2] with a BERT-based document ranking model that provides an end-to-end open-source search engine. Birch allows the community to replicate the state-of-the-art document ranking results presented in Yilmaz et al. (2019) and Yang et al. (2019c). Here we summarize those results, but our focus is on system architecture and the rationale behind a number of implementation design decisions, as opposed to the ranking model itself.

2 Integration Challenges

The problem we are trying to solve, and the focus of this work, is how to bridge the worlds of information retrieval and natural language processing from a software engineering perspective, for applications to document retrieval. Following the standard formulation, we assume a (potentially large) corpus D that users wish to search. For a keyword query Q, the system's task is to return a ranked list of documents that maximizes a retrieval metric such as average precision (AP). This stands in contrast to reading comprehension tasks such as SQuAD (Rajpurkar et al., 2016) and many formulations of question answering today such as WikiQA (Yang et al., 2015) and the MS MARCO QA Task (Bajaj et al., 2018), where there is no (or minimal) retrieval component. These are better characterized as "selection" tasks on (pre-determined) text passages.

Within the information retrieval community, there exists a disconnect between academic researchers and industry practitioners. Outside of a few large organizations that deploy custom infrastructure (mostly commercial search engine companies), Lucene (along with the closely-related

---

[1] http://birchir.io/
[2] http://anserini.io/

19

Proceedings of the 2019 EMNLP and the 9th IJCNLP (System Demonstrations), pages 19–24
Hong Kong, China, November 3 – 7, 2019. ©2019 Association for Computational Linguistics

projects Solr and Elasticsearch) has become the de facto platform for building real-world search applications, deployed at Twitter, Netflix, eBay, and numerous other organizations. However, many researchers still rely on academic systems such as Indri[3] and Terrier,[4] which are mostly unknown in real-world production environments. This gap hinders technology transfer and the potential impact of research results.

Even assuming Lucene as a "common denominator" that academic researchers learn to adopt, there is still one technical hurdle: Lucene is implemented in Java, and hence runs on the Java Virtual Machine (JVM). However, most deep learning toolkits today, including TensorFlow and PyTorch, are written in Python with a C++ backend. Bridging Python and the JVM presents a technical challenge for NLP/IR integration.

3 Birch

3.1 Anserini

Anserini (Yang et al., 2017, 2018) represents an attempt to better align academic researchers with industry practitioners by building a research-focused toolkit on top of the open-source Lucene search library. Further standardizing on a common platform within the academic community can foster greater replicability and reproducibility, a growing concern in the community (Lin et al., 2016).

Already, Anserini has proven to be effective and has gained some traction: For example, Nogueira and Cho (2019) used Anserini for generating candidate documents before applying BERT to ranking passages in the TREC Complex Answer Retrieval (CAR) task (Dietz et al., 2017), which led to a large increase in effectiveness. Yang et al. (2019b) also combined Anserini and BERT to demonstrate large improvements in open-domain question answering directly on Wikipedia.

3.2 Design Decisions

The architecture of Birch is shown in Figure 1, which codifies a two-stage pipeline architecture where Anserini is responsible for retrieval, the output of which is passed to a BERT-based reranker. Since our research group has standardized on PyTorch, the central challenge we tackle is: How do we integrate the deep learning toolkit with Anserini?

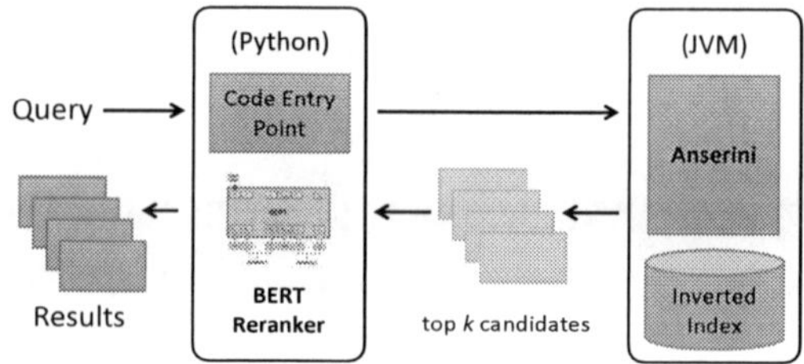

Figure 1: Architecture of Birch, illustrating a tight integration between Python and the Java Virtual Machine. The main code entry point is in Python, which calls Anserini for retrieval; candidate documents from Anserini are then reranked by our BERT models.

At the outset, we ruled out "loosely-coupled" integration approaches: For example, passing intermediate text files is not a sustainable solution in the long term. It is not only inefficient, but interchange formats frequently change (whether intentionally or accidentally), breaking code between multiple components. We also ruled out integration via REST APIs for similar reasons: efficiency (overhead of HTTP calls) and stability (imperfect solutions for enforcing API contracts, particularly in a research environment).

There are a few options for the "tightly-coupled" integration we desired. In principle, we could adopt the Java Virtual Machine (JVM) as the primary code entry point, with integration to the Torch backend via JNI, but this was ruled out because it would create two separate code paths (JVM to C++ for execution and Python to C++ for model development), which presents maintainability issues. After some exploration, we decided on Python as the primary development environment, integrating Anserini using the Pyjnius Python library[5] for accessing Java classes. The library was originally developed to facilitate Android development in Python, and allows Python code to directly manipulate Java classes and objects. Thus, Birch supports Python as the main development language (and code entry point, as shown in Figure 1), connecting to the backend JVM to access retrieval capabilities.

3.3 Models

Our document ranking approach is detailed in Yilmaz et al. (2019) and Yang et al. (2019c). We follow Nogueira and Cho (2019) in adapting BERT for binary (specifically, relevance) classification over text. Candidate documents from Anserini

---

[3] https://www.lemurproject.org/
[4] http://terrier.org/

[5] https://pyjnius.readthedocs.io/

Model	2011		2012		2013		2014	
	AP	P@30	AP	P@30	AP	P@30	AP	P@30
QL	0.3576	0.4000	0.2091	0.3311	0.2532	0.4450	0.3924	0.6182
RM3	0.3824	0.4211	0.2342	0.3452	0.2766	0.4733	0.4480	0.6339
MP-HCNN (Rao et al., 2019)	0.4043	0.4293	0.2460	0.3791	0.2896	0.5294	0.4420	0.6394
BiCNN (Shi et al., 2018)	0.4293	0.4728	0.2621	0.4147	0.2990	0.5367	0.4563	0.6806
Birch	**0.4697**	**0.5040**	**0.3073**	**0.4356**	**0.3357**	**0.5656**	**0.5176**	**0.7006**

Table 1: Results on test collections from the TREC Microblog Tracks, comparing BERT with selected neural ranking models. The first two blocks of the table contain results copied from Rao et al. (2019).

are processed individually. As model input, we concatenate the query Q and document D into a text sequence [[CLS], Q, [SEP], D, [SEP]], and then pad each text sequence in a mini-batch to N tokens, where N is the maximum length in the batch. The [CLS] vector is then taken as input to a single layer neural network. Starting from a pre-trained BERT model, we fine-tune with existing relevance judgments using cross-entropy loss. BERT inference scores are then combined with the original retrieval scores, in the simplest case, using linear interpolation.

In this simple approach, long documents pose a problem since BERT wasn't specifically designed to perform inference on long input texts. We present a simple solution: inference is applied over each sentence in a candidate document and sentence-level evidence is aggregated for ranking documents as follows:

$$S_f = a \cdot S_{doc} + (1 - a) \cdot \sum_{i=1}^{n} w_i \cdot S_i \qquad (1)$$

where S_{doc} is the original document score and S_i is the i-th top-scoring sentence according to BERT; a and w_i's are parameters that need to be learned. In practice, we only consider up to the three top-scoring sentences in each document.

The intuition behind this approach comes from Zhang et al. (2018b,a), who found that the "best" sentence or paragraph in a document provides a good proxy for document relevance. From a different perspective, we are essentially implementing a form of passage retrieval.

4 Retrieval Results

4.1 TREC 2011–2014 Microblog Tracks

As originally reported in Yang et al. (2019c), Birch was evaluated on tweet test collections from the TREC Microblog Tracks, 2011 to 2014 (Lin et al.,

2014). Since tweets are short, relevance judgments can be directly used to fine-tune the BERT model (Section 3.3). For evaluation on each year's dataset, we used the remaining years for fine-tuning, e.g., tuning on 2011–2013 data, testing on 2014 data. Additional details on the fine-tuning strategy and experimental settings are described in Yang et al. (2019c).

At retrieval (inference) time, query likelihood (QL) with RM3 relevance feedback (Nasreen et al., 2004) was used to provide the initial pool of candidates (to depth 1000). Since tweets are short, we can apply inference over each candidate document in its entirety. The interpolation weight between the BERT scores and the retrieval scores was tuned on the validation data.

Experimental results are shown in Table 1, where we present average precision (AP) and precision at rank 30 (P@30), the two official metrics of the evaluation (Ounis et al., 2011). The first two blocks of the table are copied from Rao et al. (2019), who compared bag-of-words baselines (QL and RM3) to several popular neural ranking models as well as MP-HCNN, the model they introduced. The results of Rao et al. (2019) were further improved in Shi et al. (2018); in all cases, the neural models include interpolation with the original document scores. We see that Birch yields a large jump in effectiveness across all Microblog collections.

4.2 TREC 2004 Robust Track

In addition to searching short social media posts, we also examined a "traditional" document retrieval task over newswire articles. For this, we used the test collection from the TREC 2004 Robust Track (Voorhees, 2004), which comprises 250 topics over a newswire corpus of around 500K documents. Here, we provide a summary of Yilmaz et al. (2019), which contains more detailed

Model	AP	P@20	NDCG@20
BM25+RM3	0.2903	0.3821	0.4407
1S: BERT	0.3676	0.4610	0.5239
2S: BERT	**0.3697**	0.4657	0.5324
3S: BERT	0.3691	**0.4669**	**0.5325**

Table 2: Results on Robust04, where nS denotes combining scores from the top n sentences in a document.

descriptions of our approach and presents experiments on more test collections.

The additional challenge with ranking newswire articles is the lack of training data to fine-tune the BERT models, since relevance judgments are provided at the document level. That is, in the standard formulation of document ranking, a document is considered relevant if *any* part of it is relevant—but documents are typically longer than the lengths of text BERT was designed to handle. The surprising finding of Yilmaz et al. (2019) is that BERT models fine-tuned with the Microblog test collections in Section 4.1 can be *directly* applied to rank newswire documents, despite the differences in domain (social media posts vs. news articles). Furthermore, it appears that out-of-domain passage-level relevance judgments *fortuitously* available, such as the MS MARCO passage dataset (Bajaj et al., 2018) and the TREC CAR dataset (Dietz et al., 2017), are also beneficial.

Thus, it appears that BERT is able to learn *cross-domain*, *sentence-level* notions of relevance that can be exploited for ranking newswire documents. Table 2 presents an extract of results from Yilmaz et al. (2019) for Robust04, where we find that the best results are achieved by first fine-tuning on MS MARCO and then on the Microblog data. Scores from BERT are then combined with document scores (BM25+RM3) based on Eq (1). The notation "1S", "2S", and "3S" refer to aggregating scores from the top one, two, and three sentences, respectively. Including more sentences doesn't help and ranking is already quite good if we just consider the top-scoring sentence. This result, surprisingly, suggests that document ranking can be distilled into relevance prediction primarily at the sentence level. Based on the meta-analysis by Yang et al. (2019a), this is not only the highest known AP reported on the Robust04 dataset for neural models, but also exceeds the previous best known AP score of 0.3686, which is a non-neural method based on ensembles.

5 Demonstration

We demonstrate the integration of Birch with the search frontend from HiCAL (Abualsaud et al., 2018b) and interactive Google Colab notebooks.

5.1 HiCAL

The goal of the HiCAL system[6] is to help human assessors efficiently find as many relevant documents as possible in a large document collection to achieve high recall on a search task. The system comprises two main components: a Continuous Active Learning (CAL) model (Cormack and Grossman, 2014) and a search model. In the CAL model, a machine-learned classifier selects the most likely relevant document or paragraph for the assessor to judge; judgments are then fed back to retrain the classifier. In the current HiCAL implementation, Anserini provides the backend search capabilities.

For the TREC Common Core Tracks in 2017 and 2018, a small group of researchers used HiCAL to find and judge relevant documents. The runs generated based on their assessments achieved the highest AP scores among all the submitted runs for two consecutive years (Zhang et al., 2017; Abualsaud et al., 2018a). The effectiveness of the system was further demonstrated in Zhang et al. (2018a).

We further augment the Anserini backend for HiCAL with Birch in two ways: First, HiCAL can directly take advantage of improved rankings provided by BERT. Second, the top-scoring sentences can be highlighted in the document to aid in assessment. A sample screenshot is shown in Figure 2. For query 336 "black bear attacks" from Robust04, we show part of the highest-scoring document `LA081689-0039` with one of the top three sentences (according to BERT) highlighted.

5.2 Interactive Colab Notebooks

We present Google Colab[7] notebooks that make it possible for anyone to reproduce our end-to-end document retrieval pipeline in an interactive manner.[8] We make all our data and pre-trained models available, although users may also opt to rebuild them from scratch; the Colab GPU backend enables fine-tuning BERT models directly in the notebook environment.

[6]`https://github.com/hical`
[7]`https://colab.research.google.com/`
[8]To ensure long-term availability, sample notebooks are linked from the main Birch repository.

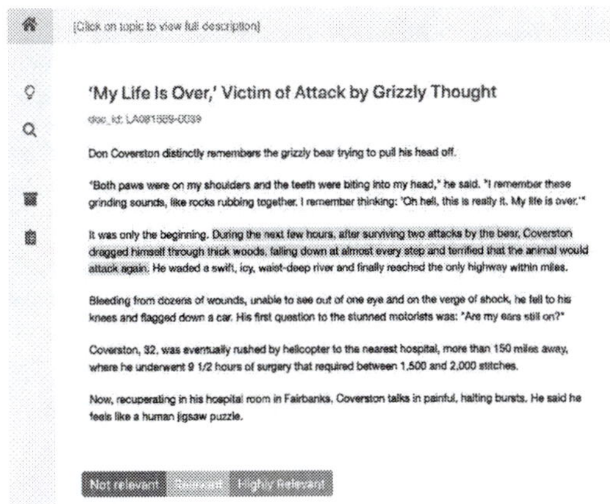

Figure 2: Screenshot of HiCAL using Birch to identify the most relevant sentences in a document retrieved for the query "black bear attacks".

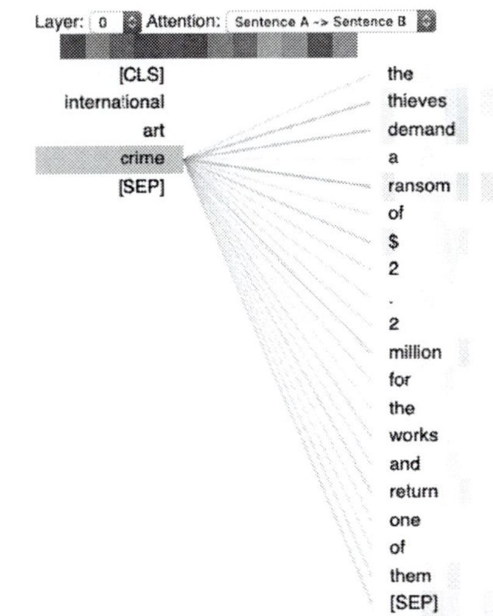

Figure 3: Screenshot of attention visualization for a sentence with a high BERT score from a document retrieved for the query "international art crime". Note the lack of exact matches with query terms.

Our notebooks are set up to allow relevance scores to be computed for an entire test collection in batch, and also to support interactive querying. When the user issues a query through the interactive notebook, candidate documents from the corpus are first retrieved using Anserini. A sentence-level dataset is created on the fly from the initial ranking by splitting each document into its constituent sentences. Each sentence is fed into our BERT model to obtain a relevance score. These relevance scores are then aggregated with document scores to rerank the candidate documents, per Eq (1). The notebook setting allows a user to step through each part of the process and examine intermediate results to gain a better understanding of our approach.

In addition, we have implemented two methods to visualize the relevant documents for a given query from a test collection, hopefully conveying even more insights. First, we generate a table that displays the document scores juxtaposed with the BERT scores of constituent sentences. Sentences with low document scores but high BERT scores (and vice versa) are highlighted, allowing the user to examine the relative contributions of exact term matching and semantic matching, as contributed by BERT. Second, we incorporate `bertviz`,[9] an open-source tool for visualizing attention in transformer models, to explore the interaction between multiple attention heads. In Figure 3, we show a sentence with a high BERT score in a document retrieved for query 322 "international art crime" from Robust04. Note that this sentence does *not*

contain any of the query terms, but yet appears to be relevant. If we examine the attention visualization for the query term "crime", we see that the model attends to obviously-related terms like "thieves", "demand", and "ransom", illustrating the semantic knowledge that is captured in the BERT model.

6   Conclusions

This paper describes the system architecture and motivation behind a straightforward application of BERT to document ranking, via sentence-level inference and simple score aggregation. With the implementation of this system, we have also overcome the technical challenge of integrating a Lucene-based backend on the JVM with PyTorch to enable development in an environment NLP researchers and practitioners are already familiar with. The fruits of our labor are released in an open-source system for the community to continue explorations in search-related tasks with BERT.

Acknowledgments

This research was supported by the Natural Sciences and Engineering Research Council (NSERC) of Canada, and enabled by computational resources provided by Compute Ontario and Compute Canada.

---

[9]https://github.com/jessevig/bertviz

23

References

M. Abualsaud, G. Cormack, N. Ghelani, A. Ghenai, M. Grossman, S. Rahbariasl, M. Smucker, and H. Zhang. 2018a. UWaterlooMDS at the TREC 2018 Common Core Track. In *TREC*.

M. Abualsaud, N. Ghelani, H. Zhang, M. Smucker, G. Cormack, and M. Grossman. 2018b. A system for efficient high-recall retrieval. In *SIGIR*, pages 1317–1320.

N. Asadi and J. Lin. 2013. Effectiveness/efficiency tradeoffs for candidate generation in multi-stage retrieval architectures. In *SIGIR*, pages 997–1000.

P. Bajaj, D. Campos, N. Craswell, L. Deng, J. Gao, X. Liu, R. Majumder, A. McNamara, B. Mitra, T. Nguyen, M. Rosenberg, X. Song, A. Stoica, S. Tiwary, and T. Wang. 2018. MS MARCO: A human generated MAchine Reading COmprehension dataset. *arXiv:1611.09268v3*.

G. Cormack and M. Grossman. 2014. Evaluation of machine-learning protocols for technology-assisted review in electronic discovery. In *SIGIR*, pages 153–162.

J. Devlin, M. Chang, K. Lee, and K. Toutanova. 2019. BERT: Pre-training of deep bidirectional transformers for language understanding. In *NAACL*, pages 4171–4186.

L. Dietz, M. Verma, F. Radlinski, and N. Craswell. 2017. TREC Complex Answer Retrieval overview. In *TREC*.

J. Lin, M. Crane, A. Trotman, J. Callan, I. Chattopadhyaya, J. Foley, G. Ingersoll, C. Macdonald, and S. Vigna. 2016. Toward reproducible baselines: The open-source IR reproducibility challenge. In *ECIR 2016*, pages 408–420.

J. Lin, M. Efron, Y. Wang, and G. Sherman. 2014. Overview of the TREC-2014 Microblog Track. In *TREC*.

S. MacAvaney, A. Yates, A. Cohan, and N. Goharian. 2019. CEDR: Contextualized embeddings for document ranking. In *SIGIR*, pages 1101–1104.

B. Mitra and N. Craswell. 2019. An introduction to neural information retrieval. *Foundations and Trends in Information Retrieval*, 13(1):1–126.

A. Nasreen, J. Allan, W. B. Croft, F. Diaz, L. Larkey, X. Li, D. Metzler, M. Smucker, T. Strohman, H. Turtle, and C. Wade. 2004. UMass at TREC 2004: Novelty and HARD. In *TREC*.

R. Nogueira and K. Cho. 2019. Passage re-ranking with BERT. *arXiv:1901.04085*.

I. Ounis, C. Macdonald, J. Lin, and I. Soboroff. 2011. Overview of the TREC-2011 Microblog Track. In *TREC 2011*.

P. Rajpurkar, J. Zhang, K. Lopyrev, and P. Liang. 2016. SQuAD: 100,000+ questions for machine comprehension of text. In *EMNLP 2016*, pages 2383–2392.

J. Rao, W. Yang, Y. Zhang, F. Ture, and J. Lin. 2019. Multi-perspective relevance matching with hierarchical ConvNets for social media search. *AAAI*, pages 232–240.

P. Shi, J. Rao, and J. Lin. 2018. Simple attention-based representation learning for ranking short social media posts. In *NAACL*, pages 2212–2217.

E. Voorhees. 2004. Overview of the TREC 2004 Robust Track. In *TREC 2004*, pages 52–69.

P. Yang, H. Fang, and J. Lin. 2017. Anserini: Enabling the use of Lucene for information retrieval research. In *SIGIR 2017*, pages 1253–1256.

P. Yang, H. Fang, and J. Lin. 2018. Anserini: Reproducible ranking baselines using Lucene. *Journal of Data and Information Quality*, 10(4):Article 16.

W. Yang, K. Lu, P. Yang, and J. Lin. 2019a. Critically examining the "neural hype": weak baselines and the additivity of effectiveness gains from neural ranking models. In *SIGIR*, pages 1129–1132.

W. Yang, Y. Xie, A. Lin, X. Li, L. Tan, K. Xiong, M. Li, and J. Lin. 2019b. End-to-end open-domain question answering with BERTserini. In *NAACL Demo*, pages 72–77.

W. Yang, H. Zhang, and J. Lin. 2019c. Simple applications of BERT for ad hoc document retrieval. *arXiv:1903.10972*.

Y. Yang, W. Yih, and C. Meek. 2015. WikiQA: A challenge dataset for open-domain question answering. In *EMNLP*, pages 2013–2018.

Z. Akkalyoncu Yilmaz, W. Yang, H. Zhang, and J. Lin. 2019. Cross-domain modeling of sentence-level evidence for document retrieval. In *EMNLP*.

H. Zhang, M. Abualsaud, N. Ghelani, A. Ghosh, M. Smucker, G. Cormack, and M. Grossman. 2017. UWaterlooMDS at the TREC 2017 Common Core Track. In *TREC*.

H. Zhang, M. Abualsaud, N. Ghelani, M. Smucker, G. Cormack, and M. Grossman. 2018a. Effective user interaction for high-recall retrieval: less is more. In *CIKM*, pages 187–196.

H. Zhang, G. Cormack, M. Grossman, and M. Smucker. 2018b. Evaluating sentence-level relevance feedback for high-recall information retrieval. *arXiv:1803.08988*.

Automatic Taxonomy Induction and Expansion

Nicolas Rodolfo Fauceglia, Alfio Gliozzo, Sarthak Dash,
Md Faisal Mahbub Chowdhury and **Nandana Mihindukulasooriya**
IBM Research AI, Yorktown Heights, NY, USA
{nicolas.fauceglia, nandana.m} @ibm.com
{gliozzo, sdash, mchowdh} @us.ibm.com

Abstract

The Knowledge Graph Induction Service (KGIS) is an end-to-end knowledge induction system. One of its main capabilities is to automatically induce taxonomies[1] from input documents using a hybrid approach that takes advantage of linguistic patterns, semantic web and neural networks. KGIS allows the user to semi-automatically curate and expand the induced taxonomy through a component called smart spreadsheet by exploiting distributional semantics. In this paper, we describe these taxonomy induction and expansion features of KGIS. A screencast video demonstrating the system is available in https://ibm.box.com/v/emnlp-2019-demo .

1 Introduction

Knowledge Graph Induction Service (KGIS) is an end-to-end knowledge graph (KG) induction system. Among other capabilities, it enables *automatic* taxonomy induction and *human-in-the-loop* curation. The output taxonomy representation can be used by downstream applications such as dialog systems and search engines.

The taxonomy is induced directly from the input documents by a combination of different approaches: one based on linguistic-patterns, another that leverages the semantic-web, and finally a novel neural network for cleaning and expanding taxonomies. The induced taxonomies are accessible through another component of the KGIS called Smart Spreadsheet (SSS), which consists of an editable interactive tabular grid where the first row contains induced *types* (aka hypernyms), and each corresponding column contains its *instances* (aka hyponyms), henceforth, simply *types* and *instances*.

Using the SSS, the user can refine the automatically induced taxonomy, both by removing wrong *types* or *instances*, and by further expanding the *instances* of a particular *type*. This is accomplished by leveraging its main features: *auto-complete* [2], *type-suggestion*, and automatic population from *semantic web* and *distant supervision* using external Knowledge Graphs (KG). KGIS also allows taxonomies to be exported in RDF/OWL representation with the terms linked to Wikidata[3] entities (Vrandečić, 2012).

We describe the use case in question in Section 2, followed by the system description for taxonomy induction component in Section 3. Then, in Section 4, we illustrate how the features of the SSS can be used for taxonomy curation and expansion. Finally, in Section 5 we conclude by discussing example outputs of the system.

2 Use Case Scenario

A typical KGIS user has a collection of documents that contain knowledge about a specific domain. The size of the collection makes human analysis or annotation impractical (slow and expensive). Therefore, the user ingests its collection into the KGIS, and fires a *KG Induction* job. Depending on the size of the collection, in minutes or a few hours the system provides the following artifacts: an annotated corpus, a terminology, a type embedding model, and different types of taxonomies that can be further refined.

---

[1]A *taxonomy* is a classification of things or concepts.

[2]The option of completing terms by selecting from a suggested list of terms on the basis of the letters that has been already typed by the user.

[3]https://www.wikidata.org

Proceedings of the 2019 EMNLP and the 9th IJCNLP (System Demonstrations), pages 25–30
Hong Kong, China, November 3 – 7, 2019. ©2019 Association for Computational Linguistics

corpus name	comments	status	modified	created	
NeurIPS papers (1987 to 2017)	from WDS	KG induced	01/07/2019 - 18:12hs	01/07/2019 - 15:12hs	
it support (4k) and wikipedia (4.5K)	from WDS	KG induced	02/07/2019 - 16:19hs	02/07/2019 - 15:08hs	
medical corpus	from WDS	KG induced	22/07/2019 - 14:07hs	22/07/2019 - 14:01hs	

Figure 1: KGIS home

3 System Description

3.1 Input processing and annotation

The input of the system is a collection of documents. The corpus creation process transforms different formats of inputs (txt, json, pdf, word, etc) into a standard document format. This is done through the *Document Conversion Service API* in IBM Cloud[TM] [4].

After corpus creation, the system annotates terms (analyzing all noun phrases). This is done through the usage of *IBM Watson® NLU API*[5]. Next, all terms that have a frequency greater than a threshold (specified by the user during *KG Induction*, see figure 3) are combined to form the terminology.

3.2 Type Models

As part of the pipeline, the system builds a *type* model, which captures *type* similarity between two given domain terms (e.g. *SVM* and *Logistic Regression* are both of type *supervised learning algorithm*). To do so, the system trains a Word2Vec model (Mikolov et al. (2013)) using Gensim[6] with a CBOW configuration of window size 2. The reason for this choice is that *type* similarity is captured by analyzing the local context around the terms. In addition, other input parameters for this model (e.g., embedding dimensions, min-frequency, learning rate, etc.), can be provided by the user while firing the *KG Induction*.

3.3 Taxonomy Induction

The Taxonomy Induction module takes the annotated corpus (see Section 3.1) and identifies *is-a* relations between pairs of terms. KGIS uses three different approaches for inducing shallow (*i.e.*, not hierarchical) taxonomies, as described in the following sections. The results of each approach are presented as an SSS where the users can manually validate the generated taxonomies and further curate them (see Section 4.

3.3.1 Pattern-Based Approach

For extracting *type-instance* relationships, i.e. *is-a* pairs, the system makes use of 24 lexico-syntactic patterns (e.g., "NP_y is a NP_x"), aka Hearst-like patterns (Hearst (1992)). Once the *is-a* pairs are extracted, the system applies the following pre-processing steps. First, the list of *is-a* pairs are represented as a graph by considering each pair as an *edge*, and the corresponding terms as nodes. The weight of each edge is the count of how often a pair has been extracted by pattern-matching.

The system excludes any cycle inside the graph; e.g. if *(x, y)*, *(y, z)* and *(z, x)* are present in the list of extracted *is-a* pairs, then all of them are discarded. KGIS also discards all edges that have a value lower than a frequency threshold f, which is specified by the user. KGIS checks all *types* and tries to identify potential proper nouns among them, using the following heuristic – a term x_1 would be considered as a proper noun if all the following three conditions hold: *(i)* it is not a substring of a *type* x_2 and vice-versa, *(ii)* x_2 is a *type* of x_1, and *(iii)* x_2 belongs to a list of *types*[7] that are known to have massive amount of proper noun *instances*. If a *type* is identified as a proper noun, KGIS discards all edges that link the term as *type* with any other term.

The next step of the pre-processing is to expand the list of pairs in the graph with likely (but not yet extracted) pairs of nested term *types* and super

---

[4]`https://cloud.ibm.com/docs/cli`
[5]`https://cloud.ibm.com/apidocs/`
`natural-language-understanding`
[6]`https://radimrehurek.com/gensim/`

[7]To be specific, "person", "place", "organization", and "name".

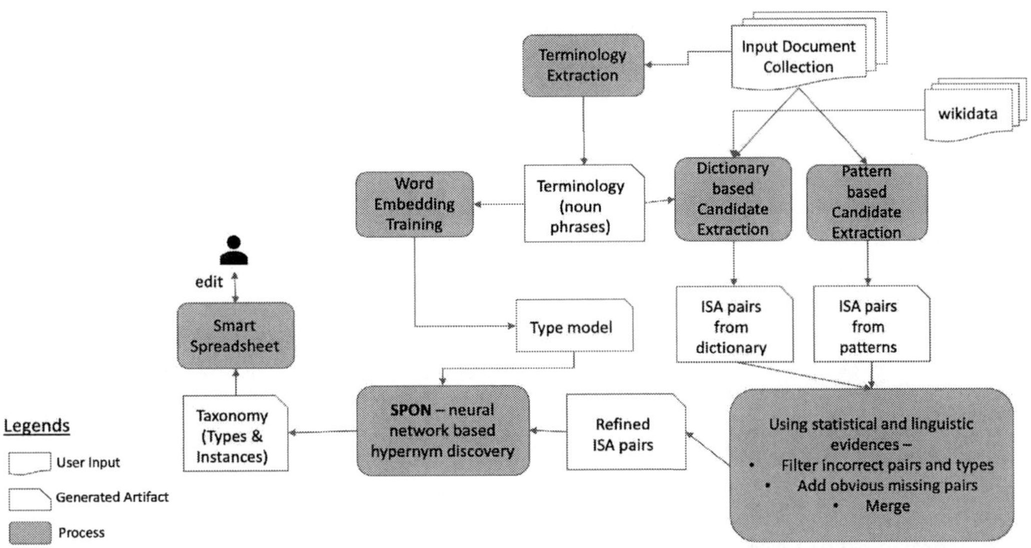

Figure 2: Taxonomy induction and expansion/curation workflow.

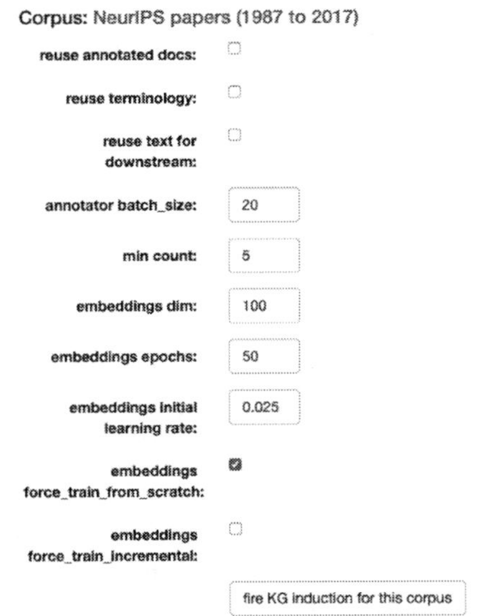

Figure 3: KG induction

term *instances*. A nested term is a term that is part of a larger term (called super term).[8] Often there are *types* that are nested terms in one or many of their *instances*. For example, the *type* "bank" is a nested term in *instances* "Capital One Bank™", "Chase Bank™" and "Bank of America™".

KGIS builds a nested term search index (Chowdhury and Farrell, 2019) using the list of remaining *is-a* pairs. For every single word $type^9$, the system identifies corresponding super terms from the index which are not already identified by the Hearst-like patterns as potential *instances*. If the *type* is the syntactic head word of one of these super terms, then KGIS adds that super term as a *type* in the list of *is-a* pairs.

The final list of pairs after all these steps is the output of the Pattern-Based approach.

3.3.2 Semantic Web Based Approach

Wikidata is a comprehensive cross-domain source of knowledge semantically represented using RDF and OWL. It contains a large amount of taxonomic information with relations such as *rdf:type* or *rdfs:subClassOf*. The semantic web based approach for candidate generation in KGIS consists on linking the terms identified in terminology extraction to Wikidata entities and discovering *is-a* relations between them using the background knowledge. Linking is done by approximate matching of the surface from of the term with the label and the aliases of the Wikidata candidate entity.

Once the initial list of *is-a* pairs is extracted, further filtering is performed to eliminate terms that might be erroneously linked. This is done by comparing the *type-instance* similarity and pairwise

---

[8]For example, the terms "IBM" and "Corporation" are nested terms in their super term "IBM Corporation".

[9]We avoid multi-word *types* as we found that exploitation of them results in significant amount of erroneous *is-a* pairs.

instance-instance similarity (using the Type model mentioned in Section 3.2) against a threshold that is provided as a parameter.

3.3.3 Neural Network Based Approach

Is-a relations are reflexive and transitive but not symmetric (Miller et al., 1990; Hearst, 1992). Using ideas from *order theory*, we can model these relations as *strict partial order* relations, i.e. a binary relation that is transitive, asymmetric and irreflexive.

We developed STRICT PARTIAL ORDER NETWORKS (SPON), a novel neural network architecture comprising of *non-negative* activations and *residual* connections designed to enforce strict partial order as a soft constraint. We use SPON as a component within the KGIS platform to model *is-a* relationships among pairs that have been generated from the approaches described in the previous Sections 3.3.1 and 3.3.2.

SPON works in three stages. In the first stage, it models the *is-a* relationships extracted in the previous steps and aims to provide a score to each individual *is-a* pair. In the second stage, it uses the same learned model in order to generate a *top-k* ranked list of *types* for every term present in the *terminology*. Finally, it ranks the accumulated *is-a* relationships generated in the previous steps according to certain *user-specified* criterion, and presents it back to the user.

Stage One. The purpose of this step is to score existing *is-a* relationships $\mathcal{T}$. This stage assumes that a true *is-a* relationship t is more likely to be inferred correctly, as opposed to a false relationship f when evaluated against a SPON model that has been trained using other *is-a* relationships i.e. $\mathcal{T} \setminus \{t, f\}$.

Following the assumption, the list of existing *is-a* relationships obtained via either Pattern based approaches or Semantic Web based approaches, are divided into *k-folds*. k independent SPON processes are then run in parallel, each process then trains upon k-2 folds, performs early stopping based on evaluations on the $(k-1)^{th}$ fold and finally generates scores for the kth fold. The results for each fold are then concatenated together to generate the output $\mathcal{O}_1$ of Stage One.

Stage Two. The purpose of this step is to generate a ranked list of *types* for all the terms extracted in the Terminology extraction step (Section 3.1), but was not included in the list of *is-a* relationships

extracted using either Pattern based or Semantic Web based approaches.

Following similar approach as of Stage One, the list of existing *is-a* relationships are divided into *k-folds*. k independent SPON processes are then run in parallel, wherein each process trains upon k-1 folds, performs early stopping based on evaluations on the $(k-1)^{th}$ fold and finally generates a ranked list of *types* for all the terms in the Terminology.

Once all the SPON processes are over, we obtain k different ranked lists of *types* for each term in the Terminology. These ranked lists are then averaged to obtain a single ranked list of *types* per term. This generated output $\mathcal{O}_2$ then behaves as output for Stage Two.

Stage Three. Concatenating the results $\mathcal{O}_1$ and $\mathcal{O}_\in$ from previous stages, we obtain an *extended* list of ranked *instances* for each *type*.

This stage, then works in two steps, in the first step all the *instances* for a given *type* whose score is less than a threshold θ are removed. In the second step, the *types* are then ranked by an average score of its *top m instances*.

Note that the parameters θ and m are entered by the user. The output of this step provides the final result for SPON component in KGIS.

4 Knowledge Curation using the Smart Spreadsheet (SSS)

The KGIS framework features a novel way of interacting with the induced knowledge called Smart Spreadsheet (SSS). The cells in an SSS correspond to the nodes in a KG [10]. In addition, within an SSS, the first row is reserved for induced *types*, and other cells in each column contain *instances* of the corresponding *type* (i.e. the term in the 1st row of the column). Functionality wise, SSS provides: *auto-complete of term names*, for easily identifying terms matching an input text; *type-suggestion*, to help the user assign a *type* to a set of *instances*, and also *suggestion of similar or related terms* given existing ones.

Each time a new taxonomy is created (Section 3.3), it is also saved as an SSS so that the user can modify it to match their business needs. In the description that follows, the example snapshots following the functionality descriptions are taken from an automatically induced taxonomy,

---

[10] cells whose content does not match the *terminology* are painted *red*

Term	Predicted types
dicoumarol	<u>drug</u>, carbohydrate, acid, person, service , ...
Planck	**person**, <u>particle</u>, physics, <u>elementary particle</u>, service, ...
Belt Line	main road, **infrastructure**, **transport infrastructure**, expressway, way, ...
relief	service, assistance, resource, support, aid, ...
honesty	<u>virtue</u>, ideal, moral philosophy, philosophy, chastity, ...
shoe	**footwear**, shoe, **footgear**, overshoe, sandal, ...
ethanol	**alcohol**, <u>fuel</u>, person, **fluid**, resource, ...
ruby	<u>language</u>, <u>precious stone</u>, <u>person</u>, resource, **stone**, ...

Table 1: Examples of ranked predictions (from left-to-right) made by our system on a set of eight *randomly* selected test queries from SemEval 2018 English dataset. *Types* predicted by SPON that match the gold annotations are highlighted in **bold**, while we use <u>underline</u> for predictions that we judge to be correct but are missing in the gold standard expected *types*.

obtained by running the steps described in Section 3.3 on a corpus of scientific papers from the NeurIPS conference.

Firstly, given a list of few terms by the user supposedly belonging to a *type*, SSS has the ability to generate additional terms belonging to the same *type* using the following three options,

- **Populate from seeds.** The embeddings for the user-entered terms are averaged together to create a *centroid* vector; and a nearest neighbor algorithm is run across all the terms in the terminology to obtain additional terms belonging to the same *type*.

- **Populate from KG Type.** This option is only available when the user has found a matching *type* from the Semantic Web (using *type* suggestion). It allows the user to get the *instances* in the target KG are of this column's *type* and are also present in the corpus' terminology.

- **Populate from KG, Distant Supervision.** This option also requires a selected KG *type*, and it is a combination of the previous two techniques: it retrieves more *instances* of the given *type* from the KG, then it combines them with the ones already in the column (seeds) and applies the same 'populate from seeds' technique.

Figure 4b shows a snapshot of the KGIS system that demonstrates the `Populate from` feature. In this example, the user enters the name of a few algorithm names as *instances*, sets *algorithm* as the *type*, then selects a few cells and right-clicks to invoke the window containing the `Populate from` feature.

In addition, SSS provides an auto-complete feature, i.e. the option of completing terms wherein the list of displayed terms conform to the Terminology extraction step as discussed in Section 3.1. For example, in figure 4a as soon as the user types the term `spectral`, the system suggests meaningful possible terms to auto-complete based on the input corpus.

5   Conclusion and Future Work

Table 1 shows the result of applying our KGIS system on the English Domain corpus of the *SemEval 2018 Hypernym Detection* shared task. Two sets of four query terms (from test set input) are chosen at random. The first four terms have corresponding *is-a* pairs in the gold annotation provided by the task organizers, whereas the final four terms do not. The right hand column presents a ranked list of *types* for each query term.

Note that the correct *types* in the gold label test set are set in bold, whereas underlined terms are the *types* which we believe to be correct. This qualitative example, together with the academic benchmark results (not reported in this demo paper) together demonstrate that our system is the state of the art in discovering *is-a* pairs from text.

In conclusion, we have introduced the `Knowledge Graph Induction Service (KGIS)`, an end-to-end knowledge induction system, which provides numerous functionalities, most notably automatic taxonomy induction. The *learned* taxonomy is instantiated via a `Smart Spreadsheet`, which allows *users* to make changes as and how they see fit. The KGIS framework reduces the need of costly human annotations (i.e. it can automatically induce

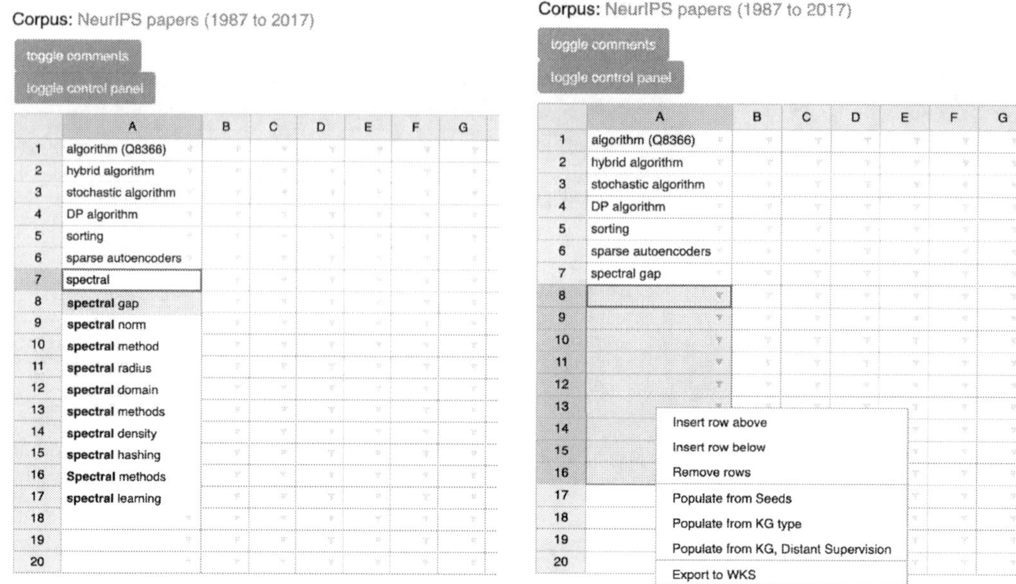

(a) AutoComplete feature in Smart Spreadsheet. (b) Smart Spreadsheet Feature: Allowing automatic population.

Figure 4: Features for Smart Spreadsheet.

taxonomies), but at the same time allows for a *human-in-the-loop* to interact with it, thereby ensuring that the user has always the final say in all the system outputs.

In the future, we plan on developing customer-centric downstream applications for using this framework. In addition, we also plan on working upon additional knowledge centric problems, such as *Unsupervised Relation Induction* to provide additional facets to our proposed framework.

References

Md. Faisal Mahbub Chowdhury and Robert Farrell. 2019. An efficient approach for super and nested term indexing and retrieval. *CoRR*, abs/1905.09761.

Marti A. Hearst. 1992. Automatic acquisition of hyponyms from large text corpora. In *COLING 1992 Volume 2: The 15th International Conference on Computational Linguistics*.

Tomas Mikolov, Ilya Sutskever, Kai Chen, Greg S Corrado, and Jeff Dean. 2013. Distributed representations of words and phrases and their compositionality. In *Advances in neural information processing systems*, pages 3111–3119.

G. A. Miller, R. Beckwith, C. Fellbaum, D. Gross, and K. J. Miller. 1990. Introduction to WordNet: an online lexical database. *International Journal of Lexicography*, 3(4):235–244.

Denny Vrandečić. 2012. Wikidata: A new platform for collaborative data collection. In *Proceedings of the 21st international conference on world wide web*, pages 1063–1064. ACM.

CFO: A Framework for Building Production NLP Systems

Rishav Chakravarti[1]   Cezar Pendus[2]   Andrzej Sakrajda[2]   Anthony Ferritto[1]
Lin Pan[1]   Michael Glass[2] Vittorio Castelli[2]   J. William Murdock[1]
Radu Florian[2]   Salim Roukos[2]   Avirup Sil[2*]

[1]IBM Watson,   [2]IBM Research AI

{rchakravarti, cpendus, ansa, panl, mrglass, vittorio, murdockj, raduf, roukos, avi}@us.ibm.com
aferritto@ibm.com

Abstract

This paper introduces a novel orchestration framework, called CFO (COMPUTATION FLOW ORCHESTRATOR), for building, experimenting with, and deploying interactive NLP (Natural Language Processing) and IR (Information Retrieval) systems to production environments. We then demonstrate a question answering system built using this framework which incorporates state-of-the-art BERT based MRC (Machine Reading Comprehension) with IR components to enable end-to-end answer retrieval. Results from the demo system are shown to be high quality in both academic and industry domain specific settings. Finally, we discuss best practices when (pre-)training BERT based MRC models for production systems.

1 Introduction

Production NLP (Natural Language Processing) and IR (information retrieval) applications often rely on a system flow consisting of multiple components that need to be woven together to build an end-to-end system (A. Ferrucci et al., 2010; Yang et al., 2019). This paper presents a novel approach for defining flow graphs and a toolkit for compiling those definitions into deploy-able production grade systems[1].

Though the framework, which we refer to as CFO (COMPUTATION FLOW ORCHESTRATOR), is well suited to a variety of use cases, we demonstrate it by creating an interactive QA (Question Answering) system that can be used both for academic benchmarking as well as industry specific use cases. The interactive system integrates SOTA (state-of-the-art) BERT-based MRC (Machine Reading Comprehension), an Elasticsearch based document retrieval component, and a deduplication & sorting component to provide end-to-end answer retrieval. We will refer to this demonstration system as GAAMA (Go Ahead, Ask Me Anything). The key contributions of this work, therefore, are to (1) introduce a novel framework for stitching together deployable NLP components, (2) demonstrate the framework with an end-to-end QA system, and (3) discuss the training steps necessary for adapting a SOTA MRC model to a data set before plugging it into the QA system.

Section 2 provides the motivations and details of the CFO framework, section 3 discusses the specific model components integrated into GAAMA, section 4 discusses experimentation to adapt the BERT-based MRC component to this system, section 5 discusses related work, and, finally, section 6 provides a conclusion and discussion of future work.

In addition, a (private) screencast video demonstration of GAAMA has been uploaded at `http://ibm.biz/gaama_demo` (along with a supplementary presentation of the CFO framework at `http://ibm.biz/gaama_cfo_demo`).

2 CFO Architecture

The CFO framework relies on two sets of system specifications to define the computation flow graph. First, each node within the graph defines its service name, input message data fields, and output message data fields using Google's Protocol Buffer Interface Definition Language[2]. Second, the orchestrator is described using a custom specification format allowing the user to declare:

1. The set of nodes (provided as containerized gRPC[3] microservices). Each node will have

---

* Corresponding author.

[1]We are actively seeking to open source the toolkit and flow definition language. If successful, we will be releasing the code to `http://ibm.biz/cfo_framework`

[2]`https://developers.google.com/protocol-buffers/`
[3]`https://grpc.io/`

Proceedings of the 2019 EMNLP and the 9th IJCNLP (System Demonstrations), pages 31–36
Hong Kong, China, November 3 – 7, 2019. ©2019 Association for Computational Linguistics

implemented a microservice according to the node's declared interface specification.

2. The set of nodes to treat as entry points to the flow graph.

3. A mapping within the flow for each *data element* comprising the input and output message interfaces for nodes.

4. For ease of deployment, the specification also provides the ability to describe deployment specific configuration settings like service ports, docker registry location etc.

Given these specification files, CFO provides a compiler to auto-generate an orchestrator node which implements the computation flow graph, a (dockerized) launch script, and a simple REST interface / GUI which provide access to the defined entry points and debug information.

The resulting design allows data flows and dependencies to be described both concisely and transparently. The flow specification allows for easy debugging and modification of how data fields enter the computation flow, get transformed, and finally outputted. This is a significant departure from traditional orchestration systems which would require parsing through source code to determine and change the route taken by data fields through the computation flow. Furthermore, the use of Protocol Buffers to describe these data fields ensures a language and platform agnostic representation that does not compromise the system's speed or ability to ensure data type correctness at compile time (as opposed to traditional JSON/XML representations which need to encode/decode from strings at run time).

Another benefit of the CFO toolkit is to auto-generate the serialization and connectivity code for each node as well as exposing the entry points via REST interfaces. Relinquishing this responsibility to the CFO toolkit frees the developer up from writing a significant amount of boilerplate code and worrying about distributed system best practices such as enforcing time outs, error propagation, latency logging, and parallelization through asynchronous calls. As an illustrative example, the auto-generated code for the GAAMA demo consists of 2,800 lines of C++ orchestration code.

Finally, the CFO toolkit generates a set of shell scripts, docker images, and config files for deploying and running the flow graph using either

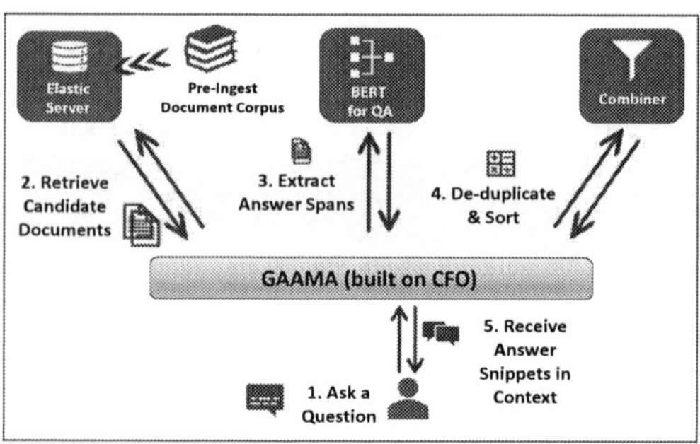

Figure 1: GAAMA System Architecture

docker-compose[4] or kubernetes[5]. This allows the generated project to be deployed both locally for debugging as well as on modern cloud infrastructure.

3 GAAMA Architecture

As a simple case study for CFO, we create a demonstration QA system consisting of four nodes: (1) an Elasticsearch[6] based IR node (2) a BERT based MRC node (3) an answer "de-duplication" node and (4) a final answer combiner node. See fig. 1 for an overview of the QA system.

As described in section 2, each component starts by declaring an interface specification allowing the underlying implementation to be swapped out without the need to modify the rest of the QA system. Next, a gRPC server is implemented with the core business logic. Auto-generated gRPC code stubs provide the core communication/serialization logic for the service layer of the server. We describe the IR and MRC nodes in further detail in the following two sections.

3.1 IR with Elasticsearch

The core business logic of the IR node uses Elasticsearch APIs to retrieve the top k documents from the appropriate corpus based on BM25, a popular variant of term frequency overlap between the query and document text (Robertson et al., 1976). Two document corpora are ingested using the standard English analyzer. The first corpus consists of Wikipedia paragraphs used for academic benchmarking and the second corpus consists of an industry dataset made up of IBM Technical Support Documentation. The user interface allows us to choose either corpus when asking

---

[4]https://docs.docker.com/compose/
[5]https://kubernetes.io/
[6]https://www.elastic.co/products/elasticsearch

questions to evaluate the system. We use "paragraphs" as the base unit of ingestion in line with (Yang et al., 2019) which shows this as an optimal pre-processing step for consumption by a MRC component.

The node's input interface, therefore, accepts query text, a hyperparameter k, and a target corpus identifier. Its output interface produces a list of document texts accompanied by retrieval scores. As discussed earlier, these interfaces are defined using protocol buffer definitions, so we follow standard steps[7] for auto-generating a gRPC server with placeholders for the custom business logic of retrieving documents. Similarly, with the server logic in place, we follow standard steps[8] to create a docker image that CFO will need to launch the gRPC server. Though we are wrapping Elasticsearch's index based retrieval implementation here, we can swap our implementation for more recent Neural IR based techniques (Craswell et al., 2017) without changing the exposed interface or the orchestration code.

3.2 MRC with BERT

The MRC node similarly wraps a BERT-for-QA model in a dockerized gRPC server which accepts a single query-document pair as its input and produces a span from the document along with a prediction score as its output. Note that CFO's orchestrator automatically realizes that the IR node produces a list of documents, while the MRC node accepts a single document at a time. So CFO will take care of calling the MRC node for each of the k retrieved documents (using asynchronous calls to parallelize requests if a configuration flag is set).

The underlying BERT-for-QA model is based on (Alberti et al., 2019). BERT (Devlin et al., 2018) is one of a series of pre-trained neural models that can be fine tuned to provide state-of-the-art results in NLP (Peters et al., 2018; Howard and Ruder, 2018; Radford et al., 2019) including on the SQuAD (Rajpurkar et al., 2018) and NQ (Kwiatkowski et al., 2019) tasks that align with our MRC based QA.

We use the Huggingface PyTorch implementation of BERT [9] which supports starting from a Base (a 12 layer, 768 hidden dimension, 12 atten-

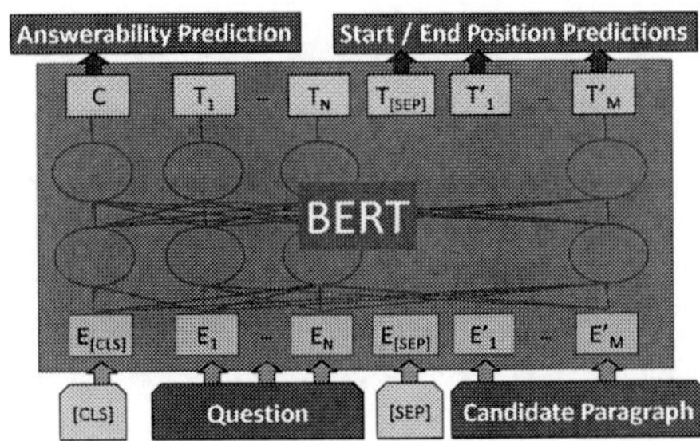

Figure 2: BERT for QA (Devlin et al., 2018)

tion head, 110M parameter transformer network) or a Large (a 24 layer, 1024 hidden dimension, 16 attention head, 340M parameter transformer network) model. An output feed forward layer is added on top of this to produce 3 sets of scores: (1) scores at each token offset marking the likelihood of an answer chunk starting at this offset (2) scores at each token offset marking the likelihood of an answer chunk ending at this offset (3) a score for the entire sequence marking the likelihood of the question being answerable given the current context.

The parameters of the entire network are fine tuned using a set of question and document pairs where annotators provide the correct start and end offsets or have marked the question-document pair as having no correct answer. Refer to fig. 2 for a visual depiction of the model and to (Alberti et al., 2019) for additional details about model architecture and implementation.

Section 4 includes practical pre-training, fine tuning, and hyperparameter optimization steps for building the final model deployed as part of GAAMA. At the time of writing, our BERT-based MRC model[10] was the best performing submission (dated 7/31/2019), outperforming the next best system by 1% on F1 on the Natural Questions public leaderboard[11].

4 Experiments

Prior to integration of the MRC node into GAAMA, we first experiment with data preparation and training of the BERT MRC model as a standalone component using dev sets provided with the NQ and SQuAD data sets (see 5 for more on these data sets). NQ is preferred for evaluat-

---

[7] https://grpc.io/docs/tutorials/
[8] https://github.com/grpc/grpc-docker-library/
[9] https://github.com/huggingface/pytorch-transformers

[10] The best performing submission to the leaderboard uses an ensemble of models using different hyperparameters rather than a single model
[11] https://ai.google.com/research/NaturalQuestions/leaderboard

	F1
Prior Work	
DecAtt + Doc Reader (Parikh et al., 2016)	31.4
BERT (Devlin et al., 2018)	50.2
BERT w/ SQuAD 1.1 (Alberti et al., 2019)	52.7
This Work	
BERT w/ U-MRC	53.6
BERT w/ U-MRC & SQuAD 1.1	54.2
BERT w/ U-MRC & SQuAD 1.1 + SQuAD 2.0 Data Aug	**54.5**

Table 1: Dev Set Performance on NQ with different pre-training & data augmentation techniques. We also report some baselines from (Alberti et al., 2019) for context

Pre-Training	EM	F1
BERT (Devlin et al., 2018)	78.7	81.9
BERT w/ U-MRC	82.2	85
BERT w/ U-MRC & NQ	**82.6**	**85.4**

Table 2: Dev Set Performance on SQuAD 2 with different pre-training strategies.

ing production systems since the questions were "naturally" generated and does not suffer from the observational bias inherent in SQuAD's data collection approach (Kwiatkowski et al., 2019). When reporting results with the SQuAD dataset, we use the methodology (and evaluation script) made available with (Rajpurkar et al., 2018). Similarly, when reporting results with the NQ dataset, we use the methodology (and evaluation script) made available with (Kwiatkowski et al., 2019). Once we are satisfied with the performance of this model, we integrate into GAAMA and evaluate manually using an internal corpus.

We use the F-score at an "optimal" threshold for the dev set[12] as the headline metric for assessing the system. Latency measurements are carried out using a random sample of examples on a system with an Intel® Xeon® E5-2690 16-core CPU, 2 Nvidia® Tesla® P100 GPUs, and 128GB of RAM.[13] We then examine the feasibility of deploying base and large models in a production environment on GPUs and CPUs.

4.1 Pre-Training & Data Augmentation

We explore two types of pre-training. The first follows (Alberti et al., 2019) by leveraging a similar task for which supervised labels are available and pre-training the model on it before moving onto fine tuning on the target dataset. Specifically, we use SQuAD 1.1 (Rajpurkar et al., 2016). Table 1 shows that this strategy can provide an absolute improvement of 2.5% over a model that starts with just the default BERT language model.

We also employ (Glass et al., 2019)'s approach to using an unsupervised auxilary task that is better aligned to our final task (i.e. MRC) than the default Masked Language Model and Next Sentence Prediction used in (Devlin et al., 2018) to pre-train the BERT models. Using the Wikipedia corpus, we create cloze style queries by masking out terms (named entities or noun phrases) in a sentence. Then we identify an answer bearing passage from the Wikipedia corpus that is relevant to the query (as identified by BM25 IR). This allows us to pre-train all layers of the BERT model including the answer extraction weights by training the model to extract the answer term from the selected passage. Like the Masked Language Model, this task relies on predicting a masked component of an input sequence, but the prediction is generated by extraction rather than generation. Table 1 labels these results as "BERT w/ U-MRC" and shows that this additional training on a MRC specific unsupervised task improves the model's final fine-tuned performance on the NQ task by 1.5%. Table 2 similarly shows the benefits of these pre-training strategies on the SQuAD 2.0 dataset.

In addition, as noted by the authors of the original BERT-for-QA submission to SQuAD (Devlin et al., 2018), there can be a benefit to fine tuning the entire network with labelled examples from multiple datasets. The last row of table 1 shows an incremental gain of 0.3% by introducing SQuAD 2.0 during the fine-tuning phase. For now, the additional data is simply shuffled into the first 80% of mini batches during the fine-tuning phase.

4.2 BERT Models & Latency

Most model settings are taken from (Alberti et al., 2019) with the exception of batch size and learning rate which are tuned using the approach from (Smith, 2018). In addition, we experiment with models trained on BERT base and BERT large to understand trade-offs between latency and accuracy. Using the hardware described in section 4, we evaluate F1 and latency on a subset of the NQ

---

[12]See `http://www.ibm.biz/confidence_thresholding` for more on choosing business specific thresholds

[13]We only use 1 P100 GPU or 8 CPU threads in latency experiments

Model	$F1$	T_{50}^G	T_{95}^G	T_{50}^C	T_{95}^C
Base	42.5	0.05	0.49	0.53	2.32
Large	50.8	0.10	0.66	1.51	6.00

Table 3: F1 and latencies for BERT base and large models running on GPU and CPU for a subset of the NQ dev set. T_K^D is the K-th percentile query latency in seconds when running on device D (GPU or CPU).

dev set[14]. In order to decrease latency, we simulate passage retrieval to send GAAMA the most relevant passage by selecting the first correct top level candidate if there is one and the first (incorrect) top level candidate if there is not. We find in table 3 that switching from base to large yields an 8.3% absolute increase in F1 in exchange for 1.3x to 2.8x increases in latency. When running GAAMA on a GPU these result in manageable 95th percentile query latencies of less than a second; whereas on the CPU the 95th percentile times are in excess of two and five seconds for base and large respectively. For large, even the median latency is greater than one and a half seconds, effectively cementing GPUs as a requirement for deploying to production environments. In future work we intend to explore network pruning or knowledge distillation techniques for potential speedups with the large model.

5   Related Work

Recently (Yang et al., 2019) proposed BERT-Serini, an end-to-end QA pipeline demo that leverages the Anserini IR toolkit (Yang et al., 2017) to look for relevant documents for a question, then uses BERT-based techniques (Devlin et al., 2018) to extract the correct answer. However, their reliance on a Lucene based IR toolkit means that constructing a NLP pipeline would either require pipeline components to be written as Lucene based plugins (which comes with a variety of constraints on programming language and structure) or writing custom orchestration code to connect components outside of the toolkit. Similar constraints are imposed by other popular NLP pipeline toolkits such as StanfordNLP (Qi et al., 2018) and Spacy[15] (both of which require development in Python with limited flexibility in training neural models with other frameworks such as Tensorflow[16]).

In contrast, CFO's inherent programming language and platform agnostic microservice architecture encourages flexibility and robustness in being able to switch out individual components without re-doing boilerplate code. In addition, CFO's out-of-the-box support for containerization provides flexibility in the compute infrastructure that can be leveraged for rapid deployment to both local and cloud environments.

This flexibility is important in a domain such as Machine Reading Comprehension (MRC) where recent advances in language-modeling based pretrained embeddings like ELMO (Peters et al., 2018) and BERT (Devlin et al., 2018) along with large scale open data sets like the Stanford Question Answering Dataset (SQuAD) 1.1 (Rajpurkar et al., 2016) and its successor SQuAD 2.0 (Rajpurkar et al., 2018) have spurred a diverse array of model architecture improvements in a short time span. Recent work has even produced systems that surpass human-level exact match accuracy on the SQuAD datasets, causing us to focus on the challenging new Natural Questions (NQ) dataset (Kwiatkowski et al., 2019) where the questions do not have any observational bias as they were not artificially created. To the best of our knowledge, there is no current software framework paper that shows its analysis on the NQ dataset and displays strong empirical performance.

UIMA (Ferrucci and Lally, 2004) is an integration framework that provides defined APIs for analyzing unstructured information and a shared data structure for storing the results of that analysis. When paired with the UIMA Asynchronous Scaleout layer (Apache UIMA Community, 2018) and the Distributed UIMA Cluster Computing tool (DUCC Team, 2013), this technology stack provides many of the same core capabilities that CFO does: pipeline orchestration, microservice deployment and management, data serialization and connectivity, etc. However, CFO is designed for modern cloud environments and includes built-in integration with docker-compose and kubernetes; the UIMA stack *can* be used with these technologies but facilities for doing so are not built-in to the stack so more development effort is needed in those contexts. Also, UIMA and CFO both require that each component expresses its data model (including input and output specifications) declaratively, but UIMA then unifies the data model of all components into a global type hierarchy, which requires some level of compatibil-

---

[14]Used 500 random examples from dev set for experiments
[15]https://spacy.io/
[16]https://www.tensorflow.org/

ity across type definitions. In contrast, CFO only requires consistency in the data model for components that directly connect to each other, and the names of corresponding types and fields do not need to match. These differences make CFO easier to use in cases where components were developed by different developers and integrated by a third party.

6 Conclusion

This paper introduces CFO, a novel methodology and toolkit for rapid development of production grade systems for use cases which can be represented as computation flow graphs. We demonstrate the use of this framework to build an end-to-end QA system composed of a SOTA MRC model that is adapted to answering "natural language questions". We also show experimentation using the NQ dataset to illustrate training techniques that can be used to build SOTA systems on top of existing pre-trained language models like BERT.

We are actively seeking to open source the CFO framework and hope that, once available, the community will be able to quickly build and deploy their own SOTA NLP components as interactive multi-component systems. We also intend on expanding GAAMA to incorporate additional QA components to improve its performance through approaches like query expansion for improved recall and network pruning for improved latency.

References

David A. Ferrucci, Eric Brown, Jennifer Chu-Carroll, James Fan, David Gondek, Aditya Kalyanpur, Adam Lally, J William Murdock, Eric Nyberg, John Prager, Nico Schlaefer, and Christopher Welty. 2010. Building Watson: An overview of the DeepQA project. *AI Magazine*, 31:59–79.

Chris Alberti, Kenton Lee, and Michael Collins. 2019. A bert baseline for the natural questions.

Apache UIMA Community. 2018. UIMA Asynchronous Scaleout: Version 2.10.3.

Nick Craswell, W Croft, Maarten de Rijke, Jiafeng Guo, and Bhaskar Mitra. 2017. Sigir 2017 workshop on neural information retrieval (neu-ir'17).

Jacob Devlin, Ming-Wei Chang, Kenton Lee, and Kristina Toutanova. 2018. Bert: Pre-training of deep bidirectional transformers for language understanding. In *NAACL-HLT*.

DUCC Team. 2013. Distributed UIMA cluster computing.

David Ferrucci and Adam Lally. 2004. UIMA: an architectural approach to unstructured information processing in the corporate research environment. *Natural Language Engineering*, 10(3-4):327348.

Michael Glass, Alfio Gliozzo, Rishav Chakravarti, Anthony Ferritto, Lin Pan, Bhargav GP Shrivatsa, Dinesh Garg, and Avirup Sil. 2019. Span selection pre-training for question answering.

Jeremy Howard and Sebastian Ruder. 2018. Universal language model fine-tuning for text classification.

Tom Kwiatkowski, Jennimaria Palomaki, Olivia Redfield, Michael Collins, Ankur Parikh, Chris Alberti, Danielle Epstein, Illia Polosukhin, Matthew Kelcey, Jacob Devlin, Kenton Lee, Kristina N. Toutanova, Llion Jones, Ming-Wei Chang, Andrew Dai, Jakob Uszkoreit, Quoc Le, and Slav Petrov. 2019. Natural questions: a benchmark for question answering research. *TACL*.

Ankur Parikh, Oscar Tckstrm, Dipanjan Das, and Jakob Uszkoreit. 2016. A decomposable attention model for natural language inference. *EMNLP*.

Matthew Peters, Mark Neumann, Mohit Iyyer, Matt Gardner, Christopher Clark, Kenton Lee, and Luke Zettlemoyer. 2018. Deep contextualized word representations. *NAACL*.

Peng Qi, Timothy Dozat, Yuhao Zhang, and Christopher D. Manning. 2018. Universal dependency parsing from scratch. CoNLL. ACL.

Alec Radford, Karthik Narasimhan, Tim Salimans, and Ilya Sutskever. 2019. Improving language understanding by generative pre-training.

Pranav Rajpurkar, Robin Jia, and Percy Liang. 2018. Know what you don't know: Unanswerable questions for squad. *arXiv preprint arXiv:1806.03822*.

Pranav Rajpurkar, Jian Zhang, Konstantin Lopyrev, and Percy Liang. 2016. Squad: 100,000+ questions for machine comprehension of text. *EMNLP*.

C S Robertson, H. Zaragoza, Stephen Robertson, and Hugo Zaragoza. 1976. The probabilistic relevance framework: Bm25 and beyond.

Leslie N. Smith. 2018. A disciplined approach to neural network hyper-parameters: Part 1 – learning rate, batch size, momentum, and weight decay.

Peilin Yang, Hui Fang, and Jimmy Lin. 2017. Anserini: Enabling the use of lucene for information retrieval research. SIGIR. ACM.

Wei Yang, Yuqing Xie, Aileen Lin, Xingyu Li, Luchen Tan, Kun Xiong, Ming Li, and Jimmy Lin. 2019. End-to-end open-domain question answering with bertserini.

Chameleon: A Language Model Adaptation Toolkit for Automatic Speech Recognition of Conversational Speech

Yuanfeng Song[1,2], Di Jiang[2], Weiwei Zhao[2]
Qian Xu[2], Raymond Chi-Wing Wong[1], Qiang Yang[1,2]
[1]Department of Computer Science and Engineering,
The Hong Kong University of Science and Technology, Hong Kong SAR, China
[2]AI Group, WeBank Co., Ltd, Shenzhen, China
`{songyf, raywong, qyang}@cse.ust.hk`
`{dijiang, davezhao, qianxu}@webank.com`

Abstract

Language model is a vital component in modern automatic speech recognition (ASR) systems. Since "one-size-fits-all" language model works suboptimally for conversational speeches, language model adaptation (LMA) is considered as a promising solution for solving this problem. In order to compare the state-of-the-art LMA techniques and systematically demonstrate their effect in conversational speech recognition, we develop a novel toolkit named Chameleon, which includes the state-of-the-art *cache-based* and *topic-based* LMA techniques. This demonstration does not only vividly visualize underlying working mechanisms of a variety of the state-of-the-art LMA models but also provide an interface for the user to customize the hyperparameters of them. With this demonstration, the audience can experience the effect of LMA in an interactive and real-time fashion. We wish this demonstration would inspire more research on better language model techniques for ASR.

1 Introduction

In recent years, conversational speech recognition attracts much research attention in both academia and industry, since it is the very premise of building intelligent conversational applications. In contemporary ASR systems, language model plays an essential role of guiding the search among the word candidates and has a decisive effect on the quality of results (Jurafsky, 2000; Xu et al., 2018). However, most commercial ASR products simply rely on a "one-size-fits-all" language model. The mismatch between training and testing scenarios becomes a huge obstacle to high-quality ASR of conversational speeches in practice. Despite its simplicity and reliability, the widely used n-gram language model suffers the drawback of limited capacity of capturing the long-distance dependencies and richer semantic information, which

greatly motivates the development of LMA techniques (Gandhe et al., 2018).

Although LMA techniques are increasingly considered as promising solutions for aforementioned limitation of n-gram language model, their effectiveness in real-life ASR tasks has never been systematically investigated so far. In this demonstration, we categorize the existing LMA models as two paradigms: the cache-based and the topic-based. The cache-based paradigm exploits historical observation by caching the previously used words in recent history, and then increases the probability of these words when predicting new words (Kuhn and De Mori, 1990; Lau et al., 1993; Chen, 2017). The topic models-based paradigm relies on the latent semantics discovered by probabilistic topic models, which are known for their ability to capture the semantic correlation between words and proven promising performance when applied to ASR systems (Chen et al., 2010; Wintrode and Khudanpur, 2014). Besides ASR, the topic models are also widely used in various applications such as word analysis (Kennedy et al., 2017), RFID data modeling (Kennedy et al., 2017), urban perception (de Oliveira Capela and Ramirez-Marquez, 2019) etc. We include a wide range of LMA techniques in Chameleon and some of them are specialized for ASR system. In Chameleon, the LMA techniques from the above two paradigms are implemented by conforming to the same APIs. Hence, the users could seamlessly switch between different LMA techniques and observe their real-time impact on ASR results. The ultimate goal of our demonstration is to provide a unique opportunity for the users to customize and experience the working mechanisms of a variety of the state-of-the-art LMA techniques in a vivid and interactive approach. We wish it will inspire more research on LMA in the field of ASR.

The rest of this paper is organized as fol-

Proceedings of the 2019 EMNLP and the 9th IJCNLP (System Demonstrations), pages 37–42
Hong Kong, China, November 3 – 7, 2019. ©2019 Association for Computational Linguistics

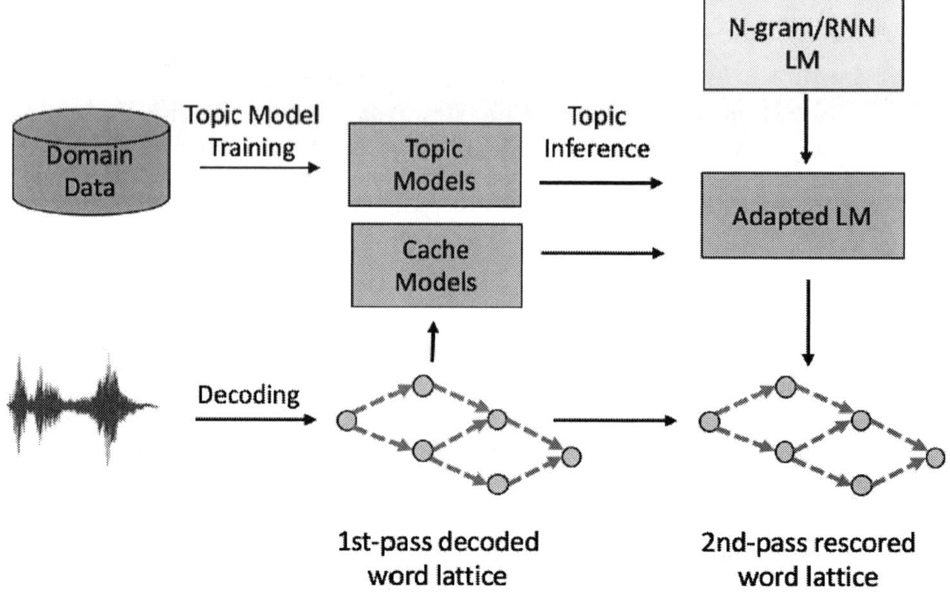

Figure 1: The Pipeline of Language Model Adaptation for ASR

lows. In Section 2, we describe the details of the Chameleon toolkit. In Section 3, we quantitatively demonstrate the performance of Chameleon, followed by the demonstration description in Section 4. Finally, we conclude this paper in Section 5.

2 Toolkit Description

In this section, we first describe the pipeline of LMA used in Chameleon, then we introduce the cache-based LMA paradigm and the topic-based LMA paradigm respectively.

2.1 Language Model Adaptation Pipeline

The pipeline of LMA used in Chameleon is illustrated in Figure 1. In the 1st-pass decoding, the system generates a word lattice containing the candidate results, which are further digested by LMA. Then the adapted language model rescores the word lattice and generate the 2nd-pass word lattice, in which the final decoding result can be straightforwardly obtained.

2.2 Cache-based Paradigm

There widely exists a phenomena named "word burstiness" in natural language such as conversational speech: if a word appears once, the same word and its semantically related words tend to appear again in the same speech (Madsen et al., 2005). Compared with basic n-gram model, the cache-based paradigm stores the recent historical information constructed by the 1st-pass decoded word lattices. Hence, it has the ability to emphasize the local context and boost the probabilities of recently seen words. The cache-based paradigm is widely used in language model, e.g. the cache model (Kuhn and De Mori, 1990) and the self-trigger models (Lau et al., 1993). In Chameleon, we implement the Trigger-based Discriminative Language Model (DLM) proposed in (Singh-Miller and Collins, 2007), which aims to find the optimal string $\mathbf{w}^*$ for a given acoustic input, denoted as $\mathbf{a}$, by the following equation:

$$\begin{aligned}
\mathbf{w}^* = \arg\max(&\alpha \log P_{LM}(\mathbf{w}) \\
&+ \log P_{AM}(\mathbf{a}|\mathbf{w}) + \langle \beta, \phi(\mathbf{a}, \mathbf{w}, \mathbf{h}) \rangle)
\end{aligned} \tag{1}$$

where P_{LM} represents a back-off n-gram language model, P_{AM} is an acoustic model, $\phi(\mathbf{a}, \mathbf{w}, \mathbf{h})$ maps the tuple $(\mathbf{a}, \mathbf{w}, \mathbf{h})$ into a feature-vector, and $\mathbf{h}$ is the history of $\mathbf{a}$ (represented as $\mathbf{h} = \{\mathbf{v_1}, \cdots, \mathbf{v_{i-1}}\}$). The parameter β is estimated using discriminative method such as perception. By caching the history of $\mathbf{a}$ and the trigger features such as the times word $\mathbf{w}$ appears in history $\mathbf{h}$, the trigger-based DLM aims to make full

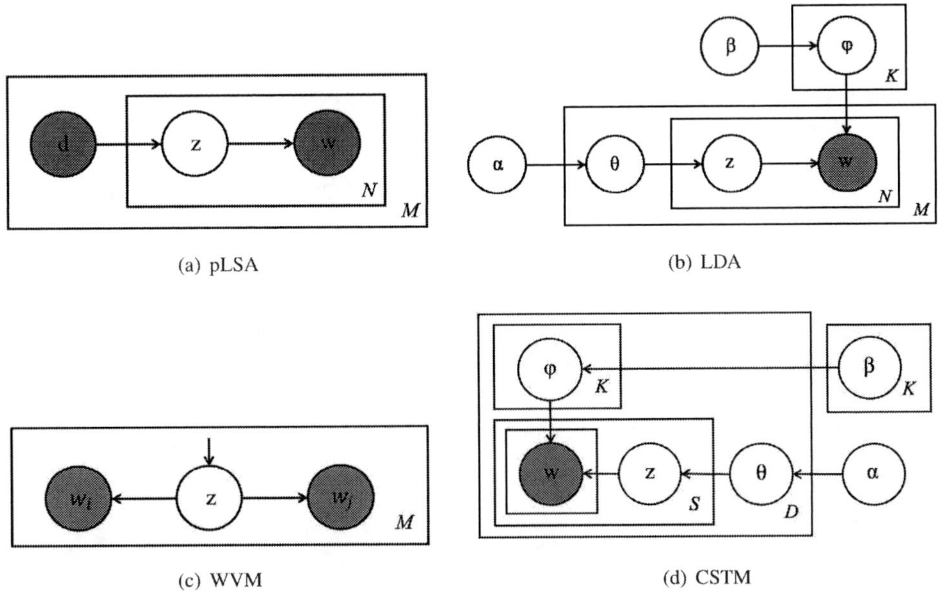

Figure 2: The Graphical Models of Topic Models Included in Chameleon

use of the local context for ASR decoding.

2.3 Topic-based Paradigm

The topic-based paradigm is mathematically defined as below:

$$P(w|c) = \sum_z P(w|z)P(z|c) \qquad (2)$$

where z is the latent topic, $P(w|z)$ is word probability given the topic and $P(z|c)$ is topic probability given the context c. Compared with the basic n-gram language models and cache-based models, the topic-based adaptation is able to predict word probability based on a long-term history and capture the long dependencies from the semantic perspective. A variety of topic models are included in Chameleon and their corresponding graphical models are illustrated in Figure 2:

- PLSA (Hofmann, 1999)

- LDA (Blei et al., 2003)

- Word Vicinity Model (WVM) (Chen et al., 2010)

- Conversational Speech Topic Model (CSTM) (Song et al., 2019)

The CSTM model is a newly designed topic model that is specialized for conversational speech. From the graphical model of CSTM in Figure 2(d), we can see that CSTM represents the words in a speech dialogue corpus D as mixtures of K "topics" and each "topic" is represented as a multinomial distribution over vocabulary of size V with Dirichlet prior β. The topic distribution θ for each speech dialogue is multinomial from a Dirichlet prior with parameter α, and each word w in a speech dialogue is drawn from a multinomial distribution of topic assignment z of the sentence it belongs to. Compared with traditional topic models such as LDA, CSTM has the ability to capture the utterance boundaries by constraining all the words in the same sentence sharing the same topic. In addition, CSTM explicitly models the "word burstiness" phenomena by allowing the word probability in the same topic varies in different documents, which is quite different from traditional topic models since their word probability in the same topic is usually fixed. The model learning process of CSTM is inspired by the inductive transfer learning mechanism (Pan and Yang, 2010) to make use of currently parallel training frameworks for LDA (Yuan et al., 2015) and well-trained open-sourced topic models (Jiang et al., 2018).

We conduct a linear interpolation between the conventional n-gram language model and the unigram model produced by the topic-based or the cache-based LMA techniques as below:

$$p_d(w|C) = \lambda P_{TM}(w|c)||P_{Cache}(w|c) \\ + (1 - \lambda)P_{LM}(w|c) \quad (3)$$

where $P_{LM}(w|c)$, $P_{TM}(w|c)$ and $P_{Cache}(w|c)$ are the probability given by n-gram language model, topic-based language model and cache-based language model respectively. λ is a trade-off parameter and empirically set by users. More sophisticated interpolation method such as (Della Pietra et al., 1992) can also be adopted for better performance.

3 Performance of Chameleon

In this section, we briefly describe the performance of some the aforementioned LMA techniques in terms of perplexity and Word Error Rate (WER). We use a custom service dataset in Mandarin Chinese with around 1000 hours dialogue speech in the experiments. 80% of speech data is used to train a full-fledged ASR system using Kaldi "chain" model, and the rest 20% of data is reserved for development and testing.

3.1 Perplexity

Figure 3 compares the perplexity (PPL) of the LMA techniques in Chameleon on testing data. In order to ensure the fairness of the comparison, all methods under study are trained based upon the transcript of the training data. We further adapt the n-gram language model with PLSA, LDA, Trigger-based DLM, WVM and CSTM respectively, which results in the following adapted language models: n-gram+PLSA, n-gram+LDA, n-gram+Trigger-based DLM, n-gram+WVM, n-gram + CSTM.

From Figure 3, we can observe that all the LMA techniques in Chameleon are effective at reducing the perplexity of testing data, indicating that they are helpful in predicting the words in testing data. Among all LMA techniques, CSTM achieves much lower perplexity than the other topic-based methods. This confirms the assumption that the latent topics discovered by CSTM provides valuable long-range dependency information of words. The superiority of CSTM over LDA shows that CSTM provides better fit for conversational data.

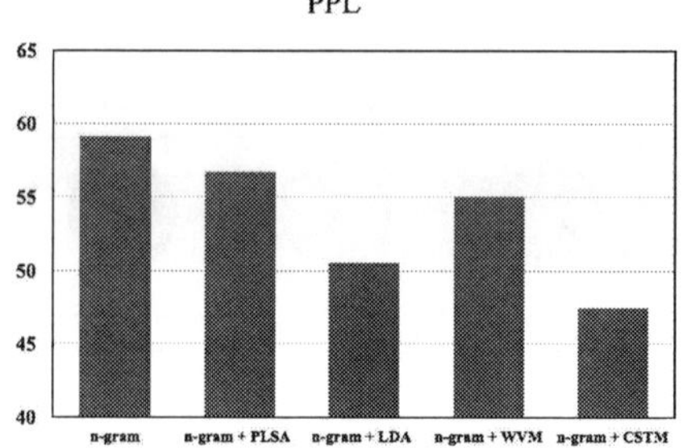

Figure 3: Perplexity Evaluation

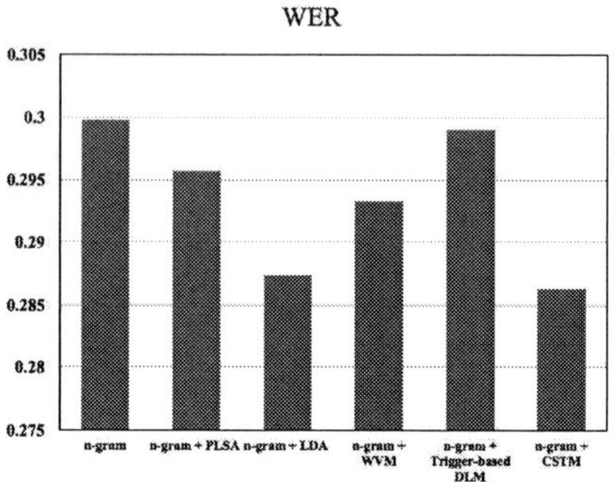

Figure 4: WER Evaluation

3.2 Lattice-rescoring

Since the ultimate goal of LMA is to improve ASR results, we further examine and compare the effectiveness of the LMA techniques in Chameleon in term of WER. Figure 4 presents the WER of all LMA techniques in Chameleon. This result shows that the LMA techniques in Chameleon is effective to reduce the errors in ASR results, indicating that utilizing the long-distance dependencies and richer semantic information is critical for ASR systems.

4 Demonstration Description

In this section, we describe the testbed ASR system and user interface of this demonstration. The goal of the demonstration is to provide a interactive approach for the users to experience the working mechanisms of a variety of the state-of-the-art LMA techniques mentioned above.

4.1 Testbed ASR System

The whole system is deployed on a machine with 314GB memory, 72 Intel Core Processor (Xeon), Tesla K80 GPU and CentOS. We trained a full-fledged ASR system based on conversational

Figure 5: The User Interface of Chameleon

speeches collected from real-life customer service in Mandarin Chinese using the Kaldi toolkit[1]. The Kaldi "chain" model is used for the acoustic model. As for conventional language models, the back-off n-gram language models are trained by SRI Language Modeling Toolkit (SRILM) (Stolcke, 2002).

4.2 User Interface

We proceed to exhibit the three steps of using Chameleon with a screenshot of the user interface illustrated in Figure 5.

Step 1: The users can either upload recorded audio files or record conversational speech in real-time through the microphone provided by our system. Optionally, the groundtruth transcript can be provided by the user for the system to evaluate the WER of different LMA techniques.

Step 2: The baseline n-gram language model together with various LMA techniques described in Section 2 can be freely chosen by the users. A horizontal slider is also provided for the users to customize the interpolation weight λ. In order to facilitate the comparison of WER and decoding results of different LMA techniques, Chameleon supports applying two LMA techniques and presents their results simultaneously in a side-by-side fashion.

Step 3: When the user clicks the "Start Decoding" button, the decoding process starts. The de-

coded results will be presented to the corresponding text area after decoding completes. If the groundtruth transcript is provided and the "Calculate WER" button is clicked, the WER of the decoded results will be calculated and presented in the interface.

5　Conclusion and Future Work

In this demonstration, we show a novel language model adaptation toolkit named Chameleon that reveals the the effectiveness and differences of the state-of-the-art LMA techniques. Through this demonstration, the audience will have a unique journey of experiencing how LMA improves the ASR performance. In the future, we plan to include more LMA techniques and investigate new topic models dedicated for conversional speech recognition. In addition, the hyperparameter tuning step can be combined with current Automatic Machine Learning (AutoML) techniques (Quanming et al., 2018) to achieve better performance and user experience.

6　Acknowledgements

This research is partially supported by HKRGC GRF 16219816. We are grateful to the anonymous reviewers for their constructive comments on this paper.

---

[1]http://kaldi-asr.org/

References

David M Blei, Andrew Y Ng, and Michael I Jordan. 2003. Latent dirichlet allocation. *Journal of machine Learning research*, 3(Jan):993–1022.

Kuan-Yu Chen, Hsuan-Sheng Chiu, and Berlin Chen. 2010. Latent topic modeling of word vicinity information for speech recognition. In *Acoustics Speech and Signal Processing (ICASSP), 2010 IEEE International Conference on*, pages 5394–5397. IEEE.

Xie Chen. 2017. Scalable recurrent neural network language models for speech recognition. In *Thesis*, pages 0–186. Cambridge.

Stephen Della Pietra, Vincent Della Pietra, Robert L Mercer, and Salim Roukos. 1992. Adaptive language modeling using minimum discriminant estimation. In *[Proceedings] ICASSP-92: 1992 IEEE International Conference on Acoustics, Speech, and Signal Processing*, volume 1, pages 633–636. IEEE.

Ankur Gandhe, Ariya Rastrow, and Bjorn Hoffmeister. 2018. Scalable language model adaptation for spoken dialogue systems. In *2018 IEEE Spoken Language Technology Workshop (SLT)*, pages 907–912. IEEE.

Thomas Hofmann. 1999. Probabilistic latent semantic analysis. In *Proceedings of the Fifteenth conference on Uncertainty in artificial intelligence*, pages 289–296. Morgan Kaufmann Publishers Inc.

Di Jiang, Yuanfeng Song, Rongzhong Lian, Siqi Bao, Jinhua Peng, Huang He, and Hua Wu. 2018. Familia: A configurable topic modeling framework for industrial text engineering. *arXiv preprint arXiv:1808.03733*.

Dan Jurafsky. 2000. *Speech & language processing*. Pearson Education India.

TF Kennedy, Robert S Provence, James L Broyan, Patrick W Fink, Phong H Ngo, and Lazaro D Rodriguez. 2017. Topic models for rfid data modeling and localization. In *2017 IEEE International Conference on Big Data (Big Data)*, pages 1438–1446. IEEE.

Roland Kuhn and Renato De Mori. 1990. A cache-based natural language model for speech recognition. *IEEE transactions on pattern analysis and machine intelligence*, 12(6):570–583.

Raymond Lau, Ronald Rosenfeld, and Salim Roukos. 1993. Trigger-based language models: A maximum entropy approach. In *1993 IEEE International Conference on Acoustics, Speech, and Signal Processing*, volume 2, pages 45–48. IEEE.

Rasmus E Madsen, David Kauchak, and Charles Elkan. 2005. Modeling word burstiness using the dirichlet distribution. In *Proceedings of the 22nd international conference on Machine learning*, pages 545–552. ACM.

Fernanda de Oliveira Capela and Jose Emmanuel Ramirez-Marquez. 2019. Detecting urban identity perception via newspaper topic modeling. *Cities*, 93:72–83.

Sinno Jialin Pan and Qiang Yang. 2010. A survey on transfer learning. *IEEE Transactions on knowledge and data engineering*, 22(10):1345–1359.

Yao Quanming, Wang Mengshuo, Jair Escalante Hugo, Guyon Isabelle, Hu Yi-Qi, Li Yu-Feng, Tu Wei-Wei, Yang Qiang, and Yu Yang. 2018. Taking human out of learning applications: A survey on automated machine learning. *arXiv preprint arXiv:1810.13306*.

Natasha Singh-Miller and Michael Collins. 2007. Trigger-based language modeling using a loss-sensitive perceptron algorithm. In *2007 IEEE International Conference on Acoustics, Speech and Signal Processing-ICASSP '07*, volume 4, pages IV–25. IEEE.

Yuanfeng Song, Di Jiang, Xueyang Wu, Qian Xu, Raymond Chi-Wing Wong, and Qiang Yang. 2019. Topic-aware dialogue speech recognition with transfer learning. In *Interspeech, Austria*.

Andreas Stolcke. 2002. Srilm-an extensible language modeling toolkit. In *Seventh international conference on spoken language processing*.

Jonathan Wintrode and Sanjeev Khudanpur. 2014. Combining local and broad topic context to improve term detection. In *Spoken Language Technology Workshop (SLT), 2014 IEEE*, pages 442–447. IEEE.

Hainan Xu, Tongfei Chen, Dongji Gao, Yiming Wang, Ke Li, Nagendra Goel, Yishay Carmiel, Daniel Povey, and Sanjeev Khudanpur. 2018. A pruned rnnlm lattice-rescoring algorithm for automatic speech recognition. In *2018 IEEE International Conference on Acoustics, Speech and Signal Processing (ICASSP)*, pages 5929–5933. IEEE.

Jinhui Yuan, Fei Gao, Qirong Ho, Wei Dai, Jinliang Wei, Xun Zheng, Eric Po Xing, Tie-Yan Liu, and Wei-Ying Ma. 2015. Lightlda: Big topic models on modest computer clusters. In *Proceedings of the 24th International Conference on World Wide Web*, pages 1351–1361. International World Wide Web Conferences Steering Committee.

Controlling Sequence-to-Sequence Models - A Demonstration on Neural-based Acrostic Generator

Liang-Hsin Shen, Pei-Lun Tai, Chao-Chung Wu, Shou-De Lin
Department of Computer Science and Information Engineering,
National Taiwan University
{laurice, b04902105, r05922042, sdlin}@csie.ntu.edu.tw

Abstract

An acrostic is a form of writing for which the first token of each line (or other recurring features in the text) forms a meaningful sequence. In this paper we present a generalized acrostic generation system that can hide certain message in a flexible pattern specified by the users. Different from previous works that focus on rule-based solutions, here we adopt a neural-based sequence-to-sequence model to achieve this goal. Besides acrostic, users can also specify the rhyme and length of the output sequences. To the best of our knowledge, this is the first neural-based natural language generation system that demonstrates the capability of performing micro-level control over output sentences.

1 Introduction

Acrostic is a form of writing aiming at hiding messages in text, often used in sarcasm or to deliver private information. In previous works, English acrostic have been generated by searching for paraphrases in WordNet's synsets (Stein et al., 2014). Synonyms that contain needed characters replace the corresponding words in the context to generate the acrostic. Nowadays Seq2Seq models have become a popular choice for text generation, including generating text from table (Liu et al., 2018), summaries (Nallapati et al., 2016), short-text conversations (Shang et al., 2015), machine translation (Bahdanau et al., 2015; Sutskever et al., 2014) and so on. In contrast to a rule-based or template-based generator, such Seq2Seq solutions are often considered more general and creative, as they do not rely heavily on pre-requisite knowledge or patterns to produce meaningful content. Although several works have presented automatic generation on rhymed text (Zhang and Lapata, 2014; Ghazvininejad et al., 2016), the works do not focus on controlling the rhyme

of the generated content. One drawback of a neural-based Seq2Seq model is that the outputs are hard to control since the generation follows certain non-deterministic probabilistic model (or language model), which makes it non-trivial to impose a hard-constraint such as acrostic (i.e. micro-controlling the position of a specific token) and rhyme. In this work, we present an NLG system that allows the users to micro-control the generation of a Seq2Seq model without any post-processing. Besides specifying the tokens and their corresponding locations for acrostic, our model allows the users to choose the rhyme and length of the generated lines. We show that with simple adjustment, a Seq2Seq model such as the Transformer (Vaswani et al., 2017) can be trained to control the generation of the text. Our demo system focuses on Chinese and English lyrics, which can be regarded as a writing style in between articles and poetry. We consider a general version of acrostic writing, which means the users can arbitrarily choose the position to place acrostic tokens. The 2-minute demonstration video can be found at https://youtu.be/9tX6ELCNMCE.

2 Model Description

Normally a neural-based Seq2Seq model is learned using input/output sequences as training pairs (Nallapati et al., 2016; Cho et al., 2014a). By providing sufficient amount of such training pairs, it is expected that the model learns how to produce the output sequences based on the inputs. Here we would like to first report a finding that a Seq2Seq model is capable of discovering the hidden associations between inputting *control signals* and outputting sequences. Based on the finding we have created a demo system to show that the users can indeed guide the outputs of a Seq2Seq model in a

Proceedings of the 2019 EMNLP and the 9th IJCNLP (System Demonstrations), pages 43–48
Hong Kong, China, November 3 – 7, 2019. ©2019 Association for Computational Linguistics

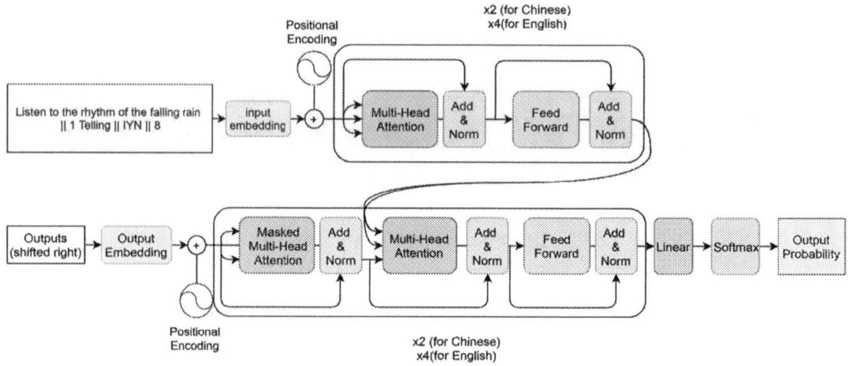

Figure 1: The structure of Transformer model.

fine-grained manner. In our demo, the users are allowed to control three aspects of the generated sequences: rhyme, sentence length and the positions of designated tokens. In other words, our Seq2Seq model not only is capable of generate next line satisfying the length and rhyme constraints provided by the user, it can also produce the exact word at a position specified by the user. The rhyme of a sentence is the last syllable of the last word in that sentence. The length of a sentence is the number of tokens in that sentence. To elaborate how our model is trained, we use three consecutive lines (denoted as S_1, S_2, S_3) of lyrics from the song "Rhythm of the Rain" as an example. Normally a Seq2Seq model is trained based on the following input/output pairs.

> S_1: Listen to the rhythm of the falling rain $\rightarrow$ S_2: Telling me just what a fool I've been

> S_2: Telling me just what a fool I've been $\rightarrow$ S_3: I wish that it would go and let me cry in vain

With some experiments on training Seq2Seq models, we have discovered an interesting fact: By appending the *control signals* in the end of the input sequences, after seeing sufficient amount of such data, the Seq2Seq model can automatically discover the association between input signals and outputs. Once the associations are identified, then we can use the *control signals* to guide the output of the model. For instance, here we append additional control information to the end of the training sequence as below

> S_1: Listen to the rhythm of the falling

rain $\parallel$ 1 *Telling* $\parallel$ *IYN* $\parallel$ 8 $\rightarrow$ S_2: Telling me just what a fool I've been

S_2: Telling me just what a fool I've been $\parallel$ 2 *wish* 6 *go* $\parallel$ *EYN* $\parallel$ 12 $\rightarrow$ S_3: I wish that it would go and let me cry in vain

The three types of *control signals* are separated by "$\parallel$". The first *control signal* indicates the position of the designated words. 1 *Telling* tells the system the token *Telling* should be produced at the first position of the output sequence s_2. Similarly, 2 *wish* 6 *go* means that the second/sixth token in the output sequence shall be *wish/go*. The second *control signal* is the rhyme of the target sentence. For instance, IHN corresponds to a specific rhyme (/In/) and EYN corresponds to another (/en/). Note that here we use the formal name of the rhyme (e.g. EYN) to improve readability. To train our system, any arbitrary symbol would work. The third part contains a digit (e.g. 8) to control the length of the output line.

By adding such additional information, Seq2Seq models can eventually learn the *meaning* of the *control signal* as they can produce outputs according to those signals with very high accuracy. Note that in our demo, all results are produced by our Seq2Seq model without any post-processing, nor do we provide any prerequisite knowledge about what length, rhyme or position really stands for to the model.

We train our system based on the Transformer model (Vaswani et al., 2017), though additional experiments show that other RNN-based Seq2Seq models such as the one based on GRU (Cho et al., 2014b) or LSTM would also work. The model consists of an encoder and a decoder. Our encoder

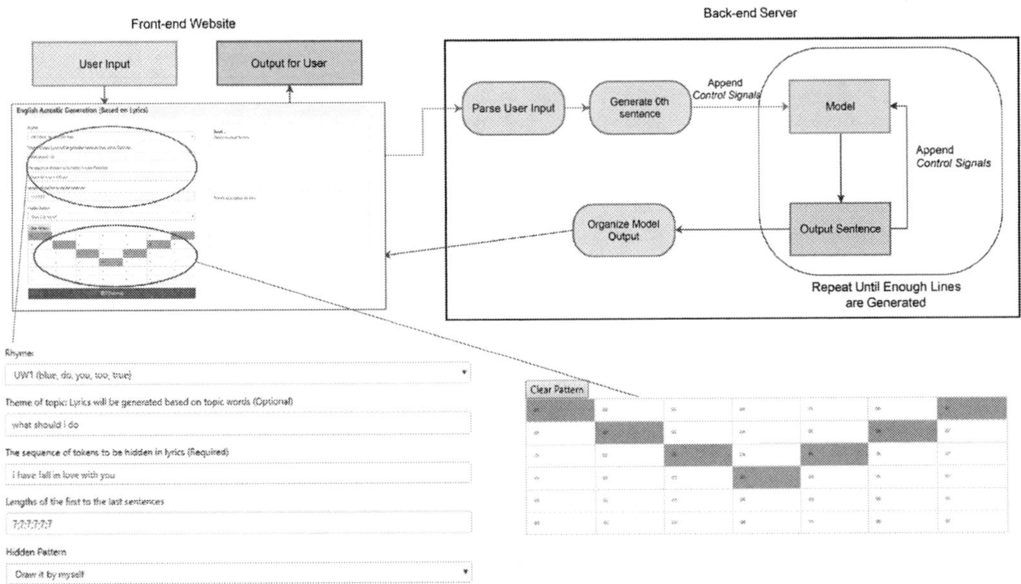

Figure 2: The structure of our acrostic generating system.

consists of two identical layers when training on Chinese lyrics and four identical layers when training on English lyrics. Each layer includes two sub-layers. The first is a multi-head attention layer and the second one is a fully connected feed-forward layer. Residual connections (He et al., 2016) are implemented between the sub-layers. The decoder also consists of two identical layers when training on Chinese lyrics and four identical layers when training on English lyrics.. Each layer includes three sub-layers: a masked multi-head attention layer, a multi-head attention layer that performs attention over the output of encoder and a fully-connected feed-forward layer. The model structure is shown in Figure 1. Note that in the original paper (Vaswani et al., 2017), Transformer consists of six identical layers for both encoder and decoder. To save resource, we start training with fewer layers than the original paper and discover that the model still performs well. Thus, we use fewer layers than the proposed Transformer model.

3 User Interface

Figure 2 illustrates the interface and data flow of our acrostic lyric generating system. First, there are several conditions (or *control signals*) that can be specified by the users:

- Rhyme: For Chinese lyrics, there are 33 different rhymes for users to choose from. As for English lyrics, there are 30 different rhymes for users to choose from.

- Theme of topic: The theme given by user is used to generate the zeroth sentence. In Chinese Acrostic demonstration, our system would pick a sentence from training set that is most similar to the user input, measured by the number of n-grams. As for English Acrostic demo, the user input of theme is directly used as the zeroth sentence.

- Length of each line: User can specify the length of every single line (separated by ;). For example, "5;6;7" means that the user wants to generate acrostic that contains 3 lines, with length equals to 5, 6, 7, respectively.

- The sequence of tokens to be hidden in the output sequences.

- Hidden Pattern: The exact positions for each token to be hidden. Apart from the common options, such as hiding in the first/last positions of each sentence or hiding in the diagonal positions, our system offers a more general and flexible way to define the pattern, realized through the *Draw It Myself* option. As shown in the bottom right corner of

Figure 2, a table based on the length of each line specified by the users is created for the users to select the positions to place acrostic tokens.

The generation is done on the server side. After receiving the *control signals* provided by users, the server first uses the given theme to search for a related line (denoted as *zeroth sequence*) from the lyric corpus, based on both sentence-level matching and character-level matching. Then the given condition of first sentence is appended to this *zeroth* sequence to serve as initial input to the Seq2Seq model for generating first line of outputs. Next, the given condition of second sentence is appended to the generated first line as input to generate the second line. The same process is repeated until all lines are generated.

4 Experiment and Results

4.1 Data set

We have two versions: one training on Chinese lyrics and one on English lyrics.

The Chinese lyrics are crawled from *Mojim lyrics site* and *NetEase Cloud*. To avoid rare characters, the vocabulary size is set to the most frequent 50,000 characters. The English lyrics are crawled from *Lyrics Freak*. The vocabulary size is set to the most frequent 50,000 words. For each line of lyrics, we first calculate its length and then retrieve the rhyme of the last token. To generate the training pairs, we randomly append to the input sequence *some tokens and their positions* of the targeting sequence as the first *control signal*, followed by the *rhyme* and then *length*. Below are two example training pairs:

> S_1: Listen to the rhythm of the *falling rain* ‖ 2 *me* 3 *just* ‖ *IYN* ‖ 8 → S_2: Telling me just what a fool I've been

> S_2: Telling me just what a fool I've been ‖ 2 *wish* 6 *go* 7 *and* ‖ *EYN* ‖ 12 → S_3: I wish that it would go and let me cry in vain

In total there are about 651,339/1,000,000 training pairs we use to train our Chinese/English acrostic systems.

4.2 Evaluation

Our system has three controllable conditions on generating acrostic: the positions of designated tokens, the rhyme of each line and the length of each line. The evaluation set consists of 30,000 lines that are not included in training data. We first evaluate how accurate the control conditions can be satisfied. As shown in Table 1, the model can almost perfectly satisfy the request from users. We also evaluate the quality of learned language model for Chinese/English lyrics. The bi-gram perplexity of original training corpus is 54.56/53.2. The bi-gram perplexity of generated lyrics becomes lower (42.33/42.34), which indicates the language model does learn a better way to represent the lyrics data. In this experiment we find that training on English lyrics is harder than training on Chinese lyrics. English has strict grammatical rules while Chinese lyrics have more freedom in forming a sentence. We also observe that the model tends to generate sentences that use the same words that appear in their previous sentences. This behavior might be learned from the repetition of lyrics lines.

4.3 Demonstration of Results

We provide our system outputs from different aspects.

The first example in Figure 3 shows that we can control the length of each line to produce a *triangle*-shaped lyrics.

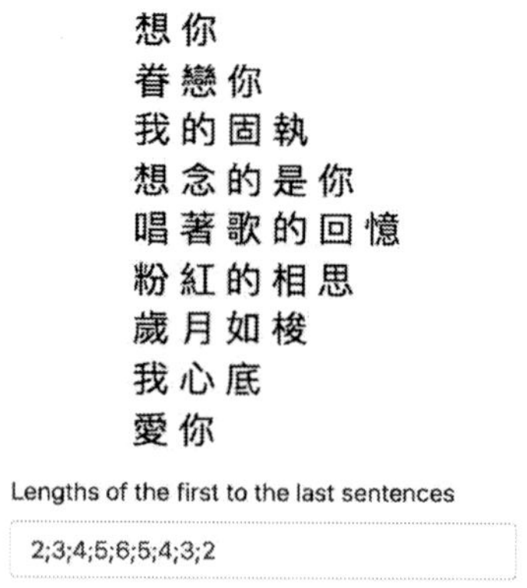

想 你
眷 戀 你
我 的 固 執
想 念 的 是 你
唱 著 歌 的 回 憶
粉 紅 的 相 思
歲 月 如 梭
我 心 底
愛 你

Lengths of the first to the last sentences

2;3;4;5;6;5;4;3;2

Figure 3: Length control of each sentence.

Second, we would like to demonstrate the results in generating acrostic. Some people use acrostic to hide message that has no resemblance with the content of the full text. We would show both English and Chinese examples generated by our system.

Figure 4 shows hiding a sentence in the first

Condition	Accuracy(Chinese)	Accuracy(English)
Character (CH) / Word (EN) Position	99.38%	98.21%
Rhyme	99.31%	97.67%
Sentence Length	99.90%	99.85%
Source	Perplexity(Chinese)	Perplexity(English)
Training data	54.56	53.2
Model generated data	42.33	42.34

Table 1: The accuracy of each condition tested on 30,000 lines and the perplexity of the original text and the text generated by our model.

word of each sentences. The sentence that being concealed in the lyrics is *I don't like you*, which is very different from the meaning of the full lyrics.

Figure 4: Message in English lyrics: *I don't like you*.

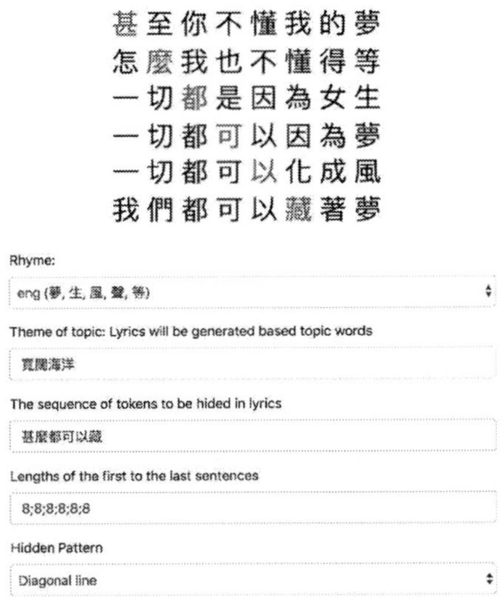

Figure 5: Hidden message in Chinese lyrics: 甚麼都可以藏 with rhyme *eng*.

Figure 5 shows a Chinese acrostic generated by our system. We hide a message 甚麼都可以藏 (Anything can be hidden) in the diagonal line of a piece of lyrics that talks about relationship and dream.

Third, we can also play with the visual shape of the designated words. Figure 6 shows an example

Figure 6: Message in English lyrics: *be the change you wish to see in the world*. To make the diamond shape clearer, the words are aligned.

of hiding a sentence in the shape of diamond in the generated lyrics. The message being concealed is *be the change you wish to see in the world*. Figure 7 shows that we can hide the message using the shape of a heart.

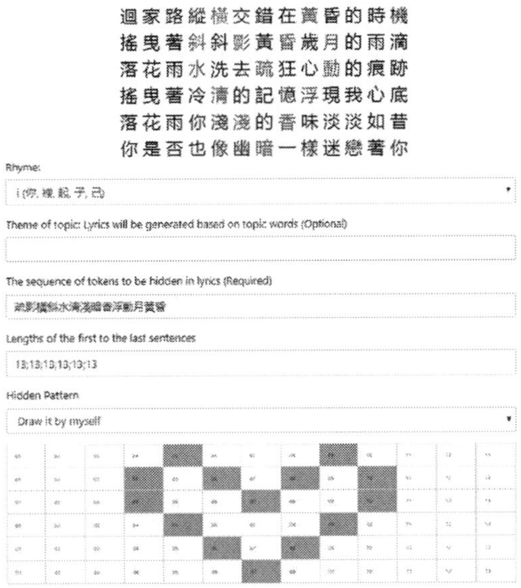

Figure 7: The designated characters form a heart. The sentence hidden in the lyrics is 疏影橫斜水清淺暗香浮動月黃昏 (The shadow reflects on the water and the fragrance drifts under the moon with the color of dusk) with rhyme *i*.

5 Conclusion

We show that by appending additional information in the training input sequences, it is possible to train a Seq2Seq model whose outputs can be controlled in a fine-grained level. This finding enables us to design and demonstrate a general acrostic generating system with various features controlled, including the length of each line, the rhyme of each line and the target tokens to be produced and their corresponding positions. Our results have shown that the proposed model not only is capable of generating meaningful content, it also follows the constraints with very high accuracy. We believe that this finding can further lead to other useful applications in natural language generation.

References

Dzmitry Bahdanau, Kyunghyun Cho, and Yoshua Bengio. 2015. Neural machine translation by jointly learning to align and translate. In *3rd International Conference on Learning Representations, ICLR 2015, San Diego, CA, USA, May 7-9, 2015, Conference Track Proceedings*.

Kyunghyun Cho, Bart van Merrienboer, Çaglar Gülçehre, Dzmitry Bahdanau, Fethi Bougares, Holger Schwenk, and Yoshua Bengio. 2014a. Learning phrase representations using RNN encoder-decoder for statistical machine translation. In *Proceedings of the 2014 Conference on Empirical Methods in Natural Language Processing, EMNLP 2014, October 25-29, 2014, Doha, Qatar, A meeting of SIGDAT, a Special Interest Group of the ACL*, pages 1724–1734.

Kyunghyun Cho, Bart van Merriënboer, Çalar Gülçehre, Dzmitry Bahdanau, Fethi Bougares, Holger Schwenk, and Yoshua Bengio. 2014b. Learning phrase representations using rnn encoder–decoder for statistical machine translation. In *Proceedings of the 2014 Conference on Empirical Methods in Natural Language Processing (EMNLP)*, pages 1724–1734, Doha, Qatar. Association for Computational Linguistics.

Marjan Ghazvininejad, Xing Shi, Yejin Choi, and Kevin Knight. 2016. Generating topical poetry. In *Proceedings of the 2016 Conference on Empirical Methods in Natural Language Processing, EMNLP 2016, Austin, Texas, USA, November 1-4, 2016*, pages 1183–1191.

Kaiming He, Xiangyu Zhang, Shaoqing Ren, and Jian Sun. 2016. Deep residual learning for image recognition. In *2016 IEEE Conference on Computer Vision and Pattern Recognition, CVPR 2016, Las Vegas, NV, USA, June 27-30, 2016*, pages 770–778.

Tianyu Liu, Kexiang Wang, Lei Sha, Baobao Chang, and Zhifang Sui. 2018. Table-to-text generation by structure-aware seq2seq learning. In *Proceedings of the Thirty-Second AAAI Conference on Artificial Intelligence, (AAAI-18), the 30th innovative Applications of Artificial Intelligence (IAAI-18), and the 8th AAAI Symposium on Educational Advances in Artificial Intelligence (EAAI-18), New Orleans, Louisiana, USA, February 2-7, 2018*, pages 4881–4888.

Ramesh Nallapati, Bowen Zhou, Cícero Nogueira dos Santos, Çaglar Gülçehre, and Bing Xiang. 2016. Abstractive text summarization using sequence-to-sequence rnns and beyond. In *Proceedings of the 20th SIGNLL Conference on Computational Natural Language Learning, CoNLL 2016, Berlin, Germany, August 11-12, 2016*, pages 280–290.

Lifeng Shang, Zhengdong Lu, and Hang Li. 2015. Neural responding machine for short-text conversation. In *Proceedings of the 53rd Annual Meeting of the Association for Computational Linguistics and the 7th International Joint Conference on Natural Language Processing of the Asian Federation of Natural Language Processing, ACL 2015, July 26-31, 2015, Beijing, China, Volume 1: Long Papers*, pages 1577–1586.

Benno Stein, Matthias Hagen, and Christof Bräutigam. 2014. Generating acrostics via paraphrasing and heuristic search. In *COLING 2014, 25th International Conference on Computational Linguistics, Proceedings of the Conference: Technical Papers, August 23-29, 2014, Dublin, Ireland*, pages 2018–2029.

Ilya Sutskever, Oriol Vinyals, and Quoc V. Le. 2014. Sequence to sequence learning with neural networks. In *Advances in Neural Information Processing Systems 27: Annual Conference on Neural Information Processing Systems 2014, December 8-13 2014, Montreal, Quebec, Canada*, pages 3104–3112.

Ashish Vaswani, Noam Shazeer, Niki Parmar, Jakob Uszkoreit, Llion Jones, Aidan N. Gomez, Lukasz Kaiser, and Illia Polosukhin. 2017. Attention is all you need. In *Advances in Neural Information Processing Systems 30: Annual Conference on Neural Information Processing Systems 2017, 4-9 December 2017, Long Beach, CA, USA*, pages 6000–6010.

Xingxing Zhang and Mirella Lapata. 2014. Chinese poetry generation with recurrent neural networks. In *Proceedings of the 2014 Conference on Empirical Methods in Natural Language Processing, EMNLP 2014, October 25-29, 2014, Doha, Qatar, A meeting of SIGDAT, a Special Interest Group of the ACL*, pages 670–680.

EASSE: Easier Automatic Sentence Simplification Evaluation

Fernando Alva-Manchego
University of Sheffield
f.alva@sheffield.ac.uk

Louis Martin
Facebook AI Research
Inria
louismartin@fb.com

Carolina Scarton
University of Sheffield
c.scarton@sheffield.ac.uk

Lucia Specia
Imperial College London
l.specia@imperial.ac.uk

Abstract

We introduce EASSE, a Python package aiming to facilitate and standardise automatic evaluation and comparison of Sentence Simplification (SS) systems. EASSE provides a single access point to a broad range of evaluation resources: standard automatic metrics for assessing SS outputs (e.g. SARI), word-level accuracy scores for certain simplification transformations, reference-independent quality estimation features (e.g. compression ratio), and standard test data for SS evaluation (e.g. TurkCorpus). Finally, EASSE generates easy-to-visualise reports on the various metrics and features above and on how a particular SS output fares against reference simplifications. Through experiments, we show that these functionalities allow for better comparison and understanding of the performance of SS systems.

1 Introduction

Sentence Simplification (SS) consists of modifying the content and structure of a sentence to improve its readability while retaining its original meaning. For automatic evaluation of a simplification output, it is common practice to use machine translation (MT) metrics (e.g. BLEU (Papineni et al., 2002)), simplicity metrics (e.g. SARI (Xu et al., 2016)), and readability metrics (e.g. FKGL (Kincaid et al., 1975)).

Most of these metrics are available in individual code repositories, with particular software requirements that sometimes differ even in programming language (e.g. corpus-level SARI is implemented in Java, whilst sentence-level SARI is available in both Java and Python). Other metrics (e.g. SAMSA (Sulem et al., 2018b)) suffer from insufficient documentation or require executing multiple scripts with hard-coded paths, which prevents researchers from using them.

EASSE (Easier Automatic Sentence Simplification Evaluation) is a Python package that provides access to popular automatic metrics in SS evaluation and ready-to-use public datasets through a simple command-line interface. With this tool, we make the following contributions: (1) we provide popular automatic metrics in a single software package, (2) we supplement these metrics with word-level transformation analysis and reference-less Quality Estimation (QE) features, (3) we provide straightforward access to commonly used evaluation datasets, and (4) we generate a comprehensive HTML report for quantitative and qualitative evaluation of a SS system. We believe this package will facilitate evaluation and improve reproducibility of results in SS. EASSE is available in https://github.com/feralvam/easse.

2 Package Overview

2.1 Automatic Corpus-level Metrics

Although human judgements on grammaticality, meaning preservation and simplicity are considered the most reliable method for evaluating a SS system's output (Štajner et al., 2016), it is common practice to use automatic metrics. They are useful for either assessing systems at development stage, to compare different architectures, for model selection, or as part of a training policy. EASSE implementation works as a wrapper for the most common evaluation metrics in SS:

BLEU is a precision-oriented metric that relies on the proportion of n-gram matches between a system's output and reference(s). Previous work (Xu et al., 2016) has shown that BLEU correlates fairly well with human judgements of grammaticality and meaning preservation. EASSE uses

Proceedings of the 2019 EMNLP and the 9th IJCNLP (System Demonstrations), pages 49–54
Hong Kong, China, November 3 – 7, 2019. ©2019 Association for Computational Linguistics

SACREBLEU (Post, 2018)[1] to calculate BLEU. This package was designed to standardise the process by which BLEU is calculated: it only expects a detokenised system's output and the name of a test set. Furthermore, it ensures that the same preprocessing steps are used for the system output and reference sentences.

SARI measures how the simplicity of a sentence was improved based on the words added, deleted and kept by a system. The metric compares the system's output to multiple simplification references and the original sentence. SARI has shown positive correlation with human judgements of simplicity gain. We re-implement SARI's corpus-level version in Python (it was originally available in Java). In this version, for each operation ($ope \in \{add, del, keep\}$) and n-gram order, precision $p_{ope}(n)$, recall $r_{ope}(n)$ and F1 $f_{ope}(n)$ scores are calculated. These are then averaged over the n-gram order to get the overall operation F1 score F_{ope}:

$$f_{ope}(n) = \frac{2 \times p_{ope}(n) \times r_{ope}(n)}{p_{ope}(n) + r_{ope}(n)}$$

$$F_{ope} = \frac{1}{k} \sum_{n=[1,..,k]} f_{ope}(n)$$

Although Xu et al. (2016) indicate that only precision should be considered for the deletion operation, we follow the Java implementation that uses F1 score for all operations in corpus-level SARI.

SAMSA measures structural simplicity (i.e. sentence splitting). This is in contrast to SARI, which is designed to evaluate simplifications involving paraphrasing. EASSE re-factors the original SAMSA implementation[2] with some modifications: (1) an internal call to the TUPA parser (Hershcovich et al., 2017), which generates the semantic annotations for each original sentence; (2) a modified version of the monolingual word aligner (Sultan et al., 2014) that is compatible with Python 3, and uses Stanford CoreNLP (Manning et al., 2014)[3] through their official Python interface; and (3) a single function call to get a SAMSA score instead of running a series of scripts.

FKGL Readability metrics, such as Flesch-Kincaid Grade Level (FKGL), are commonly reported as measures of simplicity. They however only rely on average sentence lengths and number of syllables per word, so short sentences would get good scores even if they are ungrammatical, or do not preserve meaning (Wubben et al., 2012). Therefore, these scores should be interpreted with caution. EASSE re-implements FKGL by porting publicly available scripts[4] to Python 3 and fixing some edge case inconsistencies (e.g. newlines incorrectly counted as words or bugs with memoization).

2.2 Word-level Analysis and QE Features

Word-level Transformation Analysis EASSE includes algorithms to determine which specific text transformations a SS system performs more effectively. This is done based on word-level alignment and analysis.

Since there is no available simplification dataset with manual annotations of the transformations performed, we re-use the annotation algorithms from MASSAlign (Paetzold et al., 2017). Given a pair of sentences (e.g. original and system output), the algorithms use word alignments to identify deletions, movements, replacements and copies (see Fig. 1). This process is prone to some errors: when compared to manual labels produced by four annotators in 100 original-simplified pairs, the automatic algorithms achieved a micro-averaged F1 score of 0.61 (Alva-Manchego et al., 2017).

We generate two sets of automatic word-level annotations: (1) between the original sentences and their reference simplifications, and (2) between the original sentences and their automatic simplifications produced by a SS system. Considering (1) as reference labels, we calculate the F1 score of each transformation in (2) to estimate their correctness. When more than one reference simplification exists, we calculate the per-transformation F1 scores of the output against each reference, and then keep the highest one as the sentence-level score. The corpus-level scores are the average of sentence-level scores.

Quality Estimation Features Traditional automatic metrics used for SS rely on the existence and quality of references, and are often not enough to analyse the complex process of simplification. QE

---

[1] https://github.com/mjpost/sacreBLEU
[2] https://github.com/eliorsulem/SAMSA
[3] https://stanfordnlp.github.io/
stanfordnlp/corenlp_client.html

[4] https://github.com/mmautner/
readability

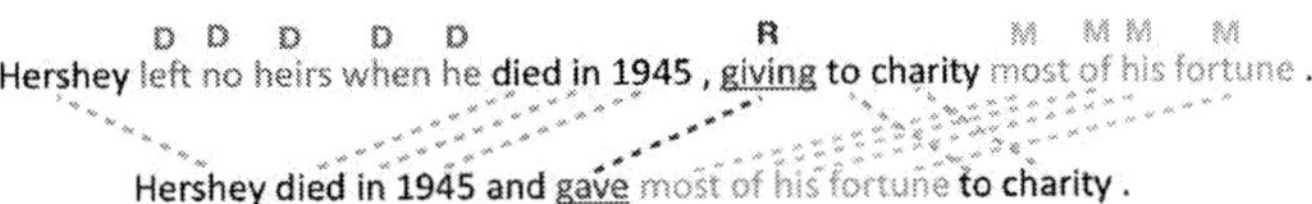

Figure 1: Example of automatic transformation annotations based on word alignments between an original (top) and a simplified (bottom) sentence. Unaligned words are DELETE. Words that are aligned to a different form are REPLACE. Aligned words without an explicit label are COPY. A word whose relative index in the original sentence changes in the simplified one is considered a MOVE.

leverages both the source sentence and the output simplification to provide additional information on specific behaviours of simplification systems which are not reflected in metrics such as SARI. EASSE uses QE features from Martin et al. (2018)'s open-source repository[5]. The QE features currently available are: the compression ratio of the simplification with respect to its source sentence, its Levenshtein similarity, the average number of sentence splits performed by the system, the proportion of exact matches (i.e. original sentences left untouched), average proportion of added words, deleted words, and lexical complexity score[6].

2.3 Access to Test Datasets

EASSE provides access to three publicly available datasets for automatic SS evaluation (Table 1): PWKP (Zhu et al., 2010), TurkCorpus (Xu et al., 2016), and HSplit (Sulem et al., 2018a). All of them consist of the data from the original datasets, which are sentences extracted from English Wikipedia (EW) articles. EASSE can also evaluate system's outputs in other custom datasets provided by the user.

PWKP Zhu et al. (2010) automatically aligned sentences in 65,133 EW articles to their corresponding versions in Simple EW (SEW). Since the latter is aimed at English learners, its articles are expected to contain fewer words and simpler grammar structures than those in their EW counterpart. The test set split of PWKP contains 100 sentences, with 1-to-1 and 1-to-N alignments (resp. 93 and 7 instances). The latter correspond to instances of sentence splitting. Since this dataset has only one reference for each original sentence,

Test Dataset	Instances	Alignment Type	References
PWKP	93	1-to-1	1
	7	1-to-N	1
TurkCorpus	359	1-to-1	8
HSplit	359	1-to-N	4

Table 1: Test datasets available in EASSE. An instance corresponds to a source sentence with one or more possible references. Each reference can be composed of one or more sentences.

it is not ideal for calculating automatic metrics that rely on multiple references, such as SARI.

TurkCorpus Xu et al. (2016) asked crowdworkers to simplify 2,359 original sentences extracted from PWKP to collect multiple simplification references for each one. This dataset was then randomly split into tuning (2,000 instances) and test (359 instances) sets. The test set only contains 1-to-1 alignments, mostly with instances of paraphrasing and deletion. Each original sentence in TurkCorpus has 8 simplified references. As such, it is better suited for computing SARI and multi-reference BLEU scores.

HSplit Sulem et al. (2018a) recognised that existing EW-based datasets did not contain sufficient instances of sentence splitting. As such, they collected four reference simplifications of this transformation for all 359 original sentences in the TurkCorpus test set. Even though SAMSA's computation does not require access to references, this dataset can be used to compute an upperbound on the expected performance of SS systems that model this type of structural simplification.

2.4 HTML Report Generation

EASSE wraps all the aforementioned analyses in a simple comprehensive HTML report that can be generated with a single command. This report compares the system output with human reference(s) using simplification metrics and

---

[5]`https://github.com/facebookresearch/`
`text-simplification-evaluation`

[6]The lexical complexity score of a simplified sentence is computed by taking the log-ranks of each word in the frequency table. The ranks are then aggregated by taking their third quartile.

QE features. It also plots the distribution of compression ratios or Levenshtein similarities between sources and simplifications over the test set. Moreover, the analysis is broken down by source sentence length in order to get insights on how the model handles short source sentence versus longer source sentences, e.g. *does the model keep short sentences unmodified more often than long sentences?* This report further facilitates qualitative analysis of system outputs by displaying source sentences with their respective simplifications. The modifications performed by the model are highlighted for faster and easier analysis. For visualisation, EASSE samples simplification instances to cover different behaviours of the systems. Instances that are sampled include simplifications with sentence splitting, simplifications that significantly modify the source sentence, output sentences with a high compression rate, those that display lexical simplifications, among others. Each of these aspects is illustrated with 10 instances. An example of the report can be viewed at `https://github.com/feralvam/easse/blob/master/demo/report.gif`.

3 Experiments

We collected publicly available outputs of several SS systems (Sec. 3.1) to evaluate their performance using the functionalities available in EASSE. In particular, we compare them using automatic metrics, and provide some insights on the reasoning behind their results (Sec. 3.2).

3.1 Sentence Simplification Systems

EASSE provides access to various SS system outputs that follow different approaches for the task. For instance, we include those that rely on phrase-based statistical MT, either by itself (e.g. PBSMT-R (Wubben et al., 2012)), or coupled with semantic analysis, (e.g. Hybrid (Narayan and Gardent, 2014)). We also include SBSMT-SARI (Xu et al., 2016), which relies on syntax-based statistical MT; DRESS-LS (Zhang and Lapata, 2017), a neural model using the standard encoder-decoder architecture with attention combined with reinforcement learning; and DMASS-DCSS (Zhao et al., 2018), the current state-of-the-art in the TurkCorpus, which is based on the Transformer architecture (Vaswani et al., 2017).

3.2 Comparison and Analysis of Scores

Automatic Metrics For illustration purposes, we compare systems' outputs using BLEU and SARI in TurkCorpus (with 8 manual simplification references), and SAMSA in HSplit. For calculating Reference values in Table 2, we sample one of the 8 human references for each instance as others have done (Zhang and Lapata, 2017).

When reporting SAMSA scores, we only use the first 70 sentences of TurkCorpus that also appear in HSplit.[7] This allows us to compute Reference scores for instances that contain structural simplifications (i.e. sentence splits). We calculate SAMSA scores for each of the four manual simplifications in HSplit, and choose the highest as an upper-bound Reference value. The results for all three metrics are shown in Table 2.

System	TurkCorpus		HSplit
	SARI	BLEU	SAMSA
Reference	49.88	97.41	54.00
PBSMT-R	38.56	**81.11**	**47.59**
Hybrid	31.40	48.97	46.68
SBSMT-SARI	39.96	73.08	41.41
DRESS-LS	37.27	80.12	45.94
DMASS-DCSS	**40.42**	73.29	35.45

Table 2: Comparison of systems' performance based on automatic metrics.

DMASS-DCSS is the state-of-the-art in TurkCorpus according to SARI. However, it gets the lowest SAMSA score, and the third to last BLEU score. PBSMT-R is the best in terms of these two metrics. Finally, across all metrics, the Reference stills gets the highest values, with significant differences from the top performing systems.

Word-level Transformations In order to better understand the previous results, we use the word-level annotations of text transformations (Table 3). Since SARI was design to evaluate mainly paraphrasing transformations, the fact that SBSMT-SARI is the best at performing replacements and second place in copying explains its high SARI score. DMASS-DCSS is second best in replacements, while PBSMT-R (which achieved the highest BLEU score) is the best at copying. Hybrid is the best at performing deletions, but is the worst at replacements, which SARI mainly measures.

---

[7] At the time of this submission only a subset of 70 sentences had been released from HSplit. However, the full corpus will soon be available in EASSE.

The origin of the TurkCorpus set itself could explain some of these observations. According to Xu et al. (2016), the annotators in TurkCorpus were instructed to mainly produce paraphrases, i.e. mostly replacements with virtually no deletions. As such, copying words is also a significant transformation, so systems that are good at performing it better mimic the characteristics of the human simplifications in this dataset.

System	Delete	Move	Replace	Copy
PBSMT-R	34.18	2.64	23.65	**93.50**
Hybrid	**49.46**	**7.37**	1.03	70.73
SBSMT-SARI	28.42	1.26	**37.21**	92.89
DRESS-LS	40.31	1.43	12.62	86.76
DMASS-DCSS	38.03	5.10	34.79	86.70

Table 3: Transformation-based performance of the sentence simplification systems in the TurkCorpus test set.

Quality Estimation Features Table 4 displays a subset of QE features that reveal other aspects of the simplification systems. For instance, the scores make it clear that Hybrid compresses the input way more than other systems (compression ratio of 0.57 vs. ≥ 0.78 for the other systems) but almost never adds new words (addition proportion of 0.01). This additional information explains the high Delete and low Replace performance of this system in Table 3. DRESS-LS keeps the source sentence unmodified 26% of the time, which does not show in the word-level analysis. This confirms that QE features are complementary to automatic metrics and word-level analysis.

System	Compression ratio	Exact matches	Additions proportion	Deletion proportion
PBSMT-R	0.95	0.1	0.1	0.11
Hybrid	**0.57**	0.03	0.01	**0.41**
SBSMT-SARI	0.94	0.11	**0.16**	0.13
DRESS-LS	0.78	**0.26**	0.04	0.26
DMASS-DCSS	0.89	0.05	0.15	0.21

Table 4: Quality estimation features, which give additional information on the output of different systems.

Report Figure 2 displays the quantitative part of the HTML report generated for the DMASS-DCSS system. The report compares the system to a reference human simplification. The "System vs. Reference" table and the two plots indicate that DMASS-DCSS closely matches different aspects of human simplifications, according to QE features. This contributes to explaining the high SARI score of the this system in Table 2.

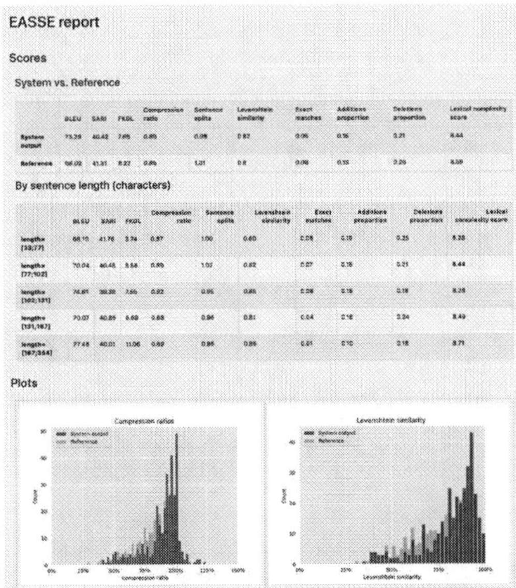

Figure 2: Overview of the HTML report for the DMASS-DCSS system (zoom in for more details).

4 Conclusion and Future Work

EASSE provides easy access to commonly used automatic metrics as well as to more detailed word-level transformation analysis and QE features which allows us to compare the quality of the generated outputs of different SS systems on public test datsets. We reported some experiments on the use of automatic metrics to obtain overall performance scores, followed by measurements of how effective the SS systems are at executing specific simplification transformations using word-level analysis and QE features. The former analysis provided insights about the simplification capabilities of each system, which help better explain the initial automatic scores.

In the future, we plan to continue developing the transformation-based analysis algorithms, so that more sophisticated transformations could be identified (e.g. splitting or subject-verb-object reordering). In addition, we expect to integrate more QE features to cover other aspects of the simplification process (e.g. depth of the dependency parse tree to measure syntactic complexity).

References

Fernando Alva-Manchego, Joachim Bingel, Gustavo Paetzold, Carolina Scarton, and Lucia Specia. 2017. Learning how to simplify from explicit labeling of complex-simplified text pairs. In *Proceedings of the Eighth International Joint Conference on Natural Language Processing (Volume 1: Long Papers)*, pages 295–305, Taipei, Taiwan. AFNLP.

Daniel Hershcovich, Omri Abend, and Ari Rappoport. 2017. A transition-based directed acyclic graph parser for ucca. In *Proceedings of the 55th Annual Meeting of the Association for Computational Linguistics (Volume 1: Long Papers)*, pages 1127–1138, Vancouver, Canada. ACL.

J.P. Kincaid, R.P. Fishburne, R.L. Rogers, and B.S. Chissom. 1975. Derivation of new readability formulas (automated readability index, fog count and flesch reading ease formula) for navy enlisted personnel. Technical Report 8-75, Chief of Naval Technical Training: Naval Air Station Memphis. 49 p.

Christopher Manning, Mihai Surdeanu, John Bauer, Jenny Finkel, Steven Bethard, and David McClosky. 2014. The stanford corenlp natural language processing toolkit. In *Proceedings of 52nd Annual Meeting of the Association for Computational Linguistics: System Demonstrations*, pages 55–60, Baltimore, Maryland. ACL.

Louis Martin, Samuel Humeau, Pierre-Emmanuel Mazaré, Éric de La Clergerie, Antoine Bordes, and Benoît Sagot. 2018. Reference-less quality estimation of text simplification systems. In *Proceedings of the 1st Workshop on Automatic Text Adaptation (ATA)*, pages 29–38, Tilburg, the Netherlands. ACL.

Shashi Narayan and Claire Gardent. 2014. Hybrid simplification using deep semantics and machine translation. In *Proceedings of the 52nd Annual Meeting of the Association for Computational Linguistics (Volume 1: Long Papers)*, pages 435–445, Baltimore, Maryland. ACL.

Gustavo H. Paetzold, Fernando Alva-Manchego, and Lucia Specia. 2017. Massalign: Alignment and annotation of comparable documents. In *Proceedings of the IJCNLP 2017, System Demonstrations*, pages 1–4, Tapei, Taiwan. ACL.

Kishore Papineni, Salim Roukos, Todd Ward, and Wei-Jing Zhu. 2002. Bleu: A method for automatic evaluation of machine translation. In *Proceedings of the 40th Annual Meeting on Association for Computational Linguistics*, ACL '02, pages 311–318, Philadelphia, Pennsylvania. ACL.

Matt Post. 2018. A call for clarity in reporting BLEU scores. In *Proceedings of the Third Conference on Machine Translation: Research Papers*, pages 186–191. Association for Computational Linguistics.

Elior Sulem, Omri Abend, and Ari Rappoport. 2018a. Bleu is not suitable for the evaluation of text simplification. In *Proceedings of the 2018 Conference on Empirical Methods in Natural Language Processing*, pages 738–744. ACL.

Elior Sulem, Omri Abend, and Ari Rappoport. 2018b. Semantic structural evaluation for text simplification. In *Proceedings of the 2018 Conference of the North American Chapter of the Association for Computational Linguistics: Human Language Technologies, Volume 1 (Long Papers)*, pages 685–696, New Orleans, Louisiana. ACL.

Md Sultan, Steven Bethard, and Tamara Sumner. 2014. Back to basics for monolingual alignment: Exploiting word similarity and contextual evidence. *Transactions of the Association for Computational Linguistics*, 2:219–230.

Ashish Vaswani, Noam Shazeer, Niki Parmar, Jakob Uszkoreit, Llion Jones, Aidan N Gomez, Ł ukasz Kaiser, and Illia Polosukhin. 2017. Attention is all you need. In I. Guyon, U. V. Luxburg, S. Bengio, H. Wallach, R. Fergus, S. Vishwanathan, and R. Garnett, editors, *Advances in Neural Information Processing Systems 30*, pages 5998–6008. Curran Associates, Inc.

Sander Wubben, Antal van den Bosch, and Emiel Krahmer. 2012. Sentence simplification by monolingual machine translation. In *Proceedings of the 50th Annual Meeting of the Association for Computational Linguistics (Volume 1: Long Papers)*, pages 1015–1024, Jeju Island, Korea. ACL.

Wei Xu, Courtney Napoles, Ellie Pavlick, Quanze Chen, and Chris Callison-Burch. 2016. Optimizing statistical machine translation for text simplification. *Transactions of the Association for Computational Linguistics*, 4:401–415.

Xingxing Zhang and Mirella Lapata. 2017. Sentence simplification with deep reinforcement learning. In *Proceedings of the 2017 Conference on Empirical Methods in Natural Language Processing*, pages 595–605, Copenhagen, Denmark. ACL.

Sanqiang Zhao, Rui Meng, Daqing He, Andi Saptono, and Bambang Parmanto. 2018. Integrating transformer and paraphrase rules for sentence simplification. In *Proceedings of the 2018 Conference on Empirical Methods in Natural Language Processing*, pages 3164–3173, Brussels, Belgium. ACL.

Zhemin Zhu, Delphine Bernhard, and Iryna Gurevych. 2010. A monolingual tree-based translation model for sentence simplification. In *Proceedings of the 23rd International Conference on Computational Linguistics*, COLING '10, pages 1353–1361, Stroudsburg, PA, USA. ACL.

Sanja Štajner, Maja Popović, Horacio Saggion, Lucia Specia, and Mark Fishel. 2016. Shared task on quality assessment for text simplification. In *Proceeding of the Workshop on Quality Assessment for Text Simplification - LREC 2016*, QATS 2016, pages 22–31, Portorož, Slovenia. ELRA.

EGG: a toolkit for research on Emergence of lanGuage in Games

Eugene Kharitonov
Facebook AI
kharitonov@fb.com

Rahma Chaabouni
Facebook AI Research / LSCP
rchaabouni@fb.com

Diane Bouchacourt
Facebook AI
dianeb@fb.com

Marco Baroni
Facebook AI / ICREA
mbaroni@fb.com

Abstract

There is renewed interest in simulating language emergence among deep neural agents that communicate to jointly solve a task, spurred by the practical aim to develop language-enabled interactive AIs, as well as by theoretical questions about the evolution of human language. However, optimizing deep architectures connected by a discrete communication channel (such as that in which language emerges) is technically challenging. We introduce EGG, a toolkit that greatly simplifies the implementation of emergent-language communication games. EGG's modular design provides a set of building blocks that the user can combine to create new games, easily navigating the optimization and architecture space. We hope that the tool will lower the technical barrier, and encourage researchers from various backgrounds to do original work in this exciting area.

1 Introduction

Studying the languages that emerge when neural agents interact with each other recently became a vibrant area of research (Havrylov and Titov, 2017; Lazaridou et al., 2016, 2018; Kottur et al., 2017; Bouchacourt and Baroni, 2018; Lowe et al., 2019). Interest in this scenario is fueled by the hypothesis that the ability to interact through a human-like language is a prerequisite for genuine AI (Mikolov et al., 2016; Chevalier-Boisvert et al., 2019). Furthermore, such simulations might lead to a better understanding of both standard NLP models (Chaabouni et al., 2019b) and the evolution of human language itself (Kirby, 2002).

For all its promise, research in this domain is technically very challenging, due to the discrete nature of communication. The latter pre-

vents the use of conventional optimization methods, requiring either Reinforcement Learning algorithms (e.g., REINFORCE; Williams 1992) or the Gumbel-Softmax relaxation (Maddison et al., 2016; Jang et al., 2016). The technical challenge might be particularly daunting for researchers whose expertise is not in machine learning, but in fields such as linguistics and cognitive science, that could contribute to this interdisciplinary research area.

To lower the starting barrier and encourage high-level research in this domain, we introduce the EGG (**E**mergence of lan**G**uage in **G**ames) toolkit. EGG aims at

1. Providing reliable building bricks for quick prototyping;
2. Serving as a library of pre-implemented games;
3. Providing tools for analyzing the emergent languages.

EGG is implemented in PyTorch (Paszke et al., 2017) and it is licensed under the MIT license. EGG can be installed from https://github.com/facebookresearch/EGG.

Notable features of EGG include: (a) Primitives for implementing single-symbol or variable-length communication (with vanilla RNNs (Elman, 1990), GRUs (Cho et al., 2014), LSTMs (Hochreiter and Schmidhuber, 1997));[1] (b) Training with optimization of the communication channel through REINFORCE or Gumbel-Softmax relaxation via a common interface; (c) Simplified configuration of the general components, such as check-pointing, optimization, Tensorboard support,[2] etc.; (d)

A screencast demonstration of EGG is available at https://vimeo.com/345470060

[1]EGG also provides an experimental support of Transformers (Vaswani et al., 2017).

[2]https://www.tensorflow.org/tensorboard

Proceedings of the 2019 EMNLP and the 9th IJCNLP (System Demonstrations), pages 55–60
Hong Kong, China, November 3 – 7, 2019. ©2019 Association for Computational Linguistics

A simple CUDA-aware command-line tool for hyperparameter grid-search.

2 EGG's architecture

In the first iteration of EGG, we concentrate on a simple class of games, involving a single, unidirectional (Sender → Receiver) message. In turn, messages can be either single-symbol or multi-symbol variable-length sequences. Our motivation for starting with this setup is two-fold. First, it corresponds to classic signaling games (Lewis, 1969), it already covers a large portion of the literature (e.g., 5 out of 6 relevant studies mentioned in Introduction) and it allows exploring many interesting research questions. Second, it constitutes a natural first step for further development; in particular, the majority of components should remain useful in multi-directional, multi-step setups.

2.1 Design principles

As different training methods and architectures are used in the literature, our primary goal is to provide EGG users with the ability to easily navigate the space of common design choices.

Building up on this idea, EGG makes switching between Gumbel-Softmax relaxation-based and REINFORCE-based training effortless, through the simple choice of a different wrapper. Similarly, one can switch between one-symbol communication and variable-length messages with little changes in the code.[3]

We aim to maintain EGG minimalist and "hackable" by encapsulating the user-implemented agent architectures, the Reinforce/GS agent wrappers and the game logic into PyTorch modules. The user can easily replace any part.

Finally, since virtually any machine-learning experiment has common pieces, such as setting the random seeds, configuring the optimizer, model check-pointing, etc., EGG pre-implements many of them, reducing the necessary amount of boiler-plate code to the minimum.

2.2 EGG design

EGG, in its first iteration, operates over the following entities. Firstly, there are two distinct agent roles: **Sender** and **Receiver**. Sender and Receiver

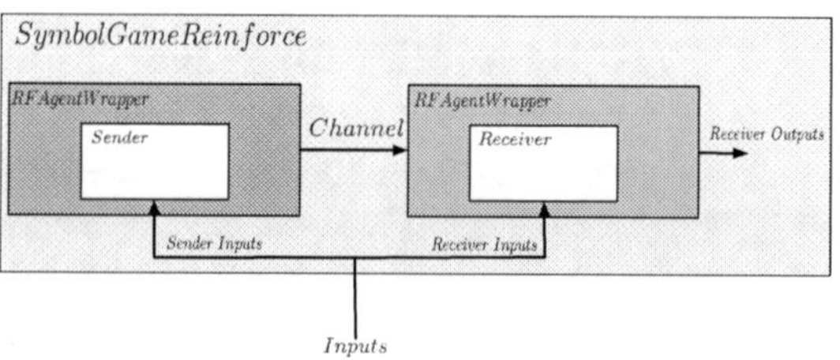

Figure 1: Example of EGG's game flow when using REINFORCE. White boxes (Sender and Receiver) represent the user-implemented agent architectures. The colored boxes are EGG-provided wrappers that implement a REINFORCE-based scenario. For example, *SymbolGameReinforce* is an instance of the Game block. It sets up single-symbol Sender/Receiver game optimized with REINFORCE. To use Gumbel-Softmax relaxation-based training instead, the user only has to change the EGG-provided wrappers.

are connected via a one-directional communication channel from the former to the latter, that has to produce the game-specific output.

The next crucial entity is **Game**. It encapsulates the agents and orchestrates the game scenario: feeding the data to the agents, transmitting the messages, and getting the output of Receiver. Figure 1 illustrates EGG's game flow in a specific example. Game applies a user-provided **loss** function, which might depend on the outputs of Receiver, the message transmitted, and the data. The value of the loss is minimized by a fourth entity, **Trainer**. Trainer also controls model checkpointing, early stopping, etc.

The Trainer and Game modules are pre-implemented in EGG. In a typical scenario, the communication method (single or multiple symbol messages) will be implemented by EGG-provided wrappers. As a result, what is left for the user to implement consists of: (a) the data stream, (b) core (non-communication-related) parts of the agents, (c) the loss. The data interface that is expected by Trainer is an instance of the standard PyTorch data loader `utils.data.DataLoader`.

To implement Sender, the user must define a module that consumes the data and outputs a tensor. On Receiver's side, the user has to implement a module that takes an input consisting of a message embedding and possibly further data, and generates Receiver's output.

Section 4 below provides examples of how to implement agents, choose communication and optimization type, and train a game.

---

[3]This also proved to be a convenient debugging mechanism, as single-symbol communication is typically simpler to train.

```python
class Sender(nn.Module):
    def __init__(self, vision, output_size):
        super(Sender, self).__init__()
        self.fc = nn.Linear(500, output_size)
        self.vision = vision

    def forward(self, x):
        with torch.no_grad():
            x = self.vision(x)
        x = self.fc(x)
        return x


class Receiver(nn.Module):
    def __init__(self, input_size):
        super(Receiver, self).__init__()
        self.fc = nn.Linear(input_size, 784)

    def forward(self, channel_input, receiver_input=None):
        x = self.fc(channel_input)
        return torch.sigmoid(x)

sender = Sender(vision, output_size)
receiver = Receiver(input_size)
```

Figure 2: MNIST game: Defining and instantiating the user-defined parts of the agents' architecture.

3 Optimizing the communication channel in EGG

EGG supports two widely adopted strategies for learning with a discrete channel, Gumbel-Softmax relaxation (used, e.g., by Havrylov and Titov (2017)) and REINFORCE (used, e.g., by Lazaridou et al. (2016)). Below, we briefly review both of them.

Gumbel-Softmax relaxation is based on the Gumbel-Softmax (GS) (aka Concrete) distribution (Maddison et al., 2016; Jang et al., 2016), that allows to approximate one-hot samples from a Categorical distribution. At the same time, GS admits reparametrization, hence allows backpropagation-based training. Suppose that Sender produces a distribution over the vocabulary, with ith symbol having probability $p_i = S(i_s)$. To obtain a sample from a corresponding Gumbel-Softmax distribution, we take i.i.d. samples g_i from the `Gumbel(0, 1)` distribution and obtain the vector y with components y_i:

$$y_i = \frac{exp((\log p_i + g_i)/\tau)}{\sum_j exp((\log p_j + g_j)/\tau)} \quad (1)$$

where τ is the temperature hyperparameter, which controls the degree of relaxation. We treat y as a relaxed symbol representation. In the case of single-symbol communication, the embedding of y is passed to Receiver. In case of variable-length messages, the embedding is also fed into a RNN cell to generate the next symbol in the message.

As a result, if Receiver and the game loss are differentiable w.r.t. their inputs, we can get gradients of all game parameters, including those of Sender, via conventional backpropagation.

REINFORCE (Williams and Peng, 1991) is a standard Reinforcement Learning algorithm. As-

sume that both agents are stochastic: Sender samples a message m, and Receiver samples its output o. Let us fix a pair of inputs, i_s, i_r, and the ground-truth output l. Then, using the log-gradient "trick", the gradient of the expectation of the loss L w.r.t. the vector of agents' parameters $\theta = \theta_s \bigsqcup \theta_r$ is:

$$\mathbb{E}_{m,o}\left[L(o, l)\nabla_\theta \log \mathbb{P}(m, o|\theta)\right] \quad (2)$$

where $\mathbb{P}(m, o|\theta)$ specifies the joint probability distribution over the agents' outputs.

The gradient estimate is found by sampling messages and outputs. A standard trick to reduce variance of the estimator in Eq. 2 is to subtract an action-independent baseline b from the optimized loss (Williams, 1992). EGG uses the running mean baseline.

Importantly, the estimator in Eq. 2 allows us to optimize agents even if the loss is not differentiable (e.g., 0/1 loss). However, if the loss is differentiable and Receiver is differentiable and deterministic, this can be leveraged by a "hybrid" approach: the gradient of Receiver's parameters can be found by backpropagation, while Sender is optimized with REINFORCE. This approach, a special case of gradient estimation using stochastic computation graphs as proposed by Schulman et al. (2015), is also supported in EGG.

4 Implementing a game

In this Section we walk through the main steps to build a communication game in EGG. We illustrate them through a MNIST (LeCun et al., 1998) communication-based autoencoding task: Sender observes an image and sends a message to Receiver. In turn, Receiver tries to reconstruct the image. We only cover here the core aspects of the implementation, ignoring standard pre- and post-processing steps, such as data loading. The full implementation can be found in an online tutorial.[4]

We start by implementing the agents' architectures, as shown in Figure 2. Sender is passed an input image to be processed by its pre-trained `vision` module, and returns its output after a linear transformation. The way Sender's output will be interpreted depends on the type of communication to be used (discussed below). Receiver gets

---

[4] https://colab.research.google.com/github/facebookresearch/EGG/blob/master/tutorials/EGG%20walkthrough%20with%20a%20MNIST%20autoencoder.ipynb

```python
sender = core.GumbelSoftmaxWrapper(sender, temperature=1.0)

receiver = core.SymbolReceiverWrapper(receiver, vocab_size,
                                      agent_input_size=400)

game = core.SymbolGameGS(sender, receiver, loss)
```

(a) Single-symbol communication, Gumbel-Softmax relaxation.

```python
sender = core.ReinforceWrapper(sender)

receiver = core.SymbolReceiverWrapper(receiver, vocab_size,
                                      agent_input_size=400)
receiver = core.ReinforceDeterministicWrapper(receiver)
game = core.SymbolGameReinforce(sender, receiver, loss, sender_entropy_coeff=0.05,
                                receiver_entropy_coeff=0.0)
```

(b) Single-symbol communication, REINFORCE.

```python
sender_rnn = core.RnnSenderGS(sender, vocab_size, emb_size, hidden_size,
                              cell="rnn", max_len=2, temperature=1.0)
receiver_rnn = core.RnnReceiverGS(receiver, vocab_size, emb_size,
                                  hidden_size, cell="rnn")
game_rnn = core.SenderReceiverRnnReinforce(sender_rnn, receiver_rnn, loss,
                                           sender_entropy_coeff=0.025,
                                           receiver_entropy_coeff=0.0)
```

(c) Variable-length communication, Gumbel-Softmax relaxation.

```python
sender_rnn = core.RnnSenderReinforce(sender, vocab_size, emb_size, hidden_size,
                                     cell="gru", max_len=2)
receiver_rnn = core.RnnReceiverDeterministic(receiver, vocab_size, emb_size,
                                             hidden_size, cell="gru")

game_rnn = core.SenderReceiverRnnGS(sender_rnn, receiver_rnn, loss)
```

(d) Variable-length communication, REINFORCE.

Figure 3: MNIST game: The user can choose different communication wrappers to switch between training regimes (Gumbel-Softmax or REINFORCE) and communication type (single-symbol or variable-length messages).

```python
trainer = core.Trainer(game=game, optimizer=optimizer,
                       train_data=train_loader,
                       validation_data=test_loader,
                       epoch_callback=None)
trainer.train(n_epochs=15)
```

Figure 4: MNIST game: Once the agents and the game are instantiated, the user must pass them to a Trainer, which implements the training/validation loop, checkpointing, etc.

an input from Sender and returns an image-sized output with pixels valued in $[0; 1]$. Again, depending on the type of channel employed, the Receiver input will have a different semantics.

In the case of one-symbol communication, Sender's output is passed through a `softmax` layer and its output is interpreted as the probabilities of sending a particular symbol. Hence, the output dimensionality defines the size of the vocabulary. In the case of variable-length messages, Sender's output specifies the initial hidden state of an RNN cell. This cell is then "unrolled" to generate a message, until the end-of-sequence symbol (`eos`) is produced or maximum length is reached. Receiver's input is an embedding of the message: either the embedding of the single-symbol message, or the last hidden state of the RNN cell that corresponds to the `eos` symbol.

Once Sender and Receiver are defined, the user wraps them into EGG-implemented wrappers which determine the communication and optimization scenarios. Importantly, the actual user-specified Sender and Receiver architectures can be agnostic to whether single-symbol or variable-length communication is used; and to whether Gumbel-Softmax relaxation- or REINFORCE-based training is performed. In Figure 3 we illustrate different communication/training scenarios: (a) single-symbol com-

munication, trained with Gumbel-Softmax relaxation, (b) single-symbol communication, trained with REINFORCE, (c) variable-length communication, trained with Gumbel-Softmax relaxation, (d) variable-length communication, trained with REINFORCE.

Once the Game instance is defined, everything is ready for training. That is, the user has to pass the game instance to `core.Trainer`, as shown in Figure 4.

We report some results obtained with the code we just described. We used the following parameters. The vision module is a pre-trained LeNet-1 (LeCun et al., 1990) instance, the maximal message length is set to 2, the communication between the agents is done through LSTM units with hidden-size 20, vocabulary size is 10. The agents are trained with REINFORCE for 15 epochs with batch size of 32, and the loss is per-pixel cross-entropy.

In Figure 5 we illustrate the language that emerges in this setup. To do this, we enumerate all possible 100 two-symbol messages x, y and input them to Receiver. We report all images that Receiver produces. The `eos` symbol is fixed to be 0, hence if the first symbol is 0 then the second symbol is ignored (top row of Figure 5).

Note that the first symbol x tends to denote digit identity: $x \in \{2, 4, 7, 8, 9\}$. In contrast, the second symbol y is either ignored ($x \in \{4, 8\}$) or specifies the style of the produced digit ($x \in \{3, 7\}$). The second symbol has the most striking effect with $x = 7$, where y encodes the rotation angle of the digit 1.

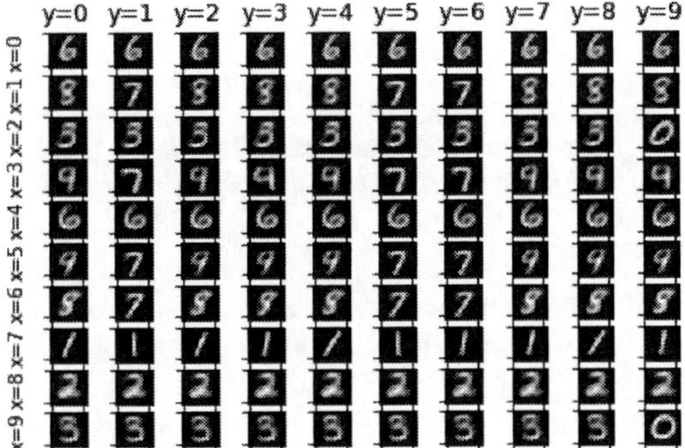

Figure 5: The emergent code-book in the MNIST auto-encoder game. After training, we feed all 100 possible two-symbol messages xy from the size-10 vocabulary to Receiver and show the returned images. The rows iterate over the first symbol x, the columns enumerate the second symbol, y. The eos symbol has id 0.

5 Some pre-implemented games

EGG contains implementations of several games. They (a) illustrate how EGG can be used to explore interesting research questions, (b) provide reference usage patterns and building blocks, (c) serve as means to ensure reproducibility of studies reported in the literature. For example, EGG incorporates an implementation of the signaling game of Lazaridou et al. (2016) and Bouchacourt and Baroni (2018). It contains code that was recently used to study the communicative efficiency of artificial LSTM-based agents (Chaabouni et al., 2019a) and the information-minimization properties of emergent discrete codes (Kharitonov et al., 2019).[5] Finally, EGG provides a pre-implemented game that allows to train agents entirely via the command line and external input/output files, without having to write a single line of Python code. We hope this will lower the learning curve for those who want to experiment with language emergence without previous coding experience.

6 Conclusion and future work

We introduced EGG, a toolkit for research on emergence of language in games. We outlined its main features design principles. Next, we briefly

---

[5]A small illustration can be run in Google Colaboratory: `https://colab.research.google.com/github/facebookresearch/EGG/blob/master/egg/zoo/language_bottleneck/mnist-style-transfer-via-bottleneck.ipynb`.

reviewed how training with a discrete communication channel is performed. Finally, we walked through the main steps for implementing a MNIST autoencoding game using EGG.

We intend to extend EGG in the following directions. First, we want to provide support for multi-direction and multi-step communicative scenarios. Second, we want to add more advanced tooling for analyzing the properties of the emergent languages (such as compositionality; Andreas 2019). We will also continue to enlarge the set of pre-implemented games, to build a library of reference implementations.

Acknowledgments

We are grateful to Roberto Dessì and Tomek Korbak for their contributions to the EGG codebase and to Serhii Havrylov for sharing his code with us.

References

Jacob Andreas. 2019. Measuring compositionality in representation learning. In *ICLR*, New Orleans, LA.

Diane Bouchacourt and Marco Baroni. 2018. How agents see things: On visual representations in an emergent language game. In *EMNLP*.

Rahma Chaabouni, Eugene Kharitonov, Emmanuel Dupoux, and Marco Baroni. 2019a. Anti-efficient encoding in emergent communication. *arXiv preprint arXiv:1905.12561*.

Rahma Chaabouni, Eugene Kharitonov, Alessandro Lazaric, Emmanuel Dupoux, and Marco Baroni. 2019b. Word-order biases in deep-agent emergent communication. In *ACL*.

Maxime Chevalier-Boisvert, Dzmitry Bahdanau, Salem Lahlou, Lucas Willems, Chitwan Saharia, Thien Huu Nguyen, and Yoshua Bengio. 2019. BabyAI: First steps towards grounded language learning with a human in the loop. In *International Conference on Learning Representations*.

Kyunghyun Cho, Bart Van Merriënboer, Caglar Gulcehre, Dzmitry Bahdanau, Fethi Bougares, Holger Schwenk, and Yoshua Bengio. 2014. Learning phrase representations using rnn encoder-decoder for statistical machine translation. *arXiv preprint arXiv:1406.1078*.

Jeffrey Elman. 1990. Finding structure in time. *Cognitive Science*, 14:179–211.

Serhii Havrylov and Ivan Titov. 2017. Emergence of language with multi-agent games: Learning to communicate with sequences of symbols. In *NIPS*.

Sepp Hochreiter and Jürgen Schmidhuber. 1997. Long short-term memory. *Neural computation*, 9(8):1735–1780.

Eric Jang, Shixiang Gu, and Ben Poole. 2016. Categorical reparameterization with Gumbel-Softmax. *arXiv preprint arXiv:1611.01144*.

Eugene Kharitonov, Rahma Chaabouni, Diane Bouchacourt, and Marco Baroni. 2019. Information minimization in emergent languages. *arXiv preprint arXiv:1905.13687*.

Simon Kirby. 2002. Natural language from artificial life. *Artificial life*, 8(2):185–215.

Satwik Kottur, José MF Moura, Stefan Lee, and Dhruv Batra. 2017. Natural language does not emerge'naturally'in multi-agent dialog. *arXiv preprint arXiv:1706.08502*.

Angeliki Lazaridou, Karl Moritz Hermann, Karl Tuyls, and Stephen Clark. 2018. Emergence of linguistic communication from referential games with symbolic and pixel input. *arXiv preprint arXiv:1804.03984*.

Angeliki Lazaridou, Alexander Peysakhovich, and Marco Baroni. 2016. Multi-agent cooperation and the emergence of (natural) language. *arXiv preprint arXiv:1612.07182*.

Yann LeCun, Bernhard E Boser, John S Denker, Donnie Henderson, Richard E Howard, Wayne E Hubbard, and Lawrence D Jackel. 1990. Handwritten digit recognition with a back-propagation network. In *NIPS*.

Yann LeCun, Léon Bottou, Yoshua Bengio, Patrick Haffner, et al. 1998. Gradient-based learning applied to document recognition. *Proceedings of the IEEE*, 86(11):2278–2324.

David Lewis. 1969. *Convention*. Harvard University Press, Cambridge, MA.

Ryan Lowe, Jakob Foerster, Y-Lan Boureau, Joelle Pineau, and Yann Dauphin. 2019. On the pitfalls of measuring emergent communication. *arXiv preprint arXiv:1903.05168*.

Chris J Maddison, Andriy Mnih, and Yee Whye Teh. 2016. The concrete distribution: A continuous relaxation of discrete random variables. *arXiv preprint arXiv:1611.00712*.

Tomas Mikolov, Armand Joulin, and Marco Baroni. 2016. A roadmap towards machine intelligence. In *International Conference on Intelligent Text Processing and Computational Linguistics*, pages 29–61. Springer.

Adam Paszke, Sam Gross, Soumith Chintala, Gregory Chanan, Edward Yang, Zachary DeVito, Zeming Lin, Alban Desmaison, Luca Antiga, and Adam Lerer. 2017. Automatic differentiation in pytorch. In *NIPS-W*.

John Schulman, Nicolas Heess, Theophane Weber, and Pieter Abbeel. 2015. Gradient estimation using stochastic computation graphs. In *NIPS*.

Ashish Vaswani, Noam Shazeer, Niki Parmar, Jakob Uszkoreit, Llion Jones, Aidan N Gomez, Łukasz Kaiser, and Illia Polosukhin. 2017. Attention is all you need. In *NIPS*.

Ronald J Williams. 1992. Simple statistical gradient-following algorithms for connectionist reinforcement learning. *Machine learning*, 8(3-4):229–256.

Ronald J Williams and Jing Peng. 1991. Function optimization using connectionist reinforcement learning algorithms. *Connection Science*, 3(3):241–268.

Entity resolution for noisy ASR transcripts

Arushi Raghuvanshi **Varsha Embar**[‡] **Vijay Ramakrishnan**[‡]
Lucien Carroll **Karthik Raghunathan**
Cisco Systems
[‡]authors contributed equally

Abstract

Large vocabulary domain-agnostic Automatic Speech Recognition (ASR) systems often mistranscribe domain-specific words and phrases. Since these generic ASR systems are the first component of most voice assistants in production, building Natural Language Understanding (NLU) systems that are robust to these errors can be a challenging task. In this paper, we focus on handling ASR errors in named entities, specifically person names, for a voice-based collaboration assistant. We demonstrate an effective method for resolving person names that are mistranscribed by black-box ASR systems, using character and phoneme-based information retrieval techniques and contextual information, which improves accuracy by 40.8% on our production system. We provide a live interactive demo to further illustrate the nuances of this problem and the effectiveness of our solution.[1]

1 Introduction

General purpose ASR has improved by a large margin in recent years, with a reported word error rate (WER) of less than 10% for English voice search queries (Chiu et al., 2018). However for domain-specific vocabularies, uncommon terms like proper nouns, non-native English accents, and noisy acoustic settings, the WER is still high. Since ASR is the first component in a spoken dialog system, errors introduced in the recognized transcript cascade to downstream natural language understanding (NLU) components, leading to unsatisfactory user experiences. While building a domain-specific ASR system could address this problem (Gao et al., 2001; Zhao et al., 2018), doing so requires prohibitively high amounts of data and resources. Therefore, using a generic black-box ASR system and handling mistranscriptions

as a post processing step is a more practical approach for most industry applications.

One such application affected by cascading ASR errors is *entity resolution*. It involves **identifying** and **linking** different references for the same real world object to a canonical form. For task-oriented dialog systems, robust entity resolution is a challenging task because users generally refer to entities informally using abbreviations and aliases, rather than official standardized names, and for many applications, entities tend to be domain-specific, uncommon terms that are most often mistranscribed (Laurent et al., 2014).

Consider an office voice assistant that helps employees start a call with a colleague by name. The assistant needs to 1) identify the name in the user query and 2) resolve it to an employee within the company. For instance, in a query *Call John please* the extracted person name entity *John* could resolve to *John Scott Edwardson (ID: 576253)*.

While popular English names like *John* or *David* are recognized by generic ASR systems with high accuracy, less common or non-English names are often mistranscribed. For example, *Dial into **Dorlis's** meeting* may get transcribed as *Dial into **doorless is** meeting*, where the person name entity is incorrectly transcribed as common English words. Similarly, *Call **Nguyen*** may be transcribed as *Call **Newman***, where the person name entity is incorrectly transcribed as a different and more common name. In the first case, the assistant fails to identify an entity to place a call and in the second it has the wrong name, leading to a call to the wrong person. In either case, it appears unintelligent to the end user.

ASR vendors provide some room for domain personalization in the form of "hints", i.e. a list of expected phrases the ASR system can bias its hypotheses towards. The number of allowed hints is usually capped at a relatively small number (e.g.

---

[1]https://vimeo.com/345579360

61

Proceedings of the 2019 EMNLP and the 9th IJCNLP (System Demonstrations), pages 61–66
Hong Kong, China, November 3 – 7, 2019. ©2019 Association for Computational Linguistics

500) and does not scale to the full set of domain-specific vocabulary required (e.g. a few thousand employee names in a company).

In this paper, we propose a scalable, unsupervised solution for tackling the problem of entity resolution of named entities in noisy ASR transcripts for an enterprise collaboration assistant. We demonstrate improvements on the task by utilizing text and phoneme information retrieval techniques along with contextual and personalization information available in an enterprise setting. This approach can easily be extended to other domains,[2] as demonstrated in MindMeld, our open source conversational AI platform.

2   Related Work

Previous work on entity resolution for noisy text mostly deals with spelling errors (Bassil and Semaan, 2012), ambiguous terms, or noise induced through style of writing (like in social media platforms) (Campbell et al., 2016). The problem of noise induced through ASR errors is different in nature. Some systems use a wide range of features like lexical, syntactic, phonetic and semantic features to identify presence of ASR errors in transcripts, asking the user to clarify the intended meaning when an error is detected (Hazen et al., 2002; Prasad et al., 2012; Marin et al., 2015). To detect out of vocabulary (OOV) name errors, a multi-task recurrent neural network language model was used by (Cheng et al., 2015).

Using a ranking mechanism on the n-best hypotheses generated by one or more ASR modules is another popular approach used in dialog systems (Morbini et al., 2012). Re-ranking systems like (Corona et al., 2017) make use of a language model and semantic parsing features, but ignore any OOV words encountered, losing valuable information. While these approaches improve downstream tasks like entity recognition (Zhai et al., 2004; Hakkani-Tür et al., 2006), they cannot correct to words that do not exist in one of the hypothesized transcripts.

While these methods are not directly applicable to our problem, we extend some of the features and ideas discussed in these papers for entity resolution.

3   Approach

Given a noisy ASR transcript of a user query that potentially contains named entities, our goal is to identify the span of text that corresponds to an entity and resolve each identified span to a canonical value that can be looked up in a database.

Our dialog system consists of a set of classifiers, information retrieval components and a dialogue manager as described in Raghuvanshi et al. (2018). We use MindMeld[3] to build and train the intent classifier and entity recognizer with crowd-sourced data for all the intents handled by the assistant including "call by name" which includes "person name" entities. Since we operate on a narrow domain, the model learns to rely on the patterns of surrounding common English words, which are generally transcribed correctly, to detect entity spans which may be mistranscribed.

For entity resolution, we store the organization's employee database, metadata, and extracted features in an inverted index which we describe in 3.1. At inference time, for each detected person name entity span, we extract the same features from the span along with metadata and use information retrieval methods to retrieve a ranked list of the most likely matching canonical names.

3.1   Features

Our system utilizes four broad feature categories. We describe each below and provide the implementation.[4]

3.1.1   Textual Similarity

For text-based retrieval, we leverage normalization, character n-grams, word n-grams, and edge n-grams. Exact matching is essential for resolving names that are already correctly transcribed. Matching against normalized text accounts for capitalization variations and special characters (e.g. *Oleary* to *O'Leary*). Character n-grams account for spelling variations which are common in entities like person names (e.g. *Ashley* to *Ashlee*). Word or token n-grams are useful for partial name matching (e.g. *Carly Rae* to *Carly Rae Jepsen*). We observed that the phonemes at the edges of tokens tend to contribute more to our notion of phonetic similarity than some of the middle phonemes

---

(e.g. *Monica* seems more similar to *Malika* than *Sonic*). Using edge n-grams accounts for this.

In addition, the index contains domain-specific metadata of synonyms or in our case, common nicknames. For example *Sid* is populated as a common nickname for *Siddharth*, *Teddy* for *Theodore* and *Bob* for *Robert*. This information matches colloquial name utterances to the formal "given" and "family" names in the index.

3.1.2 Phonetic Similarity

In many cases, relying solely on text matching will return results that are phonetically different from the original utterance. For example, *Gaurav Sharma* is transcribed as *quarter shawarma*, which is textually more similar to *Carter Warmac* than the original name, but phonetically quite different. In order to correct uncommon names for which the mistranscriptions are often beyond simple text variations, phonetic features are essential.

As we are leveraging third party ASR systems via APIs, we do not have direct access to the phonetic information from the original audio. Instead, we use techniques to recover the phonetic representation of the transcribed text. We use double metaphone (Philips, 2000) as well as grapheme-to-phoneme (G2P) representations (Daelemans and van den Bosch, 1997) to generate our phonetic features. Double metaphone is an algorithm that maps tokens to approximate phonetic representations using rules and heuristics developed primarily for English names, but extended to Chinese, Romance, and Slavic languages. The G2P toolkit in CMU Sphinx[5] is a sequence-to-sequence deep learning model that maps text to a phonetic representation. Its coverage and accuracy is dependent on the training data, which consists of common English words as well as person names. We found that the two representations had complementary information, and we benefit from using both.

While this feature is essential, no phonetic encoding technique is perfect, and the same name may have different phonetic representations when spoken by people with different accents. Therefore, it is important to balance it with the other feature categories.

3.1.3 n-best Transcripts

Almost all off-the-shelf ASR systems return a ranked *n*-best list of multiple possible transcripts.

The *n*-best entity spans, extracted from each of the alternate transcripts, provide additional phonetic information about the original audio. In some cases, the exact correct name may even exist in one of the lower ranked transcripts. The reliability of each hypothesis generally decreases as we go down the *n*-best list, so while all *n*-best spans contribute to selecting the final candidate, our weighting scheme ensures that matches against higher ranked alternates have a larger impact.

Consider an utterance *Helen* which was mistranscribed to *Ellen*, but in the *n*-best list (*Ellen, Hellen, Helena, Hella, Hello, Helen*), all of the other hypotheses start with an 'H', and the original utterance *Helen* exists as one of the lower ranked hypotheses. By utilizing the *n*-best list in conjunction with phonetic similarity features, our retrieval method has a better chance of correcting to *Helen*.

3.1.4 Personalization Features

The personalization features are highly domain and user specific, but have a high impact on the precision of our model. For the use case of calling a person, we capitalize on the observation that a user is more likely to call someone they often interact with or who is close to them in the organization hierarchy. The caller's identity can be determined by a variety of methods including authentication, device pairing, face recognition, or speaker identification. Based on information like the interaction frequency between employees, we generate a personalization factor from the user's identity to help match the entity span to the intended name.

The personalization features are generalizable across different domains. For instance, consider a food ordering use-case where the user Alice is trying to order a dish called "Dabo Kolo". Based on personalized knowledge that Alice regularly orders Ethopian cuisine in San Francisco, we can accordingly boost relevant dish search matches even if it was mistranscribed to "Debbie Carlo".

3.2 Hyperparameter Tuning

We used a combination of manual and random walk tuning to learn the optimum weights of the different features. Quantitative evaluation is based on whether the correct name exists in the top 1 or top 5 ranked results. For the random walk tuning, we define an objective function that optimizes the recall score over these features.

As a production application, we are concerned with not only recall, but also the relevance of the

---

[5]`https://github.com/cmusphinx/`
`g2p-seq2seq`

other top results, and how egregious the errors are when the correct name is not found. For tuning on these qualitative factors, we rely on manual analysis.

4 Data and Experimental Setup

We test our technique on a crowd-sourced dataset of audio transcripts for the "call by name" intent. The name used in each transcript was sampled from $\sim$100 k employees in the directory of a global company with up to 10 speakers for each name. We used Google Speech-to-Text[6] to collect 10-best ASR transcripts for each sample. Table 1 gives the overall stats and name type distribution of the evaluation dataset.

Table 1: Summary of dataset used for evaluation

# Samples	# First Names	# Full Names
2915	1234	1681

For evaluating the personalization features, we augment the data with four different settings. For each name span in the dataset, we record the entity resolution accuracy for each of the following scenarios:

1. **Same team**: the caller directly works with the person they are trying to call
2. **Same department**: the caller is a few hops away from the person they are trying to call
3. **Different department**: the caller has no previous interaction and is far removed from the person they are trying to call
4. **No information**: the system is unable to identify the caller

This ensures that the system is not over-optimizing for close interaction distances and users are still able to call people who they have little or no previous interaction with. We report the recall averaged across these interaction distance settings.

Assuming that a person can only call someone within the company, we populate the index with all $\sim$100 k employees. For each entry, we have a unique identifier, the full name of the employee, common nicknames for the name, as well as the job title and location. We also have an interaction corpus which contains information on the previous interaction history of users and the organizational hierarchy which is used to generate a "personalization score" between any two users in the index.

We evaluate our system using the IR metric of recall at n (R@n). We report numbers for $n = 1$ and $n = 5$. R@1 evaluates the effectiveness of the entity resolver by measuring the quality of the top result, while R@5 gives the likelihood with which the user can find the correct entity at least within the top 5 suggestions provided by the system.

5 Results and Discussion

Our approach significantly improves the recall of recovering the correct name from a noisy ASR transcript. The final setup gives a 40.8% improvement of R@1 over the baseline (Table 2). Table 3 breaks down the recall of the system by the interaction distances. For the most common scenario—that of users calling those they often interact with—the improvement is even larger. Because these four categories of caller distance are equally weighted in the optimization process, increased recall in the cases of same team/department leads to lower recall in the different department cases, where personalization features are generally misleading.

Table 2: Evaluation of the entity resolver with addition of different features

Features	R@1	R@5
+ Textual Features	0.100	0.120
+ Phonetic Features	0.255	0.347
+ n-best List	0.326	0.454
+ Personalization	**0.508**	**0.627**

Table 3: Performance of the final system based on the distance between the caller and the callee

Caller Distance	R@1	R@5
Same team	**0.765**	**0.864**
Same department	0.659	0.777
No information	0.326	0.454
Different department	0.281	0.412

The name resolution improvement converts an unusable product to a reasonably intelligent one with significantly less cost and computation than alternate approaches of building a domain-specific ASR. The remaining names that are not correctly resolved in the top position, often appear in one of the following ranked positions that a user can scroll between, as illustrated by the R@5 metric, or the name can be resolved by a follow-up query.

[6]https://cloud.google.com/speech-to-text/

We also present the WER of the transcripts in Table 4. While the entity resolution recall metric is more relevant, the ASR metric of WER illustrates the magnitude of errors in the original ASR transcriptions and further reinforces the effectiveness of our system. We compare the full user query transcripts from the ASR system with the transcript where recognized name spans are replaced with the top ranked name string from our entity resolution model. We find that using our IR entity resolution approach we get a relative WER reduction of 29.0% on name tokens and 12.0% on the full query. Note that this additionally demonstrates that this approach can be extended beyond entity resolution to the task of ASR correction with compelling results, particularly for correcting mistranscriptions of domain-specific entities.

Table 4: WER comparison before and after ASR correction

Model	Name WER	Transcript WER
ASR transcripts	$86.0 \pm 1.6\%$	$40.8 \pm 0.6\%$
IR entity correction	$61.1 \pm 0.7\%$	$35.9 \pm 0.4\%$

5.1 Qualitative Analysis

We performed manual evaluation while tuning the system, and found several broad categories of ASR errors that appeared often. We analyze some of them and discuss features of our ranking approach that help correct for those errors. These examples can be visualized in our interactive UI.

- Language model of generic ASR systems incorrectly biases to common vocabulary.

```
Gold: Prasanth Reddy
ASR: croissant ready
```

In these cases, n-best lists are often the most important feature, since the less common name tokens usually appear in one of the alternate transcripts.

- ASR model mistranscribes to similar phonetically but textually different tokens.

```
Gold: Kiran Prakash's
ASR: Corrine precautious
```

In these cases, the phonetic features like double metaphone and G2P are important, as they allow us to match at a phonetic level.

- Entities are mistranscribed to other entities.

```
Gold: Didi
ASR: Stevie
```

Here, contextual features are the key. Names are often mistranscribed to other more popular valid names. A single ASR transcript may be a correctly transcribed name or a mistranscription of another name, but personalization and the set of n-best transcripts provide evidence of the correct transcription. In this example, if a user had actually said *Stevie*, we shouldn't only return people whose name is *Didi*. However, if the intended person is *Didi*, which is consistently mistranscribed to *Stevie*, we need a way to recover that correct name. The personalization factor can boost names like *Didi* towards the top of the ranked list, instead of only returning names like *Stevie* or *Steven*. The n-best list can also help determine the confidence of the name. If all of the transcripts contain *Stevie*, then that is likely what the user actually said. But if the n-best results contain many terms which start with 'D', then it is more likely the user said something else and we can use this combined with other signals to recover the correct name.

- Some phonemes are not recognized due to noisy audio.

```
Gold: Mahojwal
ASR: my jaw
```

There are many cases where some phonemes are dropped or added in the mistranscription. Again, tuning to account for this type of noise is a balancing act, since we don't want our system to hallucinate sounds that don't exist in the original utterance, but it needs to have enough leeway that it can recover the correct name from noisy transcripts where a phoneme may be dropped or added. Fuzzy matching of both characters and phonemes are useful for correcting these cases.

Another error category is when the context words i.e, words surrounding the name in a query, are fused with the name token. For example, *connect me with Heather* gets transcribed as *connect Merriweather*. In such cases, the phonemes of the name span in the transcript are different from those of the intended name. While we do not evaluate our method on such transcripts in this paper, they form an important error category in the real world. Fuzzy matching of characters and phonemes can help correct these cases.

The interactive demo UI enables exploration of these errors and of which features help correct for them, as shown in the video submission.

6 Conclusion

We present a novel approach for handling ASR errors in entity resolution, highlighting the advantages of using contextual features for the task. Our proposed approach shows promising results when resolving error-prone domain-specific entities in noisy ASR transcripts against an index of up to hundreds of thousands of terms. Our results on the use case of person name resolution for voice calling can generalize to many other use cases with a fixed set of resolvable terms, such as restaurant names for food ordering, song titles in a music player, or the resolution of actor names in a movie browsing voice assistant.

Acknowledgments

This work has benefited from the comments, code, and UI design contributions of Marvin Huang, Chris Liu, Jui-Pin Wang, Chad Oakley, Qian Yu.

References

Youssef Bassil and Paul Semaan. 2012. ASR context-sensitive error correction based on Microsoft n-gram dataset. *Journal of Computing*, 4(1):34–42.

William M Campbell, Lin Li, C Dagli, Joel Acevedo-Aviles, K Geyer, Joseph P Campbell, and C Priebe. 2016. Cross-domain entity resolution in social media. *arXiv preprint arXiv:1608.01386*.

Hao Cheng, Hao Fang, and Mari Ostendorf. 2015. Open-domain name error detection using a multi-task RNN. In *Proceedings of the 2015 EMNLP*, pages 737–746.

Chung-Cheng Chiu, Tara N Sainath, Yonghui Wu, Rohit Prabhavalkar, Patrick Nguyen, Zhifeng Chen, Anjuli Kannan, Ron J Weiss, Kanishka Rao, Katya Gonina, Navdeep Jaitly, Bao Li, Jan Chorowski, and Michiel Bacchiani. 2018. State-of-the-art speech recognition with sequence-to-sequence models. In *2018 IEEE ICASSP*.

Rodolfo Corona, Jesse Thomason, and Raymond Mooney. 2017. Improving black-box speech recognition using semantic parsing. In *Proceedings of the 8th IJCNLP*, volume 2, pages 122–127.

Walter M. P. Daelemans and Antal P. J. van den Bosch. 1997. Language-independent data-oriented grapheme-to-phoneme conversion. In Jan P. H. van Santen, Joseph P. Olive, Richard W. Sproat, and Julia Hirschberg, editors, *Progress in Speech Synthesis*, pages 77–89. Springer New York, New York.

Yuqing Gao, Bhuvana Ramabhadran, Julian Chen, Hakan Erdogan, and Michael Picheny. 2001. Innovative approaches for large vocabulary name recognition. In *2001 IEEE ICASSP*, volume 1, pages 53–56.

Dilek Hakkani-Tür, Frédéric Béchet, Giuseppe Riccardi, and Gokhan Tur. 2006. Beyond ASR 1-best: Using word confusion networks in spoken language understanding. *Computer Speech & Language*, 20(4):495–514.

Timothy J Hazen, Theresa Burianek, Joseph Polifroni, and Stephanie Seneff. 2002. Recognition confidence scoring for use in speech understanding systems. *Computer Speech & Language*, 16:49–67.

Antoine Laurent, Sylvain Meignier, and Paul Deléglise. 2014. Improving recognition of proper nouns in ASR through generating and filtering phonetic transcriptions. *Computer Speech & Language*, 28(4):979–996.

Alex Marin, Mari Ostendorf, and Ji He. 2015. Learning phrase patterns for ASR name error detection using semantic similarity. In *INTERSPEECH-2015*, pages 1423–1427.

Fabrizio Morbini, Kartik Audhkhasi, Ron Artstein, Maarten Van Segbroeck, Kenji Sagae, Panayiotis Georgiou, David R Traum, and Shri Narayanan. 2012. A reranking approach for recognition and classification of speech input in conversational dialogue systems. In *2012 IEEE SLT*, pages 49–54. IEEE.

Lawrence Philips. 2000. The double metaphone search algorithm. *C/C++ Users J.*, 18(6):38–43.

Rohit Prasad, Rohit Kumar, Sankaranarayanan Ananthakrishnan, Wei Chen, Sanjika Hewavitharana, Matthew Roy, Frederick Choi, Aaron Challenner, Enoch Kan, Arvind Neelakantan, and Premkumar Natarajan. 2012. Active error detection and resolution for speech-to-speech translation. In *IWSLT 2012*.

Arushi Raghuvanshi, Lucien Carroll, and Karthik Raghunathan. 2018. Developing production-level conversational interfaces with shallow semantic parsing. In *Proceedings of the 2018 EMNLP: System Demonstrations*, pages 157–162.

Lufeng Zhai, Pascale Fung, Richard Schwartz, Marine Carpuat, and Dekai Wu. 2004. Using n-best lists for named entity recognition from Chinese speech. In *Proceedings of HLT-NAACL 2004: Short Papers*, pages 37–40.

Yong Zhao, Jinyu Li, Shixiong Zhang, Liping Chen, and Yifan Gong. 2018. Domain and speaker adaptation for Cortana speech recognition. In *2018 IEEE ICASSP*, pages 5984–5988.

EUSP: An Easy-to-Use Semantic Parsing PlatForm

Bo An, Bo Chen, Xianpei Han, Le Sun
State Key Laboratory of Computer Science
Institute of Software, Chinese Academy of Sciences, Beijing, China
{anbo, chenbo, xianpei, sunle}@iscas.ac.cn

Abstract

Semantic parsing aims to map natural language utterances into structured meaning representations. We present a modular platform, EUSP (Easy-to-Use Semantic Parsing Plat-Form), that facilitates developers to build semantic parser from scratch. Instead of requiring a large amount of training data or complex grammar knowledge, in our platform developers can build grammar-based semantic parser or neural-based semantic parser through configure files which specify the modules and components that compose semantic parsing system. A high quality grammar-based semantic parsing system only requires domain lexicons rather than costly training data for a semantic parser. Furthermore, we provide a browser-based method to generate the semantic parsing system to minimize the difficulty of development. Experimental results show that the neural-based semantic parser system achieves competitive performance on semantic parsing task, and grammar-based semantic parsers significantly improve the performance of a business search engine.

1 Introduction

Artificially intelligent applications have been emerging in various forms, such as intelligent retrieval, personal assistants, intelligent customer service robot, etc. Most of the existing intelligent applications are capable of understanding user natural language utterance and returning accurate information. One of the core components of these systems is the semantic parser, which maps natural language utterances into formal meaning representations that facilitate the computer to process. Therefore, it is critically desirable to design an easy-to-use platform that facilitates developers to quickly build a high quality semantic parsing system for various domains and applications.

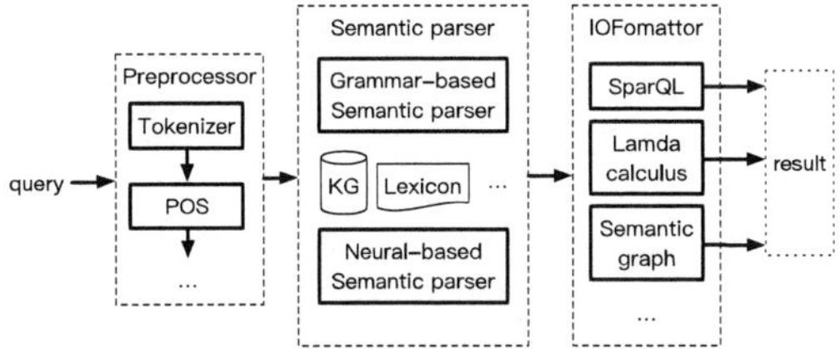

Figure 1: The framework of EUSP platform.

There are mainly two lines of work for semantic parsing: grammar-based semantic parsing and neural-based semantic parsing. Grammar-based semantic parsers employ a set of grammars and lexicons to generate meaning representations for a given utterance. The grammar is a set of expert defined rules to compose the semantic units into candidate meaning representations, which is based on the principle of compositionality (Pelletier, 1994). However, to implement grammar-based semantic parsing system the developers have to understand the complex grammar. What's worse, these parsers require an amount of training dataset that is hard to annotate and only work in a specific domain. Neural semantic parsers convert the utterance directly to meaning representations, like lambda-calculus (Dong and Lapata, 2016) and semantic graph (Chen et al., 2018). One of the major advantages of neural semantic parsing is that the model is trained in an end-to-end way without requiring the developers to understand the complex theory. Unfortunately, neural semantic parser requires a large amount of training data to achieve competitive performance. Thus, it is significantly and crucially desirable to develop a platform for helping developers build semantic parsing systems without requiring complex grammar or costly training data.

To address the above challenges, we present an easy-to-use semantic parsing platform (EUSP), which aims to help developers to build a seman-

Proceedings of the 2019 EMNLP and the 9th IJCNLP (System Demonstrations), pages 67–72
Hong Kong, China, November 3 – 7, 2019. ©2019 Association for Computational Linguistics

tic parser from scratch quickly. EUSP provides two kinds of complementary models: grammar-based semantic parser and neural-based semantic parser. The grammar-based semantic parser achieves competitive performance without training data, while neural-based semantic parsing is more generalizable. The advantages of our platform are trifold:

- Flexibility: it provides two kinds of semantic parsing methods (grammar-based and neural-based).

- Cold-Start and Continuous Optimizable: the grammar-based parser only needs domain lexicons, and both of grammar-based and neural-based semantic parsers can be optimized with training data.

- Plug and play: the generated semantic parser is an independent module and can be plugged in the original system without much modification. And it could produce various formats of outputs, like lambda-calculus and SparQL (Sirin and Parsia, 2007), etc.

2   Related Work

Semantic parsing can benefit to many intelligent applications, like intelligent retrieval, personal assistant, etc. There exists a range of semantic parsing toolkits, such as SEMPRE [1] (Berant et al., 2013) and RASA_NLU [2]. Unfortunately, most of these toolkits require both linguistic expertise and a large amount of annotated data. CRUISE (Shen et al., 2018) provide an utterance generation system to reduce the human workload of data annotation. However, CRUISE focuses on spoken language understanding. In this paper, we present a platform for building semantic parsing system quickly and easily.

3   EUSP Platform Overview

EUSP [3], a modular platform, consists of various modules, such as tokenizer, syntax parsing, semantic parsing. Data is passed between different modules in Json format. And developers can use configure files to create different semantic parser by customizing different modules.

3.1   EUSP Workflow

The framework is shown in Figure 1, EUSP has three main components: preprocessor, semantic parser and QueryIO formatter, we will detailed describe these components in the following sections.

(i) Preprocessor component consists of various modules (tokenizer, name entity recognizer (NER), syntax parser, etc) to generate useful information for each utterance, including tokens, candidate entities, POS and syntax tree.

(ii) Semantic parser component includes two kinds of semantic parsers: grammar-based and neural-based. The grammar-based parser consists of modules of lexicon recognizer, grammar composer, scorer, reranker and trainer. The neural-based semantic parser is implemented based on our Seq2Action model (Chen et al., 2018), which generates the semantic graph directly from the utterance (with entity recognized).

(iii) IOformatter component generates different formats of output based on the result of semantic parser component, such lambda-calculus.

3.2   Preprocessor component

To extract useful information for semantic parsing, EUSP firstly employs Stanford Tokenizer (Manning et al., 2014) to divide an utterance into a sequence of tokens. Then, a string-based entity linking algorithm (Blanco et al., 2015) is utilized to link the tokens with the domain lexicons, which generate the candidate name entities for semantic parsing. Finally, we use Stanford CoreNLP (Manning et al., 2014) to generate the part-of-speech tags (POS) and constituency parse tree for the given sequence of tokens.

3.3   Semantic parser component

The semantic parser component consists of two kinds of semantic parsing methods, we will illustrate them in this section.

3.3.1   Grammar-based Semantic Parser

The framework of grammar-based semantic parser is illustrated in Figure 2, it consists of four modules: lexicon, grammar, scorer and reranker.

Lexicon module consists of lexicon entries which map the tokens to pre-defined types or functions. For example, the word "texas" triggers the function of {"EntityAttribute": "State"} and the word "states" triggers the function of {"EntityType": "State"}. The lexicon is defined as Figure 3, where 'Token' represents the token

[1]https://nlp.stanford.edu/software/sempre/
[2]https://github.com/RasaHQ/rasa_nlu
[3]http://39.98.248.207:8000/nluweb

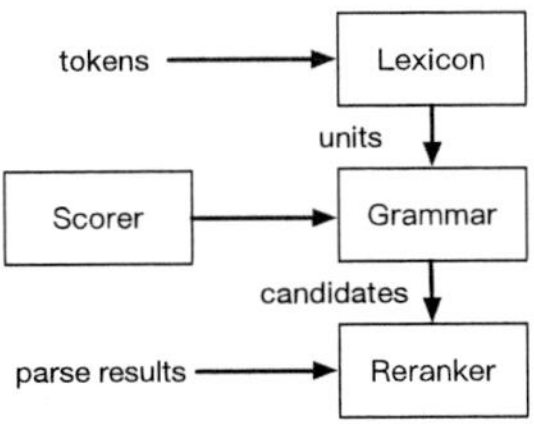

Figure 2: The framework of grammar-based semantic parser component.

which triggers the lexicon entry, and one token could trigger several lexicon entries; 'TokenType' is the type of the entity, includes *EntityClass, Attribute, AttributeValue, Value, Comparator, Combination, Aggregator and NULLQuery*; 'QueryValue' is the triggered value of the token, such as *AttributePredicate, EntityFunction*; 'NormalizedTokenValue' refers normalization of some tokens; 'DataType' refers to the types of values, include *String, Int, Double, Boolean*; 'Score' refers to the score of the lexicon entry.

The domain lexicons are the key resource for building semantic parser, in most case, EUSP only needs coarse-grained domain lexicons, such as the cell lexicon from Sogou [4].

Grammar module decides whether two kinds of tokens can be composed and the result of composition. For example, the grammar rule *EntityFunction ∧ AttributePredicate → AttributeValueFunction* means 'AttributeValueFunction' can be composed by 'EntityFunction' and 'AttributePredicate'. Most of the grammar rules are pre-defined, and developers don't need to modify them. However, if the pre-defined grammar rules contradict with the constraints of KG, the grammar rules should comply with the constraints of knowledge graph (KG). Thus we define two constraints of of the grammar rules: (i) **Attribute constraint**: a 'EntityFunction' and a 'AtttributePredict' can be composed only if the entity type has the specific attribute. (ii) **Value constraint**: the type value of 'AtttributePredict' must be the same as 'AttributeValue'.

Scorer module computes the confidence of each parsed results of the given utterance. Due to the ambiguity of the language, an utterance may produce many different results. To resolve the above issue, we calculate the confidences of the parse results based on the composition features of

different grammar rules as Formula (1).

$$score(R) = F(R) \cdot W_{parser} \qquad (1)$$

where $F(R)$ is the feature vector of the parse result R; W_{parser} refers to the trainable weight vector of features.

Reranker module further improves the parse results by incorporating the global features of the parse results, includes the size of tokens, the layers of the composition, the coverage of the grammar, etc. And the final confidence of a produced parse result is calculated as Formula (2).

$$score_{Reranker}(R) = F_{global}(R) \cdot W_{rank} \qquad (2)$$

where F_{global} refers to the global feature vector of the result and W_{rank} refers to the weight vector of global features, which is also trainable. And the final parse result is the one with maximum $score_{Reranker}(R)$.

3.3.2 Neural-based Semantic Parser

In this paper, we implement the neural-based semantic parser based on Seq2Action (Chen et al., 2018), which directly convert the utterance to semantic graph, and both structural constraints and semantic constraints are applied to ensure the parse result confirms with domain-specific schema. The framework of Seq2Action is illustrated in Figure 4. It is worth mentioning that we implement various neural-based semantic parsing algorithms (such as Seq2Seq, Seq2Tree, Coarse2Fine), developers can specify any one of them through the configure file.

3.4 IOformatter component

To support more natural language applications, EUSP platform implements an IOformatter component, which can generate various kinds of semantic representations for different usage, such as SQL, lambda-calculus, frame semantic, etc.

4 Training Semantic Parser

Grammar-based Semantic Parser

It is worth mentioning that the grammar-based semantic parser in our platform can generate high quality results for many application (such as intelligent retrieval, recommendation) without training data. If the developers have enough training data, the grammar-based semantic parser can be further improved by optimizing the score of lexicon entries, the weight vector W_{parser} and W_{rank}. The

---

[4]https://pinyin.sogou.com/dict/

Figure 3: The format of lexicons.

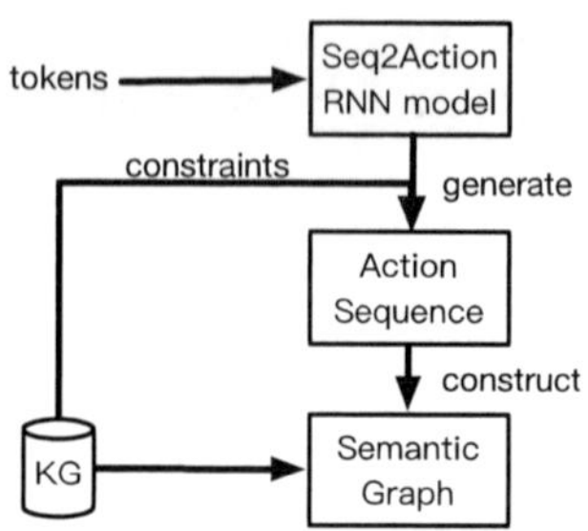

Figure 4: The framework of Seq2Action.

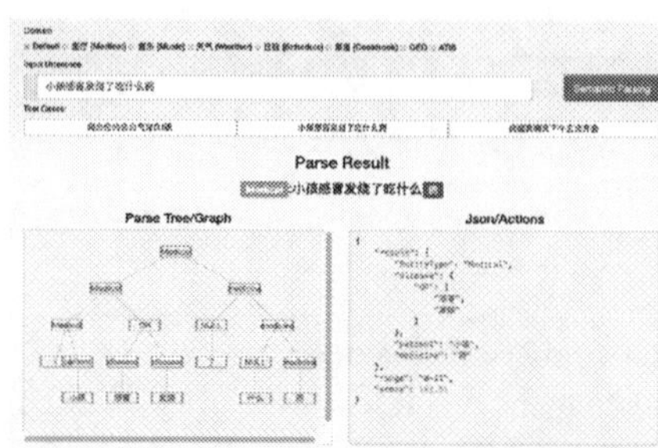

Figure 5: The UI of grammar-based semantic parser.

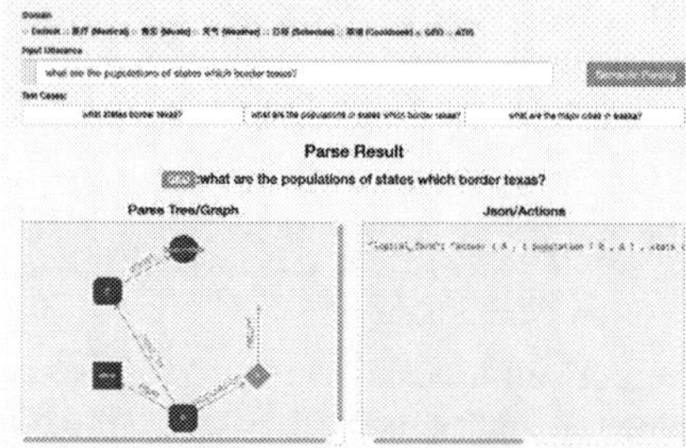

Figure 6: The UI of neural-based semantic parser.

system uses a mini-batch gradient-based discriminant online learning algorithm (Collins, 2002). The training process is as Formula (3).

$$g(S) = F(R) - F(T)$$
$$g(S_1, ..., S_k) = (g(S_1) + ... + g(S_k))/k \quad (3)$$
$$W_{t+1} = W_t - \alpha * g(S_1, ..., S_k)$$

where $F(T)$ is the annotated result of an utterance S; k is the number of instances in a mini-batch; W_t is the parameters at t-th iteration; α is the learning rate and g is the gradient which is calculated based on SGD.

Neural-based Semantic Parser

The parameters of Seq2Action in our model include RNN parameters W^s, W^a, U_w, word embeddings ϕ^x and action embeddings ϕ^y. The parameters are estimated based on training data. Given an utterance X and action sequence Y (the components of semantic graph), we maximize the likelihood of the generated sequence of actions. And the objective function is defined as Formula (4). We employ standard stochastic gradient descent algorithm to update the parameters.

$$L = \sum_{i=1}^{n} log P(Y_i|X_i) \quad (4)$$

4.1 Building Semantic Parser

To facilitate the developers to build the semantic parser system for their applications, our platform provides two methods to generate the semantic parsers: the toolkit-based building method and the browser-based building method.

The proposed toolkit consists of all the components and modules needed for building a domain specific semantic parsing system. The developers could quickly build a domain semantic parser accord to the instructions of the toolkit with the domain dependent lexicon.

Furthermore, our platform provides a more easy-to-use way to build their semantic parser. We provide a web page that the developers can upload their domain lexicons and specify some key information of the semantic parser (or default values), and our platform will generate a compressed file with the lexicon entries, grammar rules and parsing engine. And developers can deploy the semantic parser with necessary environment, like JDK and Python development environment.

And we offer user friendly interfaces for developers to build and test their semantic parsers like Figure 5 and Figure 6.

5 Experimental Evaluation

In this section, we implement neural semantic parser and grammar semantic parser based on EUSP platform for English and Chinese respectively. We compare our method with several state-of-the-art neural semantic parsers as well as the baselines without leveraging constraints. Furthermore, we deploy our grammar-based semantic parser in a Chinese business search engine to verify its value.

5.1 Neural-based Semantic Parser Results

We assess the performance of our method and compare it with previous methods. We conduct experiments on two datasets: GEO and ATIS.

GEO contains natural language questions about 494 US geography paired with corresponding Prolog database queries. Following (Zettlemoyer and Collins, 2005), we use the standard 600/280 instance splits for training/test.

ATIS contains natural language questions of a flight database, with each question is annotated with a lambda calculus query. Following (Zettlemoyer and Collins, 2007), we use the standard 4473/448 instance splits for training/test.

We use 200 hidden units and 100 dimensional word vectors for sentence encoding. And we initialize all parameters by uniformly sampling within the interval $[-0.1, 0.1]$. We train our model for a total of 30 epochs with an initial learning rate of 0.1, and halve the learning rate every 5 epochs after epoch 15. We replace word vectors for words occurring only once with a universal word vector. We evaluate different systems using the standard accuracy metric, and the accuracies on different datasets are obtained.

Results

We compare our method with state-of-the-art neural based systems on both datasets. Because all systems using the same train/test splits, we directly use the reported best performances from their original papers for fair comparison.

For our method, we train our model with three settings: the first one is the basic sequence-to-action model without constraints Seq2Act; the second one adds structure constraints in decoding Seq2Act (+C1); the third one is the full model which adds both structure and semantic constraints Seq2Act (+C1+C2). The overall results are shown in Table 1.

From Table 1 we can see that: 1) Our method achieved comparative performances on both datasets. 2) By leveraging knowledge base schema during decoding, semantic constraints are effective for semantic parsing. Compared to Seq2Act and Seq2Act (+C1), the Seq2Act (+C1+C2) achieves the best performance on both datasets. This is because semantic constraints can further filter semantic illegal actions using selectional preference and consistency between types.

Model	GEO	ATIS
Seq2Seq Models		
(Jia and Liang, 2016)	85.0	76.3
(Jia and Liang, 2016)* (+data)	89.3	83.3
(Dong and Lapata, 2016) 2Seq	84.6	84.2
(Dong and Lapata, 2016)2Tree	87.1	84.6
(Dong and Lapata, 2018)	88.2	87.7
(Dong and Lapata, 2018)+oracle sketch	93.9	95.1
Seq2Action Models		
Seq2Act	87.5	84.6
Seq2Act (+C1)	88.2	85.0
Seq2Act (+C1+C2)	88.9	85.5

Table 1: Test accuracies on GEO and ATIS datasets, where * indicates systems with extra resources are used

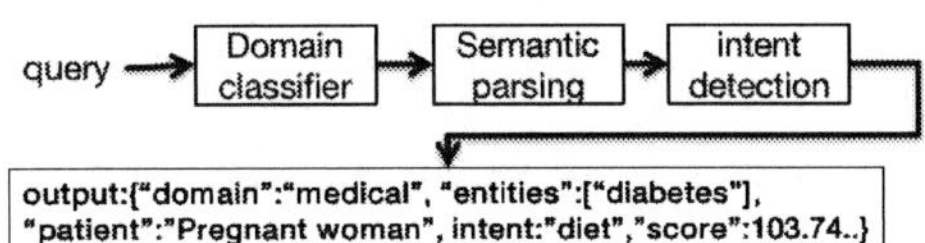

Figure 7: The illustrate of semantic parser for search engine.

5.2 Grammar-based Semantic Parser Results

In this section, we implement grammar-based semantic parser for improving a Chinese intelligent retrieval performance.

Evaluation definition

In this paper, our system parses the user query and outputs useful information for the search engine, such as the entities, user intents and confidences. And the search engine can directly link to the entities and relations in the knowledge graph, instead of just depending on the word features, and present more relevant information or pages to the user.

Evaluation We use the following evaluation metrics: (1) **pageviews coverage (PV)** : the coverage rate of pageviews of one domain; (2) **entity recall (Recall)**: the recall of the entity in the queries; (3) **classification accuracy (Acc)**: the intent classification accuracy of the queries; (4) **DCG**: discounted cumulative gain.

Experimental Settings

Due to the fact that most of the lexicon entries are domain specific and most of user queries and income refer to some top domains, such as medical, entertainment, thus we conduct experiments on three domains: medical, entertainment and novel. And we implement three semantic parsers based on the lexicons of these domains. The overall framework of this task is illustrated in Figure 7.

As showed in Figure 7, there are three components in our system: (i) We first use a domain classifier to filter out the queries that don't belong the domain, we implement the classifier based on SVM with word tfidf features and word embeddings. (ii) Then, the semantic parser component parses the queries and produces the entities, attributes, confidences, etc. (iii) Finally, the intent detection component identifies the intent of the queries based on the information generated above.

Results

We deploy our system in the pipeline of the business search engine and give the parse results to the search engine instead of plain queries. We compare our system with the baseline search engine without leveraging the parse results. To evaluate the benefit of our system for the search engine, we randomly select 2000 real user queries as input, and manually evaluate the results from the search engine. Table 2 presents our results. Overall, we observe that by incorporating our semantic parsing system all of the metrics of the search engine improved in all of the domains by a large margin. Most importantly, all of three domain semantic parsers are built only based on domain lexicons without training data for semantic parsers.

Domain	PV	Recall	Acc	DCG
Medical	1.5%	22.5%	85%	1.53
Medical + SP	**3.0%**	**39.1%**	**98%**	**1.63**
Entertainment	2.4%	26.1%	87%	1.49
Entertainment + SP	**4.9%**	**40.2%**	**99%**	**1.61**
Novel	1.6%	36.0%	90%	1.58
Novel + SP	**2.3%**	**46.1%**	**99%**	**1.67**

Table 2: The overall results of the search engine, where +SP indicates systems with leveraging results from semantic parser.

6   Conclusion

We have presented an easy-to-use platform for building domain semantic parsers from scratch, without requiring developers to understand the complex theory of semantic parsing. To reduce the requirement of training data for semantic parser, the grammar-based semantic parser can be generated only based on domain dependent lexicons without requiring training data. Although we only validate our model in search engines, our platform is universal and can be easily embedded in applications such as question answering and dialogue.

Acknowledgments

This work is supported by the National Natural Science Foundation of China under Grants no. 61433015, 61572477 and 61772505.

References

Jonathan Berant, Andrew Chou, Roy Frostig, and Percy Liang. 2013. Semantic parsing on freebase from question-answer pairs. In *Proceedings of the 2013 Conference on Empirical Methods in Natural Language Processing*, pages 1533–1544.

Roi Blanco, Giuseppe Ottaviano, and Edgar Meij. 2015. Fast and space-efficient entity linking for queries. In *Proceedings of the Eighth ACM International Conference on Web Search and Data Mining*, pages 179–188. ACM.

Bo Chen, Le Sun, and Xianpei Han. 2018. Sequence-to-action: End-to-end semantic graph generation for semantic parsing. In *Proceedings of the 56th Annual Meeting of the Association for Computational Linguistics*.

Michael Collins. 2002. Discriminative training methods for hidden markov models: Theory and experiments with perceptron algorithms. In *Proceedings of Empirical methods in natural language processing*, pages 1–8.

Li Dong and Mirella Lapata. 2016. Language to logical form with neural attention. *arXiv preprint arXiv:1601.01280*.

Li Dong and Mirella Lapata. 2018. Coarse-to-fine decoding for neural semantic parsing. *arXiv preprint arXiv:1805.04793*.

R. Jia and P. Liang. 2016. Data recombination for neural semantic parsing. In *Association for Computational Linguistics (ACL)*.

Christopher Manning, Mihai Surdeanu, John Bauer, Jenny Finkel, Steven Bethard, and David McClosky. 2014. The stanford corenlp natural language processing toolkit. In *Proceedings of the 52th Annual Meeting of the Association for Computational Linguistics: system demonstrations*, pages 55–60.

Francis Jeffry Pelletier. 1994. The principle of semantic compositionality. *Topoi*, 13(1):11–24.

Yilin Shen, Avik Ray, Abhishek Patel, and Hongxia Jin. 2018. Cruise: Cold-start new skill development via iterative utterance generation. In *Proceedings of ACL 2018, System Demonstrations*, pages 105–110.

Evren Sirin and Bijan Parsia. 2007. Sparql-dl: Sparql query for owl-dl. In *OWLED*, volume 258. Citeseer.

Luke Zettlemoyer and Michael Collins. 2007. Online learning of relaxed ccg grammars for parsing to logical form. In *Proceedings of the Joint Conference on Empirical Methods in Natural Language Processing and Computational Natural Language Learning*.

Luke S. Zettlemoyer and Michael Collins. 2005. Learning to map sentences to logical form: Structured classification with probabilistic categorial grammars. In *Conference on Uncertainty in Artificial Intelligence*.

FAMULUS: Interactive Annotation and Feedback Generation for Teaching Diagnostic Reasoning

Jonas Pfeiffer[1], Christian M. Meyer[1], Claudia Schulz[1],
Jan Kiesewetter[2], Jan Zottmann[2], Michael Sailer[3], Elisabeth Bauer[3],
Frank Fischer[3], Martin R. Fischer[2], Iryna Gurevych[1]

[1] Ubiquitous Knowledge Processing (UKP) Lab, Technische Universität Darmstadt, Germany
[2] Institute of Medical Education, University Hospital, LMU München, Germany
[3] Chair of Education and Educational Psychology, LMU München, Germany
`http://famulus-project.de`

Abstract

Our proposed system FAMULUS helps students learn to diagnose based on automatic feedback in virtual patient simulations, and it supports instructors in labeling training data. Diagnosing is an exceptionally difficult skill to obtain but vital for many different professions (e.g., medical doctors, teachers). Previous case simulation systems are limited to multiple-choice questions and thus cannot give constructive individualized feedback on a student's diagnostic reasoning process. Given initially only limited data, we leverage a (replaceable) NLP model to both support experts in their further data annotation with automatic suggestions, and we provide automatic feedback for students. We argue that because the central model consistently improves, our interactive approach encourages both students and instructors to recurrently use the tool, and thus accelerate the speed of data creation *and* annotation. We show results from two user studies on diagnostic reasoning in medicine and teacher education and outline how our system can be extended to further use cases.

1 Introduction

Motivation. Supporting students in learning has been the life purpose of many teachers throughout history. With the growing number of people who choose an academic path, it becomes increasingly important to leverage automatic methods to guide students and give them individualized feedback.

However, existing systems for technology-enhanced learning, mostly address skills on recalling, explaining, and applying knowledge, e.g., in automatically generated language learning exercises (Madnani et al., 2016) and math word problems (Koncel-Kedziorski et al., 2016). More complex cognitive tasks such as diagnostic reasoning require analytic and decision-making skills, for which there are yet only few solutions, even though diagnostic skills are vital for many professions (e.g., medical doctors searching for a therapy, teachers identifying potential mental disorders at an early stage, engineers diagnosing a machine failure, etc.).

Training diagnostic skills is hard and typically relies on time-consuming and hard-to-control live role-plays. Online case simulations involving so-called *virtual patients* crystallized as an effective alternative to role-playing games (Berman et al., 2016; Jin et al., 2018). In case simulations, students collect information on a virtual patient across multiple screens, e.g., from patient–doctor dialogs, lab results, and medical imaging. To date, the students formulate their final diagnosis by means of multiple-choice questions, which are easy to assess, but prevent important analyses of the effectiveness and the efficiency of the diagnostic reasoning process. This is why we propose to complement multiple-choice questions with prompts asking for explanations of the students' thought process. The open-form textual explanations enable good insight into the diagnostic reasoning process rather than only its result, leaving room for constructive methodological feedback. However, the text analysis and feedback generation components are highly complex and require advanced Natural Language Processing (NLP) techniques.

Contributions. To tackle this task, we propose our FAMULUS system to generate individual feedback on the students' diagnostic skills. FAMULUS integrates (a) state-of-the-art neural sequence labeling models to generate individualized feedback, incorporated in our novel NeuralWeb service, and (b) a corpus construction tool enabling interactive model training with (c) an existing tool for conducting case simulations. The backbone of our system is a sequence labeling approach to identify fine-grained diagnostic entities (e.g., *liver values*, *blood pressure*) and epistemic activities (Fischer et al.,

Proceedings of the 2019 EMNLP and the 9th IJCNLP (System Demonstrations), pages 73–78
Hong Kong, China, November 3 – 7, 2019. ©2019 Association for Computational Linguistics

Textaufgabe

Die Körperliche Untersuchung war unauffällig. Allerdings waren im Labor die Entzündungswerte und Leberwerte auffällig. Der dicke Tropfen war negativ, daher war Malaria als Diagnose ausgeschlossen. Die Hepatitis Serologie war positiv und damit die Diagnose gesichert.

Vielen Dank für Ihre Antwort!

Fallübersicht

Die 36-jährige Frau Hoffmann stellt sich vor, mit einem seit einer Woche bestehenden grippalen Infekt. Als zusätzliche Symptome gibt sie Abgeschlagenheit, Appetitverlust, Übelkeit und Diarrhoe an. Sie war vor einem Monat ins Sansibar, vor der Reise wurde eine Gelbfieberimpfung durchgeführt.

Rückmeldung zu Differentialdiagnose

Bei einem einwöchigen grippalen Infekt mit Gliederschmerzen und Abgeschlagenheit wäre zunächst eine Influenza-Infektion denkbar gewesen. Für einen grippalen Infekt ist die Symptomatik allerdings zu langanhaltend, da dieser meist nach 3 Tagen abklingt.

Bei einer Diarrhoe hättest du auch eine Darmerkrankung, wie die Gastroenteritis, vermuten sollen.

Nicht schlecht, dass du eine Tropenkrankheit differentialdiagnostisch in Betracht gezogen hast. Möglich wären zB. Malaria, Dengue Fieber, Cholera etc.

Figure 1: Excerpt of the generated feedback (bottom) to a student's explanation of her/his diagnostic process (top). Blue responses are covered by the text and highlighted in yellow. Black responses are not covered by the diagnosis.

2014) such as *drawing conclusions* and *evidence evaluation*, in German text. We have previously published the scientific foundation of our system (Schulz et al., 2018b,a, 2019a), but introduce the technical aspects of the system for the first time. Additionally, for the first time, we evaluate its applicability to real-time use cases. Our evaluation results on the prediction quality and the annotation effectiveness are based on two user studies with German medicine (Med) and teacher education (TEd) students. We show how instructors are relieved from the burden of pre-annotating huge amounts of data by our interactive annotation workflow, and we discuss the generated individualized feedback that helps students acquire diagnostic skills. Finally, we explain how our system can be obtained, re-used, and extended to further use cases.

2 Case Simulation Example

Imagine a Med student training her/his skills with our system. She/he receives information about a virtual patient: The 36 years old Ms. Hoffmann reports about a common cold lasting for about one week. In an interview, she mentions abnormal fatigue, diminished appetite, nausea, and diarrhea. Further questioning reveals that she stayed in Sansibar about a month ago. Prior to her travel, she was vaccinated against yellow fever.

Based on such inputs and further lab results, the student explains her/his diagnosis (see Figure 1): "Physical examination was clinically unremarkable. But the lab results show noticeable inflammation markers and liver values. Thick blood film was negative, therefore Malaria was excluded as a diagnosis. Hepatitis serology was positive, which assures the diagnosis."

In order to automatically provide feedback, we define a set of *diagnostic classes* covering fine-grained diagnostic entities related to the case (e.g.,

names of diseases, medical examinations, therapies) manually defined by domain experts, and epistemic activities (Fischer et al., 2014) that characterize the reasoning process. As epistemic activity classes, we use *hypothesis generation* (HG; the derivation of possible answers to the problem), *evidence generation* (EG; the derivation of evidence, e.g., through deductive reasoning or observing phenomena), *evidence evaluation* (EE; the assessment of whether and to which degree evidence supports an answer to the problem), and *drawing conclusions* (DC; the aggregation and weighing of evidence and knowledge to derive a final answer to the problem) discussed by Schulz et al. (2019a).

FAMULUS analyzes the previously mentioned diagnostic text and returns feedback on multiple important aspects related to the case. It successfully detects all aspects verbalized in the text (e.g., the discussion of tropical diseases; marked in blue in Figure 1). Aspects that are not addressed in the text are discussed and provide additional input to what the student has missed (e.g., that the differential diagnosis should consider a potential bowel disease due to the diarrhea). For the present example, the student correctly diagnoses a Hepatitis variant (correct would be Hepatitis A), which is positively acknowledged in the generated feedback. In the supplementary video material, we show two original German diagnostic texts and the corresponding feedback generated by our system.

3 System Architecture

FAMULUS consists of three intercommunicating components introduced in this section.

3.1 NeuralWeb

NeuralWeb[1] is a Python-based web service that communicates with all other components and thus

---

[1] github.com/UKPLab/emnlp2019-NeuralWeb

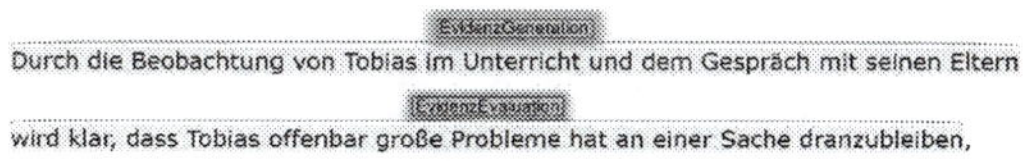

Figure 2: Annotation suggestion (grey) and accepted suggestion (orange) in the INCEpTION platform.

resembles the core of our system. It is responsible for interactive training and prediction of the diagnostic classes and for the generation of individualized feedback. We divide its functionality in a *model* and a *feedback DB* part, encompassed by a *wrapper class* that can be easily adapted for new machine learning methods and case studies.

Model. The wrapper class includes a loading function which leverages the downstream model architecture and copies the respective weights into memory. The supported neural architectures are written in Keras[2], and PyTorch[3] and are therefore easy to adapt. NeuralWeb currently provides a recent BiLSTM architecture (Reimers and Gurevych, 2017) implemented in Keras and Flair (Akbik et al., 2018) implemented in PyTorch, which holds the current state of the art on many sequence-labeling tasks. A prediction function of the wrapper preprocesses a text (sentence splitting and tokenization using NLTK) and leverages the pre-trained model to predict and return the diagnostic classes.

NeuralWeb additionally enables automatic retraining of the model within the framework which is useful when new data has been generated and annotated, improving the model automatically. This functionality is currently implemented for the Keras-based model.

Feedback DB. The output of the model is a set of discrete diagnostic class labels, which hardly yield valuable feedback for users. It is thus essential to provide an additional description, indicating whether or not the diagnosis is correct, what is missing, and if the diagnostic process is sound. We thus introduce a Feedback DB, which includes descriptive text snippets written by experts. These descriptions are associated with diagnostic classes predicted by the model and a specific case study. For example the patient in case 1 *has* Hepatitis A, whereas the patient in case 2 *does not*. The feedback for a student who diagnoses Hepatitis A thus needs to be different with respect to the case she/he currently works on. The Feedback DB is

an independent resource queried by the wrapper class. With respect to the predicted labels, the corresponding feedback text will be generated. FAMULUS finally returns the labeled texts spans of the diagnostic text together with the feedback text indicating the reasons for the prediction.

3.2 INCEpTION

Expert annotation by instructors is required due to the complexity of labeling diagnostic texts. For this reason, we leverage the INCEpTION text annotation platform (Klie et al., 2018) which enables interactive semantic annotation. The *recommender* system which provides instructors with automatically generated annotation suggestions is one of the key functionalities of the platform. Suggestions can be obtained from various integrated classifiers as well as from external sources such as NeuralWeb. The platform uses the user feedback (accepted/rejected annotations) as well as user-created annotations to continually improve the classifiers. We leverage this functionality to create an efficient interactive annotation process for our diagnostic classes and thus to create training data for our NLP models. Figure 2 shows an example of the labeling process with suggestions by our pre-trained model.

3.3 CASUS

CASUS[4] is an interactive system designed for case simulations with virtual patients. It incorporates all aspects necessary for conducting diagnostic case simulations (i.e., videos, images, text, audio integration). Students receive information relevant for solving the case. They are subsequently required to formulate their diagnosis in multiple-choice questions and our new, free-text prompts, directly integrated in CASUS. After submission, CASUS presents the feedback received from NeuralWeb.

While CASUS is a sophisticated proprietary simulation tool, we would like to stress that this is not a requirement. FAMULUS can be used with any open-source front-end tool providing a text box and communicating with NeuralWeb to print out the individualized feedback. We provide a simple version of such a tool in our GitHub repository together with NeuralWeb.

4 FAMULUS Process

The FAMULUS system consists of an interactive learning cycle connecting the three components

---

[2]keras.io
[3]pytorch.org

[4]www.instruct.eu

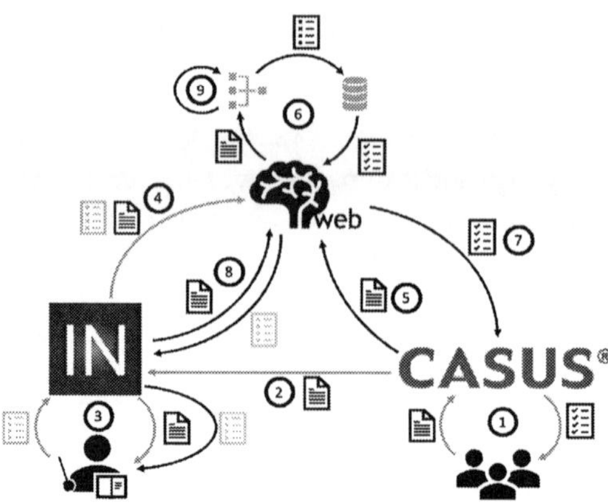

Figure 3: FAMULUS process for annotating data, training models, and generating individualized feedback. During the cold-start phase, only the blue edges are used, until enough labeled data exists to train a model.

introduced in §3 and illustrated in Figure 3.

Cold-Start. Because a small initial set of annotated data is necessary to train a preliminary model in NeuralWeb, ① few pilot users first submit their diagnoses to the CASUS system. In this cold-start phase, the users either do not receive *any* feedback or a *default* feedback text. For our experiments, all users receive a default gold diagnosis written by experts, for the users to compare their results manually. ② The students' diagnostic texts are sent to INCEpTION, where ③ instructors label the data according to the predefined annotation schema. ④ The gold labels (visualized in green) are stored and sent to NeuralWeb. Using this labeled training data, we can train our models to automatically predict the diagnostic classes found in a given text.

Warm-Run. After an initial model has been trained, a new set of users can benefit from the trained model to receive individualized feedback. ① Similarly to the cold-start phase, users work through the case study and submit their diagnosis to the CASUS system. ⑤ Instead of receiving a default feedback, the diagnosis is sent to NeuralWeb. ⑥ NeuralWeb processes the text through the trained model and generates individualized feedback with regards to the Feedback DB. ⑦ The individualized feedback is sent back to CASUS which visualizes it for the user.

Like in the cold-start phase, ② the diagnostic text is also sent to INCEpTION. ⑧ But instead of relying solely on the instructor, the trained model in NeuralWeb predicts preliminary annotations (de-

		EG	EE	HG	DC
Med	BiLSTM	71.60	80.20	69.28	65.32
Med	UB	85.61	90.25	86.37	85.58
TEd	BiLSTM	78.53	78.87	57.16	61.77
TEd	UB	93.29	90.71	81.77	82.11

Table 1: Individual macro-F1 scores following Schulz et al. (2019a) for each of the epistemic activities. The BiLSTM uses FastText embeddings (Bojanowski et al., 2017). This architecture is equal to Flair when only using FastText embeddings. UB reports the human upper bound (inter-annotator agreement) indicating room for improvement.

noted in yellow) which are additionally presented to the instructor (see Figure 2). ③ These predictions should increase the labeling speed, as in many cases, the instructor simply has to accept the suggestions the model has predicted. ④ The validated (green) labels are sent back to NeuralWeb and ⑨ the model can be interactively retrained for each additional data point which has been labeled.

5 Evaluation

We employ our proposed FAMULUS architecture in two studies yielding 1,107 Med and 944 TEd diagnostic texts written for eight distinct cases per domain. While a full analysis of the two studies is beyond the scope of this paper, we focus on three research questions highly relevant to the systemic aspects of FAMULUS: (1) the quality of the predicted diagnostic classes, (2) the computation time of the prediction and feedback generation system to assess the applicability of our system in real-time applications, and (3) the benefits of providing annotation suggestions to the instructors.

Prediction quality. In Table 1, we report the performance of the BiLSTM implementation for predicting epistemic activities in the Med and TEd data. As we can see, the difficulty of predicting the classes varies between different activities. Despite some room for improvement with respect to the human upper bound (UB) based on inter-rater agreement, the interactive nature of FAMULUS helps in succeeding in this attempt by continually improving the model when new data is available.

We conduct similar experiments for the prediction of fine-grained diagnostic entities, but omit a comprehensive discussion due to space limitations.

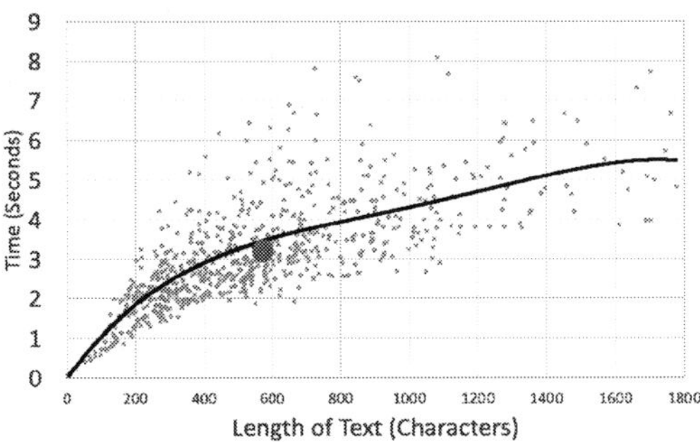

Figure 4: Prediction time for the submitted diagnostic texts of TEd students. The illustrated model is Flair with character and Flair embeddings, hidden size 256, 2 layer BiLSTM with CRF-head. The red dot indicates the mean time and length of 3.15 seconds and 562 characters respectively. The trendline is illustrated in black. The experiment was conducted on a 13-inch 2017 MacBook Pro with i7 Processor and 16GB RAM.

Computation time. In order to present the feasibility of deploying FAMULUS in a real-time scenario, we plot the inference times of the submitted diagnostic texts in Figure 4. The inference time includes sentence splitting, tokenization, model prediction, and feedback generation using the Feedback DB. We find that on average the submitted texts have a length of 562 characters with an average inference time of 3.15 seconds on a common desktop machine. The different inference times for similar text lengths are due to variable sentence lengths, as longer sentences require more inference time. We batch all sentences of one diagnostic text and pass them through the model simultaneously. As we can see in the graph, the automatic feedback generation does not surpass 9 seconds. This is intuitively faster than any human is able to read, process, and output feedback text, even by leveraging prewritten descriptions. This demonstrates the effectiveness and scalability of FAMULUS in a real-time scenario.

Annotation suggestions. To evaluate the effects of providing annotation suggestions, we have conducted an extensive study (Schulz et al., 2019b) considering annotation time, annotation quality, potential biases, and the ease of use. To this end, we asked five Med and four TEd instructors to annotate diagnostic texts. Two of the instructors per domain did not receive any suggestions. For the remaining instructors, we provided suggestions in multiple phases using different models and setups. Overall,

we find positive effects yielding a speed-up of 34 to 42 seconds per annotated text. The instructors accept 56 % (Med) and 54 % (TEd) of the annotations. While we observe a slightly higher inter-annotator agreement if instructors receive suggestions, we also study whether the instructors' decisions are influenced by the suggestions, but only observe a negligible effect.

6 Dissemination

In this section, we introduce how the components of our system can be obtained and linked with each other. Additionally, we discuss multiple use cases that can benefit from our architecture.

Availability. The NeuralWeb component is the heart of our system and has been newly developed for our purposes. We make NeuralWeb available as open-source software in our GitHub repository under the Apache License 2.0. We integrate the annotation suggestions generated by our system into the INCEpTION annotation tool, which is available as open-source software under the Apache License 2.0. To conduct the case simulations, we use the CASUS system which can be obtained from its publisher Instruct. We provide a simple but free alternative to CASUS which includes only the necessary functionality for the FAMULUS system, which is to write the diagnostic text and visualize feedback. This system, together with connection functionalities to INCEpTION and CASUS, can be found in our NeuralWeb repository.

For using FAMULUS, a server or virtual machine is needed on which the system is deployed. A thorough description can be found in our GitHub repository, including the respective URLs and ports that need to be adapted.

Use cases. Our proposed architecture is primarily useful to prepare and conduct case simulations that train diagnostic skills based on text analysis and automated feedback generation methods. Besides developing new cases for the Med and TEd domains which is the subject of our research, case simulations can be useful for students in engineering (e.g., diagnosing a machine failure), law (investigating evidence in a lawsuit), economy (optimizing business processes), and many more.

In order to leverage the FAMULUS system, three prior steps need to be made, independent of our system: (1) Expert instructors develop a set of case studies, for which they provide all necessary information. The case study can be integrated into a simulation tool such as CASUS or provided in printed form. (2) The instructors define an annotation schema, i.e. what kinds of diagnostic classes should be annotated (e.g., observations of teachers in a classroom). (3) As the individualized feedback can vary from case to case, corresponding descriptions need to be defined by the instructors.

7 Conclusion

In this paper, we have introduced FAMULUS, a case simulation system integrating interactive data acquisition and model training, and individualized feedback generation for students' explanations of diagnostic reasoning processes. Our analysis shows how FAMULUS helps experts in annotating data fast and reliable while successfully predicting entities and activities occurring in diagnostic texts. FAMULUS is applicable in real-time scenarios and generates feedback much faster than humans. While we focus specifically on diagnostic case simulations in medicine and teacher education, we outline the steps necessary to adapt our approach to many other disciplines requiring the training of diagnostic skills. We open-source all components necessary to employ FAMULUS in new case studies, hoping to encourage more research in this area.

Acknowledgments

This work has been supported by the German Federal Ministry of Education and Research (BMBF) under the reference 16DHL1040 (FAMULUS).

References

Alan Akbik, Duncan Blythe, and Roland Vollgraf. 2018. Contextual string embeddings for sequence labeling. In *Proceedings of the 27th COLING*, pages 1638–1649.

Norman B. Berman, Steven J. Durning, Martin R. Fischer, Soren Huwendiek, and Marc M. Triola. 2016. The Role for Virtual Patients in the Future of Medical Education. *Academic Medicine: Journal of the Association of American Medical Colleges*, 91(9):1217–1222.

Piotr Bojanowski, Edouard Grave, Armand Joulin, and Tomas Mikolov. 2017. Enriching Word Vectors with Subword Information. *Transactions of the Association for Computational Linguistics*, 5:135–146.

Frank Fischer, Ingo Kollar, Stefan Ufer, Beate Sodian, Heinrich Hussmann, Reinhard Pekrun, Birgit Neuhaus, Birgit Dorner, Sabine Pankofer, Martin R.

Fischer, Jan-Willem Strijbos, Moritz Heene, and Julia Eberle. 2014. Scientific Reasoning and Argumentation: Advancing an Interdisciplinary Research Agenda in Education. *Frontline Learning Research*, 4:28–45.

Lifeng Jin, David King, Amad Hussein, Michael White, and Douglas Danforth. 2018. Using Paraphrasing and Memory-Augmented Models to Combat Data Sparsity in Question Interpretation with a Virtual Patient Dialogue System. In *Proceedings of the Thirteenth Workshop on Innovative Use of NLP for Building Educational Applications (BEA)*, pages 13–23.

Jan-Christoph Klie, Michael Bugert, Beto Boullosa, Richard Eckart de Castilho, and Iryna Gurevych. 2018. The INCEpTION platform: Machine-assisted and knowledge-oriented interactive annotation. In *Proceedings of the 27th COLING: System Demonstrations*, pages 5–9.

Rik Koncel-Kedziorski, Subhro Roy, Aida Amini, Nate Kushman, and Hannaneh Hajishirzi. 2016. MAWPS: A Math Word Problem Repository. In *Proceedings of the 2016 Conference of the NAACL*, pages 1152–1157.

Nitin Madnani, Jill Burstein, John Sabatini, Kietha Biggers, and Slava Andreyev. 2016. Language Muse: Automated Linguistic Activity Generation for English Language Learners. In *Proceedings of the 54th Annual Meeting of the ACL: System Demonstrations*, pages 79–84.

Nils Reimers and Iryna Gurevych. 2017. Reporting Score Distributions Makes a Difference: Performance Study of LSTM-networks for Sequence Tagging. In *Proceedings of the 2017 Conference on EMNLP*, pages 338–348.

Claudia Schulz, Christian M. Meyer, and Iryna Gurevych. 2019a. Challenges in the Automatic Analysis of Students' Diagnostic Reasoning. In *Proceedings of the 33rd AAAI*, pages 6974–6981.

Claudia Schulz, Christian M. Meyer, Jan Kiesewetter, Michael Sailer, Elisabeth Bauer, Martin R. Fischer, Frank Fischer, and Iryna Gurevych. 2019b. Analysis of Automatic Annotation Suggestions for Hard Discourse-Level Tasks in Expert Domains. In *Proceedings of the 57th Annual Meeting of the ACL*, pages 2761–2772.

Claudia Schulz, Christian M. Meyer, Michael Sailer, Jan Kiesewetter, Elisabeth Bauer, Frank Fischer, Martin R. Fischer, and Iryna Gurevych. 2018a. Challenges in the Automatic Analysis of Students' Diagnostic Reasoning. arXiv:1811.10550.

Claudia Schulz, Michael Sailer, Jan Kiesewetter, Elisabeth Bauer, Fischer Fischer, Martin R. Fischer, and Iryna Gurevych. 2018b. Automatic recommendations for data coding: A use case from medical and teacher education. In *Proceedings of the 14th IEEE International Conference on e-Science*, pages 364–365.

Gunrock: A Social Bot for Complex and Engaging Long Conversations

**Dian Yu, Michelle Cohn, Yi Mang Yang, Chun-Yen Chen, Weiming Wen
Jiaping Zhang, Mingyang Zhou, Kevin Jesse, Austin Chau, Antara Bhowmick
Shreenath Iyer, Giritheja Sreenivasulu, Sam Davidson, Ashwin Bhandare, Zhou Yu**
University of California, Davis
{dianyu, mdcohn, yimyang, abtchen, wmwen, jpzhang, minzhou, krjesse}@ucdavis.edu
{amchau, abhowmick, shriyer, s.giritheja, ssdavidson, asbhandar, joyu}@ucdavis.edu

Abstract

Gunrock is the winner of the 2018 Amazon Alexa Prize, as evaluated by coherence and engagement from both real users and Amazon-selected expert conversationalists. We focus on understanding complex sentences and having in-depth conversations in open domains. In this paper, we introduce some innovative system designs and related validation analysis. Overall, we found that users produce longer sentences to Gunrock, which are directly related to users' engagement (e.g., ratings, number of turns). Additionally, users' backstory queries about Gunrock are positively correlated to user satisfaction. Finally, we found dialog flows that interleave facts and personal opinions and stories lead to better user satisfaction.

1 Introduction

Amazon Alexa Prize (Ram et al., 2018) provides a platform to collect real human-machine conversation data and evaluate performance on speech-based social conversational systems. Our system, Gunrock (Chen et al., 2018)[1] addresses several limitations of prior chatbots (Vinyals and Le, 2015; Zhang et al., 2018; Fang et al., 2018) including inconsistency and difficulty in complex sentence understanding (e.g., long utterances) and provides several contributions: First, Gunrock's multi-step language understanding modules enable the system to provide more useful information to the dialog manager, including a novel dialog act scheme. Additionally, the natural language understanding (NLU) module can handle more complex sentences, including those with coreference. Second, Gunrock interleaves actions to elicit users' opinions and provide responses to create an in-depth, engaging conversation; while a related

strategy to interleave task- and non-task functions in chatbots has been proposed (Rudnicky, 2019), no chatbots to our knowledge have employed a fact/opinion interleaving strategy. Finally, we use an extensive persona database to provide coherent profile information, a critical challenge in building social chatbots (Zhang et al., 2018). Compared to previous systems (Fang et al., 2018), Gunrock generates more balanced conversations between human and machine by encouraging and understanding more human inputs (see Table 1 for an example).

User_1:	let's chat
Gunrock_1:	Hi, this is an Alexa Prize Socialbot. It's nice to talk to you again, George. I think last time we were talking about movies. Would you like to talk about it now?
User_2:	sure [SPL] that would be great
Gunrock_2:	By the way, I love to discover new movies. I recently watched Crazy Rich Asians because someone told me it was hilarious. What movie would you recommend to me?
User_3:	ha [SPL] it's a tough question [SPL] i don't think i have a good one to recommend [SPL] wait [SPL] i think that *stars born* is good
Gunrock_3:	Yes I remember watching *a star is born*. Hmm. If you had to rate this movie from 1 to 10, what would it be?
User_4:	ten
Gunrock_4:	A perfect 10! You have to tell me more. What was so exceptional? When I watched it, the music design really stood out to me.
User_5:	when i watched it the music was amazing [SPL] and bradley cooper was super talented in the movie [SPL] i really like him
Gunrock_5:	You've got me wanting to watch the movie again. Ouu, Maybe you will find this interesting. Bradley Cooper claimed that his dream was to be a director before he got into acting and this was his directorial debut ...

Table 1: An example conversation between Gunrock and a human user (User). Text in red represents ASR errors while text in green represents ASR correction. [SPL] represents a split of the sentences from a sequence of words from ASR.

---

[1] https://gunrock-ucdavis.weebly.com/
2018-system-demonstration.html

Proceedings of the 2019 EMNLP and the 9th IJCNLP (System Demonstrations), pages 79–84
Hong Kong, China, November 3 – 7, 2019. ©2019 Association for Computational Linguistics

2 System Architecture

Figure 1 provides an overview of Gunrock's architecture. We extend the Amazon Conversational Bot Toolkit (CoBot) (Khatri et al., 2018) which is a flexible event-driven framework. CoBot provides ASR results and natural language processing pipelines through the Alexa Skills Kit (ASK) (Kumar et al., 2017). Gunrock corrects ASR according to the context (§2.1) and creates a natural language understanding (NLU) (§2.2) module where multiple components analyze the user utterances. A dialog manager (DM) (§2.3) uses features from NLU to select topic dialog modules and defines an individual dialog flow. Each dialog module leverages several knowledge bases (§2.4). Then a natural language generation (NLG) (§2.5) module generates a corresponding response. Finally, we markup the synthesized responses and return to the users through text to speech (TTS) (§2.6). While we provide an overview of the system in the following sections, for detailed system implementation details, please see the technical report (Chen et al., 2018).

2.1 Automatic Speech Recognition

Gunrock receives ASR results with the raw text and timestep information for each word in the sequence (without case information and punctuation). Keywords, especially named entities such as movie names, are prone to generate ASR errors without contextual information, but are essential for NLU and NLG. Therefore, Gunrock uses domain knowledge to correct these errors by comparing noun phrases to a knowledge base (e.g. a list of the most popular movies names) based on their phonetic information. We extract the primary and secondary code using The Double Metaphone Search Algorithm (Philips, 2000) for noun phrases (extracted by noun trunks) and the selected knowledge base, and suggest a potential fix by code matching. An example can be seen in User_3 and Gunrock_3 in Table 1.

2.2 Natural Language Understanding

Gunrock is designed to engage users in deeper conversation; accordingly, a user utterance can consist of multiple units with complete semantic meanings. We first split the corrected raw ASR text into sentences by inserting break tokens. An example is shown in User_3 in Table 1. Meanwhile, we mask named entities before segmentation so that a named entity will not be segmented into multiple parts and an utterance with a complete meaning is maintained (e.g.,"i like the movie a star is born"). We also leverage timestep information to filter out false positive corrections. After segmentation, our coreference implementation leverages entity knowledge (such as person versus event) and replaces nouns with their actual reference by entity ranking. We implement coreference resolution on entities both within segments in a single turn as well as across multiple turns. For instance, "him" in the last segment in User_5 is replaced with "bradley cooper" in Table 1. Next, we use a constituency parser to generate noun phrases from each modified segment. Within the sequence pipeline to generate complete segments, Gunrock detects (1) topic, (2) named entities, and (3) sentiment using ASK in parallel. The NLU module uses knowledge graphs including Google Knowledge Graph [2] to call for a detailed description of each noun phrase for understanding.

In order to extract the intent for each segment, we designed MIDAS, a human-machine dialog act scheme with 23 tags and implemented a multi-label dialog act classification model using contextual information (Yu and Yu, 2019). Next, the NLU components analyzed on each segment in a user utterance are sent to the DM and NLG module for state tracking and generation, respectively.

2.3 Dialog Manager

We implemented a hierarchical dialog manager, consisting of a high level and low level DMs. The former leverages NLU outputs for each segment and selects the most important segment for the system as the central element using heuristics. For example, "i just finished *reading* harry potter," triggers Sub-DM: Books. Utilizing the central element and features extracted from NLU, input utterances are mapped onto 11 possible topic dialog modules (e.g., movies, books, animals, etc.), including a backup module, retrieval.

Low level dialog management is handled by the separate topic dialog modules, which use modular finite state transducers to execute various dialog segments processed by the NLU. Using topic-specific modules enables deeper conversations that maintain the context. We design dialog flows in each of the finite state machines, as well. Dia-

---

[2] https://developers.google.com/
knowledge-graph/

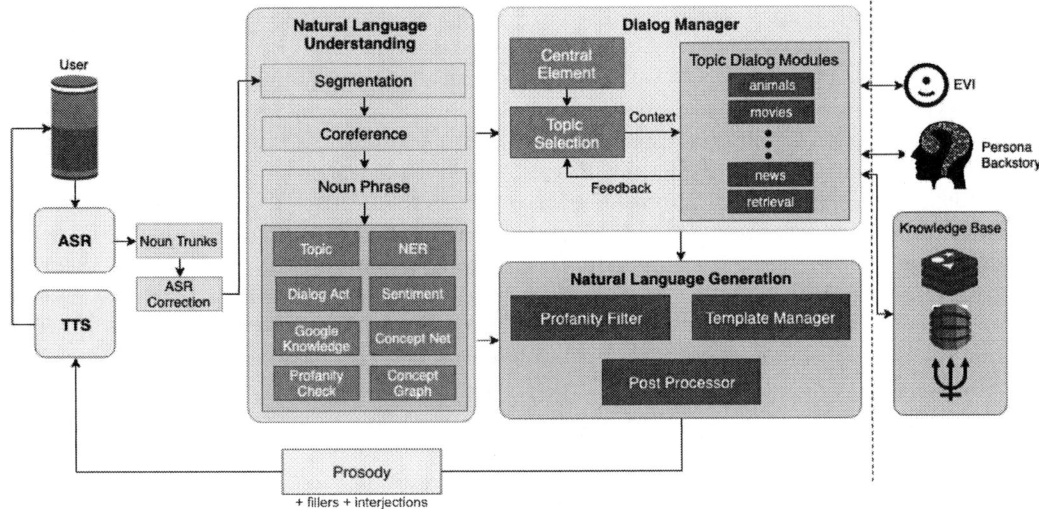

Figure 1: Gunrock system architecture

log flow is determined by rule-based transitions between a specified fixed set of dialog states. To ensure that our states and transitions are effective, we leverage large scale user data to find high probability responses and high priority responses to handle in different contexts. Meanwhile, dialog flow is customized to each user by tracking user attributes as dialog context. In addition, each dialog flow is adaptive to user responses to show acknowledgement and understanding (e.g., talking about pet ownership in the animal module). Based on the user responses, many dialog flow variations exist to provide a fresh experience each time. This reduces the feeling of dialogs being scripted and repetitive. Our dialog flows additionally interleave facts, opinions, experiences, and questions to make the conversation flexible and interesting.

In the meantime, we consider feedback signals such as "continue" and "stop" from the current topic dialog module, indicating whether it is able to respond to the following request in the dialog flow, in order to select the best response module. Additionally, in all modules we allow mixed-initiative interactions; users can trigger a new dialog module when they want to switch topics while in any state. For example, users can start a new conversation about movies from any other topic module.

2.4 Knowledge Databases

All topic dialog modules query knowledge bases to provide information to the user. To respond to general factual questions, Gunrock queries the EVI factual database [3], as well as other up-to-date scraped information appropriate for the submodule, such as news and current showing movies in a specific location from databases including IMDB. One contribution of Gunrock is the extensive Gunrock Persona Backstory database, consisting of over 1,000 responses to possible questions for Gunrock as well as reasoning for her responses for roughly 250 questions (see Table 2). We designed the system responses to elicit a consistent personality within and across modules, modeled as a female individual who is positive, outgoing, and is interested in science and technology.

User1:	do you like jeopardy?
Gunrock1:	Sure I like Jeopardy, especially when Watson competed.
User2:	why?
Gunrock2:	I'm so impressed with the capabilities of a supercomputer.

Table 2: Example interaction between Gunrock and a human user (User) querying Gunrock's backstory.

2.5 Natural Language Generation

In order to avoid repetitive and non-specific responses commonly seen in dialog systems (Li et al., 2015), Gunrock uses a template manager to select from a handcrafted response templates based on the dialog state. One dialog state can map to multiple response templates with simi-

---

[3]https://www.evi.com/

lar semantic or functional content but differing surface forms. Among these response templates for the same dialog state, one is randomly selected without repetition to provide variety unless all have been exhausted. When a response template is selected, any slots are substituted with actual contents, including queried information for news and specific data for weather. For example, to ground a movie name due to ASR errors or multiple versions, one template is "Are you talking about {movie_title} released in {release_year} starring {actor_name} as {actor_role}?". Module-specific templates were generated for each topic (e.g., animals), but some of the templates are generalizable across different modules (e.g., "Whats your favorite [movie | book | place to visit]?")

In many cases, response templates corresponding to different dialog acts are dynamically composed to give the final response. For example, an appropriate acknowledgement for the users response can be combined with a predetermined follow-up question.

2.6 Text To Speech

After NLG, we adjust the TTS of the system to improve the expressiveness of the voice to convey that the system is an engaged and active participant in the conversation. We use a rule-based system to systematically add interjections, specifically Alexa Speechcons, and fillers to approximate human-like cognitive-emotional expression (Tokuhisa and Terashima, 2006). For more on the framework and analysis of the TTS modifications, see (Cohn et al., 2019).

3   Analysis

From January 5, 2019 to March 5, 2019, we collected conversational data for Gunrock. During this time, no other code updates occurred. We analyzed conversations for Gunrock with at least 3 user turns to avoid conversations triggered by accident. Overall, this resulted in a total of 34,432 user conversations. Together, these users gave Gunrock an average rating of 3.65 (median: 4.0), which was elicited at the end of the conversation ("On a scale from 1 to 5 stars, how do you feel about talking to this socialbot again?"). Users engaged with Gunrock for an average of 20.92 overall turns (median 13.0), with an average of 6.98 words per utterance, and had an average conversation time of 7.33 minutes (median: 2.87 min.). We conducted three

principal analyses: users' response depth (§3.1), backstory queries (§3.2), and interleaving of personal and factual responses (§3.3).

3.1   Response Depth: Mean Word Count

Two unique features of Gunrock are its ability to dissect longer, complex sentences, and its methods to encourage users to be active conversationalists, elaborating on their responses. In prior work, even if users are able to drive the conversation, often bots use simple yes/no questions to control the conversational flow to improve understanding; as a result, users are more passive interlocutors in the conversation. We aimed to improve user engagement by designing the conversation to have more open-ended opinion/personal questions, and show that the system can understand the users' complex utterances (See §2.2 for details on NLU). Accordingly, we ask if users' speech behavior will reflect Gunrock's technical capability and conversational strategy, producing longer sentences.

We assessed the degree of conversational depth by measuring users' mean word count. Prior work has found that an increase in word count has been linked to improved user engagement (e.g., in a social dialog system (Yu, 2016)). For each user conversation, we extracted the overall rating, the number of turns of the interaction, and the user's per-utterance word count (averaged across all utterances). We modeled the relationship between word count and the two metrics of user engagement (overall rating, mean number of turns) in separate linear regressions.

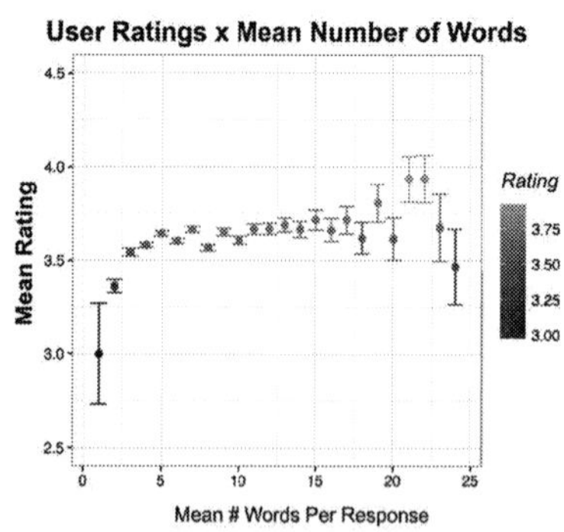

Figure 2: Mean user rating by mean number of words. Error bars show standard error.

Results showed that users who, on average, produced utterances with more words gave significantly higher ratings (β=0.01, *SE*=0.002, *t*=4.79,

$p<0.001$[4](see Figure 2) and engaged with Gunrock for significantly greater number of turns (β=1.85, SE=0.05, t=35.58, $p<0.001$) (see Figure 2). These results can be interpreted as evidence for Gunrock's ability to handle complex sentences, where users are not constrained to simple responses to be understood and feel engaged in the conversation – and evidence that individuals are more satisfied with the conversation when they take a more active role, rather than the system dominating the dialog. On the other hand, another interpretation is that users who are more talkative may enjoy talking to the bot in general, and thus give higher ratings in tandem with higher average word counts.

3.2 Gunrock's Backstory and Persona

We assessed the user's interest in Gunrock by tagging instances where the user triggered Gunrock's backstory (e.g., "What's your favorite color?"). For users with at least one backstory question, we modeled overall (log) Rating with a linear regression by the (log) 'Number of Backstory Questions Asked' (log transformed due to the variables' non-linear relationship). We hypothesized that users who show greater curiosity about Gunrock will display higher overall ratings for the conversation based on her responses. Overall, the number of times users queried Gunrock's backstory was strongly related to the rating they gave at the end of the interaction (log:β=0.10, SE=0.002, t=58.4, $p<0.001$)(see Figure 3). This suggests that maintaining a consistent personality — and having enough responses to questions the users are interested in — may improve user satisfaction.

3.3 Interleaving Personal and Factual Information: Animal Module

Gunrock includes a specific topic module on animals, which includes a factual component where the system provides animal facts, as well as a more personalized component about pets. Our system is designed to engage users about animals in a more casual conversational style (Ventola, 1979), eliciting follow-up questions if the user indicates they have a pet; if we are able to extract the pet's name, we refer to it in the conversation (e.g., "Oliver is a great name for a cat!", "How long have you had Oliver?"). In cases where the user does not indicate that they have a pet, the system solely provides animal facts. Therefore, the animal module can serve as a test of our interleaving strategy: we hypothesized that combining facts and personal questions — in this case about the user's pet — would lead to greater user satisfaction overall.

We extracted conversations where Gunrock asked the user if they had ever had a pet and categorized responses as "Yes", "No", or "NA" (if users did not respond with an affirmative or negative response). We modeled user rating with a linear regression model, with predictor of "Has Pet' (2 levels: Yes, No). We found that users who talked to Gunrock about their pet showed significantly higher overall ratings of the conversation (β=0.15, SE=0.06, t=2.53, p=0.016) (see Figure 4). One interpretation is that interleaving factual information with more in-depth questions about their pet result in improved user experience. Yet, another interpretation is that pet owners may be more friendly and amenable to a socialbot; for example, prior research has linked differences in personality to pet ownership (Kidd and Kidds, 1980).

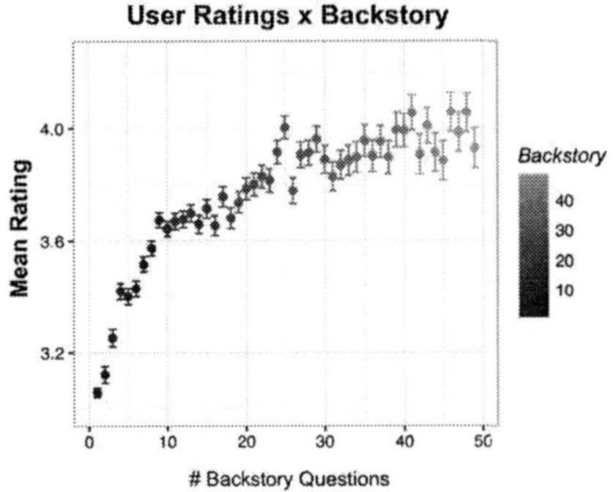

Figure 3: Mean user rating based on number of queries to Gunrock's backstory. Error bars show standard error.

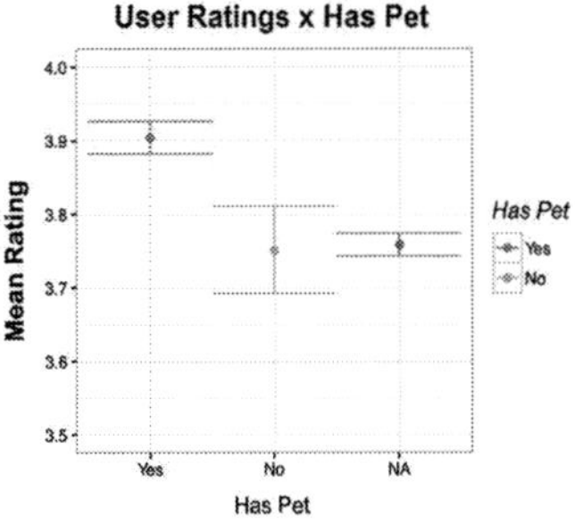

Figure 4: Mean user rating based 'Has Pet'. Error bars show standard error.

---

[4] β = Unstandardized Beta Coefficient, SE = Standard Error, t = T value, p = P value

4   Conclusion

Gunrock is a social chatbot that focuses on having long and engaging speech-based conversations with thousands of real users. Accordingly, our architecture employs specific modules to handle longer and complex utterances and encourages users to be more active in a conversation. Analysis shows that users' speech behavior reflects these capabilities. Longer sentences and more questions about Gunrocks's backstory positively correlate with user experience. Additionally, we find evidence for interleaved dialog flow, where combining factual information with personal opinions and stories improve user satisfaction. Overall, this work has practical applications, in applying these design principles to other social chatbots, as well as theoretical implications, in terms of the nature of human-computer interaction (cf. 'Computers are Social Actors' (Nass et al., 1994)). Our results suggest that users are engaging with Gunrock in similar ways to other humans: in chitchat about general topics (e.g., animals, movies, etc.), taking interest in Gunrock's backstory and persona, and even producing more information about themselves in return.

Acknowledgments

We would like to acknowledge the help from Amazon in terms of financial and technical support.

References

Chun-Yen Chen, Dian Yu, Weiming Wen, Yi Mang Yang, Jiaping Zhang, Mingyang Zhou, Kevin Jesse, Austin Chau, Antara Bhowmick, Shreenath Iyer, Giritheja Sreenivasulu, Runxiang Cheng, Ashwin Bhandare, and Zhou Yu. 2018. Gunrock: Building a human-like social bot by leveraging large scale real user data. In *2nd Proceedings of Alexa Prize*.

Michelle Cohn, Chun-Yen Chen, and Zhou Yu. 2019. A large-scale user study of an alexa prize chatbot: Effect of TTS dynamism on perceived quality of social dialog. In *Proceedings of the 20th SIGdial Workshop on Discourse and Dialogue*.

Hao Fang, Hao Cheng, Maarten Sap, Elizabeth Clark, Ari Holtzman, Yejin Choi, Noah A. Smith, and Mari Ostendorf. 2018. Sounding board: A user-centric and content-driven social chatbot. *CoRR*, abs/1804.10202.

Chandra Khatri, Behnam Hedayatnia, Anu Venkatesh, Jeff Nunn, Yi Pan, Qing Liu, Han Song, Anna Gottardi, Sanjeev Kwatra, Sanju Pancholi, Ming Cheng, Qinglang Chen, Lauren Stubel, Karthik Gopalakrishnan, Kate Bland, Raefer Gabriel, Arindam Mandal, Dilek Hakkani-Tür, Gene Hwang, Nate Michel, Eric King, and Rohit Prasad. 2018. Advancing the state of the art in open domain dialog systems through the alexa prize. *CoRR*, abs/1812.10757.

Aline H Kidd and Robert M Kidds. 1980. Personality characteristics and preferences in pet ownership. *Psychological Reports*, 46(3):939–949.

Anjishnu Kumar, Arpit Gupta, Julian Chan, Sam Tucker, Björn Hoffmeister, and Markus Dreyer. 2017. Just ASK: building an architecture for extensible self-service spoken language understanding. *CoRR*, abs/1711.00549.

Jiwei Li, Michel Galley, Chris Brockett, Jianfeng Gao, and Bill Dolan. 2015. A diversity-promoting objective function for neural conversation models. *CoRR*, abs/1510.03055.

Clifford Nass, Jonathan Steuer, and Ellen R Tauber. 1994. Computers are social actors. In *Proceedings of the SIGCHI conference on Human factors in computing systems*, pages 72–78. ACM.

Lawrence Philips. 2000. The double metaphone search algorithm. *C/C++ Users J.*, 18(6):38–43.

Ashwin Ram, Rohit Prasad, Chandra Khatri, Anu Venkatesh, Raefer Gabriel, Qing Liu, Jeff Nunn, Behnam Hedayatnia, Ming Cheng, Ashish Nagar, Eric King, Kate Bland, Amanda Wartick, Yi Pan, Han Song, Sk Jayadevan, Gene Hwang, and Art Pettigrue. 2018. Conversational AI: the science behind the alexa prize. *CoRR*, abs/1801.03604.

Alexander I Rudnicky. 2019. C ha d: Chat-oriented dialog systems. In *Advanced Social Interaction with Agents*, pages 57–60. Springer.

Ryoko Tokuhisa and Ryuta Terashima. 2006. Relationship between utterances and "enthusiasm" in non-task-oriented conversational dialogue. In *Proceedings of the 7th SIGdial Workshop on Discourse and Dialogue*.

Eija Ventola. 1979. The structure of casual conversation in english. *Journal of pragmatics*, 3(3-4):267–298.

Oriol Vinyals and Quoc V. Le. 2015. A neural conversational model. *CoRR*, abs/1506.05869.

Dian Yu and Zhou Yu. 2019. Midas: A dialog act annotation scheme for open domain human machine spoken conversations. *arXiv preprint arXiv:1908.10023*.

Zhou Yu. 2016. *Situated Intelligent Interactive Systems*. Ph.D. thesis, Carnegie Mellon University.

Saizheng Zhang, Emily Dinan, Jack Urbanek, Arthur Szlam, Douwe Kiela, and Jason Weston. 2018. Personalizing dialogue agents: I have a dog, do you have pets too? *CoRR*, abs/1801.07243.

HARE: a Flexible Highlighting Annotator for Ranking and Exploration

Denis Newman-Griffis[†,‡] and **Eric Fosler-Lussier**[†]
[†]Dept. of Computer Science and Engineering, The Ohio State University, Columbus, OH
[‡]Rehabilitation Medicine Dept., Clinical Center, National Institutes of Health, Bethesda, MD
{newman-griffis.1, fosler-lussier.1}@osu.edu

Abstract

Exploration and analysis of potential data sources is a significant challenge in the application of NLP techniques to novel information domains. We describe HARE, a system for highlighting relevant information in document collections to support ranking and triage, which provides tools for post-processing and qualitative analysis for model development and tuning. We apply HARE to the use case of narrative descriptions of mobility information in clinical data, and demonstrate its utility in comparing candidate embedding features. We provide a web-based interface for annotation visualization and document ranking, with a modular backend to support interoperability with existing annotation tools.

1 Introduction

As natural language processing techniques become useful for an increasing number of new information domains, it is not always clear how best to identify information of interest, or to evaluate the output of automatic annotation tools. This can be especially challenging when target data in the form of long strings or narratives of complex structure, e.g., in financial data (Fisher et al., 2016) or clinical data (Rosenbloom et al., 2011).

We introduce HARE, a Highlighting Annotator for Ranking and Exploration. HARE includes two main components: a workflow for supervised training of automated token-wise relevancy taggers, and a web-based interface for visualizing and analyzing automated tagging output. It is intended to serve two main purposes: (1) triage of documents when analyzing new corpora for the presence of relevant information, and (2) interactive analysis, post-processing, and comparison of output from different annotation systems.

In this paper, we demonstrate an application of HARE to information about individuals' mobility status, an important aspect of functioning concerned with changing body position or location. This is a relatively new type of health-related narrative information with largely uncharacterized linguistic structure, and high relevance to overall health outcomes and work disability programs. In experiments on a corpus of 400 clinical records, we show that with minimal tuning, our tagger is able to produce a high-quality ranking of documents based on their relevance to mobility, and to capture mobility-likely document segments with high fidelity. We further demonstrate the use of post-processing and qualitative analytic components of our system to compare the impact of different feature sets and tune processing settings to improve relevance tagging quality.

2 Related work

Corpus annotation tools are plentiful in NLP research: brat (Stenetorp et al., 2012) and Knowtator (Ogren, 2006) being two heavily used examples among many. However, the primary purpose of these tools is to streamline *manual* annotation by experts, and to support review and revision of manual annotations. Some tools, including brat, support automated pre-annotation, but analysis of these annotations and corpus exploration is not commonly included. Other tools, such as Sci-KnowMine,[1] use automated techniques for triage, but for routing to experts for curation rather than ranking and model analysis. Document ranking and search engines such as Apache Lucene,[2] by contrast, can be overly fully-featured for early-stage analysis of new datasets, and do not directly offer tools for annotation and post-processing.

Early efforts towards extracting mobility information have illustrated that it is often syntactically

---

[1]https://www.isi.edu/projects/
sciknowmine/overview
[2]https://lucene.apache.org/

Proceedings of the 2019 EMNLP and the 9th IJCNLP (System Demonstrations), pages 85–90
Hong Kong, China, November 3 – 7, 2019. ©2019 Association for Computational Linguistics

	SpaCy	WordPiece
Num documents	400	
Avg tokens per doc	537	655
Avg mobility tokens per doc	97	112
Avg mobility segments per doc		9.2

Table 1: Statistics for dataset of mobility information, using SpaCy and WordPiece tokenization.

and semantically complex, and difficult to extract reliably (Newman-Griffis and Zirikly, 2018; Newman-Griffis et al., 2019). Some characterization of mobility-related terms has been performed as part of larger work on functioning (Skube et al., 2018), but a lack of standardized terminologies limits the utility of vocabulary-driven clinical NLP tools such as CLAMP (Soysal et al., 2018) or cTAKES (Savova et al., 2010). Thus, it forms a useful test case for HARE.

3 System Description

Our system has three stages for analyzing document sets, illustrated in Figure 1. First, data annotated by experts for token relevance can be used to train relevance tagging models, and trained models can be applied to produce relevance scores on new documents (Section 3.1). Second, we provide configurable post-processing tools for cleaning and smoothing relevance scores (Section 3.2). Finally, our system includes interfaces for reviewing detailed relevance output, ranking documents by their relevance to the target criterion, and analyzing qualitative outcomes of relevance scoring output (Sections 3.3-3.5); all of these interfaces allow interactive re-configuration of post-processing settings and switching between output relevance scores from different models for comparison.

For our experiments on mobility information, we use an extended version of the dataset described by Thieu et al. (2017), which consists of 400 English-language Physical Therapy initial assessment and reassessment notes from the Rehabilitation Medicine Department of the NIH Clinical Center. These text documents have been annotated at the token level for descriptions and assessments of patient mobility status. Further information on this dataset is given in Table 1. We use ten-fold cross validation for our experiments, splitting into folds at the document level.

3.1 Relevance tagging workflow

All hyperparameters discussed in this section were tuned on held-out development data in cross-

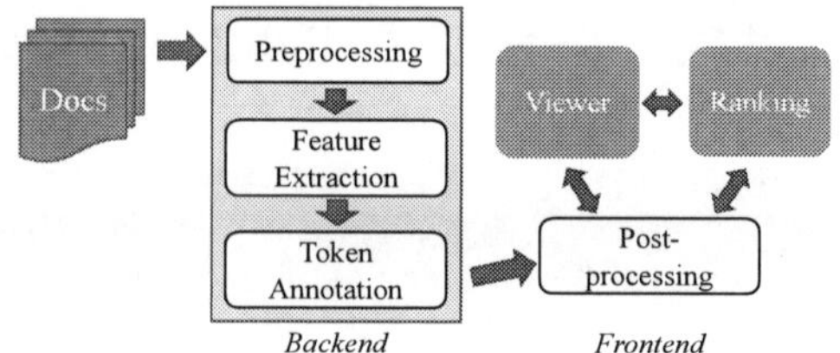

Figure 1: HARE workflow for working with a set of documents; outlined boxes indicate automated components, and gray boxes signify user interfaces.

validation experiments. We report the best settings here, and provide full comparison of hyperparameter settings in the online supplements.[3]

3.1.1 Preprocessing

Different domains exhibit different patterns in token and sentence structure that affect preprocessing. In clinical text, tokenization is not a consensus issue, and a variety of different tokenizers are used regularly (Savova et al., 2010; Soysal et al., 2018). As mobility information is relatively unexplored, we relied on general-purpose tokenization with spaCy (Honnibal and Montani, 2017) as our default tokenizer, and WordPiece (Wu et al., 2016) for experiments using BERT. We did not apply sentence segmentation, as clinical toolkits often produced short segments that interrupted mobility information in our experiments.

3.1.2 Feature extraction

Our system supports feature extraction for individual tokens in input documents using both static and contextualized word embeddings.

Static embeddings Using static (i.e., non-contextualized) embeddings, we calculate input features for each token as the mean embedding of the token and 10 words on each side (truncated at sentence/line breaks). We used FastText (Bojanowski et al., 2017) embeddings trained on a 10-year collection of physical and occupational therapy records from the NIH Clinical Center.

ELMo (Peters et al., 2018) ELMo features are calculated for each token by taking the hidden states of the two bLSTM layers and the token layer, multiplying each vector by learned weights, and summing to produce a final embedding. Combination weights are trained jointly with the token annotation model. We used a 1024-dimensional

---

[3]https://arxiv.org/abs/1908.11302

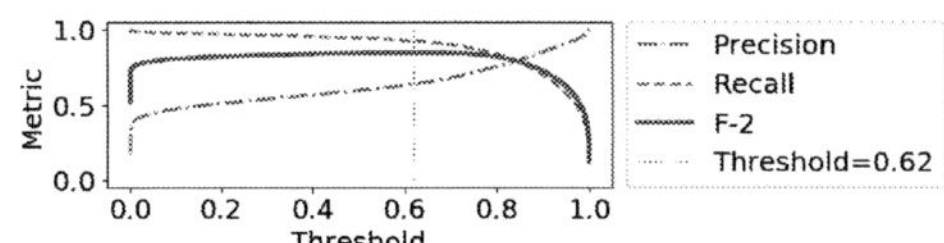

Figure 2: Precision, recall, and F-2 when varying binarization threshold from 0 to 1, using ELMo embeddings. The threshold corresponding to the best F-2 is marked with a dotted vertical line.

treatment difficulty , noting weakness in the hands and lower extremities , reporting more difficulty with performing his daily tasks . Since that time , the patient reports that he has had some

(a) No collapsing

treatment difficulty , noting weakness in the hands and lower extremities , reporting more difficulty with performing his daily tasks . Since that time , the patient reports that he has had some

(b) Collapse one blank

Figure 3: Collapsing adjacent segments illustration.

ELMo model pretrained on PubMed data[4] for our mobility experiments.

BERT (Devlin et al., 2019) For BERT features, we take the hidden states of the final k layers of the model; as with ELMo embeddings, these outputs are then multiplied by a learned weight vector, and the weighted layers are summed to create the final embedding vectors.[5] We used the 768-dimensional clinicalBERT (Alsentzer et al., 2019) model[6] in our experiments, extracting features from the last 3 layers.

3.1.3 Automated token-level annotation

We model the annotation process of assigning a relevance score for each token using a feedforward deep neural network that takes embedding features as input and produces a binomial softmax distribution as output. For mobility information, we used a DNN with three 300-dimensional hidden layers, relu activation, and 60% dropout.

As shown in Table 1, our mobility dataset is considerably imbalanced between relevant and irrelevant tokens. To adjust for this balance, for each epoch of training, we used all of the relevant tokens in the training documents, and sampled irrelevant tokens at a 75% ratio to produce a more balanced training set; negative points were re-sampled at each epoch. As token predictions are conditionally independent of one another given the embedding features, we did not maintain any sequence in the samples drawn. Relevant samples were weighted at a ratio of 2:1 during training.

After each epoch, we evaluate the model on all tokens in a held-out 10% of the documents, and calculate F-2 score (preferring recall over precision) using 0.5 as the binarization threshold of model output. We use an early stopping thresh-

old of 1e-05 on this F-2 score, with a patience of 5 epochs and a maximum of 50 epochs of training.

3.2 Post-processing methods

Given a set of token-level relevance annotations, HARE provides three post-processing techniques for analyzing and improving annotation results.

Decision thresholding The threshold for binarizing token relevance scores is configurable between 0 and 1, to support more or less conservative interpretation of model output; this is akin to exploring the precision/recall curve. Figure 2 shows precision, recall, and F-2 for different thresholding values from our mobility experiments, using scores from ELMo embeddings.

Collapsing adjacent segments We consider any contiguous sequence of tokens with scores at or above the binarization threshold to be a relevant *segment*. As shown in Figure 3, multiple segments may be interrupted by irrelevant tokens such as punctuation, or by noisy relevance scores falling below the binarization threshold. As multiple adjacent segments may inflate a document's overall relevance, our system includes a setting to collapse any adjacent segments that are separated by k or fewer tokens into a single segment.

Viterbi smoothing By modeling token-level decisions as conditionally independent of one another given the input features, we avoid assumptions of strict segment bounds, but introduce some noisy output, as shown in Figure 4. To reduce

the L leg and R leg . In addition , patient was unable to perform the unilateral stance on either leg test with eyes closed .
Functional Assessment :
Standardized testing for SBMA . Use of adult myopathy assessment tool

(a) Without smoothing

the L leg and R leg . In addition , patient was unable to perform the unilateral stance on either leg test with eyes closed .
Functional Assessment :
Standardized testing for SBMA . Use of adult myopathy assessment tool

(b) With smoothing

Figure 4: Illustration of Viterbi smoothing.

---

[4] https://allennlp.org/elmo

[5] Note that as BERT is constrained to use WordPiece tokenization, it may use slightly longer token sequences than the other methods.

[6] https://github.com/EmilyAlsentzer/clinicalBERT

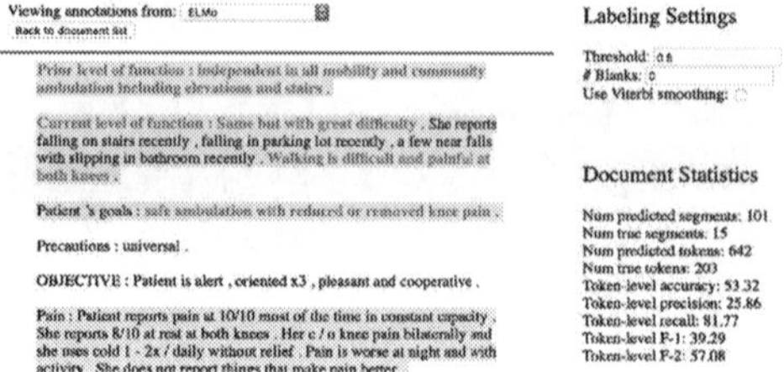

Figure 5: Annotation viewer interface.

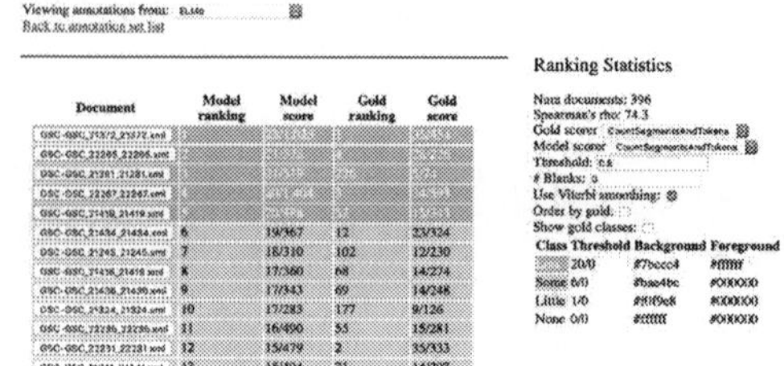

Figure 6: Ranking interface.

some of this noise, we include an optional smoothing component based on the Viterbi algorithm.

We model the "relevant"/"irrelevant" state sequence discriminatively, using annotation model outputs as state probabilities for each timestep, and calculate the binary transition probability matrix by counting transitions in the training data. We use these estimates to decode the most likely relevance state sequence R for a tokenized line T in an input document, along with the corresponding path probability matrix W, where $W_{j,i}$ denotes the likelihood of being in state j at time i given r_{i-1} and t_i. In order to produce continuous scores for each token, we then backtrace through R and assign score s_i to token t_i as the conditional probability that r_i is "relevant", given r_{i-1}. Let $Q_{j,i}$ be the likelihood of transitioning from state R_{i-1} to j, conditioned on T_i, as:

$$Q_{j,i} = \frac{W_{j,i}}{W_{R_{i-1},i-1}} \qquad (1)$$

The final conditional probability s_i is calculated by normalizing over possible states at time i:

$$s_i = \frac{Q_{1,i}}{Q_{0,i} + Q_{1,i}} \qquad (2)$$

These smoothed scores can then be binarized using the configurable decision threshold.

3.3 Annotation viewer

Annotations on any individual document can be viewed using a web-based interface, shown in Figure 5. All tokens with scores at or above the decision threshold are highlighted in yellow, with each contiguous segment shown in a single highlight. Configuration settings for post-processing methods are provided, and update the displayed annotations when changed. On click, each token will display the score assigned to it by the annotation model after post-processing. If the document being viewed is labeled with gold annota-

tions, these are shown in bold red text. Additionally, document-level summary statistics and evaluation measures, with current post-processing, are displayed next to the annotations.

3.4 Document set ranking

3.4.1 Ranking methods

Relevance scoring methods are highly task-dependent, and may reflect different priorities such as information density or diversity of information returned. In this system, we provide three general-purpose relevance scorers, each of which operates after any post-processing.

Segments+Tokens Documents are scored by multiplying their number of relevant segments by a large constant and adding the number of relevant tokens to break any ties by segment count. As relevant information may be sparse, no normalization by document length is used.

SumScores Documents are scored by summing the continuous relevance scores assigned to all of their tokens. As with the Segments+Tokens scorer, no adjustment is made for document length.

Density Document scores are the ratio of binarized relevant tokens to total number of tokens.

The same scorer can be used to rank gold annotations and model annotations, or different scorers can be chosen. Ranking quality is evaluated using Spearman's ρ, which ranges from -1 (exact opposite ranking) to +1 (same ranking), with 0 indicating no correlation between rankings. We use Segments+Tokens as default; a comparison of ranking methods is in the online supplements.

3.4.2 Ranking interface

Our system also includes a web-based ranking interface, which displays the scores and corresponding ranking assigned to a set of annotated documents, as shown in Figure 6. For ease of visual distinction, we include colorization of rows based on configurable score thresholds. Rank-

Embeddings	Smoothing	Annotation			Ranking
		Pr	Rec	F-2	ρ
Static	No	59.0	94.7	84.4	0.862
	Yes	60.5	93.7	84.3	0.899
ELMo	No	60.2	94.1	84.4	0.771
	Yes	66.5	91.4	84.8	0.886
BERT	No	55.3	93.8	82.2	0.689
	Yes	62.3	90.8	84.3	0.844

Table 2: Annotation and ranking evaluation results on mobility documents, using three embedding sources. Results are given with and without Viterbi smoothing, using binarization threshold=0.5 and no collapsing of adjacent segments. Pr=precision, Rec=recall, ρ=Spearman's ρ Pr/Rec/F2 are macro-averaged over folds, ρ is over all test predictions.

ing methods used for model scores and gold annotations (when present) can be adjusted independently, and our post-processing methods (Section 3.2) can also be adjusted to affect ranking.

3.5 Qualitative analysis tools

We provide a set of three tools for performing qualitative analysis of annotation outcomes. The first measures lexicalization of each unique token in the dataset with respect to relevance score, by averaging the assigned relevance score (with or without smoothing) for each instance of each token. Tokens with a frequency below a configurable minimum threshold are excluded.

Our other tools analyze the aggregate relevance score patterns in an annotation set. For labeled data, as shown in Figure 2, we provide a visualization of precision, recall, and F-2 when varying the binarization threshold, including identifying the optimal threshold with respect to F-2. We also include a label-agnostic analysis of patterns in output relevance scores, illustrated in Figure 7, as a way to evaluate the confidence of the annotator. Both of these tools are provided at the level of an annotation set and individual documents.

3.6 Implementation details

Our automated annotation, post-processing, and document ranking algorithms are implemented in Python, using the NumPy and Tensorflow libraries. Our demonstration interface is implemented using the Flask library, with all backend logic handled separately in order to support modularity of the user interface.

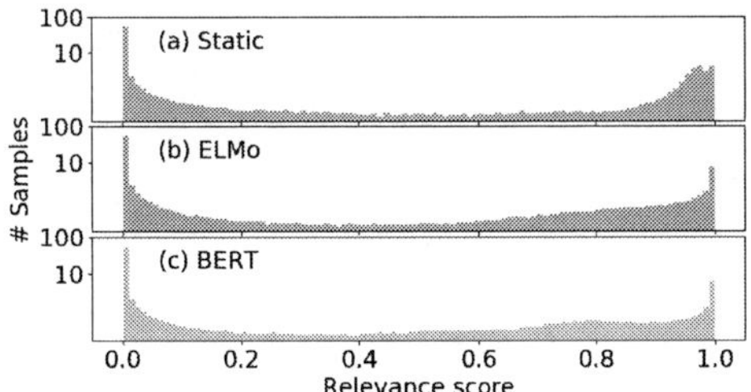

Figure 7: Distribution of token relevance scores on mobility data: (a) word2vec, (b) ELMo, and (c) BERT.

4 Results on mobility

Table 2 shows the token-level annotation and document ranking results for our experiments on mobility information. Static and contextualized embedding models performed equivalently well on token-level annotations; BERT embeddings actually underperformed static embeddings and ELMo on both precision and recall. Interestingly, static embeddings yielded the best ranking performance of $\rho = 0.862$, compared to 0.771 with ELMo and 0.689 with BERT. Viterbi smoothing makes a minimal difference in token-level tagging, but increases ranking performance considerably, particularly for contextualized models. It also produces a qualitative improvement by trimming out extraneous tokens at the start of several segments, as reflected by the improvements in precision.

The distribution of token scores from each model (Figure 7) shows that all three embedding models yielded a roughly bimodal distribution, with most scores in the ranges $[0, 0.2]$ or $[0.7, 1.0]$.

5 Discussion

Though our system is designed to address different needs from other NLP annotation tools, components such as annotation viewing are also addressed in other established systems. Our implementation decouples backend analysis from the front-end interface; in future work, we plan to add support for integrating our annotation and ranking systems into existing platforms such as brat. Our tool can also easily be extended to both multi-class and multilabel applications; for a detailed discussion, see the online supplements.

In terms of document ranking methods, it may be preferred to rank documents jointly instead of independently, in order to account for challenges such as duplication of information (common in clinical data; Taggart et al. (2015)) or subtopics.

However, these decisions are highly task-specific, and are an important focus for designing ranking utility within specific domains.

6 Conclusions

We introduced HARE, a supervised system for highlighting relevant information and interactive exploration of model outcomes. We demonstrated its utility in experiments with clinical records annotated for narrative descriptions of mobility status. We also provided qualitative analytic tools for understanding the outcomes of different annotation models. In future work, we plan to extend these analytic tools to provide rationales for individual token-level decisions. Additionally, given the clear importance of contextual information in token-level annotations, the static transition probabilities used in our Viterbi smoothing technique are likely to degrade its effect on the output. Adding support for dynamic, contextualized estimations of transition probabilities will provide more fine-grained modeling of relevance, as well as more powerful options for post-processing.

Our system is available online at `https://github.com/OSU-slatelab/HARE/`. This research was supported by the Intramural Research Program of the National Institutes of Health and the US Social Security Administration.

References

Emily Alsentzer, John Murphy, William Boag, Wei-Hung Weng, Di Jindi, Tristan Naumann, and Matthew McDermott. 2019. Publicly Available Clinical BERT Embeddings. In *Clinical NLP Workshop*, pages 72–78. ACL.

Piotr Bojanowski, Edouard Grave, Armand Joulin, and Tomas Mikolov. 2017. Enriching Word Vectors with Subword Information. *TACL*, 5:135–146.

Jacob Devlin, Ming-Wei Chang, Kenton Lee, and Kristina Toutanova. 2019. Bert: Pre-training of deep bidirectional transformers for language understanding. In *NAACL-HLT*, pages 4171–4186. ACL.

Ingrid E Fisher, Margaret R Garnsey, and Mark E Hughes. 2016. Natural Language Processing in Accounting, Auditing and Finance: A Synthesis of the Literature with a Roadmap for Future Research. *Intelligent Systems in Accounting, Finance and Management*, 23(3):157–214.

Matthew Honnibal and Ines Montani. 2017. spaCy 2: Natural language understanding with Bloom embeddings, convolutional neural networks and incremental parsing. *To appear.*

Denis Newman-Griffis and Ayah Zirikly. 2018. Embedding Transfer for Low-Resource Medical Named Entity Recognition: A Case Study on Patient Mobility. In *BioNLP*, pages 1–11. ACL.

Denis Newman-Griffis, Ayah Zirikly, Guy Divita, and Bart Desmet. 2019. Classifying the reported ability in clinical mobility descriptions. In *BioNLP*.

Philip V Ogren. 2006. Knowtator: A Protégé plug-in for annotated corpus construction. In *NAACL-HLT*, pages 273–275, New York City, USA. ACL.

Matthew E Peters, Mark Neumann, Mohit Iyyer, Matt Gardner, Christopher Clark, Kenton Lee, and Luke Zettlemoyer. 2018. Deep Contextualized Word Representations. In *NAACL-HLT*, pages 2227–2237, New Orleans, Louisiana. ACL.

S Trent Rosenbloom, Joshua C Denny, Hua Xu, Nancy Lorenzi, William W Stead, and Kevin B Johnson. 2011. Data from clinical notes: a perspective on the tension between structure and flexible documentation. *JAMIA*, 18(2):181–186.

Guergana K Savova, James J Masanz, Philip V Ogren, Jiaping Zheng, Sunghwan Sohn, Karin C Kipper-Schuler, and Christopher G Chute. 2010. Mayo clinical Text Analysis and Knowledge Extraction System (cTAKES): architecture, component evaluation and applications. *JAMIA*, 17(5):507–513.

Steven J Skube, Elizabeth A Lindemann, Elliot G Arsoniadis, Mari Akre, Elizabeth C Wick, and Genevieve B Melton. 2018. Characterizing Functional Health Status of Surgical Patients in Clinical Notes. In *AMIA Joint Summits*, pages 379–388. AMIA.

Ergin Soysal, Jingqi Wang, Min Jiang, Yonghui Wu, Serguei Pakhomov, Hongfang Liu, and Hua Xu. 2018. CLAMP – a toolkit for efficiently building customized clinical natural language processing pipelines. *JAMIA*, 25(3):331–336.

Pontus Stenetorp, Sampo Pyysalo, Goran Topić, Tomoko Ohta, Sophia Ananiadou, and Jun'ichi Tsujii. 2012. brat: a Web-based Tool for NLP-Assisted Text Annotation. In *EACL*, pages 102–107. ACL.

Jane Taggart, Siaw-Teng Liaw, and Hairong Yu. 2015. Structured data quality reports to improve EHR data quality. *Int J Med Info*, 84(12):1094–1098.

Thanh Thieu, Jonathan Camacho, and Pei-Shu Ho et al. 2017. Inductive identification of functional status information and establishing a gold standard corpus: A case study on the Mobility domain. In *BIBM*, pages 2300–2302. IEEE.

Yonghui Wu, Mike Schuster, and Zhifeng Chen et al. 2016. Google's Neural Machine Translation System: Bridging the Gap between Human and Machine Translation. *arXiv preprint arXiv:1609.08144.*

Honkling: In-Browser Personalization for Ubiquitous Keyword Spotting

Jaejun Lee, Raphael Tang, and **Jimmy Lin**

David R. Cheriton School of Computer Science
University of Waterloo

Abstract

Used for simple commands recognition on devices from smart speakers to mobile phones, keyword spotting systems are everywhere. Ubiquitous as well are web applications, which have grown in popularity and complexity over the last decade. However, despite their obvious advantages in natural language interaction, voice-enabled web applications are still few and far between. We attempt to bridge this gap with Honkling, a novel, JavaScript-based keyword spotting system. Purely client-side and cross-device compatible, Honkling can be deployed directly on user devices. Our in-browser implementation enables seamless personalization, which can greatly improve model quality; in the presence of underrepresented, non-American user accents, we can achieve up to an absolute 10% increase in accuracy in the personalized model with only a few examples.

1 Introduction

With the rapid proliferation of voice-enabled devices such as the Amazon Echo and the Apple iPhone, speech recognition systems are becoming increasingly prevalent in our daily lives. Importantly, these systems improve safety and convenience in hands-free interactions, such as using Apple's Siri to dial contacts while driving. However, a prominent drawback is that most of these systems perform speech recognition in the cloud, where a remote server receives from the device all audio to be transcribed. Clearly, the privacy and security implications are significant: servers may be accessed by other people, authorized or not. Thus, it is important to capture only the relevant speech and not all incoming audio, while providing a pleasant hands-free experience.

Enter keyword spotting systems. They solve the aforementioned issues by implementing an on-device mechanism to awaken the intelligent agent, e.g., "Okay, Google" for triggering the Google Assistant. This then allows the device to record and transmit only a limited segment of speech, obviating the need to send everything to the cloud. The task of keyword spotting (KWS) is to detect the presence of specific phrases in a stream of audio, often with the end goal of wake-word detection or simple command recognition on the device. Currently, the state of the art uses lightweight neural networks (Sainath and Parada, 2015; Tang and Lin, 2018), which can perform inference in real-time, even on low-end devices (Fernández-Marqués et al., 2018; Tang et al., 2018).

Despite the popularity of voice-enabled products, web applications have yet to make use of KWS. This is surprising, since modern web applications are supported on billions of devices ranging from desktops to smartphones. We close the gap between KWS systems and web applications by building and evaluating a JavaScript-based, in-browser KWS system. Exploiting the pervasiveness of JavaScript, our system can be deployed directly on user devices, facilitating the development of JavaScript-based, voice-enabled applications (Lee et al., 2019).

We observe, however, that the quality of our models suffers on various accents that are scarcely represented in our dataset—a problem common in speech recognition (Huang et al., 2004; Humphries et al., 1996). Fortunately, our JavaScript-based application runs completely client-side, enabling the development of personalized models. To further improve the universality of our system, we explore the benefits and costs of fine-tuning an existing KWS model on a few user-provided recordings, personalizing the application for a given user.

Our main demonstration is Honkling,[1] a novel

---

[1] http://honkling.ai

Proceedings of the 2019 EMNLP and the 9th IJCNLP (System Demonstrations), pages 91–96
Hong Kong, China, November 3 – 7, 2019. ©2019 Association for Computational Linguistics

in-browser KWS system running previous state-of-the-art models (Tang and Lin, 2018). We provide a set of comprehensive experimental results for the latency of an in-browser KWS system on a broad range of devices. We also evaluate the accuracy of KWS on various user accents and present a mechanism for in-browser user accent adaptation. On the Google Speech Commands dataset (Warden, 2018), our most accurate in-browser model achieves an accuracy of 94% while performing inference in less than 30 milliseconds. With only five user-recorded audio clips per keyword, Honkling can be fine-tuned to improve accuracy by up to an absolute 10%. Using hardware acceleration, users only need to wait for eight seconds before their Honkling becomes personalized.

2   Background and Related Work

KWS is the task of detecting a spoken phrase in audio, applicable to simple command recognition (Warden, 2018) and wake-word detection (Arik et al., 2017). Typically, KWS systems must be small footprint, since the target platforms are mobile phones, Internet-of-Things (IoT) devices, and other portable electronics. To achieve this goal, resource-efficient architectures using convolutional neural networks (CNNs) (Tang and Lin, 2018; Sainath and Parada, 2015) and recurrent neural networks (RNNs) (Arik et al., 2017) have been proposed, while other techniques make use of low-bitwidth weights (Fernández-Marqués et al., 2018; Zhang et al., 2017). However, despite the pervasiveness of modern web browsers on a broad range of devices and the availability of deep learning toolkits in JavaScript, a personalizable, on-device KWS system in web applications has not to our knowledge been explored.

In automatic speech recognition (ASR), the presence of user accents often degrades recognition quality (Huang et al., 2004; Humphries et al., 1996). Unfortunately, the solutions proposed in previous work vary depending on the underlying system, and little prior art exists using deep learning. The idea of fine-tuning neural networks to increase accuracy for a group of accents is found in Najafian et al. (2016); however, full ASR involves much larger datasets and models, and thus hours of extra training data are necessary for successful adaptation. Surprisingly, there has been little work on building KWS systems for user accent personalization.

3   Data and Models

For consistency with past results (Tang and Lin, 2018; Tang et al., 2018), we train our models on the first version of the Google Speech Commands dataset (Warden, 2018), comprising 65,000 spoken utterances for 30 short, one-second phrases. As with Tang and Lin (2018), we pick the following twelve classes: "yes", "no", "stop", "go", "left", "right", "on", "off", "up", "down", unknown, and silence. The dataset contains roughly 2,000 examples per class, including a few background noise samples of both man-made and artificial noises, e.g., washing dishes and white noise. As is standard in the speech processing literature, all audio is in 16-bit PCM, 16kHz mono-channel WAV format. We use the standard 80%, 10%, and 10% splits from the Speech Commands dataset for the training, validation, and test sets, respectively.

3.1   Input Preprocessing

First, for dataset augmentation, the input is randomly mixed with additive noise from the background noise set—this helps to decrease the generalization error and improve the robustness of the model under noise (Ko et al., 2015). Following the official TensorFlow implementation, we also apply a random time shift of $\mathrm{UNIFORM}[-100, 100]$ milliseconds (ms). For feature extraction, we compute 40-dimensional Mel-frequency cepstral coefficients (MFCCs), with a window size of 30ms and a frame shift of 10ms, yielding a final preprocessed input size of 101×40 for each one-second audio sample.

3.2   Model Architecture

We use the `res8` and `res8-narrow` architectures from Tang and Lin (2018) as starting points, which represent the prior state of the art in residual CNNs (He et al., 2016) for KWS. In both models, given the input $\mathbf{X} \in \mathbb{R}^{101 \times 40}$, we first apply a 2D convolution layer with weights $\mathbf{W} \in \mathbb{R}^{C_{out} \times 1 \times (3 \times 3)}$ and a padding of one on all sides. This step results in an output of $\tilde{\mathbf{X}} \in \mathbb{R}^{C_{out} \times 101 \times 40}$, which we then downsample using an average pooling layer with a kernel size of (4×3). Next, the output is passed through a series of three residual blocks comprising convolution and batch normalization (Ioffe and Szegedy, 2015) layers. Finally, we average pool across the channels and pass the features through a softmax across the twelve classes.

	Device	Processor	Platform	res8		res8-narrow	
				Lat. (ms)	Acc. (%)	Lat. (ms)	Acc. (%)
GPU	Desktop	GTX 1080 Ti	PyTorch	1	94.3	1	91.2
	Desktop	GTX 1080 Ti	Firefox	12	94.0	10	90.9
	MacBook Pro (2017)	Intel Iris Plus 650	Firefox	29	94.0	15	90.8
	MacBook Air (2013)	Intel HD 6000	Firefox	34	94.0	19	90.8
	Galaxy S8 (2017)	Adreno 540	Firefox	60	94.1	43	89.0
CPU	Desktop	i7-4790k (quad)	PyTorch	10	94.3	2	91.2
	MacBook Pro (2017)	i5-7287U (quad)	PyTorch	12	94.3	3	91.2
	Desktop	i7-4790k (quad)	Firefox	371	94.1	94	90.9
	MacBook Pro (2017)	i5-7287U (quad)	Firefox	361	94.0	107	90.8
	MacBook Air (2013)	i5-4260U (dual)	Firefox	485	94.0	115	90.8
	Galaxy S8 (2017)	Snapdragon 835 (octa)	Firefox	1105	94.1	265	89.0

Table 1: Latency (lat.; 90th percentile) and accuracy (acc.) results on different platforms for the `res8-*` models.

In the previous description, we are free to choose C_{out} to dictate the expressiveness and computational footprint of the model; `res8` and `res8-narrow` choose 45 and 19, respectively. In total, `res8` contains 110K parameters and incurs 30 million multiplies per second of audio, while `res8-narrow` uses 19.9K parameters and incurs 5.7 million multiplies.

4 Honkling

Training neural networks in JavaScript from scratch is ill-advised due to poorly optimized computation routines such as matrix multiplication. Therefore, we use the official PyTorch model implementations[2] at training time. At inference time, weights are transferred from PyTorch to a web application implemented in TensorFlow.js.[3] Since the official implementation utilizes LibROSA (McFee et al., 2015) for audio feature extraction, we instead use Meyda (Rawlinson et al., 2015), a JavaScript version of LibROSA. However, unlike Python, which is well suited for developing audio processing applications, in-browser JavaScript presents challenges in manipulating audio; for example, many browsers restrict the sample rate of input audio to 44.1kHz only. Due to such restrictions, the processed audio in JavaScript differ from MFCCs extracted by LibROSA. Therefore, we have patched Meyda comprehensively to minimize the mismatches.

Overall, we successfully enable KWS functionality in browsers without any server-side inference. Since the audio data is quickly processed within the browser, it is much more efficient than transferring data over the network for inference. Furthermore, users are now freed from

security and privacy implications, such as eavesdropping of network traffic and collection of personal speech data.

Measured with our university WiFi connection, the average latency to Google servers is about 25ms with a standard deviation of 20ms. Network latency is much higher for transferring audio data. With a server written in Python, we measure an average latency of 481ms with a standard deviation of 183ms for one second of 16kHz mono-channel audio data. With in-browser inference, we achieve a pure client-side architecture that does not suffer from variable network latency.

The two main metrics for our KWS application are accuracy and inference latency. To be consistent with previous work, our experiments use the same test set. We conduct experiments on desktop, laptop, and smartphone configurations to demonstrate the feasibility of our system on a broad range of devices. These include the following: a desktop with 16GB RAM, an i7-4790k CPU, and a GTX 1080 Ti; two laptop configurations, the MacBook Pro (2017), with a quad-core i5-7287U CPU and an Intel Iris Plus 650 GPU, and the MacBook Air (2013), with a dual-core i5-4260U CPU and an Intel HD 6000 GPU; the Galaxy S8 as our smartphone configuration. Given this wide range of devices, we decide to include results from Firefox only, but Honkling is also available on other browsers. Since TensorFlow.js is GPU capable, experiments are conducted both with and without GPU acceleration, which can be toggled in the browser settings.

Table 1 summarizes 90th percentile latency and recognition accuracy results for both `res8` and `res8-narrow` on various devices. Note that results with the PyTorch implementation on our laptop and desktop setups are included to compare

<hr>

[2] `http://honk.ai`
[3] `https://js.tensorflow.org`

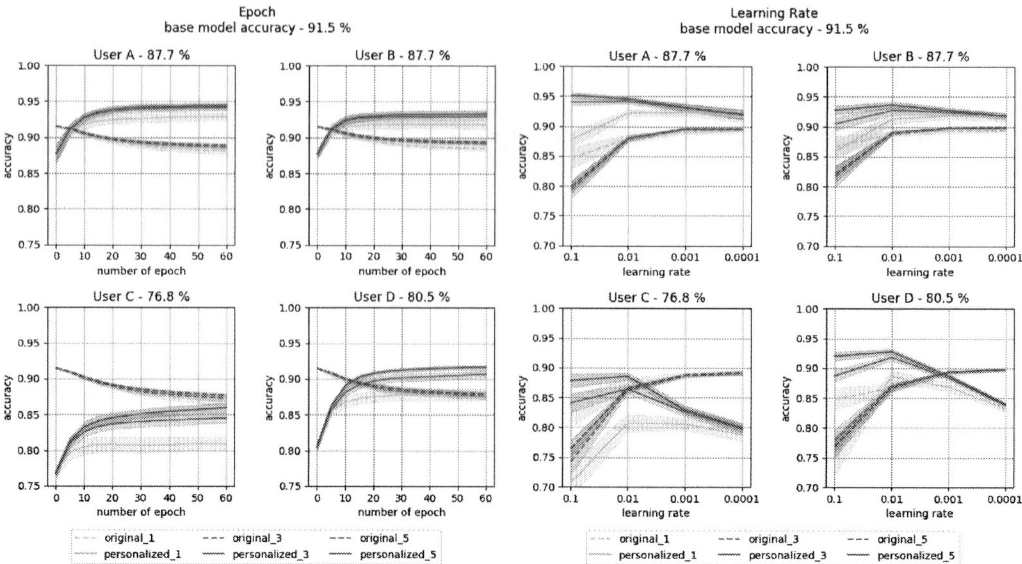

Figure 1: Accuracy varying the number of epochs (left) and the learning rate (right), with 95% confidence intervals (shaded). `original_*` and `personalized_*` denote accuracy on the original and user test sets.

with our in-browser configurations. The original implementation achieves an accuracy of 94.3% for `res8` and 91.2% for `res8-narrow` (see the first few rows in Table 1). Slight differences are observed across platforms due to a mismatch of MFCC computations between LibROSA and Meyda. However, the accuracy for each model is consistent on every platform, confirming that our in-browser implementation is robust.

Even though latency is processor dependent, the `res8-narrow` model performs inference in real time on every platform. Given that these delays are perceived by humans to be near instantaneous (Miller, 1968), our system is sufficient for real-time interactive web applications.

5 Personalization and Accent Adaptation

JavaScript applications run fully client-side and are cross-device compatible, meaning that they can be deployed directly on user devices, which enables seamless personalization. In this paper, to design a cross-device, cross-*human* KWS system, we extend Honkling to adapt to various user accents that are uncommon in the primarily American-accented dataset.

To measure the effects of different user accents on the KWS quality of Honkling, we evaluate the accuracy of `res8-narrow` on datasets comprised of recordings from different people. In

these experiments, there are four participants: A, B, C, and D. Users A and B are native speakers of Canadian English while C has a British accent and D has a Korean accent. From each person, we collected 50 recordings for each of the twelve classes, setting aside 40 recordings of each class to construct a test set of 480 samples. We conduct evaluations on the same twelve classes.

To quantify the amount of effort required from the user for personalization, we begin by finding the minimum number of recordings that leads to improvements in accuracy. Next, we experiment with different numbers of epochs and learning rates. Since we have shown that our JavaScript implementation reproduces the PyTorch implementation with minimal differences, unless indicated otherwise the following experiments are conducted using PyTorch for convenience.

We report accuracy metrics under two different sets of conditions: `original_*` and `personalized_*`, denoting accuracy on the original test set and the user test set, respectively (see Figure 1, dashed and solid lines). For each condition, we conduct experiments with three variations of training data size. The number that follows each name denotes the number of recordings per keyword in the fine-tuning dataset. To reduce the effects of outliers, we report averaged results from 60 experiments with different ran-

	Device	Processor	Platform	Number of Recordings		
				1	3	5
GPU	Desktop	GTX 1080 Ti	PyTorch	0.2 sec	0.2 sec	0.2 sec
	Desktop	GTX 1080 Ti	Firefox	3.9 sec	5.9 sec	7.6 sec
	MacBook Pro (2017)	Intel Iris Plus 650	Firefox	7.2 sec	12.6 sec	27.0 sec
CPU	Desktop	i7-4790k (quad)	PyTorch	3.3 sec	6.0 sec	8.0 sec
	MacBook Pro (2017)	i5-7287U (quad)	PyTorch	2.0 sec	5.9 sec	10.7 sec
	Desktop	i7-4790k (quad)	Firefox	25.4 min	75.8 min	128.1 min
	MacBook Pro (2017)	i5-7287U (quad)	Firefox	29.5 min	86.3 min	139.2 min

Table 2: Average in-browser fine-tuning efficiency for `res8-narrow` under different configurations.

dom seeds, where the training data is constructed by randomly selecting the appropriate number of recordings from the fine-tuning set. The test set stays the same for each experiment.

Fine-tuning progress across epochs. In Figure 1, we include in the labels of the plots both the accuracy of the base model and the accuracy on each user test set. The left half of the figure shows the fine-tuning progress across epochs, with the learning rate fixed to 0.01. As expected, accuracy on the user test set is lower than on the original test set prior to fine-tuning. For users A and B, the differences are only a few percent, which seems acceptable in practice. However, the model achieves an accuracy of only 76.8% and 80.5% for users C and D, respectively, demonstrating the need for personalization.

As fine-tuning proceeds across epochs, accuracy on the user recordings increases while accuracy on the original data decreases. We observe diminishing returns with more epochs; 50 epochs seem to be sufficient to maximize accuracy. After convergence, the models generally achieve higher accuracy on the user recordings than on the original data, thus demonstrating successful adaptation. We find that a single recording per keyword is sufficient for personalization, as the fine-tuned models exhibit higher accuracy on the user recordings for every user except user C.

Fine-tuning dataset size. Since more training data leads to a better representation of a user's speech patterns, it is no surprise that an increase in accuracy is observed as more recordings are added to the dataset; compare `personalized_{1,3,5}` in Figure 1.

However, we find that the accuracy converges rapidly after a mere five recordings per keyword; such a trend is evident for every user. Concretely, the accuracy gap between one and three recordings is substantially greater than the gap be-

tween three and five, suggesting that each additional recording provides rapidly diminishing returns. Although using one sample per keyword helps, results suggest that having at least three recordings is desirable, since the marginal benefit of two more recordings is quite large; in user C's case (see Figure 1, bottom left), we observe an absolute improvement of almost 10 points.

Learning rate. In this experiment, we fix the number of epochs to 25 and perform grid search on the learning rate from 0.1 to 0.0001, stepping by a factor of ten—see the right half of Figure 1. Among the four different learning rates, we find that choosing 0.01 consistently leads to the best accuracy on user recordings for all three variations of training data size.

Efficiency and application evaluation. Bringing all the previous threads together, Honkling supports in-browser personalization by fine-tuning with user recordings. As we find that the number of recordings has a high correlation with the quality of personalization, users have the option to choose the number of recordings. Once recording is completed, the base model is fine-tuned with the best hyperparameter settings, for 50 epochs with a learning rate of 0.01. The fine-tuned model is then stored in the browser. At startup, Honkling loads the stored model if it exists so users can keep the application personalized even after the current browser session ends.

Table 2 summarizes the in-browser fine-tuning efficiency for `res8-narrow` on the 2017 MacBook Pro and our desktop. We average results over ten trials, where fine-tuning data is randomly selected from the four user datasets from the previous experiment. To be consistent with our previous study on in-browser inference efficiency, we conduct the experiments in Firefox. From the results, we find that, unsurprisingly, personalization time increases with the data size. Since training data size correlates with the final accuracy, users have the option to trade off time and quality. Fortunately, GPU acceleration can significantly decrease fine-tuning time. The same process that consumes up to 2.3 hours on a CPU can be completed within 27 seconds on a GPU. With a GTX 1080 Ti, only 8 seconds are necessary to achieve personalization with Honkling.

6 Conclusion

In this paper, we realize a new paradigm for serving neural network applications by implementing Honkling, a JavaScript-based, in-browser KWS system. On the popular Google Speech Commands dataset, our model achieves an accuracy of 94% while maintaining an inference latency of less than 30 milliseconds on modern devices. The purely client-side architecture allows our application to be efficient and cross-device compatible, with the additional benefit of supporting user personalization. Since many speech-based systems suffer from accuracy degradation caused by differences in accents and speaking styles, we support per-user personalization in Honkling. Based on a small-scale study, we observe a substantial increase in accuracy after spending only a short amount of time fine-tuning on a few sample recordings. These results pave the way for future web applications that seamlessly support built-in speech-based interactions.

Acknowledgments

This research was supported by the Natural Sciences and Engineering Research Council (NSERC) of Canada.

References

Sercan O. Arik, Markus Kliegl, Rewon Child, Joel Hestness, Andrew Gibiansky, Chris Fougner, Ryan Prenger, and Adam Coates. 2017. Convolutional recurrent neural networks for small-footprint keyword spotting. *INTERSPEECH*.

Javier Fernández-Marqués, W.-S. Tseng Vincent, Sourav Bhattachara, and Nicholas D. Lane. 2018. BinaryCmd: Keyword spotting with deterministic binary basis. *SysML*.

Kaiming He, Xiangyu Zhang, Shaoqing Ren, and Jian Sun. 2016. Deep residual learning for image recognition. *CVPR*.

Chao Huang, Tao Chen, and Eric Chang. 2004. Accent issues in large vocabulary continuous speech recognition. *International Journal of Speech Technology*, 7:141–153.

Jason J. Humphries, Philip C. Woodland, and David J. B. Pearce. 1996. Using accent-specific pronunciation modelling for robust speech recognition. *International Conference on Spoken Language Processing*.

Sergey Ioffe and Christian Szegedy. 2015. Batch normalization: Accelerating deep network training by reducing internal covariate shift. *ICML*.

Tom Ko, Vijayaditya Peddinti, Daniel Povey, and Sanjeev Khudanpur. 2015. Audio augmentation for speech recognition. *INTERSPEECH*.

Jaejun Lee, Raphael Tang, and Jimmy Lin. 2019. Universal voice-enabled user interfaces using JavaScript. *IUI*.

Brian McFee, Colin Raffel, Dawen Liang, Daniel P. W. Ellis, Matt McVicar, Eric Battenberg, and Oriol Nieto. 2015. librosa: Audio and music signal analysis in Python. *Python in Science Conference*.

Robert B. Miller. 1968. Response time in man-computer conversational transactions. *Fall Joint Computer Conference, Part I*.

Maryam Najafian, Saeid Safavi, John H. L. Hansen, and Martin Russell. 2016. Improving speech recognition using limited accent diverse British English training data with deep neural networks. *International Workshop on Machine Learning for Signal Processing*.

Hugh Rawlinson, Nevo Segal, and Jakub Fiala. 2015. Meyda: An audio feature extraction library for the web audio API. *Web Audio Conference*.

Tara N. Sainath and Carolina Parada. 2015. Convolutional neural networks for small-footprint keyword spotting. *INTERSPEECH*.

Raphael Tang and Jimmy Lin. 2018. Deep residual learning for small-footprint keyword spotting. *ICASSP*.

Raphael Tang, Weijie Wang, Zhucheng Tu, and Jimmy Lin. 2018. An experimental analysis of the power consumption of convolutional neural networks for keyword spotting. *ICASSP*.

Pete Warden. 2018. Speech Commands: A dataset for limited-vocabulary speech recognition. *arXiv:1804.03209*.

Yundong Zhang, Naveen Suda, Liangzhen Lai, and Vikas Chandra. 2017. Hello edge: Keyword spotting on microcontrollers. *arXiv:1711.07128*.

IFlyLegal: A Chinese Legal System for Consultation, Law Searching, and Document Analysis

Ziyue Wang[†], Baoxin Wang[†], Xingyi Duan[†], Dayong Wu[†], Shijin Wang[†§], Guoping Hu[†], Ting liu[‡]

[†]State Key Laboratory of Cognitive Intelligence, iFLYTEK Research, Beijing, China
[‡]Research Center for Social Computing and Information Retrieval,
Harbin Institute of Technology, Harbin, China
[§]iFLYTEK AI Research (Hebei), LangFang, China
[†]{zywang27,bxwang2,xyduan,dywu2,sjwang3,gphu}@iflytek.com
[‡]tliu@ir.hit.edu.cn

Abstract

Legal Tech is developed to help people with legal services and solve legal problems via machines. To achieve this, one of the key requirements for machines is to utilize legal knowledge and comprehend legal context. This can be fulfilled by natural language processing (NLP) techniques, for instance, text representation, text categorization, question answering (QA) and natural language inference, etc. To this end, we introduce a freely available Chinese Legal Tech system (IFlyLegal) that benefits from multiple NLP tasks. It is an integrated system that performs legal consulting, multiway law searching, and legal document analysis by exploiting techniques such as deep contextual representations and various attention mechanisms. To our knowledge, IFlyLegal is the first Chinese legal system that employs up-to-date NLP techniques and caters for needs of different user groups, such as lawyers, judges, procurators, and clients. Since Jan, 2019, we have gathered 2,349 users and 28,238 page views (till June, 23, 2019).

1 Introduction

The term Legal Tech refers to legal technologies that apply computer technologies to legal services, such as legal consultation and judicial document analysis. Such techniques are able to ease the load of legal workers and provide easily accessible services for clients. Recently, researchers are concentrating on enhancing Legal Tech with NLP techniques (e.g., named entity recognition (Yin et al., 2018), sequence labeling (Yan et al., 2018)). Studies have proven that NLP techniques are markedly effective regarding several legal tasks, for instance, charge prediction (Hu et al., 2018) and law area classification (Sulea et al., 2017).

In industry, the majority of legal consultation products are merely platforms that redirect users to actual lawyers other than solving problems with a

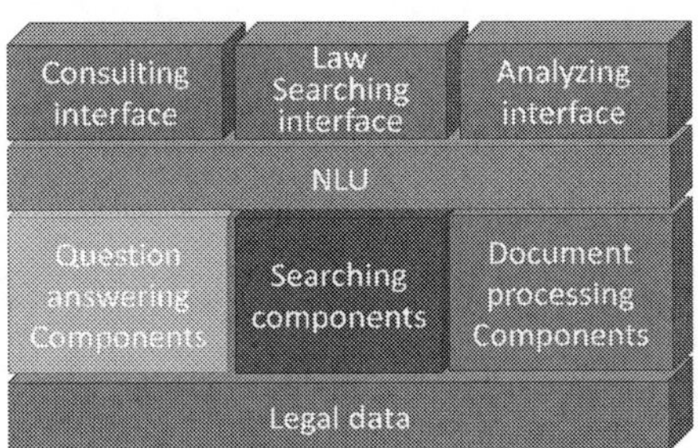

Figure 1: Architecture of the legal system

compact and efficient intelligent system. The partially automated ones, however, tend to have single functionality, either document analysis like case description analysis, or information acquiring like law searching and legal consultancy. Despite of plentiful advances in NLP, most of industrial applications remain constructed in conventional information retrieval (IR) manner or highly rely on hand-crafted responses. They do not take advantage of the most advanced algorithms in NLP and deep learning and fail to cater for the following needs: (i) flexibility: being flexible to comprehend various forms of questions or queries; (ii) diversity: being able to generate different and customized replies according to slight changes of input queries; (iii) accuracy: being able to deliver responses that correctly answer the input questions.

In this paper, we present an integrated system that adapts functionalities such as consultation and document analysis to legal context. Taking advantage of recent advances in NLP, the legal system can act as an artificial lawyer for clients and as an assistant for legal workers. It is a practical system for answering legal questions, performing law searching in multiple modes, and analyzing case descriptions. First, by coupling question-answering and scoring models with external legal knowledge such as statutes and legal commonsense, we design an architecture especially for

Proceedings of the 2019 EMNLP and the 9th IJCNLP (System Demonstrations), pages 97–102
Hong Kong, China, November 3 – 7, 2019. ©2019 Association for Computational Linguistics

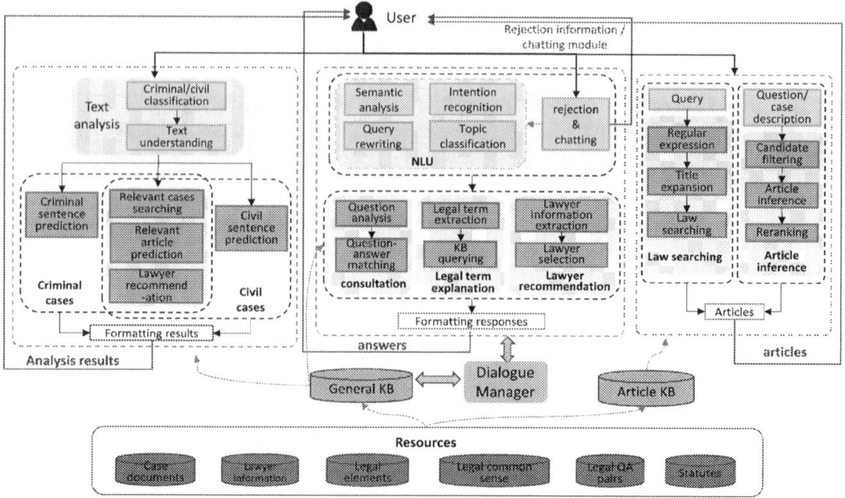

Figure 2: An illustration of the legal system

providing professional solutions to legal issues. Second, inspired by natural language inference task, we build a dedicated module to solving problems with statutes only, namely natural language article inference. Last but not least, we construct an analysis module to comprehend cases, predict judicial sentences, and retrieve similar cases.

The main contributions of this work lie in the followings: 1. It integrates the multiple legal services, consultation, law searching and document analysis, into a single application; 2. We propose a new task, natural language article inference, which replies to legal questions with a sets of possible articles of law only; 3. All the utilized models achieve practicable results.

2   Related Work

The current automated legal consultation applications usually rely on retrieving relevant text information from pre-constructed database containing legal question-answer pairs using text features such as TF-IDF and bag-of-words (BoW). Do et al. (2017) proposed QA models for legal consultation, and Hang (2017) preformed legal question classification with deep convolutional neural network trained in multi-task manner.

Law searching is an unneglectable demand of legal workers such as lawyers and procurators, as they need to support their views with sufficient articles. In industry, article retrieval applications simply parse inputs into phrases and adopt common IR approaches. Academically, Zhang et al. (2017) built a Chinese legal consultation sys-

tem to improve the precision of retrieving articles and predicting sentences by exploiting legal precedents when performing logical reasoning.

Legal document analysis is frequently viewed as text representation and classification task. Hu et al. (2018) introduces few-shot attributes to enrich the information of mapping from case descriptions to charges, and Sulea et al. (2017) used multiple SVM classifiers as an ensemble to perform law area classification.

3   Chinese Legal-tech System

The presented system consists of the following blocks: consultation, law searching and case analysis. We will go into these blocks at length in this section. Throughout the system, the LTP toolkit (Che et al., 2010) is employed for Chinese word segmentation, named entity recognition and semantic parsing tasks. The overall system architecture is depicted in Figure 1. As this paper focuses on legal context processing, we will provide details for principal modules related to legal services and omit the others like chit-chat. For better understanding, we will discuss experiments, user studies and use cases in the following sections.

3.1   Consultation Block

This block is responsible for legal QA. It contains four modules, one of which is called intention recognition and natural language understanding (NLU) module that filters out chit-chats, recognizes intentions of inputs, and analyzes the queries. The other three, namely general legal consulting, legal term explaining, and lawyer recommending, are subsequent modules that response to legal consultation concerning the recognized intention. This block accepts short questions appealing for legal support and outputs literal replies to the questions. We extract text containing legal issues from public corpus (e.g., Wikipedia), and automatically collect web text from Chinese legal forums and online communities for pre-training language models.

Intention Recognition and NLU module is the basis of consultation block. It functions as the combination of a gate and a converter. As we focus on legal scope, this module only admits legal related content, meanwhile it rejects and redirects the rest to an external chit-chat module. This is achieved by a binary classifier that assigns label "chat" or "legal" to each input. Then, the admitted inputs are analyzed and rewritten for consultation using pre-trained models and predefined features.

General Legal Consulting is an indispensable module for a legal aid system. Following the idea of general QA system (Quaresma and Rodrigues, 2005), we trained an end-to-end QA model especially for legal consulting using data collected from online forums and communities. Note that a legal consultation system should give neutral replies, biased comments are thoroughly removed. This module roles as a virtual lawyer who analyze queries and response with appropriate answers.

Furthermore, the consultation block has two complementary modules called legal Term explanation and lawyer recommendation that compensate the general legal consulting module with extra useful information. If a legal term appears by itself as a query, it will be detected by intention recognition module and fed into legal term explanation module for detail descriptions. Lawyer recommendation module is personalized with regards to users' preferred features, for example, lawyer's location and statistical winning percentage.

3.2 Law Searching Block

Aiming to work as a legal assistant, this block performs law searching in three manners. One is query-based law searching that follows the idea of standard IR approaches. Another is document-based law searching that reads long documents and retrieves applicable articles. The last is a novel task, natural language based law searching. We will discuss it in detail in the next paragraph.

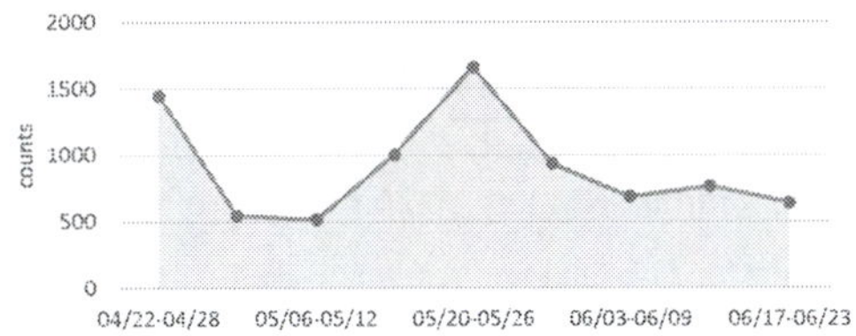

(a) Total Page Views (per week).

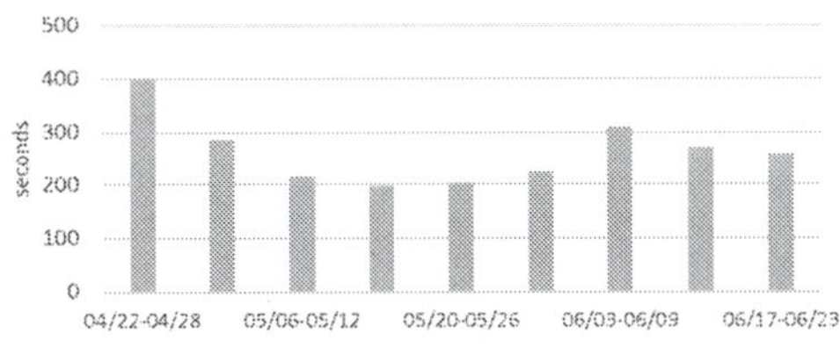

(b) Average Viewing Time (per week).

Figure 3: User studies on cumulative page views (a) and average viewing time (b) for the recent two months (from April 22 to June 23)

Article inference is a natural language based law searching approach without formatting the queries. It is a challenging task on account that the number of related statutes to a given question sometimes remains unclear even if answered by experienced lawyers, and that there are different laws and regulations stating the same fact but focusing on different aspects. Undoubtedly, we can simply pair up the input question with all the statutes and perform one-way sentence matching, i.e. deducing articles from a question. Nevertheless, this will result in tremendous amount of sentence pairs due to countless articles of various levels and from different provinces and cities, which makes it impossible to response immediately.

To address this issue, we need to generate a set of candidate statutes to narrow down the searching space and improve the predicting accuracy. We part the article inference task into two consecutive phases. Firstly, we train a law-level classifier that categorizes inputs into 267 in-force Chinese laws and extract articles from the top 3 resulting laws as a coarse candidate set. The total number of this set could go beyond a thousand since some laws contain over 400 articles. So far, the candidate space is still too large to achieve instant response. We use a bidirectional LSTM architecture employing four perspective features from (Wang et al., 2017) as an intermediate article inference model in article-level to obtain a fine-grained candidate set. Secondly, we slightly adapt the BERT model (Devlin et al., 2018) so that it becomes more sensitive

Metrics	p@1(%)	p@3(%)
Automatic	42.67	23.56
Human (Partial)	90.00	75.56
Human (Exact)	76.67	52.22

Table 1: The final test results of article inference task. Human evaluation is contains three level, not match, partially match and exact match.

Models	p%	r%	f%
vanilla RNN	80.11	80.81	80.64
BiMPM	87.05	84.82	85.92
BERT	90.57	87.76	89.14

Table 2: The results of article inference (Test set positive:negative=1:4). **BiMPM** uses 4 perspective features from Wang et al. (2017). **BERT** here is adapted from Devlin et al. (2018).

to legal context. More concretely, the BERT-base Chinese model is trained for another 300,000 steps with 20% of all the question-article pairs. Then, the model is fine-tuned for final article inference task with the training data that has 1 correct article out of 5 on average. In practice, we feed the fine-grained candidate set obtained from phase one to the fine-tuned BERT and get the inference results. Eventually, 3 most probable articles are displayed and mapped to the names of laws accordingly.

Query-based law searching provides retrievals to queries asking for certain laws or as detailed as certain statutes, which is the basic function for a law searching application. It is achieved by retrieving a set of articles with IR system and weighting and ranking by multiple features like textual similarity, priority and validity of laws. **Document-based law searching** returns articles with respect to a piece of case description. It reads and analyzes case description and returns related articles ordered by relevance to the description. In practice, it can act as a fast candidate article pool for a particular case in court trials. The difference between this module and article inference lies in the inputs where document-based searching deals with massive formal text written by law experts while article inference tackles arbitrary short oral questions coming from daily life.

3.3 Case Analysis Block

Case description is an essential component of a judicial document. It states the facts involved in a case, including sequence of events, people presenting during the event, consequences, etc. This block reads and comprehends case descriptions

Functional Modules	Accuracy%
Civil+criminal article prediction	78.0
Civil/criminal classification	95.5
Criminal accusation prediction	98.2
Civil cause prediction	84.3

Table 3: The results of analysis modules.

and reports the analysis results in different formats including statistical graphs of sentences, similar cases, relevant statutes and recommended lawyers.

Civil/Criminal Classification is a preliminary task of case analyzing, since the judging criteria and sentences varies with categories of cases. Cases are generally divided into two classes, civil and criminal. A civil case happens between citizens and the penalty usually excludes the term of imprisonment, while in a criminal case the defendant is prosecuted by public prosecution organ and would be sent to jail if proven guilty. This is a binary classification task fulfilled by pre-trained word vectors and 1-layer convolutional neural network using case description data.

Case Analysis involves civil case analysis and criminal case analysis. The results of both categories contains lists of similar cases, relevant articles and recommended lawyers together with their professional history. For sentences prediction, civil case analysis outputs the possibilities of accuser/defendant winning the lawsuit. The prediction section of criminal case is also known as automatic sentencing that models the sentencing results given a paragraph of criminal case description. The sentences contain the predicted accusation, term of imprisonment and the legal grounds, i.e. the articles of criminal law. We adopt the disconnected recurrent neural network described in Wang (2018) for automatic sentencing task.

4 Experiments and User Study

We conduct experiments on all modules and will report some important results in this section. User studies on cumulative page views and average viewing times are presented in figure 3. For the consultation block, the testset contains 2000 questions with varying legal topics. The corresponding replies are automatically obtained by the system. The retrievals are manually scored between 1 to 5, where 1 represents irrelevant answers and 5 stands for the best matches. The system achieves an average precision of 80% for the top 1 retrievals.

We compare the results of article inference task

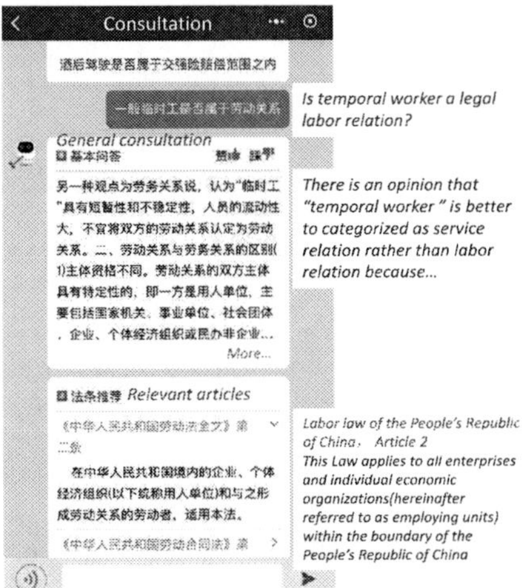

Figure 4: Use case 1: use case of consultation block.

Figure 5: Use case 2: use case of law searching block.

regarding different models and list them in Table 2. Statistics show that the vanilla RNN is able to properly predict the article from the given candidates, but is much inferior to the other complicated models. Yet, it is not the final result for the task in practice due to the inconsistencies between the distributions of experimental and real data. The manually created dataset has one correct article out of 5 candidates on average. In reality, surprisingly, it almost equals to pick up the only one correct answer out of 600, making it an extremely challenging task. We evaluate the results of 200 arbitrary questions by precision@n in two ways, automatic and manual, and report in Table 1. Regardless of disappointing automatically evaluated results, manual evaluation reveals the practicability of the models and proves that they are able to figure out most of the answers.

The testset for the analysis block is automatically extracted from the original court documents, where categories are indicated in the titles and information like the relevant articles and sentences are always listed at the end. We evaluate the performance of analysis block with respects to the following tasks: (i) civil and criminal article prediction; (ii) binary classification of civil and criminal cases; (iii) accusation prediction for criminal cases and (iv) cause prediction for civil cases, which is the counterpart of accusation as to criminal cases. The results are listed in Table 3.

5 Use Cases

In this section, we will present cases illustrating the three blocks, consultation, law searching and

case analysis. Also, we encourage readers to try IFlyLegal via scanning the QR code in figure 7.

Figure 4 is a use case of the consultation block. The inputs can be arbitrary questions as long as they contain legal issues, such as "How to divide common property after divorce?" and "Is temporal worker a legal labor relation?". A proper answer will be delivered along with a set of applicable statutes. Figure 5 displays part of the law searching results for the tested input "Criminal Law Article 200". It will be recognized as "Criminal Law" plus a further restriction on the number of article, "Article 200". Figure 6 demonstrates the results of case analysis block with a screen-shot of the predicted sentences. The other information can be found in the screencast.

6 Conclusion and Future works

We present a system called iFlyLegal for automated legal QA, multi-way law searching, and multi-perspective legal document analysis. The system is built upon a combination of classical text features and deep learning techniques in NLP. We conduct sufficient experiments and report important results in this paper. To help understand our system, we illustrate several use cases with snapshots and necessary literal explanation. These cases also prove that our system is capable to fulfill user demands.

Taking into consideration the need for ease of access, the system is demonstrated in form of WeChat Mini Program, which is compact, portable and freely available. Yet we will develop a web-based version for those who prefer access-

(a) Input Interface.   (b) Predicted Sentences.

Figure 6: Use Case 3: use case of analysis block. (a) is the case description. (b) present the predicted sentences.

Figure 7: Mini program QR code of IFlyLegal (scanning via WeChat). We also provide a screencast for readers who do not have a Wechat.

ing via computers. During maintaining, the models and topology behind would be improved along with our researches. Although neural network is regarded as "black box", we are currently working on the explainability of our models and trying to present users with evidences to the model-generated outputs so as to be convincing. IFlyLegal is an integrated and multi-functional system, whose build-in modules are complex and can be separated and adapted for different tasks such as text categorization and natural language inference. We intend to turn iFlyLegal into an NLP platform for legal AI research to cater for the boosting needs of NLP techniques in legal industrial and explore other valuable research topics of legal NLP. In the future, we will investigate into adapting the NLP research platform to other languages.

Acknowledgments

The authors would like to thank all the reviewers for their insight reviews. This paper is funded by National Key R&D Program of China (No.2018YFC0807701).

References

Wanxiang Che, Zhenghua Li, and Ting Liu. 2010. Ltp: A chinese language technology platform. In *Proceedings of the 23rd International Conference on Computational Linguistics: Demonstrations*, pages 13–16. Association for Computational Linguistics.

Jacob Devlin, Ming-Wei Chang, Kenton Lee, and Kristina Toutanova. 2018. Bert: Pre-training of deep bidirectional transformers for language understanding. *arXiv preprint arXiv:1810.04805*.

Phong-Khac Do, Huy-Tien Nguyen, Chien-Xuan Tran, Minh-Tien Nguyen, and Minh-Le Nguyen. 2017. Legal question answering using ranking svm and deep convolutional neural network. *arXiv preprint arXiv:1703.05320*.

Nga Tran Anh Hang. 2017. Applying deep neural network to retrieve relevant civil law articles. In *Proceedings of the Student Research Workshop associated with RANLP*, pages 46–48.

Zikun Hu, Xiang Li, Cunchao Tu, Zhiyuan Liu, and Maosong Sun. 2018. Few-shot charge prediction with discriminative legal attributes. In *Proceedings of the 27th International Conference on Computational Linguistics*, pages 487–498.

Paulo Quaresma and Irene Pimenta Rodrigues. 2005. A question answer system for legal information retrieval. In *JURIX*, pages 91–100.

Octavia-Maria Sulea, Marcos Zampieri, Shervin Malmasi, Mihaela Vela, Liviu P Dinu, and Josef van Genabith. 2017. Exploring the use of text classification in the legal domain. *arXiv preprint arXiv:1710.09306*.

Baoxin Wang. 2018. Disconnected recurrent neural networks for text categorization. In *Proceedings of the 56th Annual Meeting of the Association for Computational Linguistics (Volume 1: Long Papers)*, volume 1, pages 2311–2320.

Zhiguo Wang, Wael Hamza, and Radu Florian. 2017. Bilateral multi-perspective matching for natural language sentences. *arXiv preprint arXiv:1702.03814*.

Yukun Yan, Daqi Zheng, Zhengdong Lu, and Sen Song. 2018. Zooming network. *arXiv preprint arXiv:1810.02114*.

Xiaoxiao Yin, Daqi Zheng, Zhengdong Lu, and Ruifang Liu. 2018. Neural entity reasoner for global consistency in ner. *arXiv preprint arXiv:1810.00347*.

Ni Zhang, Yi-Fei Pu, Sui-Quan Yang, Ji-Liu Zhou, and Jin-Kang Gao. 2017. An ontological chinese legal consultation system. *IEEE Access*, 5:18250–18261.

INMT: Interactive Neural Machine Translation Prediction

Sebastin Santy[1]   **Sandipan Dandapat[2]**   **Monojit Choudhury[1]**   **Kalika Bali[1]**

[1] Microsoft Research, Bangalore, India
[2] Microsoft R&D, Hyderabad, India
{t-sesan, sadandap, monojitc, kalikab}@microsoft.com

Abstract

In this paper, we demonstrate an Interactive Machine Translation interface, that assists human translators with on-the-fly hints and suggestions. This makes the end-to-end translation process faster, more efficient, and creates high-quality translations. We augment the OpenNMT backend with a mechanism to accept the user input and generate conditioned translations.[1][2]

1   Introduction

Machine Translation (MT) has witnessed several leaps of advancements and is now capable of producing human level translations (Läubli et al., 2018). However, a single source sentence can be translated into multiple forms, often varying in expression (Halliday, 1978), formality (Heylighen and Dewaele, 1999) or context. Several real-world documents such as books and news require such translations. Even with performance of state-of-the-art MT systems being at par with humans, current MT systems are useful only for information assimilation (Hutchins, 2009). Wider dissemination of translated content requires substantial manual post processing, and saves only a little time compared to a fully manual human translation. Combining the pros of both human and machine translation can potentially lead to streamlining of the translation process by assisting humans with producing high quality translations quicker.

This Machine Assisted Translation can be either done through Post Editing (PE) or Interactive Translation Prediction (ITP). In PE tools such as MateCat (Federico et al., 2014), the translator is provided with a complete translation and is asked to edit tokens which they feel are not appropriate. There are no suggestions provided by the machine beyond the initial gist. Interactive Translation started off with TransType (Langlais et al., 2000), which uses a rule-based translation system. With the introduction of Statistical Machine Translation, it became easier to provide richer phrase based suggestions, which led to creation of tools such as CASMACAT (Alabau et al., 2014)[3] and LILT[4]. Green et al. (2014) extensively researched the user experience of such systems and compared between manual and assisted translation using various metrics. The current method of constrained decoding, in particular coupled with the advent of Neural Machine Translation (NMT), was put forward by Wuebker et al. (2016) and Knowles and Koehn (2016). All these studies have shown that ITP provides improved translation quality compared to PE, and also suggest that human translators prefer ITP over PE. However, due to heavy resource (parallel data) requirements, the available ITP systems work only for a handful of resource-rich languages such as Spanish, Chinese, French and German.

In this paper, we present a proof-of-concept interactive translation system between English and five Indic languages (Bengali, Hindi, Malayalam, Tamil and Telugu) using state-of-the-art NMT models. As Indian languages are resource poor, we could use only 100-1500 thousand parallel sentences for training. There are prominent syntactic differences between Indic languages and English such as the basic word order, which requires substantial replanning of the translation suggestions in real time. These characteristics make ITP a challenging problem for English to/from Indic languages. To the best of our knowledge, this is the first ITP for Indic languages, and the only publicly available Neural ITP system.

Proceedings of the 2019 EMNLP and the 9th IJCNLP (System Demonstrations), pages 103–108
Hong Kong, China, November 3 – 7, 2019. ©2019 Association for Computational Linguistics

2 Advantages of ITP

Interactive translation is beneficial to human translators and translation seekers alike:

• Faster turnaround of document translations
The gisting and suggestion (refer Interface Overview 5) helps the translator breeze through the translation task with minimal typing. Our preliminary study suggests that regular users use relatively very less number of keystrokes in ITP as compared to both manual typing and the PE process.

• High quality translation due to human-machine interaction
Language is inherently divergent and human translators cannot quickly enumerate all acceptable variants of a translation. On the other hand, in general, machine translation has not yet reached human quality though it can provide a number of variants. Combining the strengths of both of human and machine through interaction helps in getting higher quality translations compared to the individual processes. Another interesting usecase of interactive MT is in low resource settings where NMT is not able to churn out the most fluent translation. However, along with human help, this can lead to producing better translations, as compared to other mixed-initiative processes like post-editing often used in computer assisted translation tools.

• Opens translation tasks to non-expert translators
Expert human translators are often scarce for a large number of language pairs and are expensive to hire. In some countries (such as in the Indian subcontinent) it is easy to find multilingual speakers with native and near-native proficiency in multiple languages, and interactive MT systems enable non-expert translators to perform translation tasks through gisting and suggestions. The requirements of less proficiency also makes such a system more amenable to a non-expert large crowdsourced setting where the objective can be to gather more data for low resource languages.

3 Methods

3.1 Neural Machine Translation

Neural MT paradigms, starting from Seq2Seq (Bahdanau et al., 2014) to the current state-of-the-art Transformer-based architec-tures (Vaswani et al., 2017), use an encoder-decoder combination along with attention which helps in correct alignment of the tokens.

At time step t, the conditional probability of generating output token y_t given the full input sequence $\mathbf{x}$ and the previously output tokens $y_1, ..., y_{t-1}$ is:

$$p(y_t|y_1, ..., y_{t-1}, \mathbf{x}) = g(y_{t-1}, s_t, c_t) \qquad (1)$$

where g is a non-linearity function and s_t and c_t are the hidden state and context vector, respectively. The vector c_t is a weighted average of all encoder hidden states with weights generated by the attention mechanism. We use sparsemax (Martins and Astudillo, 2016) attention instead of the usual soft-max attention as it helps in focusing on specific source tokens similar to hard attention but still be-ing differentiable. This is done in order to help with word coverage visualization.

3.2 Interactive Neural Machine Translation

In INMT, instead of conditioning the prediction of each token on the previous model predictions $\{y_1, ..., y_{t-1}\}$ (as is done above), we condition based on the partial input from the human transla-tor $\{y'_1, ..., y'_{t-1}\}$. This results in a new conditional probability equation:

$$p(y_t|y'_1, ..., y'_{t-1}, \mathbf{x}) = g(y'_{t-1}, s_t, c_t) \qquad (2)$$

For producing multiple suggestions based on the partial input, we rely on beam search decoding which features in all current NMT architectures. It selects the most probable full translation for a given input sentence. If and when the translator diverges from this full translation, a new beam search is conducted from the partial input prefix till end of sentence is encountered. A full beam search (till end of sentence) is done only for gist-ing. In case of suggestion, we do beam search of maximum length of 2. Beam search has been criti-cized for its lack of diversity (Gimpel et al., 2013), which is why, showing full sentence suggestions from beam search will present the translator with very similar suggestions. Beam search with length of 2 will produce bigrams with reasonable diver-sity.

3.3 Character-Level Search

We use a word level sequence modelling for NMT in this task, which does not allow partial words

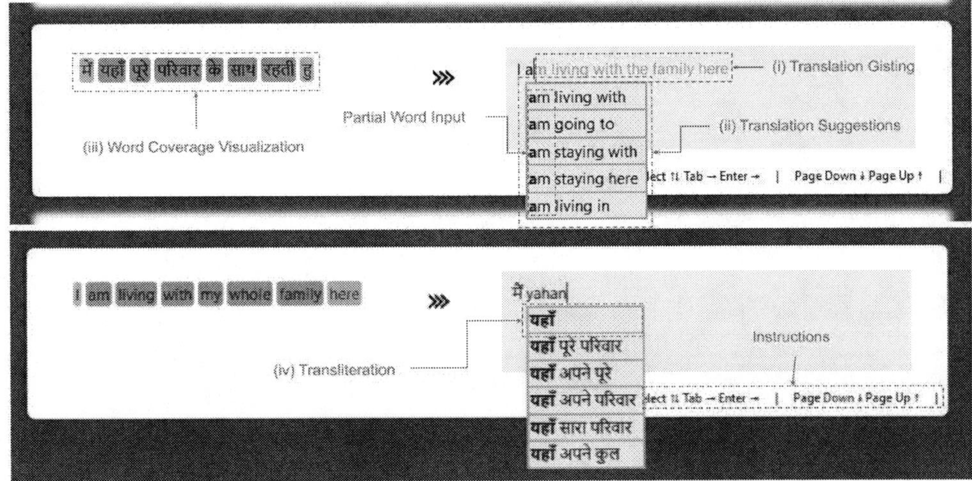

Figure 1: Example sentence being translated. (a) Hindi to English and (b) English to Hindi.

to be input inherently. We introduce two different techniques to help with character level suggestions:

• Start with Partial Word Prefix

During beam search, at each timestep each word in the vocabulary is assigned a score for k times, where k is the beam width. We mask the vocabulary set for words which only star with the partial word prefix input by the translator. This helps in getting top-k words which start with the intended prefix.

• Closest to Partial Word Prefix

We also devise a edit distance-based (Yujian and Bo, 2007) algorithm to rerank the beams which not only helps in suggesting sentences with partial word inputs but also helps in cases where the translator makes spelling mistakes for complex words. The latter algorithm already includes tokens which are limited by the former, but the former is faster due to lesser search complexity. We provide an option for the translator to select either one.

4 System Overview

We use OpenNMT (Klein et al., 2017), an open source neural machine translation toolkit to build the MT system.[5] We write a new interactive translation mechanism to accept the user input and do constrained decoding, which is plugged on top of this toolkit. This helps in keeping up with the state-of-the-art models and other updates released through the toolkit and still keeping the interaction functional. The primary advantage of using OpenNMT as our translation backend is that it is highly efficient, modular, extensible and well documented. In order to add new models (e.g. extending to new languages etc.) into this system, the models have to be trained based on OpenNMT instructions. If the target language uses a non-Latin script and users wish to use an Latin keyboard, the developer has to add an API to help with transliteration. In our case, we use the openly available Quillpad Indic Transliteration service for Indic languages.[6] There is also a default support for ISO romanizations (like ITRANS for Indic Languages) which can help with transliterations, though it might not be particularly convenient for non-Latin.

We use the Django framework (Python) for server purposes. The system makes use of the PyTorch (Paszke et al., 2017) version of OpenNMT for its ease of use. The interface, which is described below is made with JQuery (JavaScript) and communicates with the server through sockets - for interactive typing as they are faster and AJAX requests for all other calls.

5 Interface Overview

The interface is designed similar to MateCat (Federico et al., 2014) which is a open-source

---

Word Coverage and Translation Gisting	Suggestions	Keystrokes
उसी प्रकार मानसिक स्वास्थ्य के लिए ज्ञान की प्राप्ति आवश्यक है Similarly , knowledge for mental health is necessary .	Similarly , In the The knowledge Thus , So the	↓ ↓ Enter ←
उसी प्रकार मानसिक स्वास्थ्य के लिए ज्ञान की प्राप्ति आवश्यक है **In the** same way , knowledge of knowledge is essential for mental health	same way	Tab Tab Tab Tab
उसी प्रकार मानसिक स्वास्थ्य के लिए ज्ञान की प्राप्ति आवश्यक है **In the same way , knowledge** of knowledge is essential for mental health	of knowledge is essential is necessary for mental	↑
उसी प्रकार मानसिक स्वास्थ्य के लिए ज्ञान की प्राप्ति आवश्यक है **In the same way , knowledge is** essential for mental health	is essential for is necessary for is required to	Enter ←
उसी प्रकार मानसिक स्वास्थ्य के लिए ज्ञान की प्राप्ति आवश्यक है **In the same way , knowledge is essential for mental health**		Page ↓

Table 1: Translation workflow when translating from "उसी प्रकार मानसिक स्वास्थ्य के लिए ज्ञान की प्राप्ति आवश्यक है" to "In the same way , knowledge is essential for mental health". The bold black text shows the current state of user input, the gray text shows gisting and suggestions. 10 keystrokes are required when using interactive typing, whereas for manual typing 60 keystrokes will be required (Refer Keystroke Reduction 6.2)

freely available web-based post-editing translation software. In our interface, the user is able to upload documents in the format they choose, or just input free-flowing text. The user then has to select the source and target language. The next page will show tokenized sentences from the input corpus on the left with a corresponding right column where the user is expected to add the translation. Figure 1 shows how the interface looks. For each translation we use 2 different techniques to assist in the translation flow:

(i) Translation gisting
Gisting the user with a full sentence translation will prime the translator with a quick translation with very less cognitive load. Users have much less cognitive load when it comes to spotting errors in the gisting, than trying to mentally structure the translations. This accelerates the translator's initial time taken.

(ii) Translation suggestion
Gisting is not expected to always be what the translator ideally wants. This would mean that the translator needs to change the default gist which the translation engine provides. Based on the context of the previous sentence, the translation engine also sends a maximum of 5 suggestions from which the user can choose to select to move forward with the translation. If the user can find nothing from either the gist or suggestion, the translator can choose to type. The user still does not need to type the complete word, the

suggestions are assigned a score based on the edit-distance between the partial input and the tokens in the decoding lattice. The suggestions are then re-ranked taking into account both the edit-distance score along with the beam score.

Furthermore, we provide mechanisms which allow increased throughput of translations as below:

(iii) Word Coverage Visualization
The standard NMT architectures use attention to correctly align the words from source to target. We use sparsemax attention rather than softmax, as it allows us to attend to a specific word in context while translating. This helps in an appropriate visualization of word coverage which the translator can use to their benefit to validate whether they have correctly translated the sentence (cf. Table 1).

(iv) Transliteration
Languages, except the European ones generally have a non-Latin script. Translators especially non-expert ones usually use English keyboards to type. Usually they are assisted with some browser plugin like Google input tools which helps them in transliterating whatever they type in English to the target language. Here they use English characters as phones rather than as actual English words. However, such plugins deteriorates the experience when it comes to such

an interactive interface, where each character is used for translation and such post-replacement of English to target language cannot work properly. For experimentation, we use an openly available transliteration API (Quillpad) for Indic Languages.

Through multiple design iterations and feedback from our pre-pilot study, it was observed that certain keyboard commands are naturally helpful for the translator to breeze through translations. Options available are:

- `Tab` : To get the next word from the selection

- `Enter ←` : To get all the words from the selection.

- `↑` `↓` : To alter the selection between multiple suggestions.

- `Page ↑` `Page ↓` : To traverse from one sentence to another.

- `End` : To end the translation process and download the translated document.

The system is designed in such a way that translators never need to take their hands off from the keyboard. This helps in faster typing and selection of suggestions.

6 Experiments

We use parallel corpus from OPUS (Tiedemann, 2012) to build our NMT model for 5 different Indic Languages and English (en). These 5 Indic Languages include Bengali (bn), Hindi (hi), Malayalam (ml), Tamil (ta) and Telugu (te). The training data from OPUS contain 100-1500 thousand parallel sentences each for the mentioned Indic languages. All our models have been tested on the Indic Language Dataset (Post et al., 2012)[7] which contains around 1000 parallel sentences with each sentence having 4 English references. This helps us measure multi-reference BLEU score which is often useful for relatively free word order languages.

We take inspiration from Aharoni et al. (2019) to build a multilingual many-to-one and one-to-many indic neural MT system based on the state of the art transformer architecture (Vaswani et al.,

---

[7]The widely used WMT testset is only available for Hindi. Thus, to make the testset uniform across language we do not use WMT testset for our experiments.

2017). We use the recommended set of parameters for transformers from Vaswani et al. (2017) to get comparable results. We conduct multiple simulation experiments to show the efficacy of our system.

6.1 BLEU Score Analysis

BLEU (Papineni et al., 2002) scores are the current standard to evaluate MT performance. We measure the BLEU score of the generated gist after a certain fraction - x% of words of the intended translation has been provided. Table 2 shows the average BLEU score for each language pair at different values of x. As we can see, after 40% of the sentence has been provided by the user, rest of the gist is almost always perfectly correct.

	Data Size	0%	10%	20%	40%
bn-en	1.1M	25.31	27.54	35.68	54.03
hi-en	1.5M	40.64	42.06	47.90	62.18
ml-en	897K	19.76	21.95	29.84	49.88
ta-en	428K	18.71	20.90	27.05	44.55
te-en	104K	11.92	14.57	21.17	41.98

Table 2: Multi-BLEU Score with x% of partial input

The difference in performance for different languages is presumably because of the amount of resources available for each of them.

6.2 Keystroke Reduction

Keystroke Reduction algorithmically compares the minimum number of keystrokes required when typing interactively versus the same when manually typing. Interactive typing accounts for the keystrokes made when navigating through like `↑`, `↓`, `Tab`, `Enter ←` each of which is one keystroke, whereas for manual typing, number of keystrokes is determined by the number of characters in the sentence. This allows us to get an approximate idea of how many keystrokes are being saved while using interactive typing. We observe a reduction of around 30% keystrokes for all the above mentioned languages.

7 Conclusion and Future Work

The system currently provides an interface for interactive machine translation with a latency of less than 0.5 seconds. However, a real-time interactive application should focus on keeping latency to the minimum. Network calls are the primary latency bottleneck for web-based applications. We are currently working on adding support for front-end deep learning frameworks such as TensorflowJS to do heavy lifting for network intensive components like dropdown suggestions on client side.

References

Roee Aharoni, Melvin Johnson, and Orhan Firat. 2019. Massively multilingual neural machine translation. *arXiv preprint arXiv:1903.00089.*

Vicent Alabau et al. 2014. Casmacat: A computer-assisted translation workbench. In *Proceedings of the Demonstrations at the 14th Conference of the European Chapter of the Association for Computational Linguistics*, pages 25–28.

Dzmitry Bahdanau, Kyunghyun Cho, and Yoshua Bengio. 2014. Neural machine translation by jointly learning to align and translate. *arXiv preprint arXiv:1409.0473.*

Marcello Federico et al. 2014. The matecat tool. In *Proceedings of COLING 2014, the 25th International Conference on Computational Linguistics: System Demonstrations*, pages 129–132.

Kevin Gimpel, Dhruv Batra, Chris Dyer, and Gregory Shakhnarovich. 2013. A systematic exploration of diversity in machine translation. In *Proceedings of the 2013 Conference on Empirical Methods in Natural Language Processing*, pages 1100–1111.

Spence Green, Jason Chuang, Jeffrey Heer, and Christopher D Manning. 2014. Predictive translation memory: A mixed-initiative system for human language translation. In *Proceedings of the 27th annual ACM symposium on User interface software and technology*, pages 177–187. ACM.

Michael Alexander Kirkwood Halliday. 1978. *Language as social semiotic: The social interpretation of language and meaning.* Hodder Arnold.

Francis Heylighen and Jean-Marc Dewaele. 1999. Formality of language: definition, measurement and behavioral determinants. *Interner Bericht, Center "Leo Apostel", Vrije Universiteit Brüssel.*

John Hutchins. 2009. Multiple uses of machine translation and computerised translation tools. *Machine Translation*, pages 13–20.

Guillaume Klein, Yoon Kim, Yuntian Deng, Jean Senellart, and Alexander M Rush. 2017. Opennmt: Open-source toolkit for neural machine translation. *arXiv preprint arXiv:1701.02810.*

Rebecca Knowles and Philipp Koehn. 2016. Neural interactive translation prediction. In *Proceedings of the Association for Machine Translation in the Americas*, pages 107–120.

Philippe Langlais, George Foster, and Guy Lapalme. 2000. Transtype: a computer-aided translation typing system. In *ANLP-NAACL 2000 Workshop: Embedded Machine Translation Systems.*

Samuel Läubli, Rico Sennrich, and Martin Volk. 2018. Has machine translation achieved human parity? a case for document-level evaluation. *arXiv preprint arXiv:1808.07048.*

Andre Martins and Ramon Astudillo. 2016. From softmax to sparsemax: A sparse model of attention and multi-label classification. In *International Conference on Machine Learning*, pages 1614–1623.

Kishore Papineni, Salim Roukos, Todd Ward, and Wei-Jing Zhu. 2002. Bleu: a method for automatic evaluation of machine translation. In *Proceedings of the 40th annual meeting on association for computational linguistics*, pages 311–318. Association for Computational Linguistics.

Adam Paszke et al. 2017. Automatic differentiation in pytorch. In *NIPS-W.*

Matt Post, Chris Callison-Burch, and Miles Osborne. 2012. Constructing parallel corpora for six indian languages via crowdsourcing. In *Proceedings of the Seventh Workshop on Statistical Machine Translation*, pages 401–409. Association for Computational Linguistics.

Jörg Tiedemann. 2012. Parallel data, tools and interfaces in opus. In *Lrec*, volume 2012, pages 2214–2218.

Ashish Vaswani, Noam Shazeer, Niki Parmar, Jakob Uszkoreit, Llion Jones, Aidan N Gomez, Łukasz Kaiser, and Illia Polosukhin. 2017. Attention is all you need. In *Advances in neural information processing systems*, pages 5998–6008.

Joern Wuebker, Spence Green, John DeNero, Sasa Hasan, and Minh-Thang Luong. 2016. Models and inference for prefix-constrained machine translation. In *Proceedings of the 54th Annual Meeting of the Association for Computational Linguistics (Volume 1: Long Papers)*, volume 1, pages 66–75.

Li Yujian and Liu Bo. 2007. A normalized levenshtein distance metric. *IEEE transactions on pattern analysis and machine intelligence*, 29(6):1091–1095.

Joey NMT: A Minimalist NMT Toolkit for Novices

Julia Kreutzer
Computational Linguistics
Heidelberg University
kreutzer@cl.uni-heidelberg.de

Joost Bastings
ILLC
University of Amsterdam
bastings@uva.nl

Stefan Riezler
Computational Linguistics & IWR
Heidelberg University
riezler@cl.uni-heidelberg.de

Abstract

We present Joey NMT, a minimalist neural machine translation toolkit based on PyTorch that is specifically designed for novices. Joey NMT provides many popular NMT features in a small and simple code base, so that novices can easily and quickly learn to use it and adapt it to their needs. Despite its focus on simplicity, Joey NMT supports classic architectures (RNNs, transformers), fast beam search, weight tying, and more, and achieves performance comparable to more complex toolkits on standard benchmarks. We evaluate the accessibility of our toolkit in a user study where novices with general knowledge about Pytorch and NMT and experts work through a self-contained Joey NMT tutorial, showing that novices perform almost as well as experts in a subsequent code quiz. Joey NMT is available at https://github.com/joeynmt/joeynmt.

1 Introduction

Since the first successes of neural machine translation (NMT), various research groups and industry labs have developed open source toolkits specialized for NMT, based on new open source deep learning platforms. While toolkits like OpenNMT (Klein et al., 2018), XNMT (Neubig et al., 2018) and Neural Monkey (Helcl and Libovický, 2017) aim at readability and extensibility of their codebase, their target group are researchers with a solid background in machine translation and deep learning, and with experience in navigating, understanding and handling large code bases. However, none of the existing NMT tools has been designed primarily for readability or accessibility for novices, nor has anyone studied quality and accessibility of such code empirically. On the other hand, it is an important challenge for novices to understand how NMT is implemented, what features each toolkit implements exactly, and which

toolkit to choose in order to code their own project as fast and simple as possible.

We present an NMT toolkit especially designed for novices, providing clean, well documented, and minimalistic code, that is yet of comparable quality to more complex codebases on standard benchmarks. Our approach is to identify the core features of NMT that have not changed over the last years, and to invest in documentation, simplicity and quality of the code. These core features include standard network architectures (RNN, transformer, different attention mechanisms, input feeding, configurable encoder/decoder bridge), standard learning techniques (dropout, learning rate scheduling, weight tying, early stopping criteria), and visualization/monitoring tools.

We evaluate our codebase in several ways: Firstly, we show that Joey NMT's comment-to-code ratio is almost twice as high as other toolkits which are roughly 9-10 times larger. Secondly, we present an evaluation on standard benchmarks (WMT17, IWSLT) where we show that the core architectures implemented in Joey NMT achieve comparable performance to more complex state-of-the-art toolkits. Lastly, we conduct a user study where we test the code understanding of novices, i.e. students with basic knowledge about NMT and PyTorch, against expert coders. While novices, after having worked through a self-contained Joey NMT tutorial, needed more time to answer each question in an in-depth code quiz, they achieved only marginally lower scores than the experts. To our knowledge, this is the first user study on the accessibility of NMT toolkits.

2 Joey NMT

2.1 NMT Architectures

This section formalizes the Joey NMT implementation of autoregressive recurrent and fully-

Proceedings of the 2019 EMNLP and the 9th IJCNLP (System Demonstrations), pages 109–114
Hong Kong, China, November 3 – 7, 2019. ©2019 Association for Computational Linguistics

attentional models.

In the following, a source sentence of length l_x is represented by a sequence of one-hot encoded vectors $\mathbf{x}_1, \mathbf{x}_2, \ldots, \mathbf{x}_{l_x}$ for each word. Analogously, a target sequence of length l_y is represented by a sequence of one-hot encoded vectors $\mathbf{y}_1, \mathbf{y}_2, \ldots, \mathbf{y}_{l_y}$.

2.1.1 RNN

Joey NMT implements the RNN encoder-decoder variant from Luong et al. (2015).

Encoder. The encoder RNN transforms the input sequence $\mathbf{x}_1, \ldots, \mathbf{x}_{l_x}$ into a sequence of vectors $\mathbf{h}_1, \ldots, \mathbf{h}_{l_x}$ with the help of the embeddings matrix E_{src} and a recurrent computation of states

$$\mathbf{h}_i = \mathrm{RNN}(E_{src}\,\mathbf{x}_i, \mathbf{h}_{i-1}); \qquad \mathbf{h}_0 = \mathbf{0}.$$

The RNN consists of either GRU or a LSTM units. For a bidirectional RNN, hidden states from both directions are are concatenated to form $\mathbf{h}_i$. The initial encoder hidden state $\mathbf{h}_0$ is a vector of zeros. Multiple layers can be stacked by using each resulting output sequence $\mathbf{h}_1, \ldots, \mathbf{h}_{l_x}$ as the input to the next RNN layer.

Decoder. The decoder uses input feeding (Luong et al., 2015) where an attentional vector $\tilde{\mathbf{s}}$ is concatenated with the representation of the previous word as input to the RNN. Decoder states are computed as follows:

$$\mathbf{s}_t = \mathrm{RNN}([E_{trg}\,\mathbf{y}_{t-1}; \tilde{\mathbf{s}}_{t-1}], \mathbf{s}_{t-1})$$

$$\mathbf{s}_0 = \begin{cases} \tanh(W_{bridge}\,\mathbf{h}_{l_x} + \mathbf{b}_{bridge}) & \text{if bridge} \\ \mathbf{h}_{l_x} & \text{if last} \\ \mathbf{0} & \text{otherwise} \end{cases}$$

$$\tilde{\mathbf{s}}_t = \tanh(W_{att}[\mathbf{s}_t; \mathbf{c}_t] + \mathbf{b}_{att})$$

The initial decoder state is configurable to be either a non-linear transformation of the last encoder state ("bridge"), or identical to the last encoder state ("last"), or a vector of zeros.

Attention. The context vector $\mathbf{c}_t$ is computed with an attention mechanism scoring the previous decoder state $\mathbf{s}_{t-1}$ and each encoder state $\mathbf{h}_i$:

$$\mathbf{c}_t = \sum_i a_{ti} \cdot \mathbf{h}_i$$

$$a_{ti} = \frac{\exp(\mathrm{score}(\mathbf{s}_{t-1}, \mathbf{h}_i))}{\sum_k \exp(\mathrm{score}(\mathbf{s}_{t-1}, \mathbf{h}_k))}$$

where the scoring function is a multi-layer perceptron (Bahdanau et al., 2015) or a bilinear transformation (Luong et al., 2015).

Output. The output layer produces a vector $\mathbf{o}_t = W_{out}\,\tilde{\mathbf{s}}_t$, which contains a score for each token in the target vocabulary. Through a softmax transformation, these scores can be interpreted as a probability distribution over the target vocabulary $\mathcal{V}$ that defines an index over target tokens v_j.

$$p(y_t = v_j \mid x, y_{<t}) = \frac{\exp(\mathbf{o}_t[j])}{\sum_{k=1}^{|\mathcal{V}|} \exp(\mathbf{o}_t[k])}$$

2.1.2 Transformer

Joey NMT implements the Transformer from Vaswani et al. (2017), with code based on *The Annotated Transformer* blog (Rush, 2018).

Encoder. Given an input sequence $\mathbf{x}_1, \ldots, \mathbf{x}_{l_x}$, we look up the word embedding for each input word using $E_{src}\mathbf{x}_i$, add a position encoding to it, and stack the resulting sequence of word embeddings to form matrix $X \in \mathbb{R}^{l_x \times d}$, where l_x is the sentence length and d the dimensionality of the embeddings.

We define the following learnable parameters:[1]

$$A \in \mathbb{R}^{d \times d_a} \quad B \in \mathbb{R}^{d \times d_a} \quad C \in \mathbb{R}^{d \times d_o}$$

where d_a is the dimensionality of the attention (inner product) space and d_o the output dimensionality. Transforming the input matrix with these matrices into new word representations H

$$H = \underbrace{\mathrm{softmax}\left(XA\,B^{\top}X^{\top}\right)}_{\text{self-attention}} XC$$

which have been updated by attending to all other source words. Joey NMT implements multi-headed attention, where this transformation is computed k times, one time for each head with different parameters A, B, C.

After computing all k Hs in parallel, we concatenate them and apply layer normalization and a final feed-forward layer:

$$H = [H^{(1)}; \ldots; H^{(k)}]$$
$$H' = \text{layer-norm}(H) + X$$
$$H^{(\text{enc})} = \text{feed-forward}(H') + H'$$

We set $d_o = d/k$, so that $H \in \mathbb{R}^{l_x \times d}$. Multiple of these layers can be stacked by setting $X = H^{(\text{enc})}$ and repeating the computation.

---

[1]Exposition adapted from Michael Collins `https://youtu.be/jfwqRMdTmLo`

Decoder. The Transformer decoder operates in a similar way as the encoder, but takes the stacked target embeddings $Y \in \mathbb{R}^{l_y \times d}$ as input:

$$H = \underbrace{\text{softmax}\left(YA\,B^\top Y^\top\right)}_{\text{masked self-attention}} YC$$

For each target position attention to future input words is inhibited by setting those attention scores to $-inf$ before the softmax. After obtaining $H' = H + Y$, and before the feed-forward layer, we compute multi-headed attention again, but now between intermediate decoder representations H' and final encoder representations $H^{(\text{enc})}$:

$$Z = \underbrace{\text{softmax}\left(H'A\,B^\top H^{(\text{enc})\top}\right)}_{\text{src-trg attention}} H^{(\text{enc})}C$$

$$H^{(\text{dec})} = \text{feed-forward}(\text{layer-norm}(H' + Z))$$

We predict target words with $H^{(\text{dec})}W_{out}$.

2.2 Features

In the spirit of minimalism, we follow the 80/20 principle (Pareto, 1896) and aim to achieve 80% of the translation quality with 20% of a common toolkit's code size. For this purpose we identified the most common features (the bare necessities) in recent works and implementations.[2] It includes standard architectures (see §2.1), label smoothing, dropout in multiple places, various attention mechanisms, input feeding, configurable encoder/decoder bridge, learning rate scheduling, weight tying, early stopping criteria, beam search decoding, an interactive translation mode, visualization/monitoring of learning progress and attention, checkpoint averaging, and more.

2.3 Documentation

The code itself is documented with doc-strings and in-line comments (especially for tensor shapes), and modules are tested with unit tests. The documentation website[3] contains installation instructions, a walk-through tutorial for training, tuning and testing an NMT model on a toy task[4], an overview of code modules, and a detailed API documentation. In addition, we provide thorough

---

[2]We refer the reader to the additional technical description in `https://arxiv.org/abs/1907.12484`: Table 6 in Appendix A.1 compares Joey NMT's features with several popular NMT toolkits and shows that Joey NMT covers all features that those toolkits have in common.

[3]`https://joeynmt.readthedocs.io`

[4]Demo video: `https://youtu.be/PzWRWSIwSYc`

Counts	OpenNMT-py	XNMT	Joey NMT
Files	94	82	20
Code	10,287	11,628	2,250
Comments	3,372	4,039	1,393
Comment/Code Ratio	0.33	0.35	**0.62**

Table 1: Python code statistics for OpenNMT-py (commit hash `624a0b3a`), XNMT (`a87e7b94`) and Joey NMT (`e55b615`).

answers to frequently asked questions regarding usage, configuration, debugging, implementation details and code extensions, and recommend resources, such as data collections, PyTorch tutorials and NMT background material.

2.4 Code Complexity

In order to facilitate fast code comprehension and navigation (Wiedenbeck et al., 1999), Joey NMT objects have at most one level of inheritance. Table 1 compares Joey NMT with OpenNMT-py and XNMT (selected for their extensibility and thoroughness of documentation) in terms of code statistics, i.e. lines of Python code, lines of comments and number of files.[5] OpenNMT-py and XNMT have roughly 9-10x more lines of code, spread across 4-5x more files than Joey NMT . These toolkits cover more than the essential features for NMT (see §2.2), in particular for other generation or classification tasks like image captioning and language modeling. However, Joey NMT's comment-to-code ratio is almost twice as high, which we hope will give code readers better guidance in understanding and extending the code.

2.5 Benchmarks

Our goal is to achieve a performance that is comparable to other NMT toolkits, so that novices can start off with reliable benchmarks that are trusted by the community. This will allow them to build on Joey NMT for their research, should they want to do so. We expect novices to have limited resources available for training, i.e., not more than one GPU for a week, and therefore we focus on benchmarks that are within this scope. Pretrained models, data preparation scripts and configuration files for the following benchmarks will be made available on `https://github.com/joeynmt/joeynmt`.

---

[5]Using `https://github.com/AlDanial/cloc`

System	Groundhog RNN		Best RNN			Transformer	
	en-de	lv-en	layers	en-de	lv-en	en-de	lv-en
NeuralMonkey	13.7	10.5	1/1	13.7	10.5	–	–
OpenNMT-Py	18.7	10.0	4/4	22.0	13.6	–	–
Nematus	23.9	14.3	8/8	23.8	14.7	–	–
Sockeye	23.2	14.4	4/4	25.6	15.9	27.5	18.1
Marian	23.5	14.4	4/4	25.9	16.2	27.4	17.6
Tensor2Tensor	–	–	–	–	–	26.3	17.7
Joey NMT	23.5	14.6	4/4	26.0	15.8	27.4	18.0

Table 2: Results on WMT17 `newstest2017`. Comparative scores are from Hieber et al. (2018).

WMT17. We use the settings of Hieber et al. (2018), using the exact same data, pre-processing, and evaluation using WMT17-compatible Sacre-BLEU scores (Post, 2018).[6] We consider the setting where toolkits are used out-of-the-box to train a Groundhog-like model (1-layer LSTMs, MLP attention), the 'best found' setting where Hieber et al. train each model using the best settings that they could find, and the Transformer base setting.[7] Table 2 shows that Joey NMT performs very well compared against other shallow, deep and Transformer models, despite its simple code base.[8]

IWSLT14. This is a popular benchmark because of its relatively small size and therefore fast training time. We use the data, pre-processing, and word-based vocabulary of Wiseman and Rush (2016) and evaluate with SacreBLEU.[9] Table 3 shows that Joey NMT performs well here, with both its recurrent and its Transformer model. We also included BPE results for future reference.

System	de-en
Wiseman and Rush (2016)	22.5
Bahdanau et al. (2017)	27.6
Joey NMT (RNN, word)	27.1
Joey NMT (RNN, BPE32k)	27.3
Joey NMT (Transformer, BPE32k)	31.0

Table 3: IWSLT14 test results.

3 User Study

The target group for Joey NMT are novices who will use NMT in a seminar project, a thesis, or an internship. Common tasks are to re-implement a paper, extend standard models by a small novel element, or to apply them to a new task. In order to evaluate how well novices understand Joey NMT, we conducted a user study comparing the code comprehension of novices and experts.

3.1 Study Design

Participants. The novice group is formed of eight undergraduate students with a Computational Linguistics major that have all passed introductory courses to Python and Machine Learning, three of them also a course about Neural Networks. None of them had practical experience with training or implementing NMT models nor PyTorch, but two reported theoretic understanding of NMT. They attended a 20h crash course introducing NMT and Pytorch basics.[10] Note that we did not teach Joey NMT explicitly in class, but the students independently completed the Joey NMT tutorial.

As a control group (the "experts"), six graduate students with NMT as topic of their thesis or research project participated in the study. In contrast to the novices, this group of participants has a solid background in Deep Learning and NMT, had practical experience with NMT. All of them had previously worked with NMT in PyTorch.

Conditions. The participation in the study was voluntary and not graded. Participants were not allowed to work in groups and had a maximum

---

[6] BLEU+case.mixed+lang.[en-lv|en-de]+numrefs.1+smooth.exp+test.wmt17+tok.13a+version.1.3.6

[7] Note that the scores reported for other models reflect their state when evaluated in Hieber et al. (2018).

[8] Blog posts like Rush (2018) and Bastings (2018) also offer simple code, but they do not perform as well.

[9] BLEU+case.lc+numrefs.1+smooth.exp+tok.none+version.1.3.6

[10] See §**??** in the supplemental material of `https://arxiv.org/abs/1907.12484` for details.

time of 3h to complete the quiz. They had previously locally installed Joey NMT[11] and could browse the code with the tools of their choice (IDE or text editor). They were instructed to explore the Joey NMT code with the help of the quiz, informed about the purpose of the study, and agreed to the use of their data in this study. Both groups of participants had to learn about Joey NMT in a self-guided manner, using the same tutorial, code, and documentation. The quiz was executed on the university's internal e-learning platform. Participants could jump between questions, review their answers before finally submitting all answers and could take breaks (without stopping the timer). Answers to the questions were published after all students had completed the test.

Question design. The questions are not designed to test the participant's prior knowledge on the topic, but to guide their exploration of the code. The questions are either free text, multiple choice or binary choice. There are three blocks of questions:[12]

1. **Usage of Joey NMT** : nine questions on how to interpret logs, check whether models were saved, interpret attention matrices, pre-/postprocess, and to validate whether the model is doing what it is built for.

2. **Configuring Joey NMT** : four questions that make the users configure Joey NMT in such a way that it works for custom situations, e.g. with custom data, with a constant learning rate, or creating model of desired size.

3. **Joey NMT Code**: eighteen questions targeting the detailed understanding of the Joey NMT code: the ability to navigate between python modules, identify dependencies, and interpret what individual code lines are doing, hypothesize how specific lines in the code would have to get changed to change the behavior (e.g. working with a different optimizer). The questions in this block were designed in a way that in order to find the correct answers, every python module contained in Joey NMT had to be visited at least once.

Every question is awarded one point if answered correctly. Some questions require manual grading, most of them have one correct answer. We record overall completion time and time per question.[13]

3.2 Analysis

Total duration and score. Experts took on average 77 min to complete the quiz, novices 118 min, which is significantly slower (one-tailed t-test, $p < 0.05$). Experts achieved on average 82% of the total points, novices 66%. According to the t-test the difference in total scores between groups is significant at $p < 0.05$. An ANOVA reveals that there is a significant difference in total duration and scores within the novices group, but not within the experts group.

Per question analysis. No question was incorrectly answered by everyone. Three questions (#6, #11, #18) were correctly answered by everyone–they were appeared to be easiest to answer and did not require deep understanding of the code. In addition, seven questions (#1, #13, #15, #21, #22, #28, #29) were correctly answered by all experts, but not all novices–here their NMT experience was useful for working with hyperparameters and peculiarities like special tokens. However, for only one question, regarding the differences in data processing between training and validation (#16), the difference between average expert and novice score was significant (at $p < 0.05$). Six questions (#9, #18, #21, #25, #31) show a significantly longer average duration for novices than experts. These questions concerned post-processing, initialization, batching, end conditions for training termination and plotting, and required detailed code inspection.

LME. In order to analyze the dependence of scores and duration on particular questions and individual users, we performed a linear mixed effects (LME) analysis using the R library `lme4` (Bates et al., 2015). Participants and questions are treated as random effects (categorical), the level of expertise as fixed effect (binary). Duration and score per question are response variables.[14] For both response variables the variability is higher

---

[11]Joey NMT commit hash `0708d596`, prior to the Transformer implementation.

[12]`https://arxiv.org/abs/1907.12484` contains the full list of questions, complete statistics and details of the LME analysis.

[13]Time measurement is noisy, since full minutes are measured and students might take breaks at various points in time.

[14]Modeling expertise with higher granularity instead of the binary classification into expertise groups (individual variables for experience with PyTorch, NMT and background in deep learning) did not have a significant effect on the model, since the number of participants is relatively low.

depending on the question than on the user (6x higher for score, 2x higher for time). The intercepts of the fixed effects show that novices score on average 0.14 points less while taking 2.47 min longer on each question than experts. The impact of the fixed effect is significant at $p < 0.05$.

3.3 Findings

First of all, we observe that the design of the questions was engaging enough for the students because all participants invested at least 1h to complete the quiz voluntarily. The experts also reported having gained new insights into the code through the quiz. We found that there are significant differences between both groups: Most prominently, the novices needed more time to answer each question, but still succeeded in answering the majority of questions correctly. There are larger variances within the group of novices, because they had to develop individual strategies to explore the code and use the available resources (documentation, code search, IDE), while experts could in many cases rely on prior knowledge.

4 Conclusion

We presented Joey NMT, a toolkit for sequence-to-sequence learning designed for NMT novices. It implements the most common NMT features and achieves performance comparable to more complex toolkits, while being minimalist in its design and code structure. In comparison to other toolkits, it is smaller in size and but more extensively documented. A user study on code accessibility confirmed that the code is comprehensibly written and structured. We hope that Joey NMT will ease the burden for novices to get started with NMT, and can serve as a basis for teaching.

Acknowledgments

We would like to thank Sariya Karimova, Philipp Wiesenbach, Michael Staniek and Tsz Kin Lam for their feedback on the early stages of the code and for their bug fixes. We also thank the student and expert participants of the user study.

References

Dzmitry Bahdanau, Philemon Brakel, Kelvin Xu, Anirudh Goyal, Ryan Lowe, Joelle Pineau, Aaron C. Courville, and Yoshua Bengio. 2017. An actor-critic algorithm for sequence prediction. In *ICLR*.

Dzmitry Bahdanau, Kyunghyun Cho, and Yoshua Bengio. 2015. Neural machine translation by jointly learning to align and translate. In *ICLR*.

Joost Bastings. 2018. The annotated encoder-decoder with attention.

Douglas Bates, Martin Mächler, Ben Bolker, and Steve Walker. 2015. Fitting linear mixed-effects models using lme4. *Journal of Statistical Software*, 67(1):1–48.

Jindřich Helcl and Jindřich Libovický. 2017. Neural Monkey: An Open-source Tool for Sequence Learning. *PBML*.

Felix Hieber, Tobias Domhan, Michael Denkowski, David Vilar, Artem Sokolov, Ann Clifton, and Matt Post. 2018. The sockeye neural machine translation toolkit at amta 2018. In *AMTA*.

Guillaume Klein, Yoon Kim, Yuntian Deng, Vincent Nguyen, Jean Senellart, and Alexander Rush. 2018. Opennmt: Neural machine translation toolkit. In *AMTA*.

Thang Luong, Hieu Pham, and Christopher D. Manning. 2015. Effective approaches to attention-based neural machine translation. In *EMNLP*.

Graham Neubig, Matthias Sperber, Xinyi Wang, Matthieu Felix, Austin Matthews, Sarguna Padmanabhan, Ye Qi, Devendra Sachan, Philip Arthur, Pierre Godard, John Hewitt, Rachid Riad, and Liming Wang. 2018. XNMT: The extensible neural machine translation toolkit. In *AMTA*.

Vilfredo Pareto. 1896. *Cours d'économie politique: professé á l'Université de Lausanne*, volume 1. F. Rouge.

Matt Post. 2018. A call for clarity in reporting BLEU scores. In *WMT*.

Alexander Rush. 2018. The annotated transformer.

Ashish Vaswani, Noam Shazeer, Niki Parmar, Jakob Uszkoreit, Llion Jones, Aidan N Gomez, Łukasz Kaiser, and Illia Polosukhin. 2017. Attention is all you need. In *NeurIPS*.

Susan Wiedenbeck, Vennila Ramalingam, Suseela Sarasamma, and Cynthia L Corritore. 1999. A comparison of the comprehension of object-oriented and procedural programs by novice programmers. *Interacting with Computers*, 11(3):255–282.

Sam Wiseman and Alexander M. Rush. 2016. Sequence-to-sequence learning as beam-search optimization. In *EMNLP*, Austin, Texas.

Journalist-in-the-Loop: Continuous Learning as a Service for Rumour Analysis

Twin Karmakharm   **Nikolaos Aletras**   **Kalina Bontcheva**

Department of Computer Science
University of Sheffield, UK

`[t.karmakharm, n.aletras, k.bontcheva]@sheffield.ac.uk`

Abstract

Automatically identifying rumours in social media and assessing their veracity is an important task with downstream applications in journalism. A significant challenge is how to keep rumour analysis tools up-to-date as new information becomes available for particular rumours that spread in a social network.

This paper presents a novel open-source web-based rumour analysis tool that can continuous learn from journalists. The system features a rumour annotation service that allows journalists to easily provide feedback for a given social media post through a web-based interface. The feedback allows the system to improve an underlying state-of-the-art neural network-based rumour classification model. The system can be easily integrated as a service into existing tools and platforms used by journalists using a REST API.

1 Introduction

Identifying rumours and assessing their veracity in social media is an important task with downstream applications in journalism (Zubiaga et al., 2018a). Such tools can be used to make journalists more productive and also have the potential to be valuable tools in informing the public about the veracity of rumours especially during political crises and pre-electoral periods (Tsakalidis et al., 2018).

Individual and collaborative manual approaches to rumour analysis do not scale due to the large volume and velocity of user generated content (Konstantinovskiy et al., 2018). On the other hand, automatic machine learning-based approaches are often falling short on accuracy, when presented with previously unseen rumours (Zubiaga et al., 2018a).

Current rumour analysis practices also tend to entail journalists making decisions using a disparate set of tools, such as Google reverse image search, Tweetdeck, or more experimental machine learning-based rumour or video analysis algorithms. Even the latest research projects in these areas, e.g. PHEME (Derczynski and Bontcheva, 2014), InVID (Teyssou et al., 2017), Hoaxy (Shao et al., 2016), envisage the computer algorithms as intelligence augmentation tools for the journalists, used to scale up their abilities to deal with a large volume, velocity, and variety of social content with uncertain veracity.

Even though large amounts of new human insights and evidence accumulate over time, journalists cannot use this to improve their tools since the machine learning models behind them are not updatable. This is a major limitation on the practical usefulness of these tools, since our latest research (Lukasik et al., 2015) on rumour stance and veracity classification, for example, demonstrated that giving the machine learning models as few as just ten human-labelled examples from a newly emerging rumour can improve the algorithm accuracy by at least 10%.

Therefore, not only journalists can benefit from using machine intelligence to improve their productivity, but also the underlying algorithms can get smarter, if only journalists could feed back the new evidence in a way that enables the tools to learn from such new data.

This paper presents a new open source web service for rumour analysis[1] that can improve over time by using feedback from journalists. The main user requirement is for journalists to invest minimal time and effort providing the additional manual feedback which in turn will yield productivity gains from the more accurate machine learning models. From a technological perspective, the assumption being tested is that continuous learning and human which computation techniques can

---

[1] `https://tweetveracity.gate.ac.uk`

115

Proceedings of the 2019 EMNLP and the 9th IJCNLP (System Demonstrations), pages 115–120
Hong Kong, China, November 3 – 7, 2019. ©2019 Association for Computational Linguistics

be used to underpin an easy to use misinformation analysis interface for journalists. Due to this being a prototype project, we focus initially on rumour analysis and only on Twitter.

To test this hypothesis, we have built a prototype web service that brings together state-of-the-art machine learning-based algorithms for rumour detection (Aker et al., 2019). Journalists are able to access the service via a web-based application interface from their desktop or mobile devices and monitor and verify emerging rumours in social media. The web application uses the machine learning algorithms, in order to quickly gather and present journalists with evidence around the narratives being monitored, e.g. how fast is the rumour spreading and which are the users who are most affected; who are the key proponents; is the rumour attracting polarised opinions and discussions; how likely is the rumour to be true. Our main aim is to support much more complex types of analysis, than just focusing on the veracity of an individual piece of information, e.g. has an image or a video been tampered with.

2 Related Work

In 2016 alone, the Duke Reporters Lab reported a 50% increase in global fact-checking by media and independent fact-checking organisations.[2] Journalists and news editors currently use largely manual processes for analysis, investigation, and verification of social media and other online content. A limited number of production quality tools are currently available to support them in the individual steps of this process, with much of the technology still in research and experimental phases.

In more detail, existing projects and tools are mostly focused on images/video forensics and verification (e.g. InVID (Teyssou et al., 2017), RE-VEAL[3]), crowdsourced verification (e.g. Check-Desk[4], Veri.ly[5]), fact-checking claims made by politicians (e.g. Politifact[6], FactCheck.org[7], Full-Fact[8]), citizen journalism (e.g. Citizen Desk), repositories of checked facts/rumours/websites (e.g. Emergent (Ferreira and Vlachos, 2016),

FactCheck [7] , Decodex[9]), or pre-trained machine learning models and tools, which however cannot be adapted by the journalists to new data (e.g. PHEME (Derczynski and Bontcheva, 2014), REVEAL[3]).

There are also existing tools for visualising and analysing online rumours which are related to the user interface of our system:

- RumorLens (Resnick et al., 2014) is a prototype aimed at citizens and journalists, to help detect rumours early, then classify posts as spreading or correcting the given rumour, and also visualising its spread. A human-in-the-loop learning showed good results on the tweet retrieval task. This motivated us to propose extending this approach to other rumour and misinformation analysis tasks.

- TwitterTrails (Metaxas et al., 2015) is an interactive, web-based tool that visualises the origin and propagation characteristics of a rumour and its refutation, on Twitter. Another visualisation-based framework for studying rumour propagation is RumourFlow (Dang et al., 2016).

- Hoaxy (Shao et al., 2016) is a recent open-source tool focused on visualising and searching over claims and fact checks. Such sophisticated visualisations are out of scope of our system, but relevant open-source visualisation tools, e.g. from Hoaxy, could be integrated in the future.

- CrossCheck[10] was a collaborative rumour checking project led by First Draft and Google News Lab, during the French elections. Its output was a useful dataset of false or unverified rumours.

- Meedan's Check[4] is an open-source breaking news verification platform, which however does not support continuously updated machine learning methods.

- ClaimBuster (Hassan et al., 2017) is a tool which gathered volunteer and expert-based claim annotations to train machine learning methods for claim classification (factual vs non-factual). In contrast, we propose a service where rumour annotation is carried out as a side effect of the journalist workflow, as well as having a wider range of machine learning methods, for different rumour analysis tasks.

However, to the best of our knowledge, the above tools do not consider using feedback provided by journalists to continuously update their underlying rumour classification models.

3 Journalist-in-the-Loop System Overview

The system is an integration of state-of-the-art machine learning algorithms for detecting emerging rumours; analysing the online narratives around them for stance and temporal evolution; and automatic veracity classification. The starting point are our open source algorithms from the PHEME project (Derczynski and Bontcheva, 2014) adapted to fit the learning paradigm, so the models evolve as more journalist-labelled data comes in.

The core of the rumour analysis service consists of three main parts: (1) a rumour classification system; (2) a rumour annotation service; and (3) a database which stores the training data required by the classification system and allows the system to be updated continuously using the newly annotated rumours. The diagram in Fig. 1 provides an overview of the system.

4 Rumour Classification System

The rumour classification system contains and manages the model that is used for classifying new unseen rumours. The system is built on top of the PyTorch[11] deep learning framework and consists of three components.

First, the data processing component is used to transform text into a representation suitable for the Rumour Classification Model where its inputs and outputs are described in Section 4.1. If there are many annotations provided by the user for the same piece of rumour, the system chooses the most frequent one. The processed text is then transformed into a set of matrices that can be directly used in the model training process.

Second, the model training component trains and validates the model using the available annotated rumours dataset prepared by the data pro-

cessing component. The dataset is randomised and split in to training (80%) and testing (20%) sets. In this case, there is no validation dataset as there is currently no further tuning of hyperparameters, hence more data is dedicated for training the model instead. Once the training is complete, the model's parameters are then saved to be used in the next stage.

Finally, the prediction component offers an interface for making predictions on new unseen rumours which is used directly by the Rumour Annotation Service as described in Section 5. The component uses the stored model's parameters from the last stage.

4.1 Rumour Classification Model

The model used in the Rumour Classification System is based on the state-of-the-art rumour veracity classification algorithm of Aker et al. (2019). It is a recurrent network which classifiers Twitter rumours into three categories, true, false or unverified. A diagram of the model can be seen in Fig. 2.

The model takes three inputs. First input is the source tweets, the text is cleaned and tokenized before being fed into the network. The second input are the recurring terms that occur frequently and which are associated to each veracity category (e.g. the word 'live' has strong association with true rumours). In this case, only the recurring terms that are associated with false rumours are used as they are shown to give the best result. The third input is the stance related to the tweet obtained from the comments associated with the tweet. The stance are proportions of associated tweets which either support the original tweet, denies it or are neutral (e.g. further questions or simply making comments without supporting or denying).

The tokenized source tweets and recurring terms are embedded using the pre-trained Google news word2vec model (Mikolov et al., 2013). The embedded source tweets and recurring terms are then fed into an attention layer that uses the recurring terms to weight the importance of the source tweet words. The output of the attention layer is fed into a Long-Short Term Memory (LSTM) layer (Hochreiter and Schmidhuber, 1997) that generates a single 10-feature vector. The LSTMs output feature vector is concatenated with the stance input and fed in to a dense layer

---

[11]https://pytorch.org

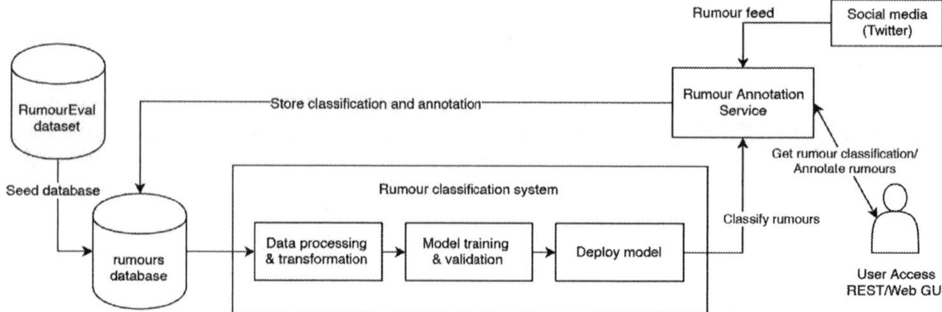

Figure 1: Data flow diagram of the rumour classification service.

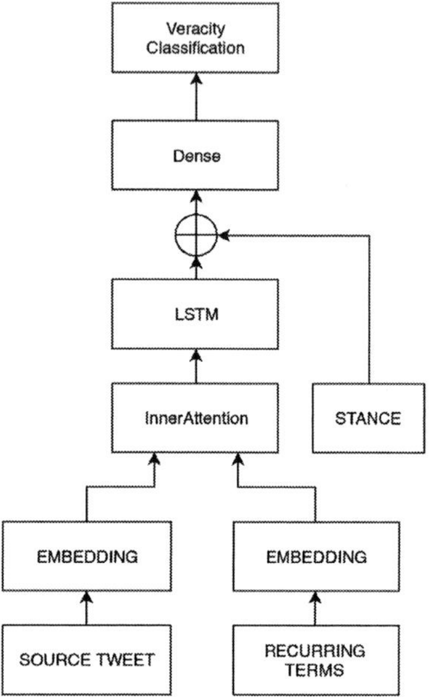

Figure 2: Network diagram of the rumour veracity model.

for a three-category classification output.

4.2 Data and Initial Results

The initial data source used for seeding the rumour veracity classification model is the RumourEval2017 dataset (Derczynski et al., 2017) which is derived from the PHEME dataset (Zubiaga et al., 2018b). The RumourEval2017 dataset contains 325 Twitter conversation threads discussing rumours with respect to eight different man-made events like Germanwings Air Crash, Charlie Hebdo, Ottowa Shootings, etc. Each thread in the dataset is annotated as true, false or unverified. Also each reply to a source tweet is annotated with one of the labels: supporting, denying, questioning and commenting. It is split into training, development and test set as in the RumourEval2017 challenge with 272, 25 and 28 rumours respectively. The dataset has a majority class baseline of 0.429.

Evaluation is performed by comparing against several state-of-the-art approaches – NileTMRG (Enayet and El-Beltagy, 2017), Branch LSTM (Zubiaga et al., 2018b), Multi-task Learning (Kochkina et al., 2018), vanilla LSTM (without inner-attention), LSTM with soft attention (Bahdanau et al., 2014) and our Inner-Attention algorithm. The algorithms achieved F-1 scores of 0.539, 0.558, 0.491, 0.528, 0.496, 0.616 and accuracy of 0.571, 0.571, 0.5, 0.537, 0.5, and 0.607 respectively. We expect the results should improve as more data is added to the training set through the Rumour Annotation Service. Further analysis and discussion of the algorithm and its evaluation can be found in Aker et al. (2019).

5 Rumour Annotation Service

The Rumour Annotation Service part provides the functionality needed for annotating rumours and storing them in a database. It has a role of an interface for interacting with users. It retrieves the social media posts, classifies them using the Rumour Classification System and sends this information back to the user. Since journalists' time is precious, we focus on scenarios where they are asked to label no more than ten to fifteen examples per rumour. Journalists will optionally be able to provide further examples if this fit their workflow.

The service can be accessed through a web Graphical User Interface (GUI) front-end (Fig. 3) that can be used standalone or as REST API which makes it possible to be easily incorporated into existing journalist platforms and tools. As long as

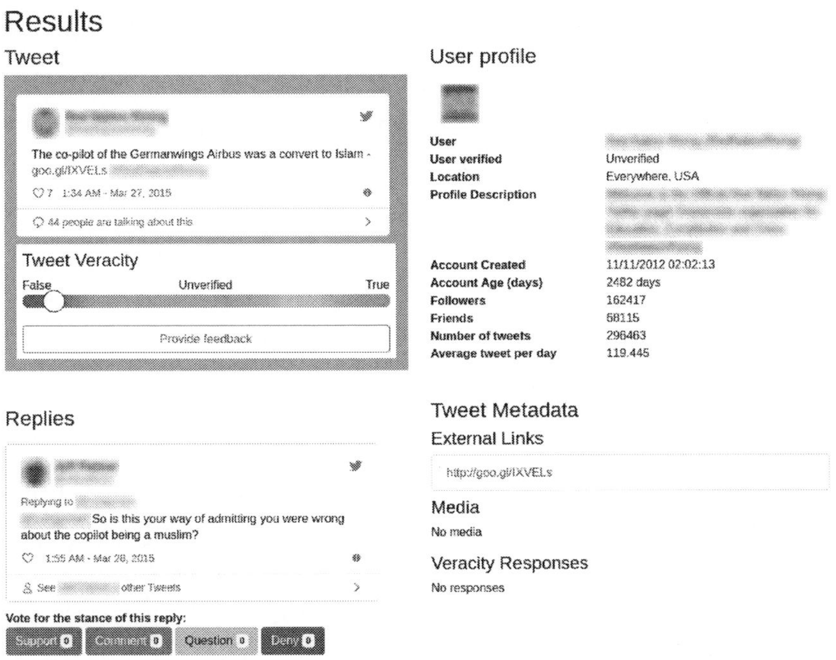

Figure 3: A screenshot of the web-based interface. The source tweet is shown on the top left. The veracity classification is displayed below the tweet on a single axis scale that ranges between False (red), Unverified (grey) and True (green). Metadata about the tweet is shown on the right. Replies to the tweet are shown on the bottom left where journalists can annotate the stance of each reply.

a journalist chooses to annotate a rumour, it will be instantly stored into the database, allowing the classification system to get updated regularly by leveraging the newly annotated rumours.

The journalist can currently make two types of annotations. Firstly, annotations on the veracity of the rumour itself. Whether it is true, false, or unverified, and are encouraged to provide evidence for making this claim. Secondly, they can annotate on the stance of the responses to the rumour. The stance of the response can either be to support the claim, deny the claim, or to offer further questions or comments, which we currently regard as neutral stance. When creating a dataset for re-training with user-provided annotations, each tweet, for both rumour veracity and stance classification, uses the class with the majority vote. Each tweet must also have 50% or more votes in the majority category to be used.

6   Conclusion and Future Work

This paper presented an open source web service for analysis of rumours on social media. The system uses a state-of-the-art deep neural network model (Aker et al., 2019) to classify Twitter rumours and allows journalists to provide annotated feedback to the system allowing the predictions to be improved as it is used.

In the future, we intend to also integrate a rumour stance classifier. User credibility will be taken into account to affect the influence of their annotations by analysing the accuracy and quality of provided evidence. In this demo, we focused only on the Twitter platform but we plan to offer support for other social media platforms, such as Reddit and 4chan. Finally, as new rumour classification models are developed, they could easily be integrated into the system to provide an ensemble of predictions.

Acknowledgements

This research was supported by a Google DNI Prototype project and the WeVerify project (partially funded by the European Commission under contract number 825297).

References

Ahmet Aker, Alfred Sliwa, Fahim Dalvi, and Kalina Bontcheva. 2019. Rumour verification through recurring information and an inner-attention mechanism. *Online Social Networks and Media*, 13:100045.

Dzmitry Bahdanau, Kyunghyun Cho, and Yoshua Bengio. 2014. Neural machine translation by jointly learning to align and translate. *arXiv preprint arXiv:1409.0473*.

Anh Dang, Abidalrahman Moh'd, Evangelos Milios, and Rosane Minghim. 2016. What is in a rumour: Combined visual analysis of rumour flow and user activity. In *Proceedings of the 33rd Computer Graphics International*, CGI '16, pages 17–20, New York, NY, USA. ACM.

L Derczynski and Kalina Bontcheva. 2014. Pheme: Veracity in digital social networks. *CEUR Workshop Proceedings*, 1181:19–22.

Leon Derczynski, Kalina Bontcheva, Maria Liakata, Rob Procter, Geraldine Wong Sak Hoi, and Arkaitz Zubiaga. 2017. Semeval-2017 task 8: Rumoureval: Determining rumour veracity and support for rumours. *Proceedings of the 11th International Workshop on Semantic Evaluation (SemEval-2017)*.

Omar Enayet and Samhaa R El-Beltagy. 2017. Niletmrg at semeval-2017 task 8: Determining rumour and veracity support for rumours on twitter. In *Proceedings of the 11th International Workshop on Semantic Evaluation (SemEval-2017)*, pages 470–474.

William Ferreira and Andreas Vlachos. 2016. Emergent: a novel data-set for stance classification. In *Proceedings of the 2016 conference of the North American chapter of the association for computational linguistics: Human language technologies*, pages 1163–1168.

Naeemul Hassan, Anil Nayak, Vikas Sable, Chengkai Li, Mark Tremayne, Gensheng Zhang, Fatma Arslan, Josue Caraballo, Damian Jimenez, Siddhant Gawsane, Shohedul Hasan, Minumol Joseph, and Aaditya Kulkarni. 2017. Claimbuster: the first-ever end-to-end fact-checking system. *Proceedings of the VLDB Endowment*, 10:1945–1948.

Sepp Hochreiter and Jürgen Schmidhuber. 1997. Long short-term memory. *Neural computation*, 9(8):1735–1780.

Elena Kochkina, Maria Liakata, and Arkaitz Zubiaga. 2018. All-in-one: Multi-task learning for rumour verification. *arXiv preprint arXiv:1806.03713*.

Lev Konstantinovskiy, Oliver Price, Mevan Babakar, and Arkaitz Zubiaga. 2018. Towards automated factchecking: Developing an annotation schema and benchmark for consistent automated claim detection.

Michal Lukasik, Trevor Cohn, and Kalina Bontcheva. 2015. Estimating collective judgement of rumours in social media. *ArXiv*, abs/1506.00468.

Panagiotis Takas Metaxas, Samantha Finn, and Eni Mustafaraj. 2015. Using twittertrails.com to investigate rumor propagation. In *Proceedings of the 18th ACM Conference Companion on Computer Supported Cooperative Work & Social Computing*, CSCW'15 Companion, pages 69–72, New York, NY, USA. ACM.

Tomas Mikolov, Ilya Sutskever, Kai Chen, Greg S Corrado, and Jeff Dean. 2013. Distributed representations of words and phrases and their compositionality. In *Advances in neural information processing systems*, pages 3111–3119.

Paul Resnick, Samuel Carton, Souneil Park, Yuncheng Shen, and Nicole Zeffer. 2014. Rumorlens: A system for analyzing the impact of rumors and corrections in social media. In *Proc. Computational Journalism Conference*, pages 10121–0701.

Chengcheng Shao, Giovanni Luca Ciampaglia, Alessandro Flammini, and Filippo Menczer. 2016. Hoaxy: A platform for tracking online misinformation. In *Proceedings of the 25th International Conference Companion on World Wide Web*, WWW '16 Companion, pages 745–750, Republic and Canton of Geneva, Switzerland. International World Wide Web Conferences Steering Committee.

Denis Teyssou, Jean-Michel Leung, Evlampios Apostolidis, Konstantinos Apostolidis, Symeon Papadopoulos, Markos Zampoglou, Olga Papadopoulou, and Vasileios Mezaris. 2017. The invid plug-in: Web video verification on the browser. In *Proceedings of the First International Workshop on Multimedia Verification*, MuVer '17, pages 23–30, New York, NY, USA. ACM.

Adam Tsakalidis, Nikolaos Aletras, Alexandra I Cristea, and Maria Liakata. 2018. Nowcasting the stance of social media users in a sudden vote: The case of the Greek Referendum. In *Proceedings of the 27th ACM International Conference on Information and Knowledge Management*, CIKM, pages 367–376.

Arkaitz Zubiaga, Ahmet Aker, Kalina Bontcheva, Maria Liakata, and Rob Procter. 2018a. Detection and resolution of rumours in social media: A survey. *ACM Computing Surveys (CSUR)*, 51(2):32.

Arkaitz Zubiaga, Elena Kochkina, Maria Liakata, Rob Procter, Michal Lukasik, Kalina Bontcheva, Trevor Cohn, and Isabelle Augenstein. 2018b. Discourse-aware rumour stance classification in social media using sequential classifiers. *Information Processing & Management*, 54(2):273–290.

LIDA: Lightweight Interactive Dialogue Annotator

Edward Collins
Wluper Ltd.
London, United Kingdom
ed@wluper.com

Nikolai Rozanov
Wluper Ltd.
London, United Kingdom
nikolai@wluper.com

Bingbing Zhang
Wluper Ltd.
London, United Kingdom
bingbing@wluper.com

Abstract

Dialogue systems have the potential to change how people interact with machines but are highly dependent on the quality of the data used to train them. It is therefore important to develop good dialogue annotation tools which can improve the speed and quality of dialogue data annotation. With this in mind, we introduce LIDA, an annotation tool designed specifically for conversation data. As far as we know, LIDA is the first dialogue annotation system that handles the entire dialogue annotation pipeline from raw text, as may be the output of transcription services, to structured conversation data. Furthermore it supports the integration of arbitrary machine learning models as annotation recommenders and also has a dedicated interface to resolve inter-annotator disagreements such as after crowdsourcing annotations for a dataset. LIDA is fully open source, documented and publicly available [1].

1 Introduction

Of all the milestones on the road to creating artificial general intelligence perhaps one of the most significant is giving machines the ability to converse with humans. Dialogue systems are becoming one of the most active research areas in Natural Language Processing (NLP) and Machine Learning (ML). New, large dialogue datasets such as MultiWOZ (Budzianowski et al., 2018) have allowed data-hungry deep learning algorithms to be applied to dialogue systems, and challenges such as the Dialogue State Tracking Challenge (DSTC) (Henderson et al., 2014) and Amazon's Alexa Prize (Khatri et al., 2018) encourage competition among teams to produce the best systems.

The quality of a dialogue system dependents on the quality of the data used to train the system.

Creating a high-quality dialogue dataset incurs a large annotation cost, which makes good dialogue annotation tools essential to ensure the highest possible quality. Many annotation tools exist for a range of NLP tasks but none are designed specifically for dialogue with modern usability principles in mind - in collecting MultiWOZ, for example, Budzianowski et al. (2018) had to create a bespoke annotation interface.

In this paper, we introduce LIDA, a web application designed to make dialogue dataset creation and annotation as easy and fast as possible. In addition to following modern principles of usability, LIDA integrates best practices from other state-of-the-art annotation tools such as INCEpTION (Klie et al., 2018), most importantly by allowing arbitrary ML models to be integrated as annotation recommenders to suggest annotations for data. Any system with the correct API can be integrated into LIDA's back end, meaning LIDA can be used as a front end for researchers to interact with their dialogue systems and correct their responses, then save the interaction as a future test case.

When data is crowdsourced, it is good practice to have multiple annotators label each piece of data to reduce noise and mislabelling (Deng et al., 2009). Once you have multiple annotations, it is important to be able to resolve conflicts by highlighting where annotators disagreed so that an arbiter can decide on the correct annotation. To this end, LIDA provides a dedicated interface which automatically finds where annotators have disagreed and displays the labels alongside a percentage of how many annotators selected each label, with the majority annotated labels selected by default.

1.1 Main Contributions

Our main contributions with this tool are:

---

[1] https://github.com/Wluper/lida

121

Proceedings of the 2019 EMNLP and the 9th IJCNLP (System Demonstrations), pages 121–126
Hong Kong, China, November 3 – 7, 2019. ©2019 Association for Computational Linguistics

Annotation Tool	Turn/Dialogue Seg-mentation	Classification Labels	Edit Dialogues/Turns	Recommenders	Inter-Annotator Disagreement Resolution	Language
LIDA	YES	YES	YES	YES	YES	PYTHON
INCEpTion (Klie et al., 2018)	NO	YES	NO	YES	YES/NO[4]	JAVA
GATE (Cunningham, 2002)	NO	YES	NO	NO	YES/NO[5]	JAVA
TWIST (Pluss, 2012)	YES	NO	YES	NO	NO	-
BRAT (Stenetorp et al., 2012)	NO	YES	NO	YES	NO	PYTHON
DOCCANO[3]	NO	YES	NO	NO	NO	PYTHON
DialogueView (Heeman et al., 2002)	YES	YES	YES	NO	NO	TcK/TK

Table 1: Annotator Tool Comparison Table
Turn/Dialogue Segmentation: segment raw text into turns and dialogues. Classification Labels: label classification data. Edit Dialogues/Turns: allow users to add/edit/delete new turns or dialogues. Recommenders: ML models to suggest annotations. Inter-Annotator Disagreement Resolution: whether the system has an interface to resolve disagreements between different annotators. Language: what programming language the system uses

- A modern annotation tool designed specifically for task-oriented conversation data

- The first dialogue annotator capable of handling the full dialogue annotation pipeline from turn and dialogue segmentation through to labelling structured conversation data

- Easy integration of dialogue systems and recommenders to provide annotation suggestions

- A dedicated interface to resolve inter-annotator disagreements for dialogue data

2   Related Work

Various annotation tools have been developed for NLP tasks in recent years. Table 1 compares LIDA with other recent annotation tools. TWIST (Pluss, 2012) is a dialogue annotation tool which consists of two stages: turn segmentation and content feature annotation. Turn segmentation allows users to highlight and create new turn segments from raw text. After this, users can annotate sections of text in a segment by highlighting them and selecting from a predefined feature list. However, this tool doesn't allow users to specify custom annotations or labels and doesn't support classification or slot-value annotation. This is not compatible with modern dialogue datasets which require such annotations (Budzianowski et al., 2018).

INCEpTION (Klie et al., 2018) is a semantic annotation platform for interactive tasks that require semantic resources like entity linking. It provides machine learning models to suggest annotations and allows users to collect and model knowledge directly in the tool. GATE (Cunningham, 2002) is an open source tool that provides predefined solutions for many text processing tasks. It is powerful because it allows annotators to enhance the provided annotation tools with their own Java code, making it easily extensible and provides an enormous number of predefined features. However, GATE is a large and complicated tool with a significant setup cost - its instruction manual alone is over 600 pages long[2]. Despite their large feature sets, INCEpTION and GATE are not designed for annotating dialogue and cannot display data as turns, an important feature for dialogue datasets.

BRAT (Stenetorp et al., 2012) and Doccano[3] are web-based annotation tools for tasks such as text classification and sequence labeling. They have intuitive and user-friendly interfaces which aim to make the creation of certain types of dataset such as classification or sequence labelling datasets as fast as possible. BRAT also supports annotation suggestions by integrating ML models. However, like INCEpTION[4] and GATE[5], they are not designed for annotating dialogues and do not support generation of formatted conversational data from a raw text file such as may be output by a transcription service. LIDA aims to fill these gaps by providing a lightweight, easy-to-setup annotation tool which displays data as a series of dialogues, supports integration of arbitrary ML models as recommenders and supports segmentation of raw text into dialogues and turns.

DialogueView (Heeman et al., 2002) is a tool for dialogue annotation. However, the main use-cases are not focused on building dialogue systems, rather it is focused on segmenting recorded conversations. It supports annotating audio files as well as discourse segmentation - hence, granular labelling of the dialogue, recommenders, inter-

---

[2] https://gate.ac.uk/sale/tao/tao.pdf

[3] https://github.com/chakki-works/doccano

[4] Getting the scores is available as a plugin: https://dkpro.github.io/dkpro-statistics/dkpro-agreement-poster.pdf - resolving the issues seems to be not supported

[5] Again inter-annotator score calculation capabilities are available as separate plug-in https://gate.ac.uk/releases/gate-5.1-beta1-build3397-ALL/doc/tao/splitch10.html - however support for resolutions is not apparent

annotator agreement, and slot-value labelling is not possible with DialogueView.

3 System Overview

LIDA is built according to a client-server architecture with the front end written in standard web languages (HTML/CSS/JavaScript) that will run on any browser. The back end written in Python using the Flask[6] web framework as a RESTful API.

The main screen which lists all available dialogues is shown in Figure 3, in the Appendix. The buttons below this list allow a user to add a blank or formatted dialogue file. Users can also drag and drop files in this screen to upload them. The user is then able to add, delete or edit any particular dialogue. There is also a button to download the whole dataset as a JSON file on this page. Clicking on a dialogue will take users to the individual dialogue annotation screen shown in Figure 1.

LIDA uses the concept of a "turn" to organise how a dialogue is displayed and recorded. A turn consists of a query by the user followed by a response from the system, with an unlimited number of labels allowed for each user query. The user query and system response are displayed in the large area on the left of the interface, while the labels for each turn are shown in the scrollable box on the right. There are two forms that these labels can currently take which are particularly relevant for dialogue: multilabel classification and slot-value pair.

An example of multilabel classification is whether the user was informing the system or requesting a piece of information. An example of a slot-value pair is whether the user mentioned the type of restaurant they'd like to eat at (slot: restaurant-type) and if so what it was (value: italian, for example). The front-end code is written in a modular form so that it is easy for researchers using LIDA to add custom types of labels and annotations, such as sequence classification, to LIDA.

Once annotation is complete, users can resolve inter-annotator disagreements on the resolution screen. Here, each dialogue is listed along with the number of different people who have annotated it. More annotations can be added by dragging and dropping dialogue files into this screen. When the user clicks on one of these dialogues, they are taken to the resolution screen shown in Figure 2. Here, all of the disagreements in a dialogue are

listed and the label which annotators disagreed on is also shown. The label most frequently selected by annotators is assigned as correct by default, and the arbiter can accept this annotation simply by pressing "Enter" or else re-label the data item. Once the arbiter has checked an annotation, it is displayed as "Accepted" in the error list and the dialogue file automatically saved.

3.1 Use Cases

3.1.1 Experimenting with Dialogue Systems

While generic evaluation metrics are important for understanding the performance of a dialogue system, another important method of evaluation is to talk to the dialogue system and see if it gives subjectively satisfying results. This gives the researcher insight into which part of the system most urgently needs improvement faster than performing more complex error analysis. However, if the user talks to their dialogue system through a terminal interface, they have no way of correcting the system when it answers incorrectly. The researcher should be able to record every interaction they have with their system and correct the predictions of the system easily and quickly. That way, the researcher will be able to use each previous recorded interaction as a test case for future versions of their system.

LIDA is designed with this in mind - a dialogue system can be integrated in the back end so that it will run whenever the user enters a new query in the front end. The user will then be able to evaluate whether the system gave the correct answer and correct the labels it gets wrong using the front end. LIDA will record these corrections and allow the user to download the interaction with their dialogue system with the corrected labels so that it can be used as a test case in future versions of the system.

3.1.2 Creating a New Dialogue Dataset

Users can create a blank dialogue on LIDA's home screen, then enter queries in the box shown at the bottom of Figure 1. Along with whole dialogue systems, arbitrary ML models can be added as recommenders in the back end. Once the user hits "Enter", the query is run through the recommender models in the back end and the suggested annotations displayed for the label. If no recommender is specified in the back end, the label will be left blank. Users can delete turns and navigate between them using "Enter" or the arrow keys. The

---

[6]http://flask.pocoo.org/

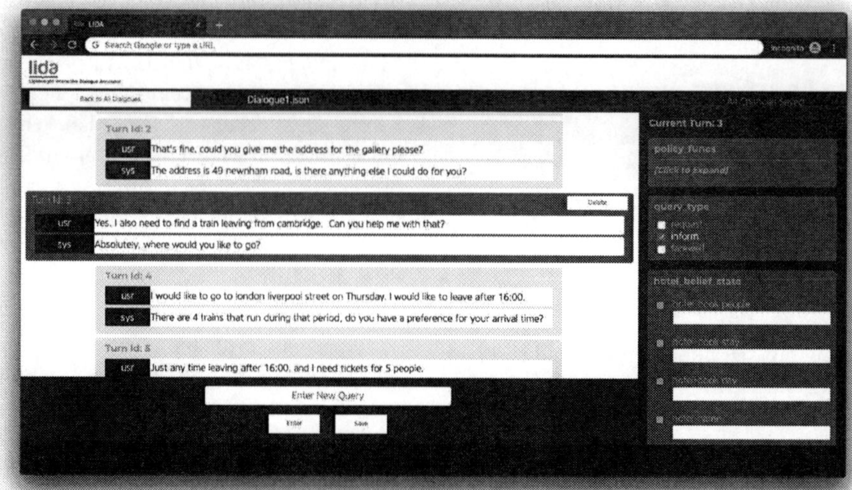

Figure 1: Turn List : A list of turns for one specific dialogue, users can add new turns, delete turns, edit utterances and annotate labels here.

name of the dialogue being annotated can be seen next to the "Back" button at the top left of the screen and can be edited by clicking on it.

3.1.3 Annotating An Existing Dataset

Datasets can be uploaded via drag-and-drop to the home screen of the system, or paths can be specified in the back end if the system were being used for crowdsourcing. Datasets can be in one of two forms, either a ".txt" file such as may be produced by a transcription service, or a formatted ".json" file, a common format for dialogue data (Budzianowski et al., 2018; Henderson et al., 2014). Once the user has uploaded their data, their dialogue(s) will appear on the home screen. The user can click on each dialogue and will be taken to the single dialogue annotation screen shown in Figure 1 to annotate it. If the user uploaded a text file, they will be taken to a dialogue and turn segmentation screen. Following the same constraints imposed in MultiWOZ (Budzianowski et al., 2018) and DSTC (Henderson et al., 2014), this turn segmenter assumes that there are only two participants in the dialogue: the user and the system, and that the user asks the first query. The user separates each utterance in the dialogue by a blank line, and separates dialogues with a triple equals sign ("==="). Once the user clicks "Done", the text file will automatically be parsed into the correct JSON format and each query run through the recommenders in the back-end to obtain anno-

tation suggestions.

3.1.4 Resolving Annotator Disagreement

Researchers could use LIDA's main interface to crowdsource annotations for a dialogue dataset. Once they have several annotations for each dialogue, they can upload these to the inter-annotator resolution interface of LIDA. The disagreements between annotators will be detected, with a percentage shown beside each label to show how many annotators selected it. The label with the highest percentage of selections is checked by default. The arbiter can accept the majority label simply by pressing "Enter" and can change errors with the arrow keys to facilitate fast resolution. This interface also displays an averaged (over turns) version of Cohen's Kappa (Cohen, 1960), the total number of annotations, total number of errors and averaged (over turns) accuracy.

3.2 Features[7]

Specifying Custom Labels LIDA's configuration is controlled by a single script in the back end. This script defines which labels will be displayed in the UI and is easy to extend. Users can define their own labels by altering this configuration script. If a user wishes to add a new label, all they need to do is specify the label's name, its type

---

[7]We refer the reader to visit the public repository for a full documentation `https://github.com/Wluper/lida`.

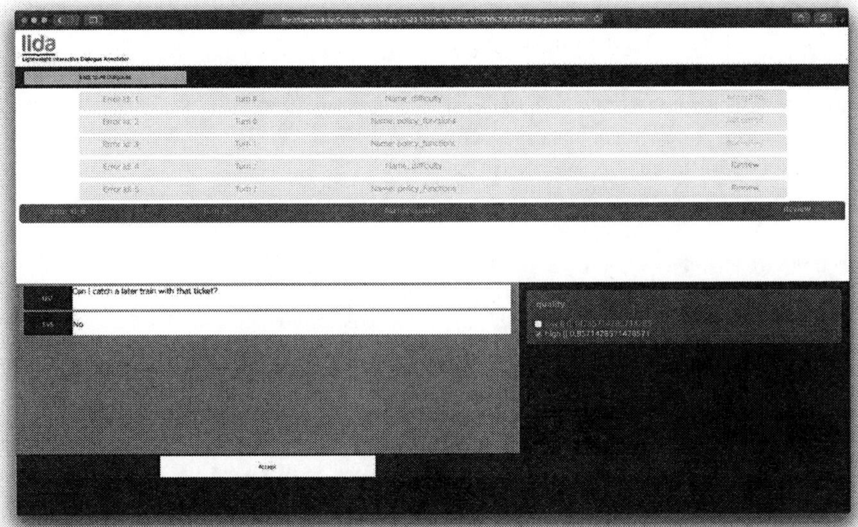

Figure 2: Screenshot of the inter-annotator disagreement resolution screen.

(classification or slot-value pair, currently) and the possible values the classification can take. Alongside the label specification, they can also specify a recommender to use for the label values. The label will then automatically be displayed in the front end. Note that labels in uploaded datasets will only be displayed if the label has an entry in the configuration file.

Custom Recommenders When creating a dialogue dataset from scratch, LIDA is most powerful when used in conjunction with recommenders which can suggest annotations for user queries to be corrected by the annotator. State-of-the-art tools such as INCEpTION (Klie et al., 2018) emphasise the importance of being able to use recommenders in annotation systems. Users can specify arbitrary ML models to use for each label in LIDA's back end. The back end is written in Python, the de facto language for machine learning, so researchers can directly integrate models written in Python to the back end. This is in contrast to tools such as INCEpTION (Klie et al., 2018) and GATE (Cunningham, 2002) which are written in Java and so require extra steps to integrate a Python-based model. To integrate a recommender, the user simply provides an instantiated Python object in the configuration file that has a method called "transform" that takes a single string and returns a predicted label.

Dialogue and Turn Segmentation from Raw Data When uploading a .txt file, users can segment each utterance and each dialogue with a simple interface. This means that raw dialogue data with no labels, such as obtained from a transcription service, can be uploaded and processed into a labelled dialogue. Segmented dialogues and turns are automatically run through every recommender to give suggested labels for each utterance.

4 Evaluation

Table 1 shows a comparison of LIDA to other annotation tools. To our knowledge, LIDA is the only annotation tool designed specifically for dialogue systems which supports the full pipeline of dialogue annotation from raw text to labelled dialogue to inter-annotator resolution and can also be used to test the subjective performance of a dialogue system.

To test LIDA's capabilities, we designed a simple experiment: we took a bespoke dataset of 154 dialogues with an average of 3.5 turns per dialogue and a standard deviation of 1.55. The task was to assign three classification labels to each user utterance in each dialogue. Each annotator was given a time limit of 1 hour and told to annotate as many dialogues as they could in that time. We had six annotators perform this task, three of whom were familiar with the system and three of whom had never seen it before.

These annotators annotated an average of 79 dialogues in one hour with a standard deviation of 30, which corresponds to an average of 816.5 individual annotations. The annotators who had never seen the system before annotated an average of 60 dialogues corresponding to an average of 617 individual annotations.

Once we had these six annotations, we performed a second experiment whereby a single arbiter resolved inter-annotator disagreements. In one hour, the arbiter resolved 350 disagreements and noted that resolution was slowest when resolving queries with a high degree of disagreement.

These results show that LIDA provides fast annotation sufficient for collecting large scale data. At the recorded pace of the annotators who had not seen the system before, 100 workers could create a dialogue dataset of 6000 dialogues with approximately $6000 * 3.5 = 21000$ turns with three annotations per turn in one hour. In large scale collections, such as MultiWOZ (Budzianowski et al., 2018) where 1249 workers were used, much larger datasets with richer annotations could be created. Clearly annotation quantity will depend on the difficulty of the task, length of dialogue and number of labels to be assigned to each utterance but our results suggest that a high speed is achievable.

5 Conclusion

We present LIDA, an open source, web-based annotation system designed specifically for dialogue data. LIDA implements state-of-the-art annotation techniques including recommenders, fully customisable labels and inter-annotator disagreement resolution. LIDA is the only dialogue annotation tool which can handle the full pipeline of dialogue dataset creation from turn and dialogue segmentation to structured conversation data to inter-annotator disagreement resolution.

Future work will look at adding new label types to LIDA, adding the possibility to have more than two actors in the conversation, a centralised admin page, additional labelling (e.g. co-reference resolution) and in general enhancing usability as users provide feedback. Our hope is that this work will find applications and usability beyond what we have outlined and developed so far and that with a community effort a modern and highly accessible tool will become widely available.

References

Paweł Budzianowski, Tsung-Hsien Wen, Bo-Hsiang Tseng, Iñigo Casanueva, Stefan Ultes, Osman Ramadan, and Milica Gašić. 2018. Multiwoz-a large-scale multi-domain wizard-of-oz dataset for task-oriented dialogue modelling. *arXiv preprint arXiv:1810.00278*.

Jacob Cohen. 1960. A coefficient of agreement for nominal scales. *Educational and psychological measurement*, 20(1):37–46.

Hamish Cunningham. 2002. Gate, a general architecture for text engineering. *Computers and the Humanities*, 36(2):223–254.

Jia Deng, Wei Dong, Richard Socher, Li-Jia Li, Kai Li, and Li Fei-Fei. 2009. Imagenet: A large-scale hierarchical image database. In *2009 IEEE conference on computer vision and pattern recognition*, pages 248–255. Ieee.

Peter A. Heeman, Fan Yang, and Susan E. Strayer. 2002. DialogueView - an annotation tool for dialogue. In *Proceedings of the Third SIGdial Workshop on Discourse and Dialogue*, pages 50–59, Philadelphia, Pennsylvania, USA. Association for Computational Linguistics.

Matthew Henderson, Blaise Thomson, and Jason D Williams. 2014. The second dialog state tracking challenge. In *Proceedings of the 15th Annual Meeting of the Special Interest Group on Discourse and Dialogue (SIGDIAL)*, pages 263–272.

Chandra Khatri, Behnam Hedayatnia, Anu Venkatesh, Jeff Nunn, Yi Pan, Qing Liu, Han Song, Anna Gottardi, Sanjeev Kwatra, Sanju Pancholi, et al. 2018. Advancing the state of the art in open domain dialog systems through the alexa prize. *arXiv preprint arXiv:1812.10757*.

Jan-Christoph Klie, Michael Bugert, Beto Boullosa, Richard Eckart de Castilho, and Iryna Gurevych. 2018. The inception platform: Machine-assisted and knowledge-oriented interactive annotation. In *Proceedings of the 27th International Conference on Computational Linguistics: System Demonstrations*, pages 5–9.

Brian Pluss. 2012. Twist dialogue annotation tool. http://mcs.open.ac.uk/nlg/non-cooperation/resources/user-guide.pdf.

Pontus Stenetorp, Sampo Pyysalo, Goran Topić, Tomoko Ohta, Sophia Ananiadou, and Jun'ichi Tsujii. 2012. Brat: a web-based tool for nlp-assisted text annotation. In *Proceedings of the Demonstrations at the 13th Conference of the European Chapter of the Association for Computational Linguistics*, pages 102–107. Association for Computational Linguistics.

LINSPECTOR WEB: A Multilingual Probing Suite for Word Representations

Max Eichler, Gözde Gül Şahin & Iryna Gurevych
Research Training Group AIPHES and UKP Lab
Department of Computer Science
Technische Universität Darmstadt
Darmstadt, Germany
`max.eichler@gmail.com, {sahin,gurevych}@ukp.tu-darmstadt.de`

Abstract

We present LINSPECTOR WEB, an open source multilingual inspector to analyze word representations. Our system provides researchers working in low-resource settings with an easily accessible web based probing tool to gain quick insights into their word embeddings especially outside of the English language. To do this we employ 16 simple linguistic probing tasks such as gender, case marking, and tense for a diverse set of 28 languages. We support probing of static word embeddings along with pretrained AllenNLP models that are commonly used for NLP downstream tasks such as named entity recognition, natural language inference and dependency parsing. The results are visualized in a polar chart and also provided as a table. LINSPECTOR WEB is available as an offline tool or at `https://linspector.ukp.informatik.tu-darmstadt.de`.

1 Introduction

Natural language processing (NLP) has seen great progress after the introduction of continuous, dense, low dimensional vectors to represent text. The field has witnessed the creation of various word embedding models such as monolingual (Mikolov et al., 2013), contextualized (Peters et al., 2018), multi-sense (Pilehvar et al., 2017) and dependency-based (Levy and Goldberg, 2014); as well as adaptation and design of neural network architectures for a wide range of NLP tasks. Despite their impressive performance, interpreting, analyzing and evaluating such black-box models have been shown to be challenging, which even led to a set of workshop series (Linzen et al., 2018).

Early works for evaluating word representations (Faruqui and Dyer, 2014a,b; Nayak et al., 2016) have mostly focused on English and used either the word similarity or a set of downstream tasks. However datasets for either of those tasks do not exist for many languages, word similarity tests do not necessarily correlate well with downstream tasks and evaluating embeddings on downstream tasks can be too computationally demanding for low-resource scenarios. To address some of these challenges, Shi et al. (2016); Adi et al. (2017); Veldhoen et al. (2016); Conneau et al. (2018) have introduced *probing tasks*, a.k.a. *diagnostic classifiers*, that take as input a representation generated by a fully trained neural model and output predictions for a linguistic feature of interest. Due to its simplicity and low computational cost, it has been employed by many studies summarized by Belinkov and Glass (2019), mostly focusing on English. Unlike most studies, Köhn (2015) introduced a set of multilingual probing tasks, however its scope has been limited to syntactic tests and 7 languages. More importantly it is not accessible as a web application and the source code does not have support to probe pretrained downstream NLP models out of the box.

Given the above information, most of the lower-resource non-English academic NLP communities still suffer from (1) the amount of required human and computational resources to search for the right model configuration, and (2) the lack of diagnostics tools to analyze their models to gain more insights into what is captured. Recently, Şahin et al. (2019) proposed 16 multilingual probing tasks along with the corresponding datasets and found correlations between certain probing and downstream tasks and demonstrated their efficacy as diagnostic tools. In this paper, we employ these datasets to develop LINSPECTOR WEB that is designed to help researchers with low-resources working on non-English languages to (1) analyze, interpret, and visualize various layers of their pretrained AllenNLP (Gardner et al.,

Proceedings of the 2019 EMNLP and the 9th IJCNLP (System Demonstrations), pages 127–132
Hong Kong, China, November 3 – 7, 2019. ©2019 Association for Computational Linguistics

	#Lang	#Task-Type	Web	Offline	Static	Models	Layers	Epochs
(Faruqui and Dyer, 2014a)	4	10-WST	×	×	×			
(Nayak et al., 2016)	1	7-DT	×	×	×			
(Köhn, 2015)	7	7-PT		×	×			
Ours	28	16-PT	×	×	×	×	×	×

Table 1: Features of previous evaluation applications compared to Ours (LINSPECTOR WEB). #Lang: Number of supported languages, #Task-Type: Number and type of the tasks, where WST: Word similarity tasks, DT: Downstream Tasks, PT: Probing Tasks. Static: Static word embeddings and Models: Pretrained downstream models.

2018) models at different epochs and (2) measure the performance of static word embeddings for language-specific linguistic properties. To the best of our knowledge, this is the first web application that (a) performs online probing; (b) enables users to upload their pretrained downstream task models to automatically analyze different layers and epochs; and (c) has support for 28 languages with some of them being extremely low-resource such as Quechuan.

2 Previous Systems

A now retired evaluation suite for word embeddings was wordvectors.org (Faruqui and Dyer, 2014a). The tool provided evaluation and visualization for antonyms, synonyms, and female-male similarity; and later it was updated to support German, French, and Spanish word embeddings (Faruqui and Dyer, 2014b). For a visualization the user could enter multiple tokens and would receive a 2 dimensional chart to visualize the cosine distance between the tokens. Therefore it was limited by the amount of tokens, a human could enter and analyze. VecEval (Nayak et al., 2016) is another web based suite for static English word embeddings that perform evaluation on a set of downstream tasks which may take several hours. The visualization is similar to LINSPEC-TOR WEB reporting both charts and a table. Both web applications do not support probing of intermediate layers of pretrained models or the addition of multiple epochs. Köhn (2015) introduced an offline, multilingual probing suite for static embeddings limited in terms of the languages and the probing tasks. A comparison of the system features of previous studies is given in Table 1.

3 LINSPECTOR WEB

Our system is targeted at multilingual researchers working with low-resource settings. It is designed as a web application to enable such users to probe their word representations with minimal effort and computational requirements by simply uploading a file. The users can either upload their **pretrained static embeddings files** (e.g. word2vec (Mikolov et al., 2013), fastText (Bojanowski et al., 2016), GloVe (Pennington et al., 2014)); [1] or their **pretrained archived AllenNLP models**. In this version, we only give support to AllenNLP, due to its high usage rate by low-resource community and being up-to-date, i.e., containing state-of-the-art models for many NLP tasks and being continuously maintained at the Allen Institute for Artificial Intelligence (Gardner et al., 2018).

3.1 Scope of Probing

We support 28 languages from very diverse language families. [2] The multilingual probing datasets (Şahin et al., 2019) used in this system are language-specific, i.e., languages with a gender system are probed for gender, whereas languages with a rich case-marking system are probed for case. The majority of the probing tasks probe for morpho-syntactic properties (e.g. case, mood, person) which have been shown to correlate well with syntactic and semantic parsing for a number of languages, where a small number of tasks probe for surface (e.g. word length) or semantic level properties (e.g. pseudoword). Finally, there are two morphological comparison tasks (Odd-/Shared Morphological Feature) aiming to find the unique distinct/shared morphological feature between two tokens, which have been shown to correlate well with the NLI task. The current probing tasks are type-level (i.e., do not contain ambiguous words) and are filtered to keep only the frequent words. These tasks are (1) domain independent and (2) contain valuable information encoded via subwords in many languages (e.g. the Turkish

---

[1] Since our probing datasets are publicly available, fastText embeddings for unknown words in our dataset can be generated by the user locally via the provided functions in (Şahin et al., 2019).

[2] Arabic, Armenian, Basque, Bulgarian, Catalan, Czech, Danish, Dutch, English, Estonian, Finnish, French, German, Greek, Hungarian, Italian, Macedonian, Polish, Portuguese, Quechuan, Romanian, Russian, Serbian, Serbo-Crotian, Spanish, Swedish, Turkish and Vietnamese

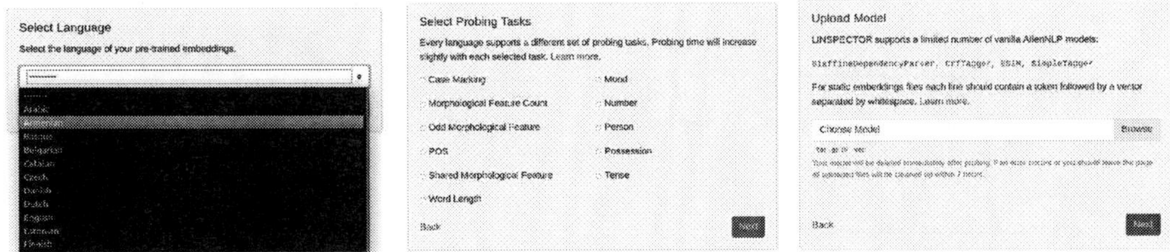

Figure 1: **Left**: Language selection, **Middle**: Probing task selection, **Right**: Uploading model.

word *gelemeyenlerden* "he/she is one of the folks who can not come" encodes sentence-level information). [3]

3.2 Features: Models, Layers and Epochs

We support the following classifier architectures implemented by AllenNLP: BiaffineDependencyParser (Dozat and Manning, 2016), CrfTagger (Sutton et al., 2007), SimpleTagger (Gardner et al., 2018), ESIM (Chen et al., 2017). BiaffineDependencyParser and CrfTagger are highlighted as the default choice for dependency parsing and named entity recognition by (Gardner et al., 2018), while ESIM was picked as one of two available natural language inference models, and SimpleTagger support was added as the entry level AllenNLP classifier to solve tasks like parts-of-speech tagging.

The users can choose the layers they want to probe. This allows the users to analyze what linguistic information is captured by different layers of the model *(e.g., POS information in lower layers, semantic information in higher levels)*. It is possible to select any AllenNLP encoder layer for classifiers with token, sentence, or document based input and models with dual input (e.g. ESIM: premise, hypothesis) that allow probing of selected layers depending on their internal architecture as described in Sec. 4.2. Additionally a user can specify up to 3 epochs for probing to inspect what their model learns and forgets during training. This is considered a crucial feature as it provides insights on learning dynamics of models (Saphra and Lopez, 2019). For instance, a user diagnosing a pretrained NLI task, can probe for the tasks that have been shown to correlate well (Mood, Person, Polarity, and Tense) (Şahin et al., 2019) for additional epochs, and analyze how their

performance evolves during training. After the diagnostic classifiers are trained and tested on the specified language, model, layer, and epochs, the users are provided with (1) accuracies of each task visualized in a polar chart, (2) a table containing accuracy and loss for each probing test, and (3) in case of additional epochs, accuracies for other epochs are overlaid on the chart and columns are added to the table for easy comparison as shown in Fig. 2-Right.

The uploaded model files are deleted immediately after probing, however the results can be saved or shared via a publicly accessible URL. The project is open source and easily extendable to additional languages, probing tasks and AllenNLP models. New languages can be added simply by adding train, dev, and test data for selected probing tasks and adding one database entry. Similarly new probing tasks can be defined following (Şahin et al., 2019). In case the new tasks differ by input type, a custom AllenNLP dataset reader and classifier should be added. It can be extended to new AllenNLP models by adding the matching predictor to the supported list or writing a custom predictor if the model requires dual input values (e.g. ESIM). Finally, other frameworks (e.g. ONNX format) can be supported by adding a method to extract embeddings from the model.

4 System Description

LINSPECTOR WEB is based on the Python Django framework [4] which manages everything related to performance, security, scalability, and database handling.

4.1 Frontend

First, the user selects the language of the model and a number of probing tests they want to perform. The probing test selection menu will vary with the selected language. Next the user has to

---

[3] Users can choose probing tasks either intuitively or rely on earlier studies e.g., that show a linguistic feature has been beneficial for the downstream task. Therefore not every probing task is needed during a specific evaluation.

[4] https://www.djangoproject.com

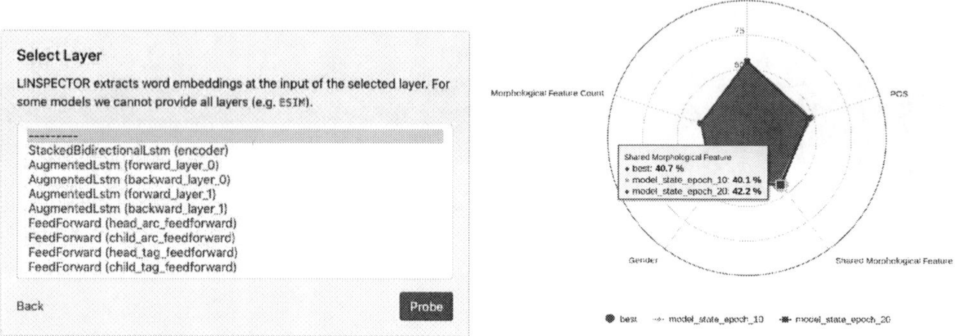

Figure 2: **Left**: Layer selection example, **Right**: Polar chart result shown for different epochs for pretrained Arabic BiaffineDependencyParser.

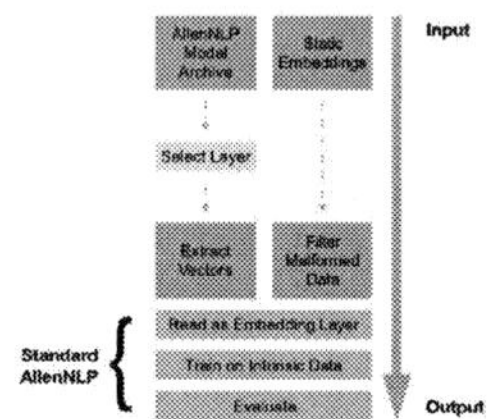

Figure 3: Backend architecture

upload an archived AllenNLP model or a static embeddings file. The input pipeline is shown in Fig. 1. The upload is handled asynchronously using custom AJAX code to support large files, prevent timeouts, and give the user some progress feedback. The backend detects if an uploaded file is an archived AllenNLP model and provides a list of layers if that is the case as shown in Fig. 2-Left. Probing is handled asynchronously by the backend. A JSON API endpoint gives progress feedback to the frontend which displays a progress bar and the currently executed probing test to the user. Finally results are displayed in an interactive chart and a table. For the user interface, we use the Bootstrap framework [5] that provides us with modern, responsive, and mobile compatible HTML and CSS. The visualization is done using the Highcharts library. [6]

4.2 Backend

The structure of the backend system is shown in Fig. 3 and the main components are explained below.

Layers: To get a list of layers an archived AllenNLP model is loaded using a standard AllenNLP API. Since every AllenNLP classifier inherits from the PyTorch (Paszke et al., 2017) class `torch.nn.Module`, we gather two levels of immediate submodules using the `named_children()` API. First we extract high level AllenNLP modules including all `Seq2SeqEncoder`, `Seq2VecEncoder`, and `FeedForward` modules by testing each submodule for a `get_input_dim()` method. Then we extract low level modules which can be either AllenNLP modules e.g. `AugmentedLstm` or PyTorch modules e.g. `Linear` by testing for the attributes `input_size` or `in_features`. All those modules are then returned as available probing layers. We require the input dimension later and since there is no standard API we have to exclude some submodules. [7] Finally we don't support models that require additional linguistic information such as POS tags.

Getting Embeddings: PyTorch modules allow us to register forward hooks. A hook is a callback which receives the module, input, and output every time an input is passed through the module. For AllenNLP models we register such a callback to the selected encoding layer. Then each time a token is passed through the model, it passes through the encoder and the callback receives the input vector. The most reliable way to pass tokens through a model is using AllenNLP predic-

---

[7]By analyzing the AllenNLP codebase and PyTorch modules used in their sample configurations, we decided to support modules providing their dimension using `get_input_dim()`, `input_size`, or `in_features`; which may change with future versions of AllenNLP.

---

tors. There is a matching predictor for every model which are regularly tested and updated. We gather all tokens from our intrinsic probing data and pass it through the predictor. For every token the forward hook is called in the background which then provides us with the vector. The token and vector are then written to a temporary file. During the embedding extraction, the progress is reported back to the frontend periodically in 30 steps. For static embeddings all lines that match the embedding dimension are written to a temporary file and malformed data is removed.

Probing: Finally the gathered embeddings are loaded as a pretrained non-trainable embedding layer for a single linear layer custom build AllenNLP classifier. The classifier is trained and evaluated using the intrinsic probing data for the specified probing test. We use 20 epochs with early stopping, a patience of 5, and gradient clipping of 0.5. The evaluation accuracy and loss are then returned. For contrastive probing tasks (Odd-/Shared Morphological Feature) a similar linear classifier that takes concatenated tokens as input, is used.

Asynchronous probing is handled using the Python Celery framework [8], the RabbitMQ message broker [9], and the Eventlet execution pool [10]. When the user starts probing, a new Celery task is created in the backend which executes all probing tasks specified by the user asynchronously and reports the progress back to the frontend. Finally the results are saved in a PostgreSQL or SQLite-database using the Django Celery Results application.

4.3   Tests

We have trained BiaffineDependencyParser, CrfTagger, SimpleTagger, and ESIM AllenNLP models for Arabic, Armenian, Czech, French, and Hungarian with varying dimensions. We have tested the intrinsic probing data, layer selection, consistency of metrics, contrastive and non-contrastive classifiers, and all probing tests for multiple combinations of languages, dimensions, and AllenNLP models. Static embeddings are tested using pretrained fastText files for the same languages. In addition, the file upload was tested with files up to 8 GB over a DSL 50k connection.

4.4   Training Times

The LINSPECTOR WEB server is hosted in university data center with a state-of-the-art internet connection which allows for fast upload speeds. Therefore, the overall upload speed mostly depends on the users connection. For a single probing task, embedding extraction, training, and evaluation is around a few minutes.

5   Conclusion

Researchers working on non-English languages under low-resource settings have lacked a tool that would assist with model selection via providing linguistic insights, to this date. To address this, we presented LINSPECTOR WEB, an open source, web-based evaluation suite with 16 probing tasks for 28 languages; which can probe pretrained static word embeddings and various layers of a number of selected AllenNLP models. The tool can easily be extended for additional languages, probing tasks, probing models and AllenNLP models. LINSPECTOR WEB is available at `https://linspector.ukp.informatik.tu-darmstadt.de` and the source code for the server is released with `https://github.com/UKPLab/linspector-web` along with the installation instructions for the server. The system is currently being extended to support contextualized word embeddings with contextualized probing tasks using the Universal Dependency Treebanks (Nivre et al., 2019).

6   Acknowledgements

This work has been supported by the DFG-funded research training group "Adaptive Preparation of Information form Heterogeneous Sources" (AIPHES, GRK 1994/1), and also by the German Federal Ministry of Education and Research (BMBF) under the promotional reference 01UG1816B (CEDIFOR) and as part of the Software Campus program under the promotional reference 01IS17050.

References

Yossi Adi, Einat Kermany, Yonatan Belinkov, Ofer Lavi, and Yoav Goldberg. 2017. Fine-grained analysis of sentence embeddings using auxiliary prediction tasks. In *ICLR 2017, Toulon, France, April 24-26, 2017, Conference Track Proceedings.*

---

[8] `http://www.celeryproject.org`
[9] `https://www.rabbitmq.com`
[10] `https://eventlet.net`

Yonatan Belinkov and James Glass. 2019. Analysis methods in neural language processing: A survey. *TACL*, 7:49–72.

Piotr Bojanowski, Edouard Grave, Armand Joulin, and Tomas Mikolov. 2016. Enriching word vectors with subword information. *CoRR*, abs/1607.04606.

Qian Chen, Xiaodan Zhu, Zhen-Hua Ling, Si Wei, Hui Jiang, and Diana Inkpen. 2017. Enhanced LSTM for natural language inference. In *ACL 2017, Vancouver, Canada, July 30 - August 4, Volume 1: Long Papers*, pages 1657–1668.

Alexis Conneau, Germán Kruszewski, Guillaume Lample, Loïc Barrault, and Marco Baroni. 2018. What you can cram into a single \$&!#* vector: Probing sentence embeddings for linguistic properties. In *ACL 2018, Melbourne, Australia, July 15-20, 2018, Volume 1: Long Papers*, pages 2126–2136.

Timothy Dozat and Christopher D. Manning. 2016. Deep biaffine attention for neural dependency parsing. *CoRR*, abs/1611.01734.

Manaal Faruqui and Chris Dyer. 2014a. Community evaluation and exchange of word vectors at wordvectors.org. In *ACL 2014, June 22-27, 2014, Baltimore, MD, USA, System Demonstrations*, pages 19–24.

Manaal Faruqui and Chris Dyer. 2014b. Improving vector space word representations using multilingual correlation. In *EACL 2014, April 26-30, 2014, Gothenburg, Sweden*, pages 462–471.

Matt Gardner, Joel Grus, Mark Neumann, Oyvind Tafjord, Pradeep Dasigi, Nelson Liu, Matthew Peters, Michael Schmitz, and Luke Zettlemoyer. 2018. Allennlp: A deep semantic natural language processing platform.

Arne Köhn. 2015. What's in an embedding? analyzing word embeddings through multilingual evaluation. In *EMNLP 2015, Lisbon, Portugal, September 17-21, 2015*, pages 2067–2073.

Omer Levy and Yoav Goldberg. 2014. Dependency-based word embeddings. In *ACL 2014, June 22-27, 2014, Baltimore, MD, USA, Volume 2: Short Papers*, pages 302–308.

Tal Linzen, Grzegorz Chrupała, and Afra Alishahi. 2018. Proceedings of the 2018 emnlp workshop blackboxnlp: Analyzing and interpreting neural networks for nlp. Association for Computational Linguistics.

Tomas Mikolov, Ilya Sutskever, Kai Chen, Greg Corrado, and Jeffrey Dean. 2013. Distributed representations of words and phrases and their compositionality. In *NIPS 2013 - Volume 2*, NIPS'13, pages 3111–3119.

Neha Nayak, Gabor Angeli, and Christopher D Manning. 2016. Evaluating word embeddings using a representative suite of practical tasks. In *RepEval@ACL*, pages 19–23.

Joakim Nivre, Mitchell Abrams, Željko Agić, and et al. 2019. Universal dependencies 2.4. LINDAT/CLARIN digital library at the Institute of Formal and Applied Linguistics (ÚFAL), Faculty of Mathematics and Physics, Charles University.

Adam Paszke, Sam Gross, Soumith Chintala, Gregory Chanan, Edward Yang, Zachary DeVito, Zeming Lin, Alban Desmaison, Luca Antiga, and Adam Lerer. 2017. Automatic differentiation in PyTorch. In *NIPS Autodiff Workshop*.

Jeffrey Pennington, Richard Socher, and Christopher Manning. 2014. Glove: Global vectors for word representation. In *EMNLP)*, pages 1532–1543, Doha, Qatar. Association for Computational Linguistics.

Matthew E. Peters, Mark Neumann, Mohit Iyyer, Matt Gardner, Christopher Clark, Kenton Lee, and Luke Zettlemoyer. 2018. Deep contextualized word representations. In *NAACL-HLT 2018, New Orleans, Louisiana, USA, June 1-6, 2018, Volume 1 (Long Papers)*, pages 2227–2237.

Mohammad Taher Pilehvar, José Camacho-Collados, Roberto Navigli, and Nigel Collier. 2017. Towards a seamless integration of word senses into downstream NLP applications. In *ACL 2017, Vancouver, Canada, July 30 - August 4, Volume 1: Long Papers*, pages 1857–1869.

Gözde Gül Şahin, Clara Vania, Ilia Kuznetsov, and Iryna Gurevych. 2019. Linspector: Multilingual probing tasks for word representations. *arXiv preprint arXiv:1903.09442*.

Naomi Saphra and Adam Lopez. 2019. Understanding learning dynamics of language models with SVCCA. In *NAACL-HLT 2019, Minneapolis, MN, USA, June 2-7, 2019, Volume 1 (Long and Short Papers)*, pages 3257–3267.

Xing Shi, Inkit Padhi, and Kevin Knight. 2016. Does String-Based Neural MT Learn Source Syntax? In *EMNLP 2016, Austin, Texas, USA, November 1-4, 2016*, pages 1526–1534.

Charles A. Sutton, Andrew McCallum, and Khashayar Rohanimanesh. 2007. Dynamic conditional random fields: Factorized probabilistic models for labeling and segmenting sequence data. *Journal of Machine Learning Research*, 8:693–723.

Sara Veldhoen, Dieuwke Hupkes, and Willem H. Zuidema. 2016. Diagnostic classifiers revealing how neural networks process hierarchical structure. In *Proceedings of the Workshop on Cognitive Computation: Integrating neural and symbolic approaches @NIPS 2016), Barcelona, Spain, December 9, 2016.*

MAssistant: A Personal Knowledge Assistant for MOOC Learners

Lan Jiang   **Shuhan Hu**   **Mingyu Huang**   **Zhichun Wang**[*]
Jinjian Yang   **Xiaoju Ye**   **Wei Zheng**
Beijing Normal University, Beijing, P. R. China, 100875
`https://kg.bnu.edu.cn`

Abstract

Massive Open Online Courses (MOOCs) have developed rapidly and attracted large number of learners. In this work, we present MAssistant system, a personal knowledge assistant for MOOC learners. MAssistant helps users to trace the concepts they have learned in MOOCs, and to build their own concept graphs. There are three key components in MAssistant: (i) a large-scale concept graph built from open data sources, which contains concepts in various domains and relations among them; (ii) a browser extension which interacts with learners when they are watching video lectures, and presents important concepts to them; (iii) a web application allowing users to explore their personal concept graphs, which are built based on their learning activities on MOOCs. MAssistant will facilitate the knowledge management task for MOOC learners, and make the learning on MOOCs easier.

1 Introduction

Massive Open Online Courses (MOOCs) have experienced a rapid development since 2012. Many MOOC platforms have been launched, including Coursera[1], edX[2], and Udacity[3] etc. MOOCs have become increasingly popular, and attracted millions of online users. By 2018, Coursera has enrolled 37 million students, and the total number of MOOC learners all over the world has reached 100 million[4]. Compared to traditional online learning courses, MOOCs provide a new and flexible way for people to acquire knowledge and skills.

MOOC lectures are mainly delivered in short videos, each video covers a specific topic. When taking courses on MOOC platforms, learners will meet important concepts in video lectures. Usually, learners will take notes about the important concepts, and figure out key relations among them. After finishing one or several courses, revisiting and organizing the learned concepts is very important for learners to build their own knowledge system. To facilitate the knowledge management task for MOOC learners, we build a personal knowledge assistant system called MAssistant. MAssistant has a large-scale concept graph built from open data, which covers concepts and their relations in various domains. MAssistant can identify and record important concepts in MOOC lectures for its users, and provide user-friendly interfaces to allow users to annotate and explore concepts they have learned. By interacting with users during their learning activities on MOOCs, MAssistant is able to generate a personal concept graph for each user, which contains inter-connected concepts, lectures and courses.

MAssistant can be accessed at `https://kg.bnu.edu.cn`. There is also a screencast at `https://youtu.be/X40X1T9fNJg` which demonstrates the usage of our system. We believe that MAssistant can make the study easier for MOOC learners.

2 System Architecture

Figure 1 shows the overall architecture of our MAssistant system. In the backend of our system, a concept graph and a database are used to support the functions of MAssistant. The concept graph is built from several open datasets, including Wikipedia[5], WikiData[6], MultiWiBi[7], and WordNet[8]. It contains concepts and their rela-

---

[*] Corresponding author: Z.Wang(zcwang@bnu.edu.cn)

[1] https://www.coursera.org
[2] https://www.edx.org
[3] https://www.udacity.com
[4] https://www.classcentral.com/report/moocs-stats-and-trends-2018/

[5] https://www.wikipedia.org
[6] https://www.wikidata.org/
[7] http://wibitaxonomy.org
[8] https://wordnet.princeton.edu

Proceedings of the 2019 EMNLP and the 9th IJCNLP (System Demonstrations), pages 133–138
Hong Kong, China, November 3 – 7, 2019. ©2019 Association for Computational Linguistics

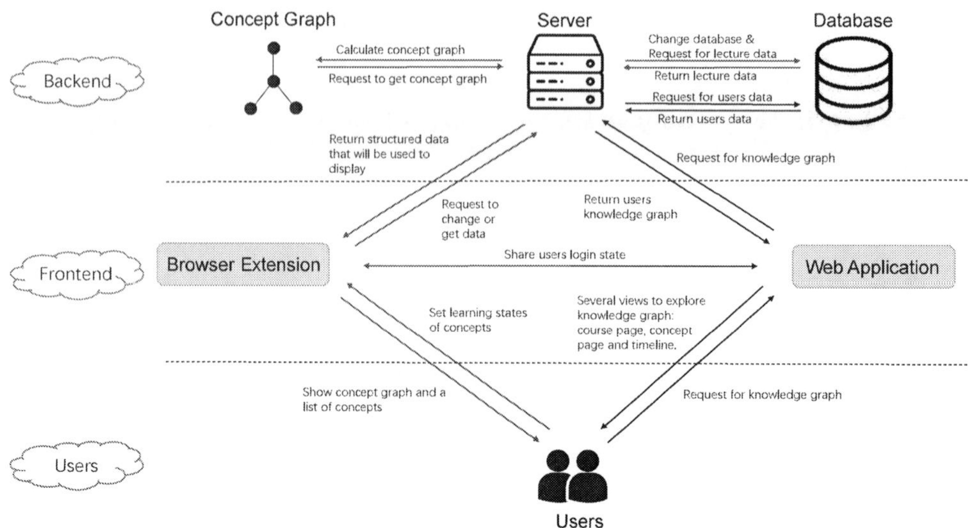

Figure 1: System architecture of MAssistant

tions in various domains, and serves as the key basis of our system. There is also a concept linking component associated with the concept graph, which identifies and links concepts in courses to the concept graph. The database is used to store user-specific information on concepts and courses. Learned concepts and courses are all recorded in the database for each user. Users' personal concept graphs are subgraphs of the system's concept graph, which are generated based on the user-specific information in the database. In the frontend, our system uses a browser extension and a web application to offer users helpful functions on tracing concepts in MOOCs. The browser extension interacts with users when they are watching video lectures, and the web application allows users to explore their personal concept graphs after leaving MOOC platforms.

3   User Interfaces

Figure 2 shows the overview of MAssistant's user interfaces. MAssistant interacts with users via a browser extension and a web application. This section introduces them in detail.

3.1   Browser Extension

The browser extension is installed in the browser, which can be used by users when they are taking MOOC lectures. When watching a video lecture, the user can click the icon of the extension, which will activate a popup window in the upper right corner of the browser. The popup window shows important concepts in the current lecture opened in the browser, and let users do simple annotations on concepts. As shown in Figure 2, the window of browser extension shows a concept timeline and a concept graph to users.

Concept Highlights in Timeline. When a user opens the webpage of a video lecture in the browser, the browser extension of MAssistant extracts important concepts from the transcript of the video, and presents them in a timeline to the user. The concepts are listed by the order in which they appear in the video. Users can quickly get an overview of the concepts mentioned in the lecture, which helps them to well understand the knowledge structure of the lecture. Users can click the concept in the timeline, and a webpage in our web application will be opened to show more information on the concept.

Concept Graph with Learning States. The browser extension visualizes a small concept graph illustrating important relations among concepts. By right clicking on the concepts in the graph, users can easily annotate the concepts in one of three states: *leanred*, *learning*, and *tolearn*. *Learned* concepts are those learners have already mastered; concepts in *tolearn* state are unfamiliar to the learners; concepts in *learning* state are those that the learners are learning but haven't mastered

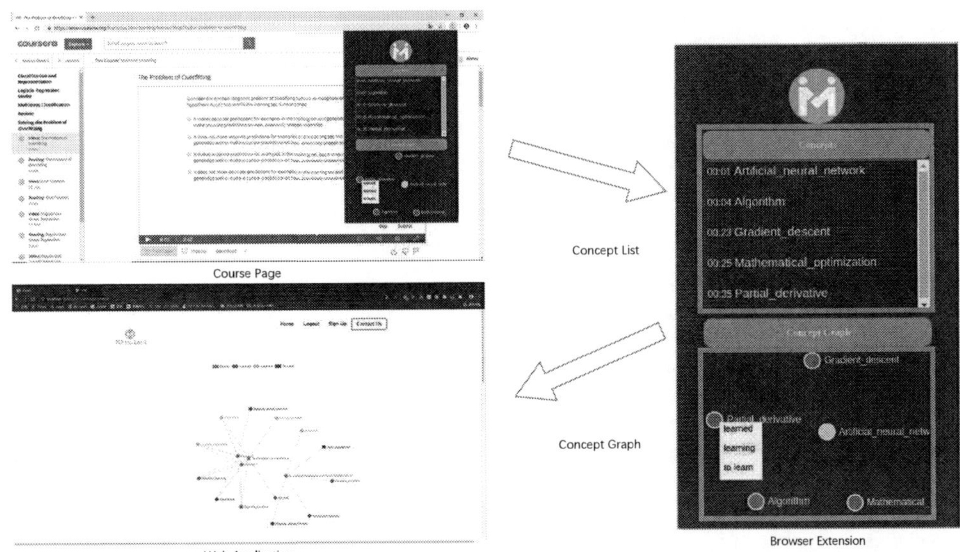

Figure 2: Overview of MAssistant's interfaces

yet. MAssistant will record users' annotations on the concepts, and later users can get a summary of their knowledge states in the web application.

3.2 Web Application

The web application provides users with their personal concept graphs, which contains all the MOOCs and concepts they have learned. MAssistant presents several views to users to explore their concept graphs, including a visualization of concept graph, a course page, a concept page and a study timeline.

Visualization of concept graph. As shown in Figure 2, the homepage of MAssistant visualizes a personal concept graph for a login user. The graph contains all the MOOC lectures and concepts that the user has learned so far. Lectures are nodes in gray in the graph. Concepts are in three colors, each of which identifies a different learning state of the concept. If a concept appears in a lecture, there is a link between them in the graph. This concept graph is a personalized one, different users get distinct graphs built from their own learning experiences on MOOCs. When clicking on the nodes in the concept graph, users will be directed to pages of the corresponding courses or concepts.

Course page. The course page shows lectures and concepts in the courses a user has learned. For each course, a tree structure is generated in the course page, which organizes lectures and concepts in it. Figure 3 shows an example of the tree for the *Machine Learning* course in Coursera. The root of the tree is the course *Machine Learning*, the inner nodes are lectures in the course, the leaf nodes are concepts in the corresponding lectures. The concepts are also in colors, representing their learning states of the current user. By clicking the lecture nodes or concept nodes, the user will be directed to the MOOC platforms or the concept page in our web application.

Concept page. The concept page shows detailed information of a specific concept. As shown in Figure 4, there are three sections in the concept page. The first section shows the definition of the concept, which is obtained from Wikipedia. The second section visualizes important concept relations of the current one. Three kinds of relations are shown, including *IsA*, *Prerequisite*, and *RelatedTo*. Details about how concepts' relations are established will be introduced in Section 4.

Study Timeline. The study timeline displays all the MOOC lectures a user has taken in the order of the occurrence time, as shown in Figure 5. Concepts are also outlined together with the lectures in which they appeared. Users can review the learning history in their study timelines.

Figure 3: Tree structure showing lectures and concepts in a course

4 Concept Graph of MAssistant

The basis of MAssistant system is a large-scale concept graph. This section introduces how this concept graph is built and how the lectures are linked to the concept graph.

4.1 Creating Concepts

To build a concept graph covering concepts in various domains, data from Wikipedia is used as the knowledge source. Wikipedia contains huge number of articles and rich links among them. Each article in Wikipedia describes a subject with texts and structured tables. In this work, we consider each Wikipedia page describing a concept, and create a concept in our concept graph from every Wikipedia page. Some pages in Wikipedia are created for administration purposes, they are excluded from our concept graph. By the above method, 17,688,418 concepts are created in the concept graph.

4.2 Creating Relations

We consider three kinds of relations between concepts to be useful and important for knowledge learning. They are *IsA*, *Prerequisite*, and *RelatedTo*. *IsA* relation defines the hierarchy of concepts, which is indispensable for helping learners to organize the learned concepts. *Prerequisite* relation identifies the dependencies between concepts in the learning process, which tells the learning orders of concepts. *RelatedTo* relation connects highly related concepts in the concept graph, which is helpful for recommending new concepts to the learners. There are 7,054,983 *IsA* relations, 15,614,563 *Prerequisite* relations, and 823,494,078 *RelatedTo* relations in the concept graph. The methods of creating these relations are introduced as follows.

IsA Relation. Several approaches have been proposed to extract *IsA* relations from Wikipedia. Some approaches focus on extracting *IsA* relations from the category network of Wikipedia, others obtain *IsA* relations from Wikipedia articles. Among the previous approaches, MultiWiBi (Flati et al., 2016) automatically creates concept hierarchy by integrating the taxonomy of Wikipedia pages and categories in multiple languages. The taxonomy built by MultiWiBi has high quality and coverage. We use the *IsA* relations in MultiWiBi to establish *IsA* relations among concepts in our concept graph. We also obtain *IsA* relations from WordNet and Wikidata, and import them to our concept graph. For WordNet, we treat nouns in it as concepts, and extract *hypernym-hyponym* relations in WordNet as *IsA* relations among concepts. For WikiData, we treat each item as a concept, and extract *instance of* and *subclass of* relations as *IsA* relations. After obtaining *IsA* relations from WordNet and Wikidata, we first match their con-

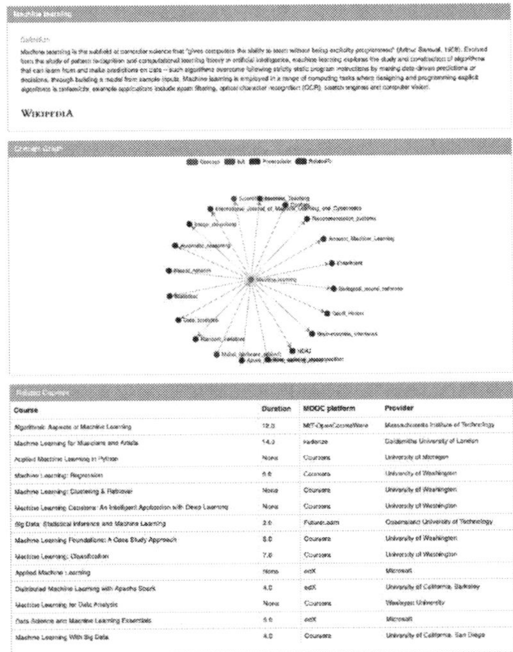

Figure 4: Concept page in MAssistant

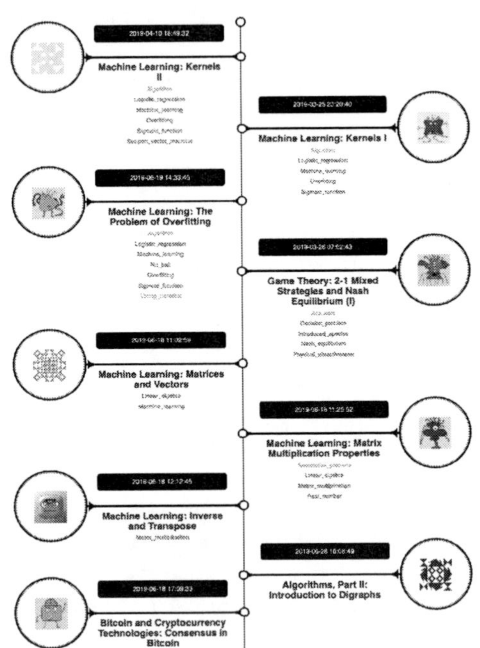

Figure 5: Study timeline in MAssistant

Table 1: Features for discovering prerequisite relations between concepts A and B

Features	Explanation
RefD	Reference distance of A and B in Wikipedia (Liang et al., 2015).
In degree	The in degree of A/B in Wikipedia.
Out degree	The out degree of A/B in Wikipedia.
#Links	Number of links from A/B to B/A.
Link proportion	The proportion of common in-links shared by A and B.
NGD	The normalized Google Distance between A and B (Milne and Witten, 2008) .
#Cooccurrence	Number of times that A and B appearing in the same MOOC lectures.

cepts with those in our concept graph, and then add the *IsA* relations to the concept graph.

Prerequisite Relation *Prerequisite* relations between concepts can be discovered from Wikipedia links (Liang et al., 2015), university curriculum (Liang et al., 2017) and MOOCs (Pan et al., 2017). Mainly following the work of Liang et al. (2018), we discover *prerequisite* relations among concepts by using features computed from Wikipedia links and MOOC lectures. Table 1 outlines all the features we use. To restrict the number of candidate *prerequisite* relations, we only select concept pairs appearing in the same MOOC lectures or directly linked to each other in Wikipedia as the candidates. For each candidate concept pair, we first compute the features in Table 1, and then feed the features to a logistic regression model to determine whether they have the *prerequisite* relation. The logistic regression model is pre-trained on the Wikipedia concept map dataset built by Wang et al. (2016) .

RelatedTo Relation. *RelatedTo* relation connects concepts that have high semantic relatedness. To automatically create the *RelatedTo* relation between concepts, we compute relatedness of concepts using word embedding and network embedding techniques. More specifically, we first build a corpus containing only concepts by extracting sequences of anchor texts (concepts' names) in Wikipedia pages. Then the Skip-gram model (Mikolov et al., 2013) is used to learn embeddings of concepts in the corpus. Besides, we also build a network of concepts by using page links in Wikipedia. The node2vec model (Grover and Leskovec, 2016) is used to learn embeddings of concepts in the network. The relatedness of two concepts are computed as the average of the cosine similarities between their word embeddings and network embeddings. Two kinds of embeddings capture both textual and topological context information of concepts, we believe that combining them leads to more accurate concept relatedness. To avoid computing relatedness of all the concepts pairs, we restrict the candidate concepts of *RelatedTo* relation to those have direct links to each other in Wikipedia. Concept pairs with relatedness no less than a threshold (0.3 in our system) will be linked by *RelatedTo* relation in our concept graph.

4.3 Concept Linking

Concept linking is to identify concepts mentioned in a MOOC lecture, and link them to the target concepts in our concept graph. Concept linking is important to build connections between MOOCs and our concept graph. To achieve this task, our system first gets the transcripts of the lectures via the browser extension, and then use the DBpedia-Spotlight[9] to annotate Wikipedia links in the transcripts. Since the concepts in our concept graph are all from Wikipedia, the annotated Wikipedia links can be easily replaced with concepts in our concept graph.

Although DBpedia-Spotlight can find concepts in the transcripts with high precision, not all the detected concepts are important in the lectures. Presenting all the identified concepts to users will not help them at all. Among all the detected concepts, we need to find the key concepts in the lectures. Therefore, we use a greedy concept selection method to incrementally select concepts having high relatedness to the main subject of the lectures. First, concepts appearing in the lecture title are taken as the initial key concepts; then, the concept having the highest average relatedness to the already selected ones is incrementally added to the set of key concepts. The selection process finishes when the relatedness between the selected concepts and the new one is less than a threshold.

5 Conclusion and Future Work

This paper presents MAssistant, a personal knowledge assistant for MOOC learners. MAssistant provides users with helpful functions to trace the concepts they have learned in MOOCs, and to build their own concept graphs. MAssistant is already in service at https://kg.bnu.edu.

---

⁹https://www.dbpedia-spotlight.org

cn, and the documentation of the system is available at https://massistant.github.io.

In the future work, we will develop more functions for users to interact with MAssistant. For example, MAssistant will allow users to add or delete concepts in their personal concept graph. In addition, we will also study how to use users' annotations on concepts to improve the quality of concept relations in MAssistant system.

References

T. Flati, D. Vannella, T. Pasini, and R. Navigli. Multiwibi: The multilingual wikipedia bitaxonomy project. *Artificial Intelligence*, 241:66 – 102, 2016. ISSN 0004-3702.

A. Grover and J. Leskovec. Node2vec: Scalable feature learning for networks. In *Proceedings of the 22Nd ACM SIGKDD International Conference on Knowledge Discovery and Data Mining*, KDD '16, pages 855–864, 2016. ISBN 978-1-4503-4232-2.

C. Liang, Z. Wu, W. Huang, and C. L. Giles. Measuring prerequisite relations among concepts. In *Proceedings of the 2015 Conference on Empirical Methods in Natural Language Processing*, pages 1668–1674, Sept. 2015.

C. Liang, J. Ye, Z. Wu, B. Pursel, and C. L. Giles. Recovering concept prerequisite relations from university course dependencies. In *Proceedings of the Thirty-First AAAI Conference on Artificial Intelligence*, AAAI'17, pages 4786–4791, 2017.

C. Liang, J. Ye, S. Wang, B. Pursel, and C. L. Giles. Investigating active learning for concept prerequisite learning. In *Thirty-Second AAAI Conference on Artificial Intelligence*, 2018.

T. Mikolov, K. Chen, G. Corrado, and J. Dean. Efficient estimation of word representations in vector space. *arXiv preprint arXiv:1301.3781*, 2013.

D. Milne and I. H. Witten. An effective, low-cost measure of semantic relatedness obtained from wikipedia links. In *Proceedings of the first AAAI Workshop on Wikipedia and Artificial Intelligence*, 2008.

L. Pan, C. Li, J. Li, and J. Tang. Prerequisite relation learning for concepts in MOOCs. In *Proceedings of the 55th Annual Meeting of the Association for Computational Linguistics (Volume 1: Long Papers)*, pages 1447–1456, Vancouver, Canada, July 2017. Association for Computational Linguistics.

S. Wang, A. Ororbia, Z. Wu, K. Williams, C. Liang, B. Pursel, and C. L. Giles. Using prerequisites to extract concept maps fromtextbooks. In *Proceedings of the 25th ACM International on Conference on Information and Knowledge Management*, CIKM '16, pages 317–326, 2016. ISBN 978-1-4503-4073-1.

MedCATTrainer: A Biomedical Free Text Annotation Interface with Active Learning and Research Use Case Specific Customisation

**Thomas Searle[1], Zeljko Kraljevic[1], Rebecca Bendayan[1],
Daniel Bean[1], Richard Dobson[1,2]**
[1]Department of Biostatistics and Health Informatics,
Kings College London, London, U.K.
[2]Institute of Health Informatics, University College London,
222 Euston Road, London NW1 2DA, U.K.
{firstname.lastname}@kcl.ac.uk

Abstract

We present MedCATTrainer[1] an interface
for building, improving and customising a
given Named Entity Recognition and Linking
(NER+L) model for biomedical domain text.
NER+L is often used as a first step in deriving
value from clinical text. Collecting labelled
data for training models is difficult due to the
need for specialist domain knowledge. Med-
CATTrainer offers an interactive web-interface
to inspect and improve recognised entities
from an underlying NER+L model via active
learning. Secondary use of data for clinical research often has task and context specific criteria. MedCATTrainer provides a further interface to define and collect supervised learning
training data for researcher specific use cases.
Initial results suggest our approach allows for
efficient and accurate collection of research
use case specific training data.

1 Introduction

We present a flexible web-based open-source
use-case configurable interface and workflow for
biomedical text concept annotation - MedCAT-
Trainer[2].

Murdoch and Detsky (2013) estimates that 80%
of biomedical data is stored in unstructured text
such as Electronic health records (EHRs). Although EHRs have seen widespread global adoption, effective secondary use of the data remains
difficult (Elkin et al., 2010). However, significant progress has been made on agreement
and usage of standardised terminologies such
as the Systematized Nomenclature of Medical
Clinical Terms (SNOMED-CT) (Stearns et al.,
2001) and the Unified Medical Language System
(UMLS)(Bodenreider, 2004). Annotating EHR
text with these concept databases is often seen as

a first step in delivering data driven applications
such as precision medicine, clinical decision support or real time disease surveillance (Assale et al.,
2019).

EHR text annotation is challenging due to the
use of domain specific terms, abbreviations, misspellings and terseness. Text can also be 'copy-
pasted' from prior notes, structured tables entered
into unstructured form, content with varying temporality and scanned images of physical documents (Botsis et al., 2010). Annotation is further
complicated as researchers have task and context
specific parameters. For example, whether family history or suspected diagnoses are considered
relevant to the task.

MedCAT[3], manuscript in preparation (Zeljko
and Lucasz, 2019), is a **Med**ical **C**oncept
Annotation **T**ool that uses unsupervised machine
learning to recognise and link medical concepts
with clinical terminologies such as UMLS. Med-
CAT, like similar tools, uses a concept database to
find and link concept mentions inside of biomedical documents. In addition it has disambiguation,
spell-checking and the option for supervised learning for improved disambiguation.

We introduce a novel web based application that
supplements usage of a biomedical NER+L models, such as MedCAT. Our contributions are as follows:

1. **Concept Inspection and Addition:** an interface that to inspect the identified concepts
   from free text, and add missing concepts to an
   existing NER+L model. This interface aligns
   with MedCAT, but could also be used with
   other models that have similar capabilities.

2. **Active Learning:** an interface for active
   learning, enabling users to provide minimal

---

[1]https://www.youtube.com/watch?v=IM914DQjvSo
[2]https://github.com/CogStack/MedCATtrainer

[3]https://github.com/CogStack/MedCAT

139

Proceedings of the 2019 EMNLP and the 9th IJCNLP (System Demonstrations), pages 139–144
Hong Kong, China, November 3 – 7, 2019. ©2019 Association for Computational Linguistics

training data to assist in improving and correcting the NER+L. This interface requires that the backing NER+L system supports active learning.

3. **Clinical Research Question Specific Annotation:** a further interface for configurable use case specific annotation of identified concepts. Allowing for the collection of research question specific training data. For example, annotating specific temporal features of a concept.

2   Related Work

Outside of the biomedical domain general purpose annotation interfaces have been developed for most popular NLP tasks such as NER, NEL, relation extraction, entity normalisation, dependency parsing, chunking etc. Popular choices include open-source tools such as BRAT (Stenetorp et al., 2012) that also allows for managing the distribution, monitoring and collection of annotated corpora. General purpose tools with active learning include the commercial product Prodigy[4]. Although these tools are mature and offer advanced features they can be complex to setup and do not offer integration with existing biomedical domain NER+L systems.

Prior work on biomedical NER+L includes MetaMAP (Aronson, 2001) and CTakes (Savova et al., 2010). Both have provided interfaces to inspect recognised entities but they have not provided means to correct and amend concepts or specify further annotations for specific research questions.

Another tool for biomedical NER+L, SemEHR Wu et al. (2018), offers features to add custom pre and post processing steps and research specific use cases, but does not directly improve the NER+L model via an interface. Instead it treats the provided NER+L model as a black-box model.

3   MedCATTrainer

MedCATTrainer is a web-based interface for inspecting, adding and correcting biomedical NER+L models through active learning. An additional interface allows for research specific annotations to be defined and collected for training of supervised learning models.

The interfaces are built with Vue.js[5] for the front-end and the python[6] web framework Django[7] for the web API and integration with NER+L models such as MedCAT. We use the Django admin features to allow administrators to configure research question specific supervised learning tasks.

MedCATTrainer is deployed via a Docker[8] container. This ensures users can build, deploy and run MedCATTrainer cross-platform without lengthy build and run processes, advanced infrastructure knowledge or root access to systems. This is especially important in health informatics as hospital infrastructure is often restrictive. MedCATTrainer allows researchers to build on top of existing biomedical domain ontologies, such as UMLS, for two use cases. Firstly, improving the underlying NER+L model by adding synonyms, abbreviations, multi-token concepts and misspellings directly from the interface. Secondly, by allowing research use case specific annotations to be defined and collected for training of supervised learning models.

3.1   Concept Inspection and Addition

Figure 1a shows the 'Train Annotations' interface. Users can inspect and correct the concepts identified by the underlying NER+L model. Entities that have not been recognised can also be added to the NER+L model concept database. This allows researchers to test the learnt entity recognition/linking capabilities of the model whilst tailoring it to recognise sub-domain specific lexicon. This can include abbreviations or misspellings common to specific corpora. Figure 1b shows the form entry to add new concepts to the underlying concept database. Semantically equivalent texts can be added under the same Concept Unique Identifier along with synonyms. Advanced NER+L tools (e.g. MedCAT) learn from the contextual embeddings of words to disambiguate future occurrences. MedCATTrainer provides a textbox for entering the surrounding context tokens to assist with concept disambiguation.

3.2   Active Learning

Annotating biomedical domain text for NER+L requires expert knowledge and therefore cannot be

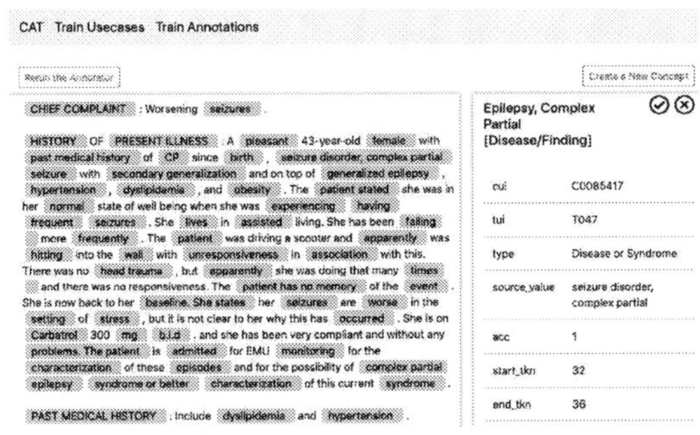

(a) The MedCATTrainer interface for viewing identified concepts by the underlying NER+L model of a publicly available[a] neurological consultation summary showing the concept metadata and active learning feedback input controls.

[a]https://bit.ly/2RLcdJx

(b) Side panel for the addition of new concepts.

Figure 1: The interfaces for inspecting annotations and the addition of concepts.

easily crowd sourced. Active learning is a common approach to provide a minimal set of high value training examples for manual annotation. Examples are valued with respect to expected improvement in classification performance once labelled and the model retrained (Settles, 2009).

We use a simple strategy of certainty based selective sampling (Lewis and Catlett, 1994) to display low confidence examples. Concretely, given a trained model $\mathbf{M}$, and the total set of annotations predicted on a new document d by model $\mathbf{M}$ is $\mathbf{L} = \{l_1, l_2, \ldots l_n\}$ where the model labelled the document with n annotations. An annotation l_i has an associated confidence c_{l_i} probability in the annotation. An annotation manager defines δ, a confidence cutoff score. The set of annotations $\mathbf{A}$ shown to an annotator is therefore $\Phi(\mathbf{L})$ where $\Phi(l_i) = c_{l_i} > \delta$.

Each human annotator is instructed to review each identified concept and provide feedback on correctness. Feedback is provided through the action of clicking the 'tick' for correct or 'cross' for incorrect as shown in the top right of Figure 1a.

If an identified concept is incorrect human annotators are asked to provide feedback, rerun the NER+L model (top left 'Rerun the Annotator'), and then confirm if the misidentified concept has been corrected. More feedback can be provided if needed. Our pilot test users found this quickly resulted in the correctly identified and linked concept as text spans often only have one or two alternative concepts.

3.3 Clinical Research Question Specific Annotation

It would be infeasible to have a clinical terminology to define every possible contextual representation of a concept. For example, disambiguation of 'seizure' for a symptom of epilepsy and 'first seizure clinic' for a clinic that provides epilepsy care or 'history of seizures' for a historical case of epilepsy.

Our second interface solves this problem by allowing clinical researchers to define use case orientated tasks and associated annotations for previously identified and linked concepts. Custom classifiers are then trained and layered over the existing NER+L model for context specific concept disambiguation. An example configured screen for 'Temporality' and 'Phenotyping' tasks for an ongoing clinical research project is shown in Figure 2 - using replacement publicly available data. The top bar lists the overall task name followed by the number of documents to be annotated. The top right corner opens the current task help document, listing annotation guidelines for this use-case.

The left panel itemises each text span, the associated Concept Unique Identifier (CUI) - that the NER+L model has identified and linked with the text, and the current value of each task specific annotation. The value 'n/a' indicates the task has not been completed for that span. Users can choose any order of the text spans to annotate. The currently selected text span is highlighted in the table and within the central text area showing the entirety of the document. Clinical notes can be

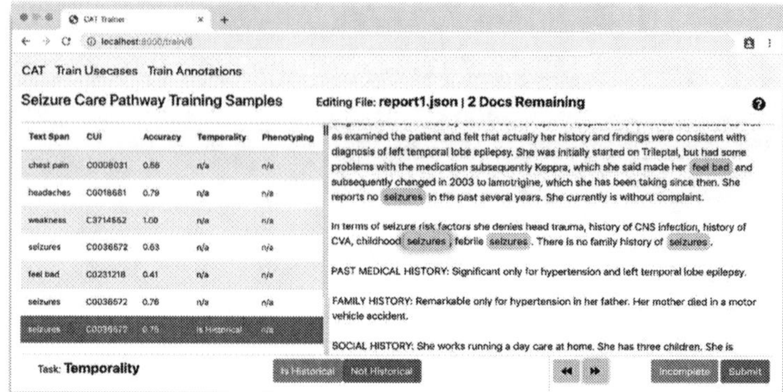

Figure 2: Task and context specific annotation interface configured for 'Temporality' and 'Phenotype' tasks

long in length. Clicking a text span from the sidebar scrolls the central text area to the corresponding span assisting human annotators in locating the span to annotate. The text area also highlights each spans current annotated value for the current task.

The bottom bottom bar lists the current task and the possible annotation values. Figure 2 shows the 'Temporality' task and the associated annotation values 'Is Historical' and 'Not Historical'. The values are in context to a seizure care pathway use case and are defined as any currently experienced mention of seizure symptoms in present clinical encounter. Use cases and associated tasks values are configurable via the admin interface.

The bottom right corner provides navigation between text spans and tasks via the arrow buttons. Navigating between spans highlights the current span to be annotated in the main left sidebar and auto scrolls to the next span in the main text area. The navigation controls here, the sidebar and the main text area allow human annotators to complete the task in any order they are comfortable.

The 'Incomplete' button marks the current document to be revisited at a later date. Samples are marked incomplete if the NER+L model has misidentified the concept or there is a genuine ambiguity. The 'Submit' button marks the document as complete. Both actions store and retrieve the next document if there is one available. If there are no more files to annotate a dialog prompts the user to return to the home screen.

Corpora are currently directly uploaded via a use case management screen. Future deployments will directly ingest documents via an elas-ticsearch[9] connector to hospital EHR deployments of CogStack (Jackson et al., 2018) an EHR ingestion, transformation and search service deployed at King's College Hospital (KCH) and South London and Maudsley(SLaM) NHS Foundation Trusts, UK.

4   Results

We ran an initial small scale pilot experiment to test the suitability of our use case specific tool to quickly and accurately collect training data labelling the temporal features of seizure symptoms. This is similar to the task shown in Figure 2. We used MIMIC3 (Johnson et al., 2016), a de-identified publicly available database of ICU admission data that includes observations, consultation and discharge summary reports. We randomly sampled 127 discharge summaries that contained one or more token occurrences that match the regular expression 'seizure|seizre|seizur|siezure', where | is an OR operator between the text tested to be present. We intentionally rely on a rule-based NER mode (i.e. the regex) here to demonstrate our tools flexibility to use possible alternatives to MedCAT if desired.

We asked 2 human non-clinical annotators to label temporal features of each occurrence in relation to a 'present', i.e. 'chief complaint: seizure' or 'historical', i.e. 'family history of seizures', mention of the term. Both took approximately 35 minutes to review all 127 documents. We achieve an percent agreement of 89% and a Cohen's Kappa $\kappa = 0.695$, Table 1. Both annotators marked some records as incomplete as they either mostly referred to non symptomatic mentions

---

[9]https://www.elastic.co/

	R1*	R2*	R1	R2
# Documents	107	117	100	100
# Concepts	351	344	317	317
# Historical	67	80	79	65
# Not Historical	276	264	238	252

Table 1: Total labelled 'seizure' symptom concepts and for each human annotator (R1, R2) for the 'temporality' task of labelling concepts that have occurred the past relative to the hospital episode. * indicates raw numbers before taking into account the intersection of notes between annotators

of seizure, i.e. 'anti-seizure meds prophylaxis' or the prevention of future seizures. This resulted in each rater having differing total documents 'submitted' as there are some document with mixes of the above occurrences. We took the intersection of submitted documents from both raters to compute the final agreement scores.

Using the collected data we fit a simple Sckit-learn[10] Random Forest (RF) classifier model demonstrating the effectiveness of the data collection in being able to easily fit a well performing model for the task of recognising temporality of seizure symptoms. We took a random 70/30 train test split, took 100 characters either side of the labelled 'seizure' occurrence, tokenized the plain text on whitespace then used a TF-IDF vectoriser with the default English stop-words list. We ran a grid search across TF-IDF and random forest classifier parameters, with a 3 fold cross validation and found the best fitting parameters: TF-IDF features 500 (range:500, 1000, 10000), RF maximum number trees of 100 range(100, 300, 500, 1000) and maximum tree depth 20 (range: 5, 20, 50, 75). We achieve an accuracy of this binary classification task of 92% and f1 score .79.

5 Discussion and Future Work

From our labelling exercise we demonstrate the speed and accuracy of our configurable use case specific interface. Strong scores across % agreement, Cohen's Kappa and trained model accuracy indicate good agreement between annotators, interpretations of the task and reasonable signal captured even with this small data set. Although, it is likely the model is over-fitting due to the size of the data set. Given the prior experiment - across two raters - gathering enough accurate data to, for

example, fine-tune a pretrained language model based classifier would be of the order of hours of manual labelling for approx 2k samples. We see this rapid labelling ability as a key strength of our interface.

We foresee that trained classifiers will likely generalise to additional research questions. For example language used to express temporality of seizures is likely to be similar to temporality of stroke or myocardial infarction.

Generally, training models across use cases will likely capture shared semantics. This suggests particular use cases would require less examples to train as annotated data or the model itself could be reused, therefore jump-starting clinical research. If a model is not performing for a new use case, further data could be collected to fine tune the model to a specific task, context or sub-domain corpora.

Clinically, domain experts in the neurology department of KCH, with varying levels of expertise (medical student to practising consultant) are scheduled to participate in the use case shown in Figure 2 in the coming months.

Our initial testing, not shown above due to space, of the active learning approach for improving the bound NER+L model suggests we can improve performance with minimal training data.

6 Conclusions

We have presented a lightweight, flexible, web-based, open-source annotation interface for biomedical domain text. MedCATTrainer is integrated with a biomedical NER+L model and allows for addition of missing concepts, improvements to the underlying NER+L model through active learning, and a configurable interface for clinical researchers to define annotations specific for their research questions. Preliminary results show promise for our interface and our approach to biomedical NER+L, which is often seen as a first step in deriving value from data sources such as electronic health records.

Acknowledgments

DMB is funded by a UKRI Innovation Fellowship as part of Health Data Research UK (MR/S00310X/1). RB is funded in part by grant MR/R016372/1 for the Kings College London MRC Skills Development Fellowship programme funded by the UK Medical Research Council

---

[10]https://scikit-learn.org/stable/index.html

(MRC) and by grant IS-BRC-1215-20018 for the National Institute for Health Research (NIHR) Biomedical Research Centre at South London and Maudsley NHS Foundation Trust and Kings College London. RD's work is supported by 1.National Institute for Health Research (NIHR) Biomedical Research Centre at South London and Maudsley NHS Foundation Trust and Kings College London. 2. Health Data Research UK, which is funded by the UK Medical Research Council, Engineering and Physical Sciences Research Council, Economic and Social Research Council, Department of Health and Social Care (England), Chief Scientist Office of the Scottish Government Health and Social Care Directorates, Health and Social Care Research and Development Division (Welsh Government), Public Health Agency (Northern Ireland), British Heart Foundation and Wellcome Trust. 3. The National Institute for Health Research University College London Hospitals Biomedical Research Centre. This paper represents independent research part funded by the National Institute for Health Research (NIHR) Biomedical Research Centre at South London and Maudsley NHS Foundation Trust and Kings College London. The views expressed are those of the author(s) and not necessarily those of the NHS, MRC, NIHR or the Department of Health and Social Care.

References

A R Aronson. 2001. Effective mapping of biomedical text to the UMLS metathesaurus: the MetaMap program. *Proc. AMIA Symp.*, pages 17–21.

Michela Assale, Linda Greta Dui, Andrea Cina, Andrea Seveso, and Federico Cabitza. 2019. The revival of the notes field: Leveraging the unstructured content in electronic health records. *Front. Med.*, 6:66.

Olivier Bodenreider. 2004. The unified medical language system (UMLS): integrating biomedical terminology. *Nucleic Acids Res.*, 32(Database issue):D267–70.

Taxiarchis Botsis, Gunnar Hartvigsen, Fei Chen, and Chunhua Weng. 2010. Secondary use of EHR: Data quality issues and informatics opportunities. *Summit Transl Bioinform*, 2010:1–5.

Peter L Elkin, Brett E Trusko, Ross Koppel, Ted Speroff, Daniel Mohrer, Saoussen Sakji, Inna Gurewitz, Mark Tuttle, and Steven H Brown. 2010. Secondary use of clinical data. *Stud. Health Technol. Inform.*, 155:14–29.

Richard Jackson, Ismail Kartoglu, Clive Stringer, Genevieve Gorrell, Angus Roberts, Xingyi Song, Honghan Wu, Asha Agrawal, Kenneth Lui, Tudor Groza, Damian Lewsley, Doug Northwood, Amos Folarin, Robert Stewart, and Richard Dobson. 2018. CogStack - experiences of deploying integrated information retrieval and extraction services in a large national health service foundation trust hospital. *BMC Med. Inform. Decis. Mak.*, 18(1):47.

Alistair E W Johnson, Tom J Pollard, Lu Shen, Li-Wei H Lehman, Mengling Feng, Mohammad Ghassemi, Benjamin Moody, Peter Szolovits, Leo Anthony Celi, and Roger G Mark. 2016. MIMIC-III, a freely accessible critical care database. *Sci Data*, 3:160035.

David D Lewis and Jason Catlett. 1994. Heterogeneous uncertainty sampling for supervised learning. In William W Cohen and Haym Hirsh, editors, *Machine Learning Proceedings 1994*, pages 148–156. Morgan Kaufmann, San Francisco (CA).

Travis B Murdoch and Allan S Detsky. 2013. The inevitable application of big data to health care. *JAMA*, 309(13):1351–1352.

Guergana K Savova, James J Masanz, Philip V Ogren, Jiaping Zheng, Sunghwan Sohn, Karin C Kipper-Schuler, and Christopher G Chute. 2010. Mayo clinical text analysis and knowledge extraction system (cTAKES): architecture, component evaluation and applications. *J. Am. Med. Inform. Assoc.*, 17(5):507–513.

Burr Settles. 2009. Active learning literature survey. Technical report, University of Wisconsin-Madison Department of Computer Sciences.

M Q Stearns, C Price, K A Spackman, and A Y Wang. 2001. SNOMED clinical terms: overview of the development process and project status. *Proc. AMIA Symp.*, pages 662–666.

Pontus Stenetorp, Sampo Pyysalo, Goran Topić, Tomoko Ohta, Sophia Ananiadou, and Jun'ichi Tsujii. 2012. BRAT: A web-based tool for NLP-assisted text annotation. In *Proceedings of the Demonstrations at the 13th Conference of the European Chapter of the Association for Computational Linguistics*, EACL '12, pages 102–107, Stroudsburg, PA, USA. Association for Computational Linguistics.

Honghan Wu, Giulia Toti, Katherine I Morley, Zina M Ibrahim, Amos Folarin, Richard Jackson, Ismail Kartoglu, Asha Agrawal, Clive Stringer, Darren Gale, Genevieve Gorrell, Angus Roberts, Matthew Broadbent, Robert Stewart, and Richard J B Dobson. 2018. SemEHR: A general-purpose semantic search system to surface semantic data from clinical notes for tailored care, trial recruitment, and clinical research. *J. Am. Med. Inform. Assoc.*, 25(5):530–537.

Kraljevic Zeljko and Roguski Lucasz. 2019. Cogstack/medcat: First release of medcat.

Memory Grounded Conversational Reasoning

Seungwhan Moon, Pararth Shah, Anuj Kumar, Rajen Subba
Facebook Assistant
`{shanemoon, pararths, anujk, rasubba@}fb.com`

Abstract

We demonstrate a conversational system which engages the user through a multi-modal, multi-turn dialog over the user's memories. The system can perform QA over memories by responding to user queries to recall specific attributes and associated media (*e.g.* photos) of past episodic memories. The system can also make proactive suggestions to surface related events or facts from past memories to make conversations more engaging and natural. To implement such a system, we collect a new corpus of memory grounded conversations, which comprises human-to-human role-playing dialogs given synthetic memory graphs with simulated attributes. Our proof-of-concept system operates on these synthetic memory graphs, however it can be trained and applied to real-world user memory data (*e.g.* photo albums, etc.) We present the architecture of the proposed conversational system, and example queries that the system supports.

1 Introduction

In the last few decades, people have been storing an increasing amount of their life's memories in the form of digital multimedia, *e.g.* photos, videos and textual posts. Retrieving one's memories from these memory banks and reminiscing about events from one's personal and professional life is a prevalent desire among many users. Traditionally, the interfaces to access these memories are either (i) keyword based search systems which demand specific keyword combinations to identify and retrieve the correct memories, or (ii) catalog based browsing systems that allow scrolling through memories across a single dimension, most commonly, time of creation. However, we posit that a more natural way of interacting with one's memories is through a flexible interface that can support fuzzy queries by referencing memories through various attributes, such as events, people,

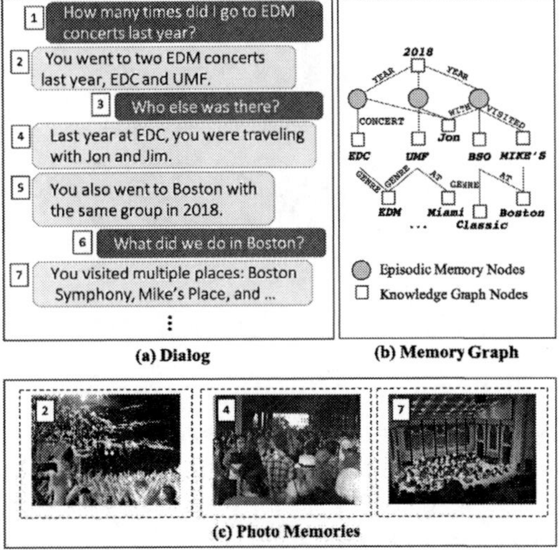

Figure 1: **Memory Grounded Conversational Reasoning** between a user and the assistant with a parallel (a) dialog and (b) memory graph pair. Dialog transitions can be captured as walks over a memory graph. (c) Some of the memories can be inferred from photos or other media, which are surfaced to the user when they are available and relevant.

locations or activities associated with them, and that can enable the user to explore other relevant memories connected through one of many dimensions, *e.g.* same group of people, same location, etc., thereby not being restricted to browsing only temporally adjacent memories.

We present a conversational system that provides a natural interface for retrieving and browsing through one's memories. The system supports conversational QA capability for open-ended querying of memories, and also supports the ability to proactively surface related memories that the user would naturally be interested in consuming. An important element of such an open-ended dialog system is its ability to ground conversations with past memories of users, making the interactions more personal and engaging.

145

Proceedings of the 2019 EMNLP and the 9th IJCNLP (System Demonstrations), pages 145–150
Hong Kong, China, November 3 – 7, 2019. ©2019 Association for Computational Linguistics

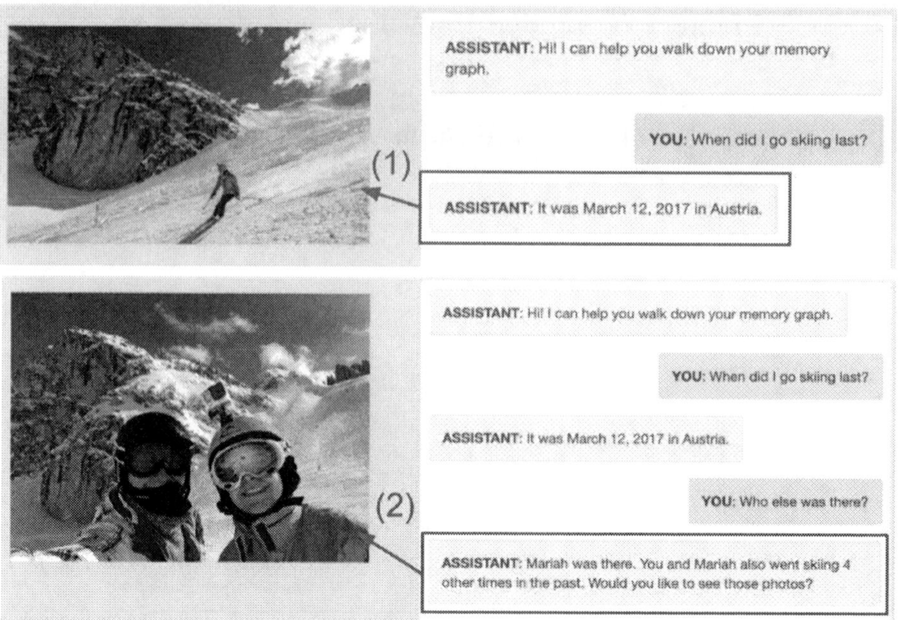

Figure 2: **Memory Walker Chatbot UI** for memory grounded conversations between a user and the assistant.

Figure 1 shows an example interaction supported by the demonstrated system, spanning multiple episodic memories that are represented as a graph composed of memory nodes and related entity nodes connected via relational edges. The example above shows three key novel features of the demonstrated system: 1) the ability of querying a personal database to answer various complex user queries (memory recall QA), 2) surfacing photos most relevant to the dialog, and 3) identifying other memories to surface that are relevant to conversational contexts, resulting in increased engagement and coherent interactions.

Our system consists of several components: First, we use the Memory Graph Networks (MGN) model, which learns natural graph paths among episodic memory nodes, conditioned over dialog contexts. MGN can introduce new memory nodes relevant to conversational contexts when memory nodes are activated as a result of graph walks. Second, the QA module takes as input user query utterances and infers correct answers given candidate memory graph nodes activated with the MGN model. Specifically, we utilize multiple sub-module nets such as CHOOSE, COUNT, etc., to support discrete reasoning questions that cannot be handled directly via graph networks. Finally, the photo recommender module then uses the MGN graph node embeddings and the generated attention scores to retrieve the most relevant photos for each dialog response.

Section 2 provides a detailed description of the system's user interface, method and data collection setup. Section 3 provides an analysis of demonstrations performed via the system, and Section 4 lists related work.

2 Memory Grounded Conversations

2.1 User Interface

The goal of the demonstrated system is to establish a natural user interface (UI) for interacting with memories. Figure 2 shows the UI of the demonstrated system, composed of two main sections: the media section (left) and the chat section (right; highlighted yellow: assistant, blue: user). This is a simple yet powerful interface for interacting with memories, for the following reasons:

Flexible. The UI enables natural language QA queries through text or voice input. This UI can be deployed in a desktop, web or mobile application, or on a connected home device like smart TVs. For each user memory recall query, the system provides a corresponding answer from the memory graph. In Figure 2 part 1, the user retrieves a memory related to an activity (skiing) through a textual question.

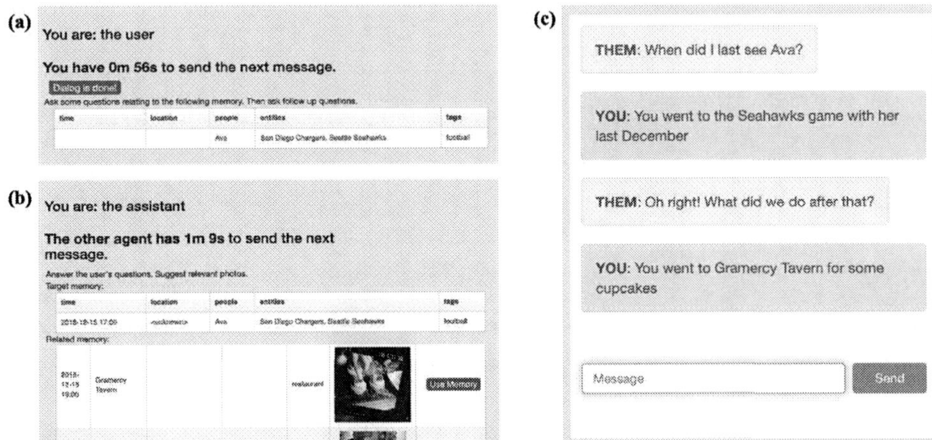

Figure 3: *Memory Dialog* **Dataset Collection Interface**, with an example. (**a**) User-playing agent is provided with partial memory information to query about. (**b**) Assistant-playing agent has the ground-truth information about the target memory as well as all related memories. (**c**) The two agents generate dialogs, grounded on the synthetic memories that they are presented with.

Visual. The UI can display visual content connected to the memories, and allow for further queries into the content of the image or video. Authors' personal photos are used in the demonstration, attached with synthetically generated memory graphs.

Contextual. The system keeps track of the conversational context within a user session, allowing the user to refer to entities present in the dialog or media. In Figure 2 part 2, the user refers to the event mentioned in the previous system response and asks a further question regarding who attended the event.

Proactive. The system can insert conversational recommendations for exploring related memories based on the system's model of which memories are naturally interesting for users to consume in a particular context. In Figure 2 part 2, the system suggests to the user other memory instances that share the same activity and set of people. The system can make the suggestions more personalized by learning the sequences in which users like to explore memories, from the user's past sessions.

2.2 Dataset: *Memory Dialog*

Synthetic Memory Graph: For the proposed system, we first bootstrap the large-scale memory collection through a synthetic memory graph generator, which creates multiple artificial episodic memory graph nodes with connections to real entities appearing on common-fact KGs (*e.g.* loca-

tions, events, public entities). We first build a synthetic social graph of users, where each user is assigned to a random interest profile as a probability distribution over the 'activity' space. We then iteratively generate a memory node and its associated attributes and entities by sampling activities, participants, locations, entities, time, *etc.* each from a manually defined ontology. Through the realistic memory graph that is synthetically generated, we avoid the need for extracting memory graphs from other structured sources (*e.g.* photo albums) which are often private or limited in size. Note also that by representing the memory database in a graph format, it allows for flexible operations required for complex QA and conversational reasoning.

Wizard-of-Oz Setup: We collect the *Memory Dialog* dataset in a Wizard-of-Oz setting (Shah et al., 2018) by connecting two crowd-workers to engage in a role-playing chat session either as a user or an assistant, with the joint goal of creating natural and engaging dialogs (Figure 3). The user-playing agent is given a memory node from the synthetic memory graph with some of the attributes hidden, and asked to initiate a conversation about those missing attributes to simulate a memory recall query. The assistant-playing agent is provided with a set of memories and photos relevant to user's questions, and is instructed to use one or more of these memories to answer the question and frame a free-form conversational response. In addition, the assistant agent is encouraged to proactively bring up any other memo-

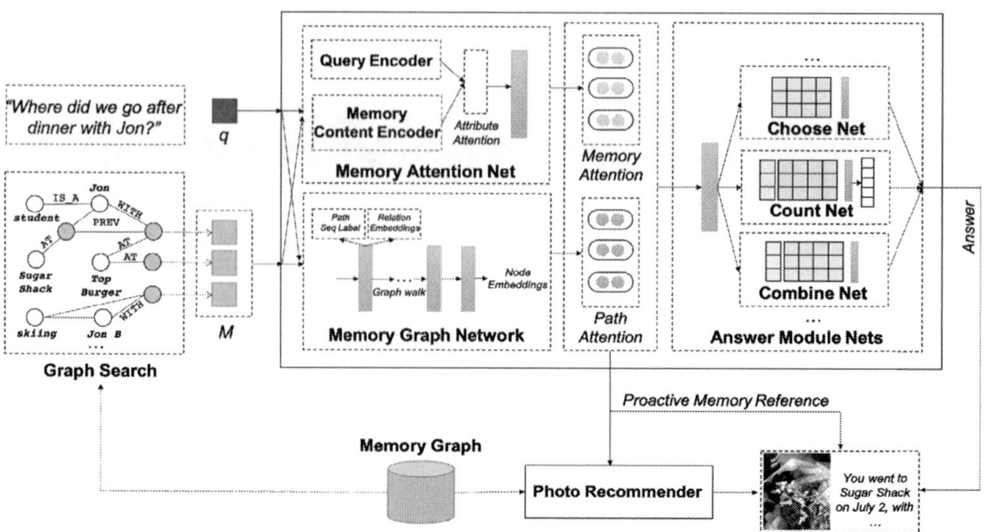

Figure 4: **Overall architecture** of the demonstrated system. Candidate memory nodes $\mathbf{m} = \{\mathbf{m}^{(k)}\}$ are provided as input memory slots for each query $\mathbf{q}$. The Memory Graph Network then traverses the memory graph to expand the initial memory slots and activate other relevant entity and memory nodes. The output paths of MGN are then used to trigger proactive memory reference, if relevant. The Answer Module executes the predicted neural programs to decode answers given intermediate network outputs. The photo recommender is then called to retrieve relevant photos (*e.g.* photos of the reference memory that includes the answer to a query).

ries relevant to conversational contexts that would make the interaction more engaging and interesting (*e.g.* memories with the same group of people, at the same location as the reference memory, etc.). The two agents continue this process to explore the given memory graph, until one of the agents decides to end the conversation.

2.3 Method

Figure 4 illustrates the overall architecture and the model components of the demonstrated system.

Input Module: For a given query $\mathbf{q}$, its relevant memory nodes $\mathbf{m} = \{\mathbf{m}^{(k)}\}_{k=1}^{K}$ for slot size K are provided as initial memory slots via graph searches. The Query Encoder then encodes the input query with a language model. Specifically, we represent each textual query with a state-of-the-art attention-based Bi-LSTM language model (Conneau et al., 2017). The Memory Encoder then encodes each memory slot based on both its structural features (graph embeddings) and contextual multi-modal features from its neighboring nodes (*e.g.* attribute values). We construct memory graph embeddings to encode structural contexts of each memory node via the graph embeddings projection approaches (Bordes et al., 2013), in which semantically similar nodes are distributed closer in the embeddings space.

Memory Graph Networks: To utilize encoded candidate memory nodes for memory recall QA and proactive memory reference, we first utilize the Memory Graph Networks (MGN) (Moon et al., 2019b). MGN stores memory graph nodes as initial memory slots, where additional contexts and answer candidates can be succinctly expanded and reached via graph traversals. For each $(\mathbf{q}, \mathbf{m}^{(k)})$ pair, MGN predicts optimal memory slot expansion steps: $\mathbf{p}^{(k)} = \{[\mathbf{p}_{e,t}^{(k)}; \mathbf{p}_{n,t}^{(k)}]\}_{t=1}^{T}$ for edge paths $\mathbf{p}_e$ and corresponding node paths $\mathbf{p}_n$. The LSTM-based sequence model is trained to learn the optimal path with ground-truth node and relation paths. The attended memory nodes are then used to answer user memory recall queries (QA module), and to predict relevant memory nodes to surface as a response to the previous conversational contexts (Recommender Module).

QA Modules: An estimated answer $\hat{\mathbf{a}} = \text{QA}(\mathbf{m}, \mathbf{q})$ is predicted given a query and MGN graph path output from initial memory slots.

We then define the memory attention to attenuate or amplify all activated memory nodes based on their compatibility with query, formulated as follows:

$$\beta = \text{MLP}(\mathbf{q}, \{\mathbf{m}^{(k)}\}, \{\mathbf{p}^{(k)}\}) \quad (1)$$

$$\alpha = \text{Softmax}(\mathbf{W}_{\beta}^{\top}\beta) \in \mathbb{R}^{K} \quad (2)$$

Question and Answer	Model Preidction	
	Top-k Answers	Other Relevant Memory Nodes
Q: *Where did Emma and I go after we watched the new Star Wars movie? // **A**: Neptune Oyster*	Neptune Oyster AMC Theatre	{Star Wars IV, John, Mar 2014, ...} {Emma, hiking, July 2017, ...}
Q: *When did I last go skiing with Emily?* **A**: *Feb 2017*	Feb 2017 Jan 2016	{skiing, Emily, Dec 2016, ...} {Emily, soccer, ...}
Q: *Show me the photos of when I went to the Dodgers game with Mia this year. // **A**: [photo 1]*	[photo 1] [photo 2]	{baseball, Mia, Dodgers, May 2016, ...} {Mia, movie, April 2018, ...}

Table 1: **Example output**: Model predictions the top-k answers and the attended memory nodes are partially shown for each question and ground-truth answer pair.

Next, the model outputs a module program $\{\mathbf{u}^{(k)}\}$ for several sub-module networks (*e.g.* CHOOSE, COUNT, ...) via the multi-layer perception module selector network, which outputs the module label probability $\{\mathbf{u}^{(k)}\}$ for each memory node:

$$\{\mathbf{u}^{(k)}\} = \mathrm{Softmax}(\mathrm{MLP}(\mathbf{q}, \{\mathbf{m}^{(k)}\})) \quad (3)$$

Each module network produces an answer vector, the aggregated result of which determines the top-k answers to be returned.

Photo Memory Recommender: The memory attention values (α) and the path outputs are then used to proactively recommend relevant photos associated with each activated memory node $\mathbf{m}^{(k)}$:

$$\{\mathbf{i}^{(k)}\} = \mathrm{Softmax}(\mathrm{MLP}(\alpha^{(k)}, \mathbf{p}^{(k)}))\forall k \quad (4)$$

where the output score is used to rank the candidate photos. Photos with the top score (above threshold) are then finally surfaced along with their memory nodes. We leave this threshold as a tunable hyper-parameter that can determine the proactive behavior of the system in introducing other relevant memories given previous conversational contexts.

3 Demonstration

Table 1 shows some of the example output from the demonstrated system given the input query and memory graph nodes. It can be seen that the model is able to predict answers by combining answer contexts from multiple components (walk path, node attention, neural modules, etc.) In general, the model successfully explores the respective single-hop or multi-hop relations within the memory graph. The activated nodes via graph traversals are then used as input for each neural module, the aggregated results of which are the final top-k answer predictions. The model also attends on other relevant memory nodes which often

have some of the key attributes shared with the target reference memory (*e.g.* same activity, people, location, etc.). At test time, we can proactively present these relevant memories to users along with their associated media contents for more engaging memory-grounded conversations.

4 Related Work

End-to-end dialog systems: There have been a number of studies on end-to-end dialog systems, often focused on task or goal oriented dialog systems such as conversational recommendations (Bordes et al., 2017; Sun and Zhang, 2018), information querying (Williams et al., 2017; de Vries et al., 2018; Reddy et al., 2018), etc. Many of the public datasets are collected via bootstrapped simulations (Bordes et al., 2017), Wizard-of-Oz setup (Zhang et al., 2018; Wei et al., 2018; Moon et al., 2019a), or online corpus (Li et al., 2016). In our work, we propose a unique setup for dialog systems called memory-grounded conversations, where the focus is on grounding human conversations with past user memories for both the goal-oriented task (memory recall QA) and the more open-ended dialogs (proactive memory reference). Our *Memory Dialog* dataset uses the popular Wizard-of-Oz setup between role-playing human annotators, where the reference memories are bootstrapped through memory graph generator.

QA Systems: Structured QA systems have been very popular due to the popularity of the fact-retrieval assistant products, which solve fact-retrieval QA queries with large-scale common fact knowledge graphs (Bordes et al., 2015; Xu et al., 2016; Dubey et al., 2018). Most of the work typically utilize an entity linking system and a QA model for predicting graph operations *e.g.* through template matching approaches, etc. For QA systems with unstructured knowledge sources (*e.g.* machine reading comprehension), the approaches that utilize Memory Networks with explicit memory slots (Weston et al., 2014; Sukhbaatar et al., 2016) are widely used for their capability of transitive reasoning. In our work, we utilize Memory Graph Networks (MGN) (Moon et al., 2019b) to store graph nodes as memory slots and expand slots via graph traversals, to effectively handle complex memory recall queries and to identify relevant memories to surface next.

Visual QA systems answer queries based on the contexts from provided images (Antol et al., 2015; Wang et al., 2018; Wu et al., 2018). Jiang et al. (2018) propose the visual memex QA task which addresses similar domains given a dataset composed of multiple photo albums. We extend the problem domain to the conversational settings where the focus is the increased engagement with users through natural multi-modal interactions. Our work also extends the QA capability by utilizing semantic and structural contexts from memory and knowledge graphs, instead of relying solely on meta information and multi-modal content available in photo albums.

References

Stanislaw Antol, Aishwarya Agrawal, Jiasen Lu, Margaret Mitchell, Dhruv Batra, C. Lawrence Zitnick, and Devi Parikh. 2015. VQA: Visual Question Answering. In *ICCV*.

Antoine Bordes, Y-Lan Boureau, and Jason Weston. 2017. Learning end-to-end goal-oriented dialog. *ICLR*.

Antoine Bordes, Nicolas Usunier, Sumit Chopra, and Jason Weston. 2015. Large-scale simple question answering with memory network. *arxiv*.

Antoine Bordes, Nicolas Usunier, Alberto Garcia-Duran, Jason Weston, and Oksana Yakhnenko. 2013. Translating embeddings for modeling multi-relational data. In *NIPS*.

Alexis Conneau, Douwe Kiela, Holger Schwenk, Loïc Barrault, and Antoine Bordes. 2017. Supervised learning of universal sentence representations from natural language inference data. In *EMNLP*.

Mohnish Dubey, Debayan Banerjee, Debanjan Chaudhuri, and Jens Lehmann. 2018. Earl: Joint entity and relation linking for question answering over knowledge graphs. *ESWC*.

Lu Jiang, Junwei Liang, Liangliang Cao, Yannis Kalantidis, Sachin Farfade, and Alexander Hauptmann. 2018. Memexqa: Visual memex question answering. *arxiv*.

Jiwei Li, Michel Galley, Chris Brockett, Georgios P Spithourakis, Jianfeng Gao, and Bill Dolan. 2016. A persona-based neural conversation model. *ACL*.

Seungwhan Moon, Pararth Shah, Anuj Kumar, and Rajen Subba. 2019a. Opendialkg: Explainable conversational reasoning with attention-based walks over knowledge graphs. *ACL*.

Seungwhan Moon, Pararth Shah, Anuj Kumar, and Rajen Subba. 2019b. Walk the memory: Memory graph networks for explainable memory-grounded question answering. *CoNLL*.

Siva Reddy, Danqi Chen, and Christopher D Manning. 2018. Coqa: A conversational question answering challenge. *arXiv preprint arXiv:1808.07042*.

Pararth Shah, Dilek Hakkani-Tur, Bing Liu, and Gokhan Tur. 2018. Bootstrapping a neural conversational agent with dialogue self-play, crowdsourcing and on-line reinforcement learning. In *NAACL*.

Sainbayar Sukhbaatar, Arthur Szlam, Jason Weston, and Rob Fergus. 2016. End-to-end memory networks. *NIPS*.

Yueming Sun and Yi Zhang. 2018. Conversational recommender system. *SIGIR*.

Harm de Vries, Kurt Shuster, Dhruv Batra, Devi Parikh, Jason Weston, and Douwe Kiela. 2018. Talk the walk: Navigating new york city through grounded dialogue. *ECCV*.

Peng Wang, Qi Wu, Chunhua Shen, Anthony Dick, and Anton van den Hengel. 2018. Fvqa: Fact-based visual question answering. *PAMI*.

Wei Wei, Quoc Le, Andrew Dai, and Jia Li. 2018. Airdialogue: An environment for goal-oriented dialogue research. In *EMNLP*.

Jason Weston, Sumit Chopra, and Antoine Bordes. 2014. Memory networks. *arXiv preprint arXiv:1410.3916*.

Jason D Williams, Kavosh Asadi, and Geoffrey Zweig. 2017. Hybrid code networks: practical and efficient end-to-end dialog control with supervised and reinforcement learning. *ACL*.

Qi Wu, Chunhua Shen, Peng Wang, Anthony Dick, and Anton van den Hengel. 2018. Image captioning and visual question answering based on attributes and external knowledge. *PAMI*.

Kun Xu, Siva Reddy, Yansong Feng, Songfang Huang, and Dongyan Zhao. 2016. Question answering on freebase via relation extraction and textual evidence. *ACL*.

Saizheng Zhang, Emily Dinan, Jack Urbanek, Arthur Szlam, Douwe Kiela, and Jason Weston. 2018. Personalizing dialogue agents: I have a dog, do you have pets too? *ACL*.

Multilingual, Multi-scale and Multi-layer Visualization of Sequence-based Intermediate Representations

Carlos Escolano[*◇], **Marta R. Costa-jussà**[*◇], **Elora Lacroux**[◇] **and Pere-Pau Vázquez**[*◇]
* TALP Research Center, ◇Universitat Politècnica de Catalunya, Barcelona
* ViRVIG Group
{carlos.escolano,marta.ruiz}@upc.edu
lacrouxelora@gmail.com,pere.pau@cs.upc.edu

Abstract

The main alternatives nowadays to deal with sequences are Recurrent Neural Networks (RNN), Convolutional Neural Networks (CNN) architectures and the Transformer. In this context, RNN's, CNN's and Transformer have most commonly been used as an encoder-decoder architecture with multiple layers in each module. Far beyond this, these architectures are the basis for the contextual word embeddings which are revolutionizing most natural language downstream applications.

However, intermediate layer representations in sequence-based architectures can be difficult to interpret. To make each layer representation within these architectures more accessible and meaningful, we introduce a web-based tool that visualizes them both at the sentence and token level. We present three use cases. The first analyses gender issues in contextual word embeddings. The second and third are showing multilingual intermediate representations for sentences and tokens and the evolution of these intermediate representations along the multiple layers of the decoder and in the context of multilingual machine translation.

1 Introduction

The Transformer (Vaswani et al., 2017) is a powerful architecture that was initially proposed to train neural machine translation. This architecture deals with variable sequences by concatenating feed-forward networks and attention-based mechanisms. While the composed modules of the Transformer may not be complex by themselves, it is the composition of several layers of these modules that make the architecture less interpretable.

We are aiming at providing a tool to give insights to the sentences and token representation from each layer in the Transformer. Far beyond the Transfomer interpretation which has become by de-facto the state-of-the-art in machine translation, our tool is able to represent intermediate representations of other sequence-based architectures such as RNNs (Bahdanau et al., 2014) or ConvS2S (Gehring et al., 2017) as well. Note that sequence-based architectures are having impact in many multimodal applications such as image captioning and speech recognition (Kaiser et al., 2017; Chan et al., 2016).

The uses of our visualization tool are quite a few varying from social bias, multilingual or linguistic analysis. In particular, we focus in analysing the gender inequalities in contextual word embeddings and the common language representation in a multilingual machine translation system.

2 Visualization tool

In this section we present a multi-scale and multi-layer visualization tool for the sequence-based architectures, available as tool[1] and as a demo[2]. The tool is implemented in Python using the Bokeh library for data visualization and the Flask library as web microfamework to embed the Bokeh dashboards on the webpage.

The tool consists in using as input fixed-representations, being a matrix of dimensions the embedding size per sentence length (in tokens). Therefore, the input data required are the sentences to be represented (*txt*), the sentence representations (*json*) and optionally the tokens embeddings (*json*). Then, a UMAP (McInnes et al., 2018) dimensionality reduction is performed to plot the representation of this multidimensional data in two dimensions. This dimensionality reduction is performed for the fixed-representations at the sentence and token level. The tool comprises two views: multi-scale intermediate repre-

---

[1]https://github.com/elorala/interlingua-visualization
[2]https://upc-nmt-vis.herokuapp.com/

151

Proceedings of the 2019 EMNLP and the 9th IJCNLP (System Demonstrations), pages 151–156
Hong Kong, China, November 3 – 7, 2019. ©2019 Association for Computational Linguistics

sentation for one layer and multi-layer sentence representation. These three views can be either monolingual or multilingual. The main page of the tool comprises these three views for the user to choose.

We describe these three views on different use cases. For the first view, we show the use cases of detection of gender bias in contextual word embeddings and common representation in multilingual machine translation. For the second view, the use case builds on layer interpretation of multi-way parallel sentences in a translation decoder and showing which layer carries out higher semantic meaning.

2.1 Multi-scale Intermediate representation

This visualization consists of two coordinated views, that encode different information through scatterplots. The one on the left shows the M sentence intermediate representations. Each dot in the sentence graph corresponds to one sentence, by hovering on a point we visualize the sentence as well as the arrows to the corresponding translation sentences, in case we are working with multilingual data. There is an option to visualize a particular sentence by writing it in the search bar. The search bar has an autocomplete feature (activated when typing two characters) and then, the user can click on the right suggestion.

The right view shows the tokens. Initially, when no sentence from the previous view is selected, this plot shows all vocabulary tokens. By brushing over one or more sentences (in left view), the right view filters out the tokens *not belonging* to the selected sentence (and the tokens that compose the parallel sentences in the other languages). Once the user selects a sentence by clicking or searching, only the words from this sentence (and its translations) remain on the chart. By hovering on a point, the user can see the text of the word, analogously to the sentences view.

Sentences and tokens can be simultaneously visualized for all languages that we are studying and we can interpret the intermediate representation in terms of both granularity levels. See Figures 4 and 5 which are as well examples of the second use case (explained as follows).

Use case 1: Gender bias in Contextual Word Embeddings. The objective of this use case is to visualize the contextual word representations on a set of occupational vocabulary. We use the ELMO implementation (Peters et al., 2018), based on RNNs and as data, we use 1019 sentences from previous work (Font and Costa-jussà, 2019) that follow the next template *I've known him/her for a long time, my friend works as a occupation.* Examples of occupations include: *accounting clerk, nurse midwife or biological scientist.* Since we have two sets: one for female templates and another for male templates, we use the two sets as if they were different languages. We visualize 2-dimensional representations of sentences and words. For sentences (see Figure 1), we see that sentences with similar professions (i.e. *financial manager, personal financial advisor*) tend to be close in the space for both female and male versions. However, when visualizing words, in the case of *financial manager*, words for female and male representation are placed in very distant points in the space as seen in Figure 2. On the contrary, words for female and male representation in the case of *personal financial advisor* are represented together as seen in Figure 3. So, we conclude that *financial* in a male/female context is differently represented if attached to *manager* but the same *financial* is similarly represented in male/female context if attached to *personal* and *advisor*. Our tool allows to visualize that contextual word embeddings encode gender biases and this conclusion is coherent with previous literature experiments (Basta et al., 2019).

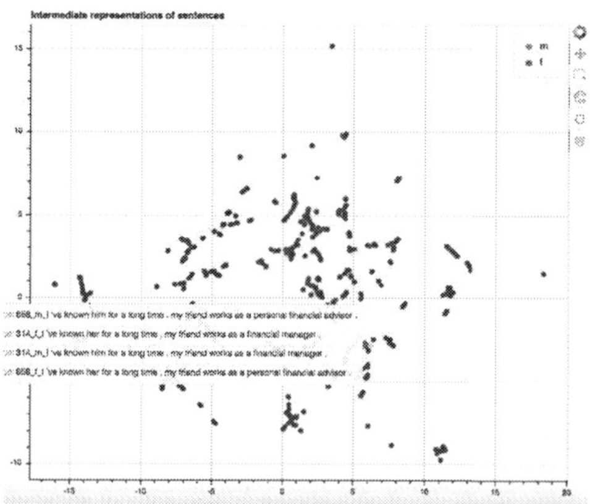

Figure 1: Contextual word embedding representation at the sentence level (sentences *I've known him/her for a long time, my friend is a financial manager/personal financial advisor*). Sentences referring to males are in green, sentences referring to females are in red.

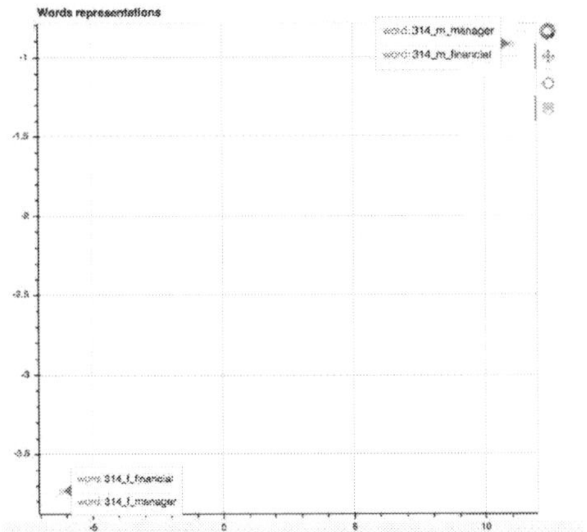

Figure 2: Contextual word embedding representation at the token level *financial manager*.

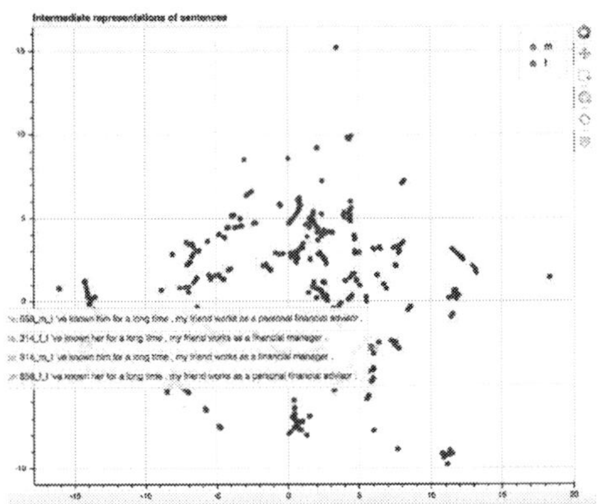

Figure 3: Contextual word embedding representation at the token level *personal financial advisor*.

Use case 2: Multilingual common representation in translation. Nowadays, there are two main architectures for multilingual neural machine translation which are a universal shared encoder and decoder and independent multiple encoders and decoders. In both cases, there is an intermediate representation where sentences that have similar meanings should be represented close in the space. For our second and third use case, we use the intermediate representations of the multilingual Transformer-based architecture presented in (Escolano et al., 2019). Basically, the architecture consists in independent encoders and decoders with a forced-interlingua space. This system is trained on data extracted from the UN (Ziemski et al., 2016) and EPPS datasets (Koehn, 2005) that provide 15 million parallel sentences

between English and Spanish and French. *newstest2012* and *newstest2013* were used as validation and test sets, respectively. These sets provide parallel data between the 3 languages.

Figure 4 shows 130 sentences extracted from the test set, in the 3 languages at hand and in the common space (at the output of the encoder). When we select a particular sentence (e.g. *people accept orders .*), for each token in the sentence selected, the user can select to visualize the token representations (e.g. *people*) as shown in Figure 5. From this visualization we conclude that the model is not able to group together sentences with the same meaning across languages.

2.2 Multi-layer sentence representation

This visualization shows T layers simultaneously for single or multiple languages in a small multiples design. This facilitates the analysis of sentence representation evolution across all the layers of the Transformer at once. See Figure 6.

On each view, we can display the sentence by hovering. In order to emphasize the distances between the translations and to have a better insight of the evolution, the link between the most dissimilar are displayed on the plots. By hovering on the lines, the user can obtain the cosine distance value computed on SciPy. On the views, only the distances superior to 1 are displayed. Even if the dimensionality reduction of UMAP does show interpretable distances (McInnes et al., 2018), showing consecutive layers of the Transformer, and seeing the evolution of the representations allows us to draw hints about the layer roles as we will see in the third use case.

Finally, the tool allows for analysis in multiple layers and languages. This means that initially, the multiple layers represented on the dashboard are in one particular language. However, the user can switch to the multiple layers from another language by using the selection tool at the top of the page. Since all views are synchronized, upon changing the language set, all of them change accordingly.

Use case 3: Multilingual Layer Interpretation in Translation Decoding Encoders and decoders in a neural machine translation system are usually composed of different layers. The role of each layer is difficult to interpret. Visualizing sentences at each of these layers can help us on identifying the sentence distance evolution giving

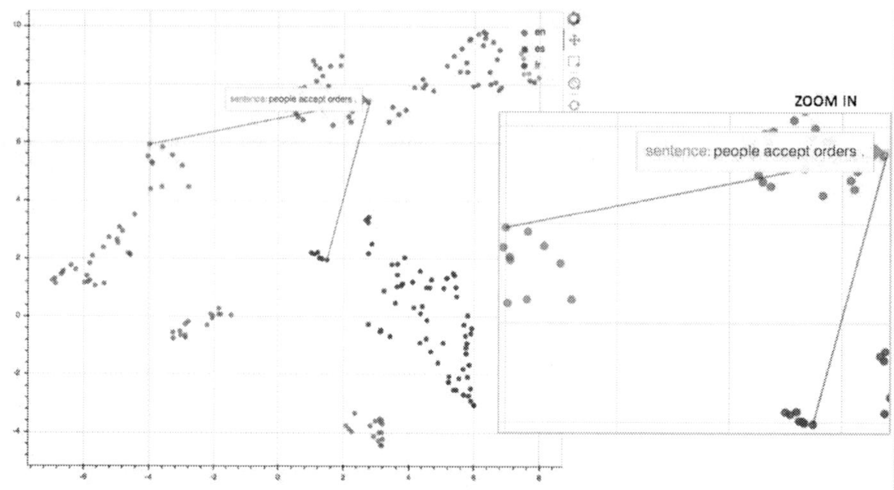

Figure 4: Multilingual common representation at the sentence level (sentence *people accept orders .*). English in red, Spanish in green and French in blue.

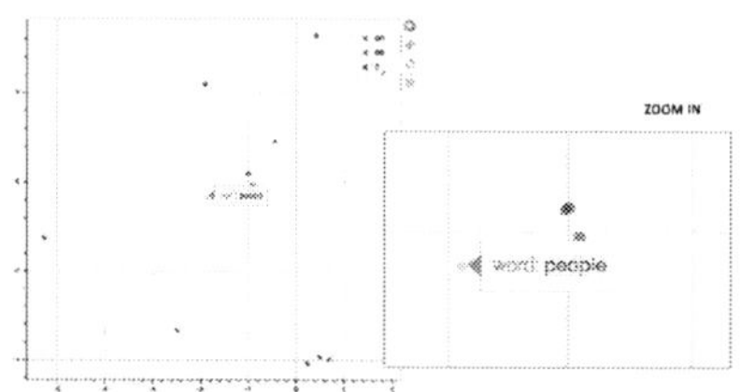

Figure 5: Multilingual common representation at the token level (token *people*).

us hints of different linguistic roles for the layers when compared between them.

In the current example, we are representing the same set and architecture as in use case 2, but for the 6 decoder layers. Figure 6 shows the plot for these layers and Figure 7 shows how it performs hovering on a point (e.g. showing sentences, *unexpected consequences.*, right) and hovering on a line (e.g. showing distance measure, left). Since we show sentences with the same meaning in different languages, we interpret that the layer that tends to better cluster sentences compared to contiguous layers is the one with higher semantic implications. From Figure 6, we conclude that higher layers in the decoder (specially 4 and 5) better group sentences (see axes values).

3 Adaptability

In this paper, we have discussed three use cases. However, our tool is highly flexible and adaptable, and it allows for a large variety of tasks. The system only requires data to be formatted as a *JSON* file following the structures defined in Figure 8.

The structure from use cases 1 and 2 defines the relation between sentence and token representations. For each token and embedding a 2-dimensional is defined, showing its coordinates in the final plots.

On the other side, the structure from use case 3 contains the representations of the layers to be plotted and it is described as an array containing the coordinates for each sentence.

This implementation allows our tool to be agnostic to factors such as vocabulary sizes and dimensionality reductions techniques, as they are applied before *JSON* creation.

4 Related Work

Given the versatility of the sequence architectures, the current tool feeds from vast research areas including contextual word embeddings, multilingual models, visualization and interpretability of sequence models, zero-shot learning. However, we just refer here to the closest and recent works.

Gender bias. Gender bias has recently been analysed in contextual word embeddings (Zhao et al., 2019; Basta et al., 2019). Our tool aims at following-up this kind of research to work towards techniques that are able to neutralize these and other social biases.

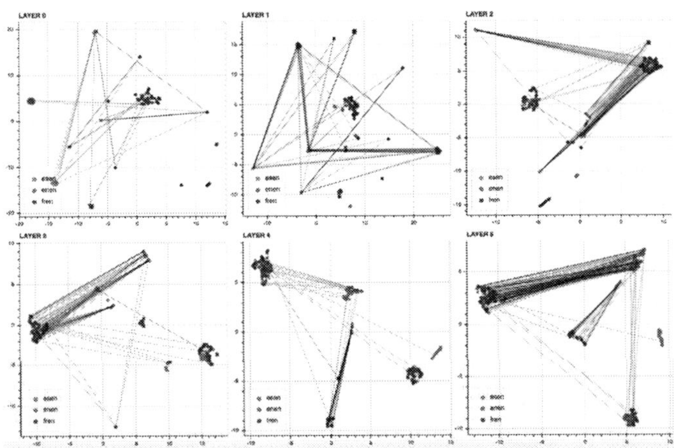

Figure 6: Decoder layer multilingual sentence representation.

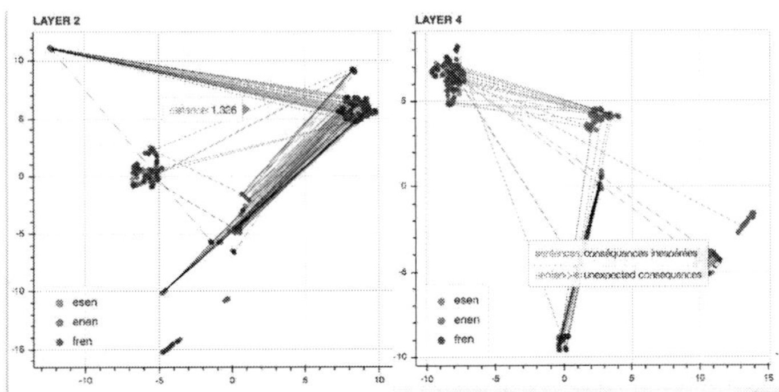

Figure 7: Decoder layer multilingual sentence representation: distance and sentences.


```
{
    "content": {
        "id": {
            "sentence": "",
            "embedding": "",
            "words": {
                "word1":"",
                "wordN":""
            }
        }
    }
}
```



```
{
    "type":"UMAP",
    "content":[
        {
            "input_source0":"",
            "input_sourceN":""
        },
        {
            "input_source0":"",
            "input_sourceN":""
        }
    ]
}
```


Figure 8: Required JSON structures: (Left) use cases 1 and 2 and (Right) use case 3

Multilinguality analysis. It is quite a common practice to visualize intermediate representations of sequence-to-sequence models (Johnson et al., 2017; Escolano et al., 2019). Our tool is not limited to this sentence representation of the intermediate representation, but it also includes the token-level representation. By simultaneously providing this two-granularity level representation we are aiming at a deeper analysis for monolingual, cross-lingual and multilingual natural language processing downstream applications in general.

Linguistic insights. (Raganato and Tiedemann, 2018) show interesting findings about syntactic and semantic behavior across Transformer layers. Following this research line, our tool can further analyse how similar sentences in multiple languages evolve in their intermediate layer representations as well as monolingual sentences with same syntactic or morphological patterns.

Finally, regarding related visualizations and demonstrations, authors in (Li et al., 2016) make an visual analysis of neural models specifically in natural language processing (but focusing on previous architectures to the Transformer), while (Vig, 2019) analyse the attention in the Transformer at multiple-scales and show different use cases on contextual word embeddings. Our tool further adds to these previous works by focusing on the intermediate representations.

5 Conclusions

We have presented an extremely flexible and adaptable visualization tool for multilingual intermediate representations of text both at the sentence and token's level. Together with our tool we have presented three use cases in the context of gender bias analysis in contextual word embeddings and for multilingual intermediate representations of machine translation.

Acknowledgements

Authors want to thank Christine Raouf Basta for sharing her expertise in contextual word embeddings. This work is supported by a Google Faculty Research Award. This work is also supported by the Spanish Ministerio de Economía y Competitividad, the European Regional Development Fund and the Agencia Estatal de Investigación, through the post-doctoral senior grant Ramón y Cajal, contracts TEC2015-69266-P and TIN2017-88515-C2-1-R(GEN3DLIVE) (MINECO/FEDER,EU), and contract PCIN-2017-079 (AEI/MINECO).

References

Dzmitry Bahdanau, Kyunghyun Cho, and Yoshua Bengio. 2014. Neural machine translation by jointly learning to align and translate. *arXiv preprint arXiv:1409.0473*.

Christine Basta, Marta R. Costa-jussà, and Noe Casas. 2019. Evaluating the underlying gender bias in contextualized word embeddings. In *Proc. of the 1st ACL Workshop on Gender Bias for Natural Language Processing*.

William Chan, Navdeep Jaitly, Quoc V. Le, and Oriol Vinyals. 2016. Listen, attend and spell: A neural network for large vocabulary conversational speech recognition. In *ICASSP*.

Carlos Escolano, Marta R. Costa-jussà, and Jos A. R. Fonollosa. 2019. From bilingual to multilingual neural machine translation by incremental training. In *Proc. of the ACL Student Research Workshop*.

Joel Escudé Font and Marta R. Costa-jussà. 2019. Equalizing gender biases in neural machine translation with word embeddings techniques. In *Proc. of the 1st ACL Workshop on Gender Bias for Natural Language Processing*.

Jonas Gehring, Michael Auli, David Grangier, Denis Yarats, and Yann N. Dauphin. 2017. Convolutional sequence to sequence learning. In *Proceedings of the 34th ICML - Volume 70*, pages 1243–1252. JMLR.org.

Melvin Johnson, Mike Schuster, Quoc V Le, Maxim Krikun, Yonghui Wu, Zhifeng Chen, Nikhil Thorat, Fernanda Viégas, Martin Wattenberg, Greg Corrado, et al. 2017. Googles multilingual neural machine translation system: Enabling zero-shot translation. *Transactions of the Association for Computational Linguistics*, 5:339–351.

Lukasz Kaiser, Aidan N Gomez, Noam Shazeer, Ashish Vaswani, Niki Parmar, Llion Jones, and Jakob Uszkoreit. 2017. One model to learn them all. *arXiv preprint arXiv:1706.05137*.

Philipp Koehn. 2005. Europarl: A parallel corpus for statistical machine translation. In *MT summit*, volume 5, pages 79–86.

Jiwei Li, Xinlei Chen, Eduard Hovy, and Dan Jurafsky. 2016. Visualizing and understanding neural models in NLP. In *Proceedings of the 2016 Conference of the North American Chapter of the Association for Computational Linguistics: Human Language Technologies*, pages 681–691, San Diego, California. Association for Computational Linguistics.

Leland McInnes, John Healy, Nathaniel Saul, and Lukas Grossberger. 2018. Umap: Uniform manifold approximation and projection. *The Journal of Open Source Software*, 3(29):861.

Matthew Peters, Mark Neumann, Mohit Iyyer, Matt Gardner, Christopher Clark, Kenton Lee, and Luke Zettlemoyer. 2018. Deep contextualized word representations. In *Proceedings of the 2018 Conference of the NAACL*, pages 2227–2237, New Orleans.

Alessandro Raganato and Jörg Tiedemann. 2018. An analysis of encoder representations in transformer-based machine translation. In *Proceedings of the 2018 EMNLP Workshop BlackboxNLP: Analyzing and Interpreting Neural Networks for NLP*, pages 287–297, Brussels, Belgium.

Ashish Vaswani, Noam Shazeer, Niki Parmar, Jakob Uszkoreit, Llion Jones, Aidan N Gomez, Łukasz Kaiser, and Illia Polosukhin. 2017. Attention is all you need. In *Advances in Neural Information Processing Systems*, pages 5998–6008.

Jesse Vig. 2019. A multiscale visualization of attention in the transformer model. In *Proc. of the ACL System Demonstrations*.

Jieyu Zhao, Tianlu Wang, Mark Yatskar, Ryan Cotterell, Vicente Ordonez, and Kai-Wei Chang. 2019. Gender bias in contextualized word embeddings. In *Proceedings of the 2019 Conference of the NAACL*, pages 629–634, Minneapolis, Minnesota.

Michal Ziemski, Marcin Junczys-Dowmunt, and Bruno Pouliquen. 2016. The united nations parallel corpus v1. 0. In *Lrec*.

MY−AKKHARA:
A Romanization-based Burmese (Myanmar) Input Method

Chenchen Ding, Masao Utiyama, and Eiichiro Sumita
Advanced Translation Technology Laboratory,
Advanced Speech Translation Research and Development Promotion Center,
National Institute of Information and Communications Technology
3-5 Hikaridai, Seika-cho, Soraku-gun, Kyoto, 619-0289, Japan
{chenchen.ding, mutiyama, eiichiro.sumita}@nict.go.jp

Abstract

MY−AKKHARA is a method used to input Burmese texts encoded in the *Unicode* standard, based on commonly accepted Latin transcription. By using this method, arbitrary Burmese strings can be accurately inputted with 26 lowercase Latin letters. Meanwhile, the 26 uppercase Latin letters are designed as shortcuts of lowercase letter sequences. The frequency of Burmese characters is considered in MY−AKKHARA to realize an efficient keystroke distribution on a QWERTY keyboard. Given that the *Unicode* standard has not been extensively used in digitization of Burmese, we hope that MY−AKKHARA can contribute to the widespread use of *Unicode* in Myanmar and can provide a platform for smart input methods for Burmese in the future. An implementation of MY−AKKHARA running in Windows is released at http://www2.nict.go.jp/astrec-att/member/ding/my-akkhara.html

1 Introduction

Burmese (Myanmar) script is an abugida system, wherein basic characters can be modified using diacritics at all directions or can be combined vertically, rather than a simple left-to-right horizontal writing (Ding et al., 2016). Details of the Burmese language can be referred to in Okell and Allott (2001), Okell (2010a,b), and Okano (2007).

Although its use is encouraged in the government and universities, the use of *Unicode* for Burmese script[1] is not currently widespread. Traditional shape-based typefaces such as *Zawgyi*[2] are preferred for daily use. The issue can be regarded as *path dependence* due to traditional typewriters, wherein the input is exactly based

---

[1] https://www.unicode.org/charts/PDF/U1000.pdf

[2] https://code.google.com/archive/p/zawgyi/downloads

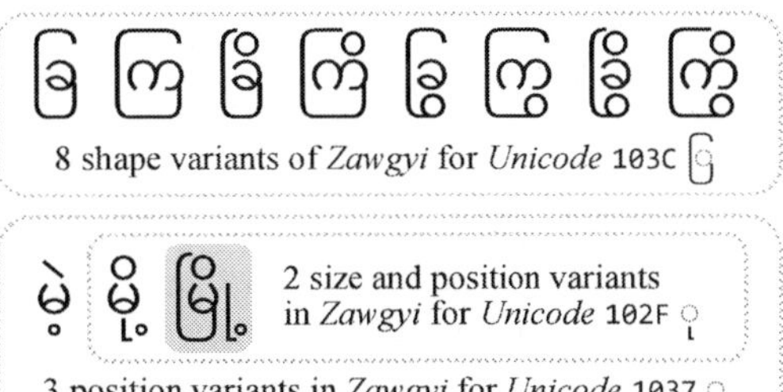

Figure 1: Shape, size, and position variants in *Zawgyi* for identical *Unicode* characters. The characters may affect each other: for those with gray background, the shape of 103C is determined by the inside combination, size and position of 102F by 103C, and the position of 1037 by 102F.

on character shape, rather than the phonetic values of characters (Fig. 1). *Zawgyi* separately encodes all possible variants of characters and diacritics, and allows users to select correct variants manually. Hence, a redundant character set becomes incompatible with the *Unicode* standard, and extra effort is required for users to utilize typeface in detail. To provide a better interface and promote *Unicode* for Burmese digitization, we design a Burmese input method referred to as MY−AKKHARA by Romanization based on the *Unicode* standard. MY−AKKHARA is generally based on the mnemonics used in *Unicode* and the *Myanmar Language Committee Transcription System* (Department of the Myanmar Language Commission, 2014). The efficiency of the key distribution on the QWERTY keyboard layout is also considered in the design of MY−AKKHARA.

The implementation of MY−AKKHARA running in Windows has been released. In this paper, we first review the default layouts of Burmese provided in Windows (Win) and Macintosh (Mac) and subsequently provide detailed descriptions of MY−AKKHARA. In addition, the keystroke distribution of different methods is compared.

157

Proceedings of the 2019 EMNLP and the 9th IJCNLP (System Demonstrations), pages 157–162
Hong Kong, China, November 3 – 7, 2019. ©2019 Association for Computational Linguistics

2 `Win` and `Mac` **Burmese Keyboards**

The keyboard layouts used to input Burmese in *Unicode* have been provided in `Win` and `Mac` operating systems. Figure 2 illustrates the default layouts of the Burmese *Unicode* keyboard in these two mainstream operating systems. Both of the layouts are a simple mapping from characters to keys. Excluding special punctuation marks and native number digits, 63 *Unicode* characters are required to represent modern standard Burmese textual data, from *Unicode* `1000` to `104F`.[3] Therefore, 26 keys with shift are not sufficient to cover the character set. In both of the layouts, extra punctuation (or digit), or alternative keys are necessary in typing.

The `Win` layout is adjusted from the traditional layout of a typewriter, by removing redundant character varieties and re-arranging the characters inputted using the `Shift`-key. Considering that this layout has a large portion of the traditional one but with a certain difference, many `Win` users are not interested in switching to this layout. Hence non-*Unicode* fonts are still inputted using the traditional keyboard in practice. Moreover, the `Mac` layout is completely redesigned based on Romanization manner, wherein the Burmese characters are arranged on the basis of their pronunciations as represented by the letters on a `QWERTY` keyboard. However, the design is inflexible, without considering the practical use of Burmese characters. Thus, the positioning of fingers when typing is tricky. The comparison of the keystroke distribution will be presented in Section 4.

3 `MY-AKKHARA`: **Proposed Input Method**

The proposed `MY-AKKHARA` is inspired by the `Mac` layout and deemed highly natural and efficient. Rather than a simple mapping between the *Unicode* characters and keys, we also facilitate character alternation processing by using the inputted Latin letters. Specifically, double keystrokes of `e`, `f`, `h`, `i`, `j`, `r`, `u`, `v`, `w`, and `y`, and the `h-` and `g`-keys at the middle of a `QWERTY` keyboard are used to alternate characters. This design naturally integrates the Romanization into the character alternation processing. The `q`-key is reserved to disambiguate in obscure cases through which the input method can precisely input any

strings with the *Unicode* Burmese characters.[4] Lowercase `a`, `o`, `x`, and 26 uppercase Latin letters are assigned as optional shortcuts. Figure 3 shows an example on the technique of inputting a Burmese string with rare and stacked characters using the proposed method.

The instruction of the proposed input method can be printed by users on an `A4` paper (Fig. 4). The proposed method can be formulated primarily through a finite-state automaton (Hopcroft et al., 2013), receiving strings comprising 23 lowercase Latin letters (excluding `a`, `o`, and `x`) and transiting among different states that represent Burmese characters. The **Appendix** provides the description of the automaton.

The shortcuts can be grouped in the following four categories:

- three lowercase letters for common combinations: `a=qevq`, `o=qiuq`, and `x=qngfq`;

- uppercase letters to save double keystrokes: `E=qee`, `F=qff`, `H=qhh`, `I=qii`, `J=qjj`, `R=qrr`, `U=quu`, `V=qvv`, `W=qww`, and `Y=qyy`;

- uppercase letters to save h/g: `B=qbh`, `C=qch`, `D=qdh`, `G=qgh`, `K=qkh`, `L=qlg`, `M=qmg`, `P=qph`, `Q=qg`, `T=qth`, and `Z=qzh`; and

- uppercase letters for other cases: `A=qegg`, `N=qny`, `O=qsr`, `S=quug`, and `X=qng`.

Lowercase letters `a`, `o`, and `x` can considerably save keystrokes. Note that the shortcuts have a preceding `q` in the implementation through which disambiguation can be realized. The recommended uppercase letters are `Y`, `H`, and `Q`, which can resolve almost all ambiguous cases when typing orthographically correct Burmese texts.

Two issues related to normalizing the encoding of the Burmese script in *Unicode* are addressed:

- `102B` is a variant of `102C`, exclusively used for narrow characters of `1001`, `1002`, `1004`, `1012`, `1015`, and `101D`. This alternation is executed automatically when typing `v` or `a` (i.e., shortcut for `ev`). However, `qv` and `qvg` can exactly input `102C` and `102B`, respectively.

- `1037` and `103A` can appear successively; however, their order is not precisely identified. `103A 1037` will always be normalized in *Unicode* into the recommended order `1037 103A`.

---

[3]Within this range, from `1040` to `104B` are Burmese digits and punctuation marks; `1022`, `1028`, `1033`, `1034`, and `1035` are not used for standard Burmese.

[4]It is possible to intentionally input orthographically incorrect Burmese strings; however, orthographically correct strings can be inputted more naturally than incorrect ones.

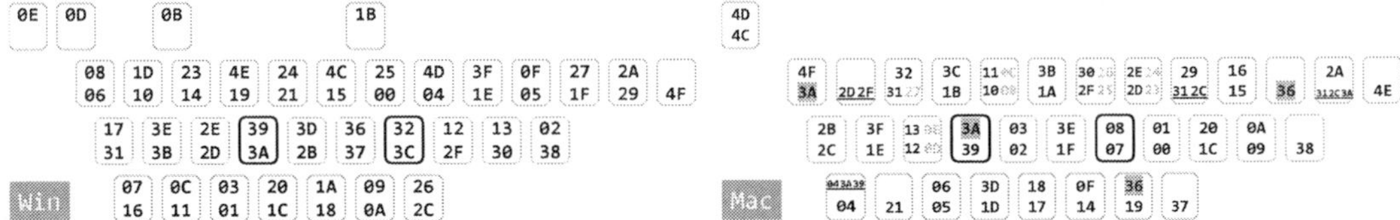

Figure 2: Default Burmese layout in `Win` (left) and `Mac` (right). Only the final two digits of *Unicode* are shown for a compact presentation. The places of `f`- and `j`-keys on a `QWERTY` keyboard are marked by bold frame. For each key, the lower character is inputted using simple keystroke, whereas the upper character requires pressing the `Shift`-key. On the `Mac` keyboard, some character combinations are mapped on one key, which is underlined in the figure. Meanwhile several rare characters require `Alt`-key, which is in gray color. Note that `103A` and `1036` marked with gray background appear two times on the `Mac` keyboard.

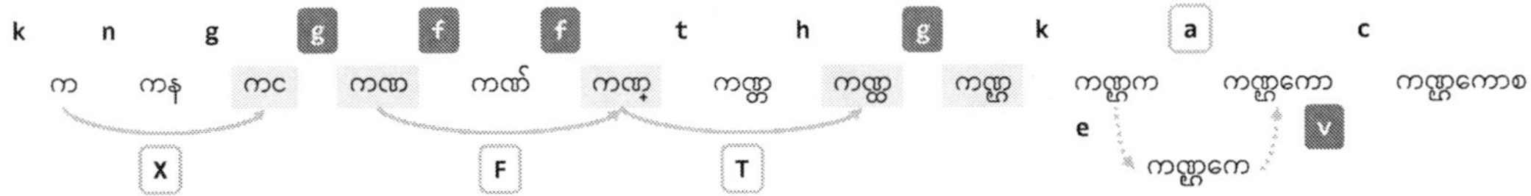

Figure 3: Example of the proposed input method. The top row is the typed Latin letters; the inputted Burmese string after each keystroke is presented in an increasing manner. Latin letters with frame are the shortcuts and those with dark background are special design that should be remembered by users. Burmese strings with gray background have a character alternation from their previous status. Although g and h are regarded as alternation operators, they are also part of the Romanization, i.e., the first g after n and h after t. The shortcuts mainly save the extra alternation by g, h and double keystroke (i.e., X, T, and F). Lowercase a is a shortcut for an extremely common character combination that can be inputted using ev.

4 Keystroke Distribution

The Burmese language has two different styles: literary and colloquial. For the literary style data, the publicly accessible Burmese dataset in the *Asian Language Treebank* (ALT) project (Riza et al., 2016) is used, containing approximately $20,000$ long sentences from news articles.[5] For the colloquial style data, we use an in-house translated Burmese version of the *Basic Travel Expression Corpus* (BTEC) (Kikui et al., 2003), comprising approximately $400,000$ daily expressions. Figures 5 and 6 show the comparison of the keystroke distribution in `Win` and `Mac` keyboards and by `MY-AKKHARA`, respectively.

The middle area of the `Mac` keyboard has not been efficiently used. Although the uppercase F can be used instead of lowercase q, the frequency of the `Shift`-key will increase considerably. The keystroke is more focused at the middle of the keyboard by `MY-AKKHARA` than that on the `Win` and `Mac` keyboards. The use of the `Shift`-key is optional in `MY-AKKHARA`, depending on the users'

preference. When the `Shift`-key is completely applied, the frequency is less than two times that of used in `Win` keyboard, and it is approximately equal to the lower bound used in `Mac` keyboard. Generally, index fingers are mostly utilized and little fingers have fewer burdens in `MY-AKKHARA`.

5 Conclusion and Future Work

In this study, a Romanization-based Burmese input method called `MY-AKKHARA` is proposed to promote the *Unicode* standard for Burmese digitization. `MY-AKKHARA` can also be regarded as a Burmese-specified, lossless coding version of Ding et al. (2018), providing a platform to develop a further fuzzy and smart Burmese input method.

References

Department of the Myanmar Language Commission. 2014. *Myanmar-English dictionary (Myanma-anggalip abidan)*, 12 edition. Ministry of Education, the Republic of the Union of Myanmar.

Chenchen Ding, Masao Utiyama, and Eiichiro Sumita. 2018. Simplified Abugidas. In *Proc. of ACL, Vol. 2*, pages 491–495.

---

[5] `http://www2.nict.go.jp/astrec-att/member/mutiyama/ALT/my-nova-170405.zip`

Consonants

1000	1001	1002	1003	1004		1009
k	kh|K	g|Q	gh|G	ng|X		nyg|Ng
1005	**1006**	**1007**	**1008**	**100A**		
c	ch|C	z	zh|Z	ny|N		
100B	**100C**	**100D**	**100E**	**100F**		
tg	thg|Tg	dg	dhg|Dg	ngg|Xg		
1010	**1011**	**1012**	**1013**	**1014**		
t	th|T	d	dh|D	n		
1015	**1016**	**1017**	**1018**	**1019**		**103F**
p	ph|P	b	bh|B	m		sg
101A	**101B**	**101C**	**101D**	**101E**		
yy|Y	rr|R	l	ww|W	s		
	101F	**1020**	**1021**			
	hh|H	lg|L	vv|V			

Independent Vowels

1022	1023	1024	1025	1026	1027	1029	102A
vv|V	ig	iig|Ig	ug	uug|Ug|S	eg	sr|O	srg|Og

Dependent Vowel Signs

102B	102C	102D	102E	102F	1030	1031	1032
vg	v	i	ii|I	u	uu|U	e	ee|E

Various Signs / Combined Vowel Signs

Various Signs					Combined Vowel Signs		
1036	1037	1038	1039	103A	102D 102F	1031 102C	1004 103A
mg|M	jj|J	j	ff|F	f	o	a	x

Dependent Consonant Signs / Various Signs

Dependent Consonant Signs				Various Signs			
103B	103C	103D	103E	104C	104D	104E	104F
y	r	w	h	nggg|Xgg	rrg|Rg	lgg|Lg	egg|A

Figure 4: Proposed input method. In each cell, the *Unicode*, the Burmese character, and the input manner are illustrated from top to bottom. For Burmese characters having more than one way to input, vertical bar is used to separate different manners.

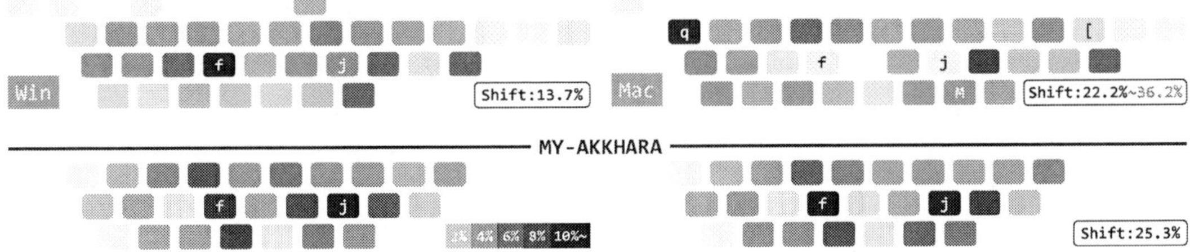

Figure 5: Keystroke distribution on the ALT literary data. The upper-left and upper-right diagrams are `Win` and `Mac` keyboards, respectively. The lower images are `MY-AKKHARA`, with `Shift` not used (left) and `Shift` completely used (right) manners, respectively. The usage frequency of the `Shift`-key is also presented. Note that `103A` and `1036` appear twice on the `Mac` keyboard. The two characters are counted by using q and [to input in the diagram, where the frequency of `Shift`-key is 22.2%. The two character can be also inputted by uppercase F and M. If they are always inputted using the `Shift`-key, then the frequency of `Shift`-key increases to 36.2%.

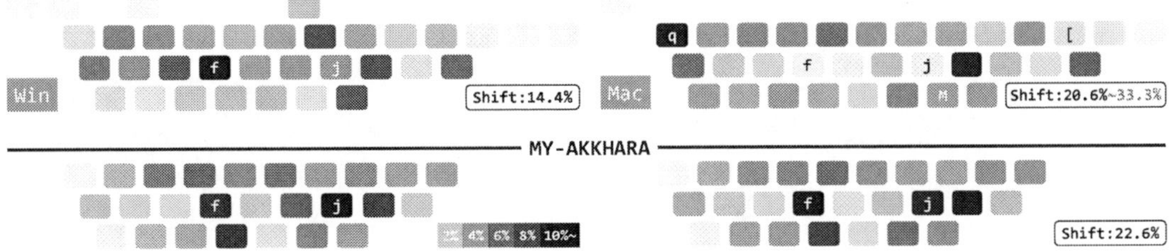

Figure 6: Keystroke distribution on the BTEC colloquial data. The configuration is the same as that of Fig. 5.

Chenchen Ding, Ye Kyaw Thu, Masao Utiyama, and Eiichiro Sumita. 2016. Word segmentation for Burmese (Myanmar). *ACM TALLIP*, 15(4):22.

John E. Hopcroft, Rajeev Motwani, and Jeffrey D. Ullman. 2013. *Introduction to Automata Theory, Languages, and Computation*, 3 edition. Pearson.

Genichiro Kikui, Eiichiro Sumita, Toshiyuki Takezawa, and Seiichi Yamamoto. 2003. Creating corpora for speech-to-speech translation. In *Proc. of EUROSPEECH*, pages 381–384.

Kenji Okano. 2007. *Colloquial Burmese (Myanmar) Grammar*. Kokusai Gogakusha. (in Japanese).

John Okell. 2010a. *Burmese – An introduction to the Spoken Language, Book 1*. Northern Illinois University Press.

John Okell. 2010b. *Burmese – An introduction to the Spoken Language, Book 2*. Northern Illinois University Press.

John Okell and Anna Allott. 2001. *Burmese / Myanmar Dictionary of Grammatical Forms*. Routledge.

Hammam Riza, Michael Purwoadi, Teduh Uliniansyah, Aw Ai Ti, Sharifah Mahani Aljunied, Luong Chi Mai, Vu Tat Thang, Nguyen Phuong Thai, Vichet Chea, Rapid Sun, Sethserey Sam, Sopheap Seng, Khin Mar Soe, Khin Thandar Nwet, Masao Utiyama, and Chenchen Ding. 2016. Introduction of the Asian language treebank. In *Proc. of O-COCOSDA*, pages 1–6.

Appendix

Figure 7 shows the overall configuration. Routes connecting the the initial (q_s) and final (q_s) states are listed in Figs. 8 – 16, where $q_n, (n \in \mathbf{N})$ are Burmese characters.[6] Although all q_n can be the final states, a separate q_e is used for clarity, and a q is marked explicitly on all the arcs to q_e.

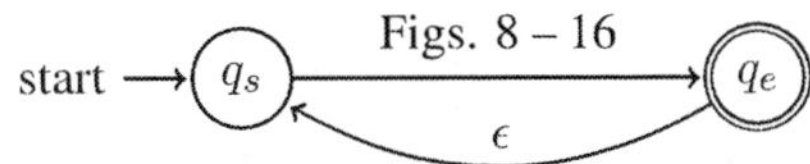

Figure 7: Overall configuration of the automaton.

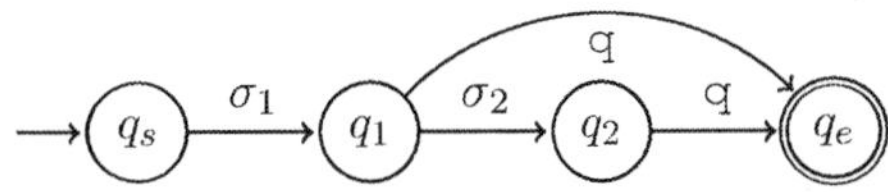

Figure 8: Simplest case. When σ_2 is h, (σ_1, q_1, q_2) can be (k, 00, 01), (g, 02, 03), (c, 05, 06), (z, 07, 08), (p, 15, 16), and (b, 17, 18). When σ_2 is g, (σ_1, q_1, q_2) is (m, 19, 36). When $\sigma_2 = \sigma_1$, (σ_1, q_1, q_2) can be (y, 3B, 1A), (w, 3D, 1C), and (h, 3E, 1D). All σ_1 are natural Romanization. When σ_2 is h, it is also a part of the Romanization.

---

[6] *Unicode* is referred to by the final two digits for brevity.

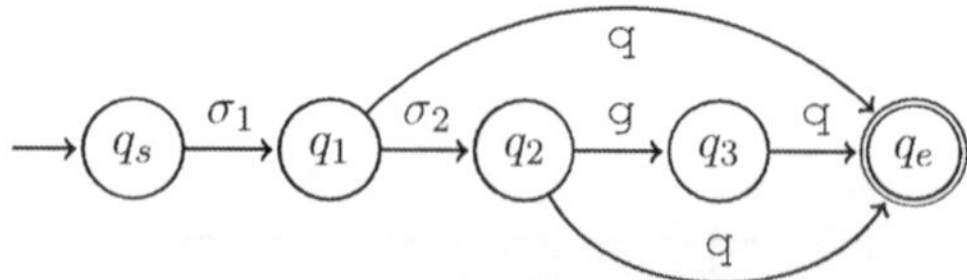

Figure 9: Two-step alternation. When (σ_1, σ_2) is (l, g), (q_1, q_2, q_3) is (1C, 20, 4E). Here, l is a natural Romanization for 101C and 1020, whereas 104E is a special abbreviated mark with l as onset. When (σ_1, σ_2) is (r, r), (q_1, q_2, q_3) is (3C, 1B, 4D), respectively. Here, r is a natural Romanization for 103C and 101B, whereas 104D is a special abbreviated mark with r as onset.

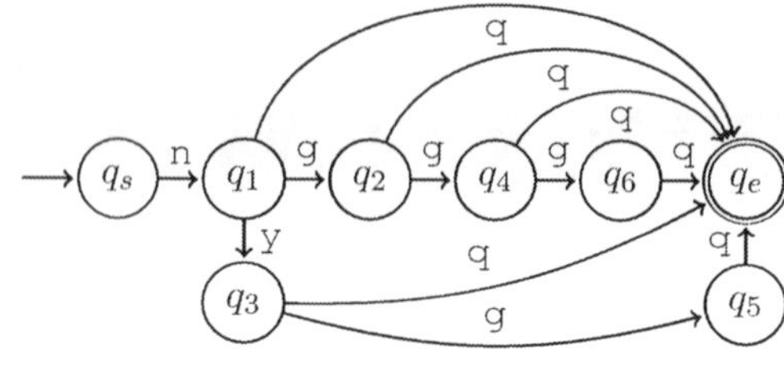

Figure 13: Most complex alternation. $(q_1, q_2, q_3, q_4, q_5, q_6)$ is (14, 04, 0A, 0F, 09, 4C). Here, n, ng and ny are the natural Romanization for 1014, 1004, and 100A, respectively. Other alternated characters are rare.

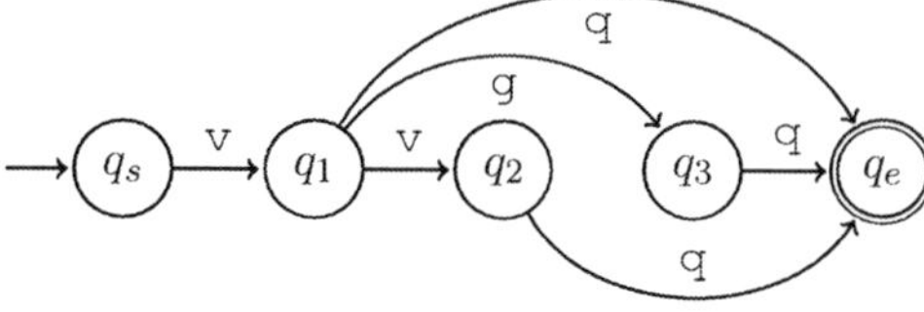

Figure 10: Alternation variant of Fig. 9. (q_1, q_2, q_3) is (2C, 21, 2B). Considering that 102C and 1021 are frequently used, the convenient v-key is assigned instead the natural Romanization by a.

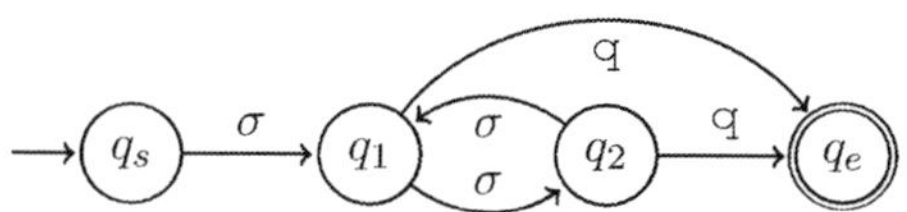

Figure 14: Doubled and looped alternation. (σ, q_1, q_2) can be (j, 38, 37), and (f, 3A, 39). Here, 1038 and 103A are remarkably frequent marks; hence convenient j- and f-keys are assigned, respectively.

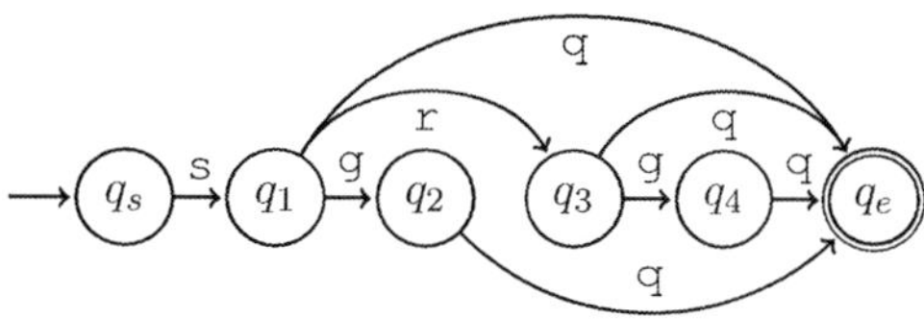

Figure 11: Alternation in Fig. 8 with an extra branch. (q_1, q_2, q_3, q_4) is (1E, 3F, 29, 2A). Here, s is a natural Romanization for 101E, whereas 103F, 1029, and 102A are extremely obscure.

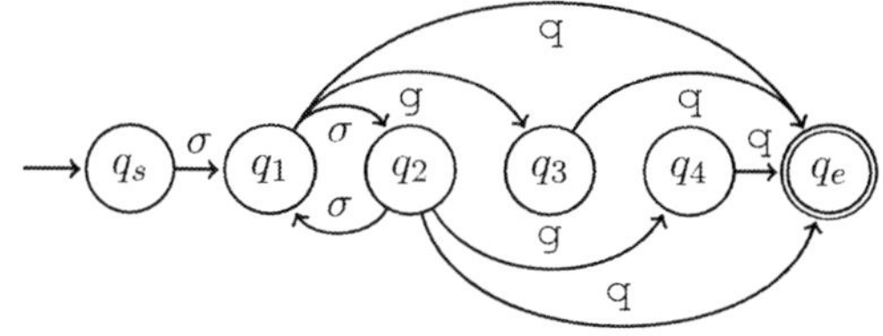

Figure 15: Combination of Figs. 12 and 14. $(\sigma, q_1, q_2, q_3, q_4)$ can be (i, 2D, 2E, 23, 24), and (u, 2F, 30, 25, 26). Here, i and u are the natural Romanization for the corresponding characters.

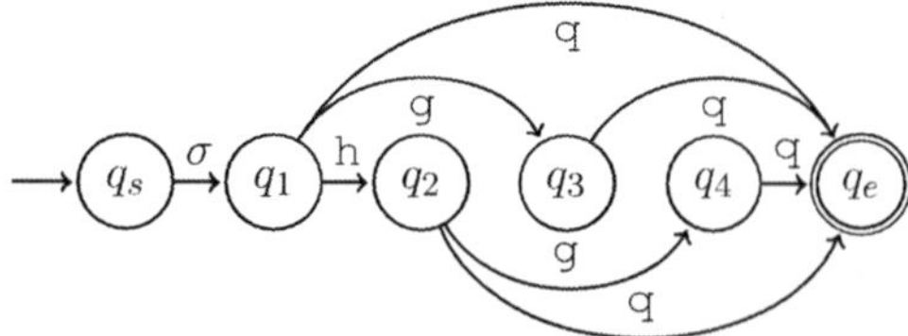

Figure 12: Alternation by h and g. $(\sigma, q_1, q_2, q_3, q_4)$ can be (t, 10, 11, 0B, 0C), and (d, 12, 13, 0D, 0E). Both t and d are the natural Romanization, and h is also a part of the Romanization.

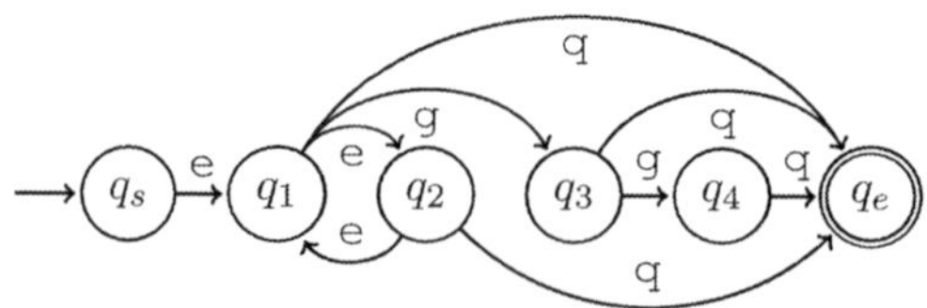

Figure 16: Alternation in Fig. 14 with an extra branch. (q_1, q_2, q_3, q_4) is (31, 32, 27, 4F). Here, e is a natural Romanization for 1031, 1032 and 1027, whereas 104F is an abbreviated mark derived from 1027.

NeuronBlocks: Building Your NLP DNN Models Like Playing Lego

Ming Gong [§]   **Linjun Shou** [§]   **Wutao Lin**[§]   **Zhijie Sang**[§]   **Quanjia Yan**[‡]

Ze Yang[§]   **Feixiang Cheng**[§]   **Daxin Jiang**[§]

[§] STCA NLP Group, Microsoft, Beijing, China

[‡] Research Center for Ubiquitous Computing Systems, ICT, CAS, Beijing, China

{migon, lisho, wutlin, zhsang, yaze, fecheng, djiang}@microsoft.com

yanquanjia17s@ict.ac.cn

Abstract

Deep Neural Networks (DNN) have been widely employed in industry to address various Natural Language Processing (NLP) tasks. However, many engineers find it a big overhead when they have to choose from multiple frameworks, compare different types of models, and understand various optimization mechanisms. An NLP toolkit for DNN models with both generality and flexibility can greatly improve the productivity of engineers by saving their learning cost and guiding them to find optimal solutions to their tasks. In this paper, we introduce NeuronBlocks[1] [2], a toolkit encapsulating a suite of neural network modules as building blocks to construct various DNN models with complex architecture. This toolkit empowers engineers to build, train, and test various NLP models through simple configuration of JSON files. The experiments on several NLP datasets such as GLUE, WikiQA and CoNLL-2003 demonstrate the effectiveness of NeuronBlocks.

1 Introduction

Deep Neural Networks (DNN) have been widely employed in industry for solving various Natural Language Processing (NLP) tasks, such as text classification, sequence labeling, question answering, etc. However, when engineers apply DNN models to address specific NLP tasks, they often face the following challenges.

- Multiple DNN frameworks, including Tensor-Flow, PyTorch, Keras, etc. It is a big overhead to learn how to program under the frameworks.
- Diverse and fast evolving DNN models, such as CNN, RNN, and Transformer. It takes big efforts to understand the intuition and maths behind these models.

- Various regularization and optimization mechanisms. To tune model performance for both quality and efficiency, model developers have to gain experience in Dropout, Normalization, Mixed precision training, etc.
- Coding and debugging complexity. Programming under DNN frameworks requires developers to be familiar with the built-in packages and interfaces. It needs much expertise to develop, debug, and optimize code.
- Platform compatibility. It requires extra coding work to run on different platforms, such as Linux/Windows, GPU/CPU.

The above challenges often hinder the productivity of engineers, and result in less optimal solutions to their given tasks. This motivates us to develop an NLP toolkit for DNN models. Before designing this NLP toolkit, we conducted a survey among engineers and identified a spectrum of three typical personas.

- The first type of engineers prefer off-the-shelf networks. Given a specific task, they expect the toolkit to suggest several end-to-end network architectures, and then they simply focus on collecting the training data, and tuning the model parameters. They hope the whole process to be extremely agile and easy.
- The second type of engineers would like to build the networks by themselves. However, instead of writing each line of code from scratch, they hope the toolkit to provide a rich gallery of reusable modules as building blocks. Then they can compare various model architectures constructed by the building blocks.
- The last type of engineers are advanced users. They want to reuse most part of the existing networks, but for critical components, they would like to make innovations and create their own modules. They hope the toolkit to have

---

[1]Code: https://github.com/Microsoft/NeuronBlocks
[2]Demo: https://youtu.be/x6cOpVSZcdo

Proceedings of the 2019 EMNLP and the 9th IJCNLP (System Demonstrations), pages 163–168

Hong Kong, China, November 3 – 7, 2019. ©2019 Association for Computational Linguistics

an open infrastructure, so that customized modules can be easily plugged in.

To satisfy the requirements of all the above three personas, the NLP toolkit has to be generic enough to cover as many tasks as possible. At the same time, it also needs to be flexible enough to allow alternative network architectures as well as customized modules. Therefore, we analyzed the NLP jobs submitted to a commercial centralized GPU cluster. Table 1 showed that about 87.5% NLP related jobs belong to a few common tasks, including sentence classification, text matching, sequence labeling, machine reading comprehension (MRC), etc. It further suggested that more than 90% of the networks were composed of several common components, such as embedding, CNN/RNN, Transformer and so on.

Tasks	Ratio
Text matching	39.4%
Sentence classification	27.3%
Sequence labeling	14.7%
MRC	6.0%
Others	12.5%

Table 1: Task analysis of NLP DNN jobs submitted to a commercial centralized GPU cluster.

Based on the above observations, we developed **NeuronBlocks**, a DNN toolkit for NLP tasks. The basic idea is to provide two layers of support to the engineers. The upper layer targets common NLP tasks. For each task, the toolkit contains several end-to-end network templates, which can be immediately instantiated with simple configuration. The bottom layer consists of a suite of reusable and standard components, which can be adopted as building blocks to construct networks with complex architecture. By following the interface guidelines, users can also contribute to this gallery of components with their own modules.

The technical contributions of NeuronBlocks are summarized into the following three aspects.

- ***Block Zoo***: categorize and abstract the most commonly used DNN components into standard and reusable blocks. The blocks within the same category can be used exchangeably.
- ***Model Zoo***: identify the most popular NLP tasks and provide alternative end-to-end network templates (in JSON format) for each task.
- ***Platform Compatibility***: support both Linux and Windows machines, CPU/GPU chips, as well as GPU platforms such as PAI[3].

---

[3] https://github.com/Microsoft/pai

2   Related Work

There are several general-purpose deep learning frameworks, such as TensorFlow, PyTorch and Keras, which have gained popularity in NLP community. These frameworks offer huge flexibility in DNN model design and support various NLP tasks. However, building models under these frameworks requires a large overhead of mastering these framework details. Therefore, higher level abstraction to hide the framework details is favored by many engineers.

There are also several popular deep learning toolkits in NLP, including OpenNMT (Klein et al., 2017), AllenNLP (Gardner et al., 2018) etc. OpenNMT is an open-source toolkit mainly targeting neural machine translation or other natural language generation tasks. AllenNLP provides several pre-built models for NLP tasks, such as semantic role labeling, machine comprehension, textual entailment, etc. Although these toolkits reduce the development cost, they are limited to certain tasks, and thus not flexible enough to support new network architectures or new components.

3   Design

Neuronblocks is built on PyTorch. The overall framework is illustrated in Figure 1. It consists of two layers: the **Block Zoo** and the **Model Zoo**. In Block Zoo, the most commonly used components of neural networks are categorized into several groups according to their functions. Within each category, several alternative components are encapsulated into standard and reusable blocks with a consistent interface. These blocks serve as basic and exchangeable units to construct complex network architectures for different tasks. In Model Zoo, the most popular NLP tasks are identified. For each task, several end-to-end network templates are provided in the form of JSON configuration files. Users can simply browse these configurations and choose one to instantiate. The whole task can be completed without any coding efforts.

3.1   Block Zoo

We recognize the following major functional categories of neural network components. Each category covers as many commonly used modules as possible. The Block Zoo is an open framework, and more modules can be added in the future.

- **Embedding Layer**: Word/character embedding and extra handcrafted feature embedding

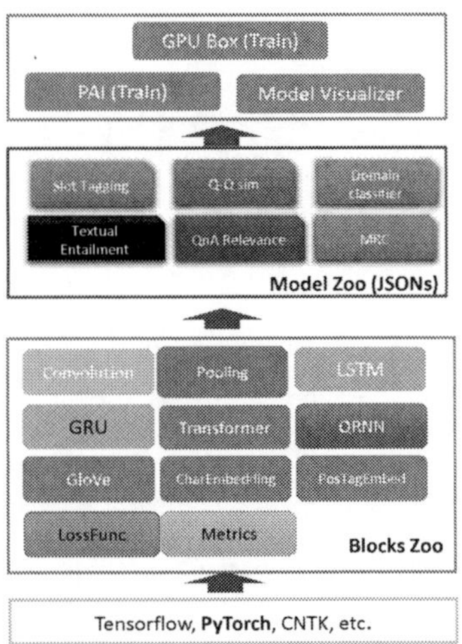

Figure 1: The overall framework of NeuronBlocks.

such as pos-tagging are supported.

- **Neural Network Layers**: Block zoo provides common layers like RNN, CNN, QRNN (Bradbury et al., 2017), Transformer (Vaswani et al., 2017), Highway network, Encoder Decoder architecture, etc. We also support multiple attention layers, such as Linear/Bi-linear Attention, Bidirectional attention flow (Seo et al., 2017), etc. Meanwhile, regularization layers such as Dropout, Layer Norm, etc are also supported.

- **Loss Function**: All built-in loss functions in PyTorch are supported.

- **Metrics**: For classification task, Area Under Curve (AUC), Accuracy, F1 metrics are supported. For sequence labeling task, F1/Accuracy are supported. For knowledge distillation task, MSE/RMSE are supported. For MRC task, ExactMatch/F1 are supported.

3.2 Model Zoo

In NeuronBlocks, we identify four types of most popular NLP tasks. For each task, we provide various end-to-end network templates.

- **Text Classification and Matching**. Tasks such as domain/intent classification, question answer matching are supported.

- **Sequence Labeling**. Predict each token in a sequence into predefined types. Common tasks include NER, POS tagging, Slot tagging, etc.

- **Knowledge Distillation** (Hinton et al., 2015). Teacher-Student based knowledge distillation is one common approach for model compression. NeuronBlocks provides knowledge distillation template to train light-weight student model to imitate heavy DNN models like BERT/GPT.

- **Extractive Machine Reading Comprehension**. Given question and passage, this task is to predict the start and end positions of the answer spans in the passage.

3.3 User Interface

NeuronBlocks provides convenient user interface[4] for users to build, train, and test DNN models. The details are described in the following.

- **I/O interface**. This part defines model input/output, such as training data, pre-trained models/embeddings, model saving path, etc.

- **Model Architecture interface**. This is the key part of the configuration file, which defines the whole model architecture. Figure 2 shows an example of how to specify a model architecture using the blocks in NeuronBlocks. To be more specific, it consists of a list of layers/blocks to construct the architecture, where the blocks are supplied in the gallery of *Block Zoo*.

- **Training Parameters interface**. In this part, the model optimizer as well as all other training hyper parameters are indicated.

3.4 Workflow

Figure 3 shows the workflow of building DNN models in NeuronBlocks. Users only need to write a JSON configuration file. They can either instantiate an existing template from *Model Zoo*, or construct a new architecture based on the blocks from *Block Zoo*. This configuration file is shared across training, test, and prediction.

For model hyper-parameter tuning or architecture modification, users just need to change the JSON configuration file. Advanced users can also contribute novel customized blocks[5] into *Block Zoo*, as long as they follow the same interface guidelines with the existing blocks. These new blocks can be further shared across all users for model architecture design. Moreover, NeuronBlocks has flexible platform support, such as GPU/CPU, GPU management platforms like PAI.

4 Experiments

To verify the performance of NeuronBlocks, we conducted extensive experiments for common

---

[4]https://github.com/microsoft/NeuronBlocks/blob/master/Tutorial.md

[5]https://github.com/microsoft/NeuronBlocks/blob/master/Contributing.md

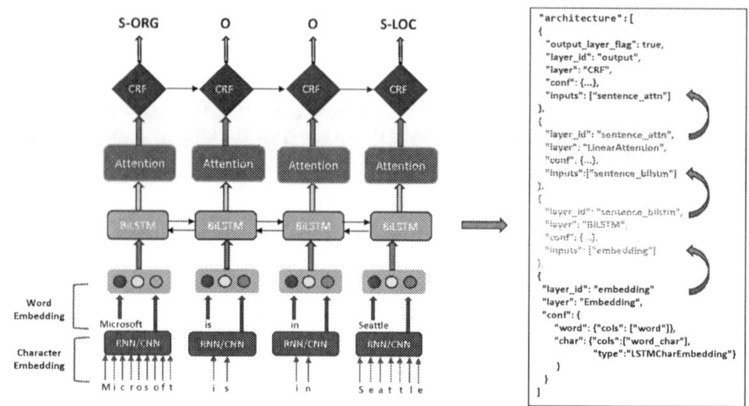

Figure 2: A Model architecture interface example of sequence labeling model in NeuronBlocks.

Results(F1-score)		WLSTM+CRF	WLSTM	WCNN+CRF	WCNN
Nochar	Literature	89.31 ± 0.1(N)	87.00(M-16) 88.49 ± 0.17(N)	88.65 ± 0.2(N)	88.50 ± 0.05(N)
	NeuronBlocks	**89.34**	**88.50**	**88.72**	**88.51**
CLSTM	Literature	90.94(L-16) 91.08 ± 0.08(N)	89.15(L-16) 90.77 ± 0.06(N)	90.48 ± 0.23(N)	90.28 ± 0.30(N)
	NeuronBlocks	**91.03**	**90.67**	**90.27**	**90.37**
CCNN	Literature	90.91 ± 0.2(C-16) 91.21(M-16) 90.87 ± 0.13(P-17) 91.11 ± 0.21(N)	89.36(M-16) 90.60 ± 0.11(N)	90.28 ± 0.09(N)	90.51 ± 0.19(N)
	NeuronBlocks	**91.38**	**90.63**	**90.41**	**90.36**

Table 2: NeuronBlocks results on CoNLL-2003 English NER testb dataset. The abbreviation (C-16)= (Chiu and Nichols, 2016), (L-16)= (Lample et al., 2016), (M-16)= (Ma and Hovy, 2016), (N)= (Yang et al., 2018), (P-17)= (Peters et al., 2017).

Model	CoLA	SST-2	QQP	MNLI	QNLI	RTE	WNLI
BiLSTM (Literature)	17.6	87.5	85.3/82.0	66.7	77.0	58.5	56.3
+Attn (Literature)	17.6	87.5	87.7/83.9	70.0	77.2	58.5	60.6
BiLSTM (NeuronBlocks)	**20.4**	**87.5**	**86.4/83.1**	**69.8**	**79.8**	**59.2**	**59.2**
+Attn (NeuronBlocks)	**25.1**	**88.3**	**87.8/83.9**	**73.6**	**81.0**	**58.9**	**59.8**

Table 3: NeuronBlocks results on GLUE benchmark development sets. As described in (Wang et al., 2019), for CoLA, we report Matthews correlation. For QQP, we report accuracy and F1. For MNLI, we report accuracy averaged over the matched and mismatched development sets. For all other tasks we report accuracy. All values have been scaled by 100. Please note that results on the development sets are reported, since GLUE does not distribute labels for the test sets.

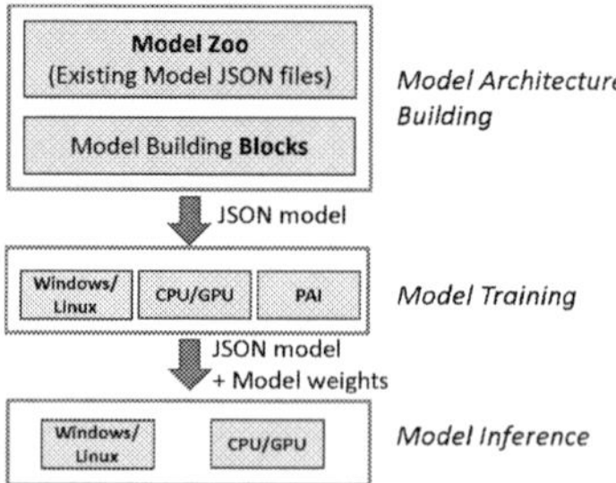

Figure 3: The workflow of NeuronBlocks.

NLP tasks on public data sets including CoNLL-2003 (Sang and Meulder, 2003), GLUE benchmark (Wang et al., 2019), and WikiQA corpus (Yang et al., 2015). The experimental results showed that the models built with NeuronBlocks can achieve reliable and competitive results on various tasks, with productivity greatly improved.

4.1 Sequence Labeling

We evaluated NeuronBlocks on CoNLL-2003 (Sang and Meulder, 2003) English NER dataset, following most works on the same task. This dataset includes four types of named entities, namely, *PERSON, LOCATION, ORGANIZATION*, and *MISC*. We adopted BIOES tagging scheme instead of IOB, as many previous works indicated meaningful improvement with BIOES scheme (Ratinov and Roth, 2009). Table 2 shows the results on CoNLL-2003 Englist testb dataset, with 12 different combinations of network layers/blocks, such as word/character embedding, CNN/LSTM and CRF. The results suggest that the flexible combination of layers/blocks in Neu-

Model	Inference Speed QPS	Parameters	Performance AUC
Teacher Model (BERT$_{base}$)	448	110M	0.9112
Student Model (BiLSTMAttn+TextCNN)	**11128**	**13.63M**	**0.8941**

Table 4: NeuronBlocks results on Knowledge Distillation task.

ronBlocks can easily reproduce the performance of original models, with comparative or slightly better performance.

4.2 GLUE Benchmark

The General Language Understanding Evaluation (GLUE) benchmark (Wang et al., 2019) is a collection of natural language understanding tasks. We experimented on the GLUE benchmark tasks using BiLSTM and Attention based models. As shown in Table 3, the models built by Neuron-Blocks can achieve competitive or even better results on GLUE tasks with minimal coding efforts.

4.3 Knowledge Distillation

In teacher-student based knowledge distillation, a lightweight student model is trained by imitating the output of heavy teacher model like BERT. We evaluated on a binary classification dataset called Domain Classification Dataset, which was collected from a commercial search engine. Each sample in this dataset consists of two parts, i.e., a query and a binary label indicating whether the query belongs to a specific domain. Table 4 shows the results, where AUC is used as the evaluation criteria and Queries per Second (QPS) is used to measure inference speed. By leveraging knowledge distillation, the student model by NeuronBlocks managed to get **24.8** times inference speedup with only small performance regression compared with BERT$_{base}$[6] fine-tuned classifier.

4.4 WikiQA

The WikiQA corpus (Yang et al., 2015) is a publicly available dataset for open-domain question answering. This dataset contains 3,047 questions from Bing query logs, each associated with some candidate answer sentences from Wikipedia. We conducted experiments on WikiQA dataset using CNN, BiLSTM, and Attention based models. The results are shown in Table 5. The models built in NeuronBlocks achieved competitive or even better results with simple model configurations.

5 Conclusion and Future Work

In this paper, we introduce NeuronBlocks, a DNN toolkit for NLP tasks built on PyTorch, targeting

Model	AUC
CNN ((Yang et al., 2015))	73.59
CNN-Cnt ((Yang et al., 2015))	75.33
CNN (NeuronBlocks)	**74.79**
BiLSTM (NeuronBlocks)	**76.73**
BiLSTM+Attn (NeuronBlocks)	**75.48**
BiLSTM+MatchAttn (NeuronBlocks)	**78.54**

Table 5: NeuronBlocks results on WikiQA.

three types of engineers, and provides a two-layer solution to satisfy the requirements from all three types of users. To be more specific, the *Model Zoo* consists of various templates for the most common NLP tasks, while the *Block Zoo* supplies a gallery of alternative layers/modules for the networks. Such design achieves a balance between generality and flexibility. Extensive experiments have verified the effectiveness of this approach. NeuronBlocks has been widely used in a product team of a commercial search engine, and significantly improved the productivity for developing NLP DNN approaches.

As an open-source toolkit, we will further extend it in various directions. The following names a few examples.

- Multi-task learning (MTL). In MTL, multiple related tasks are jointly trained so that knowledge learned in one task can benefit other tasks.

- Pre-training and fine-tuning. Deep pre-training models such as ELMo (Peters et al., 2018), GPT (Radford et al., 2018), BERT (Devlin et al., 2019) are new directions in NLP.

- Sequence generation task. Sequence generation is widely used in NLP fields such as machine translation (Bahdanau et al., 2015), text summarization (See et al., 2017), and dialogue systems (Wen et al., 2015).

- AutoML (Elsken et al., 2019). NeuronBlocks facilitates users to build models on top of *Model Zoo* and *Block Zoo*. With the integration of AutoML, the toolkit can further support automatic model architecture design.

6 Acknowledgements

We sincerely thank the anonymous reviewers for their valuable suggestions.

---

[6] https://github.com/huggingface/pytorch-transformers

References

Dzmitry Bahdanau, Kyunghyun Cho, and Yoshua Bengio. 2015. Neural machine translation by jointly learning to align and translate.

James Bradbury, Stephen Merity, Caiming Xiong, and Richard Socher. 2017. Quasi-recurrent neural networks.

Jason P. C. Chiu and Eric Nichols. 2016. Named entity recognition with bidirectional lstm-cnns. *TACL*, 4:357–370.

Jacob Devlin, Ming-Wei Chang, Kenton Lee, and Kristina Toutanova. 2019. BERT: pre-training of deep bidirectional transformers for language understanding. pages 4171–4186.

Thomas Elsken, Jan Hendrik Metzen, and Frank Hutter. 2019. Neural architecture search: A survey. *Journal of Machine Learning Research*, 20(55):1–21.

Matt Gardner, Joel Grus, Mark Neumann, Oyvind Tafjord, Pradeep Dasigi, Nelson Liu, Matthew Peters, Michael Schmitz, and Luke Zettlemoyer. 2018. Allennlp: A deep semantic natural language processing platform. *arXiv preprint arXiv:1803.07640*.

Geoffrey E. Hinton, Oriol Vinyals, and Jeffrey Dean. 2015. Distilling the knowledge in a neural network. *CoRR*, abs/1503.02531.

Guillaume Klein, Yoon Kim, Yuntian Deng, Jean Senellart, and Alexander M. Rush. 2017. Opennmt: Open-source toolkit for neural machine translation. pages 67–72.

Guillaume Lample, Miguel Ballesteros, Sandeep Subramanian, Kazuya Kawakami, and Chris Dyer. 2016. Neural architectures for named entity recognition. In *NAACL HLT 2016, The 2016 Conference of the North American Chapter of the Association for Computational Linguistics: Human Language Technologies, San Diego California, USA, June 12-17, 2016*, pages 260–270.

Xuezhe Ma and Eduard H. Hovy. 2016. End-to-end sequence labeling via bi-directional lstm-cnns-crf. In *Proceedings of the 54th Annual Meeting of the Association for Computational Linguistics, ACL 2016, August 7-12, 2016, Berlin, Germany, Volume 1: Long Papers*.

Matthew E. Peters, Waleed Ammar, Chandra Bhagavatula, and Russell Power. 2017. Semi-supervised sequence tagging with bidirectional language models. In *Proceedings of the 55th Annual Meeting of the Association for Computational Linguistics, ACL 2017, Vancouver, Canada, July 30 - August 4, Volume 1: Long Papers*, pages 1756–1765.

Matthew E. Peters, Mark Neumann, Mohit Iyyer, Matt Gardner, Christopher Clark, Kenton Lee, and Luke Zettlemoyer. 2018. Deep contextualized word representations. pages 2227–2237.

Alec Radford, Karthik Narasimhan, Tim Salimans, and Ilya Sutskever. 2018. Improving language understanding by generative pre-training. *URL https://s3-us-west-2. amazonaws. com/openai-assets/research-covers/languageunsupervised/language understanding paper. pdf.*

Lev-Arie Ratinov and Dan Roth. 2009. Design challenges and misconceptions in named entity recognition. In *Proceedings of the Thirteenth Conference on Computational Natural Language Learning, CoNLL 2009, Boulder, Colorado, USA, June 4-5, 2009*, pages 147–155.

Erik F. Tjong Kim Sang and Fien De Meulder. 2003. Introduction to the conll-2003 shared task: Language-independent named entity recognition. In *Proceedings of the Seventh Conference on Natural Language Learning, CoNLL 2003, Held in cooperation with HLT-NAACL 2003, Edmonton, Canada, May 31 - June 1, 2003*, pages 142–147.

Abigail See, Peter J. Liu, and Christopher D. Manning. 2017. Get to the point: Summarization with pointer-generator networks. pages 1073–1083.

Min Joon Seo, Aniruddha Kembhavi, Ali Farhadi, and Hannaneh Hajishirzi. 2017. Bidirectional attention flow for machine comprehension.

Ashish Vaswani, Noam Shazeer, Niki Parmar, Jakob Uszkoreit, Llion Jones, Aidan N Gomez, Łukasz Kaiser, and Illia Polosukhin. 2017. Attention is all you need. In *Advances in neural information processing systems*, pages 5998–6008.

Alex Wang, Amanpreet Singh, Julian Michael, Felix Hill, Omer Levy, and Samuel R. Bowman. 2019. GLUE: A multi-task benchmark and analysis platform for natural language understanding. In *7th International Conference on Learning Representations, ICLR 2019, New Orleans, LA, USA, May 6-9, 2019*.

Tsung-Hsien Wen, Milica Gasic, Nikola Mrksic, Pei-hao Su, David Vandyke, and Steve J. Young. 2015. Semantically conditioned lstm-based natural language generation for spoken dialogue systems. pages 1711–1721.

Jie Yang, Shuailong Liang, and Yue Zhang. 2018. Design challenges and misconceptions in neural sequence labeling. In *Proceedings of the 27th International Conference on Computational Linguistics, COLING 2018, Santa Fe, New Mexico, USA, August 20-26, 2018*, pages 3879–3889.

Yi Yang, Wen-tau Yih, and Christopher Meek. 2015. Wikiqa: A challenge dataset for open-domain question answering. In *Proceedings of the 2015 Conference on Empirical Methods in Natural Language Processing*, pages 2013–2018.

OpenNRE: An Open and Extensible Toolkit for Neural Relation Extraction

Xu Han[*], **Tianyu Gao**[*], **Yuan Yao, Demin Ye, Zhiyuan Liu**[†]**, Maosong Sun**
Department of Computer Science and Technology, Tsinghua University, Beijing, China
Institute for Artificial Intelligence, Tsinghua University, Beijing, China
State Key Lab on Intelligent Technology and Systems, Tsinghua University, Beijing, China
{hanxu17,gty16,yy18,ydm18}@mails.tsinghua.edu.cn

Abstract

OpenNRE is an open-source and extensible toolkit that provides a unified framework to implement neural models for relation extraction (RE). Specifically, by implementing typical RE methods, OpenNRE not only allows developers to train custom models to extract structured relational facts from the plain text but also supports quick model validation for researchers. Besides, OpenNRE provides various functional RE modules based on both TensorFlow and PyTorch to maintain sufficient modularity and extensibility, making it becomes easy to incorporate new models into the framework. Besides the toolkit, we also release an online system to meet real-time extraction without any training and deploying. Meanwhile, the online system can extract facts in various scenarios as well as aligning the extracted facts to Wikidata, which may benefit various downstream knowledge-driven applications (e.g., information retrieval and question answering). More details of the toolkit and online system can be obtained from http://github.com/thunlp/OpenNRE.

1 Introduction

Relation extraction (RE) aims to predict relational facts from the plain text, e.g., extracting (*Newton*, the Member of, *the Royal Society*) from the sentence "*Newton* served as the president of *the Royal Society*". Because RE models can extract structured information for various downstream applications, many efforts have been devoted to researching RE. As the rapid development of deep learning in the recent years, neural relation extraction (NRE) models show the strong ability to extracting relations and achieve great performance, which makes more and more researchers and industry developers pay attention to this field.

Although the current NRE models are effective and have been applied for various scenarios, including supervised learning paradigm (Zeng et al., 2014a; Nguyen and Grishman, 2015; Zhang et al., 2015; Zhou et al., 2016), distantly supervised learning paradigm (Zeng et al., 2015; Lin et al., 2016; Han et al., 2018b), few-shot learning paradigm (Han et al., 2018c; Gao et al., 2019; Ye and Ling, 2019; Soares et al., 2019; Zhang et al., 2019), there still lack an effective and stable toolkit to support the implementation, deployment and evaluation of models. In fact, for other tasks related to RE, there have been already some effective and long-term maintained toolkits, such as Spacy[1] for named entity recognition (NER), TagMe (Ferragina and Scaiella, 2010) for entity linking (EL), OpenKE (Han et al., 2018a) for knowledge embedding, and Stanford OpenIE (Angeli et al., 2015) for open information extraction. Hence, it becomes necessary and significant to systematically develop an efficient and effective toolkit for RE.

To this end, we develop an open and extensible toolkit for designing and implementing RE models, especially for NRE models, which is named "OpenNRE". The toolkit prioritizes operational efficiency based on TensorFlow and PyTorch, which support quick model training and validation. Meanwhile, the toolkit maintains sufficient system encapsulation and model extensibility, which can meet some individual requirements of incorporating new models. To keep the ease of use, we implement many typical RE models and provide a unified framework for their data processing, model training, and experimental evaluation. For those developers aiming at training custom

---

[*] indicates equal contribution
[†] Corresponding author: Z.Liu(liuzy@tsinghua.edu.cn)

[1] https://spacy.io

Proceedings of the 2019 EMNLP and the 9th IJCNLP (System Demonstrations), pages 169–174
Hong Kong, China, November 3 – 7, 2019. ©2019 Association for Computational Linguistics

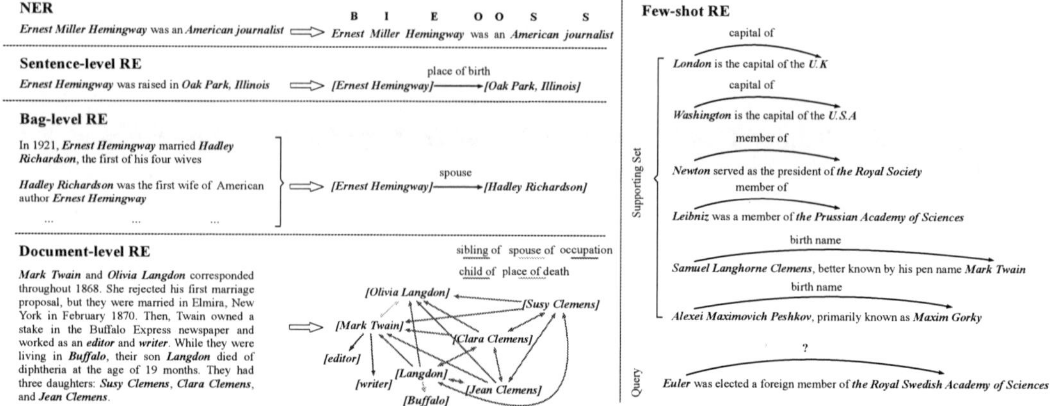

Figure 1: The examples of all application scenarios in OpenNRE.

models, they can quickly start up their RE system based on OpenNRE, without knowing too many technical details and writing tedious glue code. An online system is also available to extract structured relational facts from the text with friendly interactive interfaces and fast reaction speed. We will provide long-term maintenance to fix bugs and meet new requests for OpenNRE, and we think both researchers and industry developers can benefit from our toolkit.

2 Application Scenarios

OpenNRE is designed for various scenarios for RE, including sentence-level RE, bag-level RE, document-level RE, and few-shot RE. For completing a full pipeline of extracting structured information, we also enable OpenNRE to have the capacity of entity-oriented applications to a certain extent, e.g., NER and EL. The examples of these application scenarios are all shown in Figure 1.

2.1 Entity-Oriented Applications

For extracting structured information from plain text, it requires to extract entities from text and then predict relations between entities. In normal RE scenarios, all entity mentions have been already annotated and RE models are just required to classify relations for all annotated entity pairs. Although the entity-oriented applications are not the focus of our toolkit, we still implement specific modules for NER (Lample et al., 2016) and EL (Han et al., 2011). The NER modules can detect words or phrases (also named entity mentions) representing real-world objects. In Open-NRE, we provide two approaches for NER, one is

based on spaCy, the other is based on fine-tuning BERT (Devlin et al., 2019). The EL modules can align those entity mentions to the entities in Wikidata (Vrandečić and Krötzsch, 2014) based on TagMe (Ferragina and Scaiella, 2010).

2.2 Sentence-Level Relation Extraction

The conventional methods often handle RE in the supervised learning paradigm and extract the relation between two entities mentioned within one sentence. As shown in Figure 1, each sentence is first manually annotated with two entity mentions. Then models are required to predict the relation between those annotated entity mentions. As there are many efforts to adopt models for this setting (Zeng et al., 2014a; Zhang et al., 2015; Zhou et al., 2016), OpenNRE is specially designed for the sentence-level RE scenario.

2.3 Bag-Level Relation Extraction

The supervised RE methods suffer from several problems, especially their requirements of adequate annotated data for training. As manually labeling large amounts of data is expensive and time-consuming, Mintz et al. (2009) introduce distant supervision to automatically label large amounts of data for RE by aligning knowledge graphs and text. Although distant supervision brings sufficient auto-labeled data, it also leads to the wrong labeling problem. Considering an entity pair may occur several times in different sentences, and there is a significant probability that some of these sentences can express the relation between the entity pair. Hence Riedel et al. (2010) and Hoffmann et al. (2011) introduce to aggregate the sentences mentioning the same entity pair into a entity-pair bag. As shown in Figure 1, synthesizing the features of different sentences in a bag can provide more reliable information and result in more accurate predictions. The Bag-level setting is widely applied by various distantly supervised RE methods (Zeng et al., 2015; Lin et al., 2016; Han et al., 2018b), and thus it is also integrated into OpenNRE.

2.4 Document-Level Relation Extraction

Yao et al. (2019) have pointed out that multiple entities in documents often exhibit complex inter-sentence relations rather than intra-sentence relations. Besides, as shown in Figure 1, a large number of relational facts are expressed in multiple sentences, e.g., *Langdon* is the sibling of *Jean Clemens*. Hence, it is hard to extract these inter-sentence relations with both the sentence-level and bag-level settings. Although the document-level RE setting is not widely explored by the current work, we argue that this scenario remains an open problem for future research, and still integrate document-level RE into OpenNRE.

2.5 Few-Shot Relation Extraction

Though we can train a usable and stable RE system based on the above-mentioned scenarios, which can well predict those relations appearing frequently in data, some long-tail relations with few instances in data are still neglected. Recently, some methods have been proposed to provide a different view of this problem by formalizing RE as a few-shot learning problem (Han et al., 2018c; Gao et al., 2019; Ye and Ling, 2019; Soares et al., 2019; Zhang et al., 2019). As shown in Figure 1, each relation only have a handful of instances in the supporting set in a few-shot RE scenario, and models are required to be capable of accurately capturing relation patterns of these small amounts of training instances. Considering few-shot RE is important for handling long-tail relations, OpenNRE also provides a custom platform for further research in this direction.

3 Toolkit Design and Implementation

Our goal of designing OpenNRE is achieving the balance among system encapsulation, operational efficiency, model extensibility, and ease of use.

For system encapsulation, we build a unified underlying platform to encapsulate various data processing and training strategies, so that developers

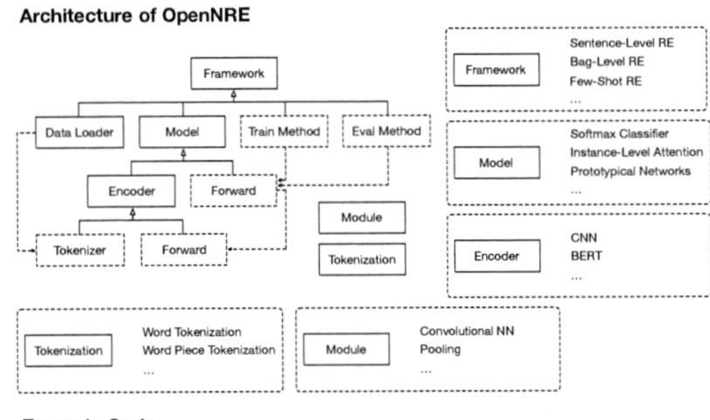

Example Code

```
rel2id = 'relation->id dictionary'
# Define encoder
sentence_encoder = nrekit.encoder.BERTEncoder(
    max_length=80, pretrain_path='bert pretrain model path')
# Define model
model = nrekit.model.SoftmaxNN(sentence_encoder, len(rel2id), rel2id)
# Define framework
framework = nrekit.framework.SentenceRE(
    train_path='path of training data',
    val_path='path of validation data',
    test_path='path of test data',
    model=model,
    ckpt='path of checkpoint',
    batch_size=64,
    max_epoch=10,
    lr=3e-5,
    opt='bert_adam')
# Train
framework.train_model()
# Test
framework.load_state_dict(torch.load(ckpt)['state_dict'])
result = framework.eval_model(framework.test_loader)
```

Figure 2: The architecture and example code of OpenNRE. The structure shows the contents of each part of OpenNRE and how they are related. Based on OpenNRE, one can use only a few lines of code to define, train and evaluate RE models of different scenarios.

can maximize the reuse of code to avoid unnecessary redundant model implementations. For operational efficiency, OpenNRE is based on Tensor-Flow and PyTorch, which enables developers to train models on GPUs. For model extensibility, we systematically implement various neural modules and some special algorithms (e.g., adversarial training (Wu et al., 2017) and reinforcement learning (Feng et al., 2018)). Hence, it is easy to implement new RE models based on OpenNRE. We also implement some typical RE models so as to conveniently train custom models for specific application scenarios.

More specifically, OpenNRE attains the above four design objects through implementing the following five components.

3.1 Tokenization

The tokenization component is responsible for tokenizing input text into several input tokens. In OpenNRE, we implement both word-level tokenization and subword-level tokenization. These two operations satisfy most tokenization demands and help developers get rid of spending too much time writing glue code for data processing. For building a new tokenizer, extending the

`BasicTokenizer` class and implementing specific tokenization operations is convenient.

3.2 Module

The module component consists of various functional neural modules for model implementation, such as the essential network layers, some pooling operations, and activation functions. In order to adapt these modules for RE scenarios, we also implement some special RE neural modules (e.g., piece-wise pooling operation (Zeng et al., 2015)). Using these atomic modules to construct and deploy RE systems has a high degree of freedom.

3.3 Encoder

The encoder is applied to encode text into its corresponding embeddings to provide semantic features. In OpenNRE, we implement the `BaseEncoder` class based on the tokenization and module components, which can provide basic functions of text tokenization and embedding lookup. By extending the `BaseEncoder` class and implementing specific neural encoding architecture, we can implement various specific encoders. In OpenNRE, we have implemented the common convolutional and recurrent neural encoders, as well as the pre-trained encoder BERT.

3.4 Model

Some developers may not require to implement and verify their own RE models, and their main demand is to easily train and deploy custom models. To this end, we also replicate several typical RE models (Zeng et al., 2015; Zhang et al., 2015). Some special algorithms for enhancing RE models are also included in the toolkit, such as attention mechanism (Lin et al., 2016), adversarial training (Wu et al., 2017), and reinforcement learning (Feng et al., 2018). On the one hand, the model component enables us to train custom models without having to understand all technical details. On the other hand, the implemented models in this model component are all tutorial examples to show how to build models with OpenNRE.

3.5 Framework

The framework module is mainly responsible for integrating other four components and supporting various functions (including data processing, model training, model optimizing, and model evaluating). In OpenNRE, for all application scenarios mentioned in Section 2, we have implemented

Model	Wiki80	SemEval
CNN	63.93	71.11
BERT	84.57	84.02
BERT-Entity	86.61	84.21

Table 1: Accuracies of various models on Wiki80 and SemEval 2010 Task-8 under the single sentence setting.

Model	F1	F1 (*)
BERT	0.880	-
BERT-Entity	0.883	0.892

Table 2: Micro F1 scores of various models on SemEval 2010 Task-8 under the sentence-level RE setting. "(*)" indicates the original results from Soares et al. (2019).

their corresponding framework. For other future potential application scenarios, we have also reserved interfaces for their implementation.

4 Experiment and Evaluation

In this section, we evaluate our toolkit on several benchmark datasets in different RE scenarios. The evaluation results show that our implementation of some state-of-the-art models with OpenNRE can achieve comparable or even better performance, as compared to the original papers.

4.1 Sentence-Level Relation Extraction

We experiment on two different encoders for sentence-level relation extraction: CNN (Zeng et al., 2014b) and BERT (Devlin et al., 2019). For CNN, we follow the setting of Nguyen and Grishman (2015), including using word and position embeddings. For BERT, we follow the setting of Soares et al. (2019). "BERT" in our paper refers to using entity markers in input and taking `[CLS]` as output. "BERT-Entity" refers to using entity markers in input and taking entity start as output like Soares et al. (2019).

We carry out experiments on two datasets of sentence-level RE: SemEval 2010 Task-8 (Hendrickx et al., 2009) and Wiki80. SemEval 2010 Task-8 contains 19 relations and 10,717 instances, 17.4% of which are with no relation. Wiki80 is derived from FewRel (Han et al., 2018c), a large scale few-shot dataset. It contains 80 relations and 56,000 instances from Wikipedia and Wikidata (Vrandečić and Krötzsch, 2014). Since Wiki80 is not an official benchmark, we directly report the results on the validation set. From Table 1 we can see that BERT-based models perform bet-

Model	5-Way 1-Shot	5-Way 5-Shot	5-Way 1-Shot (*)	5-Way 5-Shot (*)
Prototype-CNN	74.5	88.4	69.2	84.8
Prototype-BERT	80.7	89.6	-	-
BERT-PAIR	88.3	93.2	-	-

Table 3: Accuracies of various models on FewRel under the different few-shot settings. "(*)" indicates the original results taken from Han et al. (2018c).

Model	AUC	F1	AUC (*)	F1 (*)
CNN-ATT	0.333	0.397	0.318	0.380
CNN-ADV	0.337	0.406	-	-
CNN-RL	0.276	0.429	-	0.42

Table 4: AUC and F1 scores of various models on NYT10 under the bag-level RE setting. "(*)" indicates the original results taken from Lin et al. (2016) and Feng et al. (2018).

ter than the CNN model and achieve promising results on both datasets. Our implementation of BERT-Entity with OpenNRE achieves comparable results to the original work in Table 2.

4.2 Bag-Level Relation Extraction

We implement models with instance-level attention (Lin et al., 2016), adversarial training (Wu et al., 2017) and reinforcement learning (Feng et al., 2018) for bag-level relation extraction. Note that the latter two are based on the instance-level attention mechanism. We use the same CNN encoder as Section 4.1 and denote the three models as "CNN-ATT", "CNN-ADV" and "CNN-RL". We evaluate those three models on NYT10 (Riedel et al., 2010), a distantly supervised dataset based on New York Times corpus and FreeBase (Bollacker et al., 2008). Table 4 shows that our version of bag-level RE models achieves comparable or even better results than the original papers.

4.3 Few-Shot Relation Extraction

We experiment on Prototypical Networks (Snell et al., 2017) for few-shot RE. For the encoder selection, we take CNN and BERT as described in Section 4.1. We also implement a model named "BERT-PAIR", which takes one supporting sentence and one query sentence as input, and directly outputs the probability that they share the same relation with the BERT sequence classification model. The experiments are carried out on FewRel described in Section 4.1. From Table 3 we can see that for both few-shot settings, our version achieves better results than the original results from Han et al. (2018c), proving that our imple-

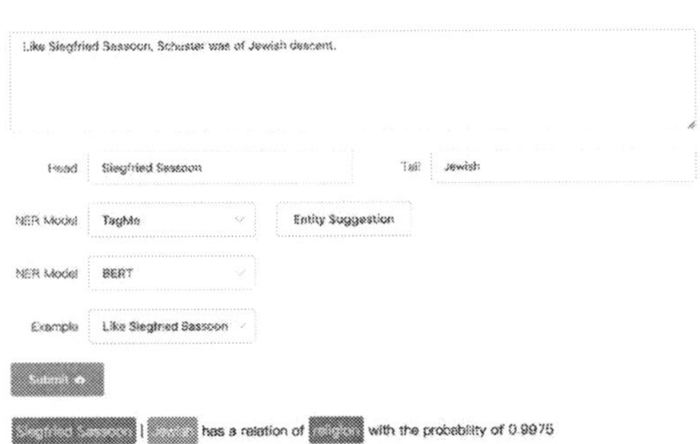

Figure 3: An example of the online system.

mentation with OpenNRE is robust.

5 Online System

Besides the toolkit, we also release an online system. As shown in Figure 3, we train a model in the sentence-level RE scenario and deploy the model for online access. The online system can be directly applied for extracting structured facts from plain text. Meanwhile, all extracted entity mentions and relations can be aligned to Wikidata.

6 Conclusion

We propose OpenNRE, an open and extensible toolkit for relation extraction. OpenNRE achieves the balance among system encapsulation, operational efficiency, model extensibility, and ease of use. Based on OpenNRE, either training custom models or quick model validation becomes easy. Some experimental results also demonstrate that the models implemented by OpenNRE are efficient and effective, which can achieve comparable or even better performance as compared to the original papers. Furthermore, an online system is also available for meeting real-time extraction without training and deploying. In the future, we will provide long-term maintenance to fix bugs and meet new requests.

Acknowledgments

This work is supported by the National Key Research and Development Program of China (No.

2018YFB1004503) and the National Natural Science Foundation of China (NSFC No. 61572273, 61772302). Han and Gao are supported by 2018 and 2019 Tencent Rhino-Bird Elite Training Program respectively. Gao is also supported by Tsinghua University Initiative Scientific Research Program.

References

Gabor Angeli, Melvin Jose Johnson Premkumar, and Christopher D Manning. 2015. Leveraging linguistic structure for open domain information extraction. In *Proceedings of ACL*.

Kurt Bollacker, Colin Evans, Praveen Paritosh, Tim Sturge, and Jamie Taylor. 2008. Freebase: a collaboratively created graph database for structuring human knowledge. In *Proceedings of SIGMOD*.

Jacob Devlin, Ming-Wei Chang, Kenton Lee, and Kristina Toutanova. 2019. BERT: pre-training of deep bidirectional transformers for language understanding. In *Proceedings of NAACL-HLT*.

Jun Feng, Minlie Huang, Li Zhao, Yang Yang, and Xiaoyan Zhu. 2018. Reinforcement learning for relation classification from noisy data. In *Proceedings of AAAI*.

Paolo Ferragina and Ugo Scaiella. 2010. TAGME: on-the-fly annotation of short text fragments (by wikipedia entities). In *Proceedings of CIKM*.

Tianyu Gao, Xu Han, Zhiyuan Liu, and Maosong Sun. 2019. Hybrid attention-based prototypical networks for noisy few-shot relation classification. In *Proceedings of AAAI*.

Xianpei Han, Le Sun, and Jun Zhao. 2011. Collective entity linking in web text: a graph-based method. In *Proceedings of SIGIR*.

Xu Han, Shulin Cao, Xin Lv, Yankai Lin, Zhiyuan Liu, Maosong Sun, and Juanzi Li. 2018a. Openke: An open toolkit for knowledge embedding. In *Proceedings of EMNLP*.

Xu Han, Pengfei Yu, Zhiyuan Liu, Maosong Sun, and Peng Li. 2018b. Hierarchical relation extraction with coarse-to-fine grained attention. In *Proceedings of EMNLP*.

Xu Han, Hao Zhu, Pengfei Yu, Ziyun Wang, Yuan Yao, Zhiyuan Liu, and Maosong Sun. 2018c. Fewrel: A large-scale supervised few-shot relation classification dataset with state-of-the-art evaluation. In *Proceedings of EMNLP*.

Iris Hendrickx, Su Nam Kim, Zornitsa Kozareva, Preslav Nakov, Diarmuid Ó Séaghdha, Sebastian Padó, Marco Pennacchiotti, Lorenza Romano, and Stan Szpakowicz. 2009. Semeval-2010 task 8: Multi-way classification of semantic relations between pairs of nominals. In *Proceedings of the Workshop on SemEval*.

Raphael Hoffmann, Congle Zhang, Xiao Ling, Luke Zettlemoyer, and Daniel S Weld. 2011. Knowledge-based weak supervision for information extraction of overlapping relations. In *Proceedings of ACL*.

Guillaume Lample, Miguel Ballesteros, Sandeep Subramanian, Kazuya Kawakami, and Chris Dyer. 2016. Neural architectures for named entity recognition. In *Proceedings of NAACL-HLT*.

Yankai Lin, Shiqi Shen, Zhiyuan Liu, Huanbo Luan, and Maosong Sun. 2016. Neural relation extraction with selective attention over instances. In *Proceedings of ACL*.

Mike Mintz, Steven Bills, Rion Snow, and Dan Jurafsky. 2009. Distant supervision for relation extraction without labeled data. In *Proceedings of ACL-IJCNLP*.

Thien Huu Nguyen and Ralph Grishman. 2015. Relation extraction: Perspective from convolutional neural networks. In *Proceedings of the NAACL-HLT*.

Sebastian Riedel, Limin Yao, and Andrew McCallum. 2010. Modeling relations and their mentions without labeled text. In *Proceedings of ECML-PKDD*.

Jake Snell, Kevin Swersky, and Richard Zemel. 2017. Prototypical networks for few-shot learning. In *Proceedings of NIPS*.

Livio Baldini Soares, Nicholas FitzGerald, Jeffrey Ling, and Tom Kwiatkowski. 2019. Matching the blanks: Distributional similarity for relation learning. In *Proceedings of ACL*.

Denny Vrandečić and Markus Krötzsch. 2014. Wikidata: a free collaborative knowledgebase. *Communications of the ACM*.

Yi Wu, David Bamman, and Stuart Russell. 2017. Adversarial training for relation extraction. In *Proceedings of EMNLP*.

Yuan Yao, Deming Ye, Peng Li, Xu Han, Yankai Lin, Zhenghao Liu, Zhiyuan Liu, Lixin Huang, Jie Zhou, and Maosong Sun. 2019. Docred: A large-scale document-level relation extraction dataset. In *Proceedings of ACL*.

Zhi-Xiu Ye and Zhen-Hua Ling. 2019. Multi-level matching and aggregation network for few-shot relation classification. In *Proceedings of ACL*.

Daojian Zeng, Kang Liu, Yubo Chen, and Jun Zhao. 2015. Distant supervision for relation extraction via piecewise convolutional neural networks. In *Proceedings of EMNLP*.

Daojian Zeng, Kang Liu, Siwei Lai, Guangyou Zhou, and Jun Zhao. 2014a. Relation classification via convolutional deep neural network. In *Proceedings of COLING*.

Daojian Zeng, Kang Liu, Siwei Lai, Guangyou Zhou, and Jun Zhao. 2014b. Relation classification via convolutional deep neural network. In *Proceedings of COLING*.

Shu Zhang, Dequan Zheng, Xinchen Hu, and Ming Yang. 2015. Bidirectional long short-term memory networks for relation classification. In *Proceedings of PACLIC*.

Zhengyan Zhang, Xu Han, Zhiyuan Liu, Xin Jiang, Maosong Sun, and Qun Liu. 2019. Ernie: Enhanced language representation with informative entities. In *Proceedings of ACL*.

Peng Zhou, Wei Shi, Jun Tian, Zhenyu Qi, Bingchen Li, Hongwei Hao, and Bo Xu. 2016. Attention-based bidirectional long short-term memory networks for relation classification. In *Proceedings of ACL*.

ParaQG: A System for Generating Questions and Answers from Paragraphs

Vishwajeet Kumar[1,3,4], **Sivaanandh Muneeswaran**[2], **Ganesh Ramakrishnan**[3], and **Yuan-Fang Li**[4]

[1]IITB-Monash Research Academy, Mumbai, India
[2]Mepco Schlenk Engineering College, Tamilnadu, India
[3]IIT Bombay, Mumbai, India
[4]Monash University, Melbourne, Australia

Abstract

Generating syntactically and semantically valid and relevant questions from paragraphs is useful with many applications. Manual generation is a labour-intensive task, as it requires the reading, parsing and understanding of long passages of text. A number of question generation models based on sequence-to-sequence techniques have recently been proposed. Most of them generate questions from sentences only, and none of them is publicly available as an easy-to-use service. In this paper, we demonstrate ParaQG, a Web-based system for generating questions from sentences and paragraphs. ParaQG incorporates a number of novel functionalities to make the question generation process user-friendly. It provides an interactive interface for a user to select answers with visual insights on generation of questions. It also employs various faceted views to group similar questions as well as filtering techniques to eliminate unanswerable questions.

1 Introduction

Asking relevant and intelligent questions has always been an integral part of human learning, as it can help assess user understanding of a piece of text (a comprehension, an article, etc.). However, forming questions manually is an arduous task. Automated question generation (QG) systems can help alleviate this problem by learning to generate questions on a large scale efficiently. A QG system has many applications in a wide variety of areas such as FAQ generation, intelligent tutoring systems, automating reading comprehension, and virtual assistants/chatbots. For a QG system, the task is to generate syntactically coherent, semantically correct and natural questions from text. Additionally, it is highly desirable that the questions are relevant to the text and are pivoted on answers present in the text. Distinct from other natural lan-

Paragraph:
Genghis Khan came to power by uniting many of the nomadic tribes of Northeast Asia. After founding the Mongol Empire and being proclaimed "Genghis Khan" , he started the Mongol invasions that resulted in the conquest of most of Eurasia . These included raids or invasions of the Qara Khitai, Caucasus, Khwarezmid Empire, Western Xia and Jin dynasties. These campaigns were often accompanied by wholesale massacres of the civilian populations - especially in the Khwarezmian and Xia controlled lands . By the end of his life, the Mongol Empire occupied a substantial portion of Central Asia and China .
Questions:
-what was the name of the invasions that resulted in the conquest of eurasia ?
Mongol invasions
-who occupied a substantial portion of central asia ?
Mongol empire
-who started the mongol empire ?
Genghis Khan

Figure 1: Example: Questions generated from the same paragraph across choices of pivotal answer(s).

guage generation tasks such as summarisation and paraphrasing, answers play an important role in question generation. Different questions can be formed from the same passage based on the choice of the *pivotal answer*. The *pivotal answer* is the span of text from the input passage around which a question is generated. The *pivotal answer* can be either selected manually by the user, automatically by the system or by a combination of the two. For example in Figure 1 it can be seen that based on different answers selected (highlighted in different colours), our system generates different questions.

Neural network-based sequence-to-sequence (Seq2Seq) models represent the state-of-the-art in question generation. Most of these models (Du et al., 2017; Kumar et al., 2018; Song et al., 2018; Kumar et al., 2019c,b) take single sentence as input, thus limiting their usefulness in real-world settings. Some recent techniques tackle the problem of question generation from paragraphs (Zhao et al., 2018). However, none of the above works is publicly available as an online service.

In this work we present ParaQG, an interactive Web-based question generation system to generate correct, meaningful and relevant questions

Proceedings of the 2019 EMNLP and the 9th IJCNLP (System Demonstrations), pages 175–180
Hong Kong, China, November 3 – 7, 2019. ©2019 Association for Computational Linguistics

from sentences, and paragraphs. Given a passage of text as input, users can manually select a set of answer spans to ask questions about (*i.e.* choose answers) from an automatically curated set of noun phrases and named entities. Questions are then generated by a combination of a (novel) sequence-to-sequence model with dynamic dictionaries, the copy mechanism (Gu et al., 2016) and the global sparse-max attention (Martins and Astudillo, 2016).

ParaQG incorporates the following main features.

1. An interactive, user-configurable Web application to automatically generate questions from a sentence, or a paragraph based on user selected answers, with visual insights on the generated questions.

2. A technique to create faceted views of the generated questions having overlapping or similar answers. Given an input passage, the same answer may appear multiple times in different spans, from which similar questions can be generated. ParaQG detects and presents the generated questions based on a grouped/faceted view of similar answer spans, thus allowing easy selection by users.

3. A novel question filtering technique based on BERT (Devlin et al., 2018) to eliminate unanswerable questions from the text.

To the best of our knowledge we are the first to propose and develop an interactive system that generates questions based on the answers selected by users. The rest of the paper is organized as follows. We discuss related work in Section 2. In Section 3, We describe the architecture of ParaQG. This is followed by details of the demonstration in Section 4 and the implementation in Section 5. Conclusion is discussed in Section 6.

2 Related Work

Automatically generating questions and answers from text is a challenging task. This task can be traced back to 1976 when Wolfe (1976) presented their system AUTOQUEST, which examined the generation of Wh-questions from single sentences. This was followed by several pattern matching (Hirschman et al., 1999) and linear regression (Ng et al., 2000) based models. These approaches are heavily dependent on either rules

or question templates, and require deep linguistic knowledge, yet are not exhaustive enough. Recent successes in neural machine translation (Sutskever et al., 2014; Cho et al., 2014) have helped address these issues by letting deep neural nets learn the implicit rules from data. This approach has inspired application of sequence-to-sequence learning to automated question generation. Serban et al. (2016) proposed an attention-based (Bahdanau et al., 2014; Luong et al., 2015) approach to question generation from a pre-defined template of knowledge base triples (subject, relation, object). We proposed multi-hop question generation (Kumar et al., 2019a) from knowledge graphs using transformers (Vaswani et al., 2017). Du et al. (2017) proposed an attention-based sequence learning approach to question generation.

Most existing work focuses on generating questions from text without concerning itself with answer generation. In our previous work (Kumar et al., 2018), we presented a pointer network-based model that predicts candidate answers and generates a question by providing a pivotal answer as an input to the decoder. Our model for question generation combines a rich set of linguistic features, pointer network-based answer selection, and an improved decoder, and is able to generate questions that are relatively more relevant to the given sentence than the questions generated without the answer signal.

Overall, the broad finding has been that it is important to either *be provided with* or *learn to choose* pivotal answer spans to ask questions about from an input passage. Founded on this observation, our system facilitates users with an option to either choose answer spans from the pre-populated set of named entities and noun phrases or manually select custom answer spans interactively. Our system, ParaQG, presented in this paper uses a novel four-stage procedure: (1) text review, (2) pivotal answer selection (3) automatic question generation pertaining to the selected answer, and (4) filtering and grouping questions based on confidence scores and different facets of the selected answer.

3 System Architecture

ParaQG generates questions from sentences and paragraphs following a four-stage interactive procedure: (a) paragraph review, (b) answer selection, (c) question generation with associated confidence score, and (d) question filtering and grouping based on answer facets. Given a paragraph, ParaQG first reviews the content automatically and then flags any unprocessable characters (e.g. Unicode characters) and URLs, which the user are prompted to edit or remove (Section 3.1). Next, the user is provided with an option to select an answer from the list of candidate answers identified by the system. Alternatively, the user can select custom answer spans from the passage to ask question about (Section 3.2). In the third step, the selected pivotal spans are encoded into the paragraph and fed to the question generation module. The question generation module is a sequence-to-sequence model with dynamic dictionaries, reusable copy attention and global sparse-max attention. This module attempts to automatically generate the most relevant as well as syntactically and semantically correct questions around the selected pivotal answers (Section 3.3). In the last step the unanswerable questions are filtered out using a BERT-based question filtering module (Section 3.4). The questions that remain are presented by grouping their associated answers. Each group of answers (which we also refer to as an answer-based facet) corresponds to some unique stem form of those answer words.

3.1 Paragraph Review

Since every sentence/word in a paragraph may not be question-worthy, it is important to filter out those that are not. Given a paragraph text, the system automatically reviews its contents to check if the paragraph contains any non-ASCII characters, URLs *etc.*, and flags them for users to edit, as illustrated in Figure 2a.

3.2 Answer Selection

ParaQG allows users to select any named entity or noun phrase present in the paragraph as a *pivotal answer*. As mentioned earlier, a user is presented with a list of all the named entities and noun phrases as extracted using the Stanford CoreNLP tagger to choose pivotal answers from. Alternatively, users can manually select a set of spans from the passage as pivotal answers, as shown in Figure 2d. The selected answer is encoded in the source sentence using the BIO (Begin, Inside, Outside) notation.

3.3 Question Generation

Similar to our previous work (Kumar et al., 2018), we encode the pivotal answer spans in the passage using BIO notation, and train a sequence-to-sequence model augmented with dynamic dictionary, copy mechanism and global sparse-max attention. Our question generation module consists of a paragraph encoder and a question decoder. The encoder represents the paragraph input as a single fixed-length continuous vector. This vector representation of the paragraph is passed to the decoder with reusable copy mechanism and sparse-max attention to generate questions.

3.4 BERT-based Question Filtering

We use the $BERT_{base}$ (Devlin et al., 2018) model to filter out unanswerable questions generated by our model. we fine-tune BERT on SQuAD 2.0(Rajpurkar et al., 2018). SQuAD 2.0 extends SQuAD with over 50000 unanswerable questions. The unanswerable questions are flagged with the attribute *is_impossible*.

We represent input question (question generated by our QG model) and the passage in a single packed sequence of tokens, while using a special token [SEP] to separate the question from the passage. Similar to (Devlin et al., 2018) we use a special classification token [CLS] at the start of every sequence. Let us denote the final hidden representation of the [CLS] token by C and the final hidden representation for the ith input token by T_i. For each unanswerable question, we represent the start and end answer index using a [CLS] token as it does not have any answer start and end index. Similar to (Devlin et al., 2018), we compare the score of no-answer span with the score of best non-null answer span to predict the answerability of a question. Score of no-answer span is calculated as: $s_{null} = S.C + E.C$ where $S \in \mathbb{R}^H$ is the vector representation of answer start index and $E \in \mathbb{R}^H$ is the vector representation of answer end index. The score of a non-null answer span is defined as $s_{i,j} = \max_{j>=i}\{S.T_i + E.T_j\}$ If the score of $s_{null} - s_{i,j} > V$, where V is a threshold calculated using a validation set, then the question is not answerable using the paragraph.

3.5 Grouped/Faceted Views of Questions

We group together all answers and their corresponding question(s) that have the same stemmed form. For example, two potential answer spans

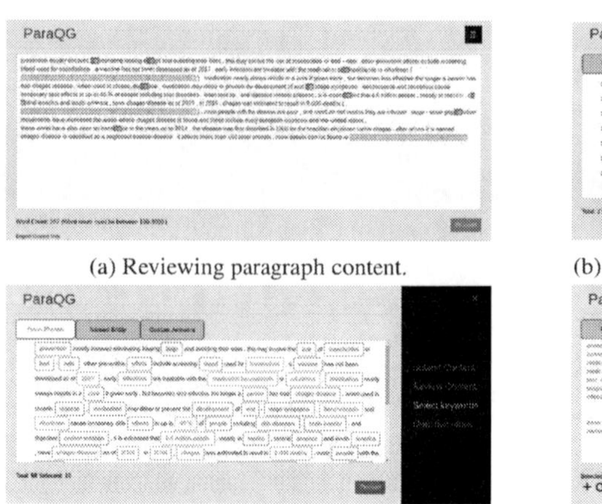

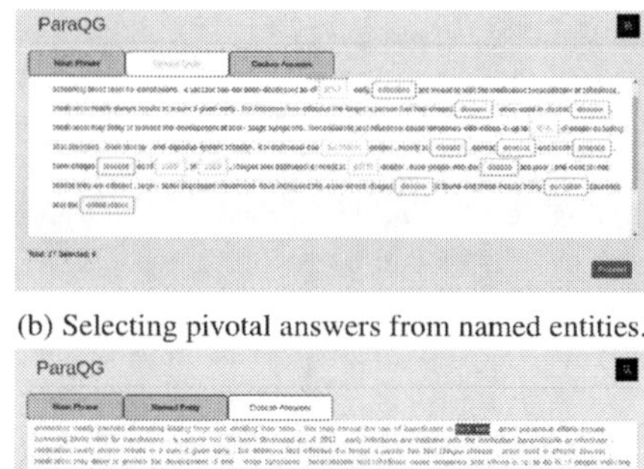

(a) Reviewing paragraph content.

(b) Selecting pivotal answers from named entities.

(c) Selecting pivotal answers from noun phrases.

(d) Interactive pivotal answer selection.

Figure 2: Main steps of ParaQG.

'switching' and 'switches' would have the same stemmed form 'switch'. Thus, the spans 'switching' and 'switches', and their associated question(s) would be grouped together under the same stemmed form 'switch'. Summarily, each such question group yields a *faceted view* of the question set. Within each group, the questions are sorted in decreasing order of their probabilities. We calculate the *intra-question probability (confidence score)* by normalizing the beam score x as: $\frac{e^x}{1+e^x}$. The final *inter-question probability* of a question-answer pair is calculated from the question with maximum intra-question probability p as: $\frac{p-min(\mathbf{P})}{max(\mathbf{P})-min(\mathbf{P})}$, where $\mathbf{P}$ is the set of maximum probability scores across answers.

4 Demonstration Details

ParaQG is available as an interactive and fully-featured Web application. A video of the ParaQG system is available at `https://youtu.be/BLChdl8kzlc`. The ParaQG system is accessible at `https://www.cse.iitb.ac.in/~vishwajeet/paraqg.html`. Important features of the Web application are discussed below.

Input and content review: A user can copy any paragraph and paste it in the text area (Fig. 2a), and subsequently will be asked to review and remove/edit unprocessable contents (Fig. 2a).

Interactive pivotal answer selection: ParaQG provides an interactive user interface for users to select pivotal answers. A user has an option to

select a pivotal answers either from a set of noun phrases or from a set of named entities present in the paragraph. To choose a pivotal answer from a set of named entities, the user can click on the *Named Entities* tab (Figure 2b). Similarly, to select a noun phrase present in the paragraph as the pivotal answer, the user can click on the *Noun Phrases* tab (Figure 2c). Once a user clicks on either of the tabs he/she will be presented with pre-highlighted noun phrases/named entities as pivotal answers. The user can subsequently deselect a pivotal answer by clicking on it.

Custom pivotal answer selection: Alternatively, the user can click on the *Custom Answers* tab (Figure 2d) and manually select the most important spans in the paragraph as the pivotal answers. The users can also select overlapping spans.

Automatic question and answer generation: Finally, the user is presented with the question generated as well as the answer to that question along with confidence score. For example for the paragraph input by the user in Figure 2b, the questions as well as the answers are generated and shown to the the user (Figure 3) along with their confidence score.

Visualization of decoder attention weights using heat maps: ParaQG also presents to the user heat maps of the decoder attention weights between words in the paragraph and words in the question generated. A user can click on the *attention weights* button next to each question (Fig-

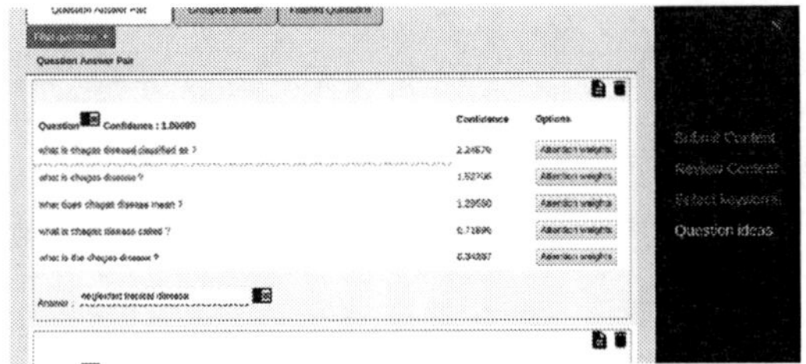

Figure 3: Editing question and answers.

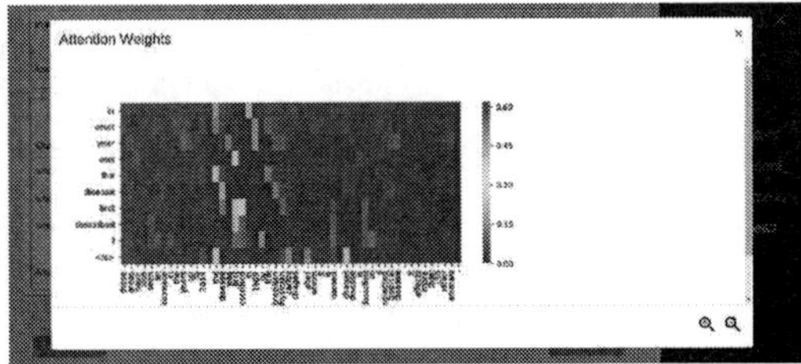

Figure 5: Attention weight visualization.

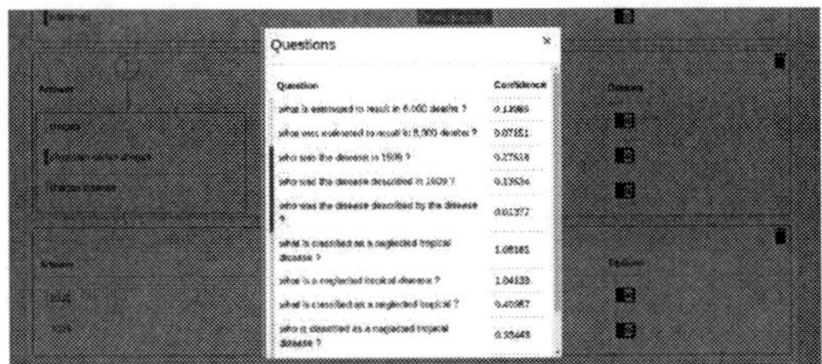

Figure 4: Filtering questions based on confidence score.

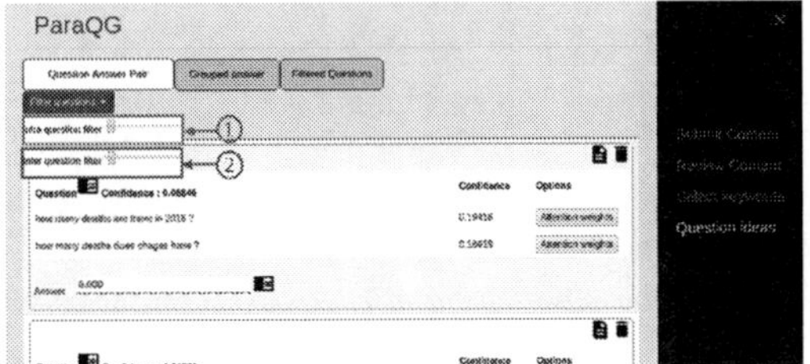

Figure 6: Clustering question based on different facets of the answer.

ure 3) to generate the attention weights heat map between words in the paragraph and words in the generated question (Fig. 5). Decoder attention weights represent the weights ParaQG gives to the words in the paragraph while generating the question words. For example, while decoding the question word "*in*", the system gives the highest weight to the paragraph word "**1909**". Similarly, the question word "*disease*" is generated by attending over the word "*disease*" in the paragraph.

Filtering and grouping questions: User can filter generated questions based on confidence scores using inter-question filter (Label 2 in figure 4) and intra-question filter (Label 1 in Fig. 4). The intra-question filter provides the user with a knob to filter questions based on the confidence score. The inter-question filter provides the user with a knob to filter low quality question-answer pairs generated from the paragraph in its entirety. We filter out unanswerable questions using our BERT-based model (explained in Section 3.4). We also group answers (and thus their associated questions) based on the stemmed form of the answer. Label 1 in Fig. 6 depicts one such answer group, whereas the generated question set is depicted by Label 2 in Fig. 6.

Editing questions with history of edits and Download generated questions and answers: If users are not satisfied with the generated ques-

tion answer pairs he/she may edit it. The system stores all version of questions and answers. Users can download the final generated set of questions and answers in JSON or text format at the end.

5   Implementation Details

ParaQG[1] comprises the frontend user interface, the backend question generator and a BERT-based question filtering module. The question generator model is implemented using the PyTorch[2] framework. We trained the question generator model on the SQuAD 1.0 (Rajpurkar et al., 2016) dataset. We use pre-trained GloVe word vectors of 300 dimension and fix them during training. We employ a 2-layer Bi-LSTM encoder and a single-layer Bi-LSTM decoder of hidden size 600. For optimization we use SGD with annealing. We set the initial learning rate to 0.1. We train the model for 20 epochs with batch size 64. Dropout of 0.3 was applied between vertical Bi-LSTM stacks. Our question generator module provide a REST API to which we can send requests and receive responses from in JSON format. The embedded Javascript is used as the template rendering engine to render the front-end of the web application along with Bootstrap 4 for responsiveness. Express is the Web application framework used for server-side on top of

---

[1]The source code is availble for download at https://github.com/sivaanandhmuneeswaran/qg-ui

[2]https://pytorch.org/

Node.js. For the BERT-based filtering module, we finetune the $BERT_{base}$ model on SQuAD 2.0 for 3 epochs, and set learning rate to 3e-5 and batch size to 12.

6 Conclusion

Question generation from text is a task useful in many application domains, yet manual generation is labour-intensive and expensive. We presented a novel online system, ParaQG, to automatically generate questions from paragraph based on pivotal answers. The system allows users to select a set of pivotal answers and then generates a ranked set of questions for each answer. ParaQG also filters out unanswerble question using a BERT-based model. ParaQG is available as a Web application, which also incorporates a novel heat map-based visualization that shows attention weights of the decoder.

References

Dzmitry Bahdanau, Kyunghyun Cho, and Yoshua Bengio. 2014. Neural machine translation by jointly learning to align and translate. *arXiv preprint arXiv:1409.0473*.

Kyunghyun Cho, Bart Van Merriënboer, Dzmitry Bahdanau, and Yoshua Bengio. 2014. On the properties of neural machine translation: Encoder-decoder approaches. *arXiv preprint arXiv:1409.1259*.

Jacob Devlin, Ming-Wei Chang, Kenton Lee, and Kristina Toutanova. 2018. Bert: Pre-training of deep bidirectional transformers for language understanding. *arXiv preprint arXiv:1810.04805*.

Xinya Du, Junru Shao, and Claire Cardie. 2017. Learning to ask: Neural question generation for reading comprehension. In *Proceedings of the 55th ACL*, pages 1342–1352. ACL.

Jiatao Gu, Zhengdong Lu, Hang Li, and Victor OK Li. 2016. Incorporating copying mechanism in sequence-to-sequence learning. In *Proceedings of the 54th ACL (Volume 1: Long Papers)*, volume 1, pages 1631–1640.

Lynette Hirschman, Marc Light, Eric Breck, and John D Burger. 1999. Deep read: A reading comprehension system. In *ACL*, pages 325–332. ACL.

Vishwajeet Kumar, Yuncheng Hua, Ganesh Ramakrishnan, Guilin Qi, Lianli Gao, and Yuan-Fang Li. 2019a. Difficulty-controllable multi-hop question generation from knowledge graphs. In *ISWC*.

Vishwajeet Kumar, N. Joshi, Arijit Mukherjee, Ganesh Ramakrishnan, and Preethi Jyothi. 2019b. Cross-lingual training for automatic question generation. In *ACL*.

Vishwajeet Kumar, Ganesh Ramakrishnan, and Yuan-Fang Li. 2018. Automating reading comprehension by generating question and answer pairs. In *PAKDD*. Springer.

Vishwajeet Kumar, Ganesh Ramakrishnan, and Yuan-Fang Li. 2019c. Putting the horse before the cart: A generator-evaluator framework for question generation from text. *SIGNLL Conference on Computational Natural Language Learning, CoNLL 2019*.

Minh-Thang Luong, Hieu Pham, and Christopher D. Manning. 2015. Effective approaches to attention-based neural machine translation. *CoRR*, abs/1508.04025.

Andre Martins and Ramon Astudillo. 2016. From softmax to sparsemax: A sparse model of attention and multi-label classification. In *ICML*, pages 1614–1623.

Hwee Tou Ng, Leong Hwee Teo, and Jennifer Lai Pheng Kwan. 2000. A machine learning approach to answering questions for reading comprehension tests. In *SIGDAT-EMNLP, ACL-Volume 13*, pages 124–132. ACL.

Pranav Rajpurkar, Robin Jia, and Percy Liang. 2018. Know what you dont know: Unanswerable questions for squad. In *ACL*, pages 784–789.

Pranav Rajpurkar, Jian Zhang, Konstantin Lopyrev, and Percy Liang. 2016. Squad: 100,000+ questions for machine comprehension of text. *arXiv preprint arXiv:1606.05250*.

Iulian Vlad Serban, Alberto García-Durán, Caglar Gulcehre, Sungjin Ahn, Sarath Chandar, Aaron Courville, and Yoshua Bengio. 2016. Generating factoid questions with recurrent neural networks: The 30m factoid question-answer corpus. *arXiv preprint arXiv:1603.06807*.

Linfeng Song, Zhiguo Wang, Wael Hamza, Yue Zhang, and Daniel Gildea. 2018. Leveraging context information for natural question generation. In *NAACL-HLT*, volume 2, pages 569–574.

Ilya Sutskever, Oriol Vinyals, and Quoc V Le. 2014. Sequence to sequence learning with neural networks. In *Advances in neural information processing systems*, pages 3104–3112.

Ashish Vaswani, Noam Shazeer, Niki Parmar, Jakob Uszkoreit, Llion Jones, Aidan N Gomez, Łukasz Kaiser, and Illia Polosukhin. 2017. Attention is all you need. In *Advances in neural information processing systems*, pages 5998–6008.

John H Wolfe. 1976. Automatic question generation from text-an aid to independent study. *ACM SIGCSE Bulletin*, 8(1):104–112.

Yao Zhao, Xiaochuan Ni, Yuanyuan Ding, and Qifa Ke. 2018. Paragraph-level neural question generation with maxout pointer and gated self-attention networks. In *EMNLP 2018*, pages 3901–3910.

PolyResponse: A Rank-based Approach to Task-Oriented Dialogue with Application in Restaurant Search and Booking

Matthew Henderson, Ivan Vulić, Iñigo Casanueva, Paweł Budzianowski, Daniela Gerz,

Sam Coope, Georgios Spithourakis, Tsung-Hsien Wen, Nikola Mrkšić, Pei-Hao Su

PolyAI Limited, London, UK

`poly-ai.com`

Abstract

We present PolyResponse, a conversational search engine that supports task-oriented dialogue. It is a retrieval-based approach that bypasses the complex multi-component design of traditional task-oriented dialogue systems and the use of explicit semantics in the form of task-specific ontologies. The PolyResponse engine is trained on hundreds of millions of examples extracted from real conversations: it learns what responses are appropriate in different conversational contexts. It then ranks a large index of text and visual responses according to their similarity to the given context, and narrows down the list of relevant entities during the multi-turn conversation. We introduce a restaurant search and booking system powered by the PolyResponse engine, currently available in 8 different languages.

1 Introduction and Background

Task-oriented dialogue systems are primarily designed to search and interact with large databases which contain information pertaining to a certain *dialogue domain*: the main purpose of such systems is to assist the users in accomplishing a well-defined task such as flight booking (El Asri et al., 2017), tourist information (Henderson et al., 2014), restaurant search (Williams, 2012), or booking a taxi (Budzianowski et al., 2018). These systems are typically constructed around rigid task-specific ontologies (Henderson et al., 2014; Mrkšić et al., 2015) which enumerate the constraints the users can express using a collection of slots (e.g., PRICE RANGE for restaurant search) and their slot values (e.g., CHEAP, EXPENSIVE for the aforementioned slots). Conversations are then modelled as a sequence of actions that constrain slots to particular values. This *explicit* semantic space is manually engineered by the system designer. It serves as the output of the natural language understanding component as well as the input to the language

generation component both in traditional modular systems (Young, 2010; Eric et al., 2017) and in more recent end-to-end task-oriented dialogue systems (Wen et al., 2017; Li et al., 2017; Bordes et al., 2017; Budzianowski et al., 2018, *inter alia*).

Working with such explicit semantics for task-oriented dialogue systems poses several critical challenges on top of the manual time-consuming domain ontology design. First, it is difficult to collect domain-specific data labelled with explicit semantic representations. As a consequence, despite recent data collection efforts to enable training of task-oriented systems across multiple domains (El Asri et al., 2017; Budzianowski et al., 2018), annotated datasets are still few and far between, as well as limited in size and the number of domains covered.[1] Second, the current approach constrains the types of dialogue the system can support, resulting in artificial conversations, and breakdowns when the user does not understand what the system can and cannot support. In other words, training a task-based dialogue system for voice-controlled search in a new domain always implies the complex, expensive, and time-consuming process of collecting and annotating sufficient amounts of in-domain dialogue data.

In this paper, we present a demo system based on an alternative approach to task-oriented dialogue. Relying on *non-generative response retrieval* we describe the *PolyResponse* conversational search engine and its application in the task of *restaurant search and booking*. The engine is trained on

---

[1] For instance, the recently published MultiWOZ dataset (Budzianowski et al., 2018) contains a total of 115,424 dialogue turns scattered over 7 target domains. Other standard task-based datasets are typically single-domain and by several orders of magnitude smaller: DSTC2 (Henderson et al., 2014) contains 23,354 turns, Frames (El Asri et al., 2017) 19,986 turns, and M2M (Shah et al., 2018) spans 14,796 turns. On the other hand, the Reddit corpus which supports our system comprises 3.7B comments spanning a multitude of topics, divided into 256M (Reddit) conversational threads and generating 727M *context-reply* pairs.

181

Proceedings of the 2019 EMNLP and the 9th IJCNLP (System Demonstrations), pages 181–186
Hong Kong, China, November 3 – 7, 2019. ©2019 Association for Computational Linguistics

hundreds of millions of real conversations from a general domain (i.e., Reddit), using an implicit representation of semantics that directly optimizes the task at hand. It learns what responses are appropriate in different conversational contexts, and consequently ranks a large pool of responses according to their relevance to the current user utterance and previous dialogue history (i.e., dialogue context).

The technical aspects of the underlying conversational search engine are explained in detail in our recent work (Henderson et al., 2019b), while the details concerning the Reddit training data are also available in another recent publication (Henderson et al., 2019a). In this demo, we put focus on the actual practical usefulness of the search engine by demonstrating its potential in the task of restaurant search, and extending it to deal with multi-modal data. We describe a PolyReponse system that assists the users in finding a relevant restaurant according to their preference, and then additionally helps them to make a booking in the selected restaurant. Due to its retrieval-based design, with the PolyResponse engine there is no need to engineer a structured ontology, or to solve the difficult task of general language generation. This design also bypasses the construction of dedicated decision-making policy modules. The large ranking model already encapsulates a lot of knowledge about natural language and conversational flow.

Since retrieved system responses are presented visually to the user, the PolyResponse restaurant search engine is able to combine text responses with relevant visual information (e.g., photos from social media associated with the current restaurant and related to the user utterance), effectively yielding a *multi-modal response*. This setup of using voice as input, and responding visually is becoming more and more prevalent with the rise of smart screens like Echo Show and even mixed reality. Finally, the PolyResponse restaurant search engine is *multilingual*: it is currently deployed in 8 languages enabling search over restaurants in 8 cities around the world. System snapshots in four different languages are presented in Figure 2, while screencast videos that illustrate the dialogue flow with the PolyResponse engine are available at: https://tinyurl.com/y3evkcfz.

2 PolyResponse: Conversational Search

The PolyResponse system is powered by a single large conversational search engine, trained on a

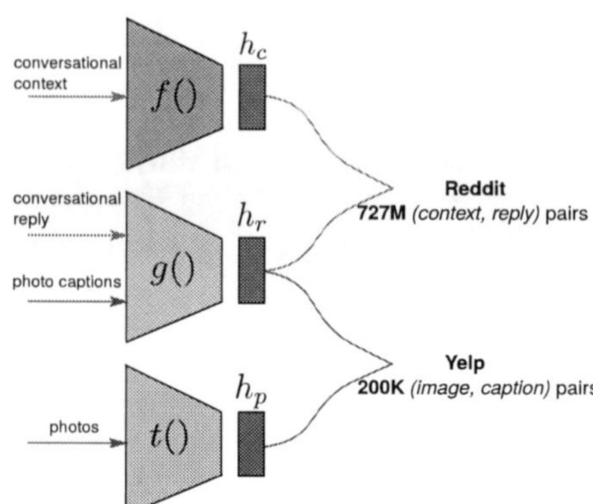

Figure 1: The PolyResponse ranking model: it encodes conversational contexts, replies, and photos to respective vectors h_c, h_r, and h_p.

large amount of conversational and image data, as shown in Figure 1. In simple words, it is a ranking model that learns to score conversational replies and images in a given conversational context. The highest-scoring responses are then retrieved as system outputs. The system computes two sets of similarity scores: **1)** $S(r, c)$ is the score of a candidate reply r given a conversational context c, and **2)** $S(p, c)$ is the score of a candidate photo p given a conversational context c. These scores are computed as a scaled cosine similarity of a vector that represents the context (h_c), and a vector that represents the candidate response: a text reply (h_r) or a photo (h_p). For instance, $S(r, c)$ is computed as $S(r, c) = Ccos(h_r, h_c)$, where C is a learned constant. The part of the model dealing with text input (i.e., obtaining the encodings h_c and h_r) follows the architecture introduced recently by Henderson et al. (2019b). We provide only a brief recap here; see the original paper for further details.

Text Representation. The model, implemented as a deep neural network, learns to respond by training on hundreds of millions *context-reply* (c, r) pairs. First, similar to Henderson et al. (2017), raw text from both c and r is converted to unigrams and bigrams. All input text is first lower-cased and tokenised, numbers with 5 or more digits get their digits replaced by a wildcard symbol #, while words longer than 16 characters are replaced by a wildcard token LONGWORD. Sentence boundary tokens are added to each sentence. The vocabulary consists of the unigrams that occur at least 10 times in a random 10M subset of the Reddit training set (see Figure 1) plus the 200K most frequent bigrams in the same random subset.

During training, we obtain d-dimensional feature representations ($d = 320$) shared between contexts and replies for each unigram and bigram jointly with other neural net parameters.[2] A state-of-the-art architecture based on transformers (Vaswani et al., 2017) is then applied to unigram and bigram vectors separately, which are then averaged to form the final 320-dimensional encoding. That encoding is then passed through three fully-connected non-linear hidden layers of dimensionality $1,024$. The final layer is linear and maps the text into the final l-dimensional ($l = 512$) representation: h_c and h_r. Other standard and more sophisticated encoder models can also be used to provide final encodings h_c and h_r, but the current architecture shows a good trade-off between speed and efficacy with strong and robust performance in our empirical evaluations on the response retrieval task using Reddit (Al-Rfou et al., 2016), OpenSubtitles (Lison and Tiedemann, 2016), and AmazonQA (Wan and McAuley, 2016) conversational test data, see (Henderson et al., 2019a) for further details.[3]

In training the constant C is constrained to lie between 0 and $\sqrt{l}$.[4] Following Henderson et al. (2017), the scoring function in the training objective aims to maximise the similarity score of context-reply pairs that go together, while minimising the score of random pairings: negative examples. Training proceeds via SGD with batches comprising 500 pairs (1 positive and 499 negatives).

Photo Representation. Photos are represented using convolutional neural net (CNN) models pretrained on ImageNet (Deng et al., 2009). We use a MobileNet model with a depth multiplier of 1.4, and an input dimension of 224×224 pixels as in (Howard et al., 2017).[5] This provides a $1,280 \times 1.4 = 1,792$-dimensional representation of a photo, which is then passed through a single hidden layer of dimensionality $1,024$ with ReLU activation, before being passed to a hidden layer of dimensionality 512 with no activation to provide the final representation h_p.

Data Source 1: Reddit. For training text representations we use a Reddit dataset similar to Al-Rfou et al. (2016). Our dataset is large and provides natural conversational structure: all Reddit data from January 2015 to December 2018, available as a public BigQuery dataset, span almost 3.7B comments (Henderson et al., 2019a). We preprocess the dataset to remove uninformative and long comments by retaining only sentences containing more than 8 and less than 128 word tokens. After pairing all comments/contexts c with their replies r, we obtain more than 727M context-reply (c, r) pairs for training, see Figure 1.

Data Source 2: Yelp. Once the text encoding sub-networks are trained, a photo encoder is learned on top of a pretrained MobileNet CNN, using data taken from the Yelp Open dataset:[6] it contains around 200K photos and their captions. Training of the multi-modal sub-network then maximises the similarity of captions encoded with the response encoder h_r to the photo representation h_p. As a result, we can compute the score of a photo given a context using the cosine similarity of the respective vectors. A photo will be scored highly if it looks like its caption would be a good response to the current context.[7]

Index of Responses. The Yelp dataset is used at inference time to provide text and photo candidates to display to the user at each step in the conversation. Our restaurant search is currently deployed separately for each city, and we limit the responses to a given city. For instance, for our English system for Edinburgh we work with 396 restaurants, 4,225 photos (these include additional photos obtained using the Google Places API without captions), 6,725 responses created from the structured information about restaurants that Yelp provides, converted using simple templates to sentences of the form such as "Restaurant X accepts credit cards.", 125,830 sentences extracted from online reviews.

PolyResponse in a Nutshell. The system jointly trains two encoding functions (with shared word embeddings) $f(context)$ and $g(reply)$ which produce encodings h_c and h_r, so that the similarity

---

[2] The model deals with out-of-vocabulary unigrams and bigrams by assigning a random id from 0 to 50,000 to each; this is then used to look up their embedding.

[3] The comparisons of performance in the response retrieval task are also available online at: `https://github.com/PolyAI-LDN/conversational-datasets/`.

[4] It is initialised to a random value between 0.5 and 1, and invariably converges to $\sqrt{l}$ by the end of training. Empirically, this helps with learning.

[5] The pretrained model downloaded from TensorFlow Slim.

[6] `https://www.yelp.com/dataset`

[7] Note that not all of the Yelp dataset has captions, which is why we need to learn the photo representation. If a photo caption is available, then the response vector representation of the caption is averaged with the photo vector representation to compute the score. If a caption is not available at inference time, we use only the photo vector representation.

$S(c, r)$ is high for all (c, r) pairs from the Reddit training data and low for random pairs. The encoding function $g()$ is then frozen, and an encoding function $t(photo)$ is learnt which makes the similarity between a photo and its associated caption high for all *(photo, caption)* pairs from the Yelp dataset, and low for random pairs. t is a CNN pretrained on ImageNet, with a shallow one-layer DNN on top. Given a new context/query, we then provide its encoding h_c by applying $f()$, and find plausible text replies and photo responses according to functions $g()$ and $t()$, respectively. These should be responses that look like answers to the query, and photos that look like they would have captions that would be answers to the provided query.

At inference, finding relevant candidates given a context reduces to computing h_c for the context c, and finding nearby h_r and h_p vectors. The response vectors can all be pre-computed, and the nearest neighbour search can be further optimised using standard libraries such as Faiss (Johnson et al., 2017) or approximate nearest neighbour retrieval (Malkov and Yashunin, 2016), giving an efficient search that scales to billions of candidate responses.

The system offers both voice and text input and output. Speech-to-text and text-to-speech conversion in the PolyResponse system is currently supported by the off-the-shelf Google Cloud tools.[8]

3 Dialogue Flow

The ranking model lends itself to the one-shot task of finding the most relevant responses in a given context. However, a restaurant-browsing system needs to support a dialogue flow where the user finds a restaurant, and then asks questions about it. The *dialogue state* for each search scenario is represented as the set of restaurants that are considered relevant. This starts off as *all the restaurants* in the given city, and is assumed to monotonically decrease in size as the conversation progresses until the user converges to a single restaurant. A restaurant is only considered valid in the context of a new user input if it has relevant responses corresponding to it. This flow is summarised here:

S1. Initialise R as the set of all restaurants in the city. Given the user's input, rank all the responses in the response pool pertaining to restaurants in R.

S2. Retrieve the top N responses $r_1, r_2, \ldots, r_N$ with corresponding (sorted) cosine similarity

scores: $s_1 \geq s_2 \geq \ldots \geq s_N$.

S3. Compute probability scores $p_i \propto \exp(a \cdot s_i)$ with $\sum_{i=1}^{N} p_i$, where $a > 0$ is a tunable constant.

S4. Compute a score q_e for each restaurant/entity $e \in R$, $q_e = \sum_{i:r_i \in e} p_i$.

S5. Update R to the smallest set of restaurants with highest q whose q-values sum up to more than a predefined threshold t.

S6. Display the most relevant responses associated with the updated R, and return to S2.

If there are multiple relevant restaurants, one response is shown from each. When only one restaurant is relevant, the top N responses are all shown, and relevant photos are also displayed. The system does not require dedicated understanding, decision-making, and generation modules, and this dialogue flow does not rely on explicit task-tailored semantics. The set of relevant restaurants is kept internally while the system narrows it down across multiple dialogue turns. A simple set of predefined rules is used to provide a templatic spoken system response: e.g., an example rule is "One review of e said r", where e refers to the restaurant, and r to a relevant response associated with e. Note that while the demo is currently focused on the restaurant search task, the described "narrowing down" dialogue flow is generic and applicable to a variety of applications dealing with similar entity search.

The system can use a set of intent classifiers to allow resetting the dialogue state, or to activate the separate restaurant booking dialogue flow. These classifiers are briefly discussed in §4.

4 Other Functionality

Multilinguality. The PolyResponse restaurant search is currently available in 8 languages and for 8 cities around the world: English (Edinburgh), German (Berlin), Spanish (Madrid), Mandarin (Taipei), Polish (Warsaw), Russian (Moscow), Korean (Seoul), and Serbian (Belgrade). Selected snapshots are shown in Figure 2, while we also provide videos demonstrating the use and behaviour of the systems at: https://tinyurl.com/y3evkcfz. A simple MT-based translate-to-source approach at inference time is currently used to enable the deployment of the system in other languages: 1) the pool of responses in each language is translated to English by Google Translate beforehand, and pre-computed encodings of their English translations are used as representations of

---

[8]https://cloud.google.com/speech-to-text/; https://cloud.google.com/text-to-speech/

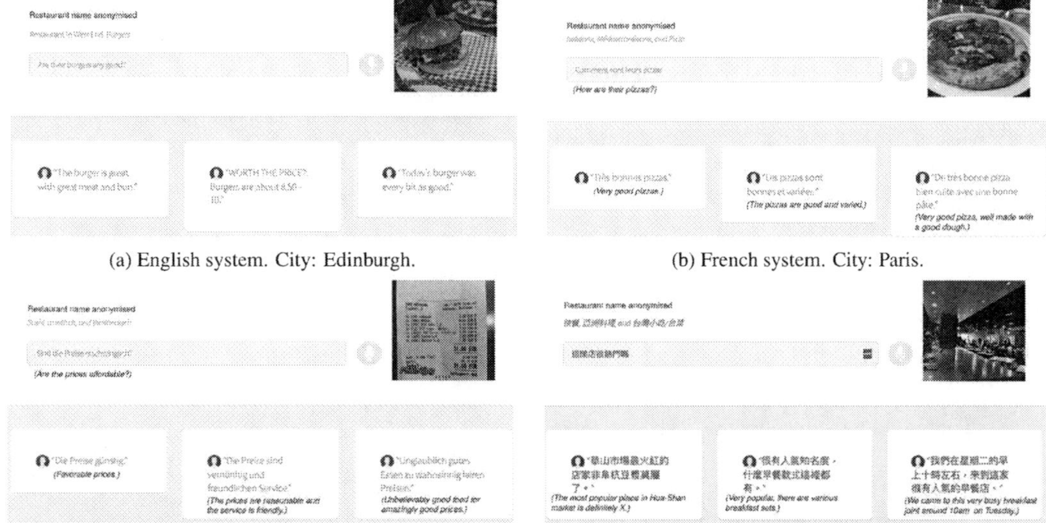

(a) English system. City: Edinburgh.

(b) French system. City: Paris.

(c) German system. City: Berlin.

(d) Mandarin system. City: Taipei.

Figure 2: Snapshots of the PolyResponse demo system for restaurant search in four different languages. Restaurant names are anonymised. Translations of non-English sentences are provided in parentheses; they are not part of the system output. The output also comprises relevant photos associated with the current restaurant.

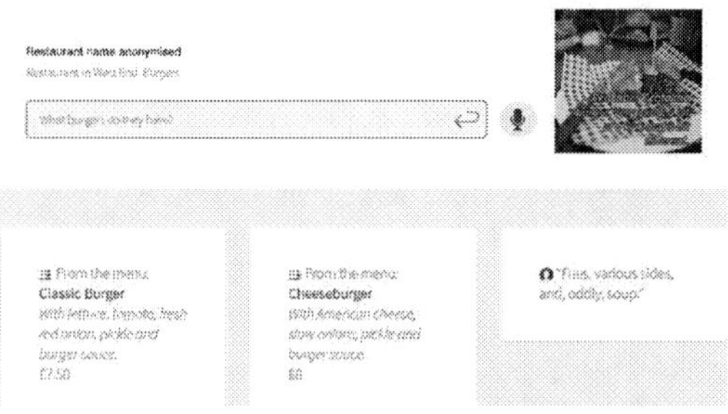

Figure 3: An example showing how the system can retrieve parts of the menu as responses to the current user utterance (if they are relevant to the utterance).

each foreign language response; 2) a provided user utterance (i.e., context) is translated to English on-the-fly and its encoding h_c is then learned. We plan to experiment with more sophisticated multilingual models in future work.

Voice-Controlled Menu Search. An additional functionality enables the user to get parts of the restaurant menu relevant to the current user utterance as responses. This is achieved by performing an additional ranking step of available menu items and retrieving the ones that are semantically relevant to the user utterance using exactly the same methodology as with ranking other responses. An example of this functionality is shown in Figure 3.

Resetting and Switching to Booking. The restaurant search system needs to support the discrete actions of restarting the conversation (i.e., resetting the set R), and should enable transferring to the slot-based table booking flow. This is achieved using two binary intent classifiers, that are run at each step in the dialogue. These classifiers make use of the already-computed h_c vector that represents the user's latest text. A single-layer neural net is learned on top of the 512-dimensional encoding, with a ReLU activation and 100 hidden nodes.[9] To train the classifiers, sets of 20 relevant paraphrases (e.g., "Start again") are provided as positive examples. Finally, when the system successfully switches to the booking scenario, it proceeds to the slot filling task: it aims to extract all the relevant booking information from the user (e.g., date, time, number of people to dine). The entire flow of the system illustrating both the search phase and the booking phase is provided as the supplemental video material.

5 Conclusion and Future Work

This paper has presented a general approach to search-based dialogue that does not rely on explicit

---

[9]Using the Reddit encoding has shown better generalisation when compared to models learned from scratch. This follows a recent trend where small robust classifiers are learned on pretrained large models (Devlin et al., 2018).

semantic representations such as dialogue acts or slot-value ontologies, and allows for multi-modal responses. In future work, we will extend the current demo system to more tasks and languages, and work with more sophisticated encoders and ranking functions. Besides the initial dialogue flow from this work (§3), we will also work with more complex flows dealing, e.g., with user intent shifts.

References

Rami Al-Rfou, Marc Pickett, Javier Snaider, Yun-Hsuan Sung, Brian Strope, and Ray Kurzweil. 2016. Conversational contextual cues: The case of personalization and history for response ranking. *CoRR*, abs/1606.00372.

Antoine Bordes, Y.-Lan Boureau, and Jason Weston. 2017. Learning end-to-end goal-oriented dialog. In *ICLR*.

Paweł Budzianowski, Tsung-Hsien Wen, Bo-Hsiang Tseng, Iñigo Casanueva, Stefan Ultes, Osman Ramadan, and Milica Gašić. 2018. MultiWOZ - A large-scale multi-domain wizard-of-oz dataset for task-oriented dialogue modelling. In *EMNLP*, pages 5016–5026.

Jia Deng, Wei Dong, Richard Socher, Li-Jia Li, Kai Li, and Fei-Fei Li. 2009. ImageNet: A large-scale hierarchical image database. In *CVPR*.

Jacob Devlin, Ming-Wei Chang, Kenton Lee, and Kristina Toutanova. 2018. BERT: Pre-training of deep bidirectional transformers for language understanding. *CoRR*, abs/1810.04805.

Layla El Asri, Hannes Schulz, Shikhar Sharma, Jeremie Zumer, Justin Harris, Emery Fine, Rahul Mehrotra, and Kaheer Suleman. 2017. Frames: A corpus for adding memory to goal-oriented dialogue systems. In *SIGDIAL*, pages 207–219.

Mihail Eric, Lakshmi Krishnan, Francois Charette, and Christopher D. Manning. 2017. Key-value retrieval networks for task-oriented dialogue. In *SIGDIAL*, pages 37–49.

Matthew Henderson, Rami Al-Rfou, Brian Strope, Yun-Hsuan Sung, László Lukács, Ruiqi Guo, Sanjiv Kumar, Balint Miklos, and Ray Kurzweil. 2017. Efficient natural language response suggestion for smart reply. *CoRR*, abs/1705.00652.

Matthew Henderson, Pawel Budzianowski, Iñigo Casanueva, Sam Coope, Daniela Gerz, Girish Kumar, Nikola Mrkšić, Georgios Spithourakis, Pei-Hao Su, Ivan Vulić, and Tsung-Hsien Wen. 2019a. A repository of conversational datasets. In *NLP4ConvAI Workshop*, pages 1–10.

Matthew Henderson, Blaise Thomson, and Steve Young. 2014. Word-based dialog state tracking with recurrent neural networks. In *SIGDIAL*.

Matthew Henderson, Ivan Vulić, Daniela Gerz, Iñigo Casanueva, Paweł Budzianowski, Sam Coope, Georgios Spithourakis, Tsung-Hsien Wen, Nikola Mrkšić, and Pei-Hao Su. 2019b. Training neural response selection for task-oriented dialogue systems. In *ACL*, pages 5392–5404.

Andrew G. Howard, Menglong Zhu, Bo Chen, Dmitry Kalenichenko, Weijun Wang, Tobias Weyand, Marco Andreetto, and Hartwig Adam. 2017. MobileNets: Efficient convolutional neural networks for mobile vision applications. *CoRR*, abs/1704.04861.

Jeff Johnson, Matthijs Douze, and Hervé Jégou. 2017. Billion-scale similarity search with GPUs. *arXiv preprint arXiv:1702.08734*.

Xiujun Li, Yun-Nung Chen, Lihong Li, Jianfeng Gao, and Asli Celikyilmaz. 2017. End-to-end task-completion neural dialogue systems. In *IJCNLP*, pages 733–743.

Pierre Lison and Jörg Tiedemann. 2016. OpenSubtitles2016: Extracting large parallel corpora from movie and TV subtitles. In *LREC*.

Yury A. Malkov and D. A. Yashunin. 2016. Efficient and robust approximate nearest neighbor search using Hierarchical Navigable Small World graphs. *CoRR*, abs/1603.09320.

Nikola Mrkšić, Diarmuid Ó Séaghdha, Blaise Thomson, Milica Gašić, Pei-Hao Su, David Vandyke, Tsung-Hsien Wen, and Steve Young. 2015. Multi-domain dialog state tracking using recurrent neural networks. In *ACL*, pages 794–799.

Pararth Shah, Dilek Hakkani-Tür, Bing Liu, and Gokhan Tür. 2018. Bootstrapping a neural conversational agent with dialogue self-play, crowdsourcing and on-line reinforcement learning. In *NAACL-HLT*, pages 41–51.

Ashish Vaswani, Noam Shazeer, Niki Parmar, Jakob Uszkoreit, Llion Jones, Aidan N. Gomez, Lukasz Kaiser, and Illia Polosukhin. 2017. Attention is all you need. In *NeurIPS*, pages 6000–6010.

Mengting Wan and Julian McAuley. 2016. Modeling ambiguity, subjectivity, and diverging viewpoints in opinion question answering systems. In *ICDM*, pages 489–498.

Tsung-Hsien Wen, David Vandyke, Nikola Mrkšić, Milica Gašić, Lina M. Rojas-Barahona, Pei-Hao Su, Stefan Ultes, and Steve Young. 2017. A network-based end-to-end trainable task-oriented dialogue system. In *EACL*, pages 438–449.

Jason D. Williams. 2012. A belief tracking challenge task for spoken dialog systems.

Steve Young. 2010. Still talking to machines (cognitively speaking). In *INTERSPEECH*, pages 1–10.

PyOpenDial: A Python-based Domain-Independent Toolkit for Developing Spoken Dialogue Systems with Probabilistic Rules

Youngsoo Jang[1*], Jongmin Lee[1*], Jaeyoung Park[1*],
Kyeng-Hun Lee[3], Pierre Lison[4], Kee-Eung Kim[1,2]

[1] School of Computing, KAIST, Daejeon, Republic of Korea
[2] Graduate School of AI, KAIST, Daejeon, Republic of Korea
[3] Samsung Electronics, Seoul, Republic of Korea
[4] Norwegian Computing Center, Oslo, Norway

{ysjang, jmlee, jypark}@ai.kaist.ac.kr,
kyenghun.lee@samsung.com, plison@nr.no, kekim@cs.kaist.ac.kr

Abstract

We present PyOpenDial, a Python-based domain-independent, open-source toolkit for spoken dialogue systems. Recent advances in core components of dialogue systems, such as speech recognition, language understanding, dialogue management, and language generation, harness deep learning to achieve state-of-the-art performance. The original OpenDial, implemented in Java, provides a plugin architecture to integrate external modules, but lacks Python bindings, making it difficult to interface with popular deep learning frameworks such as Tensorflow or PyTorch. To this end, we re-implemented OpenDial in Python and extended the toolkit with a number of novel functionalities for neural dialogue state tracking and action planning. We describe the overall architecture and its extensions, and illustrate their use on an example where the system response model is implemented with a recurrent neural network.

1 Introduction

Spoken dialogue systems (SDSs) allow interactions between users and machines through natural language conversations. These systems are composed of a broad range of components such as speech recognition, language understanding, dialogue management, language generation, and speech synthesis. Recent SDS frameworks, such as AT&T Statistical Dialogue Toolkit (Williams et al., 2010), OpenDial (Lison and Kennington, 2016), and PyDial (Ultes et al., 2017) aim to integrate these complex and diverse components through a modular architecture.

Spoken dialogue systems may either adopt symbolic or statistical approaches to perform lan-

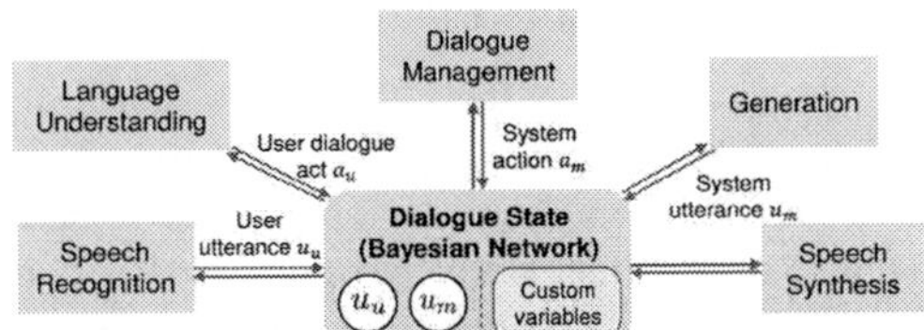

Figure 1: Information-state architecture for PyOpenDial.

guage understanding, dialogue management and language generation. Statistical approaches, including but not limited to (Young et al., 2013; Ultes et al., 2017) rely on probabilistic models of dialogue interactions and allows these models to be estimated from data. Symbolic approaches, on the other hand, model the dialogue interaction using finite-state automata or logical methods designed by the developer. Of our particular interest is OpenDial, a Java-based open-source toolkit that combines the benefits of both statistical and symbolic approaches.

In recent years, deep learning has shown to achieve promising performance results in many tasks related to dialogues, such as speech recognition (Graves et al., 2013), language understanding (Radford et al., 2018), dialogue management (Williams et al., 2017) and language generation (Yu et al., 2016). Given that one of the most popular programming languages for deep learning libraries is Python, e.g. Tensorflow (Abadi et al., 2016) and PyTorch (Paszke et al., 2017), the integration of neural conversational models would be a straightforward task if OpenDial itself was written in Python.

To this end, we developed PyOpenDial, an open-source SDS framework that re-implements OpenDial in Python and integrates a range of novel functionalities, such as the possibility to

---

*:These authors contributed equally.

This work was supported by MOTIE (KEIT No. 10063424), MSIT (IITP No. 2017-0-01779 XAI, IITP No. 2019-0-00075-001), and Samsung Research.

Proceedings of the 2019 EMNLP and the 9th IJCNLP (System Demonstrations), pages 187–192
Hong Kong, China, November 3 – 7, 2019. ©2019 Association for Computational Linguistics

track neural dialogue state and the use of Monte Carlo Tree Search for forward planning. PyOpenDial inherits the original architectural design of OpenDial, and extends the XML domain specification so that various deep learning models can be directly used for SDS components. We include the negotiation dialogue domain in (Lewis et al., 2017) as an example to show how to integrate with external components trained by deep learning.

2 Architecture

2.1 Dialogue State

PyOpenDial inherits the information-state framework in OpenDial (Larsson and Traum, 2000): All the components in the toolkit operates on the shared information state that represents the dialogue state arising from the interaction between the user and the machine (see Figure 1). The dialogue state is represented by a Bayesian network (BN), a directed graphical model for encoding the probability distribution of the dialogue state. Hence, the dialogue state consists of a factored representation of state variables on a dialogue, which are random variables, and conditional dependencies between them.

2.2 Workflow

PyOpenDial adopts the probabilistic rules used in OpenDial (Lison, 2014; Lison and Kennington, 2016) to update the dialogue state represented by a Bayesian Network during the conversation. These rules follow a *if...then...else* skeleton that map logical conditions on a subset of state variables to a probability or utility distribution on another subset of state variables. Two types of rules are provided: probability rules and utility rules. The probability rule defines the probabilistic change of state variables through a probability distribution over *effects*, each of which is an assignment on the state variables, given a logical condition of state variables. The utility rule defines utilities on the values of action variables given a logical conditions of state variables. These probabilistic rules are specified in the domain XML file. Examples are shown in Listing 1, where line 13-23 contains the probability rule and line 27-38 contains the utility rule.

These probabilistic rules can be grouped according to subtasks, such as language understanding, dialogue management, language generation and etc. Each group is defined as a *model*. Each

```
1  <initialstate>
2   <variable id="movie_rnn">
3    <value>@chatbot.MovieRNN</value>
4   </variable>
5   <variable id="music_rnn">
6    <value>@chatbot.MusicRNN</value>
7   </variable>
8  </initialstate>
9
10 <function name="gen_u_m">chatbot.generate</function>
11 <!-- User intent recognition -->
12 <model trigger="u_u">
13  <rule>
14   <case>
15    <condition>
16     <if var="u_u" value="movie" relation="contains"/>
17    </condition>
18    <effect prob="1">
19     <set var="a_u" value="movie"/>
20    </effect>
21   </case>
22       ...
23  </rule>
24 </model>
25 <!-- System utterance generation -->
26 <model trigger="a_u">
27  <rule>
28   <case>
29    <condition>
30     <if var="a_u" value="movie"/>
31    </condition>
32    <effect util="1">
33     <set var="u_m"
34      value="@gen_u_m({movie_rnn},{u_u})"/>
35    </effect>
36   </case>
37       ...
38  </rule>
39 </model>
```

Listing 1: A simple example domain XML specification for an RNN-based chat-bot. Here, u_u stands for the user utterance, a_u for the user intent and u_m for the system utterance.

model is associated with a subset of state variables, called *trigger variables*. Each model monitors the change of its trigger variables. When one or more trigger variables are updated during a conversation, the probabilistic rules on the corresponding model are applied to the dialogue state by instantiating the rule with the current dialogue state. Note that these updates may result to trigger other models, hence the procedure causes a chain of updates on the dialogue state through the probabilistic rules of the models. In summary, the workflow of PyOpenDial is basically a series of applications of probabilistic rules to the dialogue state.

Since this workflow is basically the same as in OpenDial, we refer the readers to Lison (2014), Lison and Kennington (2016), and the OpenDial toolkit website (http://www.opendial-toolkit.net) for more details on the XML specification of the domain modeling.

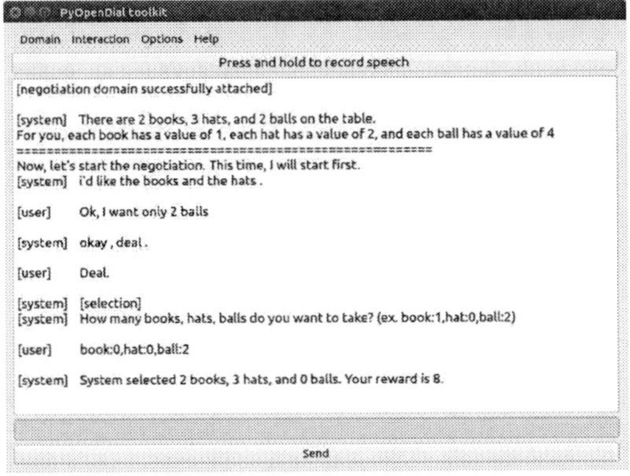

Figure 2: User interface for PyOpenDial.

2.3 Extensions to OpenDial

Custom Variable Types Neural models such as recurrent neural networks (RNNs) have become a popular choice for various dialogue processing tasks, given their capability to be trained end-to-end and infer complex latent representations of the dialogue state. In these models, the dialogue state is typically represented as a vector-valued prediction computed from a complex mapping from input to output. In contrast, the original OpenDial only supports updates on primitive data types (e.g. boolean, double, string, double array, and set) via human-readable probabilistic rules similar to decision trees. In order to overcome this limitation, we extend the specification of the dialogue state to include complex variable types and functional values to allow arbitrarily complex mappings of conditional variables, e.g. latent vectors in neural models that encode the dialogue context.

This is achieved by extending the domain XML specification to allow for variable types expressed through complex functions that can be integrated in probabilistic rules. In Listing 1, two such custom variables are defined: `movie_rnn` and `music_rnn`, which are instances of `MovieRNN` and `MusicRNN` respectively (line 2-7), representing pre-trained RNN-based generation models. Line 10 assigns `gen_u_m` to function `generate` in module `chatbot`, which executes the neural model. This particular function takes two arguments (namely the generation model and a user utterance) as input and returns the system utterance as output.

Predictive models Dialogue management is, at its core, a sequential decision-making problem,

where the goal of the system is to select actions that fulfill the system objectives while minimising associated costs. One way to achieve this objective is through forward planning, i.e. enabling the system to search for actions that yield the maximum expected utility over a given horizon. Forward planning requires the specification of predictive models (such as user simulation models) to be able to predict the consequences of the system actions on the current interaction. PyOpenDial provides the `planning-only` option to models, which makes the model triggered only when forward planning is performed. This allows the system to explicitly differentiate between observed and predicted values in the dialogue state. The specific use-case of this feature is described in Section 4 with Listing 2 (line 30).

3 Implementation

PyOpenDial is implemented in Python and is released under the MIT opensource license. The toolkit is available through the GitHub code repository at (`https://github.com/ KAIST-AILab/PyOpenDial`) [1]. The toolkit additionally provides a graphical user interface that helps fast-prototyping and test-driving the system. The graphical user interface, shown in Figure 2, displays the domain and dialogue history and take the user's next input (text or speech).

PyOpenDial implements all the core components and modules of OpenDial, including the BN inference algorithm and the probabilistic rule engine. We also introduced a number of new modules, including the Monte-Carlo tree search (MCTS) (Kocsis and Szepesvári, 2006) planner and the basic speech-to-text and text-to-speech modules using Google Speech APIs.

MCTS Planner In dialogue management, planning algorithms are often used to search for the system action that maximizes the sum of utilities in the long-term horizon so as to optimally react to the user.

The baseline planning algorithm in OpenDial is a lookahead forward planner that fully expands the search tree up to the planning horizon H:

$$Q_t(b, a) = U(b, a) + \gamma \max_{a'} \mathbb{E}_{o|b,a} \left[Q_{t+1}(b^{ao}, a') \right]$$

where b is the dialogue state, a is the value of the action variables, o is the possible observation

---

[1]More dialogue domain examples combined with deep neural networks can be found in the GitHub repository.

when taking action a in the state b, b^{ao} is the dialogue state updated from b after action a and observation o, $\gamma \in [0,1)$ is the discount factor, $U(b, a)$ is the instantaneous utility of a at the dialogue state b, and $Q_H(b, a) = 0$ for all b, a. After computing $Q_0(b, a)$ from the recursive equation, the forward planner chooses the final value of the action variable given by $\operatorname{argmax}_a Q_0(b, a)$. A major limitation of the forward planner is that the search becomes infeasible in the planning horizon as well as the branching factor (i.e. the number of candidate actions and observations).

On the other hand, MCTS combines tree search with Monte-Carlo simulation so that the search effort is non-uniformly invested into promising nodes. One of the most basic MCTS algorithms is UCT (Kocsis and Szepesvári, 2006), which performs iterative simulation on the search tree by following the UCB rule to select actions at intermediate nodes

$$\operatorname{argmax}_a \left[Q(b, a) + c\sqrt{\frac{\log N(b)}{N(b,a)}} \right]$$

where c is the exploration constant that balances exploration and exploitation trade-off, $Q(b, a)$ is the average of the sampled sum of utilities, $N(b)$ is the number of simulations performed through the dialogue state b, $N(b, a)$ is the number of times action a is selected in b. More recent versions of MCTS algorithms have shown great successes in many large sequential-decision making problems such as playing Go (Silver et al., 2016).

PyOpenDial includes an MCTS planner, and we shall demonstrate its effectiveness in the next section by comparing its performance with the forward planner, using the negotiation dialogue domain that requires long-term planning.

Google Speech Modules PyOpenDial provides new speech modules based on Google speech API: The speech recognition module that uses Google speech-to-text API and the speech synthesis module that uses Google text-to-speech API [2]. These modules can also be replaced with other custom-developed speech recognition and speech synthesis modules.

4 Application Domain

In this section, we demonstrate the aptitude of PyOpenDial using the negotiation dialogue domain (Lewis et al., 2017) as an example. In this

[2]https://cloud.google.com/text-to-speech, https://cloud.google.com/speech-to-text

```
1  <initialstate>
2   <variable id="rnn">
3    <value>@nego.NegotiationRNN</value>
4   </variable>
5   <variable id="h"><value> </value></variable>
6       ...
7  </initialstate>
8
9  <function name="gen_u_m">nego.gen_u_m</function>
10 <function name="gen_u_u">nego.gen_u_u</function>
11 <function name="reward">nego.reward</function>
12                         ...
13 <model trigger="u_u">
14  <rule>
15   <case>
16    <condition>
17     <if var="current_step" value="Negotiation"/>
18    </condition>
19    <effect util="0.001">
20     <set var="u_m" value="@gen_u_m({rnn},{h},0)"/>
21    </effect>
22       ...
23    <effect util="0.001">
24     <set var="u_m" value="@gen_u_m({rnn},{h},19)"/>
25    </effect>
26   </case>
27  </rule>
28 </model>
29
30 <model trigger="u_m" planning-only="true">
31  <rule>
32   <case>
33    <condition>
34     <if var="current_step" value="Negotiation"/>
35    </condition>
36    <effect>
37     <set var="u_u" value="@gen_u_u({rnn},{h})"/>
38    </effect>
39   </case>
40  </rule>
41 </model>
42
43 <model trigger="current_step">
44  <rule>
45   <case>
46    <condition>
47     <if var="current_step" value="Result"/>
48    </condition>
49    <effect util="@reward({rnn},{h})">
50     <set var="current_step" value="Terminated"/>
51    </effect>
52   </case>
53  </rule>
54 </model>
55                         ...
```

Listing 2: A simplified XML specification for the negotiation dialogue domain.

domain, two agents (i.e. the user and the system) negotiate on 3 types of items, and the negotiation domain has the following unique characteristics: (1) the simulated utterances of the system and the user are generated from the RNN of system and user models, which is done seamlessly thanks to Python-based implementation of the framework, (2) a long-term dialogue planning is required to get a high reward in the negotiation since the utility signal is given only at the very end of the potentially very long dialogue; thus an MCTS planner is desirable.

4.1 Domain Description

In the negotiation dialogue domain, 3 types of items (i.e. *books, hats, balls*) are divided between two agents through natural language dialogue. There is a finite amount of each item (5 to 7 total items and 1 to 4 individual items), and the agents have different utility functions that represent the agent's preference. The utility function for each agent is defined randomly while satisfying the following constraints: (1) The maximally achievable utility for each agent should be 10; (2) Each item must always have a non-zero utility for at least one agent; (3) At least one item must always have a non-zero utility for both agents. If an agreement is reached at the end of the negotiation, each agent receives a reward equal to the total utility of obtained items. If the decisions are in conflict, both agents receive a reward of 0. Figure 2 shows the negotiation dialogue example between user and system in PyOpenDial, and Listing 2 presents a simplified version of the domain XML specification.

4.2 RNN-based Natural Language Generation Model

In implementing this dialogue system, we first pretrained an RNN model that imitates negotiation dialogues between two humans, following the supervised training scheme described in (Lewis et al., 2017). This RNN model has the ability to generate natural language utterances, taking into account the previous dialogue history and the given context (i.e. value and count of each item). We use this RNN to generate candidates of system utterances (line 19-25 in Listing 2) and to generate user utterances for the user simulation model that is used during multi-horizon planning (line 37 in Listing 2). This RNN model uses PyTorch and is imported into PyOpenDial as decribed next.

4.3 Domain XML Specification

In this section, we briefly explain how the negotiation domain is specified in the XML format shown in Listing 2, which is an abbreviation of the full version distributed with PyOpenDial.

Declaration We declare `rnn` state variable, an instance of `NegotiationRNN` class (line 2-4). The class has a pre-trained RNN model, described in the previous section, as a member variable and generates actual (user or system) utterance through the RNN model. To represent the dialogue history, we also declare a state variable `h` (line 5), which maintains the user and system utterances up to the current turn. We then declare two functions, `gen_u_m` and `gen_u_u`, to generate utterances (line 9-10). `gen_u_m` is used to generate the set of candidate system utterances and `gen_u_u` is used as the user simulator in the planner to search for the best system action that maximizes the overall utility within the planning horizon. Finally, we declare the function `reward` which returns the reward at the end of the negotiation (line 11)

System Utterance Generation The utility rule specifies the utility associated with each candidate system action. In order to harness the system utterance directly generated by `NegotiationRNN` and support dialogue planning, we add 20 effects in the utility rule, each corresponding to a system utterance sampled from `NegotiationRNN`, and assign the same *immediate* utility of 0.001 (line 13-28)[3]. The actual, final utility is decided only when the negotiation has finished, and the planner described next will search for the best system utterance (among 20 candidates) using long-term planning.

Planning The planner requires a user simulation model for long-term planning. The user simulation model is given in line 30-41. Note that we set the `planning-only` tag for the user simulation model (line 30), in order to prevent the user simulation model from overwriting the actual user utterance `u_u` during planning. At the end of simulated dialogue, the final utility determined by negotiation is obtained from the python function `reward`. The variable `current_step` is set to "Terminated" to represent the end of a dialogue.

4.4 Experiments

Using the negotiation dialogue domain, we compare the performances of two planning algorithms, the forward planner and the MCTS planner, and a naive baseline that only maximizes the immediate utility without planning. The planning horizons were set to 3 for the forward planner and 7 for the MCTS planner, which made both planners take approximately same amount of search time.

As reported in Table 1, planning (using either Forward or MCTS) improves the negotiation outcome over the baseline in terms of both reward and

---

[3](Py)OpenDial includes `None` action with utility 0 by default, thus we assigned small positive utility to the generated utterances to be distinguished from the `None` action.

	Reward	Planning time (s)	% Agreed
Baseline	4.96 ± 0.12	-	81.8
Forward	5.27 ± 0.12	2.28 ± 0.05	87.3
MCTS	5.68 ± 0.12	2.03 ± 0.03	88.9

Table 1: Experimental results for the negotiation example. Baseline denotes the result of negotiation between two RNN models (without planning). Forward and MCTS represents the negotiation result between the corresponding planner and the RNN model. All the results are averaged over 3000 dialogues and report the $2\times$(standard error).

agreement rate, and the MCTS planner further outperforms the forward planner. This is mainly due to the fact that the reward signal in the negotiation domain only comes at the very end of the dialogue, thus in the early stages of the dialogue, no meaningful reward signal can be obtained within the short planning horizon of the forward planner. In contrast, MCTS performs Monte-Carlo simulations all the way towards the end of the dialogue in most cases and thus captures the final utility.

5   Conclusion

In this paper, we presented PyOpenDial, a Python-based open-source dialogue system toolkit that inherits the architectural design of OpenDial and extends the domain XML specification for integrating deep learning models.

We showed the aptitude of PyOpenDial by presenting how the negotiation dialogue domain can be implemented, seamlessly integrating with deep learning model trained for natural language generation. We also demonstrated the efficacy of the new MCTS dialogue planner, significantly outperforming the basic forward planner.

We look forward to active contribution from the developer community towards refining and improving PyOpenDial.

References

M. Abadi, P. Barham, J. Chen, Z. Chen, A. Davis, J. Dean, M. Devin, S. Ghemawat, G. Irving, M. Isard, M. Kudlur, J. Levenberg, R. Monga, S. Moore, D. G. Murray, B. Steiner, P. Tucker, V. Vasudevan, P. Warden, M. Wicke, Y. Yu, and X. Zheng. Tensorflow: A system for large-scale machine learning. In *12th USENIX Symposium on Operating Systems Design and Implementation*, pages 265–283, 2016.

A. Graves, A. Mohamed, and G. Hinton. Speech recognition with deep recurrent neural networks. In *2013 IEEE International Conference on Acoustics, Speech and Signal Processing*, 2013.

L. Kocsis and C. Szepesvári. Bandit based Monte-Carlo planning. In *European conference on machine learning*, pages 282–293, 2006.

S. Larsson and D. R. Traum. Information state and dialogue management in the TRINDI dialogue move engine toolkit. *Natural language engineering*, 6(3-4):323–340, 2000.

M. Lewis, D. Yarats, Y. Dauphin, D. Parikh, and D. Batra. Deal or no deal? end-to-end learning of negotiation dialogues. In *Proceedings of the 2017 Conference on Empirical Methods in Natural Language Processing*, pages 2443–2453, 2017.

P. Lison. *Structured Probabilistic Modelling for Dialogue Management*. PhD thesis, University of Oslo, February 2014.

P. Lison and C. Kennington. Opendial: A toolkit for developing spoken dialogue systems with probabilistic rules. In *Proceedings of ACL-2016 System Demonstrations*, pages 67–72, 2016.

A. Paszke, S. Gross, S. Chintala, G. Chanan, E. Yang, Z. DeVito, Z. Lin, A. Desmaison, L. Antiga, and A. Lerer. Automatic differentiation in PyTorch. 2017.

A. Radford, K. Narasimhan, T. Salimans, and I. Sutskever. Improving language understanding by generative pre-training. 2018.

D. Silver, A. Huang, C. J. Maddison, A. Guez, L. Sifre, G. van den Driessche, J. Schrittwieser, I. Antonoglou, V. Panneershelvam, M. Lanctot, S. Dieleman, D. Grewe, J. Nham, N. Kalchbrenner, I. Sutskever, T. Lillicrap, M. Leach, K. Kavukcuoglu, T. Graepel, and D. Hassabis. Mastering the game of Go with deep neural networks and tree search. *Nature*, pages 484–489, 2016.

S. Ultes, L. M. Rojas Barahona, P.-H. Su, D. Vandyke, D. Kim, I. n. Casanueva, P. Budzianowski, N. Mrkšić, T.-H. Wen, M. Gasic, and S. Young. PyDial: A Multi-domain Statistical Dialogue System Toolkit. In *Proceedings of ACL 2017, System Demonstrations*, pages 73–78, 2017.

J. D. Williams, I. Arizmendi, and A. Conkie. Demonstration of AT&T "let's go": A production-grade statistical spoken dialog system. In *2010 IEEE Spoken Language Technology Workshop*, 2010.

J. D. Williams, K. Asadi, and G. Zweig. Hybrid code networks: practical and efficient end-to-end dialog control with supervised and reinforcement learning. *CoRR*, abs/1702.03274, 2017.

S. Young, M. Gai, B. Thomson, and J. D. Williams. POMDP-based statistical spoken dialog systems: A review. *Proceedings of the IEEE*, 101(5), 2013.

L. Yu, W. Zhang, J. Wang, and Y. Yu. Seqgan: Sequence generative adversarial nets with policy gradient. *CoRR*, abs/1609.05473, 2016.

Redcoat: A Collaborative Annotation Tool for Hierarchical Entity Typing

Michael Stewart[✉]**, Wei Liu**[✉]**and Rachel Cardell-Oliver**
The University of Western Australia
35 Stirling Highway, Crawley, Western Australia
`michael.stewart@research.uwa.edu.au`, `wei.liu@uwa.edu.au`, and
`rachel.cardell-oliver@uwa.edu.au`

Abstract

We introduce Redcoat, a web-based annotation tool that supports collaborative hierarchical entity typing. As an annotation tool, Redcoat also facilitates knowledge elicitation by allowing the creation and continuous refinement of concept hierarchies during annotation. It aims to minimise not only annotation time but the time it takes for project creators to set up and distribute projects to annotators. Projects created using the web-based interface can be rapidly distributed to a list of email addresses. Redcoat handles the propagation of documents amongst annotators and automatically scales the annotation workload depending on the number of active annotators. In this paper we discuss these key features and outline Redcoat's system architecture. We also highlight Redcoat's unique benefits over existing annotation tools via a qualitative comparison.

1 Introduction

Recent successes of deep learning in natural language processing (NLP) is largely fuelled by high quality annotated datasets. Annotation tools provide the means to label data, and are vital for obtaining good results across a wide range of NLP tasks such as named entity recognition[1], question answering[2], and natural language inference[3]. One common underlying sub-component of these NLP tasks is entity typing, which involves identifying the type(s) of every entity in a document. Entity typing is also an enabling technique for utilising unstructured text in visualisation and knowledge discovery (Stewart et al., 2017).

Many recent entity typing taxonomies are structured in a hierarchy as opposed to a flat set of types. FIGER (Ling and Weld, 2012), for example, is a 112-class shallow hierarchy derived from Freebase. TypeNet (Murty et al., 2017), derived from Freebase and Wordnet, features over 1900 types with an average depth of 7.8. It has been shown that incorporating these hierarchies into deep learning models improves classification accuracy (Murty et al., 2018; Ren et al., 2016).

Despite the needs of deep learning algorithms for labelled data with hierarchical entity types, a review of existing annotation tools shows there is *no support for multi-label tagging using hierarchical taxonomies*. Existing annotation tools, which are designed for the labelling of entity recognition data as opposed to entity typing data, only support one label per token. These systems also *do not allow for the modification of the taxonomy during annotation*. This lack of support is especially troublesome for real-world applications that are domain specific and typically with no standard category hierarchies. A tool that can leverage the annotation efforts as knowledge elicitation for domain taxonomy creation and refinement is very much in need.

While many annotation tools claim to maximise the speed of annotation, *few tools also optimise the time it takes for a project creator to set up and distribute an annotation project*. BRAT (Rapid Annotation Tool) (Stenetorp et al., 2012), the most popular annotation tool, requires project creators to read documentation, split their data into folders, set up a web server, and email their annotators links to their respective folders.

In light of these current issues, we introduce Redcoat, a web-based collaborative annotation tool for hierarchical entity typing. Redcoat was built with four primary goals in mind:

1. *Hierarchical*: Support entity hierarchies and multi-label annotation.

2. *Flexible*: Allow hierarchy refinement during annotation.

---

[1]https://www.i2b2.org/NLP/DataSets/
[2]https://rajpurkar.github.io/SQuAD-explorer/
[3]https://nlp.stanford.edu/projects/snli/

193

Proceedings of the 2019 EMNLP and the 9th IJCNLP (System Demonstrations), pages 193–198
Hong Kong, China, November 3 – 7, 2019. ©2019 Association for Computational Linguistics

3. *Rapid*: Reduce annotation time and time taken for project creation and distribution.

4. *Easy to use*: Keep it simple and intuitive for both annotator and project owner.

This paper is structured as follows. We begin by reviewing existing annotation tools. We then outline Redcoat's key features, namely its intuitive and rapid project creation interface, annotation interface, and project dashboard. We describe Redcoat's system architecture and then present a qualitative comparison between Redcoat and existing annotation tools. Finally, we provide a link to an online demonstration of Redcoat as well as a code repository link and demonstration video.

2 Related work

Among the several open source annotation tools available, the most popular is BRAT (Stenetorp et al., 2012), a web-based annotation tool that is designed to maximise annotation speed. BRAT supports the annotation of a wide variety of NLP tasks, including entity recognition, event extraction, and POS tagging. It also offers corpus search functionality.

GATE Teamware (Bontcheva et al., 2013) is another popular web-based annotation tool. It places a stronger emphasis on user management than BRAT, allowing for multiple user roles. It also provides automatic pre-processing of documents to improve annotation speed.

WebAnno (Yimam et al., 2013), based on the BRAT editor, features a strong emphasis on crowdsourcing via the CrowdFlower platform[4]. WebAnno also allows for the annotation of several NLP tasks. Unlike BRAT, however, WebAnno uses a relational database to model users, projects, documents, and tags. This provides useful features such as project monitoring and user management.

More recent annotation tools include SAWT (Samih et al., 2016), a lightweight web-based annotation tool that aims for simplicity and ease of use. Yedda (Yang et al., 2018) offers label recommendations via machine learning and provides both command line and web-based interfaces. SANTO (Hartung et al., 2018), which is designed primarily for slot-filling tasks, enables the formation of relational structures from an ontology. It also visualises the annotations of

every user at once to help project owners monitor and curate the quality of the annotations. TALEN (Mayhew and Roth, 2018) is another recent tool that specialises in the annotation of low resource entities (i.e. where the annotators do not speak the language of the dataset). EasyTree (Tratz and Phan, 2018) is specifically designed for the annotation of dependency trees, and is integrated with Amazon Mechanical Turk crowdsourcing platform.

Several commercial annotation tools also exist, such as LightTag[5], TagTog[6], and Prodigy[7]. While these tools offer an array of features, their pricing can be prohibitive for researchers.

3 Redcoat - Key features

3.1 Intuitive and rapid project creation

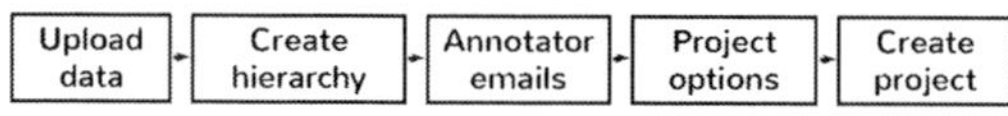

Figure 1: Redcoat's project creation process.

One of Redcoat's most notable features is its web-based project creation interface, which enables users to set up an annotation project and rapidly distribute it to a list of annotators. The process of project creation is shown in Figure 1. The project setup page allows for the user's dataset to be dragged and dropped into a web-based form. The dataset is automatically tokenised by Redcoat prior to being stored in the database.

3.1.1 Hierarchical entity categories

Unlike many annotation tools, Redcoat supports the development of hierarchical entity categories and allows for each token to be labelled with more than one type. Users may specify their entity categories as either plain text with proper indentation, or as a hierarchy using an interactive tree diagram. Figure 2 shows an example hierarchy being built by the creator of an annotation project using the interface. Users may create, rename and delete categories by right clicking on categories within the tree diagram. Users may also simply paste their categories into a text box, denoting hierarchy levels via space characters, and the tree will automatically generate based on the given text.

---

⁴*Crowdflower*. https://crowdflower.com

⁵*LightTag*. https://www.lighttag.io/
⁶*TagTog*. http://docs.tagtog.net/
⁷*Prodigy*. https://prodi.gy/

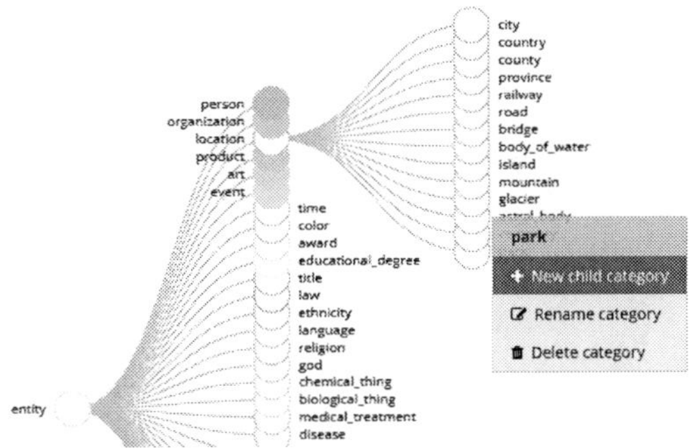

Figure 2: The category hierarchy generation window, which allows users to easily create, edit, and delete categories via an interactive tree diagram. In this example the user has loaded the FIGER preset and has right clicked on the "park" category to open the menu.

Redcoat also features three category hierarchy presets: *NER*, the standard Named Entity Recognition classes (PER, LOC, ORG, MISC), *FIGER* (Ling and Weld, 2012) (fine-grained entity recognition), and *Mining*, containing categories specific to workplace accident data in the mining industry. Selecting one of these presets via a drop-down menu instantly loads the corresponding hierarchy. UMLS[8] and SNOMED CT[9] are planned to be pre-loaded for medical dataset annotation.

3.1.2 Automatic project distribution

Project creators may specify a list of the email addresses of their annotators. Upon completion of the setup form, Redcoat sends an invitation to every valid email address in the list using Sendgrid[10], a transactional email service. Users are invited to annotate the project regardless of whether they have registered for Redcoat, preventing the need for the project creator to coordinate the creation of user accounts.

3.1.3 Document propagation

In contrast to other annotation platforms, Redcoat automatically scales the annotation load of each annotator according to the number of users that have accepted their invitations to begin annotating. The documents are not split up into distinct sets, where each user has their own set of documents to annotate; they are instead distributed to annotators on a first-come-first-serve basis. The load of each annotator therefore depends entirely on how many

annotators are actively annotating the project. If, for example, a project creator specifies 10 email addresses on the setup form, but only 5 of them accept their invitations the next day, each annotator would be required to annotate 20% of the corpus. Once the remaining 5 users accept invitation, the load per annotator drops to 10%.

The project creator may also specify the "overlap", i.e. the number of times each document should be annotated. An overlap of 2, for example, would mean each annotator would label 40% of the corpus (if 5 users have accepted invitation) and 20% of the corpus (if 10 users have accepted). Specifying an overlap value greater than 1 ensures more consistent data at the cost of annotation time.

3.2 Annotation interface

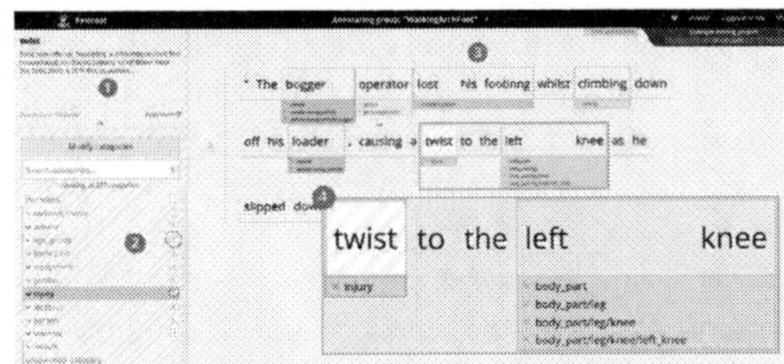

Figure 3: Redcoat's simple annotation interface. (1) shows a Wikipedia summary of the selected token. (2) is the entity categories, which may be organised in a hierarchical structure and modified during annotation. (3) is the annotation interface. (4) shows a zoomed-in view of a selection of tokens.

Redcoat offers a simple annotation interface designed to maximise the speed of annotation. This interface is shown in Figure 3. The category hierarchy is displayed in the left menu, and categories may be expanded and minimised by clicking on them. Annotators may also search for categories using the built-in search menu.

The annotation interface allows for the use of both mouse and keyboard, providing annotators with a way to rapidly annotate documents if they elect to familiarise themselves with the hotkeys associated with navigating the documents (arrow keys) and the hierarchy (W, A, S, and D). The categories in the hierarchy also have associated numerical hotkeys, circled in Figure 3, aiming to speed up annotation.

Upon annotating a token, the token is automatically labelled with all of the label's parent categories. Annotators may remove individual labels

[8]*UMLS*. https://www.nlm.nih.gov/research/umls/
[9]*SNOMED CT*. http://www.snomed.org/
[10]*Sendgrid*. https://sendgrid.com/

by clicking on the labels that appear underneath the annotated tokens.

The interface also presents an optional summary of the selected token taken from Wikipedia via the MediaWiki API[11] to reduce the need to Google search during annotation.

3.2.1 Modification of hierarchy

Redcoat allows for the modification of the category hierarchy during annotation. The extent to which the hierarchy should be modifiable is determined by the project creator. There are three options: *full permission*, whereby the hierarchy may be fully modified, *create only*, where annotators may only add new categories but may not delete them, and *no modification*. Deleted categories, along with their child categories, are removed from every annotation automatically.

The ability to modify the hierarchy is useful for domain-specific datasets for which there are no standard category hierarchies. Project creators need not worry that their hierarchy does not contain every possible category in the dataset, as it may be updated dynamically. The flexible hierarchy allows for the development of categories to be an iterative process, thereby making the annotation process help with knowledge elicitation.

3.2.2 Automatic labelling

Redcoat provides an automatic labelling process to speed up annotation. Prior to presenting the documents to the annotator, any tokens that directly correspond to categories in the hierarchy are labelled with their corresponding type(s). For example, if a document contains the words "right arm", and `body_part/arm/right_arm` is a category in the hierarchy, the token span will be labelled with `body_part/arm/right_arm`, `body_part/arm`, and `body_part`. Any incorrect labels may be deleted by the annotator. This process is implemented using regular expression parsing and does not noticeably affect load time.

3.3 Project dashboard

Redcoat's project dashboard, as shown in Figure 4a, provides a way for project creators and annotators to quickly view all projects they've created or are currently annotating. The projects list may be sorted, filtered, and searched. Upon clicking a project users are presented with a detailed summary of the entire project. Project creators

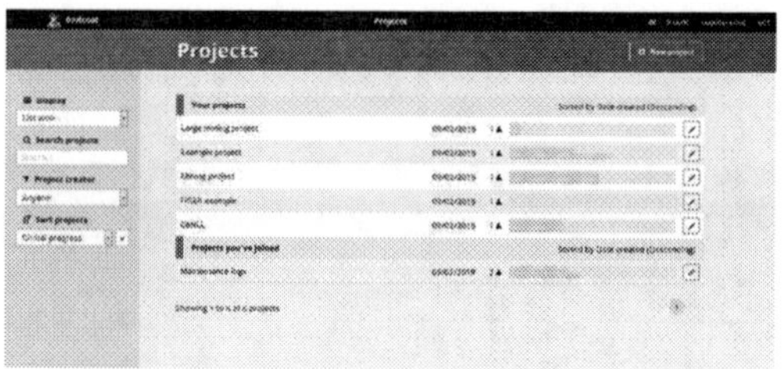

(a) Redcoat's Projects dashboard, which shows all projects the user has created and is involved in. Users may click on a project to bring up a detailed view of that project.

may view further details about their own projects, such as a list of pending/accepted invitations and a list of annotators that provides the ability to quickly download the completed annotations of the project.

3.3.1 Exporting annotations

Project creators may download annotated documents either per-annotator or for all annotators at once. At present these annotations are exported to the same JSON-based format used by state-of-the-art entity typing systems[12]. The "download all" button compiles the annotations of every user into a dataset that contains the most commonly-assigned label for each token, providing project creators with a machine-learning-ready dataset with little effort.

4 System architecture

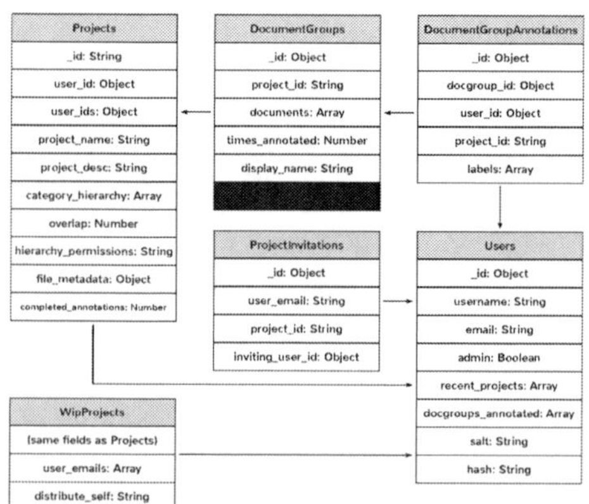

Figure 4: Redcoat's underlying MongoDB schema.

Redcoat is written in Node.js[13] and features an underlying MongoDB schema, shown in Figure 4.

[11]*MediaWiki API.* http://en.wikipedia.org/w/api.php

[12]*AFET.* https://github.com/INK-USC/AFET

[13]*Node.js.* https://nodejs.org

System	Web-based project creation	Project monitoring	Curation feature	Document propagation	Class labels		
					Dynamic	Hierarchical	Multi-label
BRAT	✗	✗	✗	✗	✗	✓	✗
GATE	✓	✓	✓	✗	✗	✗	✗
SANTO	✓	✓	✗	✗	✗	✗	✗
SAWT	✓	✓	✗	✗	✗	✗	✗
YEDDA	✓	✓	✗	✗	✗	✗	✗
WebAnno	✓	✓	✓	✗	✗	✗	✗
Redcoat	✓	✓	✓	✓	✓	✓	✓

Table 1: A comparison of existing annotation tools with Redcoat. *Dynamic* refers to the ability for any user to modify the class labels during annotation.

The `Project` model stores information related to a project. `DocumentGroup` is a set of 10 documents belonging to a particular project. The documents are stored as arrays after tokenisation. `DocumentGroupAnnotation` stores the labels a particular user has assigned to a `DocumentGroup`. `ProjectInvitations` stores the invitations of a project, and is connected to the `User` table via `user_email` as opposed to `user_id` so that the invitation persists if the user has not yet registered. Finally, the `WIPProject` model stores information about a "work in progress" project, which is transferred to a new project upon completion of the setup form. This model allows for the data the user uploads to be persistent across refreshes and devices.

The category hierarchy is stored in the `Project` model as an array. Categories are stored in the form of strings, with different hierarchy levels represented by slashes (e.g. `person`, `person/boilermaker`). This array, along with every other field in each model, is subject to schema validation in order to ensure that the data is correctly stored. The category hierarchy, in particular, is validated both client and server side using a strict validation algorithm.

The majority of the front-end Javascript is written in jQuery[14]. The category hierarchy visualisation is implemented using D3.js[15]. Several other open-source libraries are used throughout the front-end, including DataTables[16] and jsTree[17].

5 Comparison with existing tools

Table 1 provides a qualitative comparison between Redcoat and other existing annotation tools.

Web-based project creation is present in all tools except BRAT, which requires data owners to split their dataset into multiple folders and place them into the appropriate location on their remote server. Consequently, *project monitoring* is also not present in BRAT, restricting the applicability of the system for real-world projects.

Few tools have a *curation feature*, allowing owners to specify the correct tags assigned to a token across tags provided by a set of annotators. Redcoat does not provide a formal curation interface, but includes automatic curation that selects commonly-assigned labels across annotators when downloading all annotations at once. This vastly simplifies the curation process and saves project creators considerable amounts of time.

Redcoat's *document propagation* sets it apart from other tools. Annotation workload is automatically scaled depending on the number of active annotators, preventing the need to manually assign documents to annotators.

Redcoat also allows annotators to modify the class labels, and supports both hierarchical entity categories and multi-label annotation. Aside from BRAT's ability to visualise label hierarchies, these features are not present in any other annotation tool.

Our qualitative analysis shows Redcoat is a highly flexible and powerful annotation tool, offering many benefits that distinguish it from other tools. It optimises speed, flexibility and ease of use while supporting hierarchical entity categories.

6 System demonstration

A demo of Redcoat is deployed online at http://agent.csse.uwa.edu.au/redcoat/. Users may create an account via the Register button on the homepage and set up a project immediately. A video of a demonstration of the system is available at https://youtu.be/igtR8Sfi8oo.

---

¹⁴*jQuery*. https://jquery.com
¹⁵*D3.js*. https://d3js.org
¹⁶*DataTables*. https://datatables.net
¹⁷*jsTree*. https://www.jstree.com

The source code is publicly available on GitHub[18]. The Readme file outlines how to set up Redcoat locally.

7 Conclusion and future work

In this paper we have introduced Redcoat, a collaborative annotation tool for hierarchical entity typing. It supports a variety of novel features, such as the ability to model entity categories as a hierarchy, label each token with more than one label, and update the hierarchy during annotation. Users may create projects using the web-based interface and quickly distribute their project to a list of email addresses. Redcoat handles the propagation of documents amongst users and automatically scales the annotation workload depending on the number of active annotators. These features distinguish Redcoat from existing annotation tools.

While Redcoat as presented here is ready to be used, there are still features under ongoing development. We are working on incorporating our deep-learning-based entity typing algorithms to make intelligent suggestions to support continuous automatic tagging. We also plan to visualise the annotation results and activity of annotators.

8 Acknowledgements

This research was funded by an Australian Postgraduate Award Scholarship and a UWA Safety Net Top-up Scholarship. The project is also supported by ARC DP150102405 and the NVIDIA GPU academic grant program.

References

Kalina Bontcheva, Hamish Cunningham, Ian Roberts, Angus Roberts, Valentin Tablan, Niraj Aswani, and Genevieve Gorrell. 2013. Gate teamware: a web-based, collaborative text annotation framework. *Language Resources and Evaluation*, 47(4):1007–1029.

Matthias Hartung, Hendrik ter Horst, Frank Grimm, Tim Diekmann, Roman Klinger, and Philipp Cimiano. 2018. Santo: A web-based annotation tool for ontology-driven slot filling. In *Proceedings of ACL 2018, System Demonstrations*, pages 68–73. Association for Computational Linguistics.

Xiao Ling and Daniel S. Weld. 2012. Fine-grained entity recognition. In *Proceedings of the Twenty-Sixth AAAI Conference on Artificial Intelligence*, AAAI'12, pages 94–100. AAAI Press.

Stephen Mayhew and Dan Roth. 2018. Talen: Tool for annotation of low-resource entities. In *Proceedings of ACL 2018, System Demonstrations*, pages 80–86. Association for Computational Linguistics.

Shikhar Murty, Patrick Verga, Luke Vilnis, and Andrew McCallum. 2017. Finer grained entity typing with typenet. *arXiv preprint arXiv:1711.05795*.

Shikhar Murty, Patrick Verga, Luke Vilnis, Irena Radovanovic, and Andrew McCallum. 2018. Hierarchical losses and new resources for fine-grained entity typing and linking. In *Proceedings of the 56th Annual Meeting of the Association for Computational Linguistics (Volume 1: Long Papers)*, volume 1, pages 97–109.

Xiang Ren, Wenqi He, Meng Qu, Lifu Huang, Heng Ji, and Jiawei Han. 2016. Afet: Automatic fine-grained entity typing by hierarchical partial-label embedding. In *Proceedings of the 2016 Conference on Empirical Methods in Natural Language Processing*, pages 1369–1378.

Younes Samih, Wolfgang Maier, and Laura Kallmeyer. 2016. Sawt: Sequence annotation web tool. In *Proceedings of the Second Workshop on Computational Approaches to Code Switching*, pages 65–70.

Pontus Stenetorp, Sampo Pyysalo, Goran Topić, Tomoko Ohta, Sophia Ananiadou, and Jun'ichi Tsujii. 2012. Brat: a web-based tool for nlp-assisted text annotation. In *Proceedings of the Demonstrations at the 13th Conference of the European Chapter of the Association for Computational Linguistics*, pages 102–107. Association for Computational Linguistics.

Michael Stewart, Wei Liu, Rachel Cardell-Oliver, and Mark Griffin. 2017. An interactive web-based toolset for knowledge discovery from short text log data. In *International Conference on Advanced Data Mining and Applications*, pages 853–858. Springer.

Stephen Tratz and Nhien Phan. 2018. A web-based system for crowd-in-the-loop dependency treebanking. In *Proceedings of the Eleventh International Conference on Language Resources and Evaluation (LREC-2018)*.

Jie Yang, Yue Zhang, Linwei Li, and Xingxuan Li. 2018. Yedda: A lightweight collaborative text span annotation tool. In *Proceedings of ACL 2018, System Demonstrations*, pages 31–36. Association for Computational Linguistics.

Seid Muhie Yimam, Iryna Gurevych, Richard Eckart de Castilho, and Chris Biemann. 2013. Webanno: A flexible, web-based and visually supported system for distributed annotations. In *Proceedings of the 51st Annual Meeting of the Association for Computational Linguistics: System Demonstrations*, pages 1–6.

---

[18]https://github.com/Michael-Stewart-Webdev/redcoat

SEAGLE: A Platform for Comparative Evaluation of Semantic Encoders for Information Retrieval

Fabian David Schmidt,[*] Markus Dietsche,[*] Simone Paolo Ponzetto and Goran Glavaš

Data and Web Science Group
University of Mannheim
`fabian.david.schmidt@hotmail.de`
`dietsche.markus@googlemail.com`
`{simone, goran}@informatik.uni-mannheim.de`

Abstract

We introduce SEAGLE,[1] a platform for comparative evaluation of semantic text encoding models on information retrieval (IR) tasks. SEAGLE implements (1) word embedding aggregators, which represent texts as algebraic aggregations of pretrained word embeddings and (2) pretrained semantic encoders, and allows for their comparative evaluation on arbitrary (monolingual and cross-lingual) IR collections. We benchmark SEAGLE's models on monolingual document retrieval and cross-lingual sentence retrieval. SEAGLE functionality can be exploited via an easy-to-use web interface and its modular backend (micro-service architecture) can easily be extended with additional semantic search models.

1 Introduction and Motivation

Traditional IR models operate on lexical overlap and fail to identify relevance when documents and queries differently lexicalize concepts. Semantic search seeks to overcome such lexical mismatches between document and user queries (Li and Xu, 2014). Early approaches to semantic search relied on external resources like WordNet (Moldovan and Mihalcea, 2000) and Wikipedia (Strube and Ponzetto, 2006), suffering from the resource's limited coverage. More recent semantic search systems (Vulić and Moens, 2015; Litschko et al., 2018; Nogueira and Cho, 2019) remedy for those coverage issues by encoding text using distributional word vectors (i.e., word embeddings) (Mikolov et al., 2013; Bojanowski et al., 2017) and neural text encoders (Devlin et al., 2018).

While there is a plethora of semantic text encoding models, there have been few attempts to empirically compare them on IR tasks. In this

work, we aim to allow for such comparative evaluations on arbitrary IR test collections. We introduce SEAGLE, a platform for concurrent execution and comparative evaluation of semantic search models. SEAGLE implements most recently proposed (1) word embedding aggregation models (Arora et al., 2017; Rücklé et al., 2018; Yang et al., 2019; Zhelezniak et al., 2019) as well as (2) two pretraining-based text encoders (Gysel et al., 2017; Devlin et al., 2018) and allows users to evaluate them on arbitrary IR collections. Coupled with pretrained cross-lingual embedding spaces (Glavaš et al., 2019), SEAGLE also supports cross-lingual search. The platform's modular architecture based on micro-services makes it easy to extend it with additional semantic encoding models. SEAGLE is accessible via an easy-to-use web interface.

2 Semantic Representation Models

We first describe SEAGLE's semantic encoders, belonging to two categories: word embedding aggregators and pre-trained text encoders.

2.1 Word Embedding Aggregators

Word embedding aggregators encode the text by aggregating pretrained d-dimensional embeddings of its words. Formally, a document matrix $V_d \in \mathbb{R}^{N \times d}$ sequentially stacks embeddings $\mathbf{t}_i \in \mathbb{R}^d$ corresponding to tokens t_i ($i \in \{1, \cdots, N\}$) of document d from the collection D. A weight w_i is computed for every token t_i and the contribution of the embedding $\mathbf{t}_i$ to the document representation $\mathbf{d} \in \mathbb{R}^d$ is scaled according to w_i.

Continuos Bag-of-Words (CBOW) simply averages the rows of the document embedding matrix V_d. Put differently, CBOW computes the simple average of the word embeddings, i.e., it assigns equal weights (w_i=$1/N$) to all embeddings.

Term Frequency-Inverse Document Frequency

---

[*]These authors contributed equally to this paper.

[1]SEAGLE is available on GitHub and demonstrated on YouTube.

Proceedings of the 2019 EMNLP and the 9th IJCNLP (System Demonstrations), pages 199–204
Hong Kong, China, November 3 – 7, 2019. ©2019 Association for Computational Linguistics

(**TF-IDF**) aggregator computes the weight w_i as the product of term t_i's relative frequency within the document d (TF) and the inverse of proportion of documents in the collection containing t_i (IDF). The assumption is that (1) more frequent words contribute more to the document's meaning, as do (2) the terms that are more specific to the document (i.e., do not occur in many other documents).

Smooth Inverse Frequency (SIF) conflates bias-adjusted weighted word embeddings to generate document embeddings (Arora et al., 2017):

$$\mathbf{d} = \frac{1}{N} \sum_{t_i \in d} \frac{a}{a + p(t_i|D)} \mathbf{t}_i \qquad (1)$$

Weight w_i of a term t_i is a smoothed inverse of the probability of t_i under the unigram language model built from the whole collection D, with a being the smoothing factor. In the next step, common component removal (CCR) is applied to every document vector $\mathbf{d}$: let $X \in \mathbb{R}^{d \times |D|}$ be the matrix obtained by stacking vectors of all collection documents as columns. Each document vector $\mathbf{d}$ is then replaced with $\mathbf{d} - \mathbf{u}\mathbf{u}^\top \mathbf{d}$, where $\mathbf{u}$ is the left singular vector of X. CCR aims to eliminate the similarities between document vectors that originate from syntactic rather than semantic similarities.

Concatenated Power Means (CPM) generalizes the aggregation of word vectors to their chosen powers (Rücklé et al., 2018):

$$\mathbf{d}^p = \left(\frac{\mathbf{t}_1^p + \cdots + \mathbf{t}_n^p}{N} \right)^{\frac{1}{p}} \qquad (2)$$

Choices for p constitute a hyperparameter and determine the dimensionality of the resulting document embedding, as $\mathbf{d}^p$ for different p are concatenated into a final document representation. Power means can reduce a set of vectors to a geometric mean ($p = 0$), arithmetic mean ($p = 1$), minimum ($p = -\infty$), and maximum ($p = \infty$). We concatenate the last three to generate the final document embedding, and then, following the original work (Rücklé et al., 2018), perform element-wise z-normalization over document vectors $\mathbf{d}$.

Geometric Embedding (GEM) weighs word embeddings $\mathbf{t_i}$ by summing their *novelty*, *significance*, and *uniqueness* scores (Yang et al., 2019) and correcting the resulting document vectors for (document-dependent) principal components via CCR. Let $W^i = [\mathbf{t}_{i-m}, \mathbf{t}_{i-1}, \cdots, \mathbf{t}_{i+m}, \mathbf{t}_i] \in \mathbb{R}^{d \times (2m+1)}$ be the contextual window of the token t_i with m neighbours.

The *novelty score* of t_i is computed as the normalized minimal distance from from $\mathbf{t}_i$ to the subspace spanned by the vectors of context words. The *significance score* captures the semantic alignment between the vectors $\mathbf{t}_i$ and the context W^i as the similarity between $\mathbf{t}_i$ and singular vectors of W^i obtained via SVD. Intuitively, a token is more significant the more it is aligned with the context's principal components. Lastly, the *uniqueness* score quantifies the alignment between the word vector and the principal directions computed on the whole collection. A token highly aligned with collection's principal components is an uninformative word and should receive a low weight.[2]

DynaMax-Jaccard (DJ) is a non-parametric similarity measure (Zhelezniak et al., 2019). The algorithm projects stacked word embeddings of a query $\mathbf{q} \in \mathbb{R}^{M \times d}$ and stacked word embeddings of a document $\mathbf{d} \in \mathbb{R}^{N \times d}$ into the shared space $U \in \mathbb{R}^{(M+N) \times d}$. Features for $\mathbf{q}$ and $\mathbf{d}$ are then max-pooled along the rows of projections, respectively. Feature generation tests the degree of membership of $\mathbf{q}$ and $\mathbf{d}$ in U and represents an extension of set theory to real-valued vectors. Accordingly, the fuzzy Jaccard index measures the similarity between query and document representations and is computed as follows: stacked features are min- and max-pooled over rows and the sum of minima over the sum of maxima yields the fuzzy Jaccard score.

2.2 Semantic Text Encoders

BERT (Devlin et al., 2018) is a general-purpose unsupervised pretraining model based on the Transformer architecture that can dynamically predict contextualized token vectors. We integrate `bert-as-a-service` (Xiao, 2018) to infer document embeddings: we average-pool stacked token representations in each of BERT's Transformer's layers (second to fourth from the last layer) and concatenate the resulting averaged representations of each layer to obtain a document embedding d. We then element-wise z-normalize $\mathbf{d}$. Because BERT's positional encoding limits the maximal sequence length, we dissect collection documents into 256-token segments (with 32 token overlap between adjacent segments). The final document embedding $\mathbf{d}$ is the average of 256-token segments' embeddings generated by BERT.

---

[2]For more details on GEM, we refer the reader to the original work (Yang et al., 2019).

Neural Vector Space Model (NVSM) jointly learns token and document representations (Gysel et al., 2017). Specifically, during training (inference), relevant queries are modeled as CBOW embeddings of n-grams (query) sampled from the source document and then mapped via a learned transformation onto the document space. NVSM then learns its parameters (word and document embeddings; mapping), such that the mapped n-grams (queries) are most similar to the respective document representation. The model accounts for the lack of positive supervision (the number of relevance judgments is typically rather limited) via negative sampling and a contrastive maximum likelihood loss. For more details on NVSM, we refer the reader to the original work (Gysel et al., 2017).

3 Benchmarking Semantic Models

We benchmark the above semantic search models on two retrieval tasks: (1) monolingual document retrieval on the LATimes test collection (112.082 documents, 114 queries, and 2.094 positive relevance judgments) (2) cross-lingual sentence retrieval on the subset of Europarl's sentence-aligned corpora: we compile 5.000 aligned sentence translations between English (EN), Italian (IT), German (DE), and Finnish (FI). Following the specificities of each collection, we measure performance on LATimes collection in terms of NDCG@100, MAP@1000, and Precision@10; and in terms of MRR and Hits@1, 5, 10 for Europarl. We additionally evaluate BM25, a robust probabilistic retrieval model (Robertson et al., 2009) as a baseline for the monolingual document retrieval. BM25 captures only lexical overlaps between documents queries, i.e., it cannot capture any semantic alignment not originating from shared terms.

3.1 Experimental Setup

All required corpus statistics (e.g., IDF or common components) are computed offline on the document collection as a preprocessing step. For all aggregation based methods (see §2.1) we employ 300-dimensional fastText embeddings (Bojanowski et al., 2017), pretrained on Wikipedia.[3] For cross-lingual sentence retrieval, we first induce the shared bilingual word embedding spaces by projecting the EN vectors to the monolingual space of the target language (IT, DE, or

---

[3]Available at `https://fasttext.cc/docs/en/pretrained-vectors.html`

FI). To this end, following (Glavaš et al., 2019), we use 5K automatically obtained word translation pairs to induce the projection matrices by solving the Procrustes problem. We infer contextualized embeddings with pretrained BERT models using `Bert-Large, Uncased (Whole Word Masking)` and `Bert-Base, Multilingual Cased`[4] for LATimes and Europarl, respectively. Except for BERT, we lowercase and tokenize text using BlingFire.[5] For NVSM, we trim the vocabulary to 60k most frequent non-stop words and learn 512 dimensional word and document embeddings with a *tanh* activation mapping on sampled n-grams of length 16 with 10 contrastive examples.

3.2 Results

Table 1 summarizes the monolingual document retrieval and cross-lingual sentence retrieval results. NVSM yields the best retrieval performance on the monolingual document retrieval task, suggesting that reliable word and document representations can be learned from regular-size retrieval collections. Among the embedding aggregation models, SIF seems to display the best performance. The fact that BM25, a semantically unaware baseline, outperforms all semantic models on document retrieval is discouraging. However, this may merely be an artifact of the LATimes dataset: out of 2.094 relevances, the document contains some (all) query terms in 1.975 (647) cases.

The cross-lingual sentence retrieval shows that all semantic search models outperform the simple word embedding averaging. Overall, DynaMax-Jaccard (DJ) yields the strongest performance, only trailing SIF on the EN-FI evaluation. In EN-FI scenario the common component removal (CCR) step included in SIF strongly boosts the performance (SIF weighting without CCR yields merely 41.1% MRR). Our cross-lingual sentence retrieval based on the pre-trained multilingual BERT model exhibits strong performance across all three language pairs – on EN-IT and EN-DE it lags behind DJ by a small margin and substantially outperforms all other aggregators; on EN-FI it outperforms DJ but falls behind the surprisingly effective SIF (with CCR). BERT's and DJ's effectiveness, however, significantly drop in the monolingual document

---

[4]`https://github.com/google-research/bert`

[5]`https://github.com/Microsoft/BlingFire`

| Model | LATimes | | | Europarl | | | | | | | | | | | |
| | EN-EN | | | EN-IT | | | | EN-DE | | | | EN-FI | | | |
	NDCG	MAP	P@10	MRR	H@1	H@5	H@10	MRR	H@1	H@5	H@10	MRR	H@1	H@5	H@10
CBOW	28.4	18.8	14.6	59.4	52.9	66.4	71.1	55.4	48.7	62.7	67.5	38.3	30.7	46.6	52.8
TF-IDF	29.8	21.8	18.1	68.4	63.0	74.5	78.4	63.6	57.6	70.2	74.8	42.2	34.6	50.3	57.6
SIF	34.1	28.8	25.9	86.4	82.4	91.2	93.1	80.2	75.3	86.0	88.8	61.8	54.0	70.6	75.9
CPM	30.0	21.5	17.4	78.9	73.3	85.6	88.6	72.1	65.6	79.3	83.6	42.7	33.6	52.2	59.6
GEM	26.8	22.2	19.2	81.0	76.5	86.7	89.4	74.7	68.6	82.0	85.9	42.5	34.4	50.7	58.0
DJ	23.0	14.3	11.6	93.7	92.1	95.6	96.6	89.0	86.3	92.2	94.0	51.1	42.3	61.3	67.6
NVSM	31.8	34.9	29.7	–	–	–	–	–	–	–	–	–	–	–	–
BERT	20.2	12.4	11.5	87.3	84.4	90.6	92.7	87.4	84.5	90.8	92.7	56.5	49.2	64.9	71.0
BM25	38.0	42.0	32.5	–	–	–	–	–	–	–	–	–	–	–	–

Table 1: Results of the comparative evaluation of semantic search models on: (1) monolingual document retrieval (LATimes); metrics: NDCG@100, MAP@1000 and Precision@10; and (2) cross-lingual sentence retrieval (Europarl, 5K sentence pairs, EN-DE, EN-IT, and EN-FI); metrics: MRR and Hits@{1, 5, 10}.

retrieval setup where the models need to encode much longer documents.

Lastly, the complexity and runtime of the evaluated models should not be ignored. As a rule of thumb, CBOW, TF-IDF, SIF and CPM, are quite efficient and resource-light, whereas the remaining algorithms become increasingly resource-demanding and decreasingly efficient – from GEM, and DJ, which require embedding aggregation over the whole collection, over predicting vectors with BERT (one inference for each max. length token segment), to NVSM, for which any collection change warrants model retraining.

4 Architecture & Interface

SEAGLE is implemented as an application based on micro-services, consisting of a web client (see figure 1) for configuration and search and network daemons (see figure 2), one for each semantic search model. Such a modularized architecture facilitates the implementation and addition of new semantic search models (as new daemons).

4.1 SEAGLE's Architecture

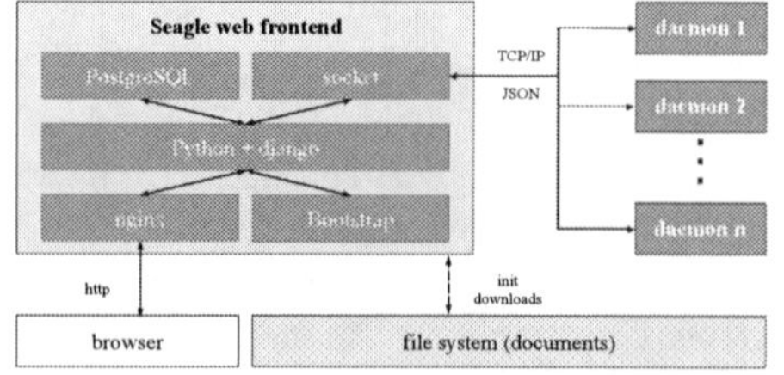

Figure 1: web front end components

Seagle is a Python application, based on the

Django[6] framework for web development. It indexes document collections (i.e., all document representations required by semantic search models) within a PostgreSQL database.[7] It runs on a nginx[8] web-server and utilises Bootstrap[9] to ensure responsiveness.

Communication between the web application and the network daemons implementing the semantic search models is conducted through web sockets via TCP/IP and a JSON API. TCP was chosen over UDP so network daemons themselves can have a increased degree of control about how many searches and initializations are executed in parallel. This becomes relevant in case of large document collections and computationally intensive algorithms.

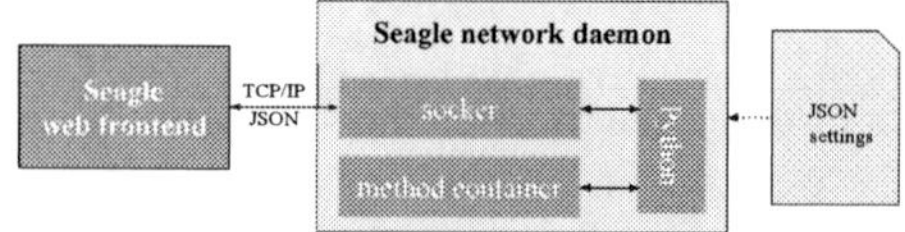

Figure 2: network daemon layout

Network Daemon Server. On the server side SEAGLE's Python-based network daemons contain the actual semantic search models. They are supplied with the document collection via the frontend and do not need to access the file system themselves. Each daemon comes with a template which implements the API and loads its settings from a local JSON file (see figure 2) containing setup information (e.g., the port on which it should run). To implement new functionality the template needs

---

[6]https://www.djangoproject.com/
[7]https://www.postgresql.org/
[8]https://www.nginx.com/
[9]https://getbootstrap.com/

to be extended with an actual method, containing the initialization function (i.e., a specification of the document indexing procedure for a particular retrieval model) and the search function (i.e., the specification of the ranking function for a particular model). In case multiple network daemons running on the same machine, they should all run on different ports.

Backend Deployment. SEAGLE daemons comprise a modular backend in which all semantic embedding models reuse I/O and evaluation functions, allowing for easy integration of additional search methods. Moreover, for efficiency, we implement all encoders using matrix and vector operations from Numpy.[10] While SEAGLE offers an easy-to-use web interface, semantic search models can be executed and evaluated from the command line.

A major benefit of the micro service architecture is its distributability on multiple machines. The main reason for multi-machine deployment of SEAGLE's backend is the computational complexity of some search models. Considering that for some models it might take hours or days to initialize (i.e., index) large document collections, the initialization process can be significantly reduced by deploying computation intensive models to different machines and running them in parallel.

4.2 SEAGLE Interface

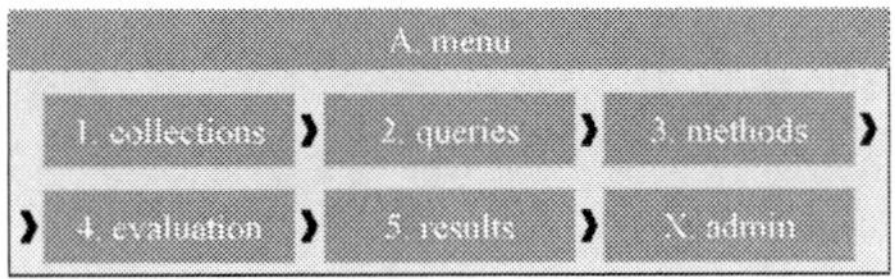

Figure 3: Components of SEAGLE's web interface

SEAGLE's web interface allows users, without programming and IR knowledge, to easily index document collections, select desired semantic search models and conduct comparative retrieval evaluations. Its core functionality is wrapped up in a easy to navigate one page layout and bundles 5 components (see figure 3):

1. Collections: Allows selection of one or multiple collections of documents on which methods are going to be evaluated.

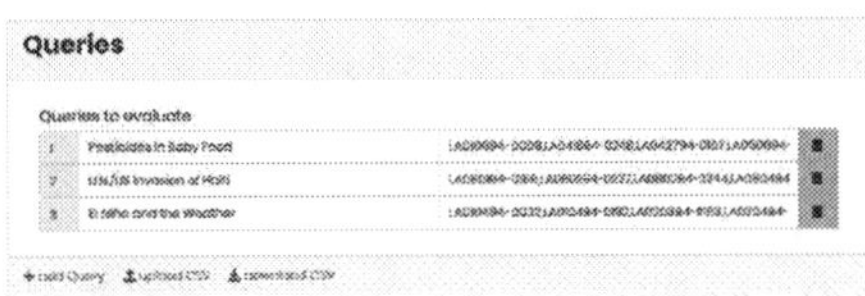

Figure 4: SEAGLE's queries component

2. Queries (see figure 4): 2.1. Manually add and remove queries (and their respective document relevance annotations); 2.2. Bundle CSV import and export & download of arbitrary number of queries with relevance annotations.

3. Methods: Select which semantic search methods to execute and evaluate.

4. Evaluation (see figure 5): 4.1. Change evaluation parameters, e.g. include or exclude evaluation metrics or specify the number of results to be shown for each method. 4.2. Contains a summary of collections, queries and methods, which are going to be evaluated along with the button triggering the evaluation process.

5. Results: 5.1. Bar charts of evaluation metrics, (e.g. MAP) or execution time per method. 5.2. A query explorer, allowing real-time exploration of executed conducted queries and top-ranked results by selected search models. (see figure 6)

Figure 5: SEAGLE's evaluation component

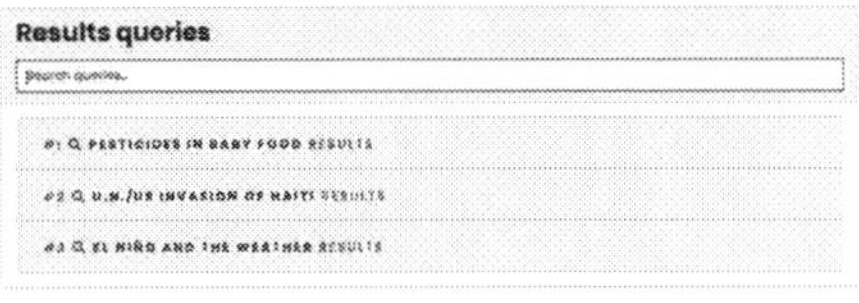

Figure 6: SEAGLE's evaluation component

---

[10]SEAGLE's reliance on Numpy routines requires a carefully tuned Numpy installation linked to fast linear algebra libraries.

Additionally, there is a quick-link component for administration (X. admin), enabling quick setup and modifications of SEAGLE's backend.

5 Conclusion

We presented SEAGLE, a platform implementing a number of strong baselines for semantic IR and allowing for their comparative evaluation on arbitrary test collections. We benchmark the implemented semantic search models on monolingual document retrieval and cross-lingual sentence retrieval tasks, offering insights into their comparative advantages and shortcomings. Our benchmarking results indicate that there is no single best-performing semantic search model for all settings and that the users must consider various factors when selecting the best model for their retrieval task.

SEAGLE offers a satisfying out-of-the-box solution for fast benchmarking of semantic retrieval models on arbitrary collections. The platform's web interface allows the user to effortlessly index document collections, select semantic search models and their hyperparameter setup, comparatively evaluate selected models and finally visualize the results for manual inspection. SEAGLE's modular architecture (based on network daemon templates) allows for fast implementation of new search models and their inclusion into comparative evaluations in a plug-and-play fashion.

Acknowledgments

We thank Leon Schüller and Siying Liu, who contributed to the original student project on which SEAGLE is based on. Additionally, we thank Hans-Peter Zorn from inovex GmbH for his feedback over the course of the same student project.

References

Sanjeev Arora, Yingyu Liang, and Tengyu Ma. 2017. A simple but tough-to-beat baseline for sentence embeddings.

Piotr Bojanowski, Edouard Grave, Armand Joulin, and Tomas Mikolov. 2017. Enriching word vectors with subword information. *Transactions of the Association for Computational Linguistics*, 5:135–146.

Jacob Devlin, Ming-Wei Chang, Kenton Lee, and Kristina Toutanova. 2018. Bert: Pre-training of deep bidirectional transformers for language understanding. *arXiv preprint arXiv:1810.04805*.

Goran Glavaš, Robert Litschko, Sebastian Ruder, and Ivan Vulić. 2019. How to (properly) evaluate cross-lingual word embeddings: On strong baselines, comparative analyses, and some misconceptions. *arXiv preprint arXiv:1902.00508*.

Christophe Van Gysel, Maarten de Rijke, and Evangelos Kanoulas. 2017. Neural vector spaces for unsupervised information retrieval. *CoRR*, abs/1708.02702.

Hang Li and Jun Xu. 2014. Semantic matching in search. *Found. Trends Inf. Retr.*, 7(5):343–469.

Robert Litschko, Goran Glavaš, Simone Paolo Ponzetto, and Ivan Vulić. 2018. Unsupervised cross-lingual information retrieval using monolingual data only. In *SIGIR*, pages 1253–1256.

Tomas Mikolov, Ilya Sutskever, Kai Chen, Gregory S. Corrado, and Jeffrey Dean. 2013. Distributed representations of words and phrases and their compositionality. In *Proceedings of NIPS*, pages 3111–3119.

Dan I Moldovan and Rada Mihalcea. 2000. Using wordnet and lexical operators to improve internet searches. *IEEE Internet Computing*, 4(1):34–43.

Rodrigo Nogueira and Kyunghyun Cho. 2019. Passage re-ranking with bert. *arXiv preprint arXiv:1901.04085*.

Stephen Robertson, Hugo Zaragoza, et al. 2009. The probabilistic relevance framework: Bm25 and beyond. *Foundations and Trends® in Information Retrieval*, 3(4):333–389.

Andreas Rücklé, Steffen Eger, Maxime Peyrard, and Iryna Gurevych. 2018. Concatenated power mean embeddings as universal cross-lingual sentence representations. *arXiv*.

Michael Strube and Simone Paolo Ponzetto. 2006. Wikirelate! computing semantic relatedness using wikipedia. In *AAAI*, volume 6, pages 1419–1424.

Ivan Vulić and Marie-Francine Moens. 2015. Monolingual and cross-lingual information retrieval models based on (bilingual) word embeddings. In *SIGIR*, pages 363–372.

Han Xiao. 2018. bert-as-service. https://github.com/hanxiao/bert-as-service.

Ziyi Yang, Chenguang Zhu, and Weizhu Chen. 2019. Zero-training sentence embedding via orthogonal basis.

Vitalii Zhelezniak, Aleksandar Savkov, April Shen, Francesco Moramarco, Jack Flann, and Nils Y. Hammerla. 2019. Don't settle for average, go for the max: Fuzzy sets and max-pooled word vectors. In *International Conference on Learning Representations*.

A Stylometry Toolkit for Latin Literature

Thomas J. Bolt,[1] **Jeffrey H. Flynt,**[2] **Pramit Chaudhuri,**[1] **Joseph P. Dexter**[3†]
[1] Department of Classics, University of Texas at Austin
[2] Department of Molecular Biosciences, University of Texas at Austin
[3] Neukom Institute for Computational Science, Dartmouth College
[†] Corresponding author: `joseph.p.dexter@dartmouth.edu`

Abstract

Computational stylometry has become an increasingly important aspect of literary criticism, but many humanists lack the technical expertise or language-specific NLP resources required to exploit computational methods. We demonstrate a stylometry toolkit for analysis of Latin literary texts, which is freely available at `www.qcrit.org/stylometry`. Our toolkit generates data for a diverse range of literary features and has an intuitive point-and-click interface. The features included have proven effective for multiple literary studies and are calculated using custom heuristics without the need for syntactic parsing. As such, the toolkit models one approach to the user-friendly generation of stylometric data, which could be extended to other premodern and non-English languages underserved by standard NLP resources.

1 Introduction

Stylometry, the quantitative analysis of writing style, is an longstanding yet active area of research in literary studies. Traditional applications of stylometry in both classical and modern literary scholarship have focused on authorship attribution and establishing relative chronology (Mosteller and Wallace, 1964; Marriott, 1979; Fitch, 1981; Vickers, 2004; Jockers and Witten, 2010; Stover et al., 2016). In recent years, new digital tools and computational methods, especially machine learning (Long and So, 2016; Dexter et al., 2017), have allowed researchers to address more fine-grained literary critical questions and have also given rise to novel frameworks for literary analysis, such as 'distant reading' and 'macroanalysis' (Moretti, 2013; Jockers, 2013; Piper, 2018; Underwood, 2019).

Much research in computational stylometry has focused on English literature due in part to the rich NLP resources available for the English language, especially high-quality syntactic parsing. NLP resources for many premodern and non-English languages are, by contrast, at an earlier stage of development or entirely lacking. Moreover, many of the academic disciplines studying these languages are smaller than for English, and thus the community of potential developers is correspondingly reduced. These factors suggest the need for user-friendly stylometric tools, which can provide a wide range of literary data for under-resourced languages and are suitable for use by humanists lacking a computational background.

Syntactic parsing, which remains at an early stage of development for Latin,[1] is not a prerequisite for the successful application of computational stylometry to literary problems. Our prior work has shown that custom heuristics can enable extraction of a wide range of features useful for the study of Latin literature, in particular syntactic markers, non-content words, and elements of sound and rhythm (Dexter et al., 2017; Chaudhuri et al., 2018). Here we report development of a point-and-click stylometry toolkit to enable easy generation of such data for a corpus containing almost all major classical Latin texts.

Other recently developed stylometry packages, such as the "stylo" R package and Lexomics, are aimed at audiences with a range of computational expertise (Eder et al., 2016; Drout et al., 2007). These packages, however, have typically been developed for general-purpose application to multiple languages instead of a single language. Focusing on the latter creates opportunities for targeting language-specific features, which often play a crucial role in literary style.

---

[1] See, for example, the recent progress of the Classical Language Toolkit (CLTK) (`www.cltk.org`) and StanfordNLP (`https://stanfordnlp.github.io/stanfordnlp/index.html`).

Proceedings of the 2019 EMNLP and the 9th IJCNLP (System Demonstrations), pages 205–210
Hong Kong, China, November 3 – 7, 2019. ©2019 Association for Computational Linguistics

The need for a point-and-click toolkit is particularly acute in classical studies. Although classical philologists have long applied stylometry to shed light on questions of authorship, relatively few studies have employed digital tools. Exceptions have tended to focus on a restricted set of features, such as relative word frequency (Stover et al., 2016) or average sentence length (Marriott, 1979; Clayman, 1981). Such limitations may be due in part to the absence of an accurate method for syntactic parsing, and in part to a more general lack of collaboration to date between classical philologists and NLP specialists. By improving the accessibility of rich philological data, our toolkit should further promote the adoption of quantitative approaches by literary critics. At the same time, the toolkit bridges the gap between classical studies and research on English, in which computational approaches are more common and are supported by a more extensive technical apparatus.

2   Toolkit

Our toolkit provides researchers working with Latin literature access to large-scale stylometric data difficult to acquire by non-computational methods and enables humanists without specialist digital training to construct custom datasets.

The design goal for the toolkit is to provide an intuitive and easy-to-use interface hosted in a web browser. The interface is point-and-click and can be used by researchers with no prior programming or NLP experience. Users can choose from over 700 Latin texts, which comprise almost all of the surviving corpus of classical Latin. The texts were originally digitized by the Perseus Digital Library and further developed by the Tesserae Project (Crane, 1996; Coffee et al., 2012). Texts can be selected by author, text, or book (roughly the ancient equivalent of a chapter). Searches can be as fine-grained as examining a single book, or as large-scale as analyzing the entire built-in corpus in one go (Figure 1).

Next, users select the stylometric features to analyze for their chosen corpus. They can run analyses using any combination of the twenty-six features (Figure 2 shows a sample output). The results are displayed on a spreadsheet in the web browser and can be downloaded as a CSV file. In addition, a user can produce simple visualizations (e.g., a bar chart comparing the values of a particular feature across a set of texts) inside the toolkit.

The ease with which the toolkit can be used does not limit its versatility. A user can create a custom corpus of texts preselected from the existing database, which is close to comprehensive for canonical material, or upload texts of their own for analysis. This latter functionality is especially important for understudied texts, such as those produced in Late Antiquity and during the Renaissance, the sum total of which far exceeds the quantity of extant classical Latin. While digital versions are available for many post-classical texts, for the most part the later periods are not well served by the prominent tools or repositories in the field, which maintain a classical focus. Our toolkit allows users to analyze any text available in electronic form. Furthermore, if a work is not available online, a user may upload a plain text file or transcribe it directly into the upload interface.

3   Features

Our feature set comprises twenty-six stylometric features across four broad syntactic and grammatical categories (pronouns and non-content adjectives, subordinate clauses, conjunctions, and miscellaneous, as listed in Table 1) and is described in detail in a previous publication (Chaudhuri et al., 2018). Some features are lexical (e.g., prepositions), while others are syntactic (e.g., sentence length) or address semantic and rhetorical aspects of the texts (e.g., superlatives and interrogative sentences). Taken together, the features offer a rich and diverse, albeit necessarily partial, profile of Latin literary style.

An important aspect of our toolkit is that it does not depend on syntactic parsing, named entity recognition, or other NLP methods that have not been developed fully for classical Latin (Erdmann et al., 2016). We employ three strategies to circumvent current technical limitations. The majority of features (*Alius*, *Idem*, *Ipse*, *Iste*, *Quidam*, Demonstrative Pronouns, Personal Pronouns, Third-Person Pronouns, *Atque* + Consonant, *Antequam*, *Cum*, *Dum*, *Priusquam*, *Quin*, *Quominus*, *Ut*, and Prepositions) are computed using hard-coded lists of almost all possible forms of the relevant Latin words. While some features (e.g., *Quin* or *Dum*) are frequencies of a single form, others (e.g., Demonstrative Pronouns) involve long lists of morphological variants. Other features are estimated based on the frequency of a

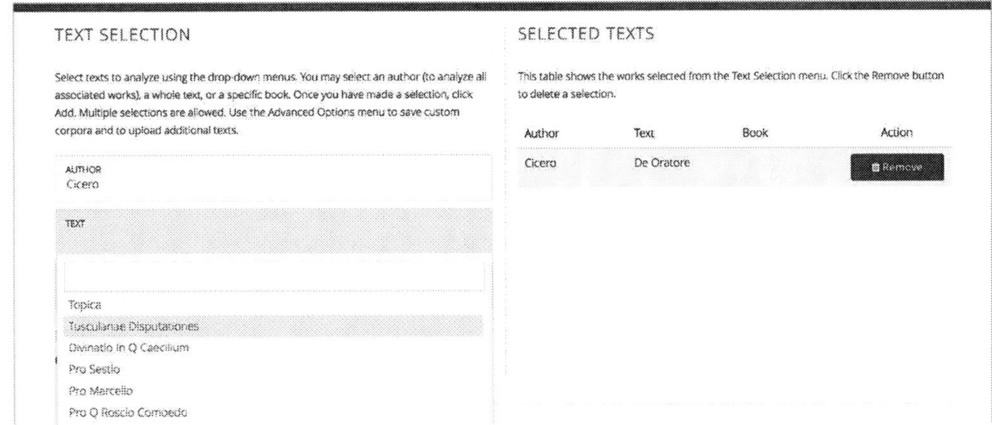

Figure 1: On the left, drop-down menu for text selection; on the right, a list of texts that have been selected.

	Text	Words	Relative Clauses	Mean Length Relative Clauses	Interrogative Sentences	Vocatives	S
403	Lucan Bellum Civile Part 9	7,077	0.29915	27.04348	0.00136	0.00017	0
404	Lucan Bellum Civile Part 10	3,508	0.27322	27.77778	0.00045	0.00005	0
405	Lucretius De Rerum Natura Part 1	7,223	0.66812	38.8	0.00055	0	0
406	Lucretius De Rerum Natura Part 2	7,562	0.6087	37.29661	0.00054	0.00002	0
407	Lucretius De Rerum Natura Part 3	7,398	0.54018	39.57635	0.00071	0.00005	0
408	Lucretius De Rerum Natura Part 4	8,622	0.56508	36.77955	0.00046	0	0
409	Lucretius De Rerum Natura Part 5	9,508	0.51299	42.15234	0.00082	0.00002	0
410	Lucretius De Rerum Natura Part 6	8,517	0.5	36.67045	0.00053	0	0
411	Manilius Astronomicon Part 1	5,880	0.44076	42.97101	0.00032	0	0
412	Manilius Astronomicon Part 2	6,244	0.44578	34.25	0.00025	0	0
413	Manilius Astronomicon Part 3	4,465	0.43646	36.16807	0.00016	0.00004	0
414	Manilius Astronomicon Part 4	6,059	0.30435	39.15686	0.00072	0	0

Figure 2: Sample output from the toolkit for a selection of Latin literary texts.

signal n-gram. For instance, all regular superlative adjectives include the n-gram *-issim-* (e.g., *largissimus*, "most abundant" or *clarissima*, "clearest"). As this n-gram is extremely rare outside of superlatives, we could curate a near-comprehensive list of exclusions (e.g., *dissimilis*, "unlike"). We use a similar strategy to capture the instances of selected gerunds and gerundives, which contain the n-grams *-ndus*, *-ndum*, *-ndarum*, or *-ndorum*. A third class of features are determined using punctuation (e.g., question marks to assess the frequency of direct interrogative sentences or to filter interrogative pronouns, which have many forms in common with relative pronouns, from relative clause counts).

The precision and recall of each of these heuristics is discussed in detail in (Chaudhuri et al., 2018). We emphasize that these approaches are not intended as a substitute for NLP, but rather as a stopgap for philologists until more substantial resources become available for classical languages. We expect that the overall usefulness of the toolkit will increase as our heuristics are rendered obsolete by improvements in part-of-speech tagging and dependency parsing for Latin.

Our features are drawn from a wide array of sources in order to maximize the capture of information pertinent to Latin literary style. Some features, such as prepositions, are inspired by studies of other languages, where they have proven useful for the characterization of genres or subgenres (Jockers, 2013). Most features, however, are based on previous studies of Latin style and are designed to capture aspects specific to the Latin language (Adams, 1972; Adams et al., 2005). For example, *atque* ("and") followed by a word beginning with a consonant is a stylistic feature that is associated with certain influential figures writing early in the tradition. When later authors employ *atque* + consonant, they do so either in imitation of these figures specifically, or to recall an archaizing style more generally.

	Feature
	Pronouns and non-content adjectives
1	*Alius*
2	*Idem*
3	*Ipse*
4	*Iste*
5	*Quidam*
6	Demonstrative Pronouns
7	Personal Pronouns
8	Third-Person Pronouns
	Conjunctions
9	*Atque* + Consonant
10	Conjunctions
	Subordinate clauses
11	*Antequam*
12	*Cum*
13	*Dum*
14	*Priusquam*
15	*Quin*
16	*Quominus*
17	Conditional Markers
18	Fraction of Sentences with Relative Clauses
19	Mean Length of Relative Clauses
	Miscellaneous
20	*Ut*
21	Interrogative Sentences
22	Mean Length of Sentences
23	Prepositions
24	Regular Superlatives
25	Selected Gerunds & Gerundives
26	Selected Vocatives

Table 1: Full set of Latin stylometric features.

4 Literary Importance

The stylometric data generated by the toolkit sheds light on a variety of literary problems. The simplest type of analysis involves a single feature calculated across a small number of texts. Past research in Ancient Greek stylometry, for instance, has shown that sentence length constitutes one meaningful difference between the early Homeric hexameter tradition and the Hellenistic tradition, since later writers use longer sentences even as they retain other core aspects such as formulaic language and meter (Clayman, 1981). Figure 3 shows the mean sentence length of most of the surviving classical Latin epics as calculated by the toolkit. Three texts, *De Rerum Natura* by Lucretius, *Astronomicon* by Manilius, and the *Georgics* by Vergil, have noticeably longer sentences on average (mean length >140 characters, compared to <125 characters for the other epics). An attractive explanation for the three anomalous texts is that they are all identified with a sub-genre of epic known as "didactic," a specific class which purports to teach its readers philosophy or a specialized technical skill, such as astrology or farming. The sentences are longer plausibly because detailed treatment of intricate philosophical or technical issues requires more complex sentences than typically more straightforward narrative action or direct speech, which represent the principal content of the other epics.

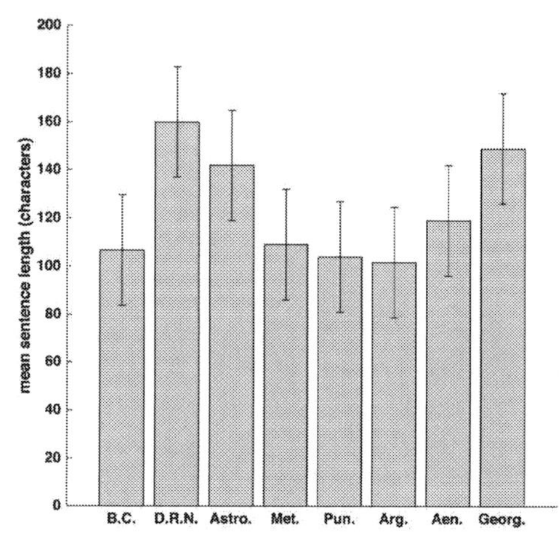

Figure 3: Mean sentence length of Latin epic poems (in characters). Error bars denote one s.d. across the eight poems.

The toolkit also reveals that Latin drama has a higher frequency of personal pronouns than other verse genres, as shown in Figure 4. This is no doubt due to drama's dialogic form: characters speak to each other directly, often employing first ("I" or "we") and second person ("you") pronouns. Many other literary genres primarily employ a narrative structure in which a narrator describes the action. This narrative type often uses third person pronouns ("he," "she," "it"), but rarely uses first or second person pronouns. Accordingly, the frequency of personal pronoun use is higher in drama. While this difference may be intuitive to a reader, the large-scale data generated by the toolkit offers quantitative evidence of a genre's formal style, which would otherwise be difficult if not impossible to calculate by hand.

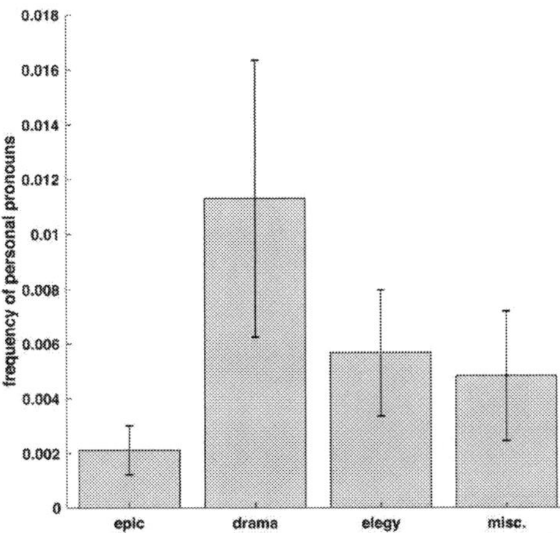

Figure 4: Mean per-character frequency of personal pronouns in the major genres of Latin literature. Error bars denote one s.d. across the texts within each of the four genres.

Finally, the toolkit can also generate input data for supervised and unsupervised machine learning analyses. In our recent study of Latin prose and verse, we trained a random forest classifier using all 26 features to distinguish the two genres with high (>97%) accuracy (Chaudhuri et al., 2018). The underlying data can now be produced easily using the toolkit, and similar datasets can be constructed for other machine learning applications.

5 Conclusion and Future Work

This paper introduces a stylometry toolkit for Latin literature, which incorporates a diverse feature set demonstrably useful for literary criticism. The toolkit includes a point-and-click interface to maximize usage among core domain specialists, principally researchers in the humanities, who may not have specialized computational training. Future versions of the toolkit will further diversify the feature set, incorporating high-frequency n-grams and sense-pauses alongside the existing categories (Fitch, 1981; Dexter et al., 2017), and will leverage expected advances in Latin NLP to improve the methods for calculation of existing features.

In related work, we have developed a similar feature set for Ancient Greek, which has been used to classify prose and verse and, at a more fine-grained level, epic and drama (Gianitsos et al., 2019). Our work on Old English has demonstrated the utility of related features for various literary and attribution studies (Neidorf et al., 2019). After extension of the current toolkit to Ancient Greek and Old English, we plan in due course to incorporate other underserved languages, in particular Bengali.

Acknowledgments

This work was conducted under the auspices of the Quantitative Criticism Lab (www.qcrit.org), an interdisciplinary group co-directed by P.C. and J.P.D. and supported by a National Endowment for the Humanities Digital Humanities Start-Up Grant (grant number HD-10 248410-16) and an American Council of Learned Societies (ACLS) Digital Extension Grant. T.J.B. was supported by an Engaged Scholar Initiative Fellowship from the Andrew W. Mellon Foundation, P.C. by an ACLS Digital Innovation Fellowship and a Mellon New Directions Fellowship, and J.P.D. by a Neukom Fellowship.

References

J.N. Adams. 1972. The language of the later books of Tacitus' *Annals*. *The Classical Quarterly*, 22(2):350–373.

J.N. Adams, M. Lapidge, and T. Reinhardt. 2005. Introduction. In J.N. Adams, M. Lapidge, and T. Reinhardt, editors, *Aspects of the Language of Latin Prose. Proceedings of the British Academy, 129*, pages 1–36. Oxford University Press, Oxford.

P. Chaudhuri, J.P. Dexter, T. Dasgupta, and K. Iyer. 2018. A small set of stylometric features differentiates Latin prose and verse. *Digital Scholarship in the Humanities*.

D.L. Clayman. 1981. Sentence length in Greek hexameter poetry. In R. Grotjahn, editor, *Hexameter Studies. Quantitative Linguistics 11*, pages 107–136. Brockmeyer, Bochum.

N. Coffee, J.-P. Koenig, S. Poornima, R. Ossewaarde, C. Forstall, and S. Jacobson. 2012. Intertextuality in the digital age. *Transactions of the American Philological Association*, 142(2):383–422.

G. Crane. 1996. Building a digital library: The Perseus Project as a case study in the humanities. In *Proceedings of the First ACM International Conference on Digital Libraries*, pages 3–10.

J.P Dexter, T. Katz, N. Tripuraneni, T. Dasgupta, A. Kannan, J.A. Brofos, J.A. Bonilla Lopez, L.A.

Schroeder, A. Casarez, M. Rabinovich, A. Haimson Lushkov, and P. Chaudhuri. 2017. Quantitative criticism of literary relationships. *Proceedings of the National Academy of Sciences USA*, 114(16):E3195–204.

M.D.C. Drout, M.J. Kahn, M.D. LeBlanc, and C. Nelson. 2007. Of dendrogrammatology: Lexomic methods for analyzing relationships among Old English poems. *Journal of English and Germanic Philology*, 110(3):301–336.

M. Eder, J. Rybicki, and M. Kestemont. 2016. Stylometry with R: A package for computational text analysis. *The R Journal*, 8(1):107–121.

A. Erdmann, C. Brown, B. Joseph, M. Janse, P. Ajaka, M. Elsner, and M.-C. de Marneffe. 2016. Challenges and solutions for Latin named entity recognition. In *Proceedings of the Workshop on Language Technology Resources and Tools for Digital Humanities (LT4DH)*, pages 85–93, Osaka, Japan.

J.G. Fitch. 1981. Sense-pauses and relative dating in Seneca, Sophocles and Shakespeare. *American Journal of Philology*, 102(3):289–307.

E.T. Gianitsos, T.J. Bolt, P. Chaudhuri, and J.P. Dexter. 2019. Stylometric classification of Ancient Greek literary texts by genre. In *Proceedings of the 3rd Joint SIGHUM Workshop on Computational Linguistics for Cultural Heritage, Social Sciences, Humanities and Literature*, pages 52–60, Minneapolis, USA.

M. Jockers. 2013. *Macroanalysis*. University of Illinois Press, Champaign, IL.

M. Jockers and D.M. Witten. 2010. A comparative study of machine learning methods for authorship attribution. *Literary and Linguistic Computing*, 25(2):215–223.

H. Long and R.J. So. 2016. Literary pattern recognition: Modernism between close reading and machine learning. *Critical Inquiry*, 42(2):235–267.

I. Marriott. 1979. The authorship of the *Historia Augusta*: Two computer studies. *Journal of Roman Studies*, 69:65–77.

F. Moretti. 2013. *Distant Reading*. Verso, London.

F. Mosteller and D.L. Wallace. 1964. *Inference and Disputed Authorship: The Federalist*. Addison-Wesley, Reading, MA.

L. Neidorf, M.S. Krieger, M. Yakubek, P. Chaudhuri, and J.P. Dexter. 2019. Large-scale quantitative profiling of the Old English verse tradition. *Nature Human Behaviour*, 3(6):560–567.

A. Piper. 2018. *Enumerations: Data and Literary Study*. University of Chicago Press, Chicago.

J. Stover, Y. Winter, M. Koppel, and M. Kestemont. 2016. Computational authorship verification method attributes a new work to a major 2nd century African author. *Journal of the Association for Information Science and Technology*, 67(1):239–243.

T. Underwood. 2019. *Distant Horizons: Digital Evidence and Literary Change*. University of Chicago Press, Chicago.

B. Vickers. 2004. *Shakespeare, Co-author: A Historical Study of Five Collaborative Plays*. Oxford University Press, Oxford.

A Summarization System for Scientific Documents

Shai Erera[1], **Michal Shmueli-Scheuer**[1], **Guy Feigenblat**[1], **Ora Peled Nakash**[2],
Odellia Boni[1], **Haggai Roitman**[1], **Doron Cohen**[1], **Bar Weiner**[1], **Yosi Mass**[1], **Or Rivlin**[1],
Guy Lev[1], **Achiya Jerbi**[1], **Jonathan Herzig**[1], **Yufang Hou**[1], **Charles Jochim**[1],
Martin Gleize[1], **Francesca Bonin**[1], **Debasis Ganguly**[1], **David Konopnicki**[1]

[1]IBM Research, [2]IBM Cloud

davidko@il.ibm.com

Abstract

We present a novel system providing summaries for Computer Science publications. Through a qualitative user study, we identified the most valuable scenarios for discovery, exploration and understanding of scientific documents. Based on these findings, we built a system that retrieves and summarizes scientific documents for a given information need, either in form of a free-text query or by choosing categorized values such as scientific tasks, datasets and more. Our system ingested 270,000 papers, and its summarization module aims to generate concise yet detailed summaries. We validated our approach with human experts.

1 Introduction

The publication rate of scientific papers is ever increasing and many tools such as Google Scholar, Microsoft Academic and more, provide search capabilities and allow researchers to find papers of interest. In Computer Science, and specifically, natural language processing, machine learning, and artificial intelligence, new tools that go beyond search capabilities are used to monitor[1], explore (Singh et al., 2018), discuss and comment[2] publications. Yet, there is still a high information load on researchers that seek to keep up-to-date. Summarization of scientific papers can mitigate this issue and expose researchers with adequate amount of information in order to reduce the load.

Many tools for text summarization are available[3]. However, such tools target mainly news or simple documents, not taking into account the characteristics of scientific papers i.e., their length and complexity.

A summarization system for scientific publications requires many underlying technologies: first, extracting structure, tables and figures from PDF documents, then, identifying important entities, and, finally, generating a useful summary. We chose to provide summarization as part of a search system as it is the most common interface to consume scientific content, regardless of the task.

Use-cases. We identified the most valuable scenarios for scientific paper usage through a qualitative user study. We interviewed six potential users: a PhD student, two young researchers, two senior researchers, and a research strategist, all in the NLP domain. Users were asked to describe when do they access scientific papers, how often does it happens, how do they explore content, and finally, what are their pain-points with current tools. Top scenarios were, by order of frequency, (1) keeping updated on current work, (2) preparing a research project/grant request, (3) preparing related works when writing a paper, (4) checking the novelty of an idea, and (5) learning a new domain or technology. While (2), (3), (4), and (5) are important, it seems that they happen only a few times a year, whereas scenario (1) happens on a daily/weekly basis. All users mentioned information overload as their main problem, and, foremost, the efforts incurred by reading papers. Thus, we decided to focus on scenario (1). We further asked the users to describe: (a) how do they search and (b) the strategy they use to decide whether they want to read a paper. For (a), users mentioned searching by using either keywords, entities (e.g., task name, dataset name, benchmark name), or citation. In this scenario, users are familiar with their research topic, and hence can be very focused. Some examples queries were "state of the art results for *SQUAD*" or "using *BERT* in *abstractive summarization*". For (b), users first read the title, and if

---

[1]arxiv-sanity.com
[2]groundai.com/
[3]github.com/miso-belica/sumy, ivypanda.com/online-text-summarizer

Proceedings of the 2019 EMNLP and the 9th IJCNLP (System Demonstrations), pages 211–216
Hong Kong, China, November 3 – 7, 2019. ©2019 Association for Computational Linguistics

relevant, continue to the abstract. Here, users mentioned, that in many cases, they find the abstract not informative enough in order to determine relevance. Hence the importance of summarization for helping researchers understand the gist of a paper without the need to read it entirely or even opening the PDF file.

Approach and Contribution. We present a novel summarization system for Computer Science publications, named IBM Science Summarizer, which can be useful foremost to the ACL community, and to researchers at large. It produces summaries focused around an information need provided by the user - a natural language query, scientific tasks (e.g., "Machine Translation"), datasets or academic venues. IBM Science Summarizer summarizes the various sections of a paper independently, allowing users to focus on the relevant sections for the task at hand. In doing so, the system exploits the various entities and the user's interactions, like the user query, in order to provide a relevant summary. We validated our approach with human experts. The system is available at: https://ibm.biz/sciencesum.

2 Related Work

Numerous tools support the domain of scientific publications including search, monitoring, exploring and more. For automatic summarization, efforts mostly concentrated on automated generation of survey papers (Jha et al., 2015; Jie et al., 2018). Surveyor (Jha et al., 2015) considers both content and discourse of source papers when generating survey papers. CitationAS (Jie et al., 2018) automatically generates survey papers using citation content for the medical domain. The main differences between these systems and ours is that they create summaries from multi-documents, while our tool summarizes individual papers and supports query-focused summaries.

For supporting the ACL community, CL Scholar (Singh et al., 2018) presents a graph mining tool on top of the ACL anthology and enables exploration of research progress. TutorialBank (Fabbri et al., 2018) helps researchers to learn or stay up-to-date in the NLP field. Recently, paperswithcode[4] is an open resource for ML papers, code and leaderboards. Our work is complementary to these approaches and provide the first

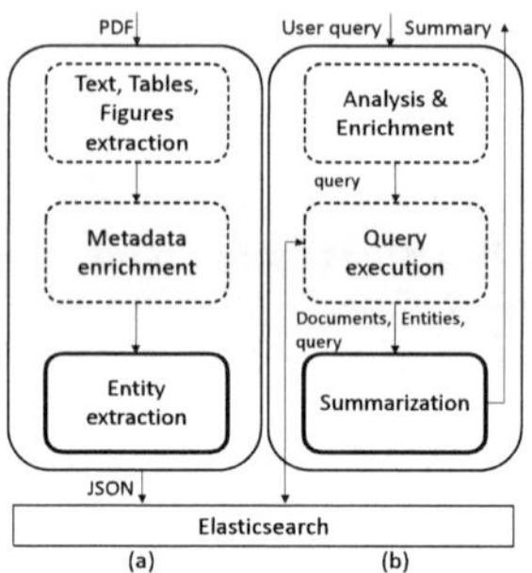

Figure 1: IBM Science Summarizer Framework.

tool for automatic summarization and exploration of scientific documents.[5]

3 System Overview

IBM Science Summarizer's main purpose is to support discovery, exploration and understanding of scientific papers by providing summaries. The system has two parts. First, an ingestion pipeline parses and indexes papers' content from arXiv.com and ACL anthology, as depicted in Figure 1(a). Second, a search engine (backed up by a UI), supports search and exploration, coupled with summarization, as shown in Figure 1(b).

Figure 2 shows the user-interface for IBM Science Summarizer. Users interact with the system by posing natural language queries, or by using filters on the metadata fields such as conference venue, year, and author, or entities (e.g., tasks, datasets)[6]. User experience is an important usability factor. Thus, our UI provides indicators to help users explore and understand results. Specifically, associating a comprehensive structure with each result allows users to navigate inside content in a controlled manner: each section shows clearly the elements that are computed by the system (section summary, detected entities, etc.) and the elements that are directly extracted from the original paper. This clear distinction allows users to have visibility into the systems' contributions (Flavian et al., 2009).

4 Ingestion Pipeline

Our system contains 270,000 papers from arXiv.org ("Computer Science" subset) and the

---

[4]paperswithcode.com/

[5]For clarity, more related works are referred to in the various sections of this paper.

[6]In this case, there is no user query.

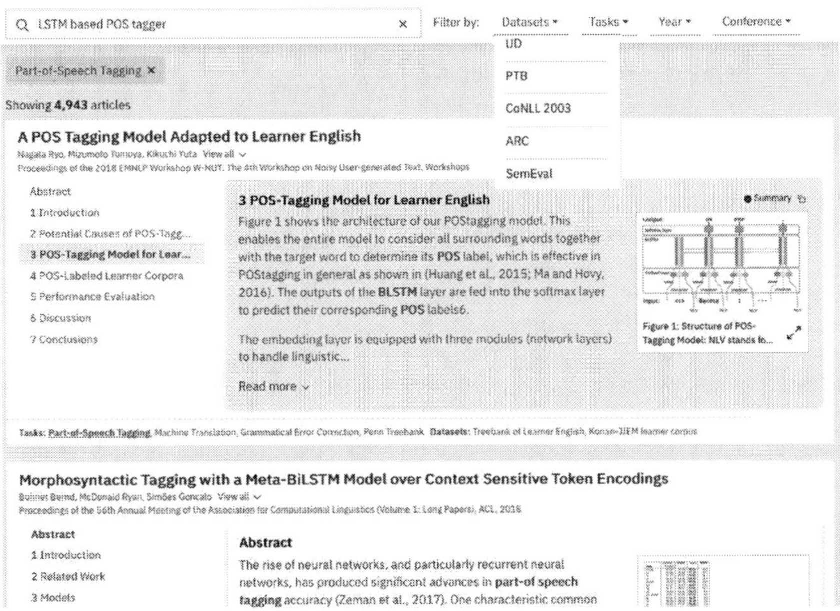

Figure 2: IBM Science Summarizer UI.

ACL anthology[7]. The ingestion pipeline consists of paper acquisition, extracting the paper's text, tables and figures and enriching the paper's data with various annotations and entities.

Paper Parsing. We use Science-Parse[8] to extract the PDF text, tables and figures. Science-Parse outputs a JSON record for each PDF, which among other fields, contains the title, abstract text, metadata (such as authors and year), and a list of the sections of the paper, where each record holds the section's title and text. We have merged sub-sections into their containing sections and this resulted in about 6-7 merged sections per article (e.g., see Fig. 2). Science-Parse also supports extracting figures and tables into an image file, as well as caption text.

In addition, we detect figure and table references in the extracted text. We extract tasks, datasets and metric (see details below). Finally, we use Elasticsearch[9] to index the papers, where for each paper we index its title, abstract text, sections text and some metadata.

Entities Extraction. Entities in our system are of three types, *task* (e.g., "Question Answering"), *dataset* (e.g., "SQuAD2.0"), and *metric* (e.g., "F1"). We utilize both a dictionary-based approach and learning-based approach as follows. First, we adopted the manual curated dictionaries of paperswithcode[5]. Since those dictionaries may not cover all evolving topics, we further developed a module that automatically extracts entities. Differently from previous work on information extraction from scientific literature which mainly focused on the abstract section (Gábor et al., 2018; Luan et al., 2018), we analyze the entire paper and extract the above three types of entities that are related to the paper's main research findings. We cast this problem as a textual entailment task: we treat paper contents as *text* and the targeting *Task-Dataset-Metric (TDM)* triples as *hypothesis*. The textual entailment approach forces our model to focus on learning the similarity patterns between *text* and various triples. We trained our module on a dataset consisting of 332 papers in the NLP domain, and it achieves a macro-F1 score of 56.6 and a micro-F1 score of 66.0 for predicting TDM triples on a testing dataset containing 162 papers (Hou et al., 2019). In total, our system indexed 872 tasks, 345 datasets, and 62 metrics from the entire corpus.

---

[7]We removed duplication between the two by using Jaccard similarity on the titles and authors.

[8]github.com/allenai/science-parse

[9]https://www.elastic.co

5 Summarization

This module generates a concise, coherent, informative summary for a given scientific paper that covers the main content conveyed in the text. The summary can either be focused around a query, or query agnostic (a generic summary)[10]. Scientific papers are complex: they are long, structured, cover various subjects and the language may be quite different between sections, e.g., the introduction is quite different than the experiments section. To ensure our summarizer assigns sufficient attention to each of these aspects we have opted to generate a standalone summary for each section. This way we summarize a shorter, more focused text, and the users can navigate more easily as they are given the structure of the paper. Each of these section-based summaries are eventually composed together into one paper summary.

Scientific papers summarization goes back more than thirty years. Some of these works focus on summarizing content (Paice, 1981; Paice and Jones, 1993), while others focused on citation sentences (citation-aware summarization) (Elkiss et al., 2008; Qazvinian and Radev, 2008; Abu-Jbara and Radev, 2011). Recently, Yasunaga et al. (2019) released a large-scale dataset, *Scisumm-Net*, including summaries produced by humans for over 1000 scientific papers using solely the papers abstract and citations. While citations data encompasses the impact of the paper and views from the research community, it is not available for newly-published papers, and tends to lead to high level and shorter summaries (*Scisumm-Net* average summary length is 151 words). We opted to focus on more extensive, detailed summaries which do not rely on citations data. As mentioned above, the inputs to the summarization module are an (optional) query and entities (task, dataset, metric), and the relevant papers returned by the search/filtering (see Fig. 2). Given a retrieved paper and the optional query Q (or entity), we describe next how a summary is produced for each section D in the paper.

Query Handling. If present, Q can either be short and focused or verbose. If short, it is expanded using query expansion (Xu et al., 2009). This pseudo-relevance feedback transforms Q into a profile of 100 unigram terms, obtained from an-alyzing the top papers that are returned from our corpus as a response to the given query. Alternatively, in the case of a verbose query, a *Fixed-Point* term weighting schema (Paik and Oard, 2014) is applied in order to rank the terms of the query.

Alternatively, if only filtering is applied and there is no query, the keyphrases of the paper are extracted and used as a surrogate for the query. In this case, all keywords in the generated query are given the same weight.

Pre-Processing. Sentences are segmented using the *NLTK* library and each sentence is tokenized, lower cased and stop words are removed. Then, each sentence is transformed into a unigrams and bi-grams *bag-of-words* representations, where each *n-gram* is associated with its relative frequency in the text.

Summarization Algorithm. In general, summaries can either be extractive or an abstractive. In the extractive case, a summary is generated by selecting a subset of sentences from the original input. Abstractive summarizers, on the other hand, can also paraphrase input text. In many cases, extractive summarization generates grammatical and focused summaries while abstractive techniques require heavy supervision, are limited to short documents and may transform meaning (Gambhir and Gupta, 2017).

In our system, summarization is applied on D using a state-of-the-art unsupervised, extractive, query focused summarization algorithm, inspired by (Feigenblat et al., 2017), whose details are briefly described as follows. The algorithm gets a paper section, a natural language query Q, a desired summary length (in our case, 10 sentences[11]), and a set of entities associated with the query E_Q. The output S is a subset of sentences from D selected through an unsupervised optimization scheme. To this end, the sentence subset selection problem is posed as a multi-criteria optimization problem, where several summary quality objectives are be considered. The selection is obtained using the *Cross Entropy (CE)* method (Rubinstein and Kroese, 2004). Optimization starts by assigning a uniform importance probability to each sentence in D. Then, CE works iteratively, and, at each iteration, it samples summaries using a learnt distribution over the sentences, and

---

[10]Note that in order to optimize the response time, the production system currently offers query agnostic summaries.

[11]We leave the study of variable-length section summaries for future work.

evaluates the quality of these summaries by applying a target function. This function takes into account several quality prediction objectives, which (for simplicity) are multiplied together. The learning process employs an exploration-exploitation trade-off in which the importance of a sentence is a fusion between its importance in previous iterations and its importance in the current one.

The following five summary quality predictors are used by Feigenblat et al. (2017): query saliency, entities coverage, diversity, text coverage and sentence length. *Query saliency* measures to what extent the summary contains query related terms as expressed by the cosine similarity between the unigrams *bag-of-words* representation of the summary and the query terms. *Entities coverage* measures to what extent the set of entities identified in a summary shares the same set of entities with E_Q, measured by the Jaccard similarity between the sets. The aim of this objective is to produce a summary that is more aligned with the information need provided explicitly (as a filter specified by the user) or implicitly (learnt from the query terms). *Diversity* lays towards summaries with a diverse language model using the entropy of the unigrams *bag-of-words* representation of the summary. *Text coverage* measures the summary coverage of D as measured by cosine similarity between the bi-gram bag-of-words representation of a summary and D. Finally, the length objective biases towards summaries that include longer sentences, which tend to be more informative.

6 Human Evaluation

IBM Science Summarizer summarization paradigm is section-based, i.e., each section is summarized independently, and then all sections' summaries are combined into the paper's summary. In order to evaluate this paradigm, we approached 12 authors from the NLP community, and asked them to evaluate summaries of two papers that they have co-authored (preferably as the first author). For each paper, we generated two summaries of two types: the *section-based* summary as described above, and a second summary generated using the same algorithm but ignoring sections (i.e., treating the paper content as flat text), a *section-agnostic* summary. For the section-based summary, each section's summary length was fixed to 10 sentences. The length of the section-agnostic summary was defined as the length of the section-based summary. In total 24 papers, and 48 summaries were evaluated.

Tasks. The authors evaluated summaries of each summary type, section-agnostic and section-based (in random order), by performing the following 3 tasks per summary: (1) for each sentence in the summary, we asked them to indicate whether they would consider it as a part of a summary of their paper (i.e., precision oriented measure); (2) we asked them to evaluate how well each of the sections of the paper is covered in the summary (i.e., coverage/recall); and (3) we asked them to globally evaluate the quality of the summary. For tasks (2) and (3) we used a 1-5 scale, ranging from very bad to excellent, 3 means good.

Analysis. The objective of the analysis is to find quantitative scores for each summary type to facilitate a comparison between them. For task (1), for each paper, we calculated the precision scores of the two summary types, and then computed the average score for each summary type across all papers. For task (2), we calculated an average score for each paper and summary type by averaging over the sections scores. Then, we obtained the average of these scores for each summary type across all papers. Finally, for task (3), we simply averaged the scores given by the authors to each summary type. To further quantify the evaluation, we analyzed how well each summary type did for each of the 3 tasks. For that we counted the number of times that each summary type scored better than the other, and then divided by the total number of papers, to obtain the "% wins".

Results. Table 1 summarizes the results across the 3 tasks. For example, for task (2), for 68% of the papers, the section-based summary was scored higher, while, for 22% the section-agnostic summary was scored higher (for 10% of the papers, the summaries were scored equally). The average score for section-based summaries was 3.32 with standard deviation of 0.53. Notably, the quality of the section-based summaries significantly outperforms the section-agnostic summaries on all 3 tasks, supporting our proposed paradigm.

7 Conclusion

We presented IBM Science Summarizer, the first system that provides researchers a tool to systematically explore and consume summaries of scientific papers. As future work, we plan to add

Task	Section-agnostic		Section-based	
	% wins	Avg. score (std)	% wins	Avg. score (std)
(1)	37	0.54 (0.17)	63	0.6 (0.18)†
(2)	22	3 (0.56)	68	3.32 (0.53) †
(3)	4.5	2.86 (0.56)	36	3.22 (0.61) ‡

Table 1: Tasks results for section-agnostic, and section-based. † - The results were significant with $p < 0.05$. ‡- The results were significant with $p < 0.005$.

support for additional entities e.g., methods, and to increase our corpus to include more papers. Finally, we plan to provide this tool to the community as an open service and conduct an extensive user study about the usage and quality of the system, including automatic evaluation of the summaries.

References

Amjad Abu-Jbara and Dragomir Radev. 2011. Coherent citation-based summarization of scientific papers. In *Proceedings of the 49th Annual HLT*, HLT '11, pages 500–509. Association for Computational Linguistics.

Aaron Elkiss, Siwei Shen, Anthony Fader, Güneş Erkan, David States, and Dragomir Radev. 2008. Blind men and elephants: What do citation summaries tell us about a research article? *J. Am. Soc. Inf. Sci. Technol.*, 59(1):51–62.

Alexander Fabbri, Irene Li, Prawat Trairatvorakul, Yijiao He, Weitai Ting, Robert Tung, Caitlin Westerfield, and Dragomir Radev. 2018. Tutorialbank: A manually-collected corpus for prerequisite chains, survey extraction and resource recommendation. In *Proceedings of the 56th ACL*, pages 611–620.

Guy Feigenblat, Haggai Roitman, Odellia Boni, and David Konopnicki. 2017. Unsupervised query-focused multi-document summarization using the cross entropy method. In *Proceedings of the 40th International ACM SIGIR*, pages 961–964.

Carlos Flavian, Raquel Gurrea, and Carlos Orus. 2009. Web design: a key factor for the website success. *Journal of Systems and Information Technology*, 11(2):168–184.

Kata Gábor, Davide Buscaldi, Anne-Kathrin Schumann, Behrang QasemiZadeh, Haïfa Zargayouna, and Thierry Charnois. 2018. Semeval-2018 task 7: Semantic relation extraction and classification in scientific papers. In *Proceedings SemEval@NAACL-HLT 2018*, pages 679–688.

Mahak Gambhir and Vishal Gupta. 2017. Recent automatic text summarization techniques: A survey. *Artif. Intell. Rev.*, 47(1):1–66.

Yufang Hou, Charles Jochim, Martin Gleize, Francesca Bonin, and Debasis Ganguly. 2019. Identification of tasks, datasets, evaluation metrics, and numeric scores for scientific leaderboards construction. volume arXiv:1906.09317.

Rahul Jha, Reed Coke, and Dragomir Radev. 2015. Surveyor: A system for generating coherent survey articles for scientific topics. In *Proceedings of the Twenty-Ninth AAAI*, AAAI'15, pages 2167–2173.

Wang Jie, Zhang Chengzhi, Zhang Mengying, and Deng Sanhong. 2018. Citationas: A tool of automatic survey generation based on citation content*. *Journal of Data and Information Science*, 3(2).

Yi Luan, Luheng He, Mari Ostendorf, and Hannaneh Hajishirzi. 2018. Multi-task identification of entities, relations, and coreference for scientific knowledge graph construction. In *Proceedings of EMNLP 2018*, pages 3219–3232.

C. D. Paice. 1981. The automatic generation of literature abstracts: An approach based on the identification of self-indicating phrases. In *Proceedings of the 3rd Annual ACM SIGIR*, SIGIR '80, pages 172–191.

Chris D. Paice and Paul A. Jones. 1993. The identification of important concepts in highly structured technical papers. In *Proceedings of the 16th Annual International ACM SIGIR*, SIGIR '93, pages 69–78, New York, NY, USA. ACM.

Jiaul H. Paik and Douglas W. Oard. 2014. A fixed-point method for weighting terms in verbose informational queries. CIKM '14, pages 131–140, New York, NY, USA. ACM.

Vahed Qazvinian and Dragomir R. Radev. 2008. Scientific paper summarization using citation summary networks. In *Proceedings of the 22Nd International Conference on Computational Linguistics - Volume 1*, COLING '08, pages 689–696.

Reuven Y. Rubinstein and Dirk P. Kroese. 2004. *The Cross Entropy Method: A Unified Approach To Combinatorial Optimization, Monte-carlo Simulation*. Springer-Verlag, Berlin, Heidelberg.

Mayank Singh, Pradeep Dogga, Sohan Patro, Dhiraj Barnwal, Ritam Dutt, Rajarshi Haldar, Pawan Goyal, and Animesh Mukherjee. 2018. Cl scholar: The acl anthology knowledge graph miner. In *Proceedings of the NAACL 2018*.

Yang Xu, Gareth J.F. Jones, and Bin Wang. 2009. Query dependent pseudo-relevance feedback based on wikipedia. In *Proceedings of the 32Nd International ACM SIGIR*, pages 59–66.

Michihiro Yasunaga, Jungo Kasai, Rui Zhang, Alexander Richard Fabbri, Irene Li, Dan Friedman, and Dragomir R. Radev. 2019. Scisummnet: A large annotated corpus and content-impact models for scientific paper summarization with citation networks. In *AAAI 2019*.

A System for Diacritizing Four Varieties of Arabic

Hamdy Mubarak **Ahmed Abdelali** **Kareem Darwish** **Mohamed Eldesouki**
Younes Samih **Hassan Sajjad**
{hmubarak,aabdelali}@qf.org.qa
Qatar Computing Research Institute, HBKU Research Complex, Doha 5825, Qatar

Abstract

Short vowels, aka diacritics, are more often omitted when writing different varieties of Arabic including Modern Standard Arabic (MSA), Classical Arabic (CA), and Dialectal Arabic (DA). However, diacritics are required to properly pronounce words, which makes diacritic restoration (a.k.a. diacritization) essential for language learning and text-to-speech applications. In this paper, we present a system for diacritizing MSA, CA, and two varieties of DA, namely Moroccan and Tunisian. The system uses a character level sequence-to-sequence deep learning model that requires no feature engineering and beats all previous SOTA systems for all the Arabic varieties that we test on.

1 Introduction

Most varieties of Arabic are typically written without short vowels, aka diacritics, and readers need to recover such diacritics to properly pronounce words. Modern Standard Arabic (MSA) and Classical Arabic (CA) use two types of diacritics, namely: core-word diacritics, which specify lexical selection, and case endings, which generally indicate syntactic role. Conversely, Arabic Dialects mostly use core-word diacritics and usually use a silence diacritic (sukun) for case-endings. For example, given the present tense MSA and CA verb "yfhm"[1] can be diacritized as "yafoham" (meaning: "he understands") or "yufah~im" ("he explains"). Both can accept dammah (u), fatHa (a), or sukun (o) as grammatical case endings according to surrounding context. The equivalent version in some Arabic dialects is "byfhm", which can be diacritized as "biyifohamo" ("he understands") or "biyofah~imo" ("he explains"). This highlights the complexity of the task of recovering

the diacritics, a prerequisite for Language Learning (Asadi, 2017) and Text to Speech (Sherif, 2018) among other applications.

In this paper, we present a system that employs a character-based sequence-to-sequence model (seq2seq) (Britz et al., 2017; Cho et al., 2014; Kuchaiev et al., 2018) for diacritizing four different varieties of Arabic. We use the approach described by Mubarak et al. (2019), which they applied to MSA only, to build a system that effectively diacritizes MSA, CA, and and two varieties of Dialectal Arabic (DA), namely Moroccan (MA) and Tunisian (TN). Our system beats all previously reported SOTA results for the aforementioned varieties of Arabic. The underlying approach treats diacritic recovery as a translation problem, where a sequential encoder and a sequential decoder are employed with undiacritized characters as input and diacritized characters as output. The system is composed of four main componenets, namely: 1) a web application that efficiently handles concurrent user diacritization requests; 2) a text tokenization and cleaning module based on Farasa (Abdelali et al., 2016), a SOTA Arabic NLP toolkit; 3) Arabic variety identifier based on a fastText (Joulin et al., 2016), a deep learning classification toolkit, to properly ascertain the appropriate diacritization model; and 4) a Neural Machine Translation (NMT) based architecture, based on OpenNMT (Klein et al., 2017), to translate sequences of undiacritized characters to diacritized sequences.

The contributions in this paper are:

- We deploy a web-based system that diacritizes four varieties of Arabic (MSA, CA, DA-MA, and DA-TN) with appropriate RESTful API.

- We employ one architecture to effectively diacritize the different varieties. The model re-

---

[1]Buckwalter Arabic transliteration scheme is used throughout the paper.

217

Proceedings of the 2019 EMNLP and the 9th IJCNLP (System Demonstrations), pages 217–222
Hong Kong, China, November 3 – 7, 2019. ©2019 Association for Computational Linguistics

quires no feature engineering or external resources such as segmenters or POS taggers. Our system surpasses SOTA results for all varieties of Arabic that we test on.

- We created large training and test datasets for CA that are highly consistent. We plan to make the test set, which is composed of 5,000 sentences (400k words) publicly available.

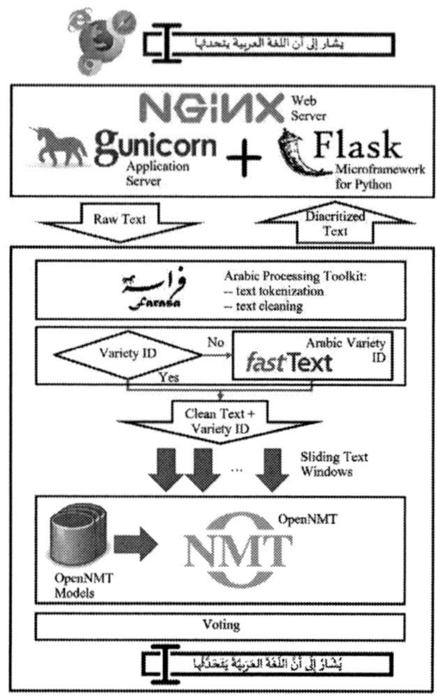

Figure 1: System architecture

2 System Architecture

2.1 Web Application

Figure 1 showcases the component of our demo. In a web browser, the user submits a sentence to diacritize. An instance of NGiNX web server receives the user request and routes it to the underlying application server. The application server is composed of two parts, namely "Flask" and "GUnicorn" (a.k.a. Green Unicorn). Flask is a web framework that deploys Python-based web application. Due to Flask's load restriction, where it does not handle concurrent requests and lacks security, we use GUnicorn, which is a web server gateway interface, as an interface between NGINX and Flask to handle concurrent requests and to properly handle security issues. Gunicorn converts NGINX requests into Python objects, which

are usable by the Flask frameworks. We make the diacritizer available as a web application and a web service that are freely accessible at: `https://bit.ly/2IdFRVE`.

2.2 Arabic Preprocessing

Flask deploys our diacritization application, which is composed of multiple components. The first component is Farasa segmenter (Abdelali et al., 2016), which is a SOTA publicly available Arabic processing toolkit. From the Farasa utilities, we use tokenization and text cleaning. Tokenization processes the text stream character by character to produce individual tokens composed of letters and numbers. Normalization maps Hindi numbers to Arabic numbers, converts non-Arabic extended Arabic script letters, such as those from Farsi or Urdu, to the closest Arabic letters, and removes all non-Arabic letters and numbers.

2.3 Arabic Variety Identification

The user may explicitly specify the variety of Arabic that they have entered. Available options include MSA, CA, DA-MA, and DA-TN. If the user does not specify the variety of Arabic, we employ a variety ID classifier. For this, we use a character-based deep-leaning classifier using fastText (Joulin et al., 2016) with character segments ranging between 3 and 6 grams, a learning rate of 0.05, and 50 training epochs. we opted to use characters for classification instead of words because Arabic is a complex language with a rich morphology, and many prefixes and suffixes can be attached to words. Also for dialectal Arabic, words can be written in many different accepted ways due to the lack of a standard orthography.

2.4 Diacritization

For diacritization, Mubarak et al. (2019) show the effectiveness of using Neural Machine Translation (NMT) framework to properly diacritize MSA while recovering both core-word diacritics and case-endings jointly and without the need for any feature engineering. We use their approach to train diacritizers for MSA, and we extend their work to train diacritizers for CA, DA-MA, and DA-TN. The method is composed of three component:
The first component produces overlapping **sliding window** sequences of n words. Diacritization requires that word and character orderings are preserved. Thus, the NMT model needs to be constrained to avoid word and character re-ordering,

insertion, and deletions. As in Mubarak et al. (2019), we enforce these constraints using a sliding window strategy, where the model is trained and tested on consecutive text windows of fixed length of 7 words.

The second component is an **NMT model**, which translates undiacritized sequences of characters to diacritized sequences. We use the OpenNMT implementation. Formally, given a word sequence w_i in source sentence S_{src}, we want to map it to the diacritized word w_i' in target sentence S_{trg} such that:

$$S_{src} = w_0, w_1, w_2, ..., w_n$$
$$S_{trg} = w_0', w_1', w_2', ..., w_n' \quad (1)$$

and:

$$w_i = c_0, c_1, .., c_m \quad c \in \{C, L\}.$$
$$C : Arabic\ characters$$
$$w_i' = c_0 v_0, c_1 v_1, .., c_m v_m \quad v \in \{V, \varnothing\} \quad (2)$$
$$V : Arabic\ diacritics$$

The third is a **voting component**. Since a word may appear in multiple consecutive windows, we get multiple diacritized versions of every word. This allows us to use voting to select the most common diacritized form for a word. In case of a tie, we favor the window in which the word appears exactly in the middle. Table 1 provides an example for a three words sentence "ktb Alwld Aldrs" (the boy wrote the lesson) with a 3 word sliding window.

Source	Target
<s>_ <s>_ k t b	<s>_ <s>_ ka ta ba
<s>_ k t b _ A l w l d	<s>_ ka ta ba _ A lo wa la du
k t b _ A l w l d _ A l d r s	ka ta ba _ A lo wa la du _ A l d~a ro sa
A l w l d _ A l d r s _ <e>	A lo wa la du _ A l d~a ro sa _ <e>
A l d r s _ <e> _ <e>	A l d~a ro sa _ <e> _ <e>

Table 1: Example sentence: "ktb Alwld Aldrs" with context window size of 3. Symbols "<s>" and "<e>" are added to mark start and end of the sentence.

3 Data and Training

For **MSA**, we used a diacritized corpus of 4.5m words for training (Darwish et al., 2017; Mubarak et al., 2019). This corpus covers different genres such as politics, economy, religion, sports, society, etc. And for testing, we used the freely available WikiNews corpus (Darwish et al., 2017) which contains 18.3k words and covers multiple genres.

For **CA**, we obtained a classical diacritized corpus of 65m words from a publisher. We used 5k random sentences (400k words) for testing, and we used the remaining words for training. We are making the test set available at: `https://bit. ly/2KuOvkN`.

For **DA**, we used the corpora described in (Darwish et al., 2018), which is composed of two diacritized translations of the New Testament into Moroccan (DA-MA) and Tunisian (DA-TN). These corpora contain 166k and 157k words respectively. For each dialect, we split the diacritized corpora into 70/10/20 for training/validation/testing splits respectively. Our splits exactly match those of Abdelali et al. (2018). We used 5-fold cross validation.

Table 3 lists the details of the training and test sets including the unique diacritized and undiacritized tokens and the percentage of OOVs in the test set that don't appear in the training set. For MSA and CA, we randomly used 10% of the training set for validation and the rest for training.

3.1 Training

For variety identification, given the diacritization training sets, we trained the classifier using 7,000 random sentences from each corpus and we used 1,000 sentences for testing. As the testing sequences increase in length (more input words), the accuracy of the classifier increases as in Table 2.

Input length	5	10	15	20
Accuracy	93.8	98.5	99.0	99.1

Table 2: Arabic variety identification per input length

When building the diacritization models, we used the OpenNMT-tf implementation for training with the hyperparameters suggested in the OpenNMT website[2]. We used two RNN layers of size 500 each and embeddings of size 300. We ran 1M training epochs for each system, which took on average 8 to 24 hours per system.

4 Evaluation and Analysis

For evaluation, we report on the results of evaluating the models as well as the performance of the deployed system.

4.1 System Results

Table 4 summarizes the results per dataset and compares our system to other SOTA systems on

---

[2] `https://github.com/OpenNMT/OpenNMT-tf`

	Word	Train		Test		
		Total	Uniq	Total	Uniq	OOV%
MSA	Diac.	4.5m	333k	18.3k	7.9k	5.0
	Undiac.		209k		6.8k	3.3
CA	Diac.	65.6m	489k	409k	39k	3.6
	Undiac.		254k		29k	2.3
DA-MA	Diac.	151k	16.3k	15.4k	4.1k	19.5
	Undiac.		15.9k		4.0k	19.0
DA-TN	Diac.	142k	17.2k	15.3k	4.4k	21.5
	Undiac.		16.6k		4.3k	20.7

Table 3: Number of words in training and test data for MSA, CA, and DA

identical test sets. WER is computed at word-level, and hence the whole word is counted as an error if a single character therein receives an incorrect diacritic. Since we did not have access to systems that are specially tuned for CA, we compared our system to Farasa (Darwish et al., 2017), which was tuned for MSA. As the results clearly show, using the NMT model at character level consistently produced better results than all SOTA systems. This confirms the previous conclusions of (Mubarak et al., 2019) about the superiority of using a character based seq2seq model for diacritization. While previously published results using DNN BiLSTM approaches have improved the results over other machine learning approaches; NMT invariably reduced the errors further – between 25% to 60%.

	Setup	WER%
MSA	**Our System**	**4.5**
	Microsoft ATKS (Said et al., 2013)	12.3
	Farasa (Darwish et al., 2017)	12.8
	RDI (Rashwan et al., 2015)	16.0
	MADAMIRA (Pasha et al., 2014)	19.0
	MIT (Belinkov and Glass, 2015)	30.5
CA	**Our System**	**3.7**
	Farasa (Darwish et al., 2017)	12.8
DA-MA	**Our System**	**1.4**
	Bi-LSTM DNN (Abdelali et al., 2018)	2.7
	CRF (Darwish et al., 2018)	2.9
DA-TN	**Our System**	**2.5**
	Bi-LSTM DNN (Abdelali et al., 2018)	3.6
	CRF (Darwish et al., 2018)	3.8

Table 4: Results and comparison of full diacritization systems.

4.2 System Performance

The system is running on a Microsoft Azure virtual machine with 4 CPU cores and 16 gigabytes of memory. The system does not require a GPU for decoding. We configured the application server to handle 100 concurrent requests, with each request containing a text sentence. In our testing, the system is able to process 10,000 requests in 14.9 seconds with zero failures. In other words, the server is able to handle 672 requests per second, with each request finishing in 149 milliseconds on average. Implementing memory mapped files to minimize disk access would further speed up the processing of requests and enhance the performance of the system.

4.3 Error Analysis

For **MSA**: we randomly selected 100 word-core and 100 case-ending errors to ascertain the most common error types. For case-endings, the top 4 error types were: long-distance dependency (e.g. coordination or verb subj/obj), which is an artifact of using limited context – 24% of errors; confusion between different syntactic functions (e.g. N N vs. N ADJ or V Subj vs. V Obj) – 22%; wrong selection of morphological analysis (e.g. present tense vs. past tense) – 20%; and named entities (NEs) – 16%. For long distance dependencies, increasing context size may help in some case, but may introduce additional errors. Perhaps combining multiple context sizes may help. As for word-cores, the top 4 errors were: incorrect selection for ambiguous words, where most of these errors were related to active vs. passive voice – 60%; NEs – 32%; borrowed words – 4%; and words with multiple valid diacritized words – 4%.

For **CA**: We randomly selected 100 errors and the top 4 error types, which summed up to 85% of errors, were: wrong diacritized form selection – 36% of errors (e.g. "Almalik" (the king) vs. "Almalak" (the angel)); long-distance dependency (e.g. coordination or verb subj/obj as in "jA' Alnby mlk", (an angel came to the prophet) where the object preceded the subject) – 32%; confusion between different syntactic functions (e.g. N N vs. N ADJ) – 9%; confusion between different suffixes or prefixes, (e.g. "katabta" (you wrote) vs. "katabat" (she wrote)) – 8%. We also found that in 7% of the differences, the diacritizations of both the reference and system output were in fact correct (e.g. "jinAzp" and "janAzp" (funeral)).

For **DA**: We manually inspected 100 random errors. The bulk of these errors (71%) came from confusing the vowels a, i, and u, with sukun or sukun-shaddah. This is normal due to the high fre-

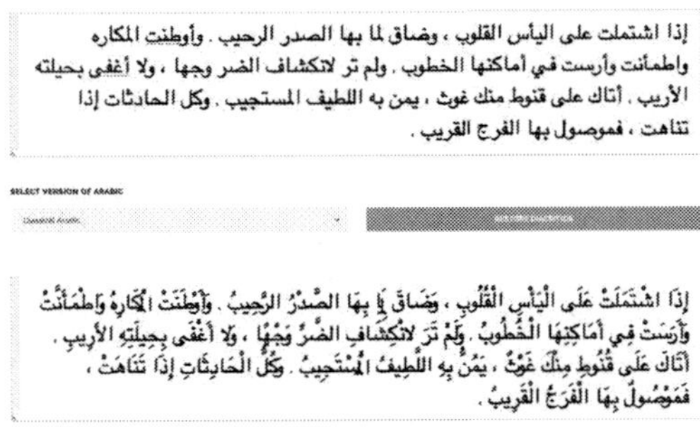

Figure 2: Screenshot for the demo site `https://bit.ly/2IdFRVE`

quency of sukkun in both Moroccan and Tunisian dialects compared to other varieties of Arabic (Abdelali et al., 2018). In about 8% of the cases, which involved NEs, the gold reference was not consistently diacritized, making it difficult for the system to learn properly. In an additional 5%, the system hallucinated producing output that is completely untethered from the source material (e.g. "$ayaTino" (the devil) vs. "$iTnino" (non-word)). These type of errors are likely an artifact of the seq2seq model. We plan to handle these errors in future by aligning input and output words and make sure that output letters are exactly the same as input, and by handling special characters that sometimes appear in DA. The remaining errors (16%) were due to erroneous selections, where for example, the system confused between feminine and masculine pronouns (e.g. "noti" (you: Fem.) vs. "nota" (you: masc.)).

5   Related Work

While the bulk of Arabic diacritic recovery research was devoted to MSA diacritization, work on CA and DA is still scarce. This can be attributed to many factors, primarily the absence of large standard resources.

In early experiments on **CA** diacritization by Gal (2002) and Elshafei et al. (2006), they used the Qur'anic text, composed of 18,623 diacritized words, and a Hidden Markov Model. Gal (2002) reported a word error rate (WER) of 14%, and Elshafei et al. (2006) reported a character error rate of 2.5%. As for **DA**, a number of systems designed either solely for diacritization or that supports the diacritization among other functionalities. Linguistic Data Consortium (LDC) CallHome corpus, containing 160K words worth

of transcripts of informal Egyptian Arabic was among the earlier resources used for DA. Employed technologies varied from manually crafted rules (Vergyri and Kirchhoff, 2004), finite state transducer and support vector machine (Habash et al., 2012; Khalifa et al., 2017; Jarrar et al., 2017), Conditional Random Fields (Darwish et al., 2018), and Deep Neural Networks (Abdelali et al., 2018). While there is no standard dataset for evaluation, recent reported performance on Moroccan and Tunisian was a WER of 2.7% and 3.6% respectively (Abdelali et al., 2018).

Similarly, for **MSA**, LDC Arabic Treebank (Part 2)[3] and its successor Part 3 (ATB3) v 1.0 and 3.2 were used with a myriad of technologies (Habash and Rambow, 2007; Pasha et al., 2014; Abandah et al., 2015) that combines SVM classifier and Recurrent Neural Networks. Abandah et al. (2015) reported a WER of 9.07% using a neural architecture consisting of two Recurrent Neural network layers with 250 nodes each. Darwish et al. (2017) used a corpus of 4.5m fully diacritized words to train an SVM classifier that achieved a 12.76% WER.

In sum, three resources were explored for diacritics recovery, namely:
– For CA: Qura'nic text with 18k words.
– For DA: LDC CallHome with 160k words; the Moroccan and Tunisian Bibles with 166k and 157k words respectively.
– For MSA: LDC Arabic Treebank with 340k words (v3.2); and a proprietary corpus of 4.5m words (Darwish et al., 2017).

6   Conclusion

In this paper, we introduced a system for diacritizing four different varieties of Arabic, namely MSA, CA, DA-TN, and DA-MA. The system employs a character based seq2seq model without the need for any feature engineering while beating other SOTA systems. The system is deployed as a web application with corresponding RESTful API. Our WER results respectively for MSA, CA, DA-MA, and DA-Tunisian are: 4.5%, 3.7%, 1.4%, and 2.5%. We plan to extend the system by integrating diacritization models for other dialects and to make the system more robust to handle different kinds of input texts with special characters, which are prevalent in tweets.

---

[3]`https://catalog.ldc.upenn.edu/LDC2004T02`

References

Gheith A. Abandah, Alex Graves, Balkees Al-Shagoor, Alaa Arabiyat, Fuad Jamour, and Majid Al-Taee. 2015. Automatic diacritization of arabic text using recurrent neural networks. *International Journal on Document Analysis and Recognition (IJDAR)*, 18(2):183–197.

Ahmed Abdelali, Mohammed Attia, Younes Samih, Kareem Darwish, and Hamdy Mubarak. 2018. Diacritization of maghrebi arabic sub-dialects. *arXiv preprint arXiv:1810.06619*.

Ahmed Abdelali, Kareem Darwish, Nadir Durrani, and Hamdy Mubarak. 2016. Farasa: A fast and furious segmenter for arabic. In *Proceedings of NAACL-HLT 2016 (Demonstrations)*, pages 11–16. Association for Computational Linguistics.

Ibrahim A. Asadi. 2017. Reading arabic with the diacritics for short vowels: vowelised but not necessarily easy to read. *Writing Systems Research*, 9(2):137–147.

Yonatan Belinkov and James Glass. 2015. Arabic diacritization with recurrent neural networks. In *Proceedings of the 2015 Conference on Empirical Methods in Natural Language Processing*, pages 2281–2285, Lisbon, Portugal.

Denny Britz, Anna Goldie, Thang Luong, and Quoc Le. 2017. Massive Exploration of Neural Machine Translation Architectures. *ArXiv e-prints*.

Kyunghyun Cho, Bart Van Merriënboer, Caglar Gulcehre, Dzmitry Bahdanau, Fethi Bougares, Holger Schwenk, and Yoshua Bengio. 2014. Learning phrase representations using rnn encoder-decoder for statistical machine translation. *arXiv preprint arXiv:1406.1078*.

Kareem Darwish, Ahmed Abdelali, Hamdy Mubarak, Younes Samih, and Mohammed Attia. 2018. Diacritization of moroccan and tunisian arabic dialects: A CRF approach. In *OSACT 3: The 3rd Workshop on Open-Source Arabic Corpora and Processing Tools*, page 62.

Kareem Darwish, Hamdy Mubarak, and Ahmed Abdelali. 2017. Arabic diacritization: Stats, rules, and hacks. In *Proceedings of the Third Arabic Natural Language Processing Workshop*, pages 9–17.

Moustafa Elshafei, Husni Al-Muhtaseb, and Mansour Alghamdi. 2006. Statistical methods for automatic diacritization of arabic text. In *The Saudi 18th National Computer Conference. Riyadh*, volume 18, pages 301–306.

Ya'akov Gal. 2002. An HMM approach to vowel restoration in arabic and hebrew. In *Proceedings of the ACL-02 workshop on Computational approaches to Semitic languages*, pages 1–7. Association for Computational Linguistics.

Nizar Habash, Ramy Eskander, and Abdelati Hawwari. 2012. A morphological analyzer for egyptian arabic. In *SIGMORPHON 2012*, pages 1–9. ACL.

Nizar Habash and Owen Rambow. 2007. Arabic diacritization through full morphological tagging. In *HLT-NAACL*, pages 53–56.

Mustafa Jarrar, Nizar Habash, Faeq Alrimawi, Diyam Akra, and Nasser Zalmout. 2017. Curras: an annotated corpus for the palestinian arabic dialect. *Language Resources and Evaluation*, 51(3):745–775.

Armand Joulin, Edouard Grave, Piotr Bojanowski, Matthijs Douze, Hérve Jégou, and Tomas Mikolov. 2016. Fasttext.zip: Compressing text classification models. *arXiv preprint arXiv:1612.03651*.

Salam Khalifa, Sara Hassan, and Nizar Habash. 2017. A morphological analyzer for gulf arabic verbs. *WANLP 2017*, page 35.

G. Klein, Y. Kim, Y. Deng, J. Senellart, and A. M. Rush. 2017. OpenNMT: Open-Source Toolkit for Neural Machine Translation. *ArXiv e-prints*.

Oleksii Kuchaiev, Boris Ginsburg, Igor Gitman, Vitaly Lavrukhin, Carl Case, and Paulius Micikevicius. 2018. Openseq2seq: extensible toolkit for distributed and mixed precision training of sequence-to-sequence models. *arXiv preprint arXiv:1805.10387*.

Hamdy Mubarak, Ahmed Abdelali, Hassan Sajjad, Younes Samih, and Kareem Darwish. 2019. Highly effective arabic diacritization using sequence to sequence modeling. In *Proceedings of NAACL-HLT 2019*.

Arfath Pasha, Mohamed Al-Badrashiny, Mona Diab, Ahmed El Kholy, Ramy Eskander, Nizar Habash, Manoj Pooleery, Owen Rambow, and Ryan M Roth. 2014. Madamira: A fast, comprehensive tool for morphological analysis and disambiguation of arabic. In *LREC-2014*, Reykjavik, Iceland.

Mohsen Rashwan, Ahmad Al Sallab, M. Raafat, and Ahmed Rafea. 2015. Deep learning framework with confused sub-set resolution architecture for automatic arabic diacritization. In *IEEE Transactions on Audio, Speech, and Language Processing*, pages 505–516.

Ahmed Said, Mohamed El-Sharqwi, Achraf Chalabi, and Eslam Kamal. 2013. A hybrid approach for arabic diacritization. In *Natural Language Processing and Information Systems*, pages 53–64, Berlin, Heidelberg.

Youssef Sherif. 2018. Arabic tacotron text to speech.

Dimitra Vergyri and Katrin Kirchhoff. 2004. Automatic diacritization of arabic for acoustic modeling in speech recognition. In *Proceedings of the workshop on computational approaches to Arabic script-based languages, COLING'04*, pages 66–73, Geneva, Switzerland.

Tanbih: Get To Know What You Are Reading

Yifan Zhang[1], Giovanni Da San Martino[1], Alberto Barrón-Cedeño[2], Salvatore Romeo[1],
Jisun An[1], Haewoon Kwak[1], Todor Staykovski[3], Israa Jaradat[4], Georgi Karadzhov[5],
Ramy Baly[6], Kareem Darwish[1], James Glass[6], Preslav Nakov[1]

[1]Qatar Computing Research Institute, HBKU, [2]Università di Bologna, Forlì, Italy
[3]Sofia University [4]University of Texas at Arlington, [5]SiteGround Hosting EOOD
[6]MIT Computer Science and Artificial Intelligence Laboratory
{yzhang,gmartino,sromeo,jan,hkwak,kdarwish,pnakov}@hbku.edu.qa
a.barron@unibo.it, todorstaykovski@gmail.com, {baly,glass}@mit.edu
israa.jaradat@mavs.uta.edu, gogokaradjov@gmail.com

Abstract

We introduce *Tanbih*, a news aggregator with intelligent analysis tools to help readers understanding what is behind a news story. Our system displays news grouped into events and generates media profiles that show the general factuality of reporting, the degree of propagandistic content, hyper-partisanship, leading political ideology, general frame of reporting, and stance with respect to various claims and topics of a news outlet. In addition, we automatically analyze each article in order to detect whether it is propagandistic and to determine its stance with respect to a number of controversial topics.

1 Introduction

Nowadays, more and more readers consume news online. The reduced costs and, generally speaking, the less strict regulations with respect to the standard press, have led to the proliferation of online news media. However, this does not necessarily entail that readers are exposed to a plurality of viewpoints as news consumed via social networks are known to reinforce the bias of the user (Flaxman et al., 2016) because of filtering bubbles and echo chambers. Moreover, visiting multiple websites to gather a more comprehensive analysis of an event might be too time-consuming for the average reader.

News aggregators —such as Flipboard[1], News Lens[2] and Google News[3]—, gather news from different sources and, in the case of the latter two, cluster them into events. In addition, News Lens displays all articles about an event in a timeline and provides additional information, such as summary of the event and a description for each entity mentioned in an article.

While these news aggregators help readers to get a more comprehensive coverage of an event, some of the sources might be unknown to the user, and thus he/she could naturally question the validity and the trustworthiness of the information provided. Deep analysis of the content published by news outlets has been performed by expert journalists. For example, Media Bias/Fact Check[4] provides reports on the bias and factuality of reporting of entire news outlets, whereas Snopes[5], Politifact,[6] and FactCheck[7] are popular fact-checking websites. All these manual efforts cannot cope with the rate at which news contents are produced.

Here, we propose *Tanbih*, a news platform that displays news grouped into events and provides additional information about the articles and their media source in order to promote media literacy. It automatically generates profiles for the news media with reports on their factuality, leading political ideology, hyper-partisanship, use of propaganda, and bias. Furthermore, *Tanbih* automatically categorizes articles in English and Arabic, flags potentially propagandistic ones, and examines their framing bias.

2 System Architecture

The architecture of *Tanbih* is sketched in Figure 1. The system consists of three main components: an online streaming processing pipeline for data collection and article level analysis, offline processing for event and media source level analysis, and a website for delivering news to the users. The online streaming processing pipeline continuously retrieves articles in English and Arabic, which are then translated, categorized, and analyzed for their general frame of reporting and use of propaganda.

---

[1]http://flipboard.com
[2]http://newslens.berkeley.edu
[3]http://news.google.com.

[4]http://mediabiasfactcheck.com
[5]http://www.snopes.com/
[6]http://www.politifact.com/
[7]http://www.factcheck.org/

223

Proceedings of the 2019 EMNLP and the 9th IJCNLP (System Demonstrations), pages 223–228
Hong Kong, China, November 3 – 7, 2019. ©2019 Association for Computational Linguistics

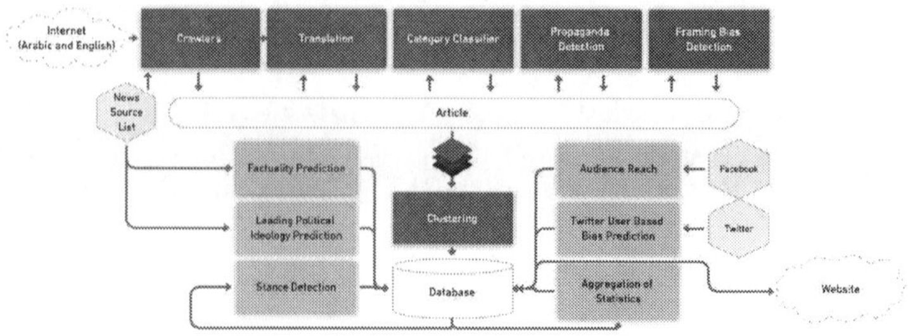

Figure 1: The architecture of *Tanbih*. The arrows indicate the information flow.

We perform clustering on the articles that have been collected every 30 minutes. The offline processing includes factuality prediction, leading political ideology detection, audience reach and Twitter user based bias prediction at the media level, and stance detection and aggregation of statistics at the article level, e.g., propaganda index (see Section 2.3) for each news medium. The offline processing does not have strict time requirements, and thus the choice of the models we develop favors accuracy over speed.

In order to run everything in a streaming and scalable fashion, we use KAFKA[8] as a messaging queue and Kubernetes[9], thus ensuring scalability and fault-tolerant deployment. In the following, we describe each component of the system. We have open-sourced the code for some of those, and we plan to do that for the remaining ones in the near future.

2.1 Crawlers and Translation

Our crawlers collect articles from a growing list of sources[10], which currently includes 155 RSS feeds, 82 Twitter accounts and two websites. Once a link to an article has been obtained from any of these sources, we rely on the Newspaper3k Python library to extract its contents.[11] After deduplication based on both URL and text content, our crawlers currently download 7k-10k articles per day. As of present, we have more than 700k articles stored in our database. We use QCRI's Machine Translation (Dalvi et al., 2017) to translate English content into Arabic and vice versa. Since translation is performed offline, we select the most accurate system in Dalvi et al. (2017), i.e., the neural-based one.

2.2 Section Categorization

We built a model to classify an article into one of six news sections: Entertainment, Sports, Business, Technology, Politics, and Health. We built a corpus using the New York Times articles from the FakeNews dataset[12] published between January 1, 2000 and December 31, 2017. We extracted the news section information embedded in the article URL and we used a total of 538k articles for training our models using TF.IDF representation. On a test set of 107k articles, our best-performing logistic regression model achieved F_1 scores of $0.82, 0.58, 0.80$, and 0.90 for Sports, Business, Technology, and Politics, respectively. The overall F_1 for the baseline was 0.497.

2.3 Propaganda Detection

We developed a propaganda detection component to flag articles that could be potentially propagandistic, i.e., purposefully biased to influence its readers and ultimately to pursue a specific agenda. Given a corpus of news that is labelled as propagandistic/non propagandistic (Barrón-Cedeño et al., 2019), we train a maximum entropy classifier on 51k articles, represented with various style-related features, such as character n-grams and a number of vocabulary richness and readability measures, and we obtain state-of-the-art F_1=82.89 on a separate test set of 10k articles. We refer to the score $p \in [0, 1]$ of the classifier as *propaganda index*, and we define the following propaganda labels, which we use to flag articles (see Figure 2; right news): very unlikely ($p < 0.2$), unlikely ($0.2 \leq p < 0.4$), somehow ($0.4 \leq p < 0.6$), likely ($0.6 \leq p < 0.8$), and very likely ($p \geq 0.8$).

---

[8]http://kafka.apache.org
[9]http://kubernetes.io
[10]http://www.tanbih.org/about
[11]http://newspaper.readthedocs.io

---

[12]http://github.com/several27/
FakeNewsCorpus

2.4 Framing Bias Detection

Framing is a central concept in political communication, which intentionally emphasizes or ignores certain dimensions of an issue (Entman, 1993). In *Tanbih*, we infer the frames of news articles, thus making them explicit. In particular, we use the Media Frames Corpus (MFC) (Card et al., 2015) to train a fine-tuned BERT model to detect topic-agnostic media frames. For training, we use a small learning rate of 0.0002, a maximum sequence length of 128, and a batch size of 32. Our model, when trained on 11k articles from MFC, achieved an accuracy of 66.7% on a test set of 1,138 articles. This is better than the previously reported state-of-the-art (58.4%) on a subset of MFC (Ji and Smith, 2017).

2.5 Factuality of Reporting and Leading Political Ideology of a Source

The factuality of reporting and the bias of an information source are key indicators that investigative journalists use to judge the reliability of information. In *Tanbih*, we model the factuality and the bias at the media level, learning from the Media Bias/Fact Check (MBFC) website, which covers over 2,800 news outlets. The model improves over our recent research (Baly et al., 2018, 2019; Dinkov et al., 2019), and combines information from articles published by the target medium, from their Wikipedia page accounts, from their social media accounts (Twitter, Facebook, Youtube) as well as from the social media accounts of the users who interact with the medium. We model factuality on a 3-point scale (*low*, *mixed* and *high*), with 80.1% accuracy (baseline 46.0%), and bias on a 7-point *left*-to-*right* scale, with 69% accuracy (baseline 24.7%), and also on a 3-point scale, with 81.9% accuracy (baseline 37.1%).

2.6 Stance Detection

Stance detection aims to identify the relative perspective of a piece of text with respect to a claim, typically modeled using labels such as *agree*, *disagree*, *discuss*, and *unrelated*. An interesting application of stance detection is medium profiling with respect to controversial topics. In this setting, given a particular medium, the stance for each article is computed with respect to a set of predefined claims. The stance of a medium is then obtained by aggregating the article-level stances. In *Tanbih*, the stance is used to profile media sources.

We implemented our stance detection model as fine-tuning of BERT on the FNC-1 dataset from the *Fake News Challenge*[13]. Our model outperformed the best submitted system (Hanselowski et al., 2018), obtaining an $F_{1_{macro}}$ of 75.30 and an F_1 of $69.61, 49.76, 83.01$, and 98.81 for *agree*, *disagree*, *discuss*, and *unrelated*, respectively.

2.7 Audience Reach

User interactions on Facebook enable the platform to generate comprehensive user profiles for gender, age, income bracket, and political preferences. After marketers have determined a set of criteria for their target audience, Facebook can provide them with an estimate of the size of this audience on its platform. As an illustration, there are about 160K Facebook users who are 20 years old, are very liberal, are female, and have an interest in The New York Times. In *Tanbih*, we use the political leaning of Facebook users who follow a news medium as a feature to potentially improve media bias and factuality prediction; we also show it in the media profiles. To get the audience of each news medium, we use Facebook's Marketing API to extract the demographic data of the medium's audience with a focus on audience members who reside in USA and their political leanings (ideology): (*Very Conservative, Conservative, Moderate, Liberal, and Very Liberal*).[14]

2.8 Twitter User-Based Bias Classification

Controversial social and political issues may spur social media users to express their opinion through sharing supporting newspaper articles. Our intuition is that the bias of news sources can be inferred based on the bias of social media users. For example, if articles from a news source are strictly shared by left- or right-leaning users, then the source is likely left- or right-leaning, respectively. Similarly, if it is being cited by both groups, then it is likely closer to the center. We used an unsupervised user-based stance detection method on different controversial topics in order to find core groups of right- and left-leaning users (Darwish et al., 2019). Given that the stance detection produces clusters with nearly perfect purity ($> 97\%$ purity), we used the identified core users to train a deep learning-based classifier, fastText, using the accounts that they retweeted as features to further tag more users.

---

[13]http://www.fakenewschallenge.org/
[14]These are only available for US-based Facebook users.

Next, we computed a valence score for each news outlet and for each topic. The valence scores range between -1 and 1, with higher absolute values indicating being cited with greater proportion by one group as opposed to the other. The score is calculated as follows (Conover et al., 2011):

$$V(u) = 2 \frac{\frac{tf(u,C_0)}{total(C_0)}}{\frac{tf(u,C_0)}{total(C_0)} + \frac{tf(u,C_1)}{total(C_1)}} - 1 \qquad (1)$$

where $tf(u, C_0)$ is the number of times (term frequency) item u is cited by group C_0, and $total(C_0)$ is the sum of the term frequencies of all items cited by C_0. $tf(u, C_1)$ and $total(C_1)$ are defined in a similar fashion. We subdivided the range between -1 and 1 into 5 equal size ranges and we assigned the labels *far-left*, *left*, *center*, *right*, and *far-right* to those ranges.

2.9 Event Identification / Clustering

The clustering module aggregates news articles into stories. The pipeline is divided into two stages: (*i*) local topic identification and (*ii*) long-term topic matching for story generation.

For step (*i*), we represent each article as a TF.IDF vector, built from the title and the body concatenated. The pre-processing consists of casefolding, lemmatization, punctuation and stopword removal. In order to obtain the preliminary clusters, in stage (*i*), we compute the cosine similarity between all article pairs in a predefined time window. We set $n = 6$ as the number of days withing a window with an overlap of three days. The resulting matrix of similarities for each window is then used to build a graph $G = (V, E)$, where V is the set of vertices, i.e., the news articles, and E is the set of edges. An edge between two articles $\{d_i, d_j\} \in V$ is drawn only if $sim(d_i, d_j) \geq T_1$, with $T_1 = 0.31$. We selected all parameters empirically on the training part of the corpus from (Miranda et al., 2018). The sequence of overlapping local graphs is merged in the order of their creation, thus generating stories from the topics. After merging, a community detection algorithm is used in order to find the correct assignment of the nodes into clusters. We used one of the fastest modularity-based algorithms: the Louvain method (Blondel et al., 2008).

For step (*ii*), the topics created from the preceding stage are merged if the cosine similarity $sim(t_i, t_j) \geq T_2$, where t_i (t_j) is the mean of all vectors belonging to topic i (j), with $T_2 = 0.8$.

Figure 2: The *Tanbih* main page.

The model achieved state-of-the-art performance on the testing partition of the corpus from Miranda et al. (2018): an F_1 of 98.11 and an $F_{1_{BCubed}}$ of 94.41.[15] As a comparison, the best model described in (Miranda et al., 2018) achieved an F_1 of 94.1. See Staykovski et al. (2019) for further details.

3 Interface

The home page of *Tanbih*[16] displays news articles grouped into stories (see the screenshot in Figure 2). Each story is displayed as a card. The users can go back and forth between the articles from the same event by clicking on the left/right arrows below the title of the article. A propaganda label is displayed if the article is predicted to be likely propagandistic. Such an example is shown on the right of Figure 2. The source of each article is displayed with the logo or the avatar of the respective news organization, and it links to a special profile page for this organization (see Figure 3). On the top-left of the home page, *Tanbih* provides language selection buttons, currently English and Arabic only, to switch the language the news are display in. Finally, a search box in the top-right corner allows the user to find the profile page of a particular news medium of interest.

On the media profile page (Figure 3a), a short extract from the Wikipedia page of the medium is displayed on the top, with recently published articles on the right-hand side. The profile page includes a number of statistics automatically derived from the models in Section 2. We use as an example Figure 3, which shows screenshots of the profile of CNN.[17]

---

[15] $F_{1_{BCubed}}$ is an evaluation measure specifically designed to evaluate clustering algorithms (Amigó et al., 2009).

[16] http://www.tanbih.org

[17] Here is a direct link to the profile: http://www.tanbih.org/media/1

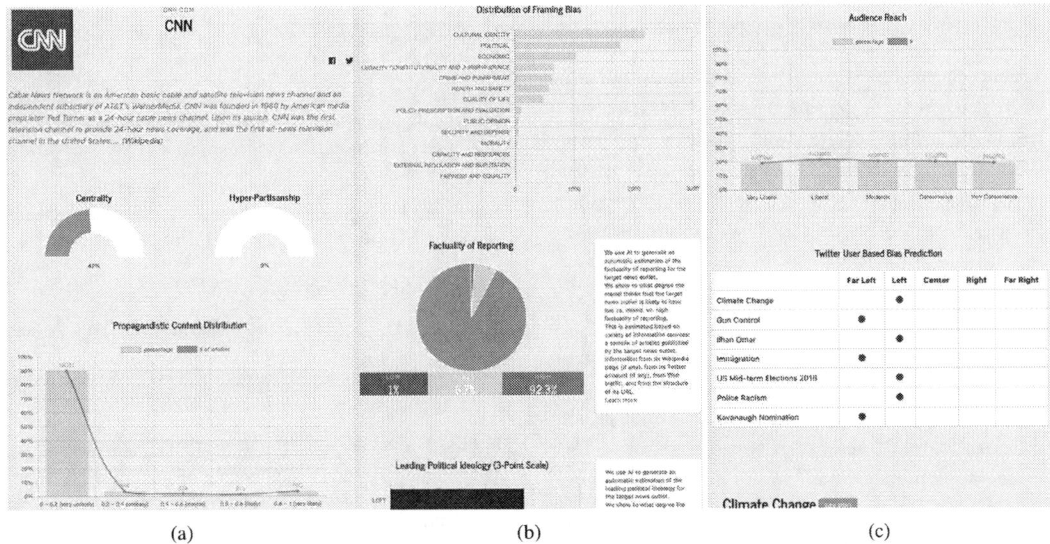

Figure 3: A partial screenshot of the media profile page for CNN in *Tanbih*.

The first two charts in Figure 3a show the centrality and the hyper-partisanship (we can see that CNN is estimated to be fairly central and low in hyper-partisanship) and the distribution of propagandistic articles (CNN publishes mostly non-propagandistic articles).

Figure 3b shows the overall framing bias distribution for the medium (CNN focuses mostly on cultural identity and politics), and the factuality of reporting (CNN is mostly factual). The profile also shows the leading political ideology of the medium on a 3-point and also on a 7-point scale.

Figure 3c shows the audience reach of the medium and the bias classification according to users' retweets (see Section 2.8). We can see that CNN is popular among readers with all political views, although it tends to have a left-leaning ideology on the topics listed. The profile also features reports on the stance of CNN with respect to a number of topics.

Finally, *Tanbih* features pages about specific topics. These are accessible via the search box on the top-right of *Tanbih*'s main page. An example is given in Figure 4, which shows the topic page for the Khashoggi's murder. Recent stories about this topic are listed on the top of the page, followed by statistics such as the number of countries, the number of articles, and the number of media reporting on it. A map shows how much reporting there is on the event per country, which allows users to get an idea of how important the topic is there.

Figure 4: A partial screenshot of the topic page for the Khashoggi Murder in *Tanbih*.

The topic page further features charts showing (*i*) the top countries in terms of coverage of the event, both in absolute and in relative numbers with respect to the total number of articles published, and (*ii*) the media sources that published most propagandistic content on the topic, again both in absolute and in relative terms with respect to the total number of articles published by the respective medium on the topic. Finally, the topic page displays plots showing the overall distribution of propagandistic articles and of the overall framing bias when reporting on the topic.

4 Conclusions and Future Work

We have introduced *Tanbih*, a news aggregator that performs media-level and article-level analysis of the news aiming to help users better understand what they are reading. *Tanbih* features factuality prediction, propaganda detection, stance detection, leading political ideology identification, media framing bias detection, event clustering, and machine translation.

In future work, we plan to include more media sources, especially from non-English speaking regions and to add interactive components, e.g., letting users ask a question about a specific topic. We also plan to add sentence-level and sub-sentence-level annotations for checkworthiness (Jaradat et al., 2018) and fine-grained propaganda (Da San Martino et al., 2019).

Acknowledgements

This research is part of the Tanbih project,[18] which aims to limit the effect of "fake news", propaganda and media bias by making users aware of what they are reading. It is developed in collaboration between the Qatar Computing Research Institute (QCRI), HBKU and the MIT Computer Science and Artificial Intelligence Laboratory (CSAIL).

References

Enrique Amigó, Julio Gonzalo, Javier Artiles, and Felisa Verdejo. 2009. A comparison of extrinsic clustering evaluation metrics based on formal constraints. *Inf. Retr.*, 12(4):461–486.

Ramy Baly, Georgi Karadzhov, Dimitar Alexandrov, James Glass, and Preslav Nakov. 2018. Predicting factuality of reporting and bias of news media sources. In *Proc. of EMNLP'18*, pages 3528–3539.

Ramy Baly, Georgi Karadzhov, Abdelrhman Saleh, James Glass, and Preslav Nakov. 2019. Multi-task ordinal regression for jointly predicting the trustworthiness and the leading political ideology of news media. In *Proc. of NAACL-HLT'19*, pages 2109–2116.

Alberto Barrón-Cedeño, Giovanni Da San Martino, Israa Jaradat, and Preslav Nakov. 2019. Proppy: Organizing news coverage on the basis of their propagandistic content. *Information Processing and Management*, 56(5):1849–1864.

Vincent D Blondel, Jean-Loup Guillaume, Renaud Lambiotte, and Etienne Lefebvre. 2008. Fast unfolding of communities in large networks. *Journal of Statistical Mechanics: Theory and Experiment*, 2008(10):P10008.

Dallas Card, Amber E Boydstun, Justin H Gross, Philip Resnik, and Noah A Smith. 2015. The media frames corpus: Annotations of frames across issues. In *Proc. of ACL '15*, pages 438–444.

Michael Conover, Jacob Ratkiewicz, Matthew R Francisco, Bruno Gonçalves, Filippo Menczer, and Alessandro Flammini. 2011. Political polarization on Twitter. In *Proc. of ICWSM'11*, pages 89–96.

Giovanni Da San Martino, Seunghak Yu, Alberto Barron-Cedeno, Rostislav Petrov, and Preslav Nakov. 2019. Fine-grained analysis of propaganda in news articles. In *Proc. of EMNLP'19*.

Fahim Dalvi, Yifan Zhang, Sameer Khurana, Nadir Durrani, Hassan Sajjad, Ahmed Abdelali, Hamdy Mubarak, Ahmed Ali, and Stephan Vogel. 2017. QCRI live speech translation system. In *Proc. of EACL'17*, pages 61–64.

Kareem Darwish, Peter Stefanov, Michaël J Aupetit, and Preslav Nakov. 2019. Unsupervised user stance detection on Twitter. In *Proc. of ICWSM'20*.

Yoan Dinkov, Ahmed Ali, Ivan Koychev, and Preslav Nakov. 2019. Predicting the leading political ideology of Youtube channels using acoustic, textual and metadata information. In *Proc. of INTERSPEECH'19*.

Robert M Entman. 1993. Framing: Toward clarification of a fractured paradigm. *Journal of communication*, 43(4):51–58.

Seth Flaxman, Sharad Goel, and Justin M Rao. 2016. Filter bubbles, echo chambers, and online news consumption. *Public opinion quarterly*, 80(S1):298–320.

Andreas Hanselowski, Avinesh P.V.S., Benjamin Schiller, Felix Caspelherr, Debanjan Chaudhuri, Christian M. Meyer, and Iryna Gurevych. 2018. A retrospective analysis of the fake news challenge stance-detection task. In *Proc. of COLING'18*, pages 1859–1874.

Israa Jaradat, Pepa Gencheva, Alberto Barrón-Cedeño, Lluís Màrquez, and Preslav Nakov. 2018. ClaimRank: Detecting check-worthy claims in Arabic and English. In *Proc. of NAACL-HLT '18*, pages 26–30.

Yangfeng Ji and Noah A. Smith. 2017. Neural discourse structure for text categorization. In *Proc. ACL'17*, pages 996–1005.

Sebastião Miranda, Arturs Znotins, Shay B. Cohen, and Guntis Barzdins. 2018. Multilingual clustering of streaming news. In *Proc. of EMNLP'18*, pages 4535–4544.

Todor Staykovski, Alberto Barrón-Cedeño, Giovanni Da San Martino, and Preslav Nakov. 2019. Dense vs. sparse representations for news stream clustering. In *Proc. of Text2story'19*, pages 47–52.

---

[18]http://tanbih.qcri.org/

TEASPN: Framework and Protocol
for Integrated Writing Assistance Environments

Masato Hagiwara[1] **Takumi Ito[2,3]** **Tatsuki Kuribayashi[2,3]**
Jun Suzuki[2,4] **Kentaro Inui[2,4]**
[1]Octanove Labs LLC   [2]Tohoku University   [3]Langsmith Inc.   [4]RIKEN AIP
masato@octanove.com
{t-ito, kuribayashi, jun.suzuki, inui}@ecei.tohoku.ac.jp

Abstract

Language technologies play a key role in assisting people with their writing. Although there has been steady progress in e.g., grammatical error correction (GEC), human writers are yet to benefit from this progress due to the high development cost of integrating with writing software. We propose TEASPN[1], a protocol and an open-source framework for achieving integrated writing assistance environments. The protocol standardizes the way writing software communicates with servers that implement such technologies, allowing developers and researchers to integrate the latest developments in natural language processing (NLP) with low cost. As a result, users can enjoy the integrated experience in their favorite writing software. The results from experiments with human participants show that users use a wide range of technologies and rate their writing experience favorably, allowing them to write more fluent text.

1 Introduction

Language technologies have been playing an important role in assisting people in writing natural language texts, such as essays, emails, business documents, and academic papers. There has been considerable progress on writing assistance technologies (or *WATs* in short) in the past few decades in fields such as NLP and computer-aided language learning (CALL). For example, in one of such areas, grammatical error correction (GEC) (Leacock et al., 2010), new models and systems are developed and published month after month, breaking the previous evaluation records and advancing state of the art. The recent development in neural language models enabled the com-

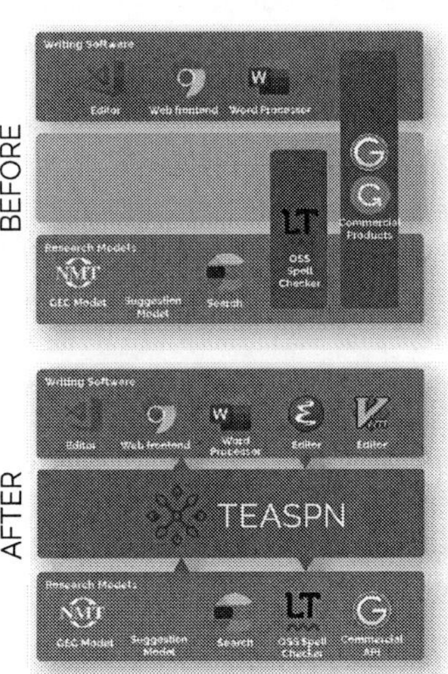

Figure 1: Writing software before and after TEASPN.

pletion of a prompt with long, realistic looking yet coherent passages (Radford et al., 2019).

However, real-world users such as writers who can and should benefit the most from WATs are yet to reap the fruits from these research efforts. Aside from a small number of commercial products, notably Grammarly[2] and Smart Compose (Chen et al., 2019), and research systems such as WriteAhead (Yen et al., 2015; Chang and Chang, 2015) and CroVeWA (Soyer et al., 2015), we see few examples of user-facing applications and experiments that make use of recent development in WATs. Many models are confined in research implementations that are not easily accessible to end users and the larger society. WATs, however, are not truly useful until they are integrated into user-facing writing applications such as editors and word processors (collectively called *writing software* in this paper) and interact with end users in a dynamic and intuitive manner. This "great divide" (see Figure 1 BEFORE) between applica-

---

[1]See https://www.teaspn.org/demo for the screencast and https://www.teaspn.org/ for more general info about TEASPN.

[2]https://www.grammarly.com/

Proceedings of the 2019 EMNLP and the 9th IJCNLP (System Demonstrations), pages 229–234
Hong Kong, China, November 3 – 7, 2019. ©2019 Association for Computational Linguistics

tions and academia is not unique in the domain of writing assistance, but a widespread phenomenon across many fields in machine learning and NLP, as pointed out by Wagstaff (2012).

One cause of this "great divide" is the high development cost for integrating and bridging both sides. Since there is a wide range of WATs, it is impractical, if not impossible, for developers of writing software to support all types of such technologies that come in different packages in different programming languages. Similarly, since there is a large selection of writing software, WAT researchers and developers cannot afford to offer their solutions in such a way that most writing software packages can benefit from them. If there are N types of writing software and M types of WATs, there can be $N \times M$ combinations between the two sides. As a result, writers often need to rely on many different writing software solutions and switch between many different applications and websites (search engines, grammar checkers, dictionaries and thesauri, etc.) in order to complete their tasks.

In this paper, we propose TEASPN (Text Editing Assistance Smartness Protocol for Natural Language; pronounced "teaspoon"), a protocol and a framework for achieving integrated writing assistance environments, as a solution to this "great divide" problem (Figure 1 AFTER). Inspired by and built upon Language Server Protocol (LSP)[3], a similar protocol for integrating software development environments, TEASPN provides an open protocol that standardizes the way writing software and WATs communicate with each other. We also released the TEASPN SDK (software development kit) as an open source library, which eases the cost of making WATs compatible with TEASPN. As a result, by using TEASPN,

- Developers of writing software can easily integrate state-of-the-art WATs into their editors and word processors just by following the protocol.
- Developers and researchers of WATs can support major writing software applications without worrying about the development cost, just by using the TEASPN SDK.
- Writers can benefit from integrated writing experience provided by their favorite writing software and WATs.

Finally, we implemented a demo TEASPN server that integrates WATs using latest developments in NLP (e.g., a neural language model and seq2seq-based paraphrasing) and ran experiments with real human writers to verify the framework's effectiveness. The experimental results demonstrated that our integrated writing assistance system developed with TEASPN provides better writing experience for human writers.

2   Related Work

Writing assistance   Use of language technologies for assisting writing in a second language (L2) has been extensively explored, especially for non-native English speakers. One of the most active research areas is GEC (Leacock et al., 2010), where several new models are published every year and commercial systems such as Grammarly are actively developed. Other research-based systems include WriteAhead (Yen et al., 2015; Chang and Chang, 2015), an interactive writing environment that provides users with grammatical patterns mined from large corpora, and CroVeWA (Soyer et al., 2015), a crosslingual sentence search system for L2 writers. FLOW (Chen et al., 2012) is another writing assistance system that allows users to type in their first languages (L1) and suggests words and phrases in L2. Running syntactic analysis and visualizing sentence structures have also been explored for L2 reading assistance (Faltin, 2003; Srdanović, 2011).

In addition to L2 learners, the use of technologies for assisting human translators has also been a focus of research. TransType (Langlais et al., 2000) is a translation assistance system that suggests completions for the text to the human translator in an interactive manner. In SemEval 2014, van Gompel et al. (2014) presented an L2 writing assistance task where systems find the proper translation of a word given a context in L2. Other writing assistance systems (not necessarily L2 learners) include assisting users with composing an email by auto-completion (Chen et al., 2019) and reply suggestion (Kannan et al., 2016).

LSP   The $N \times M$ problem mentioned in Section 1 is not unique to writing assistance. In software development, there can be N different types of integrated development environments (IDEs) and M different programming languages, making the integration cost proportionally expensive to $N \times M$. LSP solved this problem by proposing an open protocol that standardizes the way IDEs communicate with servers that offer language smartness technologies such as syntax checking and completion. As of today, LSP is widely adopted and supported by more than 70 servers and 20 development environments.

Since there is a large overlap between authoring in programming and natural languages, we built TEASPN as a "fork" of LSP. There are a few features that we need to design and implement specifically for writing assistance, namely, syntax highlighting and external resource search, which makes TEASPN incompatible with LSP. However, we re-purposed many LSP data models and features for TEASPN. Being able to leverage existing resources for LSP gives TEASPN a great head start for a wide adoption.

Protocols for NLP Language Grid (Ishida, 2006) is a platform where language providers (e.g., translation systems) and linguistic resources (e.g., dictionaries) are connected via semantic Web technologies to provide language services to communities. The NLP Interchange Format (NIF) (Hellmann et al., 2012) is a standard that aims to achieve interoperability between different NLP tools and resources by defining an RDL/OWL-based format. Although these projects have seen some real-world success, their adoption is quite limited as of this writing, compared to the aforementioned LSP, which powers at least a couple of millions of developers worldwide both for Visual Studio Code (VS code)[4] and Atom[5]. We believe the key to the wide adoption of any protocol is the focus on the right scope, practicality, and ease of development, which are the guiding principles for TEASPN.

3 TEASPN

3.1 Overview

TEASPN adopts a client-server architecture (Figure 2), where a client (writing software such as an editor or a word processor) communicates with a server that provides WATs. The client and the server communicate over the TEASPN protocol, an HTTP-like protocol which uses JSON-RPC (remote procedure call)[6] to encode the message body.

[4]https://code.visualstudio.com/blogs/
2017/11/16/connect
[5]https://blog.atom.io/2016/03/28/
atom-reaches-1m-users.html
[6]http://www.jsonrpc.org/

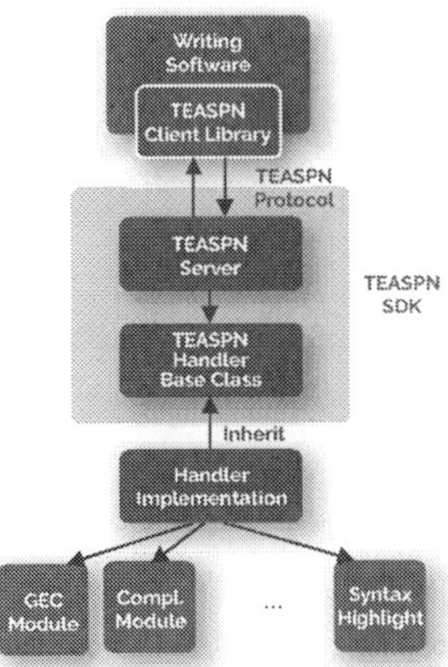

Figure 2: Architecture of TEASPN.

Requests can be sent in both directions, which are often triggered by some events (such as user input) and can be responded with additional data (such as results of GEC). TEASPN clients and servers can be written in any programming language as long as they conform to the protocol.

3.2 Features

By integrating a large selection of WATs in a single platform, TEASPN makes them available to writers at their fingertips and is expected to improve writing effectiveness. Table 1 shows the list of WATs that are supported by TEASPN. Notice that the list includes a wide range of WATs that have been extensively investigated the literature (e.g., GEC and search) as well as the ones that are less explored (e.g., syntax highlighting and jump).

Although we were able to build many WAT features upon existing ones from LSP, there were two features that we needed to design from scratch specifically for TEASPN—syntax highlighting and search. While syntax highlighting is usually handled on the client side for programming languages using shallow lexical analysis, syntactic analyses of natural language can be too costly and complex to be handled solely by the client. Therefore, we defined a new type of request and related type declarations so that it can be handled by the server.

The second feature, search, enables writers to search external linguistic resources. While the search feature for LSP is limited to the files in the same workspace, writers of natural language texts often need to consult a wide variety of resources such as corpora and dictionaries.

Feature	Description
Syntax highlighting	Highlighting parts of text
Grammatical error detection (GED)	Detecting typological and grammatical errors
Grammatical error correction (GEC)	Automatically correcting issues detected by GED
Completion	Completing or suggest succeeding text
Text rewriting	Rewriting part of text (paraphrasing, translation, etc.)
Jump	Jumping to other locations (coreference, definitions, etc.)
Hover	Showing extra information about the location (e.g., definition)
Search	Searching external resources such as corpora and dictionaries

Table 1: WATs supported by TEASPN.

3.3 Developers of Writing Software

By adopting TEASPN, developers of writing software can easily integrate WATs into their editors and word processors. The fact that a large number of IDEs and editors already support LSP helps to a great extent. For example, in the sample TEASPN client implementation[7] we provide for VS Code, we needed to modify less than 200 lines of Type-Script code to make it compatible with the TEASPN protocol while leveraging the existing library for LSP. We were also able to implement preliminary TEASPN clients for Atom and Sublime text[8] with little modification to existing code.

3.4 Developers of WATs

Developers and researchers of WATs can make their technologies available to major writing software just by using TEASPN without writing any client code. To facilitate the development process, we released the TEASPN SDK, which includes a library and a sample TEASPN server implementation in Python, one of the most popular programming languages for developing language technologies as of late. The library takes care of low-level communication and text synchronization with the client, letting WAT developers just inherit the TEASPN handler base class and focus on implementing the missing core NLP logic. As an example, Figure 3 shows a simplified code snippet for implementing completion. Notice the brevity of the code. We also provide a simple yet working TEASPN server implementation in the SDK for reference to accelerate the development.

4 Experiments and Implementation

4.1 Experiments

In this section, we develop a demo TEASPN system and investigate its effectiveness through ex-

```
@overrides
def get_completion_list(
        self, position: Position) -> CompletionList:
    """Handle autocomplete."""
    offset = self._position_to_offset(position)
    context = self._text[:offset]

    items = []
    # ... add completion items ...
    return CompletionList(isIncomplete=True, items=items)
```

Figure 3: Code snippet for computing completion

periments with end-users (writers) in order to answer the following research question:

Does the integrated writing assistance environment developed with TEASPN provide better writing experience and help write better texts?

To explore the effectiveness of integrated writing assistance environment, we compared the following two conditions. In the **INTEGRATED** condition, participants used an editor (VS Code) equipped with TEASPN, where many WATs were available, while in the **BASELINE** condition, they used the same editor with no WATs activated, while being allowed to use any other writing tools outside the editor (e.g., Grammarly and Web dictionaries). The BASELINE condition was set up to simulate the real situation that writers face, where writing assisting technologies are implemented separately outside the editor.

The participants of our experiments consist of twelve college students or researchers in NLP with a diverse L1 distribution: Bengali: 1, Chinese: 1, Croatian: 1, German: 1, Hindi: 1, Japanese: 6, Spanish: 1. They were directed to go through two writing sessions, one for each condition mentioned above, during which they wrote English text within five sentences in response to two different prompts: (i) *write about an activity you enjoy, such as a hobby*, and (ii) *write about your hometown*. The prompts and the writing environments were combined randomly. Before the writing sessions came an instruction session, where

---

[7] https://github.com/teaspn/teaspn-sdk
[8] https://www.sublimetext.com/

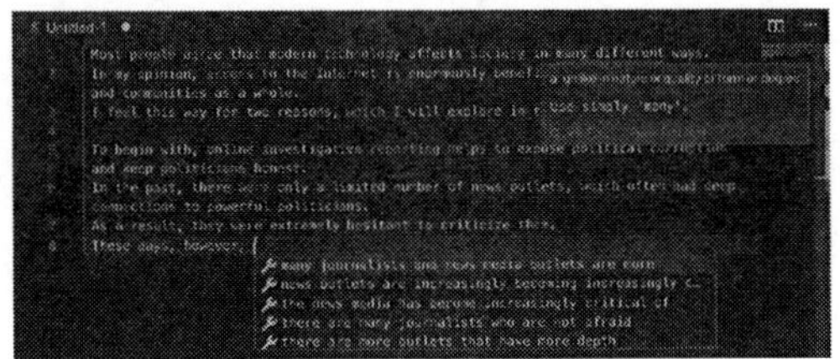

Figure 4: Screenshot of our demo system.

the authors of this paper showed the participants all the features of the demo system for a demonstration purpose. After the writing sessions, they were asked questions regarding their writing experience. Because the focus of this experiment is to evaluate the integrated writing assistance environment, participants are instructed not to consider the performance of individual WATs.

4.2 Implementation of the Demo System

We implemented a demo system using the TEASPN framework which has all of the features shown in Table 1. See Figure 4 for the screenshot.

For syntax highlighting, we used the dependency parser SpaCy[9]. Head tokens with specific dependency relation[10] were highlighted in different colors. As for the GEC and GED features, we used the open-source GEC tool LanguageTool 3.2[11]. We implemented two types of completion features: one which suggests the likely next phrases given the context using a neural language model (Radford et al., 2019) and the other one which suggests a set of words consistent with the characters being typed. We built a seq2seq paraphrase model trained on PARANMT-50M (Wieting and Gimpel, 2018) for the text rewriting feature, which allows the writer to select a part of the text and chooses among paraphrases. As for the jump feature, we used a coreference resolution model[12] to jump from a selected expression to its antecedent. The hover feature shows the definition of a hovered word using WordNet[13]. Finally, we implemented a full-text search feature using the open multilingual sentence dataset Tatoeba[14] and used Elasticsearch 7.1.1[15] for indexing and search.

---

[9]https://spacy.io/

[10]ROOT, nsubj, nsubjpass, and dobj in the CLEAR style tag set.

[11]https://github.com/languagetool-org/languagetool/releases/tag/v3.2

[12]https://github.com/huggingface/neuralcoref

[13]https://wordnet.princeton.edu/

[14]https://tatoeba.org/eng/

[15]https://www.elastic.co

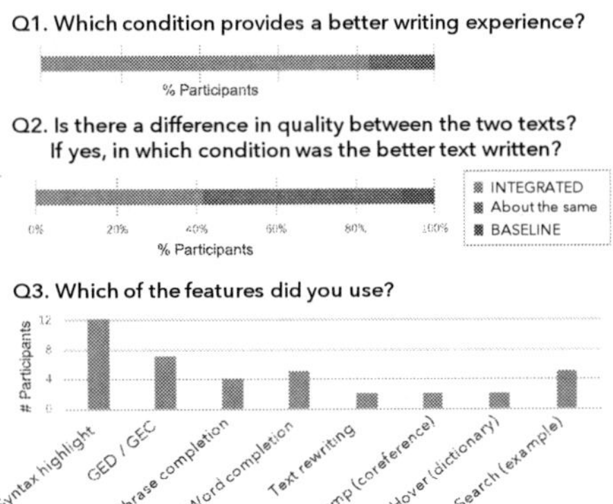

Figure 5: Response summary of the questionnaire.

Condition	Perplexity	# Chars. (mean ± std)
BASELINE	37.8	379 ± 116
INTEGRATED	26.4	335 ± 91

Table 2: Statistics of the written texts.

5 Results and Analysis

After the writing sessions, the participants responded to a questionnaire including the following questions: *Q1: Which environment provides a better writing experience?*, *Q2: Is there a difference in quality between the two texts? If yes, in which environment was the better text written?*, and *Q3: Which of the following features did you use?*

Figure 5 summarizes the responses from the participants. Ten out of twelve (83.3%) participants rated their experience favorably (Q1), and 40% believed they were able to write better texts in the INTEGRATED condition (Q2), demonstrating the effectiveness of the integrated writing assistance environment with TEASPN. The responses for Q3 show that an average participant used 3.2 WAT features in the INTEGRATED condition[16]. This suggests that the writers can benefit from an integrated environment with various WATs activated.

We ran further analyses on the texts written by the participants during the writing sessions. Table 2 shows some statistics of the written texts in the two experimental conditions. Perplexity was calculated using the pretrained GPT-2 model (small, 117M parameters) (Radford et al., 2019). The texts written in the INTEGRATED condition had lower perplexity, suggesting that the integrated writing environment helped them write

---

[16]Note that we assume that every participant used syntax highlighting, which is activated by default.

more fluent and/or typical English text. This result backs up the subjective responses from the participants indicating they were able to produce better texts in the INTEGRATED condition than the other. We also note that the texts written in the INTEGRATED condition were relatively shorter. This could be due to the fact that the participants were still spending some of their time observing and figuring out the behavior of the assisting features and spending slightly less time actually writing. We believe this trend will disappear or even reverse itself as they get more used to the integrated writing experience and the quality of the inidividual WATs improve.

6 Conclusion and Future Work

We proposed TEASPN, a framework and a protocol which standardizes the way writing software communicates with writing assistance technologies, to achieve integrated writing assistance environments. In addition, we released the TEASPN SDK as an open source library, which eases the cost of making WATs compatible with TEASPN. We developed a demo system which implements various assistance technologies based on latest NLP developments and ran experiments with human participants. The result demonstrated that they rated their integrated writing experience favorably, potentially helping them write more fluent and better text.

In future work, by making this a larger community effort, we wish to broaden the support lineup for writing software while developing various writing assistance features with TEASPN, further closing the gap between the latest developments in NLP and real-world human users.

References

Jim Chang and Jason Chang. 2015. WriteAhead2: Mining lexical grammar patterns for assisted writing. In *Proceedings of the NAACL 2015 System Demonstrations*, pages 106–110.

Mei-Hua Chen, Shih-Ting Huang, Hung-Ting Hsieh, Ting-Hui Kao, and Jason S. Chang. 2012. FLOW: A first-language-oriented writing assistant system. In *Proceedings of ACL 2012 System Demonstrations*, pages 157–162.

Mia Xu Chen, Benjamin N Lee, Gagan Bansal, Yuan Cao, Shuyuan Zhang, Justin Lu, Jackie Tsay, Yinan Wang, Andrew M. Dai, Zhifeng Chen, Timothy Sohn, and Yonghui Wu. 2019. Gmail smart compose: Real-time assisted writing.

Anne Vandeventer Faltin. 2003. Natural language processing tools for computer assisted language learning. *Linguistik Online*, 17(5):137–153.

Maarten van Gompel, Iris Hendrickx, Antal van den Bosch, Els Lefever, and Véronique Hoste. 2014. SemEval 2014 task 5 - L2 writing assistant. In *Proceedings of SemEval 2014*, pages 36–44.

Sebastian Hellmann, Jens Lehmann, and Soren Auer. 2012. NIF: An ontology-based and linked-data-aware NLP interchange format. Technical report, Working Draft.

Toru Ishida. 2006. Language Grid: An infrastructure for intercultural collaboration. In *IEEE/IPSJ Symposium on Applications and the Internet (SAINT 2006)*, pages 96–100.

Anjuli Kannan, Karol Kurach, Sujith Ravi, Tobias Kaufmann, Andrew Tomkins, Balint Miklos, Gregory S. Corrado, László Lukács, Marina Ganea, Peter Young, and Vivek Ramavajjala. 2016. Smart reply: Automated response suggestion for email. In *Proceedings of KDD 2016*.

Philippe Langlais, George Foster, and Guy Lapalme. 2000. TransType: a computer-aided translation typing system. In *ANLP-NAACL 2000 Workshop: Embedded Machine Translation Systems*.

Claudia Leacock, Martin Chodorow, Michael Gamon, and Joel Tetreault. 2010. *Automated Grammatical Error Detection for Language Learners*. Morgan & Claypool.

Alec Radford, Jeffrey Wu, Rewon Child, David Luan, Dario Amodei, and Ilya Sutskever. 2019. Language models are unsupervised multitask learners. Technical report, OpenAI.

Hubert Soyer, Goran Topić, Pontus Stenetorp, and Akiko Aizawa. 2015. CroVeWA: Crosslingual vector-based writing assistance. In *Proceedings of NAACL 2015 System Demonstrations*, pages 91–95, Denver, Colorado.

Irena Srdanović. 2011. Evaluating e-resources for Japanese language learning. In *Proceedings of eLex 2011*, pages 260–267.

Kiri Wagstaff. 2012. Machine learning that matters. In *Proceedings of the Twenty-Ninth International Conference on Machine Learning (ICML)*, pages 529–536.

John Wieting and Kevin Gimpel. 2018. ParaNMT-50M: Pushing the limits of paraphrastic sentence embeddings with millions of machine translations. In *Proceedings of ACL 2018*, pages 451–462.

Tzu-Hsi Yen, Jian-Cheng Wu, Jim Chang, Joanne Boisson, and Jason Chang. 2015. WriteAhead: Mining grammar patterns in corpora for assisted writing. In *Proceedings of ACL-IJCNLP 2015 System Demonstrations*, pages 139–144.

TellMeWhy: Learning to Explain Corrective Feedback for Second Language Learners

Yi-Huei Lai, Jason Chang
National Tsing Hua University, Hsinchu, Taiwan
`{yima, jason}@nlplab.cc`

Abstract

We present a writing prototype feedback system, *TellMeWhy*, to provide explanations of errors in submitted essays. In our approach, the sentence with corrections is analyzed to identify error types and problem words, aimed at customizing explanations based on the context of the error. The method involves learning the relation of errors and problem words, generating common feedback patterns, and extracting grammar patterns, collocations and example sentences. At run-time, a sentence with corrections is classified, and the problem word and template are identified to provide detailed explanations. Preliminary evaluation shows that the method has potential to improve existing commercial writing services.

1 Introduction

Many English essays and sentences with grammatical errors (e.g., 'We discussed about the issue.') are submitted by L2 learners to writing services every day, and an increasing number of online grammar checkers specifically target learners' essays. For example, *Write & Improve* (`writeandimprove.com`) pinpoints an error without explaining the correction. *Grammarly* (`www.grammarly.com`) corrects grammatical errors and provides context-insensitive examples using pre-compiled information.

Writing services such as *Write & Improve* and *Grammarly* typically use canned text to explain a common error. However, corrective feedback with the most useful and comprehensive explanations may contain collocations, grammar, and context-sensitive examples. These systems could provide better explanations to the user, if the context of the correction is taken into consideration.

Consider the sentence '*We discussed about the issue.*' The best explanation for the error is probably not (1) and (2) which only state the obvious

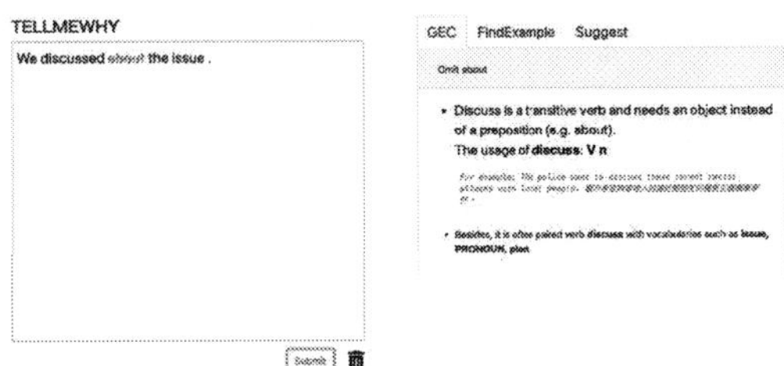

Figure 1: Example **TellMeWhy-GEC** for the error 'We discussed about the issue.'

(i.e. editing operations for a correction), but rather (3) which explains using the grammar patterns of the problem word (i.e., *discuss*) with a simple example.

(1) This word *about* may not be needed. Is your writing clearer without it? (from *Write & Improve*)
(2) The preposition seems unnecessary after the verb discussed. Consider removing the preposition. (from *Grammarly*)

Examples:

✗ The government advocated to recycling.

✓ The government advocated recycling.

(3) **discuss sth** (WITHOUT **about/on**): 'He simply refuses to discuss the matter.'

Compare **talk about, a discussion about/on**: 'They want to talk about what to do next.' (from *Longman Common Error Dictionary (Turton and Heaton, 1996)*)

We present a prototype system, *TellMeWhy*, with three functions: *GEC* (in Figure 1), *FindExample*, and *Suggest*. *Suggest* displays statistical data of erroneous and corrected usage to explain correctness; *GEC* and *FindExample* explain corrections using linguistic characteristics. With an underlying grammatical error correction (GEC) system, we will provide feedback based on the correction made by the GEC. However, if the GEC system can not detect an error, our explanation module cannot be activated. For this, *FindExample* can search for a sentence with correction edits

Proceedings of the 2019 EMNLP and the 9th IJCNLP (System Demonstrations), pages 235–240
Hong Kong, China, November 3 – 7, 2019. ©2019 Association for Computational Linguistics

and display explanations so *TellMeWhy* will not being limited by the underlying GEC system.

At run-time, *TellMeWhy* starts with a given sentence, potentially with corrections made by the underlying GEC system or submitted to *FindExample*. *TellMeWhy* then generates feedback after identifying error types, problem words, and linguistic information as described in Section 3.1. We develop explanation templates based on hand-crafted training data. In our prototype, *TellMeWhy* returns the feedback to the end user directly (Figure 1); also, the feedback can be shown to a human rater in order to assist them in rating essays.

2 Related Work

Corrective feedback on learners' writing has been an area of active research. Recently, the state-of-the-art in the research has been represented in Leacock et al. (2010) involving many automated approaches to detect a wide range of error types.

To generate explanations, most writing services adopt the approach of canned text with table lookup schemes (Andersen et al., 2013). This approach, despite providing basic explanations, is not optimal, because canned feedback tends to be superficial and context-insensitive. Additionally, canned feedback is limited to common grammatical errors, without covering lexical error types, such as word-choice errors.

Providing corrective feedback and explaining how the correction improves grammaticality and adheres to idiomatic principles (Sinclair, 1991) have long been an important research area in Teaching English as Second Language (TESOL). Bitchener et al. (2005) concluded that proper error feedback is significant in improving English writing. In this work, we focus on identifying the problem-causing word and providing a comprehensive and context-sensitive explanation based on the problem word.

In a study more closely related to our work, Nicholls (2003) describes an error coding scheme for lexicography and English Language Teaching (ELT) research based on a Cambridge Learner Corpus. Turton and Heaton (1996) compiled examples of common errors organized by problem words based on Longman Learners' Corpus. Chen et al. (2017) describes methods for providing explanations based on grammar patterns.

We used the data in Turton and Heaton (1996) as the main source of training data and adopted

(1) Classifying the error type
(2) Extracting grammar patterns, collocations as well as examples and definitions
(3) Calculating co-occurrence frequency of pairs of an edit and neighboring words
(4) Building explanation templates based on hand-crafted training data

Figure 2: Outline of the process used to train the *TellMeWhy* system

the explaining strategy proposed by Chen et al. (2017). The main difference between our work and Chen et al. (2017) is that Chen et al. (2017) provided limited error types with grammar patterns as explanation, while our method provides context-sensitive explanations of more error types.

In contrast to the existing systems on corrective feedback, *TellMeWhy* provides comprehensive explanations for multiple error types with an underlying GEC system. Additionally, to provide good explanations, a promising approach is to automatically classify the error and extract a problem word nearby to tailor the explanation to the context of the error.

3 The *TellMeWhy* System

We focus on providing comprehensive feedback on a given English sentence with corrections. The feedback is returned as an output to the end user directly. It is important to detect the potential problem-causing word and classify the error. Our goal is returning a context-sensitive explanation using the problem word and the error type to instantiate suitable explanation template and fetch reference linguistic information.

3.1 Learning to Provide Feedback

We attempt to learn to generate an informative and comprehensive explanation that matches the error and context (in particular, the problem word). Our learning process is shown in Figure 2.

In the first stage of the learning process (Step (1) in Figure 2), we analyze sentences with a correction annotated with a problem-causing word which is a word regularly causing the specific error. As we will describe in Section 3.1, we use Turton and Heaton (1996) for training. Based on an existing method, ERRANT (Bryant et al., 2017), we analyze differences between a sentence containing an error and a corrected sentence. Then we produce an error type including an edit type (insert, delete, and replace) and PoS of the edit

Table 1: top 10 error codes

Code	Gloss	Samples Sentence
1. SP	Spelling	[-Fortunaly-]{+Fortunately+}, the police found her.
2. RV	Replace v.	How to [-make-]{+create+} a better hairstyle.
3. RT	Replace prep.	We should invest more money [-to-]{+in+} education.
4. MD	Missing det.	School finishes at five in {+the+} afternoon.
5. R	Replace w.	Some people tried to enter without [-any-]{+a+} ticket.
6. RN	Replace n.	Television provides many [-advantages-]{+benefits+}.
7. FV	Form v.	The problems have been [-arised-]{+arisen+} due to overpopulation.
8. MT	Missing prep.	He apologized {+to+} her for the long delay.
9. UD	Useless det.	I have work to do. I don't have [-a-] time for anything else.
10. UT	Useless prep.	We discussed [-about-] the issue.

---

(1) Generating a set of phrase templates in the form
of PoS tags

(2) Extracting grammar patterns for all keywords
in the given corpus annotated by PoS based on
phrase templates

(3) Extracting exemplary instances for all patterns of
all keywords

Figure 3: Outline of the pattern extraction process

(e.g., *(DEL, PREP, about)*). For simplicity, we limit ourselves to Top *10* most common error types (in Table 1) in CLE-FCE (Yannakoudakis et al., 2011) and associated error types (i.e., extending error types from Top *10*, such as from replacing a word, to deleting a word or missing a word) to derive explanation templates. To sum up, we limit ourselves to provide explanation for error types related to editing a verb, adjective, noun, prepositions and function words (e.g., articles).

In the second stage of the learning algorithm (Step (2) in Figure 2), we extract reference information. First, we extract grammar patterns from Corpus of Contemporary American English (*COCA*[1]) using an existing method (in Figure 3) described in Chang and Chang (2015). Subsequently, we store examples corresponded to a keyword's grammar patterns (e.g., (discuss, V n): issue, topic, matters). Next, we build a collocation dictionary with dependency relation information using triples (e.g., (eat, V:obj:N, bananas)). The relation (e.g., V:obj:N) is produced by a dependency parser using *COCA*. Finally, we store definitions in *Online Cambridge Dictionary* to explain word-choice errors (e.g., 'accept' education). Additionally, *Online Cambridge Dictionary* gives a pair of English-Chinese definition and a guide word (e.g., TAKE, APPROVE) for each sense of a polysemous word (e.g., accept). The guide words are instrumental for us to find the closest sense between erroneous and correction words.

In the third stage of the learning algorithm (Step (3) in Figure 2), we calculate co-occurrence frequency of pairs of an edit and neighboring

---

(1) Generating skipped bigrams from a large corpus
and storing corresponded distance

(2) Filtering the collocates

(3) Filtering the distances for each collocates

Figure 4: Outline of the Smadja's process

---

words using the EF-Cambridge Open Language Database *EFCAMDAT* (Geertzen et al. (2013) and Huang et al. (2018)). Then, we use the method proposed by Smadja (1993) (in Figure 4) to calculate co-occurrence frequency of pairs of an edit and neighboring words with the goal of selecting the most potential neighboring word triggering the edit. In other words, we assume the problem-causing word as a collocate of the edit.

In the fourth and final stage of training (Step (4) in Figure 2), we formulate a feedback template for each error type, classified by *ERRANT*. For each error type, we observe and exploit the consistent patterns of feedback in Turton and Heaton (1996) to design the templates. For example, we formulate an explanation template for unnecessary preposition error with three components: problem word, grammar pattern, and example. An example feedback template is shown in Table 2. After inferencing from explanation instances of each error type, we develop type-specific templates with slots to be filled with specific information: problem words along with a grammar pattern, collocations and examples.

3.2 Run-Time Feedback

Once feedback templates have been designed and reference information for problem words has been extracted, they are stored in tables.

At run-time, users submit an essay possibly with some errors (e.g., *We discussed about the issue*). The underlying GEC system corrects the essay with edits (e.g., We discussed [-about-] the issue). Next, *TellMeWhy* determines the error type (e.g., *(DEL,PREP,about)*) and the problem word (e.g., discussed). We then produce as follows.

First, we handle corrections in the input sentence one by one. We correct an input sentence with multiple corrections to be only one correction edit temporally and iteratively. After recording the correction information (e.g., the editing type, erroneous and correction word), we also correct the only one correction because correction tags could influence a tagger to tag each word with PoS. Annotated the input sentence with PoS, we could ex-

---

[1]www.english-corpora.org/coca

Table 2: Sample correction-feedback pairs from the training collection

Problem Word	Sentence and Feedback	Analysis
discuss	✗ They would like to discuss about what to do next. ✓ They would like to discuss what to do next.	$pw = 'discuss' $edits = (DEL, PREP, about)
	discuss sth (WITHOUT **about/on**): He simply refuses to discuss the matter. There is nothing to discuss.	$gp = V n
Template	**feedback**($pw,$gp,$edits) = $pw $gp (WITHOUT $edits[2]): $example($pw,$gp)	

1 $gp denotes a grammar pattern.
2 $pw denotes a problem-trigger word.
3 $example denotes an example consisting a grammar pattern based on a problem word.

Table 3: Template for Replace a Preposition

Problem Word	Sentence and Feedback	Analysis
arm	✗ She would not stop crying until I held her on my arms. ✓ She would not stop crying until I held her in my arms.	$pw = arm $edits = (RP, PREP, on, in)
	(hold sb/sth) in your arms (NOT on): He had a great pile of books in his arms.	$gp = in N
Template	**feedback**($pw,$gp,$edits) = $gp (NOT $edits[2]): $example($pw,$gp)	

tract grammar patterns in the input sentence covering correction using the method in Figure 3.

Next, to make feedback relevant to the context, we identify the most potential problem verb, noun or adjective through the highest co-occurrence frequency of the correction and potential problem words. The problem word is then used to instantiate the explanation template and fetch reference information of grammar patterns, collocations, examples, and problem word definitions.

4 Experiment and Evaluation

TellMeWhy was designed to generate explanations containing grammar, definitions, collocations, and examples. Thus, *TellMeWhy* was trained by using the *Longman Dictionary Of Common Errors* (Turton and Heaton, 1996) as the main source of knowledge. In this section, we first present the details of training. Next, we describe common error types tested. Finally, we introduce feedback strategy and evaluate the experimental results.

4.1 Training *TellMeWhy*

We used 70% of common errors and explanations in Turton and Heaton (1996) to train *TellMeWhy*. Turton and Heaton (1996) contains a collection of approximately 2,500 common errors and explanations. Table 2 shows one sample correction-explanation pairs with a problem word and an explanation template. Additionally, we used *EF-CAMDAT*, a corpus of real learners' writings with edits by human graders and containing over 83 million words from 1 million essays written by 174,000 learners, to compute co-occurrence frequency of edits and problem words.

By analyzing a sentence with errors and their correction pairs, we produced error types including three edits: *replace*, *insert*, and *delete*, and PoS of the erroneous and correction words. We found that explaining strategies are highly related to error type. Therefore, we customized explaining strategies for each error type.

For errors related to replacing a preposition. First, we use a template (in Table 3) that shows the grammar patterns of the problem-causing word. The potential problem words are the closest noun, verb, or adjective to the erroneous preposition such as 'held' and 'arms'. We detected grammar patterns (in Figure 3) for each potential problem word (e.g., hold: V in n, arm: in N). The most relevant grammar pattern is selected by highest co-occurrence frequency of a problem word and the edit calculated in advance using *EFCAMDAT* through the method proposed by Smadja (1993). Then, we ranked collocations of an edit-problem-word pair (e.g., ([-on-]{+in+}, arm), (hold, [-on-]{+in+})) by highest co-occurrence frequency of a problem word and the edit.

As for errors related to replacing function words (e.g., articles and demonstratives), which form a closed set, we exploited feedback in Turton and Heaton (1996) and rules in Cobuild et al. (2005). Nevertheless, determiner errors related to time (e.g., in 'the' morning and at night) are difficult to handle using general determiner rules. In that case, we followed Turton and Heaton (1996) time-specific rules.

With respect to cases of replacing open-class words (i.e., verb, noun, and adjective), we handled the errors by cases: (1) spelling, (2) tense,

Table 4: Template for Replacing a Word

Problem Word	Sentence and Feedback	Analysis
abandon	✗ Since capital punishment was abandoned, the crime rate has increased. ✓ Since capital punishment was abolished, the crime rate has increased.	\$pw = abandon \$edits = (RP, VERB, abandon, abolish)
	abandon = give up a **plan, activity** or attempt to do something, without being successful: Bad weather forced them to abandon the search. Without government support, the project will have to be abandoned.	\$col[0] = [plan, activity]
Template	**feedback**(\$edits,\$col) = \$edits[2] = \$def(\$edits[2]) and usually paired with \$col[0] : \$example(\$edits[2]) \$edits[3] = \$def(\$edits[3]) and usually paired with \$col[1] : \$example(\$edits[3])	

[1] \$def denotes a definition of a word.
[2] \$col denotes a collocation of \$pw

Table 5: Scores (0-2) for explanations on top 10 error codes, generated by four systems: *TellMeWhy-GEC* (TMW-GEC),*TellMeWhy-FindExample* (TMW-FE) *Grammarly* (GL) and *Write & Improve* (W&I)

Code	Gloss	TMW-GEC	TMW-FE	GL	W&I
1. SP	Spelling	2	2	2	2
2. RV	Replace v.		1.3		
3. RT	Replace prep.	2	1.8	1	1
4. MD	Missing det.	2	1.8	1	1
5. R	Replace w.	1.67	1.8	1.71	1
6. RN	Replace n.		1.6		1
7. FV	Form v.	0.8	1	1.4	1
8. MT	Missing prep.	2	1.6	0.83	
9. UD	Useless det.	1	0.9	2	1
10. UT	Useless prep.	1.67	1.5	1	1
	Average score	1.64	1.53	1.37	1.13

Table 6: The number of testcases can be corrected by three systems: *TellMeWhy-GEC* (TMW-GEC), *Grammarly* (GL) and *Write & Improve* (W&I)

Code	Gloss	TMW-GEC	GL	W&I
1. SP	Spelling	10	10	10
2. RV	Replace v.	0	0	0
3. RT	Replace prep.	4	6	1
4. MD	Missing det.	5	6	1
5. R	Replace w.	6	7	5
6. RN	Replace n.	0	0	1
7. FV	Form v.	7	8	3
8. MT	Missing prep.	4	6	0
9. UD	Useless det.	7	9	3
10. UT	Useless prep.	9	8	3

(3) word choice errors. Spelling and tense errors associate with morphological variation and could be detected directly and explained easily as such.

A word-choice example pair of correction and feedback from Turton and Heaton (1996) is shown in Table 4. From this, we found word choice mistake is often made because users do not understand the definition of erroneous and corrected words very well. With this in mind, we first used the definitions from *Online Cambridge Dictionary* for the erroneous and corrected words (e.g., 'abandon' vs 'abolish'). To determine the contextually appropriate senses for polysemous words, we replaced erroneous and corrected words with all possible guide words (e.g., 'abandon': leave, stop; 'abolish': abolish) in *Online Cambridge Dictionary*. Second, we calculated cosine similarity between pairs of error-correction (e.g., leave-abolish and stop-abolish) using *Word2vec*. We choose the pair of senses with the highest cosine similarity to display definitions. Additionally, word-choice errors could be caused by miscollocation. We also provided related collocations with frequency to explain why the correction word is more appropriate.

4.2 Evaluation

Once we have trained *TellMeWhy* as described, we evaluated the performance using ten randomly-selected sentences for each top 10 common error type. We also evaluated problem word detection performance using Turton and Heaton (1996).

Two functions in our systems are used to evaluate explanations: *TellMeWhy-GEC* and *TellMeWhy-FindExample*. The former has an underlying GEC system. The latter is a writing examples search engine so that users can submit a sentence with known correction edits to understand why the edit makes sense; additionally, we can evaluate performance without being limited by the underlying GEC system.

One evaluation of comparison between *TellMeWhy* and other commercial systems is shown in Table 5 was evaluated by ten sentences for each error type and carried out by a linguist. A wrong explanation (such as a wrong problem word, inappropriate corrective feedback) gets zero point, while a correct explanation (i.e., identifying the problem word correctly but providing context-insensitive examples) gets one point. Explanations related to a problem word and context receive two points. However, the score of feedback on errors that *TellMeWhy-GEC*, *Grammarly*, and *Write & Improve* cannot detect does not count into the average score; besides, the correction performance of each system is shown in Table 6. The evaluation results show that *TellMeWhy* is considerably better than the existing services and able to explain more error types, such as word-choice and collocation errors, and provides context-sensitive information.

The other evaluation is the performance of problem word identification. We evaluated problem word identification using Turton and Heaton (1996) containing approximately 2,500 edit-feedback pairs. We evaluated *TellMeWhy* using the rest 30% of the dataset (i.e., 750 edit-feedback pairs). Additionally, we limited ourselves to evaluate for *Top 10* error types and extension types defined in the first stage of Section 3.1. Those types of test data account for 616 editing sentences out of 750 edit-feedback pairs. For our evaluation, we treated *keywords* organized by Turton and Heaton (1996) as ground truth. The accuracy of problem word identification is approximately 80% (493/616).

5 Future Work and Summary

In this paper, we have described a system for learning to provide corrective feedback on English sentences with corrections. The method involves classifying errors into different error types, identifying potential problem words, selecting closest senses between misuse and corrected words, and extracting collocations as well as grammar patterns. We have implemented and evaluated the method as applied to real sentences. In preliminary evaluation, we have shown that the method outperforms the existing commercial systems for many error types, especially an error triggered by a verb or adjective.

Many avenues exist for future research and improvement of our system. For example, we could extend our method to handle more error types, such as sentence patterns (e.g., One ... Another ... The other, so ... that). Collocation knowledge and selectional preference could be used to improve the explanation of word-choice error types so that explanations may contain word concepts collocating with a problem word. Additionally, better methods such as learning-based approach to identifying problem words could be implemented.

References

Øistein E Andersen, Helen Yannakoudakis, Fiona Barker, and Tim Parish. 2013. Developing and testing a self-assessment and tutoring system. In *Proceedings of the eighth workshop on innovative use of NLP for building educational applications*, pages 32–41.

John Bitchener, Stuart Young, and Denise Cameron. 2005. The effect of different types of corrective feedback on esl student writing. *Journal of second language writing*, 14(3):191–205.

Christopher Bryant, Mariano Felice, and Ted Briscoe. 2017. Automatic annotation and evaluation of error types for grammatical error correction. In *Proceedings of the 55th Annual Meeting of the Association for Computational Linguistics (Volume 1: Long Papers)*, volume 1, pages 793–805.

Jim Chang and Jason Chang. 2015. Writeahead2: Mining lexical grammar patterns for assisted writing. In *Proceedings of the 2015 Conference of the North American Chapter of the Association for Computational Linguistics: Demonstrations*, pages 106–110.

Jhih-Jie Chen, Jim Chang, Ching-Yu Yang, Mei-Hua Chen, and Jason S Chang. 2017. Extracting formulaic expressions and grammar and edit patterns to assist academic writing. *EUROPHRAS 2017: Computational and Corpus-based Phraseology: Recent Advances and Interdisciplinary Approaches*.

Collins Cobuild et al. 2005. *Collins Cobuild English Grammar*. Collins Cobuild.

Jeroen Geertzen, Theodora Alexopoulou, and Anna Korhonen. 2013. Automatic linguistic annotation of large scale l2 databases: The ef-cambridge open language database (efcamdat). In *Proceedings of the 31st Second Language Research Forum. Somerville, MA: Cascadilla Proceedings Project*.

Yan Huang, Akira Murakami, Theodora Alexopoulou, and Anna Korhonen. 2018. Dependency parsing of learner english. *International Journal of Corpus Linguistics*, 23(1):28–54.

Claudia Leacock, Martin Chodorow, Michael Gamon, and Joel Tetreault. 2010. Automated grammatical error detection for language learners. *Synthesis lectures on human language technologies*, 3(1):1–134.

Diane Nicholls. 2003. The cambridge learner corpus: Error coding and analysis for lexicography and elt. In *Proceedings of the Corpus Linguistics 2003 conference*, volume 16, pages 572–581.

John Sinclair. 1991. *Corpus, concordance, collocation*. Oxford University Press.

Frank Smadja. 1993. Retrieving collocations from text: Xtract. *Computational linguistics*, 19(1):143–177.

ND Turton and JB Heaton. 1996. Longman dictionary of common errors. new edition.

Helen Yannakoudakis, Ted Briscoe, and Ben Medlock. 2011. A new dataset and method for automatically grading esol texts. In *Proceedings of the 49th Annual Meeting of the Association for Computational Linguistics: Human Language Technologies-Volume 1*, pages 180–189. Association for Computational Linguistics.

UER: An Open-Source Toolkit for Pre-training Models

Zhe Zhao[1,2,♠]   Hui Chen[2,♣]   Jinbin Zhang[2,♣]   Xin Zhao[1,♠]   Tao Liu[1,♠]
Wei Lu[1,♠]   Xi Chen[3,♦]   Haotang Deng[2,♣]   Qi Ju[2,♣,*]   Xiaoyong Du[1,♠]

[1] School of Information and DEKE, MOE, Renmin University of China, Beijing, China
[2] Tencent AI Lab
[3] School of Electronics Engineering and Computer Science, Peking University, Beijing, China
♠{helloworld, zhaoxinruc, tliu, lu-wei, duyong}@ruc.edu.cn
♣{chenhuichen, westonzhang, haotangdeng, damonju}@tencent.com
♦{mrcx}@pku.edu.cn

Abstract

Existing works, including ELMO and BERT, have revealed the importance of pre-training for NLP tasks. While there does not exist a single pre-training model that works best in all cases, it is of necessity to develop a framework that is able to deploy various pre-training models efficiently. For this purpose, we propose an assemble-on-demand pre-training toolkit, namely Universal Encoder Representations (UER). UER is loosely coupled, and encapsulated with rich modules. By assembling modules on demand, users can either reproduce a state-of-the-art pre-training model or develop a pre-training model that remains unexplored. With UER, we have built a model zoo, which contains pre-trained models based on different corpora, encoders, and targets (objectives). With proper pre-trained models, we could achieve new state-of-the-art results on a range of downstream datasets.

1 Introduction

Pre-training has been well recognized as an essential step for NLP tasks since it results in remarkable improvements on a range of downstream datasets (Devlin et al., 2018). Instead of training models on a specific task from scratch, pre-training models are firstly trained on general-domain corpora, then followed by fine-tuning on downstream tasks. Thus far, a large number of works have been proposed for finding better pre-training models. Existing pre-training models mainly differ in the following three aspects:

1) Model encoder.

Commonly-used encoders include RNN (Hochreiter and Schmidhuber, 1997), CNN (Kim, 2014), AttentionNN (Bahdanau et al., 2014), and their combinations (Zhou et al., 2016). Recently,

Transformer (a structure based on attentionNN) is shown to be a more powerful feature extractor compared with other encoders (Vaswani et al., 2017).

2) Pre-training target (objective).

Using proper target is one of the keys to the success of pre-training. While the language model is most commonly used (Radford et al., 2018), many works focus on seeking better targets such as masked language model (cloze test) (Devlin et al., 2018) and machine translation (McCann et al., 2017).

3) Fine-tuning strategy.

Using a proper fine-tuning strategy is also important to the performance of pre-training models on downstream tasks. A commonly-used strategy is to regard pre-trained models as feature extractors (Kiros et al., 2015).

Table 1 lists 8 popular pre-training models and their main differences (Kiros et al., 2015; Logeswaran and Lee, 2018; McCann et al., 2017; Conneau et al., 2017; Peters et al., 2018; Howard and Ruder, 2018; Radford et al., 2018; Devlin et al., 2018). In additional to encoder, target, and fine-tuning strategy, corpus is also listed in Table 1 as an important factor for pre-training models.

There are many open-source implementations of pre-training models, such as Google BERT[1], ELMO from AllenAI[2], GPT and BERT from HuggingFace[3]. However, these works usually focus on the designs of either one or a few pre-training models. Due to the diversity of the downstream tasks and the computational resources constraint, there does not exist a single pre-training model that works best in all cases. BERT is one of the most widely used pre-training models. It exploits

---

* Corresponding author.

[1]https://github.com/google-research/bert
[2]https://github.com/allenai/bilm-tf
[3]https://github.com/huggingface

Proceedings of the 2019 EMNLP and the 9th IJCNLP (System Demonstrations), pages 241–246
Hong Kong, China, November 3 – 7, 2019. ©2019 Association for Computational Linguistics

Model	Corpus	Encoder	Target
Skip-thoughts	Bookcorpus	GRU	Conditioned LM
Quick-thoughts	Bookcorpus+UMBCcorpus	GRU	Sentence prediction
CoVe	English-German	Bi-LSTM	Machine translation
Infersent	Natural language inference	LSTM;GRU;CNN;LSTM+Attention	Classification
ELMO	1billion benchmark	Bi-LSTM	Language model
ULMFiT	Wikipedia	LSTM	Language model
GPT	Bookcorpus; 1billion benchmark	Transformer	Language model
BERT	Wikipedia+bookcorpus	Transformer	Cloze+sentence prediction

Table 1: 8 pre-training models and their differences. For space constraint of the table, fine-tuning strategies of different models are described as follows: Skip-thoughts, quick-thoughts, and infersent regard pre-trained models as feature extractors. The parameters before output layer are frozen. CoVe and ELMO transfer word embedding to downstream tasks, with other parameters in neural networks uninitialized. ULMFit, GPT, and BERT fine-tune entire networks on downstream tasks.

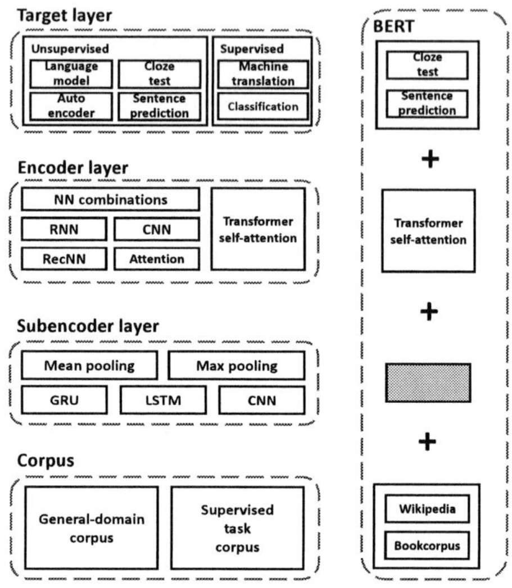

Figure 1: The architecture of UER (pre-training part). We can combine modules in UER to implement BERT model.

two unsupervised targets for pre-training. But in some scenarios, supervised information is critical to the performance of downstream tasks (Conneau et al., 2017; McCann et al., 2017). Besides, in many cases, BERT is excluded due to its efficiency issue. Based on above reasons, it is often the case that one should adopt different pre-training models in different application scenarios.

In this work, we introduce UER, a general framework that is able to facilitate the developments of various pre-training models. UER maintains model modularity and supports research extensibility. It consists of 4 components: subencoder, encoder, target, and downstream task fine-tuning. The architecture of UER (pre-training part) is shown in Figure 1. Ample modules are implemented in each component. Users could assemble different modules to implement existing models such as BERT (right part in Figure 1), or develop a new pre-training model by implementing customized modules. Clear and robust interfaces allow users to assemble (or add) modules with as few restrictions as possible.

With the help of UER, we build a Chinese pre-trained model zoo based on different corpora, encoders, and targets. Different datasets have their own characteristics. Selecting proper models from the model zoo can largely boost the performance of downstream datasets. In this work, we use Google BERT as baseline model. We provide some use cases that are based on UER, and the results show that our models can either achieve new state-of-the-art performance, or achieve competitive results with an efficient running speed.

UER is built on PyTorch and supports distributed training mode. Clear instructions and documentations are provided to help users read and use UER codes. The UER toolkit and the model zoo are publicly available at `https://github.com/dbiir/UER-py`.

2 Related Work

2.1 Pre-training for deep neural networks

Using word embedding to initialize neural network's first layer is one of the most commonly used strategies for NLP tasks (Mikolov et al., 2013; Kim, 2014). Inspired by the success of word embedding, some recent works try to initialize entire networks (not just first layer) with pre-trained parameters (Howard and Ruder, 2018; Radford et al., 2018). They train a deep neural network upon large corpus, and fine-tune the pre-trained model on specific downstream tasks. One of the most influential works among them is BERT (Devlin et al., 2018). BERT extracts text features with 12/24 Transformer layers, and exploits masked language model task and sentence prediction task as training targets (objectives). The drawback of BERT is that it requires expensive computational resources. Thankfully, Google makes its pre-trained models publicly available. So we can directly fine-tune on Google's models to achieve competitive results on many NLP tasks.

2.2 NLP toolkits

Many NLP models have tens of hyper-parameters and various tricks, and some of which exert large impacts on final performance. Sometimes it is unlikely to report all details and their effects in research paper. This may lead to a huge gap between research papers and code implementations. To solve the above problem, some works are proposed to implement a class of models in a framework. This type of work includes OpenNMT (Klein et al., 2017), fairseq (Ott et al., 2019) for neural machine translation; glyph (Zhang and Le-Cun, 2017) for classification; NCRF++ (Yang and Zhang, 2018) for sequence labeling; Hyperwords (Levy et al., 2015), ngram2vec (Zhao et al., 2017) for word embedding, to name a few.

Recently, we witness many influential pre-training works such as GPT, ULMFiT, and BERT. We think it could be useful to develop a framework to facilitate reproducing and refining those models. UER provides the flexibility of building pre-training models of different properties.

3 Architecture

In this section, we firstly introduce the core components in UER and the modules that we have implemented in each component. Figure 1 illustrates UER's framework and detailed modules (pre-training part). Modularity design of UER largely facilitates the use of pre-training models. At the end of this section, we will give some case studies to illustrate how to use UER effectively.

3.1 Subencoder

This layer learns word vectors from subword features. For English, we use character as subword features. For Chinese[4], we use radical and pinyin as subword features. As a result, the model can be aware of internal structures of words. Subword information has been explored in many NLP

tasks such as text classification (Zhang and Le-Cun, 2017) and word embedding (Joulin et al., 2016). In the pre-training literature, ELMO exploits subencoder layer. In UER, we implement RNN and CNN as subencoders, and use mean pooling or max pooling upon hidden states to obtain fixed-length word vectors.

3.2 Encoder

This layer learns features from word vectors. UER implements a series of basic encoders, including LSTM, GRU, CNN, GatedCNN, and AttentionNN. Users can use these basic encoders directly, or use their combinations. The output of an encoder can be fed into another encoder, forming networks of arbitrary layers. UER provides ample examples of combining basic encoders (e.g. CNN + LSTM). Users can also build their custom combinations with basic encoders in UER.

Currently, Transformer (a structure based on multi-headed self-attention) becomes a popular text feature extractor and is proven to be effective for many NLP tasks. We implement Transformer module and integrate it into UER. With Transformer module, we can implement models such as GPT and BERT easily.

3.3 Target (objective)

Using suitable target is the key to the success of pre-training. Many papers in this field propose their targets and show their advantages over other ones. UER consists of a range of targets. Users can choose one of them, or use multiple targets and give them different weights. In this section we introduce targets implemented in UER.

- **Language model (LM).** Language model is one of the most commonly used targets. It trains model to make it useful to predict current word given previous words.

- **Masked LM (MLM, also known as cloze test).** The model is trained to be useful to predict masked word given surrounding words. MLM utilizes both left and right contexts to predict words. LM only considers the left context.

- **Autoencoder (AE).** The model is trained to be useful to reconstruct input sequence as close as possible.

The above targets are related with word prediction. We call them word-level targets. Some works

---

[4]We don't do word segmentation on Chinese corpus. We regard each Chinese character as a word. Internal structures such as radical and pinyin are regarded as Chinese subword features.

show that introducing sentence-level task into targets can benefit pre-training models (Logeswaran and Lee, 2018; Devlin et al., 2018).

- **Next sentence prediction (NSP).** The model is trained to predict if the two sentences are continuous. Sentence prediction target is much more efficient than word-level targets. It doesn't involve sequentially decoding of words and softmax layer over entire vocabulary.

Above targets are unsupervised tasks (also known as self-supervised tasks). However, supervised tasks can provide additional knowledge that raw corpus can not provide.

- **Neural machine translation (NMT).** CoVe (McCann et al., 2017) proposes to use NMT to pre-train model. The implementation of NMT target is similar with autoencoder. Both of them involve encoding source sentences and sequentially decoding words of target sentences.

- **Classification (CLS).** Infersent (Conneau et al., 2017) proposes to use natural language inference task (three-way classification) to pre-train model.

Most pre-training models use above targets individually. It is worth trying to use multiple targets at the same time. Some targets are complementary to each other, e.g. word-level target and sentence-level target (Devlin et al., 2018), unsupervised target and supervised target. In experiments section, we demonstrate that proper selection of target is important. UER provides the flexibility to users in trying different targets and their combinations.

3.4 Fine-tuning

UER exploits similar fine-tuning strategy with ULMFiT, GPT, and BERT. Models on downstream tasks share structures and parameters with pre-training models except that they have different target layers. The entire models are fine-tuned on downstream tasks. This strategy performs robustly in practice. We also find that feature extractor strategy produces inferior results on models such as GPT and BERT.

Most pre-training works involve 2 stages, pre-training and fine-tuning. But UER supports 3 stages: 1) pre-training on general-domain corpus;

2) pre-training on downstream dataset; 3) fine-tuning on downstream dataset. Stage 2 enables models to get familiar with the distributions of downstream datasets (Howard and Ruder, 2018; Radford et al., 2018). It is also called semi-supervised fine-tuning strategy in the work of Dai and Le (2015) since stage 2 is unsupervised and stage 3 is supervised.

3.5 Case Studies

In this section, we show how UER facilitates the use of pre-training models. First of all, we demonstrate that UER can build most pre-training models easily. As shown in the following code, only a few lines are required to construct models with the interfaces in UER.

```
1   # Implementation of BERT.
2   embedding = BertEmbedding(args, vocab_size)
3   encoder = BertEncoder(args)
4   target = BertTarget(args, vocab_size)
5
6   # Implementation of GPT.
7   embedding = BertEmbedding(args, vocab_size)
8   encoder = GptEncoder(args)
9   target = LmTarget(args, vocab_size)
10
11  # Implementation of Quick-thoughts.
12  embedding = Embedding(args, vocab_size)
13  encoder = GruEncoder(args)
14  target = NspTarget(args, None)
15
16  # Implementation of InferSent.
17  embedding = Embedding(args, vocab_size)
18  encoder = LstmEncoder(args)
19  target = ClsTarget(args, None)
```

In practice, users can assemble different subencoder, encoder, and target modules without any code work. Users can specify modules through options *–subencoder*, *–encoder*, and *–target*. More details are available in quickstart and instructions of UER's github project. UER provides ample modules. Users can try different module combinations according to their downstream datasets. Besides trying modules implemented by UER, users can also develop their customized modules and integrate them into UER seamlessly.

4   Experiments

To evaluate the performance of UER, experiments are conducted on a range of datasets, each of which falls into one of four categories: sentence classification, sentence pair classification, sequence labeling, and document-based QA. BERT-base uncased English model and BERT-base Chinese model are used as baseline models. In section 4.1, UER is tested on several evaluation benchmarks to demonstrate that it can produce models as intended. In section 4.2, we ap-

Implementation	SST-2	MRPC	STS-B	QQP	MNLI	QNLI	RTE	WNLI
HuggingFace	93.0	83.8	89.4	90.7	84.0/84.4	89.0	61.0	53.5
UER	92.4	83.0	89.3	91.0	84.0/84.0	91.5	66.8	56.3

Table 2: The performance of HuggingFace's implementation and UER's implementation on GLUE benchmark.

Implementation	XNLI	LCQMC	MSRA-NER	ChnSentiCorp	nlpcc-dbqa
ERNIE	77.2	87.0	92.6	94.3	94.6
UER	77.5	86.6	93.6	94.3	94.6

Table 3: The performance of ERNIE's implementation and UER's implementation on ERNIE benchmark.

ply pre-trained models in our model zoo to different downstream datasets. Significant improvements are witnessed when proper encoders and targets are selected. For space constraint, we put some contents in UER's github project, including dataset and corpus details, system speed, and part of qualitative/quantitative evaluation results.

4.1 Reproducibility

This section uses English/Chinese benchmarks to test BERT implementation of UER. For English, we use sentence and sentence pair classification datasets in GLUE benchmark (dev set) (Wang et al., 2019). For Chinese, we use five datasets of different types: sentiment analysis, sequence labeling, question pair matching, natural language inference, and document-based QA (provided by ERNIE[5]). Table 2 and 3 compare UER's performance to other publicly available systems. We can observe that UER could match the performance of HuggingFace's and ERNIE's implementations. Results of HuggingFace and ERNIE are reported on their github projects. Results of UER can be reproduced by scripts in UER's github project.

4.2 Influence of targets and encoders

In this section, we give some examples of selecting pre-trained models given downstream datasets. Three Chinese sentiment analysis datasets are used for evaluation. They are Douban book review, Online shopping review, and Chnsenticorp datasets.

First of all, we use UER to pre-train on large-scale Amazon review corpus with different targets. The parameters are initialized by BERT-base Chinese model. The target of original BERT consists of MLM and NSP. However, NSP is not suitable for sentence-level reviews (we have to split reviews into multiple parts). Therefore we remove NSP target. In addition, Amazon reviews are at-

tached with users' ratings. To this end, we can exploit CLS target for pre-training (similar with InferSent). We fine-tune these pre-trained models (with different targets) on downstream datasets. The results are shown in Table 4. BERT baseline (BERT-base Chinese) is pre-trained upon Chinese Wikipedia. We can observe that pre-training on Amazon review corpus can improve the results significantly. Using CLS target achieves the best results in most cases.

Dataset	Douban.	Shopping.	Chn.
BERT baseline	87.5	96.3	94.3
MLM	88.1	**97.0**	95.0
CLS	**88.3**	**97.0**	**95.8**

Table 4: Performance of pre-training models with different targets.

BERT requires heavy computational resources. To achieve better efficiency, we use UER to substitute 12-layers Transformer encoder with a 2-layers LSTM encoder (embedding size and hidden size are 512 and 1024). We still use the above sentiment analysis datasets for evaluation. The model is firstly trained on mixed large corpus with LM target, and then trained on large-scale Amazon review corpus with LM and CLS targets. Table 5 lists the results of different encoders. Compared with BERT baseline, LSTM encoder can achieve comparable or even better results when proper corpora and targets are selected.

Dataset	Douban.	Shopping.	Chn.
BERT baseline	**87.5**	96.3	94.3
LSTM	80.3	94.0	88.3
LSTM+pre-training	86.5	**96.9**	**94.5**

Table 5: Performance of pre-training models with different encoders.

For space constraint, this section only uses sentiment analysis datasets as examples to analyze the influence of different targets and encoders. More tasks and pre-trained models are discussed

[5]https://github.com/PaddlePaddle/ERNIE

in UER's github project.

5 Conclusion

This paper describes UER, an open-source toolkit for pre-training on general-domain corpora and fine-tuning on downstream tasks. We demonstrate that UER can largely facilitate implementations of different pre-training models. With the help of UER, we pre-train models based on different corpora, encoders, targets and make these models publicly available. By using proper pre-trained models, we can achieve significant improvements over BERT, or achieve competitive results with an efficient training speed.

Acknowledgments

This work is supported by National Natural Science Foundation of China Grant No.U1711262 and No.61472428, 2018 Tencent Rhino-Bird Elite Training Program.

References

Dzmitry Bahdanau, Kyunghyun Cho, and Yoshua Bengio. 2014. Neural machine translation by jointly learning to align and translate. *arXiv preprint arXiv:1409.0473*.

Alexis Conneau, Douwe Kiela, Holger Schwenk, Loic Barrault, and Antoine Bordes. 2017. Supervised learning of universal sentence representations from natural language inference data. *EMNLP*.

Andrew M Dai and Quoc V Le. 2015. Semi-supervised sequence learning. In *NIPS*.

Jacob Devlin, Ming-Wei Chang, Kenton Lee, and Kristina Toutanova. 2018. Bert: Pre-training of deep bidirectional transformers for language understanding. *arXiv preprint arXiv:1810.04805*.

Sepp Hochreiter and Jürgen Schmidhuber. 1997. Long short-term memory. *Neural computation*, 9(8).

Jeremy Howard and Sebastian Ruder. 2018. Universal language model fine-tuning for text classification. *arXiv preprint arXiv:1801.06146*.

Armand Joulin, Edouard Grave, Piotr Bojanowski, and Tomas Mikolov. 2016. Bag of tricks for efficient text classification. *arXiv preprint arXiv:1607.01759*.

Yoon Kim. 2014. Convolutional neural networks for sentence classification. *EMNLP*.

Ryan Kiros, Yukun Zhu, Ruslan R Salakhutdinov, Richard Zemel, Raquel Urtasun, Antonio Torralba, and Sanja Fidler. 2015. Skip-thought vectors. In *NIPS*.

Guillaume Klein, Yoon Kim, Yuntian Deng, Jean Senellart, and Alexander M Rush. 2017. Opennmt: Open-source toolkit for neural machine translation. *ACL*.

Omer Levy, Yoav Goldberg, and Ido Dagan. 2015. Improving distributional similarity with lessons learned from word embeddings. *TACL.*, 3.

Lajanugen Logeswaran and Honglak Lee. 2018. An efficient framework for learning sentence representations. *arXiv preprint arXiv:1803.02893*.

Bryan McCann, James Bradbury, Caiming Xiong, and Richard Socher. 2017. Learned in translation: Contextualized word vectors. In *NIPS*.

Tomas Mikolov, Ilya Sutskever, Kai Chen, Greg S Corrado, and Jeff Dean. 2013. Distributed representations of words and phrases and their compositionality. In *NIPS*.

Myle Ott, Sergey Edunov, Alexei Baevski, Angela Fan, Sam Gross, Nathan Ng, David Grangier, and Michael Auli. 2019. fairseq: A fast, extensible toolkit for sequence modeling. *NAACL.*

Matthew E Peters, Mark Neumann, Mohit Iyyer, Matt Gardner, Christopher Clark, Kenton Lee, and Luke Zettlemoyer. 2018. Deep contextualized word representations. *arXiv preprint arXiv:1802.05365*.

Alec Radford, Karthik Narasimhan, Tim Salimans, and Ilya Sutskever. 2018. Improving language understanding by generative pre-training.

Ashish Vaswani, Noam Shazeer, Niki Parmar, Jakob Uszkoreit, Llion Jones, Aidan N Gomez, Łukasz Kaiser, and Illia Polosukhin. 2017. Attention is all you need. In *NIPS*.

Alex Wang, Amanpreet Singh, Julian Michael, Felix Hill, Omer Levy, and Samuel R. Bowman. 2019. GLUE: A multi-task benchmark and analysis platform for natural language understanding. In *ICLR*.

Jie Yang and Yue Zhang. 2018. Ncrf++: An open-source neural sequence labeling toolkit. *arXiv preprint arXiv:1806.05626*.

Xiang Zhang and Yann LeCun. 2017. Which encoding is the best for text classification in chinese, english, japanese and korean?

Zhe Zhao, Tao Liu, Shen Li, Bofang Li, and Xiaoyong Du. 2017. Ngram2vec: Learning improved word representations from ngram co-occurrence statistics. *EMNLP.*

Peng Zhou, Wei Shi, Jun Tian, Zhenyu Qi, Bingchen Li, Hongwei Hao, and Bo Xu. 2016. Attention-based bidirectional long short-term memory networks for relation classification. In *ACL.*, volume 2.

Visualizing Trends of Key Roles in News Articles

Chen Xia[1]*, Haoxiang Zhang[1]*, Jacob Moghtader[2], Allen Wu[2], Kai-Wei Chang[1]
[1]University of California Los Angeles, [2]Taboola
`kasinxc@cs.ucla.edu`; `haoxiangzhx@gmail.com`;
`{jacob.m, allen.wu}@taboola.com`; `kw@kwchang.net`

Abstract

There are tons of news articles generated every day reflecting the activities of key roles such as people, organizations and political parties. Analyzing these key roles allows us to understand the trends in news. In this paper, we present a demonstration system that visualizes the trend of key roles in news articles based on natural language processing techniques. Specifically, we apply a semantic role labeler and the dynamic word embedding technique to understand relationships between key roles in the news across different time periods and visualize the trends of key role and news topics change over time.

1 Introduction

Nowadays, numerous news articles describing different aspects of topics are flowing through the internet and media. Underneath the news flow, key roles including people and organizations interact with each other and involve in various events over time. With the overwhelmed information, extracting relations between key roles allows users to better understand what a key person is doing and how he/she is related to different news topics. To understand the action of key roles, we provide a semantic level analysis using semantic role labeling (SRL). To measure the trend of news topics, a word vector level analysis is supported using dynamic word embeddings.

In our system, we show that a semantic role labeller, which identifies subject, object, and verb in a sentence, provides a snapshot of news articles. Analyzing the change of verbs with fixed subject over time can track the actions of key roles. Besides, the relationships between subjects and objects reflect how key roles are involved in different events. We implemented the semantic role analyzer based on the SRL model in AllenNLP, which

formulates a BIO tagging problem (He et al., 2017) and uses deep bidirectional LSTMs to label semantic roles (Gardner et al., 2018).

On the other hand, word embeddings map words to vectors such that the embedding space captures the semantic similarity between words. We apply dynamic word embeddings to analyze the temporal changes, and leverage these to study the trend of news related to a key role. For example, President Trump is involved in many news events; therefore, he is associated with various news topics. By analyzing the association between "Trump" and other entities in different periods, we can characterize news trends around him. For example, in February 2019, "Trump" participated in the North Korea-United States Summit in Hanoi, Vietnam. The word embedding trained on news articles around that time period identifies "Trump" is closely associated with "Kim Jun Un" (the President of North Korea) and "Vietnam" (the country hosted the summit).

We create a system based on two datasets collected by Taboola, a web advertising company. 1) *Trump dataset* contains 20,833 English news titles in late April to early July 2018. 2) *Newsroom dataset* contains approximately 3 million English news articles published in October 2018 to March 2019. The former provides a controllable experiment environment to study news related to President Donald Trump, and the second provides a comprehensive corpus covering wide ranges of news in the U.S. Source code of the demo is available at `https://bit.ly/32f8k3t` and more details are in (Zhang, 2019; Xia, 2019).

2 Related Work

Various systems to visualize the transition of topics in news articles have been published. Kawai et al. (2008) detected news sentiment and visu-

---

*Equal contribution.

247

Proceedings of the 2019 EMNLP and the 9th IJCNLP (System Demonstrations), pages 247–252
Hong Kong, China, November 3 – 7, 2019. ©2019 Association for Computational Linguistics

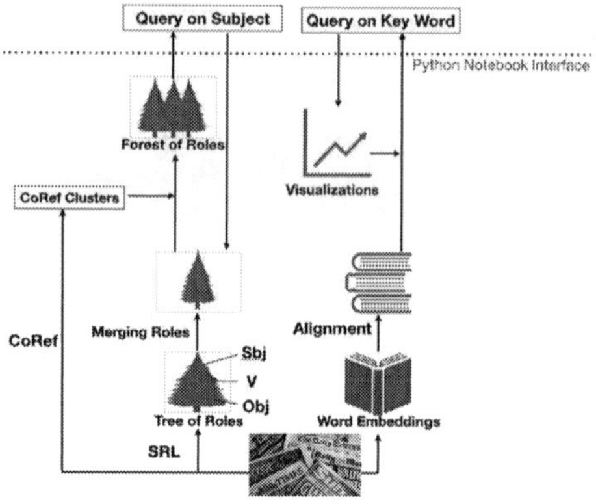

Figure 1: System Overview.

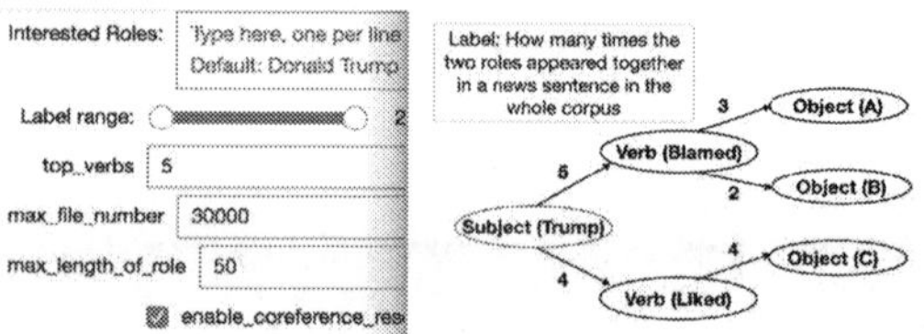

Figure 2: Tree Graph for Semantic Role Visualization.

alized them based on date and granularity such as city, prefecture, and country. Ishikawa and Hasegawa (2007) developed a system called T-Scroll (Trend/Topic-Scroll) to visualize the transition of topics extracted from news articles. Fitzpatrick et al. (2003) provided an interactive system called BreakingStory to visualize change in online news. Cui et al. (2010) introduced TextWheel to convey the dynamic natures of news streams. Feldman et al. (1998) introduced Trend Graphs for visualizing the evolution of concept relationships in large document collections. Unlike these works, our analysis focuses on the key roles in news articles. We extract semantic roles and word vectors from news articles to understand the action and visualize the trend of these key roles.

3 System Overview

To visualize the news trends, we apply semantic role analysis and word embedding techniques.

For semantic roles, we first construct a tree graph with subject as root, verbs as the first layer and objects as leaf nodes by extracting semantic roles with SRL (Gardner et al., 2018). Then we aggregate the tree graphs by collecting tree with the same subject and similar verb and object. Beyond applying simple string matching to identify same object and subject, we also apply a coreference resolution system (CoRef) to identify phrases refer to the same entity. As a result, we create a forest visualization where each tree represents the activities of a key role.

For word embeddings, we first train individual word vectors model for each month's data. However, there is no guarantee that coordinate axes of different models have similar latent seman-

tics; therefore, we perform alignment algorithm to project all the word vectors into the same space. Once the embeddings are aligned, we are able to identify the shift of association between key roles and other news concepts based on their positions in the embedding space.

3.1 Visualization by Semantic Roles

Tree Graph for Semantic Roles We provide users with a search bar to explore roles of interest. For example, when searching for *Trump*, a tree graph is presented with *Trump* as root. The second layer of the tree is all of the verbs labeled together with subject *Trump*, e.g., *blamed* and *liked* in Figure 2. The edge label represents how many times two nodes, subject (e.g, *Trump*) and Verb (e.g., *liked*), appear together in a news sentence in the corpus. The edge label reflects the total number of semantic role combination in the given dataset, which depicts the importance of a news action.

Forest Graph for Semantic Roles In news articles, President Trump have different references, such as Donald Trump, the president of the United States, and pronoun "he" – a well-known task, called coreference resolution. When generating semantic trees, the system should not look only for *Trump* but also other references. To realize this, we preprocess the dataset with CoRef system (Lee et al., 2017) in AllenNLP (Gardner et al., 2018) and generate local coreference clusters for each news article. To obtain a global view, we merge the clusters across documents together until none of them shares a common role. A visualization demo for CoRef is also provided.

In Figure 3, the CoRef system clusters "*the Philladelphia Eagles*" with "*the Eagles*", and "*Hilary*" with "*Hilary Clinton*". The red nodes are center roles, which are representative phrases. For example, "*the Philladelphia Eagles*" and "*Hilary Clinton*" are the center roles of their corresponding cluster.

We use the following three rules to determine which phrases are center roles. If phrases are

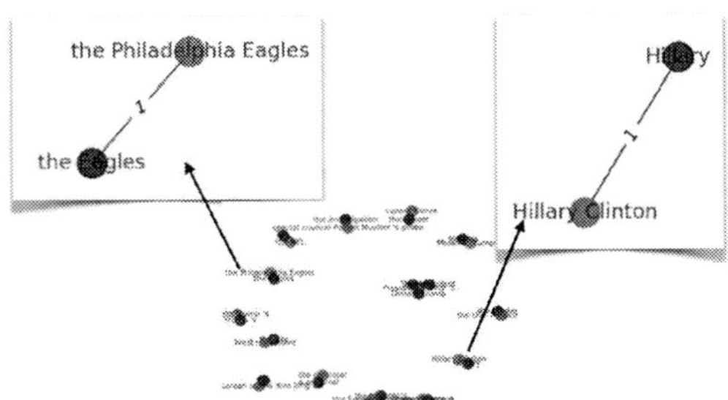

Figure 3: Coreference Resolution Clusters.

tied, the one with longest length will be se-lected: *LongestSpan* method selects the role with longest length. *WordNet* method marks spans not in the WordNet (Miller, 1998) as specific roles. *NameEntity* method marks roles in the name entity list generated by latent dirichlet allocation as spe-cific ones. Both WordNet and NameEntity meth-ods select the most frequent role as the center role.

Merging Algorithms for Semantic Roles Fi-nally, we use the following rule-based approach to merge trees with same referent subject by CoRef.

1) Merging Objects with the Same Verb To better visualize the semantic roles, we merge ob-jects with similar meaning if they are associated with same verb. To measure the similarity, we gen-erate bag-of-word representations with *TF-IDF* scores for each object. If the cosine similarity be-tween the representations of two objects is larger than a threshold, we merge the two nodes. We then sum up the frequency weights on the edges of all merging objects to form a new edge.

2) Merging Verbs with the Same Subject Verbs like *believe*, *say* and *think* convey simi-lar meanings. Merging such verbs can emphasize the key activities of the key roles. The similarity between verbs associated with the same subject is calculated by cosine similarity between word vec-tors using word2vec (Mikolov et al., 2013). In par-ticular, we merge two verbs if their cosine similar-ity is larger than a threshold. By showing a cer-tain range of edge labels, the system is also capa-ble of filtering out verbs with extreme high or low frequency such as *say*, as these verbs carry less meaningful information.

Modifier, Negative and Lemmatization While our news analysis is mainly based on subject-verb-object relations, we also consider other semantic roles identified by the SRL model. For example, we include identification of modifier so that we can recognize the difference between "resign" and "might resign". We also add negation as an extra sentiment information. Verbs have different forms and tenses (e.g., win, won, winning). If we merge all verbs with the same root form, we can obtain a larger clusters and reduce duplicated trees. How-ever, for some analysis, the tense of verbs are im-portant. Therefore, we provide Lemmatizating as an option in our system.

3.2 Dynamic Word Embeddings

Dynamic word embeddings model align word em-beddings trained on corpora collected in different time periods (Hamilton et al., 2016). It divides data into time slices and obtains the word vector representations of each time slice separately. To capture how the trends in news change monthly, we train a word2vec word embedding model on news articles collected in each month. We then apply the orthogonal Procrustes to align the em-beddings from different time periods by learning a transformation $\mathbf{R}^{(t)} \in R^{d \times d}$:

$$\mathbf{R}^{(t)} = \arg\min_{\mathbf{Q}^\top \mathbf{Q} = \mathbf{I}} \| \mathbf{W}^{(t)} \mathbf{Q} - \mathbf{W}^{(t+1)} \|,$$

where $W^{(t)} \in R^{d \times V}$ is the learned word embed-dings of each month t (d is the dimension of word vector, and V is the size of vocabulary).

N-Gram To represent named entities such as 'white house' in the word embeddings, we treat phrases in news articles as single words. The max length of phrases is set as 4 to avoid large vocabu-lary size.

Absolute Drift Inspired by Rudolph and Blei (2018), we define a metric that is suitable to detect which words fluctuate the most relative to the key word w_k. Denote $cos(w_k, w_i, t)$ as the cosine sim-ilarities between the word w_i and the key word w_k at time t. For top n words close to w_k, calculate the absolute drift of each word w_i by summing the cosine similarity differences.

$$drift(w_i) = \sum_{t=2}^{T} | \cos(w_k, w_i, t) - \cos(w_k, w_i, t-1)|$$

After finding meaningful words that fluctuate the most, cosine similarities between these words and w_k of each month can be plotted to present possi-ble useful interpretations.

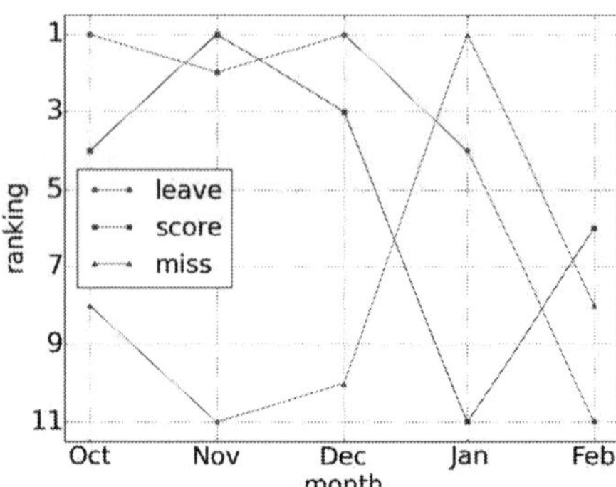

Figure 4: Action Tracking for *LeBron James*

rank	verbs for *LeBron James*	fixed main objects
1	miss	games
2	suffer	a groin strain injury
3	make	no fixed main objects
4	leave	Cleveland Cavaliers
5	lead	the team

Table 1: Verb Rankings for *LeBron James* in January

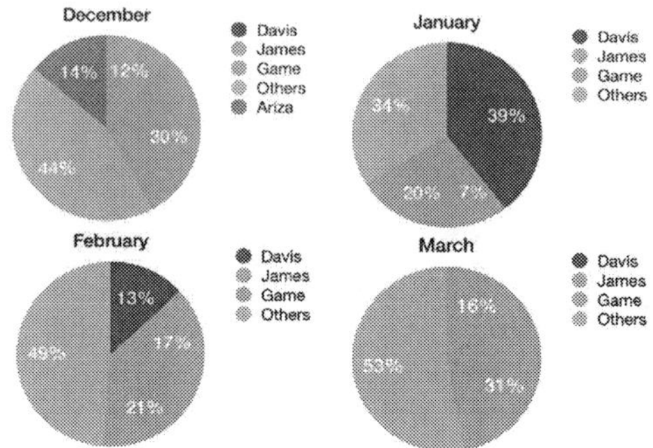

Figure 5: Breaking News Tracking on Trade Rumors.

4 Case Studies

4.1 Semantic Roles

Action Tracking on Verbs We apply semantic role labelling model to *newsroom dataset* collected from October 2018 to February 2019 on taxonomy: */sports/basketball* and search for subject *LeBron James*, a basketball player.

For each month, we generate the top frequent verbs from sentences where *LeBron James* is marked as the subject. We found that the top verbs include "Leave", "Score" and "Miss". Example sentences include: "LeBron James **leave** the Cleveland Cavaliers", "LeBron James **score** points" and "LeBron James **miss** games".

We further show the ranking of these verbs in different months in Figure 4. As results show the verb "leave" ranks at the top around October due to an earlier announcement that Lebron James will leave the Cavaliers. However, the frequency falls in January.

Meanwhile, news on *LeBron James **miss** games* ranked first and the verb "score" doesn't co-occur with LeBron James in January due to his injury.

To explain the absence, we list the top 5 frequent verbs are listed below. Verbs that occur with LeBron James only in December and January are colored in red.

From this analysis, we can see that *LeBron James* was suffering the groin strain injury in January, causing his absence of the game.

Breaking News Tracking on Objects We run our algorithm to analyze news article under the topic: */sports/basketball*, which has 75,827 peices of news title descriptions. We search *Lakers* as subject in every month and sum up all the label weights on the edges between verb and object.

$$W(V, o|S = s) = \sum_{v \in V} W(v, o|S = s), \quad (1)$$

where $W(v, o|S = s)$ denotes the weight on edges between all the verbs $v \in V$ and a specific object o under certain subject s.

We rank all objects based on Eq. (1) and the top 5 objects associated with the subject "Lakers" are: "Davis", "James", "Game", "Ariza", and "Others". We further show the pie chart to demonstrate the percentage of each object associated with "Lakers" in different months.

The purple part in Figure 5 shows that the number of news mentioning *Anthony Davis* and *Lakers* suddenly emerged and even beat *James* and *Lakers* in January but gradually decreased in February. The breaking news about Anthony and Lakers disappeared completely in March. The event happened in January and February was the trade rumors on *Davis*. After the trade deadlines, the topic eventually disappeared.

4.2 Dynamic Word Embeddings

2D Visualization The t-SNE embedding method (Maaten and Hinton, 2008) is used to visualize the word embeddings in two dimensions. First, given

Rank	Dec 2018	Jan 2019	Feb 2019	Mar 2019
1	los_angeles_lakers	los_angeles_lakers	los_angeles_lakers	los_angeles_lakers
2	lebron_james	**pelicans**	lebron_james	lebron_james
3	lonzo_ball	lebron_james	clippers	clippers
4	clippers	lonzo_ball	**pelicans**	kevin_durant
5	brandon_ingram	**anthony_davis**	boston_celtics	lonzo_ball
6	kevin_durant	cavs	kyle_kuzma	lebron
7	**anthony_davis**	boston_celtics	tobias_harris	giannis_antetokounmpo
8	raptors	rockets	**anthony_davis**	magic_johnson

Table 2: Top 5 Words closest to the Word 'lakers' in Each Month.

a word w that we are interested in, the nearest neighbors of w at different time periods are put together. Next, the t-SNE embeddings of these word vectors are calculated and visualized in a 2D plot.

Figure 6: Shifts of the Word 'Max'.

On March 10 2019, the Boeing 737 MAX 8 aircraft crashed shortly after takeoff. After this fatal crash, aviation authorities around the world grounded the Boeing 737 MAX series. Figure 6 shows that dynamic word embeddings capture this sudden trend change. In particular, before March 2019 (from when the 'max_Mar19' embedding is obtained), the word 'max' was close to different people names. When the crash happened or afterwards, the word 'max' immediately shifts to words such as 'boeing', '737' and 'grounding'.

Top Nearest Nighbors Listing the top nearest neighbors (words that have highest cosine similarities with the key word) of the key word w inside a table also shows some interesting results. For example, Table 2 confirms with Figure 5 that breaking news of *Anthony Davis* and *Lakers* happened

because of the trade rumors.

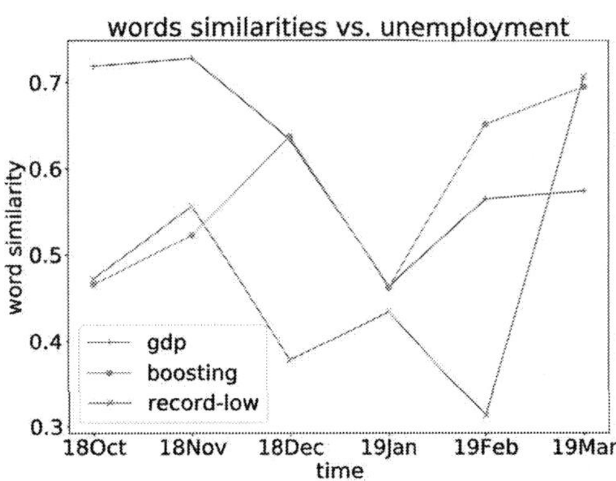

Figure 7: Cosine Similarities with 'Unemployment'.

Changing Words with Absolute Drift Figure 7 displays the cosine similarity changes with respect to 'unemployment'. One thing we can infer from this figure is that as the economy ('gdp') shows a strong signal ('boosting') in the first quarter of 2019, the unemployment rate reaches a 'record-low' position. According to National Public Radio, the first quarter's gross domestic product of U.S. grew at an annual rate of 3.2%, which is a strong improvement compared to the 2.2% at the end of last year. In addition, the Labor Department reported that 196,000 jobs were added in March, and the unemployment is near 50-year lows.

5 Conclusion

We presented a visualization system for analyzing news trends by applying semantic roles and word embeddings. We demonstrated that our system can track actions and breaking news. It can also detect meaningful words that change the most. Future work will focus on adding entity linking to subjects, providing more semantic roles information. Also, we plan to work on qualitative assessment on the quality of the trends and other word embedding models like Glove(Pennington et al., 2014).

6   Acknowledgment

This work was supported in part by a gift grant from Taboola. We acknowledge feedback from anonymous reviewers and fruitful discussions with the Taboola team at Los Angeles.

References

Weiwei Cui, Hong Zhou, Huamin Qu, Wenbin Zhang, and Steven Skiena. 2010. A dynamic visual interface for news stream analysis. In *Proceedings of the first international workshop on Intelligent visual interfaces for text analysis*, pages 5–8. ACM.

Ronen Feldman, Yonatan Aumann, Amir Zilberstein, and Yaron Ben-Yehuda. 1998. Trend graphs: Visualizing the evolution of concept relationships in large document collections. In *European Symposium on Principles of Data Mining and Knowledge Discovery*, pages 38–46. Springer.

Jean Anne Fitzpatrick, James Reffell, and Moryma Aydelott. 2003. Breakingstory: visualizing change in online news. In *CHI'03 Extended Abstracts on Human Factors in Computing Systems*, pages 900–901. ACM.

Matt Gardner, Joel Grus, Mark Neumann, Oyvind Tafjord, Pradeep Dasigi, Nelson Liu, Matthew Peters, Michael Schmitz, and Luke Zettlemoyer. 2018. Allennlp: A deep semantic natural language processing platform. *arXiv preprint arXiv:1803.07640*.

William L. Hamilton, Jure Leskovec, and Dan Jurafsky. 2016. Diachronic word embeddings reveal statistical laws of semantic change. In *Proceedings of the 54th Annual Meeting of the Association for Computational Linguistics (Volume 1: Long Papers)*, pages 1489–1501, Berlin, Germany. Association for Computational Linguistics.

Luheng He, Kenton Lee, Mike Lewis, and Luke Zettlemoyer. 2017. Deep semantic role labeling: What works and whats next. In *Proceedings of the 55th Annual Meeting of the Association for Computational Linguistics (Volume 1: Long Papers)*, pages 473–483.

Yoshiharu Ishikawa and Mikine Hasegawa. 2007. T-scroll: Visualizing trends in a time-series of documents for interactive user exploration. In *International Conference on Theory and Practice of Digital Libraries*, pages 235–246. Springer.

Yukiko Kawai, Yusuke Fujita, Tadahiko Kumamoto, Jianwei Jianwei, and Katsumi Tanaka. 2008. Using a sentiment map for visualizing credibility of news sites on the web. In *Proceedings of the 2nd ACM workshop on Information credibility on the web*, pages 53–58. ACM.

Kenton Lee, Luheng He, Mike Lewis, and Luke Zettlemoyer. 2017. End-to-end neural coreference resolution. *arXiv preprint arXiv:1707.07045*.

Laurens van der Maaten and Geoffrey Hinton. 2008. Visualizing data using t-sne. *Journal of machine learning research*, 9(Nov):2579–2605.

Tomas Mikolov, Ilya Sutskever, Kai Chen, Greg S Corrado, and Jeff Dean. 2013. Distributed representations of words and phrases and their compositionality. In *Advances in neural information processing systems*, pages 3111–3119.

George Miller. 1998. *WordNet: An electronic lexical database*. MIT press.

Jeffrey Pennington, Richard Socher, and Christopher Manning. 2014. Glove: Global vectors for word representation. In *Proceedings of the 2014 conference on empirical methods in natural language processing (EMNLP)*, pages 1532–1543.

Maja Rudolph and David Blei. 2018. Dynamic embeddings for language evolution. In *Proceedings of the 2018 World Wide Web Conference on World Wide Web*, pages 1003–1011.

Chen Xia. 2019. Extracting global entities information from news. Master's thesis, University of California, Los Angeles, California, US, 6.

Haoxiang Zhang. 2019. Dynamic word embedding for news analysis. Master's thesis, University of California, Los Angeles, California, US, 6.

VizSeq: A Visual Analysis Toolkit for Text Generation Tasks

Changhan Wang[†], Anirudh Jain*[‡], Danlu Chen[†] and Jiatao Gu[†]
[†] Facebook AI Research, [‡] Stanford University
{changhan, danluchen, jgu}@fb.com, anirudhj@stanford.edu

Abstract

Automatic evaluation of text generation tasks (e.g. machine translation, text summarization, image captioning and video description) usually relies heavily on task-specific metrics, such as BLEU (Papineni et al., 2002) and ROUGE (Lin, 2004). They, however, are abstract numbers and are not perfectly aligned with human assessment. This suggests inspecting detailed examples as a complement to identify system error patterns. In this paper, we present VizSeq, a visual analysis toolkit for instance-level and corpus-level system evaluation on a wide variety of text generation tasks. It supports multimodal sources and multiple text references, providing visualization in Jupyter notebook or a web app interface. It can be used locally or deployed onto public servers for centralized data hosting and benchmarking. It covers most common n-gram based metrics accelerated with multiprocessing, and also provides latest embedding-based metrics such as BERTScore (Zhang et al., 2019).

1 Introduction

Many natural language processing (NLP) tasks can be viewed as conditional text generation problems, where natural language texts are generated given inputs in the form of text (e.g. machine translation), image (e.g. image captioning), audio (e.g. automatic speech recognition) or video (e.g. video description). Their automatic evaluation usually relies heavily on task-specific metrics. Due to the complexity of natural language expressions, those metrics are not always perfectly aligned with human assessment. Moreover, metrics only produce abstract numbers and are limited in illustrating system error patterns. This suggests the necessity of inspecting detailed evaluation examples to get a full picture of system behaviors as

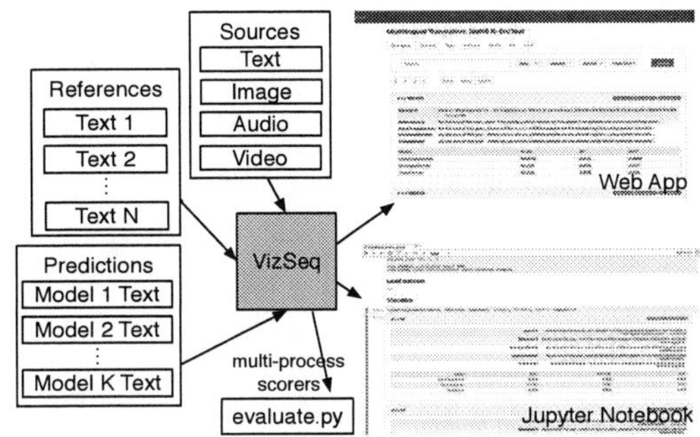

Figure 1: An overview of VizSeq. VizSeq takes multimodal sources, text references as well as model predictions as inputs, and analyzes them visually in Jupyter notebook or in a web app interface. It can also be used without visualization as a normal Python package.

well as seek improvement directions.

A bunch of softwares have emerged to facilitate calculation of various metrics or demonstrating examples with sentence-level scores in an integrated user interface: ibleu (Madnani, 2011), MTEval [1], MT-ComparEval (Klejch et al., 2015), nlg-eval (Sharma et al., 2017), Vis-Eval Metric Viewer (Steele and Specia, 2018), compare-mt (Neubig et al., 2019), etc. Quite a few of them are collections of command-line scripts for metric calculation, which lack visualization to better present and interpret the scores. Some of them are able to generate static HTML reports to present charts and examples, but they do not allow updating visualization options interactively. MT-ComparEval is the only software we found that has an interactive user interface. It is, however, written in PHP, which unlike Python lacks a complete NLP eco-system. The number of metrics it supports is also limited and the software is no longer being actively developed. Support of multiple references is not a prevalent standard across all the softwares we investigated, and

---

* Work carried out during an internship at Facebook.

[1] https://github.com/odashi/mteval

Proceedings of the 2019 EMNLP and the 9th IJCNLP (System Demonstrations), pages 253–258
Hong Kong, China, November 3 – 7, 2019. ©2019 Association for Computational Linguistics

Source Type	Example Tasks
Text	machine translation, text summarization, dialog generation, grammatical error correction, open-domain question answering
Image	image captioning, visual question answering, optical character recognition
Audio	speech recognition, speech translation
Video	video description
Multimodal	multimodal machine translation

Table 1: Example text generation tasks supported by VizSeq. The sources can be from various modalities.

Metrics	VizSeq	compare-mt	nlg-eval	MT-Compar-Eval
BLEU	✓	✓	✓	✓
chrF	✓	✓		
METEOR	✓	✓	✓	
TER	✓			✓
RIBES	✓	✓		
GLEU	✓			
NIST	✓			
ROUGE	✓	✓	✓	
CIDEr	✓		✓	
WER	✓	✓		
LASER	✓			
BERTScore	✓			

Table 2: Comparison of VizSeq and its counterparts on n-gram-based and embedding-based metric coverage.

none of them supports multiple sources or sources in non-text modalities such as image, audio and video. Almost all the metric implementations are single-processed, which cannot leverage the multiple cores in modern CPUs for speedup and better scalability.

With the above limitations identified, we want to provide a unified and scalable solution that gets rid of all those constraints and is enhanced with a user-friendly interface as well as the latest NLP technologies. In this paper, we present VizSeq, a visual analysis toolkit for a wide variety of text generation tasks, which can be used for: 1) instance-level and corpus-level system error analysis; 2) exploratory dataset analysis; 3) public data hosting and system benchmarking. It provides visualization in Jupyter notebook or a web app interface. A system overview can be found in Figure 1. We open source the software at https://github.com/facebookresearch/vizseq.

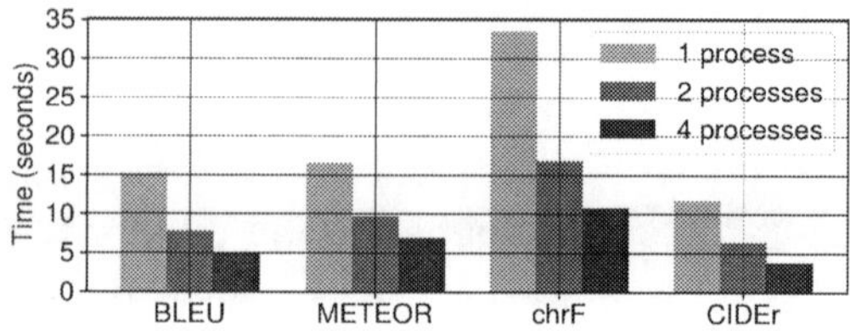

Figure 2: VizSeq implements metrics with multiprocessing speedup. Speed test is based on a 36k evaluation set for BLEU, METEOR and chrF, and a 41k one for CIDEr. CPU: Intel Core i7-7920HQ @ 3.10GHz

2 Main Features of VizSeq

2.1 Multimodal Data and Task Coverage

VizSeq has built-in support for multiple sources and references. The number of references is allowed to vary across different examples, and the sources are allowed to come from different modalities, including text, image, audio and video. This flexibility enables VizSeq to cover a wide range of text generation tasks and datasets, far beyond the scope of machine translation, which previous softwares mainly focus on. Table 1 provides a list of example tasks supported by Vizseq.

2.2 Metric Coverage and Scalability

Table 2 shows the comparison of VizSeq and its counterparts on metric coverage.

N-gram-based metrics To the extent of our knowledge, VizSeq has the best coverage of common n-gram-based metrics, including BLEU (Papineni et al., 2002), NIST (Doddington, 2002), METEOR (Banerjee and Lavie, 2005), TER (Snover et al., 2006), RIBES (Isozaki et al., 2010), chrF (Popović, 2015) and GLEU (Wu et al., 2016) for machine translation; ROUGE (Lin, 2004) for summarization and video description; CIDEr (Vedantam et al., 2015) for image captioning; and word error rate for speech recognition.

Embedding-based metrics N-gram-based metrics have difficulties in capturing semantic similarities since they are usually based on exact word matches. As a complement, VizSeq also integrates latest embedding-based metrics such as BERTScore (Zhang et al., 2019) and LASER (Artetxe and Schwenk, 2018). This is rarely seen in the counterparts.

Scalability We re-implemented all the n-gram-based metrics with multiprocessing, allowing

```python
from vizseq.scorers import
    register_scorer

@register_scorer('metric name')
def calculate_score(
    hypothesis: List[str],
    references: List[List[str]],
    n_processes: int = 2,
    verbose: bool = False
) -> Tuple[float, List[float]]:
    return corpus_score, sentence_scores
```

Figure 3: VizSeq metric API. Users can define and register their new metric by implementing this function.

users to fully utilize the power of modern multi-core CPUs. We tested our multi-process versions on large evaluation sets and observed significant speedup against original single-process ones (see Figure 2). VizSeq's embedding-based metrics are implemented using PyTorch (Paszke et al., 2017) framework and their computation is automatically parallelized on CPU or GPU by the framework.

Versatility VizSeq's rich metric collection is not only available in Jupyter notebook or in the web app, it can also be used in any Python scripts. A typical use case is periodic metric calculation during model training. VizSeq's implementations save time, especially when evaluation sets are large or evaluation is frequent. To allow user-defined metrics, we designed an open metric API, whose definition can be found in Figure 3.

2.3 User-Friendly Interface

Given the drawbacks of simple command-line interface and static HTML interface, we aim at visualized and interactive interfaces for better user experience and productivity. VizSeq provides visualization in two types of interfaces: Jupyter notebook and web app. They share the same visual analysis module (Figure 4). The web app interface additionally has a data uploading module (Figure 9) and a task/dataset browsing module (Figure 10), while the Jupyter notebook interface gets data directly from Python variables. The analysis module includes the following parts.

Example grouping VizSeq uses sentence tags to manage example groups (data subsets of different interest, can be overlapping). It contains both user-defined and machine-generated tags (e.g. labels for identified languages, long sentences, sentences with rare words or code-switching). Metrics will be calculated and visualized by different

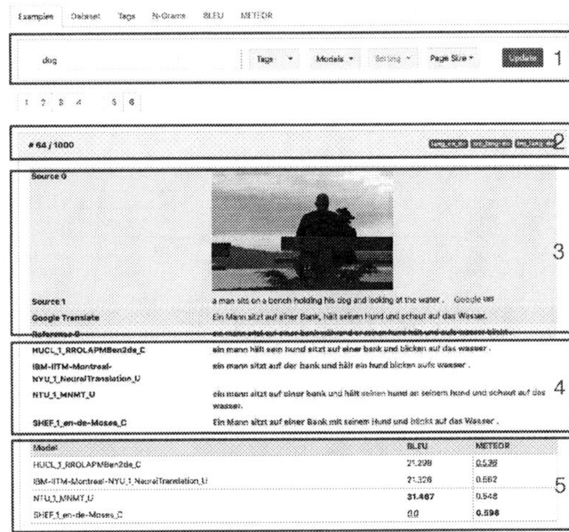

Figure 4: VizSeq example viewing. (1) keyword search box, tag and model filters, sorting and page size options; (2) left: example index, right: user-defined tags (blue) and machine-generated tags (grey); (3) multi-modal sources and Google Translate integration; (4) model predictions with highlighted matched (blue) and unmatched (red) n-grams; (5) sentence-level scores (highest ones among models in boldface, lowest ones in italics with underscore).

example groups as a complement to scores over the entire dataset.

Example viewing VizSeq presents examples with various sentence-level scores and visualized alignments of matched/unmatched reference n-grams in model predictions. It also has Google Translate integration to assist understanding of text sources in unfamiliar languages as well as providing a baseline translation model. Examples are listed in multiple pages (bookmarkable in web app) and can be sorted by various orders, for example, by a certain metric or source sentence lengths. Tags or n-gram keywords can be used to filter out examples of interest.

Dataset statistics VizSeq provides various corpus-level statistics, including: 1) counts of sentences, tokens and characters; 2) source and reference length distributions; 3) token frequency distribution; 4) list of most frequent n-grams (with links to associated examples); 5) distributions of sentence-level scores by models (Figure 5, 6 and 7). Statistics are visualized in zoomable charts with hover text hints.

Data export Statistics in VizSeq are one-click exportable: charts into PNG or SVG images (with

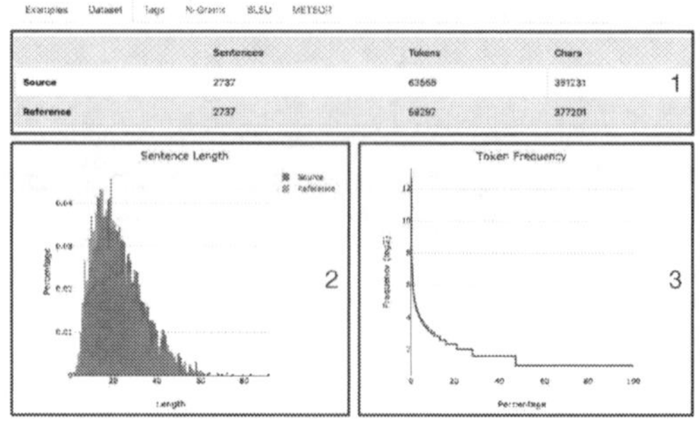

Figure 5: VizSeq dataset statistics. (1) sentence, token and character counts for source and reference sentences; (2) length distributions of source and reference sentences; (3) token frequency distribution. Plots are zoomable and exportable to SVG or PNG images.

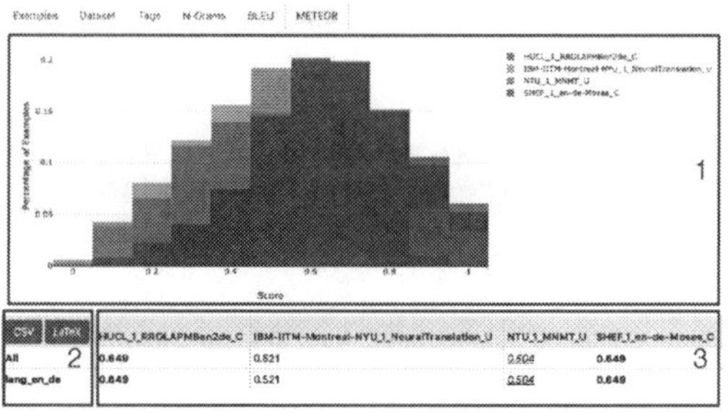

Figure 6: VizSeq dataset statistics: most frequent n-grams (n=1,2,3,4). Each listed n-gram is clickable to show associated examples in the dataset.

users' zooming applied) and tables into CSV or LaTeX (copied to clipboard).

2.4 Data Management and Public Hosting

VizSeq web app interface gets new data from the data uploading module (Figure 9) or a RESTful API. Besides local deployment, the web app back-end can also be deployed onto public servers and provide a general solution for hosting public benchmarks on a wide variety of text generation tasks and datasets.

In VizSeq, data is organized by special folder structures as follows, which is easy to maintain:

```
<task>/<eval set>/source_*.{txt,zip}
<task>/<eval set>/reference_*.txt
<task>/<eval set>/tag_*.txt
<task>/<eval set>/<model>/prediction.txt
<task>/<eval set>/__cfg__.json
```

When new data comes in, scores, n-grams and machine-generated tags will be pre-computed and cached onto disk automatically. A file monitoring and versioning system (based on file hashes, sizes or modification timestamps) is employed to detect file changes and trigger necessary updates on pre-computed results. This is important for supporting evaluation during model training where model predictions change over training epochs.

3 Example Use Cases of VizSeq

We validate the usability of VizSeq with multiple tasks and datasets, which are included as examples in our Github repository:

- WMT14 English-German[2]: a classic medium-size dataset for bilingual machine translation.

- Gigaword[3]: a text summarization dataset.

- COCO captioning 2015 (Lin et al., 2014): a classic image captioning dataset where VizSeq can present source images with text targets.

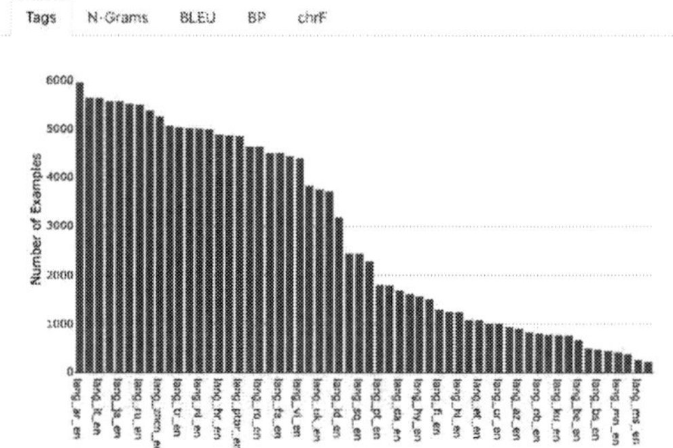

Figure 7: VizSeq corpus-level metric viewing. (1) distributions of sentence-level scores by models; (2) one-click export of tabular data to CSV and LaTeX (copied to clipboard); (3) corpus-level and group-level (by sentence tags) scores (highest ones among models in boldface, lowest ones in italics with underscore).

Figure 8: VizSeq sentence tag distribution view. In this example, tags are source-target language directions in a multilingual machine translation dataset.

---

[2]http://www.statmt.org/wmt14/translation-task.html
[3]https://github.com/harvardnlp/sent-summary

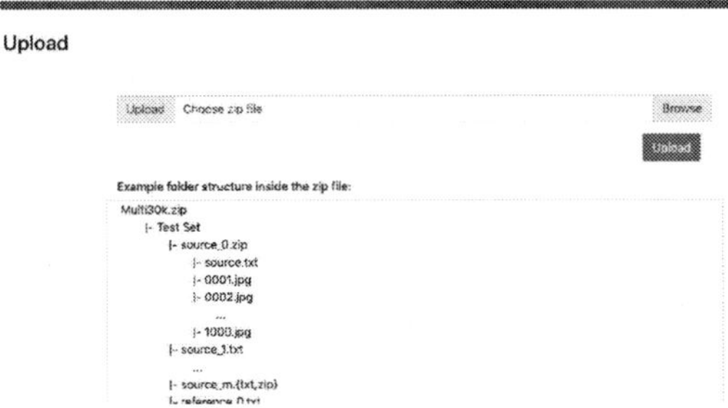

Figure 9: VizSeq data uploading. Users need to organize the files by given folder structures and pack them into a zip file for upload. VizSeq will unpack the files to the data root folder and perform integrity checks.

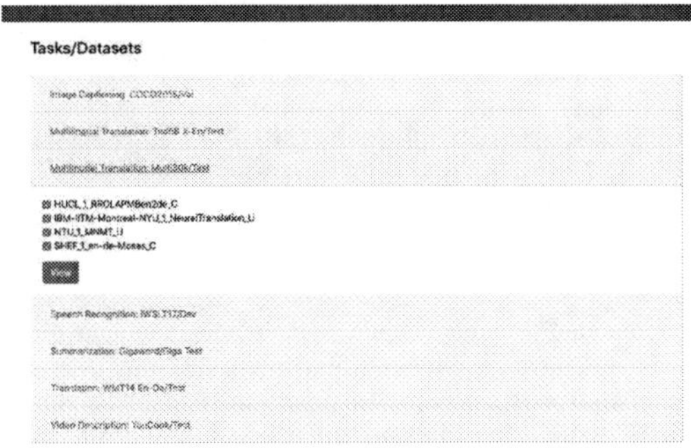

Figure 10: VizSeq task/dataset browsing. Users need to select a dataset and models of interest to proceed to the analysis module.

- WMT16 multimodal machine translation task 1[4]: English-German translation with an image the sentences describe. VizSeq can present both text and image sources, and calculate the official BLEU, METEOR and TER metrics.

- Multilingual machine translation on TED talks dataset (Ye et al., 2018): translation from 58 languages into English. VizSeq can use language directions as sentence tags to generate score breakdown by languages. The test set has as many as 165k examples, where VizSeq multi-process scorers run significantly faster than single-process ones. The integrated Google Translate can help with understanding source sentences in unfamiliar languages.

- IWSLT17 English-German speech translation[5]: VizSeq can present English audios with English transcripts and German text translations.

- YouCook (Das et al., 2013) video description: VizSeq enables inspecting generated text de-

scriptions with presence of video contents.

4 Related Work

With the thrive of deep learning, task-agnostic visualization toolkits such as Tensorboard[6], visdom[7] and TensorWatch[8], have emerged in need of monitoring model statistics and debugging model training. Model interpretability is another motivation for visualization. In NLP, softwares have been developed to interpret model parameters (e.g. attention weights) and inspect prediction generation process: LM (Rong and Adar, 2016), OpenNMT visualization tool (Klein et al., 2018) and Seq2Seq (Strobelt et al., 2019). For machine translation, toolkits are made to perform metric calculation and error analysis: ibleu (Madnani, 2011), MTEval [9], MT-ComparEval (Klejch et al., 2015), nlg-eval (Sharma et al., 2017), Vis-Eval Metric Viewer (Steele and Specia, 2018) and compare-mt (Neubig et al., 2019).

5 Conclusion

In this paper, we present VizSeq, a visual analysis toolkit for {text, image, audio, video}-to-text generation system evaluation, dataset analysis and benchmark hosting. It is accessible as a web app or a Python package in Jupyter notebook or Python scripts. VizSeq is currently under active development and our future work includes: 1) enabling image-to-text and video-to-text alignments; 2) adding human assessment modules; 3) integration with popular text generation frameworks such as fairseq[10], opennmt[11] and tensor2tensor[12].

Acknowledgments

We thank the anonymous reviewers for their comments. We also thank Ann Lee and Pratik Ringshia for helpful discussions on this project.

References

Mikel Artetxe and Holger Schwenk. 2018. Massively multilingual sentence embeddings for zero-shot cross-lingual transfer and beyond. *arXiv preprint arXiv:1812.10464.*

---

[4]https://www.statmt.org/wmt16/multimodal-task.html
[5]https://sites.google.com/site/iwsltevaluation2017

[6]https://github.com/tensorflow/tensorboard
[7]https://github.com/facebookresearch/visdom
[8]https://github.com/microsoft/tensorwatch
[9]https://github.com/odashi/mteval
[10]https://github.com/pytorch/fairseq
[11]https://github.com/OpenNMT/OpenNMT-py
[12]https://github.com/tensorflow/tensor2tensor

Satanjeev Banerjee and Alon Lavie. 2005. Meteor: An automatic metric for mt evaluation with improved correlation with human judgments. In *Proceedings of the acl workshop on intrinsic and extrinsic evaluation measures for machine translation and/or summarization*, pages 65–72.

Pradipto Das, Chenliang Xu, Richard F Doell, and Jason J Corso. 2013. A thousand frames in just a few words: Lingual description of videos through latent topics and sparse object stitching. In *Proceedings of the IEEE conference on computer vision and pattern recognition*, pages 2634–2641.

George Doddington. 2002. Automatic evaluation of machine translation quality using n-gram co-occurrence statistics. In *Proceedings of the second international conference on Human Language Technology Research*, pages 138–145. Morgan Kaufmann Publishers Inc.

Hideki Isozaki, Tsutomu Hirao, Kevin Duh, Katsuhito Sudoh, and Hajime Tsukada. 2010. Automatic evaluation of translation quality for distant language pairs. In *Proceedings of the 2010 Conference on Empirical Methods in Natural Language Processing*, pages 944–952. Association for Computational Linguistics.

Guillaume Klein, Yoon Kim, Yuntian Deng, Vincent Nguyen, Jean Senellart, and Alexander M. Rush. 2018. Opennmt: Neural machine translation toolkit.

Ondřej Klejch, Eleftherios Avramidis, Aljoscha Burchardt, and Martin Popel. 2015. Mt-compareval: Graphical evaluation interface for machine translation development. *The Prague Bulletin of Mathematical Linguistics*, 104(1):63–74.

Chin-Yew Lin. 2004. Rouge: A package for automatic evaluation of summaries. *Text Summarization Branches Out*.

Tsung-Yi Lin, Michael Maire, Serge Belongie, James Hays, Pietro Perona, Deva Ramanan, Piotr Dollár, and C Lawrence Zitnick. 2014. Microsoft coco: Common objects in context. In *European conference on computer vision*, pages 740–755. Springer.

Nitin Madnani. 2011. ibleu: Interactively debugging and scoring statistical machine translation systems. In *2011 IEEE Fifth International Conference on Semantic Computing*, pages 213–214. IEEE.

Graham Neubig, Zi-Yi Dou, Junjie Hu, Paul Michel, Danish Pruthi, and Xinyi Wang. 2019. compare-mt: A tool for holistic comparison of language generation systems. *arXiv preprint arXiv:1903.07926*.

Kishore Papineni, Salim Roukos, Todd Ward, and Wei-Jing Zhu. 2002. Bleu: a method for automatic evaluation of machine translation. In *Proceedings of the 40th annual meeting on association for computational linguistics*, pages 311–318. Association for Computational Linguistics.

Adam Paszke, Sam Gross, Soumith Chintala, Gregory Chanan, Edward Yang, Zachary DeVito, Zeming Lin, Alban Desmaison, Luca Antiga, and Adam Lerer. 2017. Automatic differentiation in PyTorch. In *NIPS Autodiff Workshop*.

Maja Popović. 2015. chrf: character n-gram f-score for automatic mt evaluation. In *Proceedings of the Tenth Workshop on Statistical Machine Translation*, pages 392–395.

Xin Rong and Eytan Adar. 2016. Visual tools for debugging neural language models. In *Proceedings of ICML Workshop on Visualization for Deep Learning*.

Shikhar Sharma, Layla El Asri, Hannes Schulz, and Jeremie Zumer. 2017. Relevance of unsupervised metrics in task-oriented dialogue for evaluating natural language generation. *CoRR*, abs/1706.09799.

Matthew Snover, Bonnie Dorr, Richard Schwartz, Linnea Micciulla, and John Makhoul. 2006. A study of translation edit rate with targeted human annotation. In *Proceedings of association for machine translation in the Americas*, volume 200.

David Steele and Lucia Specia. 2018. Vis-eval metric viewer: A visualisation tool for inspecting and evaluating metric scores of machine translation output. In *Proceedings of the 2018 Conference of the North American Chapter of the Association for Computational Linguistics: Demonstrations*, pages 71–75.

Hendrik Strobelt, Sebastian Gehrmann, Michael Behrisch, Adam Perer, Hanspeter Pfister, and Alexander M Rush. 2019. Seq2seq-vis: A visual debugging tool for sequence-to-sequence models. *IEEE transactions on visualization and computer graphics*, 25(1):353–363.

Ramakrishna Vedantam, C Lawrence Zitnick, and Devi Parikh. 2015. Cider: Consensus-based image description evaluation. In *Proceedings of the IEEE conference on computer vision and pattern recognition*, pages 4566–4575.

Yonghui Wu, Mike Schuster, Zhifeng Chen, Quoc V Le, Mohammad Norouzi, Wolfgang Macherey, Maxim Krikun, Yuan Cao, Qin Gao, Klaus Macherey, et al. 2016. Google's neural machine translation system: Bridging the gap between human and machine translation. *arXiv preprint arXiv:1609.08144*.

Qi Ye, Sachan Devendra, Felix Matthieu, Padmanabhan Sarguna, and Neubig Graham. 2018. When and why are pre-trained word embeddings useful for neural machine translation. In *HLT-NAACL*.

Tianyi Zhang, Varsha Kishore, Felix Wu, Kilian Q Weinberger, and Yoav Artzi. 2019. Bertscore: Evaluating text generation with bert. *arXiv preprint arXiv:1904.09675*.

What's Wrong with Hebrew NLP?
And How to Make it Right

Reut Tsarfaty   Amit Seker   Shoval Sadde   Stav Klein
Open University of Israel, University Road 1, Ra'anana, Israel
{reutts,shovalsa,amitse,stavkl}@openu.ac.il

Abstract

For languages with simple morphology, such as English, automatic annotation pipelines such as spaCy or Stanford's CoreNLP successfully serve AI/DS projects in academia and the industry. For many morphologically-rich languages (MRLs), similar pipelines show sub-optimal performance that limits their applicability for text analysis in research and commerical use. The suboptimal performance is mainly due to errors in early morphological disambiguation decisions, which cannot be recovered later in the pipeline, yielding incoherent annotations on the whole. In this paper we describe the design and use of the ONLP suite, a joint morpho-syntactic parsing framework for processing Modern Hebrew texts. The joint inference over morphology and syntax substantially limits error propagation, and leads to high accuracy. ONLP provides rich and expressive output which already serves diverse academic and commercial needs. Its accompanying demo further serves educational activities, introducing Hebrew NLP intricacies to researchers and non-researchers alike.

1 Introduction

NLP pipelines for the automatic annotation of unstructured texts are at the core of language technology applications for Data Science, Text Analytics and Artificial Intelligence. For English, annotation pipelines such as spaCy (Honnibal and Montani, 2017) or Stanford's CoreNLP (Manning et al., 2014) successfully deliver the ability to automatically annotate unstructured texts with their underlying linguistic structures, including: Part-of-Speech (POS) Tags, Morphological Features, Dependency Relations, Named Entities, and so on. These annotations serve research labs, non-profit organizations and commercial endeavors in their quest to *make sense* of the vast amount of unstructured data available to them.

Universal processing pipelines such as UDPipe (Straka et al., 2016) aim to serve a range of other languages, but unfortunately, their performance on many morphologically rich languages (MRLs) (Tsarfaty et al., 2010), and in particular Semitic languages, is not on a par with their performance on English. This, in turn, greatly limits their applicability for further research and commercial use. The main reason for this sub-optimal performance on Semitic languages is that the *pipeline* design inherent in these frameworks is inappropriate for languages that exhibit extreme morphological ambiguity in their input stream. This is because errors made in morphological segmentation and disambiguation early on, jeopardize the system accuracy down the pipeline. For Hebrew, this performance gap has long been a show-stopper for advancing Language Technology and Artificial Intelligence for the Hebrew-speaking community. With this contribution, we aim to remedy this situation.

In this paper we describe the design and use of the ONLP system, a *joint* morphological-syntactic parsing framework for processing the Semitic language Modren Hebrew (Henceforth, Hebrew). The system is accurate, efficient, and provides rich and expressive output including: Segmentation, POS tags, Lemmas, Features and Labeled Dependencies. The *joint* training and inference over the different layers substantially limits error propagation, and leads in turn to speed and high accuracy. Among the technical advantages of the ONLP suite are its open license, an easy 3-step installation, and a single package with all elements included — no need to train or maintain individual components separately. The ONLP suite already serves academic and commercial projects in diverse domains. Its accompanying online demo has further proved valuable for educational purposes, exposing CS/NLP and non-CS researchers and engineers to the intricacies of Semitic NLP.

259

Proceedings of the 2019 EMNLP and the 9th IJCNLP (System Demonstrations), pages 259–264
Hong Kong, China, November 3 – 7, 2019. ©2019 Association for Computational Linguistics

2   The Linguistic Challenge

In morphologically-rich languages (MRLs), each input token may consist of multiple lexical and functional units (henceforth, *morphemes*), each of which serves a particular role in the overall syntactic or semantic representation. In Hebrew, for example, the token 'וכשמהמעבדה' corresponds to five word tokens in English, each of which carrying its distinct role: 'ו' (and, CC), 'כש' (when, REL), 'מ' (from, IN), 'ה' (the, DT), 'מעבדה' (lab, NN).[1] This means that in order to process Hebrew texts, one first needs to segment the Hebrew tokens into their constituting morphemes. At the same time, Hebrew raw tokens are highly ambiguous. A token such as: 'הקפה' may be interpreted as 'הקפה' (orbit, NN), 'קפה' + 'ה' (the+coffee, DT+NN), or 'היא' + 'של' + 'הקף' (perimeter of her, NN+POSS+PRP), etc. This is further complicated by the lack of diacritics in standardized texts, meaning that most vowels are not present, and thus out of context no reading is a-priory more likely than the others. Only *in context* the correct interpretation and segmentation become apparent.

These facts create an apparent loop in the design of NLP pipelines for Hebrew: *syntactic parsing requires morphological disambiguation – but morphological disambiguation requires syntactic context*. This apparent loop has called for the development of *joint systems* rather than *pipelines*, for Semitic languages processing (Tsarfaty, 2006; Green and Manning, 2010). This joint hypothesis has proven useful for Hebrew and Arabic phrase-structure parsing (Goldberg and Tsarfaty, 2008; Green and Manning, 2010; Goldberg and Elhadad, 2011). The ONLP suite is a *dependency-based* parsing framework implementing this joint hypothesis, over the entire morpho-syntactic search-space, as depicted in Figure 1 (More et al., 2019).

3   The Architectural Design

The core of ONLP is *YAP (Yet Another Parser)*, a morpho-syntactic parser for morphological and syntactic analysis of Hebrew Texts. YAP re-implements and extends the structure-prediction framework of Zhang and Clark (2011). We describe *YAP* in detail in More and Tsarfaty (2016) and More et al. (2019). Here we only provide a bird's eye view of the architecture.

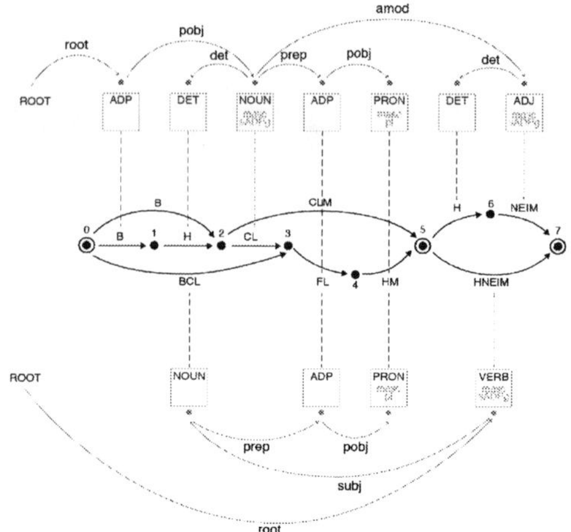

Figure 1: The Joint Morpho-Syntactic Search-Space. Lattice paths vary in length. Each lattice path can be assigned an exponential number of dependency trees.

In YAP we embrace the extreme morphological ambiguity in Hebrew. That is, we do *not* aim to resolve morphological ambiguity via pre-processing. The input to YAP is the complete *Morphological Analysis (MA)* of an input sentence x, termed here $\text{MA}(x)$. $\text{MA}(x)$ is a *lattice* structure, consisting of all possible morphological analysis possibilities of the input sentence, as seen in the middle of Figure 1. Each *lattice arc* is a tuple specifying the *start-index, end-index*, the *form* of the segment, its *part-of-speech, lemma, features*, and the *index* of the raw token the arc

originated from. An *arc* in the lattice can serve as a *node* in a syntactic dependency tree. Each contiguous path in the lattice presents one valid morphological segmentation of the sentence, for which a dependency tree can be assigned, as in Figure 1. For each path in the lattice, there is an exponential number of dependency trees that are potentially applicable.

We refer to the task of selecting the most likely lattice-path as *Morphological Disambiguation* (MD), and to the task of selecting the most likely dependency tree for a given path as *Dependency Parsing* (DEP). For an input sentence x, our goal is to *jointly* predict a single pair of $\text{MD}(x)$ and $\text{DEP}(x)$ that are consistent with one another, and form the most-likely analysis of the sentence.

The MD component is the transition-based *morphological parser* of More and Tsarfaty

---

(2016), which is formally based on the structure-prediction framework of Zhang and Clark (2011). MD accepts a sentence lattice MA(x) as input and delivers a selected sequence of arcs (morphemes) MD(x) as output. The transition-based system for MD selects arcs for MD one at a time. It decodes the lattice using beam-search, and keeps the K-best paths at each step, scored according to morpheme-level and token-level features, weighted via structured-perceptron learning.

The DEP component is a re-implementation of the Zhang and Nivre (2011) dependency parser for English, adapted for Hebrew. We assume an Arc-Eager transition system and beam-search decoding. Feature weights are learned via the structured perceptron. We employ a carefully-designed feature set that reflects linguistic properties of Hebrew such as its rich morphological paradigms, flexible word-order, agreement, etc. This provides SOTA results on Hebrew dependency parsing, albeit in Oracle (i.e., gold morphology) scenario.

Seen that both the MD and DEP realize the same formal framework and computational machinery, we can easily *unify* them and treat the morpho-synactic task as a single objective. The transition systems are combined and the beam-search decoder interleaves morphological and syntactic decisions. Now morphological decisions may be affected by syntactic content, and vice versa. The architecture is depicted in Figure 2. In More et al. (2019) we compared the performance of our joint system to our own pipeline, and to other parsing systems available for Hebrew. Our empirical results in More and Tsarfaty (2016); More et al. (2019) show significant improvements of YAP's joint model for both the morphological and syntactic tasks, over all standalone morphological or syntactic parsers available for Hebrew.

4 The Annotation Scheme

We deliver automatic morpho-syntactic annotation of Hebrew texts based on the scheme of the SPMRL Hebrew dependency treebank. The SPMRL Hebrew scheme employs the labels of Sima'an et al. (2001) for morphology and POS tags, and the Unified-SD scheme of Tsarfaty (2013) for the labeled dependencies.[2] Specifically, we deliver the following annotation layers:

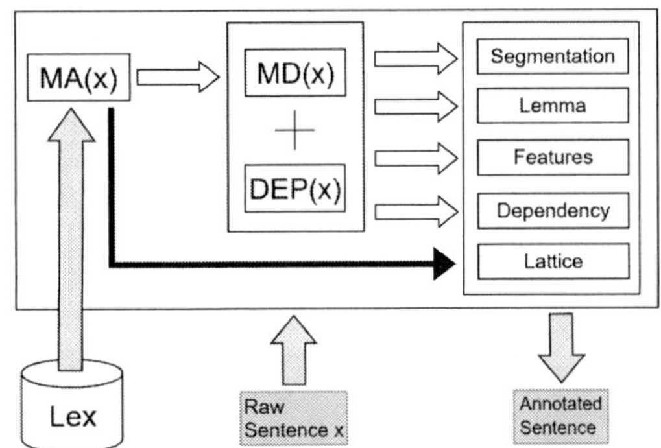

Figure 2: A bird's eye view of the Architecture

Morphological Segmentation The most basic form of analysis of Hebrew texts is the segmentation of raw tokens into multiple meaning-bearing units that we call *morphemes*.[3] Due to orthographic and phonological processes, some morphemes do not appear explicitly in the surface form. Our segmentation recovers all morphemes, both overt and covert. For example, the token 'בבית' (in the house) is segmented as 'ב' + 'ה' + 'בית'.

Part-of-Speech (POS) Tags Each morphological segment is assigned a single Part-of-Speech tag category that indicates its syntactic role. The set of tags used by the system is based on the SPMRL scheme which in turn adopts the POS labels from Sima'an et al. (2001) (detailed in our appendix).

Morphological Features Along with the POS category, we specify for each segment the properties that are signalled by inflectional morphology. The scheme encodes the following properties: **Number** [S (Singular) / P (Plural) / D (Dual)], **Gender** [F (Female) / M (Male) / F,M (both)], **Person** [1 / 2 / 3 / A (All)],[4] and **Tense** [Past, Present, Future, Imperative, Infinitive].[5]

Lemmas Each segment is also assigned a lemma, i.e., the cannonical representation of its core (uninflected) meaning.[6] For Hebrew nouns and adjectives, the lemma is chosen to be the Masculine-Singular form. For verbs, the lemma is in the Masculine-Singular-3per form in Past tense.

---

[2]With an eye for future comparability, we further developed a conversion algorithm to convert the dependency tree from Unified-SD to Universal Dependencies (UD). `https://universaldependencies.org/`

[3]In UD they are called *words*. In Hebrew NLP they are called *segments*. We use *morphemes* or *segments* herein.

[4]*A* is used in cases where all analyses are valid, such as in Beinoni form - 'אוכלת' (I/you/she eat.singular.feminine)

[5]Present-tense verbs and participles are tagged 'Beinoni'.

[6]Note that due to high morphological fusion in Hebrew, simple surface-based *stemming* will not suffice.

261

Dependency Tree The dependency tree is defined over all morphological segments and an artificial root node. It consists of a set of labeled binary relations that indicate the bi-lexical dependencies between segments. Note that the SPMRL dependency scheme, as opposed to UD, always selects *functional* heads, rather than lexical heads. The dependency labeling is based on the scheme from Tsarfaty (2013), repeated in the appendix.

Lattices As explained in section 3 above, a word can be segmented into morphemes in multiple ways, which are constrained by a broad-coverage lexicon. In addition to the parsed output, we make available for each input sentence its sentence lattice, i.e. the set of all possible segmentations for a given sentence, along with all possible morphosyntactic analyses for each arc.

5   Technical Details and Forms of Use

YAP is implemented in the Go language.[7] It requires 6GB of RAM to run, and employs a simple 3-step installation, given in the supplementray material. The input to the system is a tokenized sentence, with tokens appearing one per line, and a line break after every sentence.[8] The output is a dependency tree (where each node in the tree is a lattice arc) provided in the CoNLL-X format (Buchholz and Marsi, 2006). YAP is trained on the Hebrew section of the SPMRL shared task. It also makes use of the broad-coverage lexicon of Itai and Wintner (2008) for finding all potential lattice paths. In case of out-of-vocabulary (OOV) items, we employ a simple heuristic where we suggest the 10 most-likely analyses of rare tokens observed during training.

Simple Use | Command line From the command line, one can process one input file at a time, with a single sentence or more. The input file must be formatted with a single token per line, and an empty line denoting the end of every sentence.

Processing a file is done in 2 steps: First, run Morphological Analysis using `./yap hebma` to generate a sentence lattice containing all possible morphological breakdowns of each token. YAP will save the lattice to the file specified via the `-out` flag.

Now you can run joint Morphological Disambiguation and Dependency Parsing using `./yap joint` to jointly predict the best lattice path and corresponding dependency tree. The input to this command is the output file generated in the previous step, and there are 3 output files: one containing word segments, one containing the disambiguated lattice path, and one containing the complete dependency tree in CoNLL-X format.

Advanced Use | RESTful API YAP can run as a RESTful server that accepts parse requests. To do this simply start the server, listening on localhost port 8000. Now you can call the joint endpoint with a json object containing the list of tokens to process in the HTTP data payload. The response is a json object containing the three output levels (MA, MD and Dep). You can use jq and sed (or any other json and line processing tools) to format the (tab separated value) responses and reassemble the output. Check our appendix for an illustration.

Educational Use | The Online Demo In 2018 we decided to create an online demo of the system, for educational purposes: (i) To expose NLP/AI researchers to NLP capabilities available for Hebrew. (ii) To educate non-CS scientists and engineers who work with Hebrew data (e.g., digital humanities) on text annotations that can potentially be useful for their applications. (iii) To launch outreach activities where we teach *what is NLP* to the local community (e.g., school kids).[9]

To use the demo, simply go to `onlp.openu.ac.il` and type a Hebrew sentence in the textbox. The demo is built with Django and Bootstrap web frameworks. It sends the user's Hebrew text input to the ONLP server, which returns a CoNLL-X formatted parse along with the complete sentence lattice. Pre-processing includes pre-morphological tokenization of the input, where punctuation is being separated from the tokens. Double quotation marks are being separated from the word unless they appear before the last character of the word, to avoid over-segmentation of acronyms.[10] The tokenized sequence is then passed to the ONLP server. The CoNLL-X output is then processed into the following layers: the FORM column is concatenated and presented as "Segmented Text", and the POS, LEMMA, FEATS and DEPS are pre-

---

[7] `https://golang.org/`

[8] We assume the tokenization convention of MILA (Itai and Wintner, 2008).

[9] E.g., `https://www.youtube.com/watch?v=TFwQeoKpznA&feature=youtu.be`

[10] Acronyms in Hebrew are written with a quotation mark before the last letter, e.g. 'ארה"ב' (USA) .

	Tok	MA	MD	POS	Lem	Feats	Deps	Joint
Tasks								
MILA	✓	✓						
NITE	✓	✓	✓					
Hebrew-NLP		✓						
Adler			✓	✓		✓		
Goldberg							✓	
Pipelines								
UDPipe	✓	✓	✓	✓	✓	✓	✓	
CoreNLP	✓	✓	✓	✓	✓	✓	✓	
ONLP	✓	✓	✓	✓	✓	✓	✓	✓

Table 1: Existing Coverage for Hebrew NLP Tasks

sented in separate accordion tabs. Furthermore, the demo presents the sentence lattice which is the input to the joint parser. This is useful for debugging, and for analyzing lexical-coverage in out-of-domain scenarios.

Expert Use | Out of Domain Scenarios A bottleneck for the system in out-of-domain parsing scenarios is the coverage of the lexicon. We rely on a general-purpose lexicon containing over 500K entries. OOV words are treated via heuristics we designed, which are suitable for the general case only. However, identifying vocabulary items accurately may be critical when applying the parser to new domains with domain-specific information (medical, financial, political, etc.). Fortunately, we can extend the system with a domain-specific lexicon, thus extending the MA coverage. Due to joint inference, the availability of a better suited *lexical* analysis triggers better *lexico-syntactic* decisions on the whole.[11]

6   Related and Future Work

Hebrew NLP in general and Hebrew parsing in particular are known to be challenging, due to interesting linguistic properties, the scarcity of annotated data, and the small research community around. So, Hebrew has been seriously understudied in NLP. During the early 2000s, the MILA knowledge center was established, where the two of the main Hebrew resources for NLP were developed: the Hebrew treebank (Sima'an et al., 2001) and the Hebrew Lexicon (Itai and Wintner, 2008).

Morphological Taggers for Hebrew using local linear-context have been trained on these data and were made available for free use (Adler and Elhadad, 2006; Bar-haim et al., 2008). However, their performance was not on a par with parallel tools for English and thus insufficient for commercial use. Hebrew dependency parsing was initially

provided by Goldberg and Elhadad (2009), but the parser provided *unlabeled* dependency, and the pipeline relied on Adler's morphological tagger. This left the predicted dependency trees inaccurate and unsatisfying. *Joint* morpho-syntactic models for constituency-based parsing based on Tsarfaty (2010) showed good performance on benchmark data, but was never released for open use.

With the development of the UD treebanks collection, general frameworks such as UDPipe (Straka et al., 2016) and CoreNLP (Manning et al., 2014) have been trained on the Hebrew UD treebank, and made the model available. However, these models provide performance that is still far from satisfactory. As we also demonstrate in our screen-cast,[12] these systems make critical mistakes, even with the simplest sentences. We conjecture that this is due to their inherent pipeline assumption: initial layers of processing present many mistakes. due to the extreme morphological ambiguity, and later layers cannot recover.[13] Notably, neural-network models utilizing word embeddings, (e.g., UDPipe) also lag behind.

Table 1 shows the task-coverage of existing tools and toolkits for NLP in Hebrew, academic as well as private initiatives (NITE,Hebrew-NLP). The task-coverage of the ONLP suite we present is on a par with international standards (UDPipe, CoreNLP), and its level of performance was shown to exceed all existing models (More et al., 2019). We are currently working towards Named-Entity Recognition as well as Open Information Extraction, to be added to ONLP in the near future.

7   Conclusion

This paper presents ONLP, a complete language-processing framework for automatic annotation of Modern Hebrew Texts. The framework covers morphological segmentation, POS tags, lemmas and features, and dependency parsing, predicted jointly. The system is easy to install and to use, and we support multiple forms of usage fitting user-personas with different needs. We hope the availability of an open-source, accurate, and easy-to-use system for NLP in Hebrew will benefit the local NLP open-source community and greatly advance Hebrew language technology research and development, in academia and in the industry.

---

[11]We discuss how exactly this is executed in the appendix.

[12]https://www.youtube.com/watch?v=H6pvh1x20FQ

[13]Our detailed qualitative error analysis in More et al. (2019) indeed confirms this conjecture.

Acknowledgements

We thank the NLPH community, in particular Shay Palachi, Amit Shkolnick and Yuval Feinstein, for discussion and insightful comments. We further thank Avi Bivas (Israel Innovation Authority) and Milo Avisar for promoting NLP initiatives in Israel. This research is supported by an ISF grant (1739/26) and an ERC Starting grant (677352), for which we are grateful.

References

Meni Adler and Michael Elhadad. 2006. An unsupervised morpheme-based hmm for Hebrew morphological disambiguation. In *ACL*. The Association for Computer Linguistics.

Roy Bar-haim, Khalil Sima'an, and Yoad Winter. 2008. Part-of-speech tagging of Modern Hebrew text. *Natural Language Engineering*, 14(2):223–251.

Sabine Buchholz and Erwin Marsi. 2006. Conll-x shared task on multilingual dependency parsing. In *Proceedings of CoNLL*, pages 149–164.

Yoav Goldberg and Michael Elhadad. 2009. Hebrew dependency parsing: Initial results. In *Proceedings of the 11th International Conference on Parsing Technologies*, IWPT '09, pages 129–133.

Yoav Goldberg and Michael Elhadad. 2011. Joint Hebrew segmentation and parsing using a PCFGLA lattice parser. In *Proceedings of ACL*.

Yoav Goldberg and Reut Tsarfaty. 2008. A single framework for joint morphological segmentation and syntactic parsing. In *Proceedings of ACL*.

Spence Green and Christopher D. Manning. 2010. Better Arabic parsing: Baselines, evaluations, and analysis. In *Proceedings of COLING*.

Matthew Honnibal and Ines Montani. 2017. spaCy 2: Natural language understanding with Bloom embeddings, convolutional neural networks and incremental parsing. To appear.

Alon Itai and Shuly Wintner. 2008. Language resources for Hebrew. *Language Resources and Evaluation*, 42(1):75–98.

Christopher Manning, Mihai Surdeanu, John Bauer, Jenny Finkel, Steven Bethard, and David McClosky. 2014. The stanford corenlp natural language processing toolkit. In *Proceedings ACL: system demonstrations*, pages 55–60.

Amir More, Amit Seker, Victoria Basmova, and Reut Tsarfaty. 2019. Joint transition-based models for morpho-syntactic parsing: Parsing strategies for MRLs and a case study from modern Hebrew. *Transactions of the Association for Computational Linguistics*, 7:33–48.

Amir More and Reut Tsarfaty. 2016. Data-driven morphological analysis and disambiguation for morphologically rich languages and universal dependencies. In *Proceedings of COLING*, pages 337–348. The COLING 2016 Organizing Committee.

Khalil Sima'an, Alon Itai, Yoad Winter, Alon Altman, and N. Nativ. 2001. Building a tree-bank of Modern Hebrew text. *Traitement Automatique des Langues*, 42(2).

Milan Straka, Jan Hajic, and Jana Straková. 2016. Udpipe: Trainable pipeline for processing conll-u files performing tokenization, morphological analysis, pos tagging and parsing. In *Proceedings of the Tenth International Conference on Language Resources and Evaluation (LREC 2016)*, Paris, France. European Language Resources Association (ELRA).

Reut Tsarfaty. 2006. Integrated morphological and syntactic disambiguation for modern Hebrew. In *Proceedings ACL-CoLing Student Research Workshop*, pages 49–54, Stroudsburg, PA, USA. ACL.

Reut Tsarfaty. 2010. *Relational-realizational parsing*. Ph.D. thesis.

Reut Tsarfaty. 2013. A unified morphosyntactic scheme for stanford dependencies. In *Proceedings of ACL*.

Reut Tsarfaty, Djamé Seddah, Yoav Goldberg, Sandra Kübler, Marie Candito, Jennifer Foster, Yannick Versley, Ines Rehbein, and Lamia Tounsi. 2010. Statistical parsing of morphologically rich languages (spmrl): What, how and whither. In *Proceedings of the NAACL HLT 2010 First Workshop on Statistical Parsing of Morphologically-Rich Languages*, SPMRL '10, pages 1–12, Stroudsburg, PA, USA. Association for Computational Linguistics.

Yue Zhang and Stephen Clark. 2011. Syntactic processing using the generalized perceptron and beam search. *Computational Linguistics*, 37(1):105–151.

Yue Zhang and Joakim Nivre. 2011. Transition-based dependency parsing with rich non-local features. In *Proceedings of the ACL*, HLT '11, pages 188–193, Stroudsburg, PA, USA. ACL.

A Resources

1. Paper Appendix and Supplementary Materials:
```
https://arxiv.org/abs/1908.05453
```
2. Github:
```
https://github.com/OnlpLab/yap
```
3. Demo - Website:
```
http://onlp.openu.org.il
```
4. Demo - Screencast:
```
https://www.youtube.com/watch?v=
H6pvh1x20FQ
```
5. API Docker Image:
```
https://hub.docker.com/r/onlplab/
yap-api
```
6. SPMRL-to-UD Conversion:
```
https://github.com/OnlpLab/Hebrew_UD
```
7. ONLP Lab Website:
```
http://onlp.openu.org.il/home
```

Author Index

Association for Computational Linguistics
209 N. Eighth Street
Stroudsburg, Pennsylvania 18360

ISBN 978-1-7138-0068-2